DORLING KINDERSLEY *TRAVEL GUIDES*

PARIS

Main Contributor: ALAN TILLIER

DORLING KINDERSLEY, INC.

LONDON • NEW YORK • SYDNEY • MOSCOW • DELHI

www.dk.com

DORLING KINDERSLEY, INC.

www.dk.com

PROJECT EDITOR Heather Jones
ART EDITOR Janis Utton
EDITOR Alex Gray
US EDITORS Mary Ann Lynch, Mary Sutherland
DESIGNER Vanessa Hamilton
DESIGN ASSISTANT Clare Sullivan

CONTRIBUTORS
Chris Boicos, Michael Gibson, Douglas Johnson

PHOTOGRAPHERS
Max Alexander, Neil Lukas, Robert O'Dea

ILLUSTRATORS
Stephen Conlin, Stephen Gyapay,
Maltings Partnership

This book was produced with the assistance of
Websters International Publishers.

Reproduced by Colourscan, Singapore
Printed and bound by Dai Nippon Printing Co., (Hong Kong) Ltd

First American Edition, 1993
4 6 8 10 9 7 5
Published in the United States by
Dorling Kindersley, Inc.,
95 Madison Avenue, New York, New York 10016
Reprinted with revisions 1997, 1999, 2000

Copyright © 1993, 2000 Dorling Kindersley Limited, London

Library of Congress Cataloging-in-Publication Data
Tillier, Alan
Paris / Alan Tillier.
p. cm.
ISBN 1-56458-185-3
1. Paris (France)--Guidebooks. 2. Walking--France--Paris--
Guidebooks. 3. Amusements--France--Paris--Guidebooks. 4. Maps,
Tourist--France--Paris. I. Title.
DC708. T55 1993   92-53472
914. 4'36104839--dc20   CIP

THROUGHOUT THIS BOOK, FLOORS ARE REFERRED TO IN ACCORDANCE WITH
EUROPEAN USAGE, I.E. THE "FIRST FLOOR" IS ONE FLIGHT UP.

**The information in every
Dorling Kindersley Travel Guide is checked annually**.
Every effort has been made to ensure that this book is as up-to-
date as possible at the time of going to press. Some details,
however, such as telephone numbers, opening hours, prices,
gallery hanging arrangements and travel information are liable to
change. The publishers cannot accept responsibility for any
consequences arising from the use of this book. We value the
views and suggestions of our readers very highly. Please write to:
Editorial Director, Dorling Kindersley Travel Guides,
Dorling Kindersley, 9 Henrietta Street, London WC2E 8PS.

CONTENTS

Henri II (1547–59)

INTRODUCING PARIS

Pont Alexandre III

Opéra de Paris Bastille

The Kiss by Rodin (1886)

Sacré-Coeur in Montmartre

An island in the Bois de Boulogne

TRAVELERS' NEEDS

Noisettes of lamb

SURVIVAL GUIDE

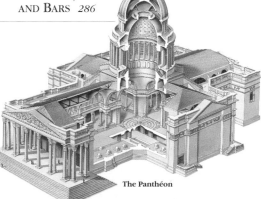

The Panthéon

HOW TO USE THIS GUIDE

THIS EYEWITNESS TRAVEL GUIDE helps you get the most from your stay in Paris with the minimum of practical difficulty. The opening section, *Introducing Paris*, locates the city geographically, places modern Paris in its historical context and explains how Parisian life changes through the year. *Paris at a Glance* is an overview of the city's attractions. The main sightseeing section of the book is section two,

Paris Area by Area, describing all the main sights with maps, photographs and detailed illustrations. In addition, five planned walks take you step-by-step through special Paris areas.

Carefully researched tips for hotels, shops, markets, restaurants, bars, sports and entertainment are found in section three, *Travelers' Needs*, and section four, *Survival Guide* has advice on everything from mailing a letter to catching the metro.

PARIS AREA BY AREA

The city has been divided into 14 sightseeing areas. Each section opens with a portrait of the area, summing up its character and history, with a list of all the sights to be covered. These are clearly located by numbers on an *Area Map*. This is followed by a large-scale *Street-by-Street Map* focusing on the most interesting part of the area. Finding your way around the section is made simple by the numbering system used throughout. This refers to the order in which sights are described on the pages throughout the section.

Sights at a Glance lists the sights in the area by category: Historic Streets and Buildings; Churches; Museums and Galleries; Monuments; Gardens, Parks and Squares; and so on.

The area covered in greater detail on the *Street-by-Street Map* is shaded red.

Travel tips help you reach the area quickly.

1 Area Map

For easy reference, the sights in each area are numbered and located on an area map. To help the visitor, the map also shows metro and mainline RER stations and parking areas.

The Conciergerie ❽ is shown on this map as well.

Color-coding on each page makes the area easy to find in the book.

Numbered circles pinpoint all the listed sights on the *Area Map*. The Conciergerie, for example, is ❽

2 Street-by-Street Map

This gives a bird's-eye view of the heart of each sightseeing area. The most important buildings are highlighted in stronger color, to help you spot them as you walk around.

A locator map shows you where you are in relation to surrounding areas. The area of the *Street-by-Street Map* is shown in red.

Photographs of facades and distinctive details of buildings help you locate the sights.

A suggested route for a walk takes in the most attractive and interesting streets in the area.

Red stars indicate the sights that no visitor should miss.

ILE DE LA CITÉ AND ILE ST-LOUIS

Street by Street: Ile de la Cité

PARIS AREA BY AREA

SIGHTS AT A GLANCE

GETTING THERE

KEY

PARIS AT A GLANCE

Each map in this section concentrates on a specific theme: *Museums and Galleries; Churches; Gardens, Parks and Squares;* and *Remarkable Parisians.* The major sights are shown on the map; other sights are described on the pages following.

Each sightseeing area is color-coded.

The theme is explored in greater detail on the pages following the map.

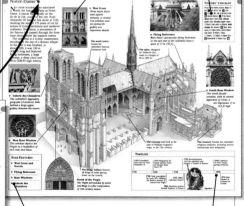

3 Detailed information on each sight

All important sights in each area are described in depth in this section. They are listed in order, following the numbering on the Area Map. *Practical information is also provided.*

4 Paris's major sights

These are given two or more full pages in the sightseeing area in which they are found. Historic buildings are dissected to reveal their interiors, and museums and galleries have color-coded floor plans to help you find important exhibits.

PRACTICAL INFORMATION

Each entry provides all the information needed to plan a visit to the sight. The key to the symbols used is on the inside back cover.

Sight number

Telephone number

Opening hours

Nearest metro station

Conciergerie ⑧

1 Quai de l'Horloge 75001.
Map 13 A3. 📞 *43 54 30 06.* Ⓜ
Cité. **Open** *Apr–Sep 9:30am–6pm daily.* 🚫 🚻

Map reference to *Street Finder* **at back of book**

Services and facilities available

Address

The Visitors' Checklist provides the practical information you will need to plan your visit.

The facade of each major sight is shown to help you spot it quickly.

Red stars indicate the most interesting architectural details of the building and the most important works of art or exhibits to be seen inside.

A timeline charts the key events in the history of the sight.

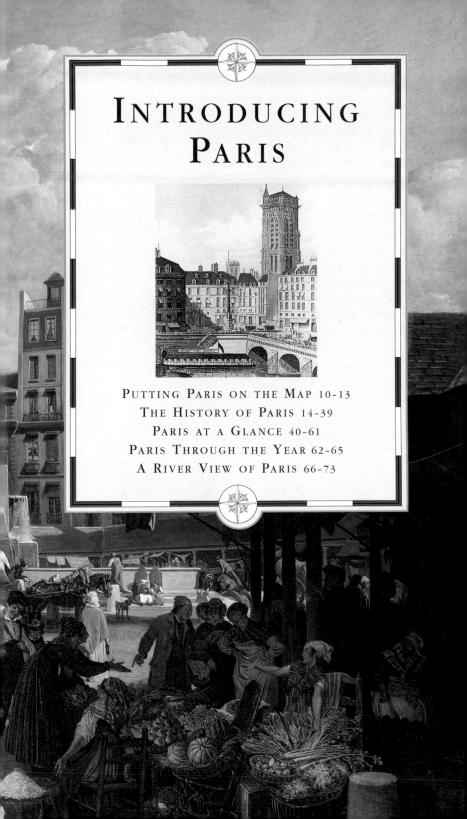

INTRODUCING
PARIS

Putting Paris on the Map

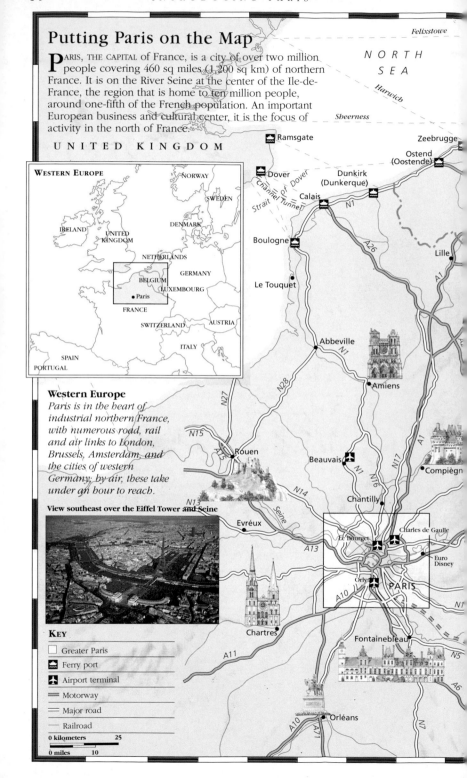

PARIS, THE CAPITAL of France, is a city of over two million people covering 460 sq miles (1,200 sq km) of northern France. It is on the River Seine at the center of the Ile-de-France, the region that is home to ten million people, around one-fifth of the French population. An important European business and cultural center, it is the focus of activity in the north of France.

UNITED KINGDOM

WESTERN EUROPE

NORWAY

SWEDEN

DENMARK

IRELAND

UNITED KINGDOM

NETHERLANDS

GERMANY

BELGIUM

LUXEMBOURG

• Paris

FRANCE

SWITZERLAND

AUSTRIA

ITALY

SPAIN

PORTUGAL

Western Europe

Paris is in the heart of industrial northern France, with numerous road, rail and air links to London, Brussels, Amsterdam, and the cities of western Germany; by air, these take under an hour to reach.

View southeast over the Eiffel Tower and Seine

Felixstowe

NORTH SEA

Harwich

Sheerness

Ramsgate

Zeebrugge

Ostend (Oostende)

Dover

Dunkirk (Dunkerque)

Channel Tunnel

Strait of Dover

Calais

N1

A26

Lille

A1

Boulogne

Le Touquet

N28

N27

Abbeville

N1

Amiens

N15

Rouen

Beauvais

N1

N16

N17

Compiègn

Evréux

Chantilly

N14

Seine

N13

Le Bourget

Charles de Gaulle

A13

Euro Disney

Orly

PARIS

A10

N1

Chartres

Fontainebleau

N5

A11

A6

A10

A71

Orléans

N2

KEY

- ☐ Greater Paris
- ⬓ Ferry port
- ✈ Airport terminal
- ═ Motorway
- ━ Major road
- — Railroad

0 kilometers   25

0 miles   10

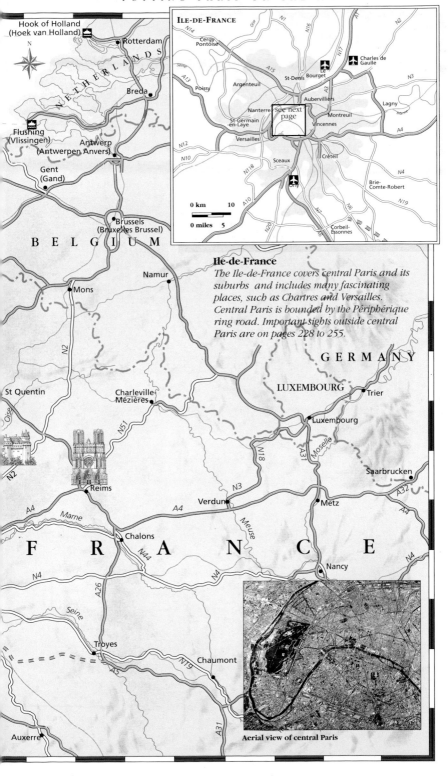

ILE-DE-FRANCE

Hook of Holland
(Hoek van Holland)

Rotterdam

NETHERLANDS

Breda

Flushing
(Vlissingen)

Antwerp
(Antwerpen Anvers)

Gent
(Gand)

Brussels
(Bruxelles Brussel)

B E L G I U M

Namur

Mons

St Quentin

Charleville-
Mézières

Reims

Chalons

F   R   A   N   C   E

Troyes

Chaumont

Auxerre

Cergy-
Pontoise

Poissy

Argenteuil

St-Denis   Bourget

Charles de
Gaulle

Aubervilliers

Nanterre   see next
page

St-Germain
-en-Laye

Versailles   Vincennes

Montreuil

Lagny

Sceaux

Orly

Créteil

Brie-
Comte-Robert

Corbeil-
Essonnes

0 km   10

0 miles   5

GERMANY

LUXEMBOURG   Trier

Luxembourg

Saarbrucken

Verdun   Metz

Nancy

Ile-de-France

*The Ile-de-France covers central Paris and its
suburbs and includes many fascinating
places, such as Chartres and Versailles.
Central Paris is bounded by the Périphérique
ring road. Important sights outside central
Paris are on pages 228 to 255.*

Aerial view of central Paris

Central Paris

THIS GUIDE DIVIDES PARIS into 14 areas, comprising central Paris and the nearby area of Montmartre. Most of the sights covered in the book lie within these areas, each of which has its own chapter. Each area contains a range of important historical and cultural sights. The sights of Montmartre, for example, reveal its village charm and colorful history as a thriving artistic enclave. In contrast, Champs-Elysées is renowned for its wide avenues, expensive fashion houses and opulent mansions. Most of the city's famous sights are within reach of the heart of the city and are easy to reach on foot or by public transportation.

PAGES 202–9
*Street Finder maps
3–4, 5, 11*

Champs-Elysées

Chaillot Quarter

0 kilometers   1

0 miles   0.5

R I V E R   S E

Invalides and Eiffel Tower Quarter

PAGES 194–201
*Street Finder maps
3, 9–10*

PAGES 182–93
*Street Finder maps
9–10, 11*

PAGES 116–33
*Street Finder maps
6, 11–12*

PAGES 134–47
*Street Finder maps
11–12*

PAGES 174–81
*Street Finder maps
15–16*

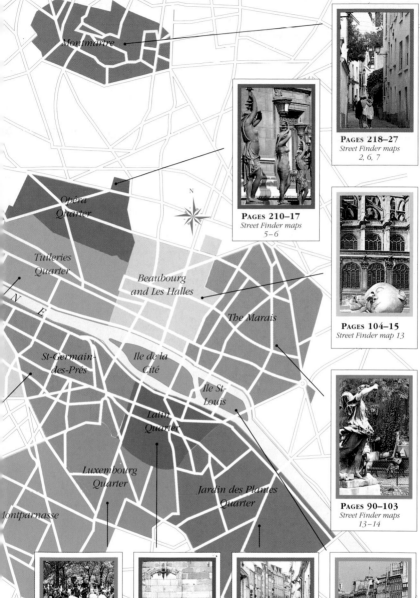

Montmartre

Opera Quarter

Tuileries Quarter

Beaubourg and Les Halles

The Marais

St-Germain-des-Prés

Ile de la Cité

Ile St-Louis

Latin Quarter

Luxembourg Quarter

Jardin des Plantes Quarter

Montparnasse

PAGES 218–27
Street Finder maps 2, 6, 7

PAGES 210–17
Street Finder maps 5–6

PAGES 104–15
Street Finder map 13

PAGES 90–103
Street Finder maps 13–14

PAGES 168–73
Street Finder maps 12, 16

PAGES 148–59
Street Finder maps 12, 13, 17

PAGES 160–7
Street Finder maps 17–18

PAGES 76–87
Street Finder maps 12–13

REPUBLIQUE FRANCAISE
LIBERTE EGALITE · FRATERNITE

THE HISTORY OF PARIS

THE PARIS CONQUERED by the Romans in 55 BC was a small flood-prone fishing village on the Ile de la Cité, inhabited by the Parisii tribe. A Roman settlement soon flourished and spread to the Left Bank of the Seine. The Franks succeeded the Romans, named the city Paris and made it the center of their kingdom.

During the Middle Ages the city flourished as a religious center, and architectural masterpieces such as Sainte-Chapelle were erected. It also thrived as a center of learning, enticing European scholars to its great university, the Sorbonne.

Paris emerged during the Renaissance and the Enlightenment as a great center of culture and ideas, and under the rule of Louis XIV became a city of immense wealth and power. But rule by the monarch gave way to rule by the people in the bloody Revolution of 1789. By the early 1800s, however, revolutionary fervor had faded, and the brilliant militarist Napoleon Bonaparte proclaimed himself Emperor of France and began pursuing his ambition to make Paris the new center of the world.

Soon after the Revolution of 1848, a radical transformation of the city began. Baron Haussmann's grand urban scheme replaced Paris's medieval slums with elegant avenues and boulevards. By the century's end, the city was the driving force of Western culture. This continued into the 20th century, interrupted only by the German military occupation of 1940 to 1944. Since then, the city has revived and expanded dramatically as it strives to be at the heart of a unified Europe.

The following pages illustrate Paris's history with snapshots of the most dramatic and significant periods in the city's evolution.

Fleur-de-lys, the royal emblem

A map of Paris (about 1845)

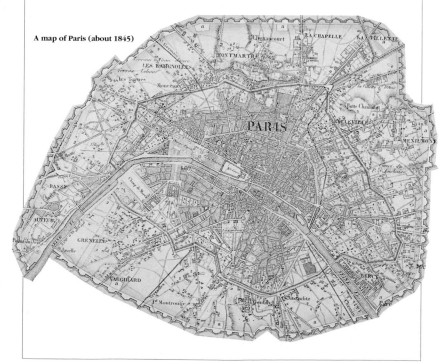

Allegory of the Republic (1848) by Dominique Louis Papety

Kings and Emperors in Paris

P ARIS BECAME the power base for the kings of France at the beginning of the Capetian dynasty, when Hugh Capet ascended the throne. Successive kings and emperors have left their mark. Many of the places mentioned in this book have royal associations: Philippe-Auguste's fortress, the Louvre Palace, is now one of the world's great museums; Henri IV's Pont Neuf bridge links the Ile de la Cité with the two banks of the Seine; and Napoleon conceived the Arc de Triomphe to celebrate his military victories. The end of the long line of kings came with the overthrow of the monarchy in 1848, during the reign of Louis-Philippe.

768–814 Charlemagne

743–751 Childéric III

716–721 Chilpéric II

695–711 Childebert II

566–584 Chilpéric I

558–562 Clotaire I

447–458 Merovich

674–691 Thierri III

655–668 Clotaire III

458–482 Childéric I

628–637 Dagobert I

954–986 Lothaire

898–929 Charles III, the Simple

884–888 Charles II, the Fat

879–882 Louis III

840–877 Charles I, the Bald

1137–80 Louis VII

987–996 Hugh Capet

1031–60 Henri I

1060–1108 Philippe I

400	500	600	700	800	900	1000	1100
MEROVINGIAN DYNASTY				**CAROLINGIAN DYNASTY**		**CAPETIAN DYNASTY**	
400	500	600	700	800	900	1000	1100

996–1031 Robert II, the Pious

986–987 Louis V

751–768 Pépin the Short

721–737 Thierri IV

711–716 Dagobert III

936–954 Louis IV, the Foreigner

691–695 Clovis III

888–898 Odo, Count of Paris

668–674 Childéric II

882–884 Carloman

637–655 Clovis II

584–628 Clotaire II

877–879 Louis II, the Stammerer

562–566 Caribert

511–558 Childebert I

814–840 Louis I, the Debonair

482–511 Clovis I

1108–37 Louis VI, the Fat

1515–47 François I

1226–70 Louis IX
(St. Louis)

1498–1515 Louis XII,
Father of his People

1483–98 Charles VIII

1422–61 Charles VII, the
Victorious

1774–93 Louis XVI

1270–85 Philippe III,
the Bold

1547–59 Henri II

1285–1314 Philippe
IV, the Fair

1559–60 François II

1316–22
Philippe V

1610–43 Louis XIII

1328–50
Philippe VI

1643–1715 Louis
XIV, the Sun King

1804–14
Napoleon I

1200	1300	1400	1500	1600	1700	1800

VALOIS DYNASTY   **BOURBON DYNASTY**

1200	1300	1400	1500	1600	1700	1800

1380–1422
Charles VI,
the Fool

1560–74
Charles IX

1814–24
Louis XVIII

1314–16
Louis X

1574–89
Henri III

1824–30
Charles X

1322–28
Charles IV, the
Fair

1364–80
Charles V,
the Wise

1589–1610
Henri IV

1830–48
Louis-Philippe I

1852–70
Napoleon III

1350–64 Jean II,
the Good

1223–26 Louis VIII, the Lion

1180–1223 Philippe II, Auguste

1461–83 Louis XI, the Spider

1715–74
Louis XV

Gallo-Roman Paris

PARIS WOULD NOT have existed without the Seine. The river provided early peoples with the means to exploit the land, forests, marshes and islands. Recent excavations have unearthed canoes dating back to 4,500 BC, well before a Celtic tribe, known as the Parisii, settled there in the 3rd century BC, in an area known as Lutetia. From 59 BC, the Romans undertook the conquest of Gaul (France). Seven years later, Lutetia was sacked by the Romans. They fortified and rebuilt it, especially the main island (the Ile de la Cité) and the Left Bank of the Seine.

Roman enamel brooch

EXTENT OF THE CITY
◻ 200 BC   ☐ Today

Bronze Age Harness
Everyday objects like harnesses continued to be made of bronze well into the Iron Age, which began in Gaul around 900 BC.

Iron Daggers
From the 2nd century BC, short swords of iron replaced long swords and were sometimes decorated with human and animal shapes.

Baths

Theater

Forum

Present-day Rue Soufflot

Glass Beads
Iron Age glass beads and bracelets have been found on the Ile de la Cité.

Fired-Clay Vase
Pale ceramics with colored decoration were common in Gaul.

N

Present-day Rue St-Jacques

TIMELINE

Helmet worn by Gaulish warriors

4500 BC Early boatmen operate from the banks of the Seine

52 BC Labienus, Caesar's lieutenant, defeats the Gauls under Camulogenes. The Parisii destroy their own city

4500	400	300	200	100 BC

Parisii gold coin minted on the Ile de la Cité

300 BC Parisii tribe settle on the Ile de la Cité

100 BC Romans rebuild the Ile de la Cité and create a new town on the Left Bank

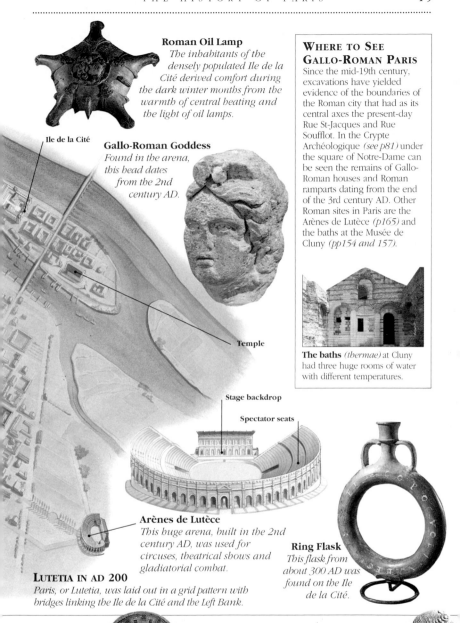

Roman Oil Lamp
The inhabitants of the densely populated Ile de la Cité derived comfort during the dark winter months from the warmth of central heating and the light of oil lamps.

Ile de la Cité

Gallo-Roman Goddess
Found in the arena, this head dates from the 2nd century AD.

WHERE TO SEE GALLO-ROMAN PARIS
Since the mid-19th century, excavations have yielded evidence of the boundaries of the Roman city that had as its central axes the present-day Rue St-Jacques and Rue Soufflot. In the Crypte Archéologique *(see p81)* under the square of Notre-Dame can be seen the remains of Gallo-Roman houses and Roman ramparts dating from the end of the 3rd century AD. Other Roman sites in Paris are the Arènes de Lutèce *(p165)* and the baths at the Musée de Cluny *(pp154 and 157)*.

The baths *(thermae)* at Cluny had three huge rooms of water with different temperatures.

Temple

Stage backdrop

Spectator seats

Arènes de Lutèce
This huge arena, built in the 2nd century AD, was used for circuses, theatrical shows and gladiatorial combat.

Ring Flask
This flask from about 300 AD was found on the Ile de la Cité.

LUTETIA IN AD 200
Paris, or Lutetia, was laid out in a grid pattern with bridges linking the Ile de la Cité and the Left Bank.

Roman floor mosaic from the Cluny baths

200 Romans add arena, baths and villas

285 Barbarians advance, Lutetia swept by fire

360 Julien, prefect of Gaul, is proclaimed emperor. Lutetia changes its name to Paris

0	100 AD	200	300	400

250 Early Christian martyr, St. Denis, beheaded in Montmartre

451 Sainte Geneviève galvanizes the Parisians to repulse Attila the Hun

485–508 Clovis, leader of the Franks, defeats the Romans. Paris becomes Christian

Medieval Paris

Manuscript illumination

THROUGHOUT THE MIDDLE AGES, strategically placed towns like Paris, positioned at a river crossing, became important centers of political power and learning. The Church played a crucial part in intellectual and spiritual life. It provided the impetus for education and for technological advances, such as the drainage of land and the digging of canals. The population was still confined mainly to the Ile de la Cité and the Left Bank. When the marshes *(marais)* were drained in the 12th century, the city was able to expand.

EXTENT OF THE CITY
- 1300
- Today

Sainte-Chapelle
The upper chapel of this medieval masterpiece (see pp88–9) was reserved for the royal family.

The Ile de la Cité, including the towers of the Conciergerie and Sainte-Chapelle, features in the pages for June.

Octagonal Table
Medieval manor houses had wooden furniture like this trestle table.

Drainage allowed more land to be cultivated.

Weavers' Window
Medieval craftsmen formed guilds, and many church windows were dedicated to their crafts.

A rural life was led by most Parisians, who worked on the land. The actual city occupied only a tiny area.

TIMELINE

512 Death of Sainte Geneviève. She is buried next to Clovis

725–732 Muslims attack Gaul

845–862 Normans attack Paris

500	700	800	900

543–556 Foundation of St-Germain-des-Prés

Golden hand reliquary of Charlemagne

800 Charlemagne crowned emperor by the pope

Notre-Dame
The great Gothic cathedrals took many years to build. Work continued on Notre-Dame from 1163 to 1334.

University Seal
The University of Paris was founded in 1215.

The Monasteries
Monks of many different orders lived in monasteries in Paris, especially on the Left Bank of the Seine.

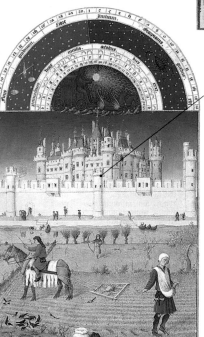

The Louvre of Charles V
with its defensive wall is seen here from the Ile de la Cité.

The Nobility
From the mid-14th century, dress was considered to be a mark of class; noble ladies wore high pointed hats.

THE MONTHS: JUNE AND OCTOBER
This illuminated prayer book and calendar, the Très Riches Heures (left and above), was made for the Duc de Berri in 1416. It shows many Paris buildings.

A MEDIEVAL ROMANCE

It was in the cloisters of Notre-Dame that the romance between the monk Abélard and the young Héloïse began. Pierre Abélard was the most original theologian of the 12th century and was hired as a tutor to the 17-year-old niece of a canon. A love affair soon developed between teacher and pupil. In his wrath, Héloïse's uncle had the scholar castrated; Héloïse took refuge in a convent for the rest of her life.

1010–22 Christians burn Jews and heretics

1167 Les Halles food market created on the Right Bank of the Seine

1253 The Sorbonne opens

Joan of Arc

1380 The Bastille fortress completed

1000	1100	1200	1300	1400

1079 Birth of Pierre Abélard

1163 Work starts on Notre-Dame cathedral

1245 Work starts on Sainte-Chapelle

1226–70 Reign of Louis IX, St. Louis

1430 Henry VI of England crowned King of France after Joan of Arc fails to defend Paris

1215 Paris University founded

Renaissance Paris

AT THE END of the Hundred Years' War with England, Paris was in a terrible state. By the time the occupying English army had left in 1453, the city lay in ruins, with many houses and trees burned. Louis XI brought back prosperity and a new interest in art, architecture, decoration and clothes. During the course of the 16th century, French kings came under the spell of the Italian Renaissance. Their architects made the first attempts at town planning, creating elegant uniform buildings and open urban spaces like the magnificent Place Royale.

Couple in fine courtly dress

EXTENT OF THE CITY

☐ 1590   ☐ Today

A Knight Preparing to Joust
The Place Royale was the setting for jousting displays well into the 17th century.

Printing Press (1470)
Religious tracts, mainly in Latin, were printed on the first press at the Sorbonne.

Jewel-encrusted Pendant
A sign of the new prosperity, jewels became an important part of dress.

Pont Notre-Dame
This bridge with its row of houses was built at the start of the 15th century. The Pont Neuf (1589) was the first bridge without houses.

PLACE ROYALE
Built by Henri IV in about 1609, Paris's first square (see p94), with grand symmetrical houses around a central open space, was the residence of the aristocracy.

TIMELINE

1453 End of the Hundred Years' War with England

François I

1516 François I invites Leonardo da Vinci to France. He brings the *Mona Lisa* with him

1450	1460	1470	1480	1490	1500	1510	1520

1469 First French printing works starts operating at the Sorbonne

1528 François I takes up residence in the Louvre

16th-Century Knife-and-Fork Set
Ornate knife-and-fork sets were used in the dining rooms of the wealthy to carve joints of meat. Diners used hands or spoons for eating.

WHERE TO SEE RENAISSANCE PARIS TODAY

Besides the Place des Vosges with its fine buildings, there are many examples of the Renaissance in Paris today. Churches include the Tour St-Jacques (p115), St-Etienne-du-Mont (p153) and St-Eustache (p114). Mansions such as the Hôtel Carnavalet (pp96–7) have recently been restored, and the staircases, courtyard and turrets of the Hôtel de Cluny (pp154–5) date from 1485 to 1896.

The rood screen of St-Etienne-du-Mont (about 1520) is of outstanding delicacy.

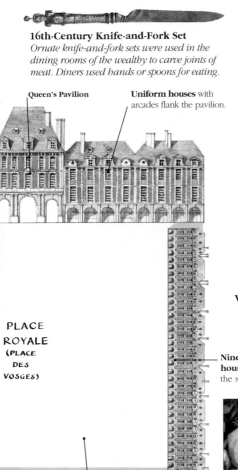

Queen's Pavilion

Uniform houses with arcades flank the pavilion.

PLACE ROYALE (PLACE DES VOSGES)

King's Pavilion

Duels were fought in the center of the square in the 17th century.

Walnut Dresser (about 1545)
Elegant carved wooden furniture decorated the homes of the wealthy.

Nine symmetrical houses line each side of the square.

Hyante and Climente
Toussaint Dubreuil and other artists took up Renaissance mythological themes.

1534 Ignatius of Loyola founds the Society of Jesus	**1546** Work starts on new Louvre palace; first stone quay built along Seine	**1559** Primitive street lanterns introduced; Louvre completed	**1572** St. Bartholomew's Day massacre of Protestants	**1589** Henri III assassinated at St-Cloud, near Paris
				1609 Henri IV begins building Place des Vosges

1530	1540	1550	1560	1570	1580	1590	1600

1547 François I dies

1534 Founding of the Collège de France

1559 Henri II killed in a Paris tournament

1533 Hôtel de Ville rebuilt

1589 Protestant Henri of Navarre converts to Catholicism, crowned as Henri IV

1589 Henri IV completes Pont-Neuf and improves capital's water supply

1610 Henri IV is assassinated by Ravaillac, a religious fanatic

The assassin Ravaillac

The Sun King's Paris

THE 17TH CENTURY in France, which became known as the *Grand Siècle* (the great century), is epitomized by the glittering extravagance of Louis XIV (the Sun King) and his court at Versailles. In Paris, imposing buildings, squares, theaters and aristocratic **hôtels** (mansions) were built. Beneath this brilliant surface lay the absolute power of the monarch. By the end of Louis' reign, the cost of his extravagance and of waging almost continuous war with France's neighbors led to a decline in the monarchy.

Emblem of the Sun King

EXTENT OF THE CITY

▨ *1657*	☐ *Today*

The Gardens of Versailles
Louis XIV devoted a lot of time to the gardens, which were designed by André Le Nôtre.

The mansard roof, with its slopes at both sides and both ends, came to typify French roofs of this period.

An open staircase rose from the internal courtyard.

Cross section of the living quarters

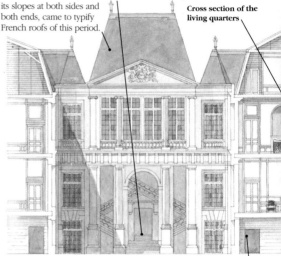

Louis XIV as Jupiter
On ascending the throne in 1661, Louis, depicted here as Jupiter triumphant, ended the civil wars that had been raging since his childhood.

The ground floor contained the servants' quarters.

Chest of Drawers
This gilded piece was made by André-Charles Boulle for the Grand Trianon at Versailles.

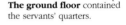

TIMELINE

1610 Louis XIII's accession marks the start of the *Grand Siècle*

Louis XIII

1624 Completion of Tuileries Palace

1631 Launch of *La Gazette,* Paris's first newspaper

Cardinal Mazarin

1643 Death of Louis XIII. Regency under control of Marie de Médicis and Cardinal Mazarin

1661 Louis XIV becomes absolute monarch. Enlargement of Château de Versailles begun

1610	1620	1630	1640	1650	1660

1622 Paris becomes an episcopal see

1629 Richelieu, Louis XIII's first minister, builds Palais Royal

1638 Birth of Louis XIV

1662 Colbert, Louis XIV's finance minister, founds Gobelins tapestry works

1614 Final meeting of the Estates Council (the main legislative assembly) before the Revolution

1627 Development of the Ile St-Louis

Weaving frame

Ceiling by Charles Le Brun
Court painter to Louis XIV, Le Brun decorated many ceilings like this one at the Hôtel Carnavalet (see p96).

Madame de Maintenon
When the queen died in 1683, Louis married Madame de Maintenon, shown here in a framed painting by Caspar Netscher.

Decorated Fan
For special court fêtes, Louis XIV often stipulated that women carry fans.

The Galerie d'Hercule
with Le Brun ceiling

Formal classical garden

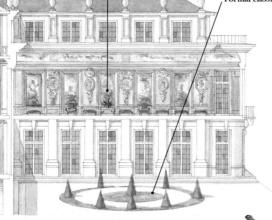

Dôme Church (1706)

HÔTEL LAMBERT (1640)
In the 17th century, the aristocracy built luxurious town houses with grand staircases, courtyards, formal gardens, coach houses and stables.

WHERE TO SEE THE SUN KING'S PARIS
Many 17th-century mansions, such as the Hôtel Lambert, still exist in Paris, but not all are open to the public. However, the Hôtel des Invalides *(p184)*, the Dôme Church *(p188)*, the Palais du Luxembourg *(p172)* and Versailles *(p248)* all give a magnificent impression of the period.

Neptune Cup
Made from lapis lazuli with a silver Neptune on top, this cup was part of Louis' vast collection of art objects.

1667 Louvre rebuilt and observatory established	**1682** Court moves to Versailles, where it stays until the Revolution	**1686** Le Procope, Paris's first café	**1702** Paris first divided into 20 arrondissements (districts)		**1715** Louis XIV dies

1670	1680	1690	1700	1710

1670 Hôtel des Invalides built

1692 Great famines due to bad harvests and wars

1689 Pont Royal built

Statue of Louis XIV at Musée Carnavalet

Paris in the Age of Enlightenment

T HE ENLIGHTENMENT, with its emphasis on scientific reason and a critical approach to existing ideas and society, was centered in the city of Paris. In contrast, nepotism and corruption were rife at Louis XV's court at Versailles. Meanwhile the economy thrived; the arts flourished as never before; and intellectuals, such as Voltaire and Rousseau, were renowned throughout Europe. In Paris, the population rose to about 650,000: town planning was developed, and the first accurate street map of the city appeared in 1787.

Bust of François Marie Arouet, known as Voltaire

EXTENT OF THE CITY

☐ *1720* ☐ *Today*

Nautical Instruments
As the science of navigation advanced, scientists developed telescopes and trigonometric instruments (used for measuring longitude and latitude).

18th-Century Wigs
These were not only a mark of fashion but also a way of indicating the wearer's class and importance.

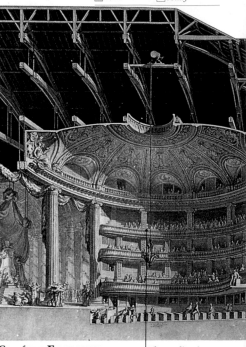

COMÉDIE FRANÇAISE
The Age of Enlightenment saw a burst of dramatic activity and the opening of new theaters, such as the Comédie Française (see p120). Today the Théâtre Français company is based here.

The auditorium, with 1,913 seats, was the largest in Paris.

TIMELINE

1734 Fontaine des Quatre Saisons built

1748 Montesquieu's *L'Esprit des Lois* (an influential work about different forms of government) published

1720	1730	1740	1750

1722 City's first fire brigade founded

Fireman

ENCYCLOPÉDIE

1751 First volume of Diderot's *Encyclopedia* published

Madame de Pompadour
Although generally remembered as the mistress of Louis XV, she was renowned as a patron of the arts and had great political influence.

Chocolate Pot
By the 18th century, bourgeois families could afford tobacco, tea, chocolate and coffee from Asia and the New World.

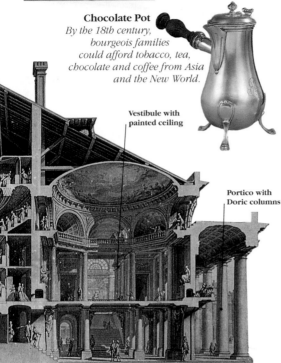

Vestibule with painted ceiling

Portico with Doric columns

The Catacombs
These were set up in 1785 as a more hygienic alternative to Paris's cemeteries (see p179).

WHERE TO SEE ENLIGHTENMENT PARIS

The district around the Rue de Lille, the Rue de Varenne and the Rue de Grenelle (pp182–3) has many luxurious town houses, or *hôtels*, which were built by the aristocracy during the first half of the 18th century. Memorabilia from the lives of the great intellectuals Voltaire and Jean-Jacques Rousseau is in the Musée Carnavalet (pp96–7), along with 18th-century interior designs and paintings.

Churches were built throughout the Enlightenment. St-Sulpice (p172) was completed in 1776.

Le Procope (p140) is the oldest café in Paris. It was frequented by Voltaire and Rousseau.

1757 First oil street lamps

1764 Madame de Pompadour dies

1774 Louis XV, great grandson of Louis XIV, dies

1778 France supports American independence

1785 David paints the *Oath of the Horatii*

1760 | 1770 | 1780

c.1760 Place de la Concorde, Panthéon and Ecole Militaire built

1762 Rousseau's *Emile* and the *Social Contract*

Rousseau, philosopher and writer, believed that humans were naturally good and had been corrupted by society

1782 First pavements built, in the Place du Théâtre Français

1783 Montgolfier brothers make the first hot-air balloon ascent

Paris During the Revolution

A plate made in celebration of the Revolution

IN 1789, MOST PARISIANS were still living in squalor and poverty, as they had since the Middle Ages. Rising inflation and opposition to Louis XVI culminated in the storming of the Bastille, the king's prison; the Republic was founded three years later. However, the Reign of Terror soon followed, when those suspected of betraying the Revolution were executed without trial: more than 60,000 lost their lives. The bloody excesses of Robespierre, the zealous revolutionary, led to his overthrow, and a new government, the Directory, was set up in 1795.

EXTENT OF THE CITY

| 1796 | Today |

The prison turrets were set on fire.

The French guards, who were on the side of the revolutionaries, arrived late in the afternoon with two cannons.

Declaration of the Rights of Man and the Citizen
The Enlightenment ideals of equality and human dignity were enshrined in the Declaration. This illustration is the preface to the 1791 Constitution.

REPUBLICAN CALENDAR
The revolutionaries believed that the world was starting again, so they abolished the existing church calendar and took September 22, 1792, the day the Republic was declared, as the first day of the new era. The Republican calendar had 12 equal months, each subdivided into three ten-day periods, with the remaining 5 days of each year set aside for public holidays. All the months of the year were given poetic names that linked them to nature and the seasons – such as fog, snow, seed time, flowers, harvest time and so on.

A colored engraving by Tresca showing *Ventôse*, the windy month (Feb 19–Mar 20), from the new Republican calendar

Drawbridge

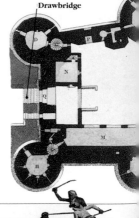

TIMELINE

1789	1790	1791	1792
Jul 14 Fall of the Bastille			
Aug 4 Abolition of feudalism			
Aug 26 Declaration of the Rights of Man and the Citizen			
Sep 17 Law of Suspects passed: the Terror begins			**Aug 10** The storming of the Tuileries

Cartoon on the three Estates: the clergy, the nobility and the awakening populace

Lafayette, Commander of the National Guard, takes his oath to the Constitution

Jul 17 Champ de Mars massacre

Apr 25 *"La Marseillaise"* composed

May 5 The Estates council meets

Jul 14 Fête de la Fédération

Paper Money
Bonds, called assignats, *were used to fund the Revolution from 1790–1793.*

"La Marseillaise"
The revolutionaries' marching song is now the national anthem.

The Sans Culottes
By 1792, the wearing of trousers instead of breeches (culottes) was a political symbol of Paris's artisans and shopkeepers.

"Patriotic" Chair
The back of this wooden chair is topped by red bonnets, symbols of revolutionary politics.

Wallpaper
Commemorative wallpaper was produced to celebrate the Revolution.

The dead and wounded totaled 171 by the end of the day.

Coin tower

Great court

Well court

Guillotine
This was used for the first time in France in April 1792.

STORMING OF THE BASTILLE
The Bastille was overrun on July 14, 1789, and the seven prisoners held there were released. The defenders (32 Swiss guards, 82 wounded soldiers and the governor) were massacred.

Jun 20 Invasion of the Tuileries	**Jan 21** Execution of Louis XVI	**Oct 16** Execution of Marie Antoinette	**Apr 5** Execution of Danton and supporters	**Aug 22** New constitution: the Directory
Aug 10 Overthrow of Louis XVI	**Autumn** Robespierre in control of Committee of Public Safety	**Nov 24** Churches closed	**Nov 19** Jacobin Club (a revolutionary pressure group) closed	

1793	1794	1795
Sep 20 Battle of Valmy	**Jul 13** Assassination of Marat, founder of *L'Ami du Peuple*, the revolutionary newspaper	*Robespierre, revolutionary and architect of the Terror*
Sep 2–6 September massacres		**Jul 27** Execution of Robespierre

Napoleonic Paris

NAPOLEON BONAPARTE WAS the most brilliant general in the French army. The instability of the new government after the Revolution gave him the chance to seize power, and in November 1799 he installed himself in the Tuileries Palace as First Consul. He crowned himself Emperor in May 1804. Napoleon established a centralized administration and a code of laws, reformed France's educational system and set out to make Paris the most beautiful city in the world. The city was endowed with grand monuments and embellished with the spoils of conquest. His power was always fragile and dependent on incessant wars. In March 1814, Prussian, Austrian and Russian armies invaded Paris, and Napoleon fled to Elba. He returned to Paris in 1815 but was defeated at Waterloo and died in exile in 1821.

Napoleon's imperial crown

EXTENT OF THE CITY
☐ *1810*   ☐ *Today*

Château Malmaison
This was the favorite home of Josephine, Napoleon's first wife.

Ladies-in-Waiting hold Josephine's train.

Opaline-Glass Clock
The decoration on this clock echoed the fashion for draperies.

Elephant Project
This monument was planned for the center of the Place de la Bastille.

Eagle's Flight
Napoleon's flight to Elba in 1814 was satirized in this cartoon.

TIMELINE

1797 Battle of Rivoli

1799 Napoleon seizes power

1800 Banque de France founded

1800 Napoleon returns from Egypt on his ship *L'Orient*

1802 Legion of Honour established

1804 Napoleon crowned

1806 Arc de Triomphe commissioned

1809 Napoleon divorces Josephine and marries Marie Louise

1812 Russian campaign ends in defeat

1814 Napoleon abdicates

1815 Waterloo; second abdication of Napoleon. Restoration of the monarchy

1821 Napoleon dies

Napoleon's death mask

1800	1805	1810	1815	1820

Bronze Table Top
Inlaid with Napoleon's portrait, this table marks the victory at Austerlitz.

Josephine kneels before Napoleon.

Napoleon holds the crown for his Empress, Josephine.

Russian Cossacks in the Palais Royale
After Napoleon's defeat and flight in 1814, Paris suffered the humiliation of being occupied by foreign troops, including Austrians, Prussians and Russians.

The Pope makes the sign of the cross.

The Arc de Triomphe du Carrousel was erected in 1806 and crowned with the horses looted from St. Mark's, Venice.

WHERE TO SEE NAPOLEONIC PARIS

Many of the grand monuments Napoleon planned for Paris were never built, but two triumphal arches, the Arc de Triomphe (pp208–9) and Arc de Triomphe du Carrousel (p122), were a major part of his legacy. La Madeleine church (p214) was also inaugurated in his reign, and much of the Louvre was rebuilt (pp122–3). Examples of the Empire style can be seen at Malmaison (p255) and at the Carnavalet (pp96–7).

NAPOLEON'S CORONATION
Napoleon's rather dramatic crowning took place in 1804. In this recreation by J. L. David, the Pope, summoned to Notre-Dame, looks on as Napoleon crowns his Empress just before crowning himself.

The Empress
Josephine was divorced by Napoleon in 1809.

1842 First railroad line between Paris and St-Germain-en-Laye opens

1825	1830	1835	1840	1845

1830 Revolution in Paris and advent of constitutional monarchy

1831 Victor Hugo's *Notre-Dame de Paris* published

Cholera epidemic hits Paris

1840 Reburial of Napoleon at Les Invalides

Napoleon's tomb

The Grand Transformation

IN 1848 PARIS SAW a second revolution that brought down the recently restored monarchy. In the uncertainties that followed, Napoleon's nephew assumed power in the same way as his uncle before him – by a *coup d'état*. He proclaimed himself Napoleon III in 1851. Under his rule Paris was transformed into the most magnificent city in Europe. He entrusted the task of modernization to Baron Haussmann. Haussmann demolished the crowded, unsanitary streets of the medieval city and created a well-ordered, well-ventilated capital within a geometrical grid of avenues and boulevards. Neighboring districts such as Auteuil were annexed, creating the suburbs.

Lamp post outside the Opéra

EXTENT OF THE CITY

☐ *1859*   ☐ *Today*

Boulevard des Italiens
This tree-lined avenue, painted by Edmond Georges Grandjean (1889), was one of the most fashionable of the new boulevards.

Arc de Triomphe

Twelve avenues formed a star (*étoile*).

AVE DE FRIEDLAND

AVE HOCHE

AVE DE WAGRAM

PLACE

AVE MAC-MAHON

AVE CARNOT

Laying the Sewers
This engraving from 1861 shows the early work for laying the sewer system (see p190) from La Villette to Les Halles. Most was the work of the engineer Belgrand.

Circular Billboard
Distinctive billboards advertised opera and theater performances.

Grand mansions were built around the Arc de Triomphe between 1860 and 1868.

TIMELINE

1851 Napoleon III declares the Second Empire

1852 Haussmann begins massive town-planning schemes

Viewing the exhibits at the World Exhibition

1855 World Exhibition

1850	1852	1854	1856	1858

20 centimes stamp showing Napoleon III

1857 The poet, Baudelaire, prosecuted for obscenity for *The Flowers of Evil*

PLACE DE L'ETOILE

The new plan for the center of Paris included redesigning the area at one end of the Champs-Elysées (Elysian Fields). Haussmann created a star of 12 broad avenues around the new Arc de Triomphe.
(The inset map shows the area as it was in 1790.)

Drinking Fountain

In 1840, 50 fountains were erected in poor areas of Paris through the generosity of the English francophile Richard Wallace.

Fields

Avenue des Champs-Elysées

Site of Arc de Triomphe

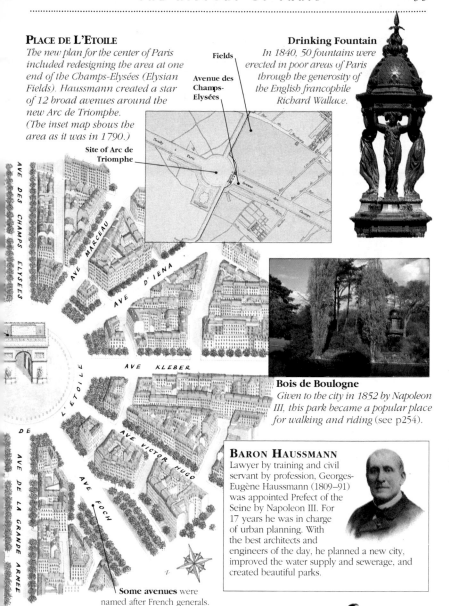

Bois de Boulogne

Given to the city in 1852 by Napoleon III, this park became a popular place for walking and riding (see p254).

BARON HAUSSMANN

Lawyer by training and civil servant by profession, Georges-Eugène Haussmann (1809–91) was appointed Prefect of the Seine by Napoleon III. For 17 years he was in charge of urban planning. With the best architects and engineers of the day, he planned a new city, improved the water supply and sewerage, and created beautiful parks.

Some avenues were named after French generals.

1861 Garnier designs new Opera House

1863 The nudity in Manet's *Le Déjeuner sur l'Herbe* causes a scandal and is rejected by the Academy *(see pp144–5)*

1867 World Exhibition

1870 Napoleon's wife, Eugénie, flees Paris at threat of war

1860	1862	1864	1866	1868

1863 Credit Lyonnais bank established

1862 Victor Hugo's epic novel of Paris's poor, *Les Misérables,* published

1868 Press censorship relaxed

1870 Start of Franco-Prussian War

The Belle Epoque

Art Nouveau pendant

THE FRANCO-PRUSSIAN War culminated in the terrible Siege of Paris. When peace came in 1871, it fell to the new government, the Third Republic, to bring about economic recovery. From about 1890, life was transformed: the automobile, airplane, movies, telephone and gramophone all contributed to the enjoyment of life, and the Belle Epoque (beautiful age) was born. Paris became a glittering city where the new style, Art Nouveau, decorated buildings and objects. The paintings of the Impressionists, such as Renoir, reflected the joie de vivre of the times, while later those of Matisse, Braque and Picasso heralded the modern movement in art.

EXTENT OF THE CITY

☐ 1895   ☐ Today

The interior was arranged as tiers of galleries around a central grand staircase.

Cabaret Poster
Toulouse-Lautrec's posters immortalized the singers and dancers of the cafés and cabaret clubs of Montmartre, where artists and writers congregated in the 1890s.

Electricity illuminated the window displays.

Windows facing the Boulevard Haussmann displayed the goods for sale.

Central Hall of the Grand Palais
The Grand Palais (pp206–7) was built to house two huge exhibitions of French painting and sculpture at the World Exhibition of 1889.

Art Nouveau Cash Register
Even ordinary objects like this cash register were beautified by the new style.

TIMELINE

1871 Third Republic established

1874 Monet paints first Impressionist picture: *Impression: Soleil levant*

Louis Pasteur

1892 Panama Canal built by Ferdinand de Lesseps, a Paris engineer

1889 Eiffel Tower built

1870	1875	1880	1885	1890

Zoo animals were shot to feed the hungry (see p224)

1870 Siege of Paris

Entrance ticket to the exhibition

1885 Louis Pasteur discovers rabies vaccine

1891 First metro station opens

1889 Great Exhibition

Citroën 5CV
France led the world in the early development of the automobile. By 1900 the Citroën began to be seen on the streets of Paris, and long-distance motor racing was popular.

WHERE TO SEE THE BELLE EPOQUE

Art Nouveau can be seen in monumental buildings like the Grand Palais and Petit Palais *(p206)*, while the Galeries Layfayette *(pp212–13)* and the Pharamond restaurant *(p300)* have beautiful Belle Epoque interiors. The Musée d'Orsay *(pp144–7)* has many objects from this period.

The glass dome could be seen from all parts of the store.

Moulin Rouge (1890)
The old, decorative windmills of Montmartre became nightclubs, like the world-famous Moulin Rouge (red windmill) (see p226).

The entrance to the metro at Porte Dauphine was the work of leading Art Nouveau designer Hector Guimard *(p226)*.

GALERIES LAFAYETTE (1906)
This beautiful department store , with its dome of colored glass and wrought iron, was a sign of the new prosperity.

The Naughty Nineties
The Lumière brothers captured the daring negligée fashions of the 1890s in the first moving images of the cinematograph.

The doorway of No. 29 Avenue Rapp *(p191)*, in the Eiffel Tower quarter, is a fine example of Art Nouveau.

1894–1906 Dreyfus Affair

Captain Dreyfus was publicly humiliated for selling secrets to the Prussians. He was later found innocent

1907 Picasso paints *Les Demoiselles d'Avignon*

1913 Proust publishes first volume of *Remembrance of Things Past*

1895	1900	1905	1910

1898 Pierre and Marie Curie discover radium

1909 Blériot flies across the English Channel

1911 Diaghilev brings the Russian ballet to Paris

1895 Lumière brothers introduce cinematography

Avant-Garde Paris

FROM THE 1920s TO THE 1940s, Paris became a mecca for artists, musicians, writers and filmmakers. The city was alive with new movements, such as Cubism and Surrealism, represented by Cézanne, Picasso, Braque, Man Ray and Duchamp. Many new trends came from **Office chair by Le Corbusier** the United States, as writers and musicians including Ernest Hemingway, Gertrude Stein and Sidney Bechet took up residence in Paris. In architecture, the geometric shapes created by Le Corbusier changed the face of the modern building.

EXTENT OF THE CITY
☐ 1940   ☐ Today

Napoleon by Abel Gance
Paris has always been a city for filmmakers. In 1927, Abel Gance made an innovative movie about Napoleon, using triple screens and wide-angle lenses.

Occupied Paris
Paris was under occupation for most of World War II. The Eiffel Tower was a favorite spot for German soldiers.

Josephine Baker
Arriving in Paris in 1925, the outlandish dancer catapulted to fame in "La Revue Nègre" wearing nothing but feathers.

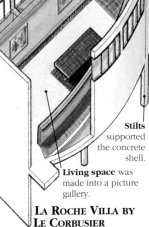

Stilts supported the concrete shell.

Living space was made into a picture gallery.

LA ROCHE VILLA BY LE CORBUSIER
Made from concrete and steel, with straight lines, horizontal windows and a flat roof, this house (1923) epitomized the new style.

Sidney Bechet
In the 1930s and 1940s, the jazz clubs of Paris resounded with the swing music of such black musicians as the saxophonist Sidney Bechet.

TIMELINE

1919 Treaty of Versailles signed in the Hall of Mirrors

1924 Olympic Games held in Paris

1924 André Breton publishes Surrealist Manifesto

1925 Art Deco style first seen at the Exposition des Arts Décoratifs

PARIS-1925

| 1914 | 1916 | 1918 | 1920 | 1922 | 1924 | 1926 | 1928 |

1914–18 World War I. Paris is under threat of German attack, saved by the Battle of the Marne. A shell hits St-Gervais-St-Protais

World War I soldier in uniform

1920 Interment of the Unknown Soldier

An eternal flame for the Unknown Soldier burns under the Arc de Triomphe

Fashion in the 1940s

After World War II, the classic look for men and women was reminiscent of military uniforms.

The roof was designed as a garden terrace.

Airmail Poster
Airmail routes developed during the 1930s, especially to French North Africa.

The bedroom was above the dining room.

The kitchen was built at the back with a sloping glass roof.

The garage was built into the ground floor.

Windows were arranged in a horizontal strip.

The old Trocadéro was changed to the Palais de Chaillot *(see p198)* for the World Exhibition.

WHERE TO SEE AVANT-GARDE PARIS

La Roche Villa is now part of the Fondation Le Corbusier *(p254)* and can be visited in the Paris suburb of Auteuil. The Musée du Cinéma *(p199)* has a retrospective of the French cinema. For fashion from this period don't miss the Musée de la Mode et du Costume *(p201)*.

***Claudine in Paris** by Colette*
The Claudine series of novels, written by Colette Willy, known simply as "Colette," was extremely popular in the 1930s.

1931 Colonial Exhibition	*A visitor to the exhibition in colonial dress*			**1937** Picasso paints *Guernica* in protest at the Spanish Civil War	**1940** World War II: Paris bombed and occupied by Nazis	
1930	1932	1934	1936	1938	1940	1942
		1934 Riots and strikes in response to the Great Depression		**1937** Palais de Chaillot built		

Symbol of Free French superimposed on the victory sign

Aug 1944 Liberation of Paris

The Modern City

In 1962, A PROGRAM of renovation was started in Paris. Run-down districts like the Marais were lovingly restored. This preservation of the past is part of the late François Mitterrand's *Grand Travaux* (great works) scheme. Access has been improved to historical monuments and art collections, such as the Grand Louvre *(see pp122–9)*

Late President François Mitterrand and the Musée d'Orsay *(see pp144–7)*. The scheme has also been responsible for the building of several monuments to the modern age, including the Opéra Bastille *(see p98)* and the Cité des Sciences *(see pp236–9)*. With these, and the magnificently modern Défense and Grande Arche, Paris is ready to enter the 21st century.

EXTENT OF THE CITY
☐ *1959*   ☐ *Today*

La Grande Arche is taller and wider than Notre-Dame and runs in an axis linking the Arc de Triomphe and the Louvre Pyramid.

Christo's Pont Neuf
To create a work of art, the Bulgarian-born artist Christo wrapped Paris's oldest bridge, the Pont Neuf, in fabric in 1985.

Simone de Beauvoir
Influential philosopher and life-long companion of J.P. Sartre, de Beauvoir fought for the liberation of women in the 1950s.

Shopping center

Citroën Goddess (1956)
With its ultramodern lines, this became Paris's most prestigious car.

TIMELINE

1945	1950	1955	1960	1965	1970	1975

1950 Construction of UNESCO, and the Musée de Radio-France

1962 André Malraux, Minister of Culture, begins renovation program of run-down districts and monuments

Ducting at the Pompidou Center

1977 Pompidou Center opens. Jacques Chirac is installed as first elected Mayor of Paris since 1871

President de Gaulle

1958 Establishment of Fifth Republic with de Gaulle as President

1964 Reorganization of the Ile de France

1968 Student riots and workers strikes in the Latin Quarter

1969 Les Halles market transfers to Rungis

1973 Construction of Montparnasse Tower and the Périphérique (ring road)

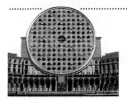

Marne La Vallée
Like a gigantic loudspeaker, this residential complex is in one of Paris's dormitory towns near Disneyland Paris.

Chanel Designs
Paris is the center of the fashion world, with important shows each year.

The Pompidou Center
The nation's collection of modern art is housed in this popular building (see pp110–13).

The Fiat Tower is one of Europe's tallest buildings.

Opéra de la Bastille
It was built in 1989 to mark the bicentenary of the fall of the Bastille.

The Défense Palace, housing the center for industry, is the oldest tower.

LA DÉFENSE
This huge business center was started on the edge of Paris in 1958. Today 30,000 people commute here from Paris's surrounding areas.

STUDENTS AT THE BARRICADES
In May 1968 Paris saw a revolution of a kind. The Latin Quarter was taken over by students and workers. What began as a protest movement against the war in Vietnam spread to other issues and became an expression of discontent with the government. President de Gaulle rode out the storm, but his prestige was severely damaged.

Rioting students clash with police

1985 Christo wraps Pont Neuf

Participant of the bi-centenary wearing the French national colors

Victorious French soccer team holding aloft the World Cup trophy in Paris

1980	1985	1990	1995	2000	2005	2010

1980 Thousands greet Pope John-Paul on his official visit

1989 Bicentenary celebrations to mark the French Revolution

1998 France hosts – and wins – the 1998 soccer World Cup tournament

PARIS AT A GLANCE

THERE ARE NEARLY 300 places of interest described in the *Area by Area* section of this book. A broad range of sights is covered: from the ancient Conciergerie and its grisly associations with the guillotine *(see p81)*, to the modern opera house, the Opéra de la Bastille *(see p98)*; from No. 3 Rue Volta *(see p103)*, one of the oldest houses in Paris, to the elegant Musée Picasso *(see pp100–101)*. To help make the most of your stay, use the following 20 pages as a time-saving guide to the best Paris has to offer. Museums and galleries, historic churches, spacious parks, gardens and squares all have sections. There are also guides to Paris's famous personalities. Each sight has a cross reference to its own full entry. Below are the top tourist attractions to start you off.

PARIS'S TOP TOURIST ATTRACTIONS

La Défense
See p255.

Sainte-Chapelle
See pp88–9.

Palace of Versailles
See pp248–53.

Pompidou Center
See pp110–13.

Musée d'Orsay
See pp144–7.

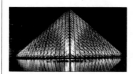

Musée du Louvre
See pp122–9.

Jardin du Luxembourg
See p172.

Eiffel Tower
See pp192–3.

Bois de Boulogne
See pp254–5.

Notre-Dame
See pp82–5.

Arc de Triomphe
See pp208–9.

The Dôme Church, adjoining the Hôtel des Invalides

Celebrated Visitors and Residents

THROUGHOUT ITS HISTORY, Paris has lured the world's greatest talents. It has been a haven for those seeking a place to express themselves and live life to the fullest. Thomas Jefferson, before becoming president of the United States in 1801, lived near the Avenue des Champs-Elysées in the 1780s and called the city "everyone's second home." Over the centuries, Paris has been one of the creative centers of the Western world. It has accommodated kings and political exiles (Americans, Russians, Chinese and Vietnamese among them) who went on to achieve power, and painters, writers, poets and musicians who became household names. All succumbed to the pull of the city's beauty; its distinctive way of life; its sense of style; and, of course, its superb gastronomy.

Marlene Dietrich *(1901–92)*
The German-born singer gave some of her best shows at the Olympia music hall (see p337).

Champs-Elysées

Chaillot Quarter

RIVER SEINE

Invalides and Eiffel Tower Quarter

Josephine Baker *(1906–75)*
The "Queen" of Paris music halls made headlines in 1925 for dancing the black bottom wearing nothing but a string of bananas. Her early performances were at the Théâtre des Champs-Elysées (see p334).

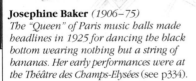

Montparnasse

Richard Wagner *(1813–83)*
After fleeing his creditors in Germany, the composer lived at No.14 Rue Jacob.

Roman Polanski *(b. 1933)*
The Polish filmmaker (left in the picture) can be seen frequently at the fashionable café La Coupole (see p311).

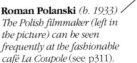

0 kilometers 1

0 miles 0.5

Montmartre

Salvador Dalí *(1904–89)*
*The Surrealist artist moved
to Paris in 1929. Later, he
was a regular at the Hôtel
Meurice at No. 228 Rue de
Rivoli (see p281). The
Espace Montmartre is
devoted to aspects of his
work (see p222).*

Pablo Picasso *(1881–1973)*
*The Spanish artist lived in
the artists' colony at the
Bateau-Lavoir (see p226).*

Vincent Van Gogh
(1853–90)
*The Dutch painter stayed
at No. 56 Rue Lepic
with his art-dealer
brother, Theo.*

Opéra Quarter

N

Tuileries Quarter

Beaubourg and Les
Halles

The Marais

St-Germain-
des-Prés

Ile de la Cité

Rudolf Nureyev *(1938–93)*
*The Russian ballet star was director
of the Ballet de l'Opéra (see p335).*

Ile St-Louis

Latin Quarter

Luxembourg
Quarter

Jardin des Plantes
Quarter

Leon Trotsky
(1879–1940)
*Before the Russian
Revolution in 1917,
leading Bolshevik
Trotsky was often seen
with Lenin in the Dôme
Café (see p311).*

Oscar Wilde *(1854–1900)*
*After his release from Reading
jail, the exiled Irish writer
died in L'Hôtel (see p281).*

Remarkable Parisians

BY VIRTUE OF ITS STRATEGIC position on the Seine, Paris has always been the economic, political and artistic hub of France. Over the centuries, many prominent and influential figures from other parts of the country and abroad have come to the city to absorb her unique spirit. In return they have left their mark: artists have brought new movements, politicians new schools of thought, musicians and filmmakers new trends and architects a new environment.

Actress Catherine Deneuve

ARTISTS

Sacré-Coeur by Utrillo (1934)

IN THE EARLY 18TH CENTURY, Jean Antoine Watteau (1684–1721) took the inspiration for his paintings from the Paris theater. Half a century later, Jean-Honoré Fragonard (1732–1806), popular painter of the Rococo, lived and died here, financially ruined by the Revolution. Later, Paris became the cradle of Impressionism. Its founders, Claude Monet (1840–1926), Pierre-Auguste Renoir (1841–1919) and Alfred Sisley (1839–99), met in a Paris studio. In 1907, Pablo Picasso

(1881–1973) painted the seminal work *Les Demoiselles d'Avignon* at the Bateau-Lavoir, *(see p226)* where Georges Braque (1882–1963), Amedeo Modigliani (1884–1920) and Marc Chagall (1887–1985) also lived. Henri de Toulouse-Lautrec (1864–1901) drank and painted in Montmartre. So did Salvador Dalí (1904–89), who frequented the Café Cyrano, center of the Surrealists. The Paris School eventually moved to Montparnasse, home to sculptors Auguste Rodin (1840–1917), Constantin Brancusi (1876–1957) and Ossip Zadkine (1890–1967).

POLITICAL LEADERS

HUGH CAPET, Comte de Paris, became King of France in 987. His palace was on the Ile de la Cité. Louis XIV, XV and XVI lived at Versailles *(see pp248–53)*, but Napoleon *(see pp30–31)* preferred the Tuileries. Cardinal Richelieu (1585–1642), the power behind Louis XIII, created the Académie Française and the Palais-Royal *(see p120)*. Today the President lives in the Palais de l'Elysée *(p207)*.

FILMS AND FILMMAKERS

PARIS HAS ALWAYS been at the heart of French cinema. The prewar and immediate postwar classics were usually made on the sets of the Boulogne and Joinville studios, where whole areas of the city were reconstructed, such as the Canal St-Martin for Marcel Carné's *Hôtel du Nord*. Jean-Luc Godard and other New Wave directors preferred to shoot outdoors. Godard's *Au Bout du Souffle* (1960) with Jean-Paul Belmondo and Jean Seberg was filmed in and around the Champs-Elysées.

Simone Signoret (1921–85) and Yves Montand (1921–91), the most celebrated couple of French cinema, were long associated with the Ile de la Cité. Many actresses, such as Catherine Deneuve (b. 1943) and Isabelle Adjani (b. 1955), live in the city to be near their couturiers.

MUSICIANS

JEAN-PHILIPPE RAMEAU (1683–1764), organist and pioneer of harmony, is associated with St-Eustache *(see p114)*. Hector Berlioz (1803–69) had his *Te Deum* first performed there in 1855, and Franz Liszt (1811–86) his *Messe Solemnelle* in 1866. A great dynasty of organists, the Couperins, gave recitals in St-Gervais–St-Protais *(see p99)*.

The stage of the Opéra *(see p215)* has seen many talents, but audiences have not always been appreciative. Richard Wagner (1813–83) had his *Tannhäuser* hooted down. George Bizet's *Carmen*

Portrait of Cardinal Richelieu by Philippe de Champaigne (about 1635)

(1838–75) was booed, as was *Peléas et Mélisande* by Claude Debussy (1862–1918).

Soprano Maria Callas (1923–77) gave triumphal performances here. The composer and conductor Pierre Boulez (b. 1925) has devoted his talent to experimental music at IRCAM near the Pompidou Center *(see p333),* which he helped to found.

The diminutive chanteuse, Edith Piaf (1915–63), known for her nostalgic love songs, began singing in the streets of Paris and then went on to tour the world. There is now a museum devoted to her life and work *(see p233).*

The Grand Trianon at Versailles, built by Louis Le Vau in 1668

built Notre-Dame and Sainte-Chapelle. Louis Le Vau (1612–70) and Jules Hardouin-Mansart (1646–1708) designed Versailles *(see pp248–53).* Jacques-Ange Gabriel (1698–1782) built the Petit Trianon *(see p249)* and the Place de la Concorde *(see p131).* Haussmann (1809–91) gave the city its boulevards *(see pp32–3).* Gustave Eiffel (1832–1923) built his tower in 1889. Nearly a century later, I.M. Pei added a distinctive landmark – the Louvre's glass pyramid entrance *(see p129),* and Dominique Perrault the new Bibliotheque Nationale de France *(see p246).*

WRITERS

F RENCH IS CALLED "the language of Molière," after playwright Jean Baptiste Poquelin (known as Molière) (1622–73), who helped create the Comédie-Française, now situated near his home in Rue Richelieu. The Left Bank's, Théâtre de l'Odéon was home to playwright Jean Racine (1639–99). It is near the statue of Denis Diderot (1713–84), who published his

L'Encyclopédie between 1751 and 1776. Marcel Proust (1871–1922), author of *Remembrance of Things Past,* lived on the Boulevard Haussmann. To the existentialists, the district of St-Germain was the only place to be *(see pp142–3).* Here Sylvia Beach welcomed James Joyce (1882–1941) to her bookshop on the Rue de l'Odéon. Ernest Hemingway (1899–1961) and F. Scott Fitzgerald (1896–1940) wrote novels in Montparnasse.

Proust by J.E. Blanche (about 1910)

SCIENTISTS

P ARIS HAS a Quartier Pasteur, a Boulevard Pasteur, a Pasteur metro and the world-famous Institut Pasteur *(see p247),* all in honor of Louis Pasteur (1822–95), the great French chemist and biologist. His apartment and laboratory are faithfully preserved. The Institut Pasteur is today home to Professor Luc Montagnier, who first isolated the AIDS virus in 1983. Discoverers of radium, Pierre (1859–1906) and Marie Curie (1867–1934), also worked in Paris. The Curies have been the subject of a long-running play in Paris, *Les Palmes de M. Schutz.*

Jean-Marie Renée as Carmen (1948)

ARCHITECTS

G OTHIC, CLASSICAL, Baroque and Modernist – all co-exist in Paris. The most brilliant medieval architect was Pierre de Montreuil (d. 1267), who

EXILED IN PARIS

The Duke and Duchess of Windsor married in France after his abdication in 1936 as King Edward VIII. The city granted them a rent-free mansion in the Bois de Boulogne. Other famous exiles have included Chou En-Lai (1898–1976), Ho Chi Minh (1890–1969), Vladimir Ilyich Lenin (1870–1924), Oscar Wilde (1854–1900) and Rudolf Nureyev (1938–93).

The Duke and Duchess of Windsor

Paris's Best: Churches

THE CATHOLIC CHURCH has been the bastion of Parisian society through time. Many of the city's churches are worth visiting. Architectural styles vary, and the interiors are often spectacular. Most churches are open during the day, and many have services at regular intervals. Paris's tradition of church music is still alive. You can spend an evening enjoying the interiors while listening to an organ recital or a classical concert *(p333)*. A more detailed overview of Paris churches is on pages 48 and 49.

Early crucifix in St-Gervais–St-Protais

La Madeleine
Built in the style of a Greco-Roman temple, this church is known for its fine sculpture.

Chaillot Quarter

Champs-Elysées

Tuileries Quarter

Invalides and Eiffel Tower Quarter

St-Germain-des-Prés

Dôme Church
This memorial to the military engineer Vauban lies in the Dôme Church, where Napoleon's remains were buried in 1840.

Sainte-Chapelle
With its fine stained glass, this chapel is a medieval jewel.

Montparnasse

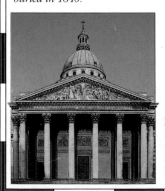

Panthéon
The Neoclassical Sainte-Geneviève, now the Panthéon, was inspired by Wren's St. Paul's Cathedral in London.

0 kilometers

0 miles   0.5

Sacré-Coeur

Above the altar in this massive basilica, the chancel vault is decorated with a vast mosaic of Christ by Luc-Olivier Merson.

Montmartre

St-Eustache

With its mixture of Gothic and Renaissance styles, this is one of the finest churches in Paris.

Opéra
Quarter

St-Paul–St-Louis

This Christ figure is one of the many rich furnishings in this Jesuit church, built in 1641 for Cardinal Richelieu.

N

Beaubourg and
Les Halles

The Marais

Ile de la Cité

Ile St-Louis

Latin Quarter

Notre-Dame

The great cathedral was left to rot after the Revolution, until Victor Hugo led a restoration campaign.

Luxembourg
Quarter

Jardin des Plantes
Quarter

St-Séverin

The west door leads to one of the finest medieval churches in the city.

Mosquée de Paris

The minaret of this 1920s mosque is 100 ft (33 m) tall.

Exploring Paris's Churches

SOME OF PARIS'S FINEST ARCHITECTURE is reflected in the churches. The great era of church building was the medieval period, but examples survive from all ages. During the Revolution (see pp28–9) churches were used as grain or weapons stores but were later restored to their former glory. Many churches have superb interiors with fine paintings and sculptures.

Facade of Eglise de la Sorbonne

MEDIEVAL

Tower of St-Germain-des-Prés

BOTH THE POINTED arch and the rose window were created in a suburb north of Paris at the Basilica de St-Denis, where most of the French kings and queens are buried. This was the first Gothic building, and it was from here that the Gothic style spread. The finest Gothic church in Paris is the city cathedral, **Notre-Dame**, tallest and most impressive of the early French cathedrals. Begun in 1163 by Bishop Maurice de Sully, it was completed in the next century by architects Jean de Chelles and Pierre de Montreuil, who added the transepts with their fine translucent rose windows. Montreuil's masterpiece is Louis IX's medieval palace chapel, **Sainte-Chapelle**, with its two-tier structure. It was built to house Christ's Crown of Thorns. Other surviving churches are **St-Germain-des-Prés**, the oldest surviving abbey church in Paris (1050); the tiny, rustic Romanesque **St-Julien-le-Pauvre**; and the Flamboyant Gothic **St-Séverin**, **St-Germain l'Auxerrois** and **St-Merry**.

RENAISSANCE

THE EFFECT of the Italian Renaissance swept through Paris in the 16th century. It led to a unique architectural style in which fine Classical detail and immense Gothic proportions resulted in an impure but attractive cocktail known as "French Renaissance." The best example in Paris is **St-Etienne-du-Mont** whose interior has the feel of a wide and light basilica. Another is **St-Eustache**, the massive market church in Les Halles, and the nave of **St-Gervais–St-Protais,** with its stained glass and carved choir stalls.

St-Gervais–St-Protais

BAROQUE AND CLASSICAL

CHURCHES and convents flourished in Paris during the 17th century, as the city expanded under Louis XIII and his son, Louis XIV. The Italian Baroque style was first seen on the majestic front of **St-Gervais–St-Protais**, built by Salomon de Brosse in 1616. The style was toned down to suit French tastes and the rational temperament of the Age of Enlightenment (see pp26–7). The result was a harmonious and monumental classicism in the form of columns and domes. One example is the **Eglise de la Sorbonne**, completed by Jacques Lemercier in 1642 for Cardinal Richelieu. Grander and more richly decorated, with a painted dome, is the church built by François Mansart to honor the birth of the Sun King at the **Val-de-Grâce** convent. The true gem of the period is Jules Hardouin-Mansart's **Dôme Church**, with its enormous gilded

---

TOWERS, DOMES AND SPIRES

The outlines of Paris's many churches have dominated her skyline since early Christian times. The Tour St-Jacques, in Gothic style, reflects the medieval love of the defensive tower. St-Etienne-du-Mont, with its pointed gable and rounded pediment, shows the transition from Gothic to Renaissance. The dome, a much-used feature of the French Baroque, was used to perfection in the Val-de-Grâce. By contrast, St-Sulpice with its severe arrangement of towers and portico is typical of the Neoclassical style. With its ornate spires, Sainte-Clothilde is a Gothic Revival church. Modern landmarks include the mosque with its minaret.

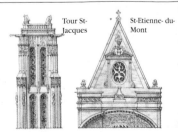

Tour St-Jacques   St-Etienne-du-Mont

Gothic   Renaissance

dome. Jesuit extravagance can be seen in **St-Paul– St Louis**, built in the style of Il Gesú in Rome. In contrast are Libéral Bruand's chapels, the **Salpêtrière** and **St-Louis-des-Invalides,** with their severe geometry and unadorned simplicity. Other fine Classical churches are **St-Joseph-des-Carmes** and the 18th-century bankers' church, **St-Roch**, with its Baroque Marian chapel.

NEOCLASSICAL

Interior of the Panthéon

AN OBSESSION with all things Greek and Roman swept France in the mid-18th century and well into the 19th century. The excavations at Pompeii (1738) and the influence of the Italian architect Andrea Palladio produced a generation of architects fascinated by the column, geometry and engineering. The best example of such a church is Jacques-Germain Soufflot's Sainte-Geneviève, now the **Panthéon**. Begun in 1773, it boasts a colonnaded dome that

was inspired by Christopher Wren's St. Paul's in London. The dome is supported by four pillars, built by Guillaume Rondelet, linking four great arches. The first colonnaded facade was Giovanni Niccolo Servandoni's **St-Sulpice**. Construction began in 1733 and consisted of a two-story portico, topped by a triangular pediment. **La Madeleine**, Napoleon's grand temple to his victorious army, was constructed on the ground plan of a Greco-Roman temple.

SECOND EMPIRE AND MODERN

FRANZ CHRISTIAN Gau's **Sainte-Clothilde** of the 1840s is the first and best example in Paris of the Gothic Revival, or *style religieux*. Showy churches were built in the new districts created by Haussmann in the Second Empire *(pp32–3)*. One of the most lovely is Victor Baltard's St-Augustin, at the intersection of the Boulevard de Malesherbes and the Boulevard de la Madeleine. Here historic detail combines with modern iron columns and girders in a soaring interior space. The great basilica of the late 19th century, **Sacré-Coeur**, was built as a gesture of religious defiance. **St-Jean l'Evangéliste** by Anatole de Baudot is an interesting modern church combining the Art Nouveau style with Islamic arches. The modern gem of Islamic architecture, the **Mosquée de Paris**, is an attractive 1920s building in the Hispanic-Moorish style. It has a grand patio inspired by the Alambra, woodwork in cedar and eucalyptus, plus a fountain.

The arches of St-Jean L'Evangéliste, reminiscent of Islamic architecture

FINDING THE CHURCHES

Val-de-Grâce

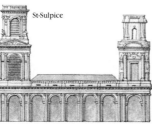

St-Sulpice

Sainte-Clothilde

Mosquée de Paris

Baroque and Classical   **Neoclassical**   **Second Empire**   **Modern**

Paris's Best: Gardens, Parks and Squares

Few cities can boast the infinite variety of styles found in Parisian gardens, parks and squares today. They date from many different periods and have been central to Parisian life for the past 300 years. The Bois de Boulogne and the Bois de Vincennes enclose the city with their lush, green open spaces, while elegant squares and landscaped gardens, such as the Jardin du *Luxembourg, brighten the inner city and provide a retreat for those craving a few moments peace from the bustling city.

Parc Monceau
This English-style park features many follies, grottoes, magnificent trees and rare plants.

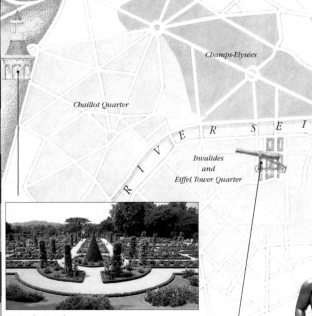

Champs-Elysées

Opéra Quarter

Chaillot Quarter

Tuileries Quarter

R I V E R   S E I N E

Invalides and Eiffel Tower Quarter

St-Germain-des-Prés

Luxembourg Quarter

Bois de Boulogne
The Bagatelle gardens, set in this wooded park, have an amazing array of flowers including the spectacular rose garden.

Montparnasse

Esplanade des Invalides
From this huge square, lined with lime trees, are some brilliant views over the docks.

Jardin des Tuileries
These gardens are renowned for ornamental ponds, terraces and the collection of bronze figures by Aristide Maillol.

Parc des Buttes-Chaumont

Once a scraggy hilltop, this park was transformed to provide open spaces for the growing city. It is now beautifully landscaped with huge cliffs revealing caves.

N

0 kilometers   1

0 miles   0.5

Square du Vert-Galant

The square, named after Henri IV's sobriquet, forms the west point of the Ile de la Cité.

Place des Vosges

Considered one of the most beautiful squares in the world, it was finished in 1612 and is the oldest square in Paris.

Beaubourg
and
Les Halles

The Marais

Ile de la
Cité

Ile St-Louis

Jardin des Plantes

The botanical garden has a vast collection of plants and flowers from around the world.

Latin Quarter

Jardin des Plantes
Quarter

Jardin du Luxembourg

This park is a favorite with Parisians wanting to escape the bustle of the Latin Quarter.

Bois de Vincennes

The flower garden in this charming park is the perfect place to relax.

Exploring Gardens, Parks and Squares

PARIS IS DOTTED with many areas of parkland, intimate gardens and attractive tree-lined squares. Each is a reminder of the French capital's illustrious past. Many squares were formed during Napoleon III's transformation of the city, creating a pleasant environment for Parisians to live in *(see pp32–3)*. This aim has been preserved right up to the present day. Paris's parks and gardens have their own character: some are ideal for a stroll; others for romance; while some provide space for sporting activities, such as a game of *boules*.

Engraving of the Jardin du Palais Royal (1645)

HISTORIC GARDENS

THE OLDEST PUBLIC gardens in Paris were made for queens of France – the **Jardin des Tuileries** for Catherine de Médicis in the 16th century and the **Jardin du Luxembourg** for Marie de Médicis in the 17th century. The Tuileries form the beginning of the axis running from the Arc du Triomphe du Carrousel through the Arc de Triomphe *(pp208–9)* to La Défense *(p255)*. These gardens retain the formality devised by landscape architect André Le Nôtre, originally for the **Palace of Versailles**. Many of the Jardin des Tuileries' original sculptures survive, as well as modern pieces, notably the bronze nudes by Aristide Maillol (1861–1944).

The Jardin du Luxembourg also has the traditional formal plan – straight paths, clipped lawns, Classical sculpture and a superb 17th-century fountain. It is shadier and more intimate than the Tuileries, with lots of seats, pony rides and puppet shows to amuse the children.

The **Jardins des Champs-Elysées**, also by Le Nôtre, were reshaped in the English style in the 19th century. They have Belle Epoque pavilions, three theaters (L'Espace Pierre Cardin, Théâtre Marigny and the Théâtre Barrault), smart restaurants – and the ghost of the novelist Marcel Proust, who once played here as a child.

A haven of peace in a busy district is the **Jardin du**

Palais Royal, built by Cardinal Richelieu in the 17th century. An elegant arcade encloses the garden. The 19th-century **Parc Monceau,** in the English picturesque style, has follies and grottoes. The flat **Jardins des Invalides** and the landscaped **Champ-de-Mars** were the grounds of the Hôtel des Invalides and the Ecole Militaire. They were the site of the Paris Universal Exhibition, whose reminder is the Eiffel Tower *(pp192–3)*.

An attractive public garden is attached to the lovely Hôtel Biron, home of the **Musée Rodin**. The 17th-century **Jardin des Plantes** is famous for its ancient trees, flowers, alpine garden, hothouses and small zoo.

19TH-CENTURY PARKS AND SQUARES

Aquatic Garden, Bois de Vincennes

THE GREAT 19th-century parks and squares owe much to Napoleon III's long exile in London before he came to power. The unregimented planting and rolling lawns of Hyde Park and the leafy squares of Mayfair inspired him to bring trees,

Relaxing in Jardin du Luxembourg

FOLLIES AND ROTUNDAS

Dramatic features of Paris's parks and gardens are the many follies and rotundas. Every age of garden design has produced these ornaments. The huge Gloriette de Buffon in the Jardin des Plantes was erected as a memorial to the great naturalist *(p166)*. It is the oldest metal structure in Paris. The pyramid in the Parc Monceau, the Oriental temple in the Bois de Boulogne and the recently restored 19th-century temple of love in the Bois de Vincennes reflect a more sentimental age. In contrast are the stark painted-concrete follies that grace the Parc de la Villette.

Egyptian pyramid

Parc Monceau

fresh air and park benches to what was then Europe's most congested and dirty capital. Under his direction, landscape gardener Adolphe Alphand turned two woods at opposite ends of the city, the **Bois de Boulogne** (known as the "Bois") and the **Bois de Vincennes**, into English-style parks with duck ponds, lakes and flower gardens. He also added a race course to the "Bois." Today it is traversed by traffic and by prostitutes at night. Its most attractive feature is the Bagatelle rose garden.

Far more pleasant are the two smaller Alphand parks, **Parc Montsouris** in the south and **Parc des Buttes-Chaumont** in the northeast. The "Buttes" (hills), a favorite with the Surrealists, was a quarry transformed into two craggy minimountains with overhanging vegetation, suspended bridge, a temple of love and a lake below.

Part of the town-planning schemes for the old city included squares and avenues with fountains, sculptures, benches and greenery. One of the best is the **Square du Vert-Galant** on the Ile de la Cité. The Avenue de l'Observatoire in the **Jardin du Luxembourg** is rich in sculptures by Jean Baptiste Carpeaux.

Fountains and sculpture in the Jardins du Trocadéro

Parc Montsouris

MODERN PARKS AND GARDENS

THE SHADY **Jardins du Trocadéro** sloping down to the river from the Palais de Chaillot were planted after the 1937 Universal Exhibition. Here is the largest fountain in Paris and fine views of the river and the Eiffel Tower.

More recent Paris gardens eschew formality in favor of wilder planting, multiple levels, mazelike paths, children's gardens and modern sculpture. Typical are the gardens in front of the **Forum des Halles**, the **Parc André-Citroën**, the **Parc de la Villette** and the Jardins Atlantique above the Gare Montparnasse.

Pleasant strolls may be taken in Paris's waterside gardens: in the modern sculpture park behind Notre-Dame (pp77–81), at the Bassin de l'Arsenal at the Bastille (pp28–9), along the quays of the Seine between the Louvre (pp122–9) and the Place de la Concorde (p70), or on the elegantly residential Ile St-Louis (pp262–3).

Jardin des Plantes — Gloriette de Buffon

Bois de Boulogne — Oriental temple

Bois de Vincennes — Temple of love

Parc de la Villette — Modern folly

Paris's Best: Museums and Galleries

SOME OF THE OLDEST, newest and finest museums and galleries to be found anywhere are in Paris – many are superb works of art in their own right. They house some of the greatest and strangest collections in the world. Some of the buildings complement their themes, such as the Roman baths and Gothic mansion that form the Musée de Cluny, or the Pompidou Center, a modern masterpiece. Elsewhere there is pleasing contrast, such as the Picassos in their gracious 17th-century museum and the Musée d'Orsay housed in its grand old railway station. Together they make a spectacular unrivaled feast for visitors.

Musée des Arts Décoratifs
Decorative and ornamental art like this Paris bathroom by Jeanne Lanvin is displayed here.

Champs-Elysées

Chaillot Quarter

R I V E R   S E I N E

Invalides and Eiffel Tower Quarter

Petit Palais
A collection of works by the 19th-century sculptor Jean-Baptiste Carpeaux is housed here, including
The Fisherman and Shell.

Musée Guimet
This 4th-century head of Buddha from India is part of a vast collection of Asian art and artifacts housed here.

Montparnasse

Musée Rodin
The museum brings together works bequeathed to the nation by sculptor Auguste Rodin, like the magnificent Gates of Hell *doors.*

Musée d'Orsay
Carpeaux's Four Quarters of the World *(1867–72) can be found among this collection of 19th-century art.*

Musée du Louvre

The museum boasts one of the world's great collections of paintings and sculpture, from the ancient civilizations to the 19th century. This Babylonian monument, the Code of Hammurabi, *is the oldest set of laws in existence.*

Pompidou Center

Paris's modern art collection from 1905 to the present day is housed here. The center also has art libraries and an industrial-design center.

N

Opéra Quarter

Beaubourg and Les Halles

The Marais

Tuileries Quarter

St-Germain-des-Prés

Ile de la Cité

Ile St-Louis

Musée Picasso

Sculptor and Model *(1931) is one of many paintings on display in Picasso's private collection, "inherited" in lieu of tax by the French government after his death in 1973.*

Latin Quarter

Luxembourg Quarter

Jardin des Plantes Quarter

Musée Carnavalet

The museum is devoted to the history of Paris. Its historic buildings surround attractive garden courtyards.

Musée de Cluny

The remains of the old Gallo-Roman baths are part of this fine museum of ancient and medieval art.

| 0 kilometers | 1 |
| 0 miles | 0.5 |

Exploring Paris's Museums and Galleries

PARIS HOLDS great treasures in its museums and art galleries. The major national art collection is to be found at the **Musée du Louvre**, which began collecting 400 years ago and is still doing so. Other important museums, such as the **Musée d'Orsay**, the **Musée Picasso** and the **Pompidou Center**, have their own treasures, but there are scores of smaller, specialized museums, each with its own interest.

Dante and Virgil in the Underworld (1822) by Delacroix, Musée du Louvre

GREEK, ROMAN AND MEDIEVAL ART

Golden altar in the Musée de Cluny

SCULPTURE from Greek and Roman times is well represented in the **Musée du Louvre**, which also has fine medieval sculptures. The major medieval collection is at the **Musée de Cluny**, a superb 15th-century mansion. Among the highlights are the Unicorn Tapestries, the Kings' Heads from Notre-Dame and the golden altar from Basel Cathedral. Adjoining the Cluny are the 3rd-century Roman baths. Remains of houses from Roman and medieval Paris can be seen in the **Crypte Archéologique** near Notre-Dame cathedral.

OLD MASTERS

THE *MONA LISA* was one of the **Musée du Louvre's** first paintings, acquired 400 years ago. It also has other fine Leonardos, which can be found along with superb Titians, Raphaels and other Italian masters. Other works include Rembrandt's *Pilgrims at Emmaüs*, Watteau's *Gilles* and Fragonard's *The Bathers*. The **Musée Cognacq-Jay** has a small but exquisite collection of paintings and drawings by 18th-century French artists. The **Musée Jacquemart-André** has works by such masters as Mantegna, Uccello, Canaletto, Rembrandt and Chardin.

IMPRESSIONIST AND POST-IMPRESSIONIST ART

INSTALLED IN A converted 19th-century railroad station, the **Musée d'Orsay** boasts the world's largest collection of art from 1848 to 1904. Admired for its fine Impressionist and Post-Impressionist collections, it also devotes substantial space to the earlier Realists and the formerly reviled 19th-century academic and "Salon" masters. There are superb selections of Degas, Manet, Courbet, Monet, Renoir, Millet, Cézanne, Bonnard and Vuillard, plus some fine Gauguins, Van Goghs and Seurats, but these have to contend with poor lighting and an intrusive stone decor.

A great ensemble of late Monets is to be found at the **Musée Marmottan** and another at the **Musée de l'Orangerie**, including Monet's last great water-lily murals (1920–5). Here also is a good collection of Cézannes and late Renoirs.

Three artists' studios and homes are now museums of their life and work. The **Musée Rodin**, in an attractive 18th-century mansion and garden, offers a complete survey of the master's sculptures, drawings and paintings. The **Musée Delacroix**, set in a garden near St-Germain-des-Prés, has sketches, prints and oils by the Romantic artist. The **Musée Gustave Moreau**, in an oppressive 19th-century town house, has an extraordinary collection of intricately painted canvases of legendary femmes fatales and dying youths. The **Petit Palais** has an interesting collection of 19th-century painting with four major Courbets, including *The Sleep*.

Dead Poet in Musée Gustave Moreau

MODERN AND CONTEMPORARY ART

AS THE INTERNATIONAL center of the avant-garde from 1900 to 1940, Paris has a great concentration of modern painting and sculpture. The Pompidou Center houses the **Musée de l'Art Moderne**, covering the period from 1905 to the present. It has a good selection of Fauvist and Cubist works. It is strong on Matisse, Rouault, Braque, Leger, Delaunay and Dubuffet, plus French Pop Art.

The **Musée d'Art Moderne de la Ville de Paris**, an elegant 1930s Neoclassical pavilion, has a smaller collection with good Delaunays, Bonnards and Fauvist paintings. The highlight is Matisse's 1932 mural *The Dance*.

Penelope by Bourdelle

The **Musée Picasso**, in a lovely 17th-century mansion, has the world's largest Picasso collection. It also has his own personal collection of the work of his contemporaries. Picasso, Matisse, Modigliani, Utrillo and late Derains make up the collection of 1920s art dealer Paul Guillaume on display at the **Musée de l'Orangerie**. For modern sculpture, the small **Musée Zadkine** has Cubist work by a minor school whose leading light was Ossip Zadkine. The **Musée Antoine Bourdelle** features the work of the sculptor Bourdelle (1861–1929), a pupil of the master sculptor Auguste Rodin.

FURNITURE, DECORATIVE ARTS AND OBJETS D'ART

PRIDE OF PLACE after painting must go to furniture and the decorative arts, contained in a plethora of museums. Fine ensembles of French furnishings and decoration are in the **Louvre** (medieval to Napoleonic) and at the **Palace of Versailles** (17th–18th century). Furniture and objets d'art from the Middle Ages to the present century are arranged in period rooms at the **Musée des Arts Décoratifs**. The **Musée d'Orsay** has a large collection of 19th-century furniture, notably Art Nouveau. A superb example of Louis XV (1715–74) and Louis XVI (1774–93) furniture and decoration is in the **Musée Nissim de Camondo**, a mansion from 1910 facing the Parc Monceau. Other notable collections are the **Musée Cognacq-Jay**; the **Musée Carnavalet** (18th century); the **Musée Jacquemart-André** (French furniture and earthenware); the **Musée Marmottan** (Empire); and **Musée d'Art Moderne de la Ville de Paris** (Art Deco).

Candelabra in the Galerie Royale

Jeweler's shop in the Carnavalet

SPECIALIST MUSEUMS

DEVOTEES OF antique sporting guns, muskets and hounds of the chase should head for the attractive Marais **Hôtel Guénégaud** (Musée de la Chasse et de la Nature). This museum also has some fine 18th-century animal paintings by Jean-Baptiste Oudry and Alexandre-François Desportes, as well as others by Rubens and Brueghel. For locksmiths, and perhaps also for burglars, the Musée Bricard in the **Hôtel Libéral Bruand** houses a large collection of antique locks and keys. Numismatists will find a coin and medallion museum in luxurious surroundings at the 18th-century Paris Mint at the **Musée de la Monnaie**. French coins are no longer minted here, but the old Mint still makes medals that are on sale. Stamps are on display at the **Musée de la Poste**. The history of postal services is also covered, as are all aspects of philately old and new, with temporary shows on current philatelic design. Antique and exotic pipes, together with smoking paraphernalia, are displayed at the **Musée de la Seita**. Sumptuous silver dinner services and other silverware can be seen at the **Galerie Royale**. They were made over a period of 150 years by the Paris firm whose founder was Charles Bouilhet-Christofle, silversmith to King Louis-Philippe and Napoleon III.

FASHION AND COSTUME

THE TWO RIVAL fashion museums in Paris are the **Musée de la Mode et de la Costume** at the Palais Galliera and the more recent national museum within the **Musée des Arts Décoratifs**. Neither displays a permanent collection, but both hold shows devoted to the great Paris couturiers, such as Saint Laurent and Givenchy. They also display fashion accessories and – more rarely – historical costumes.

Poster for the Palais Galliera

ASIAN, AFRICAN AND OCEANIAN ART

THE MAJOR collection of Asian art in France is housed at the **Musée National des Arts Asiatiques Guimet**, covering China, Tibet, Japan, Korea, Indochina, Indonesia, India and Central Asia. It includes some of the best Khmer art outside Cambodia. Renovations scheduled to finish at the end of 1999 will improve the presentation of

Sri Lankan theatrical mask

this stunning but little-known collection, reflecting the growing influence of Asian civilizations in France. The **Musée Cernuschi,** named after the banker, has a smaller but well-chosen Chinese collection, noted for its ancient bronzes and reliefs. Artifacts from the former French colonies (North and Sub-Saharan Africa, the South Pacific) are displayed at the **Musée des Arts Africains et Océaniens** in an Art Deco building near the Bois de Vincennes.

HISTORY AND SOCIAL HISTORY

Café in Musée de Montmartre

COVERING THE entire history of the city of Paris, the **Musée Carnavalet** is housed in two historic Marais *hôtels.* It has period interiors, paintings

of the city and old shop signs. There is a fascinating section covering events and artifacts from the French Revolution. The Carnavalet even has Marcel Proust's bedroom. The **Musée de l'Armée,** in the Hôtel des Invalides, recounts French military history from Charlemagne to de Gaulle. The Musée de l'Histoire de France, in the Rococo **Hôtel de Soubise,** has historical documents from the national archives on display. Famous *tableaux vivants* and characters, both current and historical, await the visitor at the **Musée Grévin** wax museum. The intriguing **Musée de Mont-**martre, overlooking Paris's last surviving vineyard, holds exhibitions on the history of Montmartre.

ARCHITECTURE AND DESIGN

THE CENTRE de la Création Industrielle holds modern and contemporary design and architecture exhibitions at the **Pompidou Center**. The **Centre de l'Architecture et de Patrimonie** has an eerie collection of plaster casts of French monumental sculpture from Roman times onward. Superb scale models of fortresses built for Louis XIV and later are on display at the **Musée des Plans-Reliefs**. The work of the celebrated Franco-Swiss architect forms

---

THE FRENCH IMPRESSIONISTS

***Impression: Sunrise* by Monet**

IMPRESSIONISM, the great art revolution of the 19th century, began in Paris in the 1860s, when young painters, influenced in part by the new art of photography, started to break with the academic values of the past. They aimed to capture the "impression" of

Monet's sketchbooks

what the eye sees at a given moment and used brushwork designed to capture the fleeting effects of light falling on a scene. Their favorite subjects were landscapes and scenes from contemporary urban life.

The movement had no founder, though Edouard Manet (1832–83) and the radical Realist painter Gustave Courbet (1819–77) both inspired many of the younger artists. Paintings of scenes of everyday life by Manet and Courbet often offended the academicians who legislated artistic taste. In 1863 Manet's *Le Déjeuner sur l'Herbe (see p144)* was exhibited at the Salon des Refusés, an exhibition set up for paintings rejected by the official Paris Salon of that year. The first time the term "Impressionist" was used to describe this new artistic movement was at another unofficial exhibition, in 1874. The name came from a painting by Claude Monet, *Impression: Sunrise,* a view of Le Havre in the mist from 1872. Monet was almost exclusively a landscape artist, influenced by the works of the English

***Harvesting* (1876) by Pissarro**

The living room of La Roche Villa by Le Corbusier (1923)

the basis of the **Fondation Le Corbusier**. The showpiece is the 1920s villa built by Le Corbusier for a friend, art collector Raoul La Roche. There is also furniture designed by Le Corbusier.

SCIENCE AND TECHNOLOGY

IN THE JARDIN des Plantes the **Muséum National d'Histoire Naturelle** has sections on paleontology, minerology,

entomology, anatomy and botany, plus a zoo and a botanical garden. In the Palais de Chaillot, the **Musée de l'Homme** is a major museum of anthropology, ethnology and prehistory with numerous African artifacts. Next door, the **Musée de la Marine** covers French naval history from the 17th century onward, with fine 18th-century models of ships and sculpted figureheads. The museum devoted to the history of science, the **Palais de la Découverte**, has a good planetarium, but it has been overshadowed by the spectacular new one at the **Cité des Sciences** in the Parc de la Villette. This vast museum is on several levels and has a spherical movie screen, the **Géode**.

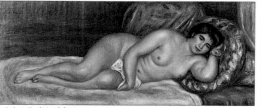

Gabrielle (1910) by Renoir

artists Constable and Turner. He always liked to paint out of doors and encouraged others to follow his example.

At the 1874 exhibition, a critic wrote that one should stand well back to see these "impressions" – the farther back the better – and that members of the establishment should retreat altogether. Other exhibitors at the show were Pierre-Auguste Renoir, Edgar Degas, Camille Pissarro, Alfred Sisley and Paul Cézanne.

There were seven more Impressionist shows up to 1886. By then the power of the Salon had waned, and the whole direction of art had changed. From then on, new movements were defined in terms of their relation to Impressionism. The leading Neo-Impressionist was Georges Seurat, who used thousands of minute dots of color to build up his paintings. It took later generations to fully

appreciate the work of the Impressionists. Cézanne was rejected all his life, Degas sold only one painting to a museum, and Sisley died unknown. Of the great artists whose genius is now universally recognized, only Renoir and Monet were ever acclaimed in their lifetimes.

Profile of a Model (1887) by Seurat

Artists in Paris

THE CITY FIRST attracted artists during the reign of Louis XIV (1643–1715), and Paris became the most sophisticated artistic center in Europe; the magnetism has persisted. During the 18th century, all major French artists lived and worked in Paris. In the latter half of the 19th century and early part of this century,

Monet's palette

Paris was the European center of modern and progressive art, and movements such as Impressionism and Post-Impressionism were founded and blossomed in the city.

BAROQUE ARTISTS

Champaigne, Philippe de (1602–74)
Coysevox, Antoine (1640–1720)
Girardon, François (1628–1715)
Le Brun, Charles (1619–90)
Le Sueur, Eustache (1616–55)
Poussin, Nicolas (1594–1665)
Rigaud, Hyacinthe (1659–1743)
Vignon, Claude (1593–1670)
Vouet, Simon (1590–1649)

ROCOCO ARTISTS

Boucher, François (1703–70)
Chardin, Jean-Baptiste-Siméon (1699–1779)
Falconet, Etienne-Maurice (1716–91)
Fragonard, Jean-Honoré (1732–1806)
Greuze, Jean-Baptiste (1725–1805)
Houdon, Jean-Antoine (1741–1828)
Oudry, Jean-Baptiste (1686–1755)
Pigalle, Jean-Baptiste (1714–85)
Watteau, Jean-Antoine (1684–1721)

Boucher's Diana Bathing (1742), typical of the Rococo style (Louvre)

1600	1650	1700	1750
BAROQUE		ROCOCO	NEOCLASSICISM
1600	1650	1700	1750

1627 Vouet returns from Italy and is made court painter by Louis XIII. Vouet revived a dismal period in the fortunes of French painting

1667 First Salon, France's official art exhibition; originally held annually, later every two years

Philippe de Champaigne's Last Supper (about 1652). His style slowly became more Classical in his later years (Louvre)

1793 Louvre opens as first national public gallery

1648 Foundation of the Académie Royale de Peinture et de Sculpture, which had a virtual monopoly on art teaching

Vouet's The Presentation in the Temple (1641), with typically Baroque contrasts of light and shade (Louvre)

NEOCLASSICAL ARTISTS

David, Jacques-Louis (1748–1825)
Gros, Antoine Jean (1771–1835)
Ingres, Jean-Auguste-Dominique (1780–1867)
Vigée-Lebrun, Elisabeth (1755–1842)

David's The Oath of the Horatii (1784), in the Neoclassical style (Louvre)

ROMANTIC AND REALIST ARTISTS
Courbet, Gustave (1819–77)
Daumier, Honoré (1808–79)
Delacroix, Eugène (1798–1863)
Géricault, Théodore (1791–1824)
Rude, Francois (1784–1855)

Courbet's The Burial at Ornans *(1850) which showed Courbet to be the foremost exponent of Realism (Musée d'Orsay)*

Rude's Departure of the Volunteers in 1792 *(1836), a tribute to the French Revolution (see p209)*

MODERN ARTISTS
Arp, Jean (1887–1966)
Balthus (b. 1908)
Brancusi, Constantin (1876–1957)
Braque, Georges (1882–1963)
Buffet, Bernard (b. 1928)
Chagall, Marc (1887–1985)
Delaunay, Robert (1885–1941)
Derain, André (1880–1954)
Dubuffet, Jean (1901–85)
Duchamp, Marcel (1887–1968)
Epstein, Jacob (1880–1959)
Ernst, Max (1891–1976)
Giacometti, Alberto (1901–66)
Gris, Juan (1887–1927)
Léger, Fernand (1881–1955)
Matisse, Henri (1869–1954)
Miró, Joan (1893–1983)
Modigliani, Amedeo (1884–1920)
Mondrian, Piet (1872–1944)
Picasso, Pablo (1881–1973)
Rouault, Georges (1871–1958)
Saint-Phalle, Niki de (b. 1930)
Soutine, Chaim (1893–1943)
Stael, Nicolas de (1914–55)
Tinguely, Jean (1925–91)
Utrillo, Maurice (1883–1955)
Zadkine, Ossip (1890–1967)

1904 Picasso settles in Paris

1886 Van Gogh moves to Paris

1874 First Impressionist exhibition

1905 Birth of Fauvism, the first of the "isms" in modern art

Giacometti's Standing Woman II *(1959), one of his many tall, thin bronze figures (see p113)*

00	1850	1900	1950
ROMANTICISM/REALISM		IMPRESSIONISM	MODERNISM
00	1850	1900	1950

1863 Manet's *Le Déjeuner sur l'Herbe* causes a scandalous sensation at the Salon des Refusés, both for its "poor moral taste" and for its broad brushstrokes. The artist's *Olympia* was thought just as outrageous, but it was not exhibited until 1865 *(see p144)*.

1938 International Surrealist exhibition in Paris

1977 Pompidou Center opens

Monet's Impression: Sunrise *(1872), which led to the name Impressionism*

Delacroix's Liberty Leading the People *(1830) romantically celebrates victory in war (Louvre).*

1819 Géricault paints *The Raft of the Medusa,* one of the greatest works of French Romanticism *(see p124)*

IMPRESSIONIST AND POST-IMPRESSIONIST ARTISTS
Bonnard, Pierre (1867–1947)
Carpeaux, Jean-Baptiste (1827–75)
Cézanne, Paul (1839–1906)
Degas, Edgar (1834–1917)
Gauguin, Paul (1848–1903)
Manet, Edouard (1832–83)
Monet, Claude (1840–1926)
Pissarro, Camille (1830–1903)
Renoir, Pierre-Auguste (1841–1919)
Rodin, Auguste (1840–1917)
Rousseau, Henri (1844–1910)
Seurat, Georges (1859–91)
Sisley, Alfred (1839–99)
Toulouse-Lautrec, Henri de (1864–1901)
Van Gogh, Vincent (1853–90)
Vuillard, Edouard (1868–1940)
Whistler, James Abbott McNeill (1834–1903)

Tinguely and Saint-Phalle's Fontaine Igor Stravinsky *(1980), a modern kinetic sculpture (Pompidou Center)*

PARIS THROUGH THE YEAR

PARIS'S PULLING POWER is strongest in spring – the season for chestnuts in blossom and tables under trees. From June Paris is slowly turned over to tourists; the city almost comes to a standstill for the French Tennis Open, and the major racetracks stage the big summer races. Next comes the July 14 Bastille Day parade down the Champs-Elysées; toward the end of the month the Tour de France ends here. Parisians then abandon the city to visitors until *la rentrée,* the return to school and work in September. October sees the Paris Jazz Festival, and as the days get shorter, the shops get ready for Christmas. Dates of events listed on the following pages may vary annually. For details consult the listings magazines or contact Allo Sports *(see p343)*. The Office du Tourisme *(see p351)* produces an annual calendar of events.

SPRING

A GOOD MANY OF the city's annual 20 million visitors arrive in the spring. It is the season for fairs and concerts, when the marathon street race is held and the outdoor temperature is pleasant. Spring is also the time when hoteliers offer weekend packages, often with tickets for jazz concerts and museum passes included.

1990 French Tennis Open, Stade Roland Garros

MARCH

Collectionamania *(last weekend)*, Espace Austerlitz, 30 Quai d'Austerlitz. Curio and object collectors' fair.
Foire du Trône *(mid-Mar–end-May)*, Bois de Vincennes *(p246)*. Large funfair.
18 Heures – 18 Francs *(first week)*, F18 for any film starting at 6pm.
Jumping International de Paris *(third week)*, Palais d'Omnisports de Paris-Bercy *(pp343–4)*. International show jumping.
Salon International d'Agriculture *(first week)*,

Parc des Expositions de Paris, Porte de Versailles. Vast farming fair.
Spring flower shows at the Bagatelle Gardens in the Bois de Boulogne *(p254)* and Parc Floral in the Bois de Vincennes *(p246)*.

APRIL

Six Nations Trophy *(early Apr)*, Parc des Princes *(p343)*. International rugby.
Musicora *(second week)*, International classical music extravaganza.
Salon de la Jeune Peinture *(for two weeks mid-month)*, Exhibition of contemporary young artists' work.
Shakespeare Garden Festival *(until Oct)*, Bois de Boulogne *(p254)*. Classic plays performed outdoors.
Paris International Marathon *(April)*, from Place de la Concorde to Château de Vincennes.
Foire de Paris *(end-Apr–1st week May)*, Paris Expo. Food, wine, homes and gardens and tourism show.

MAY

Carré Rive Gauche *(one week, mid-month)*. Exhibits at antiques dealers in St-Germain-des-Prés *(p135)*.
Football Cup Final *(second week)*, Stade de France.

Spring color, Jardin du Luxembourg

Grands Eaux Musicales *(Apr–Jun and Sep–mid-Oct: every Sun; Jul–Aug: every Sat)*, Versailles *(pp248–53)*. Open-air concerts.
French Tennis Open *(last week May–first week Jun)*, Stade Roland Garros. *(p343)*

Paris International Marathon

AVERAGE DAILY HOURS OF SUNSHINE

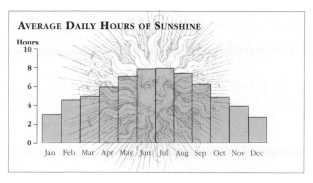

Hours
10
8
6
4
2
0

Jan Feb Mar Apr May Jun Jul Aug Sep Oct Nov Dec

Sunshine Hours
The northerly position of Paris gives it long and light summer evenings, but in winter the daylight recedes, with few truly bright days.

SUMMER

SUMMER begins with the French Tennis Open, and there are many events and festivities until July. Thereafter the French begin thinking of their own annual holiday, but there are big celebrations on Bastille Day (July 14), with military displays for the president and his guests.

Jardin du Luxembourg in summer

JUNE

Festival St-Denis Basilique St-Denis. Concerts with emphasis on large-scale choral works *(pp333–4)*.
Fête du Cinéma movies shown all over Paris for F1 *(p340)*.

Final lap of the Champs-Elysées during the 1991 Tour de France

Fête de la Musique *(21 Jun)*, all over Paris. Nightlong summer solstice celebrations with amateur and professional bands.
Flower show, Bois de Boulogne *(p254)*. Rose season in the Bagatelle Gardens.
Paris Jazz Festival *(Jun–Sep)*, Parc Floral de Paris. International jazz musicians come to play in Paris *(p337)*.
Paris Air and Space Technology Show *(mid-Jun)*, Le Bourget Airport.
Prix de Diane-Hermès *(second Sun)*, Chantilly. French equivalent of the British Ascot high society horse racing event.

JULY

Tournoi International de Pétanque, *(first weekend)*, Porte de Montreuil. International bowls. Contact the Fédération Française de Pétanque *(p343)*.
Paris Quartier d'Eté *(until mid Aug)*. Dance, music, theater, ballet.
Tour de France *(late Jul)*. Last stage of the world's greatest cycle race finishes in the Champs-Elysées.
Fêtes de Nuit au Château de Versailles *(2, 10, 17, 24 Jul, 28 Aug, 4 and 11 Sep)*. Festival of evening performances of music, dance and theatre *(p333–4)*.

March of troops on Bastille Day (July 14)

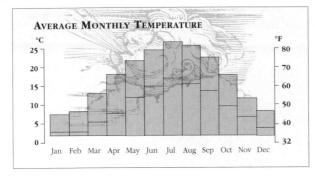

AVERAGE MONTHLY TEMPERATURE

Temperature
The chart shows the average minimum and maximum temperatures for each month. It is hottest in July and August and coolest between December and February, though Paris is rarely freezing cold. Temperatures are pleasant in the spring and autumn.

AUTUMN

SEPTEMBER SEES the start of the social season, with gala performances of new movies and parties in big houses on the Ile St-Louis. Paris is the world's largest convention center and there are a rush of shows in September, ranging from children's clothes and gifts to leisure and music. The pace barely slackens in October and November, when Parisians begin to indulge their great love for the movies. French and Hollywood stars make appearances at premieres staged on the Champs-Elysées.

The Prix de l'Arc de Triomphe (October)

SEPTEMBER

Festival d'Automne à Paris *(mid-Sep–end Dec)*, throughout Paris. Music, dance, theater *(pp333–4)*.
Journée du Patrimoine *(usually third week)*. Three hundred historic buildings, monuments, museums and ministries are open free to the public for two days.

Foire Internationale d'Art Contemporain *(one week, usually mid-month)*, Grand Palais *(p206)*. The biggest international modern and contemporary art fair in Paris.
Garçons de Café race *(one Sun mid-Jun)*, from Place de la République to Place de la Bastille *(p98)*. Dozens of waiters race with a bottle and glass balanced on a tray.

OCTOBER

Festival d'Ile-de-France *(weekends, Sep–end Oct)*. Classical, jazz and early music concerts.
Prix de l'Arc de Triomphe *(first week)*, Longchamp. An international field competes

for the richest prize in European horse-racing.
Salon de l'Automobile *(first and second weeks, every other year)*, Parc des Expositions, Porte

Jazz fusion guitarist Al di Meola playing in Paris

de Versailles 75015. Commercial car show, which alternates annually with a motorcycle show.

NOVEMBER

Paris Tennis Open *(usually Nov)*, Palais d'Omnisports de Paris-Bercy *(pp342–3)*.
Festival d'Art Sacré *(Nov–Dec 24)*, at St-Sulpice, St-Eustache and St-Germain-des-Prés churches. Religious art festival.
Mois de la Photo *(every 2 years, until Jan)*. Numerous photography shows in museums and galleries.

Autumn in the Bois de Vincennes

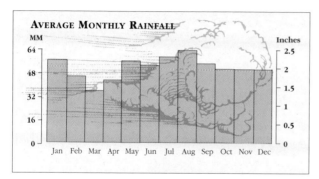

AVERAGE MONTHLY RAINFALL

MM — Inches

	Jan	Feb	Mar	Apr	May	Jun	Jul	Aug	Sep	Oct	Nov	Dec

Rainfall

August is the wettest month in Paris, as well as the hottest. In August and September you risk getting caught in storms. Sudden showers, sometimes with hail, can occur between January and April – notoriously in March. There is occasional snow in winter.

WINTER

P ARIS RARELY sees snow; winter days tend to be invigorating rather than chilly. There are jazz and dance festivals, candlelit Christmas church services and much celebrating in the streets over the New Year. After New Year, the streets seem to become slightly less congested, and on bright days the riverside quays are used as the rendezvous point of strollers and lovers.

Snow in the Tuileries, a rare occurrence

DECEMBER

Christmas illuminations *(until Jan)* in the Grands Boulevards, Opéra, Avenue Montaigne, Champs-Elysées and the Rue du Faubourg St-Honoré.
Crèche des Andes *(early Dec–early Jan)*, under a canopy in Place de l'Hôtel de Ville, Marais *(p91)*. Lifesize Christmas crèche in the South American tradition.

January fashion show

Horse and Pony Show *(first two weeks)*, Parc des Expositions, Porte de Versailles.
Midnight Mass *(Dec 24)*, Notre-Dame *(pp82–5)*.
Paris International Boat Show *(first two weeks)*, Parc des Expositions, Porte de Versailles.

JANUARY

Commemorative mass for Louis XVI *(Sun nearest to Jan 21)*, Chapelle Expiatoire, 29 Rue Pasquier 75008.
Fashion shows, summer collections. *(See Haute Couture p316.)*

FEBRUARY

Découvertes *(usually first week)*, Grand Palais *(p206)*. International art fair for new galleries and artists.
Floraisons *(all month)*, Parc Floral de Paris, Bois de Vincennes *(p254)* and Parc de Bagatelle, Bois de Boulogne *(p246)*. Displays of crocuses and snowdrops brighten the winter gloom.

PUBLIC HOLIDAYS
New Year's Day (Jan 1)
Easter Monday
Labor Day (May 1)
VE Day (May 8)
Ascension Day (6th Thu after Easter)
Whit Monday (2nd Mon after Ascension)
Bastille Day (Jul 14)
Assumption (Aug 15)
All Saints' Day (Nov 1)
Remembrance Day (Nov 11)
Christmas (Dec 25)

Eiffel Tower Christmas decorations

A RIVER VIEW OF PARIS

Sculpture on the Pont Alexandre III

THE REMARKABLE French music-hall star Mistinguett described the Seine as a "pretty blonde with laughing eyes." The river most certainly has a beguiling quality, but the relationship that exists between it and the city of Paris is far more than one of flirtation.

No other European city defines itself by its river in the same way as Paris. The Seine is the essential point of reference to the city: distances are measured from it; street numbers determined by it; and it divides the capital into two distinct areas, with the Right Bank on the north side of the river and the Left Bank on the south. These are as well defined as any of the supposedly official boundaries. The city is also divided historically, with the east more closely linked to the city's ancient roots and the west more closely linked to the 19th and 20th centuries.

Practically every building of note in Paris is either along the river or within a stone's throw. The quays are lined with fine apartments, magnificent town houses, great museums and striking monuments.

Above all, the river is very much alive. For centuries, fleets of small boats used it, but motorized land traffic stifled this once-bustling scene. Today, the river is busy with commercial barges and massive *bateaux-mouche,* pleasure boats cruising sightseers up and down the river.

The octagonal lake, in the Jardin de Luxembourg, is a favorite spot for children to sail their toy boats. The Seine is host to larger craft, including many pleasure cruisers.

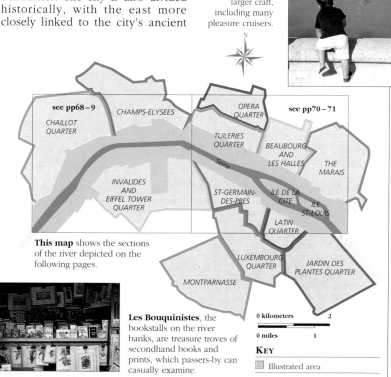

see pp68–9

CHAMPS-ELYSEES

CHAILLOT QUARTER

OPERA QUARTER

see pp70–71

TUILERIES QUARTER

BEAUBOURG AND LES HALLES

THE MARAIS

Seine

INVALIDES AND EIFFEL TOWER QUARTER

ST-GERMAIN-DES-PRES

ILE DE LA CITE

ILE ST-LOUIS

LATIN QUARTER

This map shows the sections of the river depicted on the following pages.

LUXEMBOURG QUARTER

JARDIN DES PLANTES QUARTER

MONTPARNASSE

Les Bouquinistes, the bookstalls on the river banks, are treasure troves of secondhand books and prints, which passers-by can casually examine.

0 kilometers 2

0 miles 1

KEY

☐ Illustrated area

Pont Alexandre III, encrusted with exuberant statuary

From Pont de Grenelle to Pont de la Concorde

THE SOARING monuments and grand exhibition halls along this stretch of the river are remnants of the Napoleonic era and the Industrial Revolution with its great exhibitions. The exhilarating self-confidence of the Eiffel Tower, the Petit Palais and the Grand Palais is matched by more recent buildings, such as the Palais de Chaillot, the Maison de Radio France and the skyscrapers of the Left Bank.

Palais de Chaillot
The curved wings and arching fountains make this a spectacular setting for four museums (p198).

Palais de Tokyo
Figures by Bourdelle adorn this museum (p198).

The Statue of Liberty was given to the city in 1885. It faces west, toward the original Liberty in New York.

Bateaux Parisiens
Tour Eiffel

Vedettes de Paris
Ile de France

Passerelle

Trocadéro **M**

Pont
d'Iéna

Maison de Radio France
Studios and a radio museum are housed in this imposing circular building (p200).

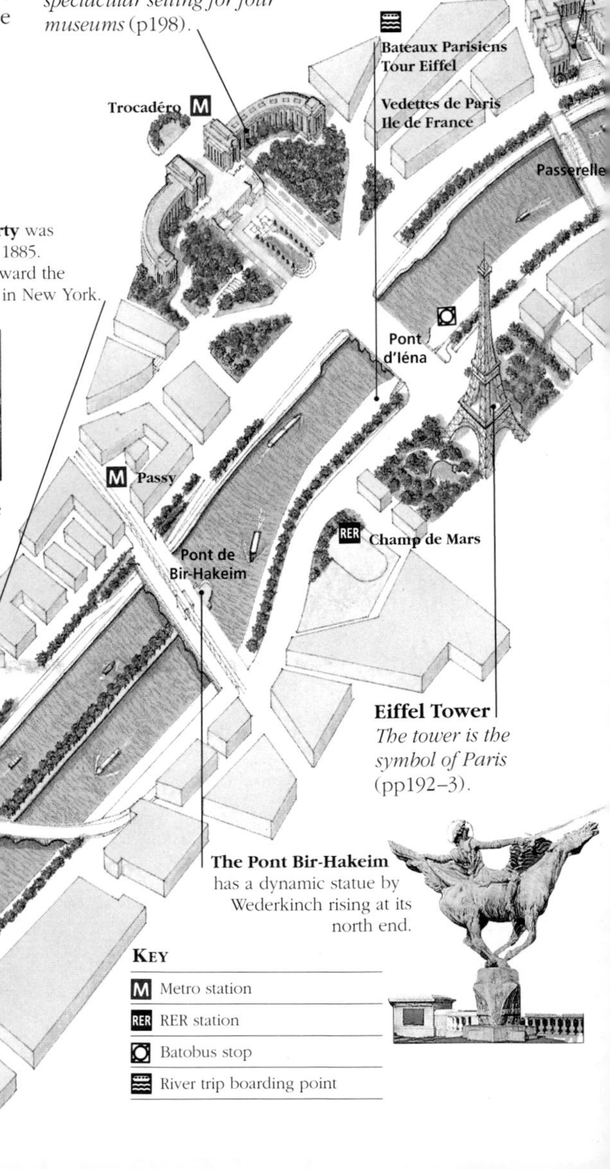

M Passy

Pont de
Bir-Hakeim

RER Champ de Mars

RER Prés. Kennedy
Radio France

Eiffel Tower
The tower is the symbol of Paris (pp192–3).

The Pont Bir-Hakeim has a dynamic statue by Wederkinch rising at its north end.

Pont de Grenelle

KEY

M	Metro station
RER	RER station
◙	Batobus stop
≋	River trip boarding point

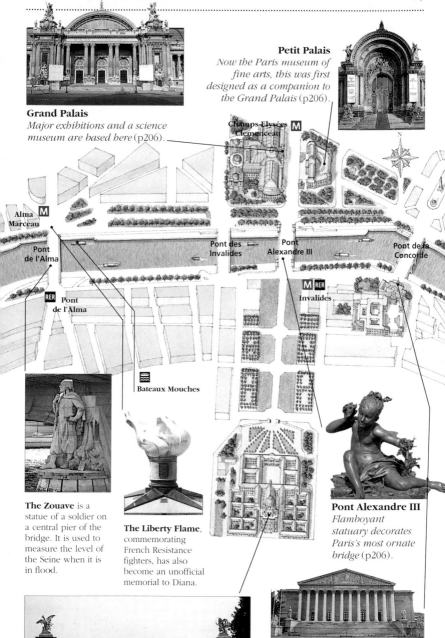

Grand Palais
Major exhibitions and a science museum are based here (p206).

Petit Palais
Now the Paris museum of fine arts, this was first designed as a companion to the Grand Palais (p206).

Champs-Elysées Clemenceau [M]

Alma Marceau [M]

Pont de l'Alma

Pont des Invalides

Pont Alexandre III

Pont de la Concorde

[RER] Pont de l'Alma

[M] [RER] Invalides

Bateaux Mouches

The Zouave is a statue of a soldier on a central pier of the bridge. It is used to measure the level of the Seine when it is in flood.

The Liberty Flame, commemorating French Resistance fighters, has also become an unofficial memorial to Diana.

Pont Alexandre III
Flamboyant statuary decorates Paris's most ornate bridge (p206).

Assemblée Nationale Palais-Bourbon
Louis XIV's daughter once owned this palace, which is now used by the Chambre des Députés as the national forum for political debate (p190).

Dôme Church
The majestic gilded dome (p188–9) is here seen from Pont Alexandre III.

From Pont de la Concorde to Pont de Sully

THE HISTORIC heart of Paris lies on the banks and islands of the east river. At its center is the Ile de la Cité, a natural stepping stone across the Seine and the cultural core of medieval Paris. Today it is still vital to Parisian life.

Jardin des Tuileries
These are in the formal style (p130).

Musée du Louvre
Before becoming the world's greatest museum and home to the Mona Lisa, this was Europe's largest royal palace (pp122–9).

Pont de la Concorde

Assemblée Nationale

Pont Solférino

Quai d'Orsay

Pont Royal

Pont du Carrousel

Pont des Arts

Musée de l'Orangerie
An important collection of 19th-century paintings is on display here (p131).

Musée d'Orsay
Paris's most important collection of Impressionist art is in this converted railroad station (pp144–7).

Bateaux Vedettes du Pont Neuf

The Pont Solférino was built in 1859 to give access to the Tuileries Gardens from the district of St-Germain-des-Prés.

The Pont des Arts, Paris's first cast-iron bridge took two years to build and was completed in 1804.

Hôtel des Monnaies
The Mint, built in 1175, has a fine coin collection in its old milling halls (p141).

Ile de la Cité
The medieval identity of this small island was almost completely erased in the 19th century by Baron Haussmann's grand scheme. Sainte-Chapelle and parts of the Conciergerie are the only buildings of the period that remain today (pp76–89).

Conciergerie
During the Revolution this building, with its distinctive towers, became notorious as a prison (p81).

The Tour de l'Horloge, a 14th-century clock tower, features the first public clock in Paris. Germain Pilon's fine carvings continue to adorn the clock face.

Ile St-Louis
This has been a desirable address since the 17th century (pp76–89).

St-Gervais–St-Protais
The oldest organ in Paris, dating from the early 17th century, is in this church (p99).

Pont Neuf
M

nt Neuf

M **Châtelet**

Hotel de Ville
M

Pont au Change

Pont Notre Dame

Cité
M

Pont d'Arcole

Pont Louis Philippe

RER M
St-Michel

Petit Pont

Pont au Double

Pont St. Louis

M **Pont Marie**

Pont Marie

Pont de Archeveche

Pont de la Tournelle

Sully Morland
M

Pont de Sully

Notre-Dame
This towering cathedral surveys the river (pp82–5).

Bateaux Parisiens

How to Take a River or Canal Trip

RIVER SEINE CRUISES on *bateaux-mouches* and *vedettes* pleasure boats operate along the main sightseeing reaches of the river, taking in many of the city's famous monuments. The Batobus river service operates as a shuttle or bus service, allowing you to get on and off anywhere along the route. The main city canal trips operate along the old industrial canal at St-Martin in the city's east.

Types of Boats
Bateaux-mouches, *the largest of the pleasure-cruise boats, are a spectacular sight, with their passenger areas enclosed in glass for excellent all-around viewing. At night, floodlights Illuminate riverbank buildings. A more luxurious version of these is used on the Bateaux Parisien cruises. The* vedettes *are smaller, more intimate boats, with viewing through glass walls. The Canauxrama canal boats are flat-bottomed.*

Pleasure-cruise boats passing under the Pont Alexandre III

SEINE CRUISES AND CANAL SHUTTLE SERVICES
The Seine cruises and shuttle services information below includes the location of boarding points, the nearest metro and RER stations and the nearest bus routes. Lunch and dinner cruises must be reserved in advance, and passengers must board them 30 minutes before departure.

ILE de FRANCE
Vedettes de Paris Ile de France Seine Cruise
A fleet of six boats, each of which has the capacity to carry an average of up to 100 passengers in comfort and style. The boarding point is:

Pont d'Iena.
Map 10 D2. **(** 01 47 05 71 29. **M** Bir Hakeim. **RER** Champ de Mars. **(bus)** 22, 30, 32, 44, 69, 72, 82, 87. **Departures** May–Oct: 10am–10pm daily (every hour); Nov–Apr: 11am–8pm daily (every hour). **Duration** 1 hr. **Dinner Cruise** 8pm Thu–Sat. **Duration** 3 hr.

CANAUXRAMA
Parc de la Villette Shuttle Service
This canal trip takes you from the Rotonde de Ledoux, in the Bassin de la Villette, to the Parc de la Villette *(see pp234–9).* The boarding points are:

13 Quai de la Loire.
Map 8 E1.
(01 42 39 15 00. **M** Jaures. **Parc de la Villette.** **M** Porte de Pantin.
Departures Jul & Aug: 11am–noon, 1:30pm–6pm Tue–Sun (every 30 min); Apr–Oct: 11am–noon, 1:30pm–6pm Sat, Sun & public hols (every 30 min) . **Duration** 15 min.

BATEAUX PARISIENS
Bateaux Parisiens Notre-Dame Seine Cruise
This is the company that also organizes the Tour Eiffel trip. This trip, however, operates only during the summer, following the same route but in the opposite direction. The boarding point is:

Porte de Montebello.
Map 13 B4. **(** 01 43 26 92 55. **M** Maubert–Mutualite, St-Michel. **RER** St-Michel. **(bus)** 24, 27, 47.
Departures May–Oct: 2:20–6:20pm daily (every hour). Also 8:20pm & 9:20pm Fri, Sat. **Duration** 1 hr.

BATEAUX PARISIENS
Bateaux Parisiens Tour Eiffel Seine Cruise
This company has a fleet of seven boats with a carrying capacity of 100 to 400 passengers. A commentary is provided in English and French. The boarding point is:

Pont d'Iena.
Map 10 D2. **(** 01 44 11 33 44. **M** Trocadéro, Bir Hakeim. **RER** Champs de Mars. **(bus)** 42, 82, 72.
Departures Easter–Oct: 10am–10:30pm daily (every 30 min); Nov–Easter: 10am–9pm Sun–Fri (every hour); 10am–10pm Sat (every 30 min). **Duration** 1 hr. **Lunch cruise** 1pm daily. **Duration** 1 hr 45min. **Dinner cruise** 8:30pm. **Duration** 2 hr 30 min. Unsuitable for children. Jacket & tie required.

Boarding Points

The boarding points for the river cruises and the Batobus services are easy to find

along the river. Here you can buy tickets, and there are such amenities as snack bars. Major cruise companies also have foreign exchange booths. There is limited parking around the points, but none near the Pont Neuf.

River boarding point

Batobus

Shuttle service. A daily pass is available. Board at:
Eiffel Tower. Map 10 D3. **M** Bir Hakeim. **Musée d'Orsay. Map** 12 D2. **M** Solferino. **Louvre. Map** 12 E2. **M** Louvre. **St-Germain-de-Prés:. Map** 12 E3. **M** St-Germaine-de-Prés. **Notre-Dame. Map** 13 B4. **M** Cité. **Hôtel de Ville. Map** 13 B4. **M** Hôtel de Ville. **Departures** Apr–Oct: 10am–7pm (9pm Jun–Aug) daily (every 25 min).

BATEAUX-MOUCHES

Bateaux-Mouches Seine Cruise

This well-known pleasure-boat company's fleet of 11 boats carries between 600 and 1,400 passengers at a time. The boarding point is:

Pont de l'Alma.
Map 10 F1. **C** 01 42 25 96 10. **M** Alma-Marceau. **RER** Pont de l'Alma. 🚌 28, 42, 49, 63, 72, 80, 92. **Departures** Mar–Nov: 10am–11:30pm daily (every 30 min); Nov–Mar: 11am, 2:30pm, 4pm, 9pm (with extra departures on Sat, Sun & public hols). **Duration** 1 hr 15 min. **Lunch cruise** Mar–Nov only.1pm Tue–Sun. **Duration** 1 hr 45 min. Children under 12, half price. **Dinner cruise** 8:30pm daily. **Duration** 2 hr 15 min. Jacket and tie required.

Vedettes du Pont Neuf

Bateaux Vedettes Pont Neuf Seine Cruise

This company runs a fleet of six 80-passenger boats. The boats are of an older style and provide a quainter cruise. The boarding point is:

Square du Vert-Galant (Pont Neuf). **Map** 12 F3. **C** 01 53 00 98 98. **M** Pont Neuf. **RER** Châtelet. 🚌 24, 27, 58, 67, 70, 72, 74, 75. **Departures** Apr–Oct: 10:30am, 11:15am, noon; 1:30pm–6:30pm, 9–10:30pm daily (every 30 min); Nov–Mar: 10:30am, 11:15am, noon, 2pm–6:30pm (every 45 min); 8pm, 10pm Mon– Wed, Fri; 10:30am, 11:15am, noon, 2pm–6:30pm, 9pm–10:30pm (every 30 min) Sat, Sun. **Duration** 1 hr.

CANAL TRIPS

The Canauxrama company operates boat cruises along the city's Canal St-Martin and along the Canal de l'Ourcq. The St-Martin journey passes along the tree-lined canal, which has nine locks, two swing bridges and eight romantic footbridges. The Canal de l'Ourcq trip travels well into the French countryside as far as the Vignely lock. The **Paris Canal Company** (01 42 40 96 97) also has a St-Martin canal trip, but this one extends beyond the canal, passing into the River Seine and traveling up as far as the Musée d'Orsay.

CANAUXRAMA

Canal St-Martin

The Canauxrama company has two 125-passenger boats that operate between the Bassin de la Villette and the Porte de l'Arsenal. The boarding points are:
Bassin de la Villette. Map 8 E1. **M** Jaures.
Porte de l'Arsenal. Map 14 E4. **M** Bastille.
C 01 42 39 15 00. **Departures**, Apr–Oct, times may vary so call to check and to make a reservation: Bassin de la Villette 9:45am and 2:45pm; Porte de l'Arsenal 9:45am and 2:30pm daily. On weekday mornings there are concessions for students, pensioners and children under 12. Children under six travel free. Concert cruises are available on chartered trips on the Canal St-Martin and the Seine. **Duration** 3 hr.

Canal de l'Ourcq

This all-day cruise extends 67 miles (108 km) north-east of Canal St-Martin. Passengers stop for their own lunch at the charming village of Claye-Souilly. The boarding point is:
Bassin de la Villette. Map 8 E1. **M** Jaures. **C** 01 42 39 15 00. **Departures** Apr–Oct: 8:30am Thu–Tue. Reservations necessary. Not suitable for children. **Duration** 8 hr 30 min.

Canal-cruise boat in the Bassin de la Villette

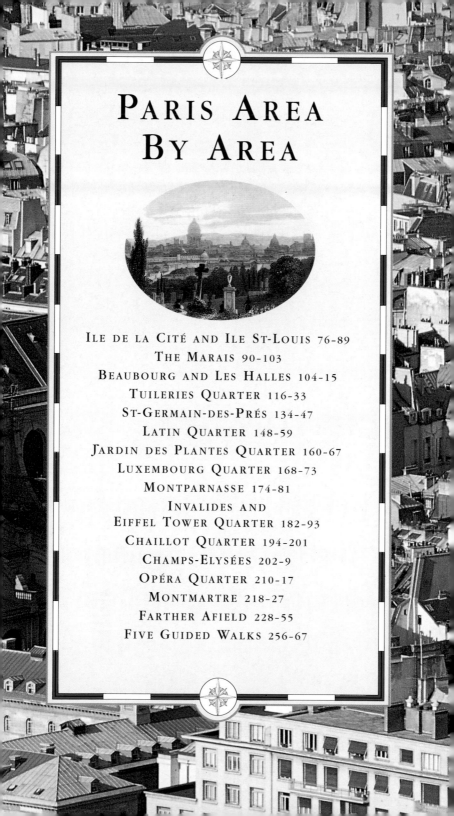

PARIS AREA BY AREA

ILE DE LA CITÉ AND ILE ST-LOUIS

THE HISTORY of the Ile de la Cité is the history of Paris. This island on the Seine was no more than a primitive village when the conquering Julius Caesar arrived in 53 BC. Ancient kings later made it the center of political power, and in medieval times it became the home of church and law. Although no longer the seat of power, the island now draws armies of tourists to its historic attractions, including the imposing Palais de Justice and the brilliant Gothic masterpiece, Notre-Dame.

The medieval huddles of tiny houses and excruciatingly narrow streets that so characterized the

The motto of the city of Paris

island at one time were swept away by the spacious thoroughfares built in the 19th century. But there are still small areas of charm and relief, among them the colorful bird and flower markets, the romantic Square du Vert-Galant and the ancient Place Dauphine.

At the eastern end of the island, the St-Louis bridge connects it to the smaller Ile St-Louis. This former swampy pastureland was transformed into an elegant 17th-century residential area. More recently, rich artists, physicians, actresses and heiresses have lived there. Its tree-lined quays are the most enchanting aspect – intimate and picturesque.

SIGHTS AT A GLANCE

Historic Buildings
Hôtel Dieu ⑥
Conciergerie ⑧
Palais de Justice ⑩
Hôtel de Lauzun ⑯

Bridges
Pont Neuf ⑫

Monuments
Mémorial des Martyrs et de la Déportation ④

Markets
Marché aux Fleurs and Marché aux Oiseaux ⑦

Squares and Gardens
Square du Jean XXIII ③
Place Dauphine ⑪
Square du Vert-Galant ⑬

Museums and Galleries
Musée de Notre-Dame de Paris ②
Crypte Archéologique ⑤
Musée Adam Mickiewicz ⑭

Churches and Cathedrals
Notre-Dame pp82–5 ①
Sainte-Chapelle pp88–9 ⑨
St-Louis-en-l'Ile ⑮

GETTING THERE

This area served by the metro station at Cité and the RER at St-Michel. The bus routes 21, 38, 47, 85 and 96 cross the Ile de la Cité, and 67, 86 and 87 cross the Ile St-Louis.

SEE ALSO

- *Street Finder*, map 12–13
- *St-Louis Walk* pp262–3
- *Where to Stay* pp278–9
- *Restaurants* pp296–8

KEY

▦	Street-by-Street map
Ⓜ	Metro station
RER	RER station
Ⓟ	Parking

0 meters   400

0 yards   400

View of the Pont Neuf and Ile de la Cité from the Pont des Arts

Street by Street: Ile de la Cité

THE ORIGINS OF PARIS are here on the Ile de la Cité, the boat-shaped island on the Seine first inhabited over 2,000 years ago by Celtic tribes. One tribe, the Parisii, eventually gave its name to the city. The island offered a convenient river crossing on the route between northern and southern Gaul and was easily defended. In later centuries the settlement was expanded by the Romans, the Franks and the Capetian kings to form the nucleus of today's city.

There is no older place in Paris, and remains of the first buildings can still be seen today in the archeological crypt under the square in front of Notre-Dame, the great medieval cathedral and place of pilgrimage for millions of visitors each year. At the other end of the island is another Gothic masterpiece, Sainte-Chapelle – a miracle of light.

★ Conciergerie
A grisly antechamber to the guillotine, this prison was much used in the Revolution **8**

The Cour du Mai
is the impressive main courtyard of the Palais de Justice.

Metro Cité

★ Sainte-Chapelle
A jewel of Gothic architecture and one of the most magical sights of Paris, Sainte-Chapelle is noted for the magnificence of its stained glass **9**

To Pont Neuf

The Quai des Orfèvres
owes its name to the goldsmiths *(orfèvres)* who frequented the area from medieval times onward.

Palais de Justice
With its ancient towers lining the quays, the old royal palace is today a massive complex of law courts. Its history extends back 16 centuries **10**

The Préfecture de Police
is the headquarters of the police and was the scene of intense battles during World War II.

The Statue of Charlemagne
commemorates the emperor who was crowned in 768. He united all the Christian peoples of the West.

0 meters	100
0 yards	100

★ **Marché aux Fleurs et Oiseaux**
The flower and bird market is a colorful, lively island sight. Paris was once famous for its flower markets, but this is now one of the last ⑦

LOCATOR MAP
See Central Paris Map pp12–13

Hôtel Dieu
Once an orphanage, this is now a city hospital ⑥

★ **Crypte Archéologique**
Deep under the square, there are remains of houses from 2,000 years ago ⑤

STAR SIGHTS

★ **Notre-Dame**

★ **Sainte-Chapelle**

★ **Conciergerie**

★ **Marché aux Fleurs et Oiseaux**

★ **Crypte Archéologique**

KEY

— — — Suggested route

The Rue Chanoinesse has had many famous residents, such as the 17th-century playwright Racine.

Musée Notre-Dame
Many exhibits tracing the cathedral's history are in this museum ②

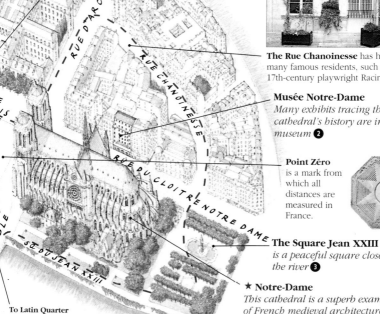

Point Zéro
is a mark from which all distances are measured in France.

The Square Jean XXIII
is a peaceful square close to the river ③

★ **Notre-Dame**
This cathedral is a superb example of French medieval architecture ①

To Latin Quarter

Notre-Dame from the Left Bank

Notre-Dame ❶

See pp82–5.

Musée de Notre-Dame de Paris ❷

10 Rue du Cloître-Notre-Dame 75004. **Map** 13 B4. **℡** 01 43 25 42 92. **M** Cité. **Open** 2:30pm–6pm Wed, Sat, Sun (last adm: 5:40pm). **Adm charge**.

FOUNDED IN 1951, this museum has exhibits and documents that commemorate and illustrate the great events in Notre-Dame's history. The displays include Gallo-Roman objects; old engravings; works of art; and the city of Paris's oldest extant Christian relic, a fine 4th-century glass cup.

A Gallo-Roman coin

Square Jean XXIII ❸

75004. **Map** 13 B4. **M** Cité.

NOTRE-DAME'S St. Stephen's door opens onto this pleasant garden square, dedicated to Pope John XXIII. The garden runs alongside the river and is an excellent place for enjoying the sculptures, rose windows and flying buttresses of the east end of the cathedral. From the 17th century, the square was occupied by the archbishop's palace, which was ransacked by rioters in 1831 and later demolished. A square was conceived as a replacement by the Prefect of Paris, Rambuteau. The Gothic-style fountain of the Virgin standing in the center of the square has been there since 1845.

Mémorial des Martyrs et de la Déportation ❹

Sq de l'Ile-de-la Cité 75004. **Map** 13 B4. **℡** 01 46 33 87 56. **M** Cité. **Open** Apr–Sep: 10am–noon, 2pm–7pm daily; Oct–Mar: 10am–noon, 2pm–5pm daily.

THE SIMPLE, modern memorial to the 200,000 French men, women and children deported to Nazi concentration camps in World War II is covered with a roll-call of names and the camps to which they were deported. Earth from these camps has been used to form small tombs. At the far end is the tomb dedicated to the Unknown Deportee.

Inside the Mémorial des Martyrs et de la Déportation

The Square du Jean XXIII behind Notre-Dame

Gallo-Roman ruins in the Crypte Archéologique

Crypte Archéologique ❺

Pl du Parvis Notre-Dame 75004. **Map** 13 A4. [01 43 29 83 51. M Cité. **Open** Apr–Sep: 10am–5:30pm daily; Oct–Mar: 10am–5pm daily (last adm: 30 min before closing). **Closed** May 1, Nov 1 & 11, Dec 25, Jan 1. **Adm charge.**

Situated on the main square (the *parvis*) in front of Notre-Dame and stretching 80 m (262 ft) underground, this crypt exhibits the remains of foundations and walls that pre-date the cathedral by several hundred years. Here are the remnants of a house from Lutèce, the settlement of the Parisii, the Celtic tribe who inhabited the island 2,000 years ago and eventually gave their name to the city.

Hôtel Dieu ❻

1 Pl du Parvis Notre-Dame 75004. **Map** 13 A4. **Not open** to the public for visits. M Cité.

On the north side of the place de Parvis Nottre-Dame is the Hôtel Dieu, the hospital serving central Paris. It was built on the site of an orphanage between 1866 and 1878. The original Hôtel Dieu, built in the 12th century and stretching across the island to both banks of the river, was demolished in the 19th century to make way for one of Baron Haussmann's urban-planning schemes.

It was here in 1944 that the Paris police courageously resisted the Germans; the battle is commemorated by a monument in Cour de 19-Août.

Paris's main flower market

Marché aux Fleurs and Marché aux Oiseaux ❼

Pl Louis-Lépine 75001. **Map** 13 A3. M Cité. **Open** 8am–6pm Mon–Sat; 8am–7pm Sun.

The yearround flower market adds color and scent to an area otherwise dominated by administrative buildings. It is the most famous and unfortunately one of the last remaining flower markets in Paris, offering a wide range of specialist varieties such as orchids. Each Sunday it makes way for the cacophony of the caged bird market.

Conciergerie ❽

1 Quai de l'Horloge 75001. **Map** 13 A3. [01 53 73 78 50. M Cité. **Open** Apr–Sep: 9:30am–6:30pm daily; Oct–Mar: 10am–5pm daily (last adm: 30 min before closing). **Closed** Jan 1, May 1, Nov 1 & 11, Dec 25. **Adm charge.** 11am, 3pm daily.

Occupying part of the lower floor of the Palais de Justice, the historic Conciergerie was originally the residence of the Comte des Cierges (Count of the Candles), the palace superintendent in charge of taxes and lodgings. He became chief gaoler when the splendid Gothic halls were transformed into a prison. Henry IV's assassin, Ravaillac, was imprisoned and tortured here.

During the Revolution it housed over 4,000 prisoners, including Marie-Antoinette, who was held in a tiny cell until her execution, and Charlotte Corday, who stabbed Revolutionary leader Marat as he lay in his bath. Ironically, the Revolutionary judges Danton and Robespierre also became "tenants" before being sent to the guillotine.

The Conciergerie has a superb four-aisled Gothic Salle des Gens d'Armes (Hall of the Men-at-Arms), where guards of the royal household once lived. The building, renovated in the 19th century, retains the 11th-century torture chamber, the Bonbec Tower and the 14th-century clock tower. Today the building is well scrubbed, and concerts and wine tastings are some of its attractions.

A portrait of Marie-Antoinette in the Conciergerie, awaiting her execution at the guillotine

Hôtel Dieu, central Paris's hospital

Notre-Dame ●

No OTHER BUILDING is so associated with the history of Paris as Notre-Dame. It stands majestically on the Ile de la Cité, cradle of the city. Pope Alexander III laid the first stone in 1163, marking the start of 170 years of toil by armies of Gothic architects and medieval craftsmen. Ever since, a procession of the famous has passed through the three main doors below the massive towers.

The cathedral is a Gothic masterpiece, standing on the site of a Roman temple. At the time it was finished, in about 1330, it was 430 ft (130 m) long and featured flying buttresses, a large transept, a deep choir and 228-ft (69-m) high towers.

★ **West Front**
Three main doors with superb statuary, a central rose window and an openwork gallery are important details.

The south tower houses the cathedral's famous Emmanuel bell.

★ **Galerie des Chimières**
The cathedral's legendary gargoyles (chimières) hide behind a large upper gallery between the towers.

★ **West Rose Window**
This window depicts the Virgin in a medallion of rich reds and blues.

The Kings' Gallery features 28 Kings of Judah above the main door gazing down.

Portal of the Virgin
The Virgin surrounded by saints and kings is a fine composition of 13th-century statues.

STAR FEATURES

★ **West Front and Portals**

★ **Flying Buttresses**

★ **Rose Windows**

★ **Galerie des Chimières**

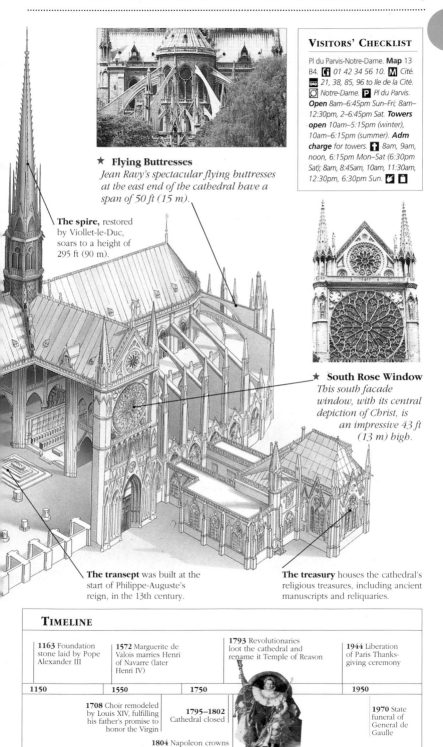

VISITORS' CHECKLIST

Pl du Parvis-Notre-Dame. **Map** 13
B4. 📞 01 42 34 56 10. Ⓜ Cité.
🚌 21, 38, 85, 96 to Ile de la Cité.
Ⓒ Notre-Dame. 🅿 Pl du Parvis.
Open 8am–6:45pm Sun–Fri; 8am–
12:30pm, 2–6:45pm Sat. **Towers
open** 10am–5:15pm (winter),
10am–6:15pm (summer). **Adm
charge** for towers. 🔔 8am, 9am,
noon, 6:15pm Mon–Sat (6:30pm
Sat); 8am, 8:45am, 10am, 11:30am,
12:30pm, 6:30pm Sun. 🎥 📷

★ **Flying Buttresses**
*Jean Ravy's spectacular flying buttresses
at the east end of the cathedral have a
span of 50 ft (15 m).*

The spire, restored
by Viollet-le-Duc,
soars to a height of
295 ft (90 m).

★ **South Rose Window**
*This south façade
window, with its central
depiction of Christ, is
an impressive 43 ft
(13 m) high.*

The transept was built at the
start of Philippe-Auguste's
reign, in the 13th century.

The treasury houses the cathedral's
religious treasures, including ancient
manuscripts and reliquaries.

TIMELINE

1163 Foundation stone laid by Pope Alexander III	**1572** Marguerite de Valois marries Henri of Navarre (later Henri IV)	**1793** Revolutionaries loot the cathedral and rename it Temple of Reason	**1944** Liberation of Paris Thanksgiving ceremony
1150	1550	1750	1950
	1708 Choir remodeled by Louis XIV, fulfilling his father's promise to honor the Virgin	**1795–1802** Cathedral closed	**1970** State funeral of General de Gaulle
	1804 Napoleon crowns himself Emperor of France	*Napoleon I*	

A Guided Tour of Notre-Dame

NOTRE-DAME'S INTERIOR grandeur is strikingly apparent in its high-vaulted central nave. This is bisected by a huge transept, at either end of which is a medieval rose window, 43 ft (13 m) in diameter. Works by major sculptors adorn the cathedral. Among them are Jean Ravy's old choir-screen carvings, Nicolas Coustou's *Pietà* and Antoine Coysevox's Louis XIV statue. In this majestic setting kings and emperors were crowned and royal Crusaders were blessed. But Notre-Dame was also the scene of turmoil. Revolutionaries ransacked it, banished religion, changed it into a temple to the Cult of Reason and then used it as a wine store. Napoleon restored religion in 1804, and architect Viollet-le-Duc later restored the buildings, replacing missing statues as well as raising the spire and fixing the gargoyles.

A jeweled chalice of Notre-Dame

⑨ North Rose Window
This 13th-century stained-glass window, depicting the Virgin encircled by figures from the Old Testament, is 69 ft (21 m) high.

⑩ View and Gargoyles
The 387 steps up the north tower lead to the famous gargoyles and magnificent views of Paris.

Stairs to the tower

Entrance

① View of Interior
From the main entrance, the view takes in the high-vaulted central nave looking down toward the huge transept, the choir and the high altar.

KEY

--- Walk route

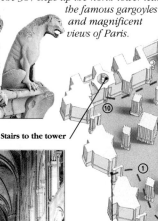

② Le Brun's "May" Paintings
These religious paintings by Charles Le Brun hang in the side chapels. In the 17th and 18th centuries, the Paris guilds presented a painting to the cathedral on May Day each year.

⑧ Carved Choir Stalls

Noted for their 18th-century carved woodwork, the choir stalls were commissioned by Louis XIV, whose statue stands behind the high altar. Among the details carved in bas-relief on the back of the high stalls are scenes from the life of the Virgin.

⑦ Louis XIII Statue

After many years of childless marriage, Louis XIII pledged to erect a high altar and to redecorate the east chancel to honor the Virgin if an heir was born to him. The future Louis XIV was born in 1638, but it took 60 years before the promises were made good. One of the surviving features from that time is the carved choir stalls.

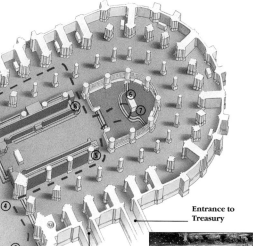

⑥ Pietà

Behind the high altar is Nicolas Coustou's Pietà, *standing on a gilded base sculpted by François Girardon.*

Entrance to Treasury

Entrance to Sacristy

⑤ Chancel Screen

A 14th-century high stone screen enclosed the chancel and provided canons at prayer with peace and solitude from noisy congregations. Some of it has survived to screen the first three north and south bays.

③ South Rose Window

Located at the south end of the transept, this window retains some of its original 13th-century stained glass. The window depicts Christ in the center, surrounded by virgins, saints and the 12 Apostles.

④ Statue of the Virgin and Child

Against the southeast pillar of the transept stands the 14th-century statue of the Virgin and Child. It was brought to the cathedral from the chapel of St. Aignan and is known as Notre-Dame de Paris (Our Lady of Paris).

The Pont Neuf, extending to the north and south of the Ile de la Cité

Sainte-Chapelle ❾

See pp88–9.

A Sainte-Chapelle decoration of angels with the Crown of Thorns

Palais de Justice ❿

4 Blvd du Palais (entrance by the Cour de Mai) 75001. **Map** 13 A3.
📞 *01 44 32 50 00.* Ⓜ *Cité.*
Open *9am–6pm Mon–Fri (seasonal variations).* 🚫 🖥 🏛

THIS HUGE BLOCK of build-ings making up the law courts stretches the entire width of the Ile de la Cité. It is a splendid sight with its old towers lining the quays. The site has been occupied since Roman times and was the seat of royal power until Charles V moved the court to the Marais in the 14th century. In April 1793 the Revolutionary Tribunal began dispensing

justice from the Première Chambre (gilded chamber). Today the site embodies Napoleon's great legacy – the French judicial system.

Place Dauphine ⓫

75001 (enter by Rue Henri-Robert).
Map 12 F3. Ⓜ *Pont Neuf, Cité.*

EAST OF PONT NEUF is this ancient square, laid out in 1607 by Henri IV and named after the Dauphin, the future Louis XIII. No. 14 is one of the few buildings to have avoided any subsequent restoration. This haven of 17th-century charm is popular with *pétanque* (boules) players and employees of the adjoining Palais de Justice.

Pont Neuf ⓬

75001. **Map** 12 F3. Ⓜ *Pont Neuf, Cité.*

DESPITE ITS name (New Bridge), this bridge is the oldest in Paris and has been immortalized by major literary and artistic figures since it was built. The first stone was laid by Henri III in 1578, but it was Henri IV who inaugurated it and gave it its name in 1607. The bridge has 12 arches and spans 912 ft (275 m). The first stone bridge to be built without houses, it heralded a new era in the relationship between the Cité and the river and has been popular ever since. Fittingly, Henri IV's statue stands in the central section.

A sculptured relief on the Palais de Justice

Henri IV in Square du Vert-Galant

Square du Vert-Galant ⑬

75001. **Map** 12 F3. **M** *Pont Neuf, Cité.*

ONE OF THE magical spots of Paris, this square bears the nickname of Henri IV. This amorous and colorful monarch did much to beautify Paris in the early 17th century, and his popularity has lasted to this day. From here there are splendid views of the Louvre and the Right Bank of the river, where Henri was assassinated in 1610. This is also the point from which the Vedettes de Paris pleasure boats depart *(see pp72–3).*

Musée Adam Mickiewicz ⑭

6 Quai d'Orléans 75004. **Map** 13 C4. **Ⓒ** *01 55 42 83 83.* **M** *Pont Marie.* **Open** *2pm–6pm Thu.* **Closed** *mid-Jul–mid-Sep, 2 weeks at Christmas and Easter, public hols.* **Adm charge.** ☑

THE POLISH Romantic poet Adam Mickiewicz, who lived in Paris in the 19th century, was a major force in Polish cultural and political life, devoting his writing to helping his countrymen who were oppressed at home and abroad. The museum – founded in 1903 by the poet's eldest son, Ladislas – and adjoining library together form probably the finest Polish collection outside Poland: paintings, books, maps, emigration archives covering the 19th and 20th centuries and, above all, Frédéric Chopin memorabilia, including his death mask.

St-Louis-en-l'Ile ⑮

19 bis Rue St-Louis-en-l'Ile 75004. **Map** 13 C4. **Ⓒ** *01 46 34 11 60.* **M** *Pont Marie.* **Open** *8am–noon, 3pm–7pm Tue–Sun.* **Closed** *public hols.* **Concerts.**

THE CONSTRUCTION of this church was begun in 1664 from plans by the royal architect Louis Le Vau, who lived on the island. It was completed and consecrated in 1726. Among its outstanding exterior features are the 1741 iron clock at the entrance and the pierced iron spire.

The interior, in the Baroque style, is richly decorated with gilding and marble. There is a statue of St. Louis holding a crusader's sword. A plaque in the north aisle, given in 1926, bears the inscription "in grateful memory of St. Louis in whose honor the City of St. Louis, Missouri is named." The church is also associated with Carthage Cathedral in Tunisia, where the body of St. Louis is buried.

A bust of Adam Mickiewicz

The interior of St.-Louis-en-l'Ile

Hôtel de Lauzun ⑯

17 Quai d'Anjou 75004. **Map** 13 C4. **M** *Pont Marie.* **Not open** to the public.

THIS SPLENDID mansion was built by Louis Le Vau in the mid-1650s for Charles Gruyn des Bordes, an arms dealer. It was sold in 1682 to the French military commander Duc de Lauzun, who was a favorite of Louis XIV. It later became a focus for Paris's Bohemian literary and artistic life. It now belongs to the city of Paris and, for those lucky enough to see inside, offers an unsurpassed insight into wealthy lifestyles in the 17th century. Charles Le Brun worked on the decoration of its magnificent paneling and painted ceilings before moving on to Versailles.

The poet Charles Baudelaire (1821–67) lived on the third floor and wrote the major part of his controversial master-piece *Les Fleurs du Mal* here in a room packed with antiques and bric-a-brac. The celebrated French Romantic poet, traveler, and critic, Théophile Gautier (1811–72), had apartments here in 1848. Meetings of the Club des Haschischines (the Hashish-Eaters' Club) took place on the premises.

Other famous residents were the Austrian poet Rainer Maria Rilke, the English artist Walter Sickert and the German composer Richard Wagner. Nowadays it is used for public receptions by the mayor of Paris.

Sainte-Chapelle ❾

ETHEREAL AND MAGICAL, Sainte-Chapelle has been hailed as one of the greatest architectural masterpieces of the Western world. In the Middle Ages the devout likened this church to "a gateway to heaven." Today no visitor can fail to be transported by the blaze of light created by the 15 magnificent stained-glass windows, separated by the narrowest of columns that soar 50 ft (15 m) to the star-studded, vaulted roof. The windows portray over 1,000 religious scenes in a kaleidoscope of red, gold, green, blue and mauve. The chapel was built in 1248 by Louis IX to house Christ's purported Crown of Thorns and other relics.

The spire
rises 245 ft (75 m) into the air. It was erected in 1853 after three previous spires burned down.

The Crown of Thorns
decorates the pinnacle as a symbol of the first relic bought by Louis IX.

★ **Rose Window**
Best seen at sunset, the religious story of the Apocalypse is told in 86 panels of stained glass. The window was a gift from Charles VIII in 1485.

STAR FEATURES

★ **Rose Window**

★ **Window of Christ's Passion**

★ **Apostle Statues**

★ **Window of the Relics**

Main Portal
The two-tier structure of the portal, the lower half of which is shown here, echoes that of the chapel.

ST. LOUIS' RELICS

Louis IX was so devout a king that he came to be known as Saint Louis. In 1239 he acquired the Crown of Thorns from the Emperor of Constantinople and then, in 1241, other relics, including a fragment of Christ's Cross. He built this beautiful chapel as a shrine to house them. Louis paid nearly three times more for the relics than he did for the whole of the construction of Sainte-Chapelle.

VISITORS' CHECKLIST

4 Blvd du Palais. **Map** 13 A3.
[01 53 73 78 50. **M** Cité.
🚌 21, 38, 85, 96 to Ile de la Cité. **RER** St.-Michel. **[O]** Notre-Dame. **P** Palais de Justice.
Open Apr–Sep: 9:30am–6:30pm; Oct–Mar: 10am–5pm daily. Last adm 30 mins before closing.
Closed Jan 1, May 1, Nov 1 & 11 & Dec 25. **Adm charge.**

The angel
once revolved so that its cross could be seen from anywhere in Paris.

UPPER CHAPEL WINDOWS

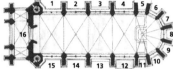

1 Genesis
2 Exodus
3 Numbers
4 Deuteronomy: Joshua
5 Judges
6 *left* Isaiah *right* Rod of Jesse
7 *left* St. John the Evangelist *right* Childhood of Christ
8 Christ's Passion
9 *left* St. John the Baptist *right* Story of Daniel
10 Ezekiel
11 *left* Jeremiah *right* Tobiah
12 Judith and Job
13 Esther
14 Book of Kings
15 Story of the Relics
16 Rose Window: The Apocalypse

Upper Chapel
The windows are a pictorial Bible, showing scenes from the Old and New Testaments.

★ Window of Christ's Passion
The Last Supper is shown here in one of the most beautiful windows in the upper chapel.

★ Apostle Statues
These magnificent examples of medieval wood carving adorn the 12 pillars of the upper chapel.

★ Window of the Relics
This shows the journey of the True Cross and the nails of the Crucifixion to Sainte-Chapelle.

Lower Chapel
Servants and commoners worshiped here, while the chapel above was reserved for the use of the king and the royal family.

THE MARAIS

THE MARAIS IS ARGUABLY the most fascinating area of Paris. A place of royal residence in the 17th century, it was mercilessly abandoned to the people during the Revolution and descended into an architectural wasteland, before being rescued in the 1960s. It was officially declared a historical monument by the Charles de Gaulle government in 1962, and its resurrection then began.

Buildings have come to life, and the area is fashionable again with new galleries and restaurants, chic fashion boutiques and cultural centers. The main streets and the narrow passageways are again bustling. Some of the traders have been driven out by high prices, but many artisans, bakers and small cafés have survived, as has the ethnic mix of Jews, former Algerian settlers, Asians and many other groups.

SIGHTS AT A GLANCE

Historic Buildings and Streets
Hôtel de Lamoignon **2**
Rue des Francs-Bourgeois **3**
Rue des Rosiers **8**
Hôtel de Ville **19**
Hôtel de Rohan **22**
No. 3 Rue Volta **25**

Churches
St-Paul–St-Louis **15**
St-Gervais–St-Protais **18**
Cloître des Billettes **20**
Notre-Dame-des-Blancs-Manteaux **21**

Museums and Galleries
Musée Carnavalet pp96–7 **1**
Musée Cognacq-Jay **4**
Maison de Victor Hugo **6**
Hôtel de Sully **7**
Hôtel de Coulanges **9**
Hôtel Libéral Bruand (Musée Bricard) **10**
Musée Picasso pp100–1 **11**
Hôtel de Sens **16**

Hôtel de Soubise **23**
Hôtel Guénégaud (Musée de la Chasse et de la Nature) **24**
Musée d'Art et d'Histoire du Judaïsme **27**

Monuments and Statues
Colonne de Juillet **13**
Mémorial du Martyr Juif Inconnu **17**

Opera Houses
Opéra de Paris Bastille **12**

Squares
Place des Vosges **5**
Place de la Bastille **14**
Square du Temple **26**

GETTING THERE
The metro stations in the area include Bastille and Hôtel de Ville. Bus route 29 travels along Rue des Francs-Bourgeois; passing by the Rue de Sévigné, where the Musée Carnavalet is located; and by the Place des Vosges.

SEE ALSO
- *Street Finder*, map 13–14
- *Where to Stay* pp278–9
- *Restaurants* pp296–8

KEY
Street-by-Street map
M Metro station
Batobus boarding point
P Parking

0 meters 400
0 yards 400

An office worker taking a break amid the statuary of the Square Georges Caïn

Street by Street: The Marais

ONCE AN AREA of marshland as its name suggests (*marais* means swamp), the Marais grew steadily in importance from the 14th century, by virtue of its proximity to the Louvre, the preferred residence of Charles V. Its heyday was in the 17th century, when it became the fashionable area for the wealthy classes. They built many grand and sumptuous mansions, the *hôtels* that still dot the Marais today. Many of these mansions have recently been restored and turned into museums. One of the most intriguing is the Carnavalet, whose exhibits trace the history of Paris from Roman times.

To the Pompidou Center

RUE BARBETTE

RUE ELZEVIR

RUE PAYENNE

RUE DES BLANCS-MANTEAUX

RUE PAVÉE

RUE MALHER

FRAN

RUE DES HOSPITALIERES ST GERVAIS

RUE DES ROSIERS

Rue des Francs-Bourgeois
This ancient street is lined with important museums ❸

Hôtel Libéral Bruand
Named after the architect who built it for his own use, this mansion now contains a museum devoted to locks ❿

Rue des Rosiers
The smell of hot pastrami and borscht wafts from restaurants and shops in the heart of the Jewish area ❽

Musée Cognacq-Jay
An exquisite collection of 18th-century paintings and furniture is shown in perfect period setting ❹

STAR SIGHTS

★ **Musée Picasso**

★ **Musée Carnavalet**

★ **Place des Vosges**

KEY

– – – Suggested route

0 meters	100
0 yards	100

Hôtel de Lamoignon
Behind the ornate doorway of this fine mansion is Paris's historical library ❷

★ Musée Picasso
The palatial home of an 17th-century salt-tax collector is the setting for the largest collection of Picassos in the world, the result of a family bequest to the state ⓫

LOCATOR MAP
See Central Paris Map pp12–13

The Hôtel le Peletier de St-Fargeau adjoins the Hôtel Carnavalet to form the Museum of Paris History.

★ Musée Carnavalet
The statue of Louis XIV in Roman dress by Coysevox is in the courtyard of the Hôtel Carnavalet ❶

Maison de Victor Hugo
Author of Les Misérables, *Victor Hugo lived at No. 6 Place des Vosges, where his house is now a museum of his life and work* ❻

To Metro Sully Morland

★ Place des Vosges
Once the site of jousting and tournaments, the historic Place des Vosges, in the very heart of the Marais, is a square of perfect symmetry ❺

Hôtel de Sully
This Renaissance hôtel was built for a notorious gambler ❼

Musée Carnavalet ❶

See pp96–7.

Hôtel de Lamoignon ❷

24 Rue Pavée 75004. **Map** 14 D3.
[*01 44 59 29 40.* **M** *St-Paul.*
Open *9:30am–6pm Mon–Sat.* **Closed**
public hols & Aug 1–15. ⊘ ☐

T HE IMPOSING Hôtel de
Lamoignon is home to the
historical library of the city of
Paris. This mansion was built
in 1584 for Diane de France,
also known as the Duchesse
d'Angoulême, daughter of
Henri II. The building is
noted for six high Corinthian
pilasters topped by a triangular
pediment and flourishes of
dogs' heads, bows, arrows
and quivers – recalling
Diane's passion for hunting.
The collection includes
documents from the French
Revolution and 80,000 prints
covering the history of Paris.

Rue des Francs-Bourgeois ❸

75003, 75004. **Map** 14 D3.
M *Rambuteau, Chemin-Vert.*

T HIS STREET is an important
thoroughfare in the heart
of the Marais, linking the Rue
des Archives and the Place

Courtyard of the Musée Carnavalet

des Vosges, with the imposing
Hôtel de Soubise at one end
and the Musée Carnavalet at
the other. The street got its
name from the *francs* (free
from taxes) – almshouses
built for the poor in 1334 at
Nos. 34 and 36. These were
later closed because of illegal
financial activities, although
the state kept its pawnshop
nearby, still there today.

Musée Cognacq-Jay ❹

Hôtel de Donon, 8 Rue Elzévir 75004.
Map 14 D3. **[** *01 40 27 07 21.* **M**
St-Paul. **Open** *10am–5:40pm Tue–Sun
(last adm: 4:30pm).* **Closed** *public hols.*
Adm charge. ⊘ ☑ *pre-book.* ☐

T HIS FINE small collection of
French 18th-century works
of art and furniture was

formed by Ernest Cognacq
and his wife, Louise Jay,
founder of La Samaritaine,
Paris's largest department
store *(see p115)*. The private
collection was bequeathed to
the city and is now housed in
the heart of the Marais at the
Hôtel de Donon–an elegant
building dating from 1575
with an 18th-century
extension and facade.

Place des Vosges ❺

75003, 75004. **Map** 14 D3.
M *Bastille, St-Paul.*

T HIS SQUARE is considered
among the most beautiful
in the world by Parisians and
visitors alike *(see pp22–3)*. Its
impressive symmetry – 36
houses, nine on each side, of
brick and stone, with deep
slate roofs and dormer
windows over arcades – is
still intact after 400 years. It
has been the scene of many
historic events over the
centuries. A three-day
tournament was held here to
celebrate the marriage of
Louis XIII to Anne of Austria
in 1615. The famous literary
hostess, Madame de Sévigné,
was born here in 1626;
Cardinal Richelieu, pillar of
the monarchy, stayed here in
1615; and Victor Hugo, the
writer, lived here for 16 years.

**A 19th-century engraving of the
Place des Vosges**

Maison de Victor Hugo 6

6 Pl des Vosges 75004.
Map 14 D3. **C** *01 42 72 10 16.*
M *Bastille.* **Open** *10am–5:40pm Tue–Sun.* **Closed** *public hols.* **Adm charge.** ∅ 🗗 *Library.*

T HE FRENCH poet, dramatist and novelist lived on the second floor of the former Hôtel Rohan-Guéménée, the largest house on the square, from 1832 to 1848. It was here that he wrote most of *Les Misérables* and completed many other famous works. On display are some reconstructions of the rooms in which he lived, pen-and-ink drawings, books and mementos from the crucially important periods in his life, from his childhood to his exile between 1852 and 1870.

Marble bust of Victor Hugo by Auguste Rodin

Hôtel de Sully 7

62 Rue St.-Antoine 75004.
Map 14 D4. **C** *01 44 61 20 00.* **M** *St-Paul.* **Open** *(courtyard only) 9am–noon, 2pm–6pm Mon–Thu; 9am–noon, 2pm–5pm Fri.* **Closed** *public hols.* 🗗 *once each month, call for details (01 44 61 21 69).*

T HIS FINE 17th-century mansion on one of Paris's oldest streets has been extensively restored, using old engravings and drawings as reference. It was built in 1624 for a notorious gambler, Petit Thomas, who lost his whole fortune in one night. The Duc de Sully, Henri IV's chief minister, purchased the house in 1634 and added some of the interior decoration as well as the Petit Sully orangery in the gardens. Today it is the head office of the Caisse Nationale des Monuments Historiques. The exterior of the *hôtel* has a late-

Late-Renaissance façade of the Hôtel de Sully

Renaissance façade. Inside there is courtyard with carved pediments, dormer windows and statues of the four seasons and sphinxes.

Rue des Rosiers 8

75004. **Map** 13 C3. **M** *St-Paul.*

T HE JEWISH quarter in and around this street is one of the most colorful areas of Paris. The street's name refers to the rosebushes within the old city wall. Jews first settled here in the 13th century, with a second wave in the 19th century from Russia, Poland and central Europe. Then, in the 1960s, Sephardic Jews arrived from Algeria. Today this area contains synagogues, bakeries and kosher restaurants, the most famous being Jo Goldenberg's *(see p322).*

Orthodox Jews in the Marai

Hôtel de Coulanges 9

35 rue des Francs Bourgeois, 75004.
Map 13 C3. **C** *01 44 61 85 85.* **M** *St-Paul.* **Open** *8:30am–6:30pm Mon–Fri.* **Closed** *public hols.* **Concerts (adm charge)** *call for times (01 42 07 22 07).*

T HIS HÔTEL IS a magnificent example of the architecture of the early 18th century. The right wing of the building, separating the courtyard from the garden, dates from the early 17th century. The hôtel was given in 1640 to Phillipe II de Coulanges, the King's counselor. Renamed the "Petit hôtel Le Tellier" in 1662 by its new owner Le Tellier, this is where the children of Louis XIV and Madame de Montespan were raised in secrecy. It is now home to the Maison de L'Europe de Paris.

Musée Carnavalet ●

Carnavalet entrance

Dᴇᴠᴏᴛᴇᴅ ᴛᴏ the history of Paris, this vast museum occupies two adjoining mansions. They include entire decorated rooms with paneling, furniture and objets d'art; many works of art such as paintings and sculptures of prominent personalities; and engravings showing Paris being built. The main building is the Hôtel Carnavalet, built as a town house in 1548 and transformed in the mid-17th century by François Mansert. The neighboring 17th-century mansion house, Hôtel le Peletier features superb interiors dating from the beginning of the 20th-century.

Marie Antionette in Mourning *(1793) Alexandre Kucharski painted her at the Temple prison after the execution of Louis XVI.*

Memorabilia in this room is dedicated to 18th-century philosophers, in particular Jean-Jacques Rousseau and Voltaire.

★ **Charles Le Brun Ceiling**
Magnificent works by the 17th-century artist decorate the former study and great hall from the Hôtel de la Rivière.

★ **Mme de Sévigné's Gallery**
The gallery includes this portrait of Madame de Sévigné, the celebrated letter writer, whose beloved home this was for the 20 years up to her death.

Sᴛᴀʀ Exʜɪʙɪᴛs

- ★ **Mme de Sévigné's Gallery**

- ★ **Charles Le Brun Ceiling**

- ★ **Hôtel d'Uzès Reception Room**

- ★ **Ballroom of the Hôtel de Wendel**

★ **Hotel d'Uzès Reception Room**
The room was created in 1761 by Claude Nicolas Ledoux. The gold-and-white paneling is from a Rue Montmartre mansion.

Entrance the museu

Second floor

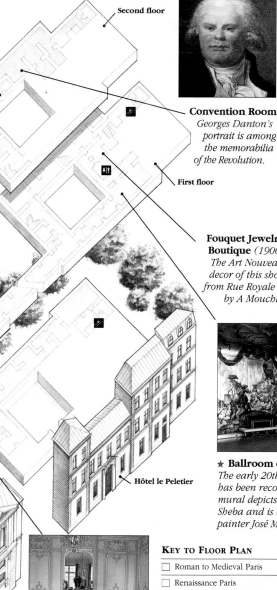

Convention Room
*Georges Danton's
portrait is among
the memorabilia
of the Revolution.*

First floor

VISITORS' CHECKLIST

23 Rue de Sévigné 75003.
Map 14 D3. 🛈 *01 42 72 21 13.*
Ⓜ *St-Paul.* 🚌 *29, 69, 76, 96
to St-Paul, Pl des Vosges.*
🅿 *Hôtel de Ville, Rue St-Antoine.*
Open *10am–5:40pm Tue–Sun
(last adm: 5:15pm).* **Closed**
public hols. **Adm charge.** 📷
🎦 *12:30pm Tue, 2:15pm Sun.* 🚻

**Fouquet Jewelry
Boutique** *(1900)
The Art Nouveau
decor of this shop
from Rue Royale is
by A Moucha.*

Hôtel le Peletier

★ Ballroom of the Hôtel de Wendel
*The early 20th-century ballroom interior
has been reconstructed. This immense
mural depicts the retinue of the Queen of
Sheba and is by the Catalan designer and
painter José María Sert y Badia.*

Louis XV Lilas Room
*This delightful room
contains art from the
Bouvier collection and
paneling from the
Hôtel de Broglie.*

KEY TO FLOOR PLAN

- ☐ Roman to Medieval Paris
- ☐ Renaissance Paris
- ☐ 17th-Century Paris
- ☐ Louis XV's Paris
- ☐ Louis XVI's Paris
- ☐ Revolutionary Paris
- ☐ First Empire to Second Empire
- ☐ Second Empire to Present
- ☐ Temporary exhibitions
- ☐ Nonexhibition space

GALLERY GUIDE
*The collection is mainly
arranged chronologically.
The Hôtel Carnavalet covers
the history of Paris up to
1789. The Renaissance is on
the ground floor, and the
exhibits covering the 17th
century to the Revolution are
on the first floor. In the Hôtel
le Peletier the second floor is
devoted to the Revolution,
the ground floor to the First
to the Second Empire, and
the first floor to the Second
Empire to the present.*

Hôtel Libéral Bruand ❿

1 Rue de la Perle 75003. **Map** 14 D3.
☎ *01 42 77 79 62.* Ⓜ *St-Paul, Chemin-Vert.* **Open** *2pm–5pm Mon, 10am–noon & 2pm–5pm Tue–Fri.* **Closed** *Aug & public hols.* **Adm charge**.

THIS SMALL private house, built by the architect Libéral Bruand for himself in 1685, is far removed, with its elegant Italianate touches, from his most famous work, the Invalides *(see pp186–7)*. The building has recently been restored and now contains the Musée Bricard, one of the most intriguing collections of its kind in the world, with locks, doorknobs and knockers from as long ago as Roman times.

Musée Picasso ⓫

See pp100–1.

Opéra de Paris Bastille ⓬

120 Rue de Lyon 75012. **Map** 14 E4.
☎ *01 40 01 17 89.* 📠 *01 43 43 96 96.* Ⓜ *Bastille.* **Open** *call for details.* **Closed** *public hols.* **Adm charge**. ♿
✉ *See **Entertainment** pp334–5.*

ONE OF THE most modern and controversial opera houses in Europe, the "people's opera" was officially opened on July 14, 1989, to

The "genius of liberty" on top of the Colonne de Juillet

coincide with the bicentennial celebrations of the fall of the Bastille. Carlos Ott's imposing building is a notable break with 19th-century opera-house design, epitomized by Garnier's opulent Opéra in the heart of the city *(see pp214–15)*. It is a massive, curved, glass building. The main auditorium seats an audience of 2,700; its design is functional and modern with black upholstered seats contrasting with the granite of the walls and the impressive glass ceiling. With its five movable stages, this opera house is a masterpiece of technological wizardry.

Colonne de Juillet ⓭

Pl de la Bastille 75004. **Map** 14 E4.
Ⓜ *Bastille.* **Not open** *to the public.*

TOPPED BY the statue of the "genius of liberty," this column of hollow bronze reaches 170 ft (51.5 m) into the sky. It is a memorial to those who died in the street battles of July 1830 that led to the overthrow of the monarch *(see pp30–31)*. The crypt contains the remains of 504 victims of the violent fighting and others who died in the 1848 revolution.

Place de la Bastille ⓮

75004. **Map** 14 E4. Ⓜ *Bastille.*

NOTHING IS NOW left of the prison *(see pp28–9)* stormed by the revolutionary mob on July 14, 1789, an event celebrated annually by the French at home and abroad. A line of paving stones from No. 5 to No. 49 Boulevard Henri IV traces the former towers and fortifications. A large, traffic-clogged square is the site of the prison's former stronghold. The square still has its old link between smart central Paris and the eastern *faubourgs* or working-class areas. Gentrification, however, is now underway with the construction of attractive cafés and a marina.

The glass facade of the Bastille Opéra

St-Paul–St-Louis ⓯

99 Rue St-Antoine 75004.
Map 14 D4. 📞 *01 42 72 30 32.*
Ⓜ *St-Paul.* **Open** *7:30am–8pm
Mon–Sat; 8am–8pm Sun.*

A JESUIT CHURCH, St-Paul–St-
Louis was a key symbol
of the society's influence from
1627, when Louis XIII laid the
first stone, to 1762 when the
Jesuits were expelled from
France. The Gesù church in
Rome served as the model
for the nave, while the 195-ft
high (60-m) dome was the
forerunner of those of the
Invalides and the Sorbonne.
Most of the church's treasures
were removed during periods
of turmoil, but Delacroix's
masterpiece, *Christ in the
Garden of Olives*, can still be
seen. The church stands on
one of the main streets of
the Marais, but can also be
approached by the ancient
Passage St-Paul.

Christ in the Garden of Olives by Delacroix in St-Paul–St-Louis

him to die of rage in 1594 on
hearing that the Protestant
Henri IV had entered Paris.
Marguerite de Valois, lodged
here by her ex-husband, Henri
IV, led a life of breathtaking
debauchery and scandal. This
culminated in the beheading
of an ex-lover, who had
dared to assassinate her
current favorite.

Hôtel de Sens ⓰

1 Rue du Figuier 75004. **Map** 13 C4.
📞 *01 42 78 14 60.* Ⓜ *Pont-Marie.*
Open *1:30pm–8:30pm Tue–Fri;
10am–8:30pm Sat.* **Closed** public hols.
Adm charge for exhibitions. 🚫 📷
by appointment only.

T HIS IS ONE of the few
medieval buildings left in
Paris. It now houses the
Forney fine arts library. In the
16th century, at the time of the
Catholic League, it was turned
into a fortified mansion and
occupied by the Bourbons, the
Guises and Cardinal de Pellevé,
whose religious fervor led

**The memorial to the unknown
Jewish martyr, dedicated in 1956**

Mémorial du Martyr Juif Inconnu ⓱

17 Rue Geoffroy-l'Asnier 75004. **Map**
13 C4. 📞 *01 42 77 44 72.* Ⓜ
Pont-Marie. **Open** *10am–1pm, 2pm–
6pm Sun–Fri.* **Adm charge.** ♿ 📷

T HE ETERNAL FLAME burning
in the crypt is the
memorial, built in 1956,
to the unknown Jewish
martyr of the Holocaust. It is
situated at the edge of the
Jewish quarter. Its striking
feature, apart from its
emotional impact, is a large
cylinder with the names of
the concentration camps. A
marble-faced building behind
the memorial at No. 17
contains the archives of the
Jewish documentation center
and a library.

St-Gervais–St-Protais ⓲

Pl St-Gervais 75004. **Map** 13 B3.
📞 *01 48 87 32 02.* Ⓜ *Hôtel de
Ville.* **Open** *6am–9pm daily.*

N AMED AFTER Gervase and
Protase, two Roman
soldiers who were martyred
by Nero, this remarkable
church dates from the 6th
century. It has the oldest
Classical facade in Paris,
which is formed of a three-
tiered arrangement of
columns: Doric, Ionic and
Corinthian. Behind its facade
lies a beautiful Gothic church
renowned for its association
with religious music. It was
for the church's fine organ
that François Couperin
(1668–1733) composed his
two masses. The church
currently has a Roman
Catholic monastic community
whose liturgy attracts people
from all over the world.

**The facade of St-Gervais–St-Protais
with its Classical columns**

**The Hôtel de Sens, now home to a
fine arts library**

Musée Picasso ⓫

ON THE DEATH of the Spanish-born artist Pablo Picasso (1881–1973), who lived most of his life in France, the French State inherited many of his works in lieu of death duties. It used them to establish the Musée Picasso, which opened in 1986. The museum is housed in a large 17th-century mansion, the Hôtel Salé, in the Marais. The original character of the Hôtel, which was built in 1656 for Aubert de Fontenay, a salt-tax collector (*salé* means "salty"), has been preserved. The breadth of the collection reflects both the full extent of Picasso's artistic development, including his Blue, Pink and Cubist periods, and his use of so many different materials.

★ **Self-Portrait**
Poverty, loneliness and the onset of winter all made the end of 1901, when this picture was painted, a particularly difficult time for Picasso.

Violin and Sheet Music
This collage (1912) is from the artist's Synthetic Cubist period.

★ **The Two Brothers**
During the summer of 1906 Picasso returned to Catalonia in Spain, where he painted this picture.

★ **The Kiss** *(1969)*
Picasso married Jacqueline Roque in 1961, and at around the same time he returned to the familiar themes of the couple and of the artist and model.

Basement

GALLERY GUIDE

The collection is mainly presented in chronological order, starting on the first floor with the Blue and Pink periods, Cubist and Neo-Classical works. Exhibitions change regularly – not all paintings are on show at any one time. On the ground floor there is a sculpture garden and works from the late 1920s to late 1930s, and from the mid-1950s to 1973.

KEY TO FLOOR PLAN

☐	Paintings
☐	Illustrations
☐	Sculpture garden
☐	Ceramics
☐	Non-exhibition space

Woman with a Mantilla *(1949)*
Picasso extended his range when he began working in ceramics in 1948.

Painter with Palette and Easel *(1928)*
This Post-Cubist portrait in oils was painted at a time when Picasso's work was verging on Surrealism.

First floor

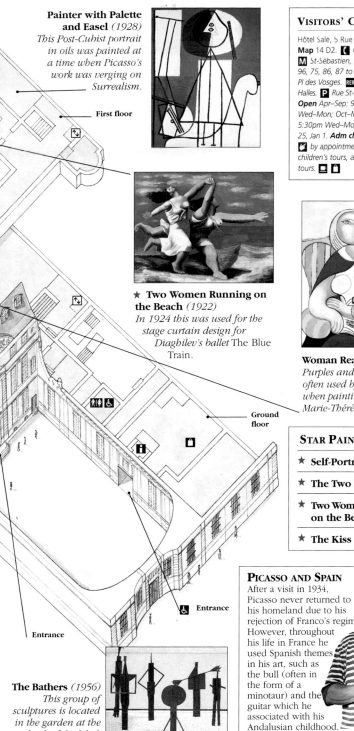

★ **Two Women Running on the Beach** *(1922)*
In 1924 this was used for the stage curtain design for Diaghilev's ballet The Blue Train.

Woman Reading *(1932)*
Purples and yellows were often used by Picasso when painting his model Marie-Thérèse Walter.

Ground floor

STAR PAINTINGS

★ **Self-Portrait**

★ **The Two Brothers**

★ **Two Women Running on the Beach**

★ **The Kiss**

Entrance

Entrance

The Bathers *(1956)*
This group of sculptures is located in the garden at the back of the hôtel.

PICASSO AND SPAIN

After a visit in 1934, Picasso never returned to his homeland due to his rejection of Franco's regime. However, throughout his life in France he used Spanish themes in his art, such as the bull (often in the form of a minotaur) and the guitar which he associated with his Andalusian childhood.

The town hall (Hôtel de Ville), overlooking a delightful square

Hôtel de Ville ⑲

4 Pl de l'Hôtel de Ville 75004. **Map** 13 B3. [C] *01 42 76 50 49.* [M] *Hôtel-de-Ville.* **Open** *for group guided tours only, call to arrange.* **Closed** *public hols, official functions.* [access] [photo]

H OME OF the city council, the town hall is a 19th-century reconstruction of the 17th-century town hall that was burned down in 1871. It is highly ornate, with elaborate stonework, turrets and statues overlooking a pedestrianized square that is a delight to stroll in, especially at night when the fountains are illuminated.

The square was once the main site for hangings, burnings and other horrific executions. It was here that Ravaillac, who assassinated Henri IV in 1610, was quartered alive, his body ripped to pieces by four strong horses.

Inside the Hôtel de Ville, a notable feature is the long Salles des Fêtes (ballroom), with adjoining salons devoted to science, the arts and literature. The impressive staircase, the decorated coffered ceilings with their chandeliers and the numerous statues and caryatids all add to the air of ceremony and pomp – a fitting power base for mayors of the city to hold elaborate banquets and receptions for foreign dignitaries in the building's grand halls.

Cloître des Billettes ⑳

24 Rue des Archives 75004. **Map** 13 B3. [C] *01 42 72 38 79.* [M] *Hôtel-de-Ville.* **Church & Cloister open** *11am–7pm daily.*

T HIS IS THE only remaining medieval cloister in Paris. It was built in 1427 for the Brothers of Charity, or *Billettes*, and three of its four original galleries are still standing. The adjoining church is a simple Classical building which replaced the monastic original in 1756.

The oldest cloister in Paris

Notre-Dame-des-Blancs-Manteaux ㉑

12 Rue des Blancs-Manteaux 75004. **Map** 13 C3. [C] *01 42 72 09 37.* [M] *Rambuteau.* **Open** *10am–1pm, 4pm–7pm daily.* **Concerts**.

T HIS CHURCH, built in 1685, takes its name from the white habits worn by the Augustinian friars who founded a convent on the site in 1258. It has a magnificent 18th-century Rococo Flemish pulpit, and its famous organ is best appreciated at one of its regular concerts of religious music.

Hôtel de Rohan ㉒

87 Rue Vieille-du-Temple 75003. **Map** 13 C2. [C] *01 40 27 62 18.* [M] *Rambuteau.* **Open** *for temporary exhibitions only.*

A LTHOUGH NOT resembling it in appearance, the Hôtel de Rohan forms a pair with the Hôtel de Soubise. It was built by the same architect, Delamair, for Armand de Rohan-Soubise, a cardinal and Bishop of Strasbourg. The *hôtel* has been home to a part of the national archives since 1927. In the courtyard over the doorway of the stables is the 18th-century sculpture *Horses of Apollo* by Robert Le Lorrain.

Horses of Apollo **by Le Lorrain**

Hôtel de Soubise ㉓

60 Rue des Francs-Bourgeois 75003.
Map 13 C2. ☎ *01 40 27 60 96.*
Ⓜ *Rambuteau.* **Open** *noon–6:45pm
Wed–Mon.* **Closed** *public hols.* **Adm
charge.** ∅

The Hôtel de Soubise

THIS IMPOSING mansion, built
from 1705 to 1709 for the
Princesse de Rohan, is one of
two main buildings housing
the national archives. (The
other is the Hôtel de Rohan.)
The Hôtel de Soubise displays
a majestic courtyard and a
magnificent interior decoration dating from 1735 to 1740
by some of the most gifted
painters of the day: Carl Van
Loo, Jean Restout, Natoire and
François Boucher.
Natoire's *rocaille* work on
the Princess's bedroom, the
Oval Salon, can still be
enjoyed by many today
because it forms part of the
museum of French history
that is now housed here.
Other exhibits include
Napoleon's will, in which he
asks for his remains to be
returned to France.

Hôtel Guénégaud ㉔

60 Rue des Archives 75003.
Map 13 C2. ☎ *01 42 72 86 43.*
Ⓜ *Hôtel de Ville.* **Open** *11am–6pm,
Tue–Sun.* **Closed** *public hols.*
Adm charge. 🚻 📷 *on payment.*

THE CELEBRATED architect
François Mansart built this
superb mansion in the mid-
17th century for Henri de

The garden of the Hôtel Guénégaud

Guénégaud des Brosses, who
was Secretary of State and
Keeper of the Seals. One
wing now contains the Musée
de la Chasse et de la Nature
(Hunting Museum) inaugur-
ated by André Malraux in
1967. The exhibits include a
fine collection of hunting
weapons from the 16th to the
19th centuries, many from
Germany and Central Europe.
There are also animal trophies
from around the world, along
with drawings and paintings
by Oudry, Rubens, Rembrandt
and Monet, and other artists.

No. 3 Rue Volta ㉕

75003. **Map** 13 C1. Ⓜ *Arts-et-
Métiers.* **Not open** *to the public.*

THIS HALF-TIMBERED four-story
house dating to 1300 was
thought to be the oldest in
Paris until 1978, when it was
found to be a 17th-century
imitation. Its sturdy structure
with beam-and-plaster ceilings
and vertical beams on the
facade is typical of Parisian
homes of the medieval period.
Originally there would have
been two shops at ground-
floor level. Trading was con-
ducted in the street from a
lowered horizontal shutter.

Square du Temple ㉖

75003. **Map** 13 C1. Ⓜ *Temple.*

A QUIET AND pleasant square
today, this was once a
fortified center of the medieval
Knights Templars. A state within a state, the area contained a
palace, a church and shops

**A 17th-century reconstruction of a
medieval house on the Rue Volta**

behind high walls and a drawbridge, making it a haven for
those who were seeking to
escape from royal jurisdiction.
Louis XVI and Marie-Antoinette
were held here after their
arrest in 1792 *(see pp28–9).*
The king left from here for his
execution on the guillotine.

Musée d'Art et
d'Histoire du
Judaïsm ㉗

Hôtel de St-Aignan, 71 rue du Temple
75003. **Map** 13 B2. ☎ *01 53 01 86
53.* Ⓜ *Rambuteau.* **Open** *11am–6pm
Mon–Fri, 10am–6pm Sun.* **Adm
charge.** ♿ 🚻 📷 📹

THIS MUSEUM celebrates the
history and culture of the
Jewish community from medieval times to the present day.
The collection of the former
Musée d'Art Juif is now here,
as well as outstanding religious works and artifacts formerly in the Musée de Cluny.

BEAUBOURG AND LES HALLES

THIS AREA OF THE Right Bank is dominated by the modernistic Forum des Halles and the Pompidou Center. These two spectacular undertakings are now the city's most thriving public areas of contact for shoppers, art lovers, students and tourists. Literally millions flow between the two squares. The new Halles is the scene for street fashion; most of the shops are underground, and the crowd strolling under the new concrete-and-glass bubbles is young. The surrounding streets are colored by popular inex-

Fountain in the Place Igor Stravinsky

pensive shops and bars. But there are still enough food shops, butchers and small markets to suggest what Les Halles must have been like in its prime as the city's thriving market. All roads around Les Halles resolutely lead to the Beaubourg area and the Pompidou Center, a no-compromise avant-garde assembly of vast pipes, ducts and cables, and one of Paris's most visible buildings. The adjoining streets, such as Rues St-Martin and Beaubourg, accommodate small contemporary art galleries housed in crooked gabled buildings.

SIGHTS AT A GLANCE

Historic Buildings and Streets
No. 51 Rue de Montmorency ⓫
Tour de Jean Sans Peur ⓬
Bourse du Commerce ⓮
Tour St-Jacques ⓱

Churches
St-Merry ❷
St-Eustache ⓭
St-Germain l'Auxerrois ⓯

Museums and Galleries
Pompidou Center pp110–13 ❶
Pavillon des Arts ❺
Vidéothèque de Paris ❼
Musée de la Poupée ❿

Modern Architecture
Forum des Halles ❽
Le Défenseur du Temps ❾

Cafés
Café Beaubourg ❹
Bistrot d'Eustache ❻

Fountains
Fontaine des Innocents ❸

Shops
La Samaritaine ⓰

GETTING THERE

Among the metro stations serving the area are Rambuteau, Hôtel de Ville, Châtelet and Les Halles. Among the bus routes passing through the area, 47 goes along Rue Beaubourg past the Pompidou Center and along Boulevard Sebastopol.

SEE ALSO

- **Street Finder**, map 13
- **Where to Stay** pp278–9
- **Restaurants** pp296–8

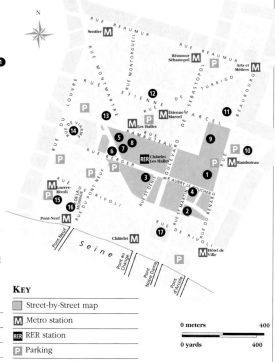

KEY

▨	Street-by-Street map
Ⓜ	Metro station
RER	RER station
Ⓟ	Parking

0 meters 400
0 yards 400

St-Eustache and sculptured head, *l'Ecoute*, by Henri de Miller

Street-by-Street: Beaubourg and Les Halles

WHEN EMILE ZOLA described Les Halles as the "belly of Paris" he was referring to the meat, vegetable and fruit market that had thrived here since 1183. Traffic congestion in the 1960s forced the market to move to the suburbs and Baltard's giant umbrella-like market pavilions were pulled down, despite howls of protest, and replaced by a shopping and leisure complex, the Forum. The conversion worked: today, Les Halles and the Pompidou Centre, which lies in the Beaubourg quarter and has been Paris's main tourist attraction ever since it opened in 1977, draw the most mixed crowds in Paris.

Pavillon des Arts
This is one of the mushroom-shaped pavilions overlooking the Forum. It houses changing exhibitions **5**

Bistrot d'Eustache
This lively café is a favorite spot for enthusiasts of both classic and modern jazz **6**

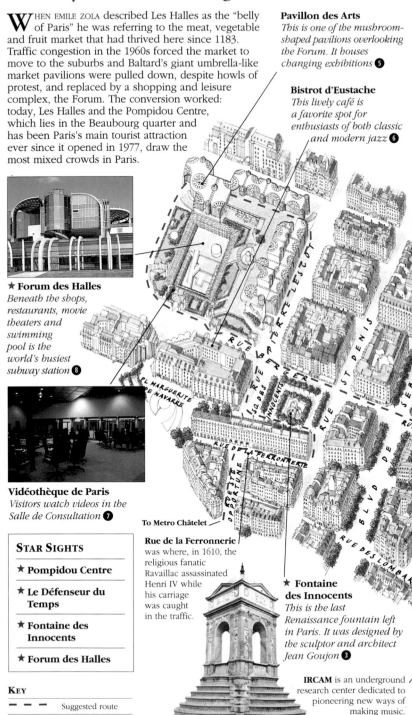

★ **Forum des Halles**
Beneath the shops, restaurants, movie theaters and swimming pool is the world's busiest subway station **8**

Vidéothèque de Paris
Visitors watch videos in the Salle de Consultation **7**

To Metro Châtelet

Rue de la Ferronnerie was where, in 1610, the religious fanatic Ravaillac assassinated Henri IV while his carriage was caught in the traffic.

★ **Fontaine des Innocents**
This is the last Renaissance fountain left in Paris. It was designed by the sculptor and architect Jean Goujon **3**

IRCAM is an underground research center dedicated to pioneering new ways of making music.

STAR SIGHTS

★ **Pompidou Centre**

★ **Le Défenseur du Temps**

★ **Fontaine des Innocents**

★ **Forum des Halles**

KEY

- - - Suggested route

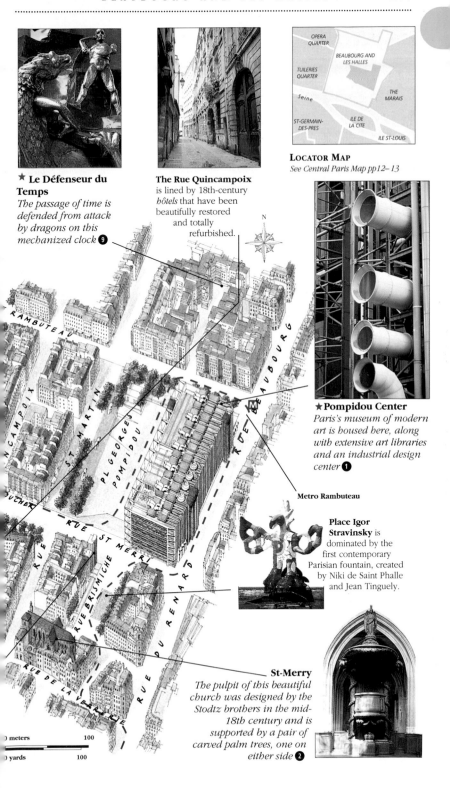

★ Le Défenseur du Temps
The passage of time is defended from attack by dragons on this mechanized clock ❾

The Rue Quincampoix is lined by 18th-century *hôtels* that have been beautifully restored and totally refurbished.

LOCATOR MAP
See Central Paris Map pp12–13

★ Pompidou Center
Paris's museum of modern art is housed here, along with extensive art libraries and an industrial design center ❶

Metro Rambuteau

Place Igor Stravinsky is dominated by the first contemporary Parisian fountain, created by Niki de Saint Phalle and Jean Tinguely.

St-Merry
The pulpit of this beautiful church was designed by the Stodtz brothers in the mid-18th century and is supported by a pair of carved palm trees, one on either side ❷

meters   100
yards   100

Pompidou Center ❶

See pp110–13.

A Nativity scene from the stained-glass windows in St-Merry

St-Merry ❷

76 Rue de la Verrerie 75004. **Map** 13 B3. **C** *01 42 71 93 93.* **M** *Hôtel-de-Ville.* **Open** *3pm–7pm daily.* 📷 *1st & 3rd Sun, pm.* **Concerts**.

THE SITE of this church dates back to the 7th century. St Médéric, the abbot of St-Martin d'Autun, was buried here at the beginning of the 8th century. The saint's name, which was eventually corrupted to Merry, was given to a chapel built nearby. The building of the church – in the Flamboyant Gothic style – was not completed until 1552. The west front is particularly rich in decoration, and the northwest turret contains the oldest bell in Paris, dating from 1331. It was the wealthy parish church of the Lombard moneylenders, who gave their name to the nearby Rue des Lombards.

Fontaine des Innocents ❸

Sq des Innocents 75001. **Map** 13 A2. **M** *Les Halles.* **RER** *Châtelet-Les-Halles.*

THIS CAREFULLY restored Renaissance fountain stands in the Square des Innocents, the area's main crossroads. Erected in 1549 on the Rue St-Denis, it was moved to its present location in the 18th century, when the square was constructed on the site of a former graveyard. Popular with the city's youth as a meeting place, the fountain is one of the landmarks of Les Halles.

Decoration on the Fontaine des Innocents

Café Beaubourg ❹

100 Rue St-Martin, 75004. **Map** 13 B2. **C** *01 48 87 63 96.* **M** *Les Halles.* **RER** *Châtelet-Les-Halles.* **Open** *8am–1am Sun–Thu; 8am–2am Fri, Sat.*

Interior of Café Beaubourg

OPENED BY Gilbert Costes in 1987, this stylish café was designed and decorated by one of France's star architects, Christian de Portzamparc, who created the impressive Cité de la Musique in the Parc de la Villette *(see p234)*. Its vast terrace is lined with comfortable red and black wicker chairs. The spacious and coolly elegant interior is decorated with rows of books, which soften its severely Art Deco ambience. The café is a favorite meeting point for art dealers from the surrounding galleries and Pompidou Center staff. It serves light meals and brunch. If the crush gets too much around Les Halles, the Café Beaubourg is the ideal place to soothe the nerves.

Pavillon des Arts ❺

101 Rue Rambuteau, Terrasse Lautréamont 75001. **Map** 13 A2. **C** *01 42 33 82 50.* **M** *Les Halles.* **Open** *3pm–7pm daily.* **RER** *Châtelet-Les-Halles.* **Open** *11.30am–6.30pm Tue–Sun.* **Closed** *public hols.* **Adm charge.** 📷 📷

IN CREATING this exhibition center in 1983, Paris opened up the newly revitalized quarter of Les Halles to the arts. Housed in the futuristic glass and steel of the Baltard Pavilion, its program of changing exhibitions often focus on unusual or rarely-seen subjects and works, drawn together from French and foreign museums. For example, past exhibitions have included Russian history as portrayed by Soviet photographers, and Surrealists recalled through their collections of Indian dolls.

Exterior of the Pavillon des Arts

Bistrot d'Eustache 6

37 Rue Berger, 75001.
Map 13 A2. **C** *01 40 26 23 20.*
M *Les Halles.* **RER** *Châtelet-Les-Halles.*
Open *9am–2am daily.* **Live jazz** Thu,
Flamenco/gypsy Fri–Sat.

THIS COMPACT café, decorated with old wood paneling and attractive mirrors, retains a feeling of Paris as it was in the 1930s and 1940s – a period when jazz venues flourished throughout the city. It is always packed on Thursday nights, when musicians squeeze into a handkerchief-sized space to play racy, guitar-led gypsy jazz. The café serves a variety of traditional French food, at all times throughout the day, and at very reasonable prices.

Terrace of the Bistrot d'Eustache

Vidéothèque de Paris 7

2 Grande Galerie, Forum des Halles
75001. **Map** 13 A2. **C** *01 44 76 62
00.* **M** *Les Halles.* **RER** *Châtelet-Les-
Halles.* **Open** *1pm–9pm Tue, Wed,
Fri–Sun; 1pm–10pm Thu.* **Closed**
public hols. **Adm charge.** 🔊 📺

AT THE VIDEOTHEQUE you can choose from thousands of feature, television, and amateur movies. All feature the city of Paris. There is footage on the history of Paris since 1895 including a remarkable newsreel of General de Gaulle avoiding sniper fire during the Liberation of Paris in 1944. There are countless movies such as Truffaut's *Baisers Volés*. Admission includes two hours' viewing of your chosen movie

in the Salle de Consultation *(see p106)* and entry to two auditoriums showing movies linked by a theme.

François Truffaut's *Baisers Volés*

Forum des Halles 8

75001. **Map** 13 A2. **M** *Les Halles.*
RER *Châtelet-Les-Halles.*

THE PRESENT Forum des Halles, known as Les Halles, was built in 1979, amid much controversy, on the site of the famous old fruit and vegetable market. The existing complex occupies 750,000 sq ft (7 ha), partly above and partly below ground. The underground levels 2 and 3 are occupied by a varied array of shops, from chic boutiques to megastores. Above ground there are well-tended gardens, pergolas and

Pygmalion by Julio Silva in the Forum des Halles

minipavilions. Also outside are the palm-shaped buildings of metal and glass which house the Pavillon des Arts and the Maison de la Poésie. The Pavillon des Arts and the Maison de la Poésie are cultural centers for contemporary art and poetry respectively.

Le Défenseur du Temps 9

Rue Bernard-de-Clairvaux 75003.
Map 13 B2. **M** *Rambuteau.*

THE MODERN Quartier de l'Horloge (Clock Quarter) is the location of Paris's newest public clock, "The Defender of Time" by Jacques Monastier. An impressive brass-and-steel mechanical sculpture, it stands 13 ft (4 m) high and weighs 1 ton. The defender battles against the elements: air, earth and water. In the shape of savage beasts, they attack him at the approach of each hour, to the accompanying sound of earthquakes, hurricanes and rough seas. At 2pm and 6pm he overcomes all three, as watching children cheer.

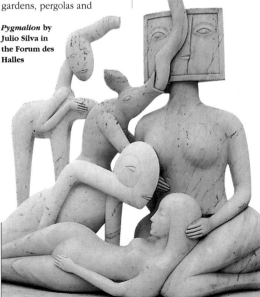

Pompidou Center ●

THE POMPIDOU IS LIKE a building turned inside out: escalators, elevators, air and water ducts and even the massive steel struts that are the building's skeleton have all been placed on the outside. This allowed the architects, Richard Rogers, Renzo Piano and Gianfranco Franchini, to create an uncluttered and flexible space within it for the Musée National d'Art Moderne and for the Pompidou's other activities. Among the schools represented in the museum are Fauvism, Cubism and Surrealism. Outside in the piazza, large crowds gather to watch the street performers. The Pompidou has been completely renovated for the new millennium.

The escalator that rises step by step up the facade overlooking the piazza runs through a glass conduit. From the top there is a spectacular view over Paris that includes Montmartre, La Défense and the Eiffel Tower.

KEY

☐ Exhibition space

☐ Nonexhibition space

GALLERY GUIDE

The permanent collections are on the fifth and fourth levels: works from 1905 to 1960 are on the former, with the latter reserved for contemporary art. The first and sixth levels are for major exhibitions of contemporary art, while the second and third levels house an information library. The lower levels make up "The Forum," the focal public area, which includes a performance center, movie theater, and children's workshop.

Portrait of the Journalist Sylvia von Harden *(1926)*
The surgical precision of Dix's style makes this a harsh caricature.

Le Cheval Majeur
This bronze horse (1914–16) by Duchamp-Villon is one of the finest examples of Cubist sculpture.

To Russia, the Asses and the Others *(1911)*
Throughout his life, Chagall drew inspiration from the small Russian town of Vitebsk, where he was born.

VISITORS' CHECKLIST

Centre d'Art et de Culture Georges Pompidou, Pl Georges Pompidou. **Map** 13 B2. **(** *01 44 78 12 33.* **M** *Rambuteau, Châtelet, Hôtel de Ville.* 🚌 *21, 29, 38, 47, 58, 69, 70, 72, 74, 75, 76, 81, 85, 96.* RER *Châtelet-Les-Halles.* **P** *Centre Georges Pompidou.* **Open** *noon–10pm Mon, Wed–Fri; 10am–10pm Sat, Sun.* **Closed** *May Day public hol.* 🚫 ♿ 📷
🍴 🖥 🏛

Sorrow of the King *(1952)*
Toward the end of his life, Matisse produced a number of collages using gouache-painted paper cutouts.

Man with a Guitar *(1914)*
Braque, along with Picasso, developed the Cubist technique of presenting many different views of the subject in one picture.

COLOR-CODING

The colored pipes that are the most striking feature at the back of the Pompidou, on rue de Renard, moved one critic to compare the building to an oil refinery. Far from being merely decorative, the colors serve to distinguish the pipes' various functions: air-conditioning ducts are blue, water pipes green, and electricity lines are painted yellow. The areas through which people move vertically (such as escalators) are colored red. The white funnels are ventilation shafts for the underground areas, and the structural beams are clad in stainless steel. The architects' idea in doing this was to enable the public to understand the way the dynamics or "metabolism" of a building function.

Exploring the Pompidou's Modern Art Collection

WITH A COLLECTION OF OVER 45,000 works of art from more than 42,000 artists, the Pompidou encompasses all of the fine arts. Since its renovation, classic disciplines – painting, sculpture, drawing, and photography – have been integrated with other media such as cinema, architecture, design, and visual and sound archives. The collections now represent a complete overview of modern and contemporary creation.

The Two Barges (1906) by André Derain

ART FROM 1905–60

THE "HISTORICAL" collections bring together the great artistic movements of the first half of the 20th century, from Fauvism to Abstract Expressionism to the changing currents of the 1950s. The rich collection of Cubist sculptures, of which the *Cheval Majeur* by Duchamp-Villon (1914–1916) is a fine example, is displayed, as well as examples of the great masters of the 20th century. Matisse, Picasso, Braque, Duchamp, Kandinsky, Léger, Miro, Giacometti, and Dubuffet command large

areas at the heart of the collection. Towards the end of his life, Matisse made several collages from cut up large sheets of paper. Among others, the museum possesses *La Tristesse du Roi* (Sorrow of the King) which he created in 1952. With *Homme à la Guitare* (Man with a Guitar), Braque demonstrates his command of the Cubist technique which he pioneered along with Picasso. Considered as one of the first, if not

the first, Abstract painter, Kandinsky transformed works inspired by nature into constructions of color and form. The museum has a large collection of the Russian painter's works, of which the Impressions (*Impressions V, Parc*, 1911) mark the end of his Expressionist period before his plunge into Abstract art with *Improvisations XIV* or *Avec l'Arc Noir* (With the Black Arc) both dating from 1912 compositions.

The collection also shows the groups and the movements on which the history of modern art is based, or by which it has been affected, including Dada, Abstract Art, and Informal. A pioneer of Informal art, Jean Fautrier is represented in the collections with *Otages* (Hostages), a commemoration of the suffering of the resistance fighters.

At the heart of this chronological progression, some newly opened spaces are a revelation. One set shows the Union des Artistes Modernes (Modern Artists Union) where architects, visual artists, and designers met in the 1920s. Another room recreates the atmosphere of André Breton's workshop in which the works of his Surrealist friends are also shown. Silent pauses have also been allowed for: the room reserved for Miro's three huge *Bleus* (Blues) gives time and space for visitors to meditate on the explosion and revolutions of modern art.

BRANCUSI'S STUDIO

Romanian by birth, Constantin Brancusi settled in Paris when he was 28, and on his death in 1957 the entire contents of his studio passed to the French State. Until quite recently these sculptures were housed a short distance from the Pompidou in a replica of the original studio. Many of the works have now been moved to the permanent exhibition space on the fourth floor of the Pompidou. At the same time a new studio, which will be part of the main building, is being constructed. This will open in 1995.

Miss Pogany (1919–20) by Constantin Brancusi

With the Black Arc (1912) by Vassily Kandinsky

The Good-bye Door (1980) by Joan Mitchell

ART SINCE 1960

THE CONTEMPORARY department opens with the 1960s and pays homage to Jean Tinguely. This sculptor/ engineer was creator of the Stravinsky fountain situated near the Center, along with Niki de Saint-Phalle. The display is organized around a central aisle from which the rooms holding the museum's collections lead off.

The 1960s saw the rise of Pop Art in America, which introduced advertising and mass-media images, along with objects from the consumer society, into art. Works by Jasper Johns, Andy Warhol, and Claes Oldenburg are in the collection. In the Rauschenberg *Oracle*, for example, products become abstract shapes. Among other works of importance are *Ghost Drums Set* by Claes Oldenburg and *Electric Chair* by Andy Warhol.

In France, the New Realists, a heterogenous group including Yves Klein, César, Arman, and others, were also interested in contemporary objects. They believed that by choosing mundane things from everyday life the artist could imbue them with artistic significance. Arman makes "accumulations,"

Raymond Hains collects wall posters in order to make abstract canvases while Jean Tinguely builds machines using materials collected.

The subtle eroticism of Balthus (Count Balthasar Klossowski de Rola) glows through *The Painter and His Model* (1980–81). In another area are ink drawings by poet-painter Henri Michaux.

Homogenous Infiltration (1966) by Joseph Beuys

The work of Herbin, who founded the Abstraction-Création group, a loosely-based association of non-figurative painters, is the focus for the work of the Geometric Abstractionists, while the Hard Edge Abstraction movement in America, which specializes in flat-colored, well-defined shapes, is represented by Ellsworth Kelly and Frank Stella. Richard Serra's *Corner Prop No. 7 (For Natalie)* (1983) and Carl André's *144 Tin Square* (1975) are just two of the several Minimalist sculptures in the collection.

The museum has a selection of figurative art by Georg Baselitz, Gilbert and George, and Anselm Kiefer, as well as art from the abstract landscape painter Joan Mitchell.

Kinetic Art, Poor Art and Conceptual Art, and new trends in figurative and

abstract painting, punctuate the route of the contemporary department's galleries.

Since the Pompidou's reopening, certain areas have been designated to bring together different disciplines around a theme and no longer around a school or movement. For example, the use of plastic materials in contemporary art is shown in the works of Jean Dubuffet, César or Claes Oldenburg and compared against the work of architects such as Richard Buckminster or Hans Hollein and designers such as Ettore Sottsass.

In its new arrangement the fourth floor offers areas allowing different aspects of the museum's collections to be discovered. They often reflect the museum's preference for the more ironic and conceptual forms. One display offered such works as Joseph Beuys's *Plight* (1985), which included a grand piano and wall and ceiling covered with about 7 tonnes of thick felt, and the video artist Nam June Paik's *Video Fish* (1979–85), in which video screens flashed manic sequences of images from behind aquaria populated by indifferent fish.

The museum gallery allows temporary exhibitions to be mounted from works held in reserve. A graphic arts exhibition room and a video area complete the arrangement. A screening room gives access to the museums' entire collection of videotapes and audio recordings of a wide range of modern artists.

Mobile on Two Planes (1955) by Alexander Calder

Ben's Store (1973) by Ben (Vautier Benjamin)

Musée de la Poupée ⑩

Impasse Berthaud 75003. **Map** 13 B2.
⦗ *01 42 72 73 11.* **Ⓜ** *Rambuteau.*
Open *10am–6pm Tue–Sun.* **Adm charge.** ⦁ *for groups, by appt.*

AN IMPRESSIVE collection of handmade dolls, from the mid-19th century to the present day, are on display in this charming museum. Thirty-six of the displays contain French dolls with porcelain heads dating from 1850 to 1950. Another 24 display windows are devoted to themed exhibitions of dolls from around the world.

Father and son, Guido and Samy Odin, who own the museum, are at your service if your doll needs medical care. The museum shop stocks everything you need to preserve and maintain these unique works of art in pristine condition. The Odins also offer comprehensive classes on doll-making for both adults and children.

A 19th-century French doll with porcelain head

No. 51 Rue de Montmorency ⑪

75003. **Map** 13 B1. **Ⓜ** *Réaumur-Sébastopol.* **Not open** *to the public.*

THIS HOUSE is considered to be the oldest in Paris, followed by No. 3 Rue Volta in the Marais quarter. No. 51 was built in 1407 by Nicolas Flamel, a writer and teacher. His house was always open to poor laborers, from whom he demanded nothing more than that they should pray for those who were dead.

The interior of St-Eustache in the 1830s

Tour de Jean Sans Peur ⑫

20 Rue Etienne-Marcel 75002.
Map 13 A1. **Ⓜ** *Etienne-Marcel.*
Not open *to the public.*

AFTER THE Duc d'Orléans had been assassinated on his orders in 1408, the Duc de Bourgogne feared reprisals. To protect himself, he had this 88-ft (27-m) tower built on to his home, the Hôtel de Bourgogne. He moved his bedroom up to the fourth floor of the tower (which was reached by climbing a flight of 140 steps) where he slept at night safe from the plots of his enemies.

No. 51 Rue de Montmorency, the oldest house in Paris

St-Eustache ⑬

Pl du Jour 75001. **Map** 13 A1.
⦗ *01 42 36 31 05.* **Ⓜ** *Les Halles.* **RER**
Châtelet-Les-Halles. **Open** *9am–7pm daily.* **Ⓟ ⦁** *10am, 6pm Tue–Fri; 6pm Mon & Sat; 9:30am, 11am, 6pm Sun.*
Organ recitals *Sun pm.*

WITH ITS GOTHIC plan and Renaissance decoration, St-Eustache is one of Paris's most beautiful churches. Its interior plan is modeled on Notre-Dame, with five naves and side and radial chapels. The 105 years (1532–1637) it took to complete the church saw the flowering of the Renaissance style, which is evident in the magnificent arches, pillars and columns. The stained-glass windows in the chancel are created from cartoons by Philippe de Champaigne.

The church has associations with many famous figures: Molière was buried here, and the Marquise de Pompadour, official mistress of Louis XV, was baptized here, as was Cardinal Richelieu.

Entrance to the Bourse du Commerce, the old corn exchange

Bourse du Commerce **⑭**

2 Rue de Viarmes 75001. **Map** 12 F2.
☎ 01 55 65 55 65. **M** Les Halles.
RER Châtelet-Les-Halles. **Open** 9am–6pm
Mon–Fri. **🛇** groups only, by appt.

COMPARED BY Victor Hugo to a jockey's cap without a peak, the old corn exchange building was built in the 18th century and remodeled in 1889. Today its huge, domed hall is filled with the hustle and bustle of the commodities market for coffee and sugar. It houses a World Trade Center and the offices of the Chambre de Commerce et d'Industrie de Paris.

St-Germain l'Auxerrois **⑮**

2 Pl du Louvre 75001.
Map 12 F2. **☎** 01 42 60 13 96.
M Louvre, Pont-Neuf.
Open 8am–8pm daily. **Organ recitals**
Sun pm, bells Wed pm.

AFTER THE Valois Court decamped to the Louvre from the Ile de la Cité in the 14th century, this became the favored church of kings, who attended mass here.

Its many historical associations include the horrific St. Bartholomew's Day Massacre on August 24, 1572, the eve of the royal wedding of Henri of Navarre and Marguerite de Valois. Thousands of Huguenots who had been lured to Paris for the wedding

were murdered as the church bell tolled. Later, after the Revolution, the church was used as a barn. Despite many restorations, it is a jewel of Gothic architecture.

La Samaritaine **⑯**

19 Rue de la Monnaie 75001.
Map 12 F2. **☎** 01 40 41 20 20.
M Pont-Neuf. **Open** 9:30am–7pm
Mon–Wed, Fri, Sat; 9:30am–10pm
Thu. **🛏 🖳 🅿** See p313.

THIS FASHIONABLE department store was founded in 1900 by Ernest Cognacq, a former street trader. Built in 1926 with a framework of iron and wide expanses of glass, La Samaritaine is an outstanding example of the Art Deco style. The renovated interior now has a fine Art Nouveau ironwork staircase and hanging galleries under a large dome. The rooftop restaurant offers some of the most spectacular views of Paris. Cognacq was also a leading collector of 18th-century art, and his collection is now on display in the Musée Cognacq-Jay in the Marais quarter (see p94).

The stylish Art Deco interior of La Samaritaine

The Tour St-Jacques with its ornate decoration

Tour St-Jacques **⑰**

Square de la Tour St-Jacques 75004.
Map 13 A3. **M** Châtelet. **Not open**
to the public.

THIS IMPOSING late Gothic tower, dating from 1523, is all that remains of an ancient church that was a rendezvous for pilgrims setting out on long journeys. The church was destroyed after the Revolution. Earlier, Blaise Pascal, the 17th-century mathematician, physicist, philosopher and writer, used the tower for barometrical experiments. There is a memorial statue to him on the ground floor of the tower. Queen Victoria passed by on her state visit in 1854, giving her name to the nearby Avenue Victoria.

The St. Bartholomew's Day Massacre (c. 1572–84) by François Dubois

TUILERIES QUARTER

THE TUILERIES AREA is bounded by the vast and harmonious expanse of the Concorde square at one end and the Grand Louvre at the other. This was once a place for kings and palaces. The Sun King (Louis XIV) lives on in the Place des Victoires, designed solely to show off his statue. But fashion kings are today's objects of admiration. In Place Vendôme, royal glitter has been replaced by the sparkle of precious stones at Cartier, Boucheron and Chaumet; by

Ornate lamppost on Place de la Concorde

the fine cut of Arab, German and Japanese bankers; and by the chic attire of women visiting the luxurious Ritz. The area is crossed by two of Paris's most magnificent shopping streets. Parallel to the Jardin des Tuileries is the long Rue de Rivoli, with arcades, expensive boutiques, bookshops and five-star hotels. And just north beyond the Rivoli is the Rue St-Honoré, another lively, extensive street, bringing together the richest and humblest in people and commerce.

SIGHTS AT A GLANCE

Historic Buildings
Palais Royal ❸
Banque de France ⓴

Museums and Galleries
Musée du Louvre pp122–9 ❶
Musée des Arts de la Mode ❾
Musée des Arts Décoratifs ⓫
Musée de l'Orangerie ⓰
Musée de la Publicité ❿
Galerie National du
Jeu de Paume ⓯
Village Royale ⓲

Churches
St-Roch ❼

Monuments and Fountains
Fontaine Molière ❻
Arc de Triomphe du Carrousel ⓬

Squares, Parks, and Gardens
Jardin du Palais Royal ❺
Place des Pyramides ❽
Jardin des Tuileries ⓮

Place de la Concorde ⓱
Place Vendôme ⓳
Place des Victoires ㉑

Theaters
Comédie Française ❹

Shops
Louvre des Antiquaires ❷
Rue de Rivoli ⓭

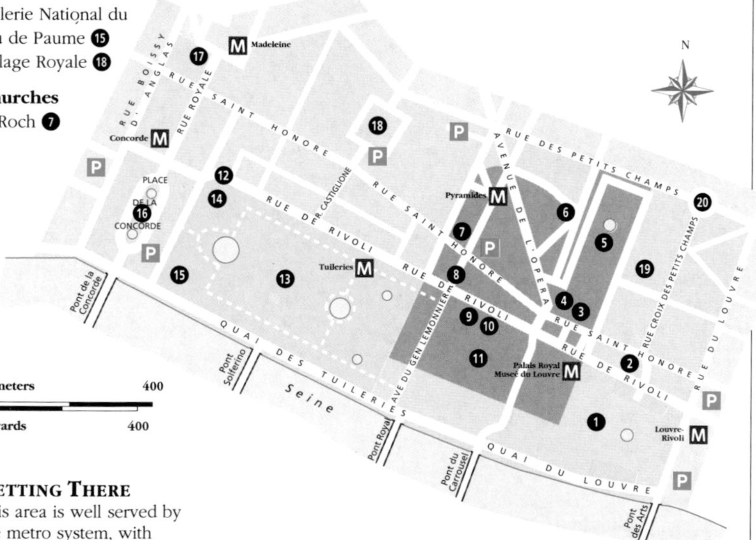

GETTING THERE
This area is well served by the metro system, with stations at Tuileries, Pyramides, Palais Royal and Louvre. There are frequent buses through the area. Routes 24 and 72 travel along the quayside, passing the Jardin des Tuileries and the Musée du Louvre.

SEE ALSO
• *Street Finder*, maps 6, 11–12
• *Where to Stay* pp278–9
• *Restaurants* pp296–8

KEY
▢ Street-by-Street map
Ⓜ Metro station
🅿 Parking

View of the Place de la Concorde and the Obelisk

Street by Street: Tuileries Quarter

ELEGANT SQUARES, formal gardens, street arcades and courtyards give this part of Paris its special character. Monuments to monarchy and the arts coexist with contemporary luxury: five-star hotels, world-famous restaurants, fashion emporiums and jewelers of international renown. Sandblasting and washing have given a new glow to the façades of the Louvre and the Palais Royal square, where Cardinal Richelieu's creation, the royal palace, is now occupied by government offices. From here the Ministry of Culture surveys the cleaning and restoration of the city's great buildings. The other former royal palace, the Louvre, is now one of the great museums of the world.

St-Roch
The papal statue stands in this remarkably long 17th-century church, unusually set on a north–south axis. St-Roch is a treasure house of religious art ⑦

Metro Pyramides

The Normandy is an elegant hotel in the Belle Epoque style, a form of graceful living that prevailed in Paris at the turn of the century.

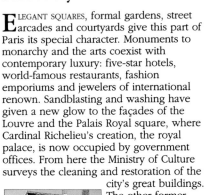

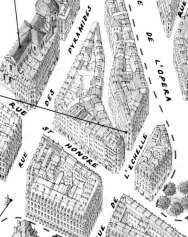

★ Jardin des Tuileries
Donkey rides are a popular attraction in these formal gardens, which were designed by the royal gardener André Le Nôtre in the 17th century ⑭

Place des Pyramides
Frémiet's gilded statue of Joan of Arc is the focus of pilgrimage for royalists ⑧

To the Quai du Louvre

Musée des Arts de la Mode
The haute couture collections that are kept in this museum have given the Louvre a new role ⑨

Musée des Arts Décoratifs
A highlight of the museum's displays of art and design is the Art Nouveau collection ⑪

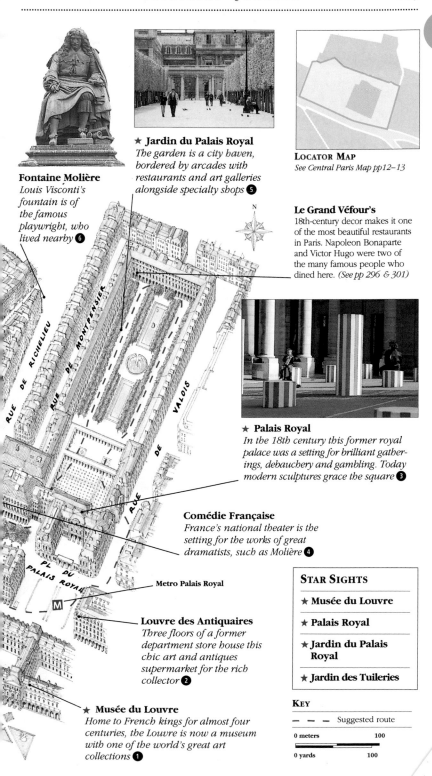

Fontaine Molière
*Louis Visconti's
fountain is of
the famous
playwright, who
lived nearby* ❻

★ Jardin du Palais Royal
*The garden is a city haven,
bordered by arcades with
restaurants and art galleries
alongside specialty shops* ❺

LOCATOR MAP
See Central Paris Map pp12–13

Le Grand Véfour's
18th-century decor makes it one
of the most beautiful restaurants
in Paris. Napoleon Bonaparte
and Victor Hugo were two of
the many famous people who
dined here. *(See pp 296 & 301)*

★ Palais Royal
*In the 18th century this former royal
palace was a setting for brilliant gatherings, debauchery and gambling. Today
modern sculptures grace the square* ❸

Comédie Française
*France's national theater is the
setting for the works of great
dramatists, such as Molière* ❹

Metro Palais Royal

Ⓜ

Louvre des Antiquaires
*Three floors of a former
department store house this
chic art and antiques
supermarket for the rich
collector* ❷

★ Musée du Louvre
*Home to French kings for almost four
centuries, the Louvre is now a museum
with one of the world's great art
collections* ❶

STAR SIGHTS

★ **Musée du Louvre**

★ **Palais Royal**

★ **Jardin du Palais Royal**

★ **Jardin des Tuileries**

KEY

– – – Suggested route

0 meters	100
0 yards	100

The five-arched Pont Royal linking the Louvre with the Left Bank

Musée du Louvre ❶

See pp122–9.

Louvre des Antiquaires ❷

2 Pl du Palais Royal 75001. **Map** 12 E2.
℡ 01 42 97 27 00. **Open** 11am–7pm
Tue–Sun (Jul & Aug Tue–Sat). **Closed**
Jan 1, Dec 25. **❙❙** ⌨ *See pp322–3.*

One of the shops in the Louvre
des Antiquaires market

A LARGE DEPARTMENT store –
the Grands Magasins du
Louvre – was converted at the
end of the 1970s into this
three-floor collection of art
galleries and antique shops.
Few bargains are found here,
but the 250 shops of this chic
market provide clues about
what *nouveaux riches*
collectors are seeking.

Palais Royal ❸

Pl du Palais Royal 75001. **Map** 12 E1.
M *Palais Royal.* **Buildings not open**
to public.

T HIS FORMER royal palace has
had a turbulent history.
Starting out in the early 17th
century as Richelieu's Palais
Cardinale, it passed to the

Crown on his death and
became the childhood home
of Louis XIV. Under the
control of the 18th-century
royal dukes of Orléans it was
the scene of brilliant gatherings, interspersed with
periods of debauchery and
gambling. The cardinal's
theater, where Molière
performed, burned down in
1763, but was replaced by the
Comédie Française. After the
Revolution, the palace
became a gambling house. It
was reclaimed in 1815 by the
future King Louis-Philippe,
one of whose librarians was
Alexandre Dumas. The
building narrowly escaped the
flames of the 1871 uprising.
  After being restored again,
between 1872 and 1876, the
palace reverted to the state,
and it now houses both the
Council of State, the supreme
legal body for administrative
matters, and its more recent
"partner," the Constitutional
Council. Another wing of the
palace is occupied by the
Ministry of Culture.

Comédie Française ❹

2 Rue de Richelieu 75001. **Map** 12 E1.
℡ 01 44 58 15 15. **M** *Palais Royal.*
Open for performances. **✦** 10:30am
Sun (01 44 58 13 16). **Adm charge.**
∅ *See **Entertainment** pp330–33.*

A stone plaque to Pierre Corneille

O VERLOOKING TWO charming,
if traffic-jammed squares
named after the writers
Colette and André Malraux,
sits France's national theater.
The company has its roots
partly in Molière's 17th-
century players. In the foyer is
the armchair in which Molière
collapsed, dying, on stage in
1673 (ironically while he was
performing *Le Malade
Imaginaire – The Hypochon-
driac*). Since the company's
founding in 1680 by Louis
XIV, the theater has enjoyed
state patronage as a center of
national culture, and it has
been based in the present
building since 1799. The
repertoire includes works of
Corneille, Racine, Molière and
Shakespeare, as well as those
of modern playwrights.

Daniel Buren's stone columns (1980s) in the Palais Royal courtyard

Jardin du Palais Royal ⑤

Pl du Palais Royal 75001. **Map** 12 F1.
Ⓜ *Palais Royal.*

THE PRESENT garden is about a third smaller than the original one, laid out by the royal gardener for Cardinal Richelieu in the 1630s. This is due to the construction, between 1781 and 1784, of 60 uniform houses bordering three sides of the square. Today restaurants, art galleries and specialty shops line the square, which maintains a strong literary history – Jean Cocteau, Colette and Jean Marais are among its famous recent residents.

Statue in the Jardin du Palais Royal

Fontaine Molière ⑥

Rue de Richelieu 75001. **Map** 12 F1.
Ⓜ *Palais Royal.*

FRANCE'S MOST famous playwright lived near here, in a house on the site of No. 40 Rue de Richelieu. The 19th-century fountain is by Louis Visconti, who also designed Napoleon's tomb at Les Invalides *(see pp188–9).*

St-Roch ⑦

296 Rue St-Honoré 75001. **Map** 12 E1.
Ⓒ *01 42 44 13 20.* Ⓜ *Tuileries.*
Open *8am–7pm daily.* **Closed** *non-religious public hols.* Ⓣ *Daily, times vary.* **Concerts.** Ⓞ

THIS HUGE church was designed by Lemercier, architect of the Louvre, and its foundation stone was laid

Vien's *St Denis Preaching to the Gauls* (1767) in St-Roch

by Louis XIV in 1653. Jules Hardouin-Mansart added the large Lady Chapel with its richly decorated dome and ceiling in the 18th century and two additional chapels extended the church to 413 ft (126 m), just short of Notre-Dame. It is a treasure house of religious art, much of it from now-vanished churches and monasteries. It also contains the tombs of the playwright Pierre Corneille, the royal gardener André Le Nôtre and the philosopher Denis Diderot. The façades reveal marks of Napoleon's attack, in 1795, on royalist troops who were defending the church steps.

Place des Pyramides ⑧

75001. **Map** 12 E1. Ⓜ *Tuileries, Pyramides.*

JOAN OF ARC, wounded nearby fighting the English in 1429, is commemorated by a 19th-century equestrian statue by the sculptor Daniel Frémiet. The statue is a rallying point for royalists.

Musée des Arts de la Mode ⑨

107 Rue de Rivoli 75001. **Map** 12 E1.
Ⓒ *01 44 55 57 50.* Ⓜ *Palais Royal, Tuileries.* **Open** *11am–6pm Tue–Fri (9pm Wed); 10am–6pm Sat, Sun.* **Adm charge.** Ⓣ

SET IN THE LOUVRE'S Pavillon de Marsan, the museum promotes one of the city's oldest, and most famous, industries – fashion.
It houses an impressive collection of *haute couture* costumes and accessories and has become an important venue of temporary exhibitions of costumes.

Schiaparelli jacket in the museum

Musée du Louvre ❶

T HE MUSÉE DU LOUVRE, containing one of the most important art collections in the world, has a history extending back to medieval times. First constructed as a fortress in 1190 by King Philippe-Auguste to protect Paris against Viking raids, it lost its imposing keep and dungeon in the reign of François I, who replaced it with a Renaissance-style building. Thereafter, four centuries of French kings and emperors improved and enlarged it. A recent addition is the main courtyard's glass pyramid entrance, from which all the galleries are reached.

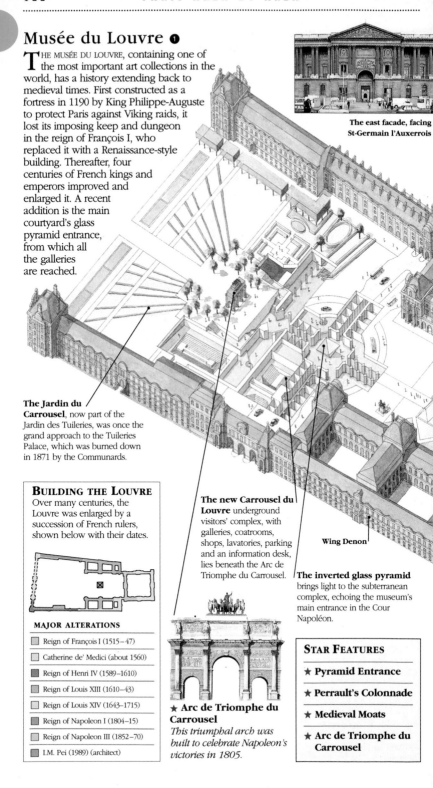

The east facade, facing St-Germain l'Auxerrois

The Jardin du Carrousel, now part of the Jardin des Tuileries, was once the grand approach to the Tuileries Palace, which was burned down in 1871 by the Communards.

BUILDING THE LOUVRE
Over many centuries, the Louvre was enlarged by a succession of French rulers, shown below with their dates.

MAJOR ALTERATIONS

☐	Reign of François I (1515–47)
☐	Catherine de' Medici (about 1560)
■	Reign of Henri IV (1589–1610)
☐	Reign of Louis XIII (1610–43)
☐	Reign of Louis XIV (1643–1715)
■	Reign of Napoleon I (1804–15)
☐	Reign of Napoleon III (1852–70)
☐	I.M. Pei (1989) (architect)

The new Carrousel du Louvre underground visitors' complex, with galleries, coatrooms, shops, lavatories, parking and an information desk, lies beneath the Arc de Triomphe du Carrousel.

Wing Denon

The inverted glass pyramid brings light to the subterranean complex, echoing the museum's main entrance in the Cour Napoléon.

★ **Arc de Triomphe du Carrousel**
This triumphal arch was built to celebrate Napoleon's victories in 1805.

STAR FEATURES

★ **Pyramid Entrance**

★ **Perrault's Colonnade**

★ **Medieval Moats**

★ **Arc de Triomphe du Carrousel**

Pavillon Richelieu

This imposing 19th-century pavilion is part of the Wing Richelieu, once home to the Ministry of Finance but now converted into magnificent galleries.

VISITORS' CHECKLIST

Map 12 E2. 01 40 20 53 17. 01 40 20 51 51. M Palais Royal, Louvre. 21, 27, 39, 48, 68, 69, 72, 75, 95. RER Châtelet-Les-Halles. Louvre. P Carrousel du Louvre (entrance via Ave du General Lemmonier); Pl du Louvre, Rue St- Honoré. **Museum open** 9am– 6pm Thu–Sun; Mon, Wed. **Hall Napoleon** (including History of the Louvre, auditorium, temporary exhibitions, restaurants, bookshop) **Open** 9am–10pm Wed–Mon. **Closed** Jan 1, Easter Mon, May 1, May 31, Jul 14, Nov 1, Dec 25. **Adm charge.** (reduced price after 3pm & all day Sun; free 1st Sun of each month). partial. call 01 40 20 52 09. **Lectures, movies, concerts.** www.louvre.fr

Cour Marly is the glass-roofed courtyard that now houses the Marly Horses (see p125).

Wing Richelieu

★Pyramid Entrance
The popular new main entrance, designed by the architect I.M. Pei, was opened in 1989.

Cour Puget

Cour Khorsabad

Wing Sully

Cour Carrée

★Perrault's Colonnade
The east facade with its majestic rows of columns was built by Claude Perrault, who worked on the Louvre with Louis Le Vau in the mid-17th century.

The Salle des Caryatides
takes its name from the statues of women created by Jean Goujon in 1550 to support the upper gallery.

Cour Napoleon

The Louvre of Charles V
In about 1360, Charles V transformed Philippe-Auguste's old fortress, with its distinctive towers and keep, into a royal residence.

★ Medieval Moats
The base of the twin towers and the drawbridge support of Philippe-Auguste's fortress can be seen in the excavated area.

The Louvre's Collection

THE LOUVRE'S TREASURES can be traced back to the collection of François I (1515–47), who purchased many Italian paintings, including the *Mona Lisa (La Gioconda)*. In Louis XIV's reign (1643–1715) there were a mere 200 works, but donations and purchases augmented the collection. The Louvre was first opened to the public in 1793 after the Revolution, and has been continually enriched ever since.

The Lacemaker
In this exquisite picture from about 1665, Jan Vermeer gives us a glimpse into everyday domestic life in Holland. The painting came to the Louvre in 1870.

The Raft of the Medusa *(1819)*
Théodore Géricault derived his inspiration for this gigantic and moving work from the shipwreck of a French frigate in 1816. The painting shows the moment when the few survivors sight a sail on the horizon.

Cour Marly

Richelieu Wing

Main entrance

GALLERY GUIDE

The main entrance is beneath the glass pyramid. From here, corridors radiate to each of the wings of the museum. The works are displayed on four floors, with the painting and sculpture collections arranged by country of origin. There are separate departments for Oriental, Egyptian, Greek, Etruscan and Roman antiquities, objets d'art and prints and drawings.

Underground visitors' complex

KEY TO FLOOR PLAN

☐	Painting
▨	Objets d'art
☐	Sculpture
▨	Antiquities
▨	Non-exhibition space

Denon Wing

★ **Venus de Milo**
Found in 1820 on the island of Milo in Greece, this ideal of feminine beauty was made in the Hellenistic Age at the end of the 2nd century BC.

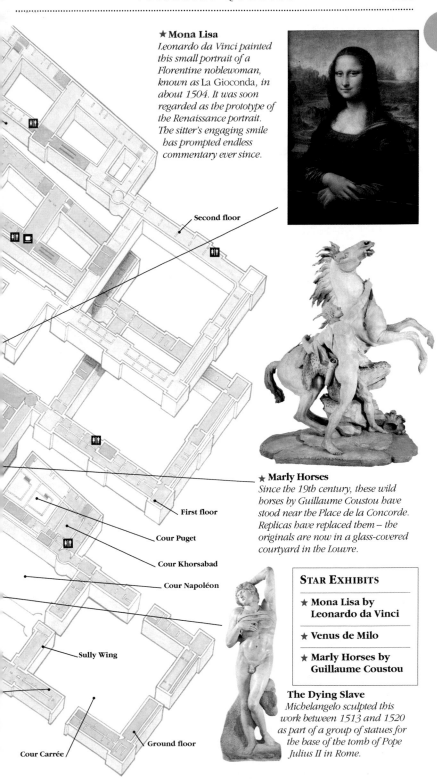

★ **Mona Lisa**
Leonardo da Vinci painted this small portrait of a Florentine noblewoman, known as La Gioconda, *in about 1504. It was soon regarded as the prototype of the Renaissance portrait. The sitter's engaging smile has prompted endless commentary ever since.*

Second floor

★ **Marly Horses**
Since the 19th century, these wild horses by Guillaume Coustou have stood near the Place de la Concorde. Replicas have replaced them – the originals are now in a glass-covered courtyard in the Louvre.

First floor

Cour Puget

Cour Khorsabad

Cour Napoléon

Sully Wing

Cour Carrée

Ground floor

STAR EXHIBITS

★ **Mona Lisa by Leonardo da Vinci**

★ **Venus de Milo**

★ **Marly Horses by Guillaume Coustou**

The Dying Slave
Michelangelo sculpted this work between 1513 and 1520 as part of a group of statues for the base of the tomb of Pope Julius II in Rome.

Exploring the Louvre's Collection

IT IS IMPORTANT NOT TO UNDERESTIMATE the size of this vast collection and useful to set a few viewing priorities before starting. The collection of European painting (1400–1900) is comprehensive and 40 percent of the works are by French artists; the selection of sculpture is less complete. The museum's antiquities – Oriental, Egyptian, Greek, Etruscan and Roman – are of world renown and offer the visitor an unrivaled range of objects. The objets d'art on display are very varied and include furniture and jewelry.

The Fortune Teller (about 1594) by Caravaggio

EUROPEAN PAINTING: 1400 TO 1900

PAINTING FROM northern Europe (Flemish, Dutch, German and English) is well covered. One of the earliest Flemish works is Jan van Eyck's *Madonna of Chancellor Rolin* (about 1435), which shows the Chancellor of Burgundy kneeling in prayer before the Virgin and Child.

Portrait of Erasmus (1523) by Hans Holbein

Hieronymus Bosch's *Ship of Fools* (1500) is a fine satirical account of the futility of human existence. In the Dutch collection, Anthony van Dyck's portrait *King Charles Out Hunting* (1635) shows Charles I of England in all his refined elegance. Jacob Jordaens, best known for scenes of gluttony and lust, reveals unusual sensitivity in his *Four Evangelists*. The saucy smile of the *Gipsy Girl* (1628) displays Frans Hals's effortless virtuosity. Rembrandt's self-portrait, his *Disciples at Emmaus* (1648) and his *Bathsheba* (1654) are examples of the artist's genius.

There is relatively little German painting, but the three major German painters of the 15th and 16th centuries are represented by important works. There is a 1493 self-portrait by Albrecht Dürer as a young artist of 22, a 1529 *Venus* by Lucas Cranach and a portrait of the great humanist scholar Erasmus by Hans Holbein. English artists include Thomas Gainsborough (*Conversation in a Park*, about

1746), Sir Joshua Reynolds (*Master Hare*, 1788) and J. M. W. Turner (*Landscape with a River and Bay in the Distance*, about 1835–40).

Many of the masterworks in the Spanish collection depict the tragic side of life: El Greco's *Christ on the Cross Adored by Donors* (1576) and Francisco de Zurbarán's *Lying-in-State of St. Bonaventura* (about 1629) with its dark-faced corpse are two of the Louvre's prize pieces. The subject of José de Ribera's *Club-Footed Boy* (1642) is a poor mute who carries a scrap of paper requesting alms. In a lighter vein, there are several portraits by Goya from the 19th century.

The museum's collection of Italian painting is large, covering the period from 1200 to 1800. The father figures of the early Renaissance, Cimabue and Giotto, are here, as are Fra Angelico, with his *Coronation of the Virgin* (1435), and Pisanello, with his delightful *Portrait of Ginevra d'Este* (about 1435). There are also a fine portrait in profile of Sigismondo Malatesta by Piero della Francesca (about 1450) and an action-packed battle scene by Paolo Uccello. Several paintings by Leonardo da Vinci, for instance, the *Virgin with the Infant Jesus and St. Anne*, are as enchanting as his *Mona Lisa*.

The Louvre's fine collection of French painting ranges from the 14th century to 1848. Paintings after this date are housed in the Musée d'Orsay (*see pp144–7*). An outstanding

Gilles or *Pierrot* (about 1717) by Jean Antoine Watteau

LEONARDO DA VINCI IN FRANCE

Leonardo, artist, engineer and scientist, was born in 1452 and became a leading figure in the Italian Renaissance. François I met Leonardo in 1515 and invited him to live and work in France. The painter brought the *Mona Lisa* with him. Already in poor health, he died three years later in the arms of the king.

Self-portrait (early 16th century)

early work is Enguerrand Quarton's *Villeneuve-les-Avignon Pietà* (1455). Another early painting shows *Gabrielle d'Estrée*, mistress of Henri IV, in her bath tub. From the 16th and 17th centuries there are several splendid works by Georges de la Tour with the dramatic torchlight effect so typical of his work.

That great 18th-century painter of melancholy, Jean Watteau, is represented, as is J.H. Fragonard, master of the Rococo. His delightful frivolity is evident in *The Bathers* from 1770. In stark contrast is the Classicism of Nicolas Poussin and the history painting of J.L. David. Most of J.D. Ingres' work is in the Musée d'Orsay, but the Louvre kept the erotic *Turkish Bath* of 1862.

EUROPEAN SCULPTURE: 1100 TO 1900

EARLY FLEMISH and German sculpture in the collection contains many masterpieces, such as Tilman Riemenschneider's *Virgin of the Annunciation* from the end of the 15th century and an unusual life-size nude of the penitent Mary Magdalen by Gregor Erhart (early 16th century). An ornate gilded-wood altarpiece of the same period exemplifies Flemish church art. An important work of Flemish sculpture is Adrian de Vries's long-limbed *Mercury and Psyche* from 1593, which was originally made for the court of Rudolph II in Prague.

The French section opens with early Romanesque works, such as the figure of Christ by a 12th-century Burgundian sculptor and a head of St. Peter. With its eight black-hooded mourners, the tomb of Philippe Pot (a high-ranking official in Burgundy) is one of the more unusual pieces. Diane de Poitiers, mistress of Henri II, had a large figure of her namesake Diana, goddess of the hunt, installed in the courtyard of her castle west of Paris. It is now in the Louvre. The works of Pierre Puget (1620–94), the great sculptor from Marseilles, have been assembled inside a glass-covered courtyard, Cour Puget. They include a figure of Milo of Crotona, the Greek athlete who got his hands caught in the cleft of a tree stump and was eaten by a lion. The wild horses of Marly now stand in the glass-roofed Cour Marly, surrounded by other masterpieces of French sculpture, including Jean-Antoine Houdon's early 19th-century busts of such famous men as Diderot and Voltaire.

The collection of Italian sculpture includes such splendid exhibits as Michelangelo's *Slaves* and Benvenuto Cellini's Fontainebleau *Nymph.*

***Tomb of Philippe Pot** (late 15th century) by Antoine le Moiturier*

ORIENTAL, EGYPTIAN, GREEK, ETRUSCAN AND ROMAN ANTIQUITIES

THE RANGE of antiquities in the Louvre is impressive. There are objects from the Neolithic period (about 6000 BC) to the fall of the Roman Empire. Important works of Mesopotamian art include the seated figure of Ebih I, from 2400 BC, and several portraits of Gudea, Prince of Lagash, from about 2255 BC. A black basalt block bearing the code of the Babylonian King Hammurabi, from about 1700 BC, is one of the world's oldest legal documents.

The warlike Assyrians are represented by delicate carvings and a spectacular reconstruction of part of Sargon II's (722–705 BC) palace with its huge, winged bulls. In the 6th century BC Darius, king of Persia, decorated the staircase of his Palace of Khorsabad with ceramic tiles depicting his personal guard of archers.

Most Egyptian art was made for the dead, providing them with the things that they needed for the afterlife. It often included vivid images of daily life in ancient Egypt. One example is the tiny funeral chapel built for a high official in about 2500 BC. It is covered with exquisite carvings: men in sailing ships, catching fish and tending cattle and fowl.

It is also possible to gain insights into family life in ancient Egypt through a number of lifelike funeral portraits, like the squatting scribe, and several sculptures

of married couples. The earliest sculpture dates from 2500 BC, the latest from 1400 BC.

From the New Kingdom, (1555–1080 BC), a special crypt dedicated to the god Osiris contains some colossal sarcophagi and a large number of mummified animals.

Some smaller objects of considerable charm include an 11-inch (29-cm) headless body of a woman, sensually outlined by the transparent veil of her dress and thought to be Queen Nefertiti (about 1365–1349 BC).

The department of Greek, Roman and Etruscan antiquities contains a vast array of fragments, among them some exceptional pieces. There is a large geometric head from the Cyclades (2700 BC) and an elegant, swan-necked bowl, quite modern in its unadorned simplicity. It is hammered out of a single gold sheet and dates from about 2500 BC. The Archaic Greek period, from the 7th to the 5th century BC, is represented by the *Auxerre Goddess,* one of the earliest-known pieces of Greek sculpture, and the *Hera of Samos* from the Ionian Islands. From the height of the Classical Greek period, (about the 5th century

***Winged Bull with Human Head** from 8th century BC, found in Khorsabad, Assyria*

***Winged Victory of Samothrace** (Greece, late 3rd–early 2nd century BC)*

BC), there are several fine male torsos and heads such as the *Laborde Head.* This head has been identified as part of the sculpture that once decorated the west pediment of the Parthenon in Athens.

The two most famous Greek statues in the Louvre, the *Winged Victory of Samothrace* and the *Venus de Milo,* belong to the Hellenistic period (late 3rd to 2nd century BC) when more naturalistic human forms were produced.

The undisputed star of the Etruscan collection is the terracotta sarcophagus of a married couple who appear

Etruscan Sarcophagus (6th century BC)

as though they are attending an eternal banquet.

The sculptures in the Roman section demonstrate the great debt owed to the art of ancient Greece: There are many fine pieces: a bust of Agrippa; a basalt head of Livia, the wife of Augustus; and a splendid, powerful bronze head of Emperor Hadrian from the 2nd century AD. This has the look of a true portrait, unlike so many Imperial heads that are uninspired and impersonal.

Squatting Scribe (Egyptian, about 2500 BC)

OBJETS D'ART

THE CATCHALL term *objets d'art* (art objects) covers a vast range of objects: jewelry, furniture, clocks, watches, sundials, tapestries, miniatures, silver and glassware, cutlery, small French and Italian bronzes, Byzantine and Parisian carved ivory, Limoges enamels, porcelain, French and Italian stoneware, rugs, snuffboxes, scientific instruments and armor. The Louvre has well over 8,000 items, from many ages and regions.

Many of these precious objects were in the Abbey of St-Denis, where the kings of France were crowned. Long before the Revolution, a regular flow of visitors had made it something of a museum. After the Revolution all the objects were removed and presented to the nation. Much was lost or stolen during the move but what remains is still outstanding.

The treasure includes a serpentine stone plate from the 1st century AD with a 9th-century border of gold and precious stones. (The plate itself is inlaid with eight golden dolphins.) There is also a porphyry vase that Suger, Abbot of St-Denis, had mounted in gold in the shape of an eagle, and the golden scepter made for King Charles V in about 1380.

The French crown jewels include the coronation crowns of Louis XV and Napoleon, scepters, swords and other accessories of the coronation ceremonies. On display is also the Regent, one of the purest diamonds in the world. It was bought in 1717 and worn by Louis XV at his coronation in 1722.

One whole room is taken up with the series of tapestries called *Hunts of Maximilian,* originally executed for Emperor Charles V

The Eagle of Suger (mid-12th century)

in 1530 after drawings by Bernard Van Orley.

The large collection of French furniture ranges from the 16th to the 19th centuries and is assembled by period or in rooms devoted to donations by distinguished collectors such as Isaac de Camondo. On display are important pieces by exceptionally prominent furniture-makers such as André-Charles Boulle, cabinetmaker to Louis XIV, who worked at the Louvre in the late 17th to mid–18th centuries. He is noted for his technique of inlaying copper and tortoiseshell. From a later date, the curious inlaid steel and bronze writing desk, created by Adam Weisweiler for Queen Marie-Antoinette in 1784, is one of the more unusual pieces in the museum's collection.

THE GLASS PYRAMID

Plans for the modernization and expansion of the Louvre were first conceived in 1981. They included the transfer of the Ministry of Finance from the Richelieu wing of the Louvre to new offices elsewhere, and a new main entrance to the museum. A Chinese-American architect, I.M. Pei, was chosen to design the changes. He designed the pyramid as both the focal point and new entrance to the Louvre. Made out of glass, it enables the visitor to see the historic buildings that surround it while allowing light down into the underground visitors' reception area.

Musée de la Publicité ⑪

Palais du Louvre, 107 Rue de Rivoli 75001. **Map** 12 E2. *01 44 55 59 60.* Ⓜ *Palais Royal, Tuileries.* **Open** *11am–6pm Tue, Thu, Fri; 11am–9pm Wed; 10am–6pm Sat & Sun.*

THE MUSEUM OF advertising, open from the end of 1999, brings together a superb collection of over 40,000 historic posters dating from the 18th century to 1949, plus around 45,000 more recent posters, and modern, multimedia advertising ranging from videos to promotional items. There is also a good reference library.

Musée des Arts Décoratifs ⑪

Palais du Louvre, 107 Rue de Rivoli 75001. **Map** 12 E2. *01 44 55 57 50.* Ⓜ *Palais Royal, Tuileries.* **Open** *11am–6pm Tue, Thu, Fri; 11am–9pm Wed; 10am–6pm Sat & Sun.* **Reference library closed** until 2001.

WITH FIVE FLOORS and over 100 rooms, this museum offers an eclectic display of decorative and ornamental art and design from the Middle Ages to the present day.

Among the highlights are Art Nouveau and Art Deco rooms, including a reconstruction of the Left Bank home of couturier Jeanne Lanvin, the interwar queen of the Parisian fashion world. Art Deco jewelry and Gallé glass are prominently featured.

Other floors show Louis XIV, XV and XVI styles of artistic decoration and furniture. The doll collection is remarkable.

Lemot's Restoration group of statues with the gilded figure of Victory

Arc de Triomphe du Carrousel ⑫

Pl du Carrousel 75001. **Map** 12 E2. Ⓜ *Palais Royal.*

BUILT BY NAPOLEON in 1806–1808 as an entrance to the former Palais des Tuileries, its marble columns are topped by soldiers of the Grande Armée. They replaced the Horses of St. Mark's, which he was forced to return in 1815, after Waterloo.

Arcades along the Rue de Rivoli

Rue de Rivoli ⑬

75001. **Map** 11 C1 & 13 A2. Ⓜ *Louvre, Palais Royal, Tuileries, Concorde.*

THE LONG ARCADES with their shops, topped by Neo-classical apartments, date back to the early 18th century,

though they were finished only in the 1850s. Commissioned by Napoleon after his victory at Rivoli, in 1797, the street completed the link between the Louvre and the Champs-Elysées, and became an important artery as well as an elegant center for commerce. The Tuileries walls were replaced by railings and the whole area opened up.

Today along the Rue de Rivoli there are makers of expensive men's shirts and bookshops toward the Place de la Concorde, and popular department stores near the Châtelet and Hôtel de Ville. Angélina's, at No. 226, is said to serve the best hot chocolate in Paris (*see p288*).

Jardin des Tuileries ⑭

75001. **Map** 12 D1. Ⓜ *Tuileries, Concorde.*

THESE FORMAL gardens were once the gardens of the old Palais des Tuileries. They are an integral part of the landscaped area running parallel to the Seine from the Louvre to the Champs-Elysées and the Arc de Triomphe.

The gardens were laid out in the 17th century by André Le Nôtre, royal gardener to Louis XIV. He created a Neo-classical garden with a broad central avenue and regularly spaced terraces and flower beds. Recent restoration has created a new garden with chestnut and lime trees.

A 17th-century engraving of the Jardin des Tuileries by G. Perelle

Galerie Nationale du Jeu de Paume **⑮**

Jardin des Tuileries, Pl de la Concorde 75008. **Map** 11 C1. **📞** *01 47 03 12 50*. **📠** *01 42 60 69 69*. **Ⓜ** *Concorde*. **Open** *noon–9:30pm Tue; noon–7pm Wed–Fri; 10am–7pm Sat, Sun*. **Closed** *Jan 1, May 1, Dec 25*. **Adm charge**. 🚫 ♿ 🎥 💻 📷 🔊

Monet's water lilies, on display in the Musée de l'Orangerie

THE JEU DE PAUME – or *réal* tennis court – was built by Napoleon III in 1851. When *réal* (royal) tennis was replaced in popularity by lawn tennis, the court was used to exhibit art. Eventually the Impressionist museum was founded on the site. In 1986, the collection was moved to the new Musée d'Orsay (in the former Orsay railway station, see pp144–7) across the river. The Jeu de Paume now shows exhibitions of contemporary art.

Entrance to the Jeu de Paume

Musée de l'Orangerie **⑯**

Jardin des Tuileries, Pl de la Concorde 75008. **Map** 11 C1. **📞** *01 42 97 48 16*. **Ⓜ** *Concorde*. **Closed** *until 2001*. **Adm charge**. 📷 ♿ 🎥 *by appointment*. 📷

CLAUDE MONET'S crowning work, the water lily series, fills the oval ground floor rooms of this museum. Known as the *Nymphéas*, the series was painted in his garden at Giverny, near Paris. This superb work is complemented well by the outstanding Walter-Guillaume collection of artists of the Ecole de Paris, from the late Impressionist era to the inter-war period. This is a remark-

able concentration of masterpieces, including a room of dramatic works by Soutine and some 14 works by Cézanne – still lifes, portraits *(Madame Cézanne)* and landscapes, such as *Dans le Parc du Château Noir*.

Renoir is represented by 24 canvases, including *Les Fillettes au Piano (Young Girls at the Piano)*. There are early Picassos, works by Henri Rousseau – notably *Le Carriole du Père Junier (Old Junier's Cart)* – Matisse and a portrait of Paul Guillaume by Modigliani. All are bathed in the natural light that flows through the windows.

Place de la Concorde **⑰**

75008. **Map** 11 C1. **Ⓜ** *Concorde*.

THIS IS ONE of Europe's most magnificent and historic squares, covering more than 20 acres (8 ha) in the middle of Paris. Starting out as Place Louis XV, for displaying a statue of the king, it was built in the mid-18th century by architect Jacques-Ange Gabriel, who chose to make it an open octagon with only the north side containing mansions.

The 3,200-year-old obelisk from Luxor

In the square's next incarnation, as the Place de la Révolution, the statue was replaced by the guillotine. The death toll in the square in two and a half years was 1,119, including Louis XVI, Marie-Antoinette (who died in view of the small, secret apartment she kept at No. 2 Rue Royale) and the revolutionary leaders Danton and Robespierre.

Renamed Concorde (originally by chastened Revolutionaries) in a spirit of reconciliation, the grandeur of the square was enhanced in the 19th century by the 3,200-year-old Luxor obelisk, two fountains and eight statues personifying French cities. It has become the culminating point of triumphal parades down the Champs-Elysées each July 14, most notably on the memorable Bastille Day of 1989 when the Revolution's bicenten-ary was celebrated by a million people and many world leaders.

Colonnaded entrance to the Village Royale

Village Royale

75008. **Map** 5 C5. **M** *Madeleine.*
Galerie Royale Open *10am–6pm*
Tue–Sat. **Closed** *public hols.*

THIS DELIGHTFUL enclave of 18th-century town houses sits discreetly between the Rue Royale and the Rue Boissy d'Anglas. The Galerie Royale is the former home of the Duchess d'Abrantès. It was converted in 1994 by architect Laurent Bourgois who has combined classical and modern in superb style, reflecting both the antique glass- and silverware on display and the contemporary glassworkers and goldsmiths

who occupy the vaults. Beneath the original glass roof in the central courtyard, a statue of the goddess Pomona is lit by fiber optics and colored with blue cabochons of Bohemian crystal. There is also a quiet, elegant Bernardaud Porcelain tearoom.

Place Vendôme

75001. **Map** 6 D5. **M** *Tuileries.*

PERHAPS THE best example of 18th-century elegance in the city, the royal square by architect Jules Hardouin-Mansart was begun in 1698. The original plan was to house academies and embassies behind the arcaded facades. However, bankers moved in and created opulent homes. Miraculously the square has remained virtually intact and is home to jewelers and bankers. Among the famous, Frédric Chopin died here in 1848 at No. 12 and César Ritz established his famous hotel at the turn of the century at No. 15.

Banque de France

39 Rue Croix des Petits Champs
75001. **Map** 12 F1. **M** *Palais Royal.*

FOUNDED BY Napoleon in 1800, France's central bank is housed in a building that was intended for quite different purposes. The 17th-century architect François Mansart designed this mansion for Louis XIII's wealthy secretary of state, Louis de la

Napoleon's statue in Place Vendôme

FORMAL GARDENS IN PARIS

The South Parterre at Versailles (see pp248–9)

FOR THE PAST 300 years, the main formal gardens in Paris have been open to the public and are a firm fixture in the city's life. Today the Jardin des Tuileries (see p130) is about to undergo extensive renovation and replanting; the Jardin du Luxembourg (see p172), the private garden of the French Senate, is still beloved of Left Bankers; and the Jardin du Palais Royal (see p121) are enjoyed by those who seek peace and privacy.

French landscaping was raised to an art form in the 17th century, thanks to Louis XIV's talented landscaper André Le Nôtre, who created the gardens of Versailles (see pp248–9). He achieved a brilliant marriage between the traditional Italian Renaissance garden and the French love of rational design.

The role of the French garden architect was not to tend nature but to transform it, pruning and planting to

The long Galerie Dorée in the Banque de France

Vrillière, with the sumptuous 164 ft (50m) long Galerie Dorée specially created for hanging his great collection of historical paintings. The house was later sold to the Comte de Toulouse, son of Louis XIV and Madame de Montespan. The building was extensively reconstructed in the 19th century after the ravages of the Revolution. The bank's most famous modern alumnus is Jacques Delors, president of the European Commission.

Place des Victoires ㉑

75002. Map 12 F1. M *Palais Royal.*

THIS CIRCLE of elegant mansions was built in 1685 solely to set off the statue of Louis XIV, which was placed in the middle, with torches burning day and night. The proportions of the buildings and even the arrangement of the surrounding streets were designed by the architect and courtier Jules Hardouin-Mansart to display the statue to its best advantage.

Unfortunately, the 1792 rebellious crowds tore down the statue in protest. A replacement, of a different style, was erected in 1822, to the detriment of the whole system of proportions of buildings to statue. Yet the square retains much of the original design, and today it is the address of major names in the fashion business, most notably Thierry Mugler, Cacharel and Kenzo.

Louis XIV on Place des Victoires

A Bagatelle garden with floral color *(see p255)*

create leafy sculptures out of trees, bushes and hedges. Complicated geometrical designs that were created in beds and paths were interspersed with pebbles and carefully thought out splashes of floral color. Symmetry and harmony were the landscaper's passwords, a sense of grandeur and magnificence his ultimate goal.

In the 17th century, as now, formal French gardens served two purposes: as a setting or backdrop for a château or palace and for enjoyment. The best view of a formal garden was from the first floor of the château, from which the combination of boxwood hedges, flowers and gravel came together in an intricate abstract pattern, a blossoming tapestry that complemented the château's interior. Paths of trees drew the eye into infinity, reminding the onlooker of how much land belonged to his host and therefore establishing his undoubted wealth. So, early on, the formal garden became a status symbol, and it still is. This is obvious in both private gardens and grand public projects. Napoleon Bonaparte completed his vista from the Jardin des Tuileries with a triumphal arch. The late President Mitterand applied the principle in building his Grand Arc de la Défense *(see pp38–9, 255)* along the same axis as the Tuileries and Arc de Triomphe.

But formal gardens were also made to be enjoyed. People in the 17th century believed that walking in the fresh air kept them in good health. There was no more perfect spot for this than a formal garden bedecked with statues and fountains. The old and infirm could be moved around in sedan chairs and people could meet one another around a boxwood hedge or quietly sit on a stone bench under the marbly gaze of the goddess Diana.

ST-GERMAIN-DES-PRÉS

T HIS AREA OF THE Left Bank is fuller and livelier, its streets and cafés more crowded, than when it was at the forefront of the city's intellectual life in the 1950s. The leading figures of the time have now gone, and the rebellious disciples have retreated to their bourgeois backgrounds. But the new philosophers are there, the radical young thinkers who emerged from the 1960s upheavals, and the area still has its major publishing houses, whose executives entertain treasured writers and agents at the celebrated cafés. But they now share the area with the haut monde, those who patronize Yves Saint Laurent's opulent premises and the elegant Rue Jacob's smart interior designers. On the south side of Boulevard St-Germain, the streets are quiet and quaint, with a selection of many good restaurants, and at the Odéon end, there are brassy cafés and a profusion of movie theaters.

Musée d'Orsay clock

SIGHTS AT A GLANCE

Historic Buildings and Streets
Palais Abbatial **2**
Boulevard St-Germain **7**
Rue du Dragon **9**
Rue de l'Odéon **11**
Cour de Rohan **13**
Cour du Commerce St-André **14**
Institut de France **16**
Ecole Nationale Supérieure des Beaux-Arts **17**
Ecole Nationale d'Administration **18**
Quai Voltaire **19**

Churches
St-Germain-des-Prés **1**

Museums and Galleries
Musée Eugène Delacroix **3**
Musée Maillol **8**
Musée de la Monnaie **15**
Musée d'Orsay pp144–7 **20**
Musée Nationale de la Légion d'Honneur **21**

Theaters
Théâtre National de l'Odéon **12**

Cafés and Restaurants
Les Deux Magots **4**
Café de Flore **5**
Brasserie Lipp **6**
Le Procope **10**

GETTING THERE
Metro stations St-Germain-des-Prés and Odéon and the RER station at Musée d'Orsay serve the area. Bus route 63 travels down Boulevard St-Germain, and 48 and 95 go along Rue Bonaparte. Routes 58 and 70 pass along Rue Mazarine.

SEE ALSO
• *Street Finder*, map 11–12
• *Where to Stay* pp278–9
• *Restaurants* pp296–8

KEY

▨	Street-by-Street map
M	Metro station
▣	Batobus boarding point
RER	RER station
P	Parking

0 meters   400
0 yards   400

The church of St-Germain-des-Prés and Les Deux Magots café

Street by Street: St-Germain-des-Prés

Organ grinder in St-Germain

AFTER WORLD WAR II, St-Germain-des-Prés became synonymous with intellectual life centered around bars and cafés. Philosophers, writers, actors and musicians mingled in the cellar nightspots and brasseries, where existentialist philosophy co-existed with American jazz. The area is now smarter than in the heyday of Jean-Paul Sartre and Simone de Beauvoir, the haunting singer Juliette Greco and the New Wave filmmakers. The writers are still around, enjoying the pleasures of sitting in Les Deux Magots, Café de Flore and other haunts. The 17th-century buildings have survived, but signs of change are evident in the affluent shops dealing in antiques, books and fashion.

Les Deux Magots
The café is famous for the patronage of celebrities such as Hemingway ❹

Café de Flore
In the 1950s, French intellectuals wrestled with new philosophical ideas in the Art Deco interior of the café ❺

RUE DU DRAGON

RUE DU SABOT

RUE DE RENNES

RUE BONAPARTE

RUE DU FOUR

Metro St-Germain-des-Prés

BLVD S

RUE BONAPARTE

Brasserie Lipp
Colorful ceramics decorate this famous brasserie frequented by politicians ❻

★ **St-Germain-des-Prés**
Descartes and the king of Poland are among the notables buried here at Paris's oldest church ❶

★ **Boulevard St-Germain**
Café terraces, boutiques, cinemas, restaurants and bookstores characterize the central section of the Left Bank's main street ❼

Picasso's sculpture *Homage to Apollinaire* is a tribute to the artist's friend, the poet Guillaume Apollinaire. It was erected in 1959, near the Café de Flore, where the poet held court.

LOCATOR MAP
See Central Paris Map pp12–13

★ Musée Delacroix
Here, Delacroix created the splendid mural, Jacob Wrestling, *for St-Sulpice.* (see p172.) **3**

STAR SIGHTS

★ **St-Germain-des-Prés**

★ **Boulevard St-Germain**

★ **Musée Delacroix**

KEY

- - - - Suggested route

| 0 meters | 100 |
| 0 yards | 100 |

Rue de Fürstenberg is a tiny square with old-fashioned street lamps and shady trees. It is often used as a film setting.

Rue de Buci was for centuries an important Left Bank street and the site of some real (royal) tennis courts. It now holds a lively market every day.

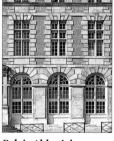

Palais Abbatial
This was the residence of abbots from 1586 till the 1789 Revolution **2**

Metro Odéon

Metro Mabillon

Marché St-Germain is an old covered food market that was opened in 1818, taking over the site of a former fairground. *(See p326.)*

Danton's statue (1889), by Auguste Paris, is a tribute to the Revolutionary leader.

St-Germain-des-Prés ❶

3 Pl St-Germain-des-Prés 75006.
Map 12 E4. **C** 01 43 25 41 71.
M St-Germain-des-Prés. **Open** 7am–
8pm daily. **Concerts.** 🎵 🅰

THIS IS THE OLDEST CHURCH in
Paris, originating in 542
when King Childebert built a
basilica to house holy relics.
This became an immensely
powerful Benedictine abbey,
which was suppressed during
the Revolution, when most of
the buildings were destroyed
by a fire in 1794. One of the
Revolution's most horrific
episodes took place in a
nearby monastery when 318
priests were hacked to death
by the mob on
September 3,
1792. The present
church dates from
about the 11th
century and was
heavily restored
in the 19th
century. One of
the three original
towers survives,
housing one of
the oldest belfries
in France. The
interior of the
church is an
interesting mix of
architectural styles,
with some 6th-
century marble
columns, Gothic
vaulting and
Romanesque
arches. Famous tombs include
those of the 17th-century
philosopher René Descartes,
the poet Nicolas Boileau and
John Casimir, king of Poland,
who later became abbot of St-
Germain-des-Prés in 1669.

*Our Lady of
Consolation* statue
in St-Germain-des-
Prés

Palais Abbatial ❷

1–5 Rue de l'Abbaye 75006.
Map 12 E4. **M** St-Germain-des-Prés.
Not open to the public.

THIS BRICK and stone palace
was built in 1586 for
Charles of Bourbon who was
cardinal-abbot of St-Germain
and, very briefly, king of
France. Ten more abbots
lived there until the Revolution, when the building was

**An ironwork detail from the
facade of the Palais Abbatial**

sold. James Pradier, the 19th-
century sculptor who was
famous for his female figures,
established a studio here. The
palace is now noted for its
mixture of building materials
and vertical windows.

Musée Eugène Delacroix ❸

6 Rue de Fürstenberg 75006.
Map 12 E4. **C** 01 44 41 86 50.
M St-Germain-des-Prés. **Open**
9:30am–5pm Wed–Mon (last adm:
4:30pm). **Adm charge.** 🅰

Eugène Delacroix

THE LEADING nonconformist
Romantic painter, Eugène
Delacroix, known for his
passionate and highly colored
canvases, lived and worked
here from 1857 to his death in
1863. Here he painted *The
Entombment of Christ* and
The Way to Calvary (which
now hang in the museum).
He also created superb
murals for the Chapel of the
Holy Angels in the nearby St-
Sulpice church, which is part
of the reason why he moved
to this area.

The first-floor apartment and
garden studio now form a
national museum, where
regular exhibitions of
Delacroix's work are held.
The apartment has a portrait
of George Sand, self-portraits,
studies for future works and
artistic memorabilia.
  The charm of Delacroix's
garden is reflected in the tiny
Fürstenberg square. With its
pair of rare catalpa trees and
old-fashioned street lamps,
the square is one of Paris's
most romantic corners.

Les Deux Magots ❹

170 Blvd St-Germain 75006.
Map 12 E4. **C** 01 45 48 55 25.
M St-Germain-des-Prés.
Open 7:30am–1:30am daily.
Closed for one week in Jan.

THE CAFÉ STILL trades on its
self-styled reputation as
the rendezvous of the literary
and intellectual elite of the
city. This derives from the
patronage of Surrealist artists
and young writers including
Ernest Hemingway in the
1920s and 1930s, and existentialist philosophers and writers
during the 1950s.
  The present clientele is
more likely to be publishers
or people-watchers than the
new Hemingway. The café's
name comes from the two
wooden statues of Chinese
commercial agents *(magots)*
that adorn one of the pillars.
This is a good place for
enjoying an old-fashioned hot
chocolate and simply
watching the world go by.

The interior of Les Deux Magots

Café de Florc ❺

172 Blvd St-Germain 75006.
Map 12 D4. ☎ *01 45 48 55 26.*
Ⓜ *St-Germain-des-Prés.* **Open** *7am–2am daily.* ♿ *restricted.*

THE CLASSIC Art Deco interior of all-red seating, mahogany and mirrors has changed little since the war. Like its rival Les Deux Magots, it has hosted most of the French intellectuals during the post-war years. Jean-Paul Sartre and Simone de Beauvoir would meet "the Family" (their cronies) here and develop their philosophy of existentialism over a drink.

A walter at the Brasserie Lipp

Brasserie Lipp ❻

151 Blvd St-Germain 75006.
Map 12 E4. ☎ *01 45 48 53 91.*
Ⓜ *St-Germain-des-Prés.* **Open** *noon–1am daily. See* **Restaurants, Cafés and Bars** *p301.*

THIRD OF THE famous cafés clustered around St-Germain-des-Prés, Brasserie Lipp combines Alsatian beer, sauerkraut and sausages (it was founded by a refugee from Alsace) with excellent coffee to produce a Left Bank fixture popular with French politicians and fashion gurus as well as visitors. Originally opened in the late 19th century, it is regarded by many as the quintessential Parisian brasserie, although the experience is more atmospheric than culinary these days. The interior is bright with ceramic tiles of parrots and cranes. Phone reservations are not accepted.

Boulevard St-Germain ❼

75006, 75007. **Map** 11 C2 & 13 C5.
Ⓜ *Solférino, Rue du Bac, St-Germain-des-Prés, Mabillon, Odéon.*

THE LEFT BANK'S most celebrated thoroughfare, over 3 km (2 miles) long, curves across three districts from the Ile St-Louis to the Pont de la Concorde. The architecture is homogeneous because the boulevard was another of Baron Haussmann's bold strokes of 19th-century urban planning, but it encompasses a wide range of different lifestyles as well as a number of religious and cultural institutions.

From the east (the low street numbers) the boulevard passes the late François Mitterrand's private town residence in the Rue de Bièvre, the Maubert-Mutualité market square, the Musée de Cluny and the Sorbonne university before crossing the lively Boulevard St-Michel.

It continues past the Ecole de Médecine and the Place de l'Odéon to St-Germain-des-Prés, with its historic church and café terraces. Fashion boutiques, movie theaters, restaurants, and bookstores give this central portion its distinctive character. It is also here that one is most likely to see a celebrity – a movie star or prize-winning author. The area is active from midday to the early morning hours.

Beyond this section the boulevard becomes more exclusively residential and then distinctly political with the Ministry of Defence and the National Assembly.

Musée Maillol ❽

59 Rue de Grenelle 75007. **Map** 11 C4. ☎ *01 42 22 59 58.* Ⓜ *Sèvres-Babylone, Rue du Bac.* **Open** *9.30am–5pm Wed–Mon.* ♿ 🅿 🏠

A FORMER MODEL to Maillol, Dina Vierny, has created this museum dedicated to the Catalan artist. All aspects of his work are here: drawings, engravings, paintings, sculpture, and decorative objects. Also displayed is Dina Vierny's private collection, in which naïve art sits alongside works by Matisse, Dufy, Picasso, and Rodin. There are also changing shows of 20th century art.

Rue du Dragon ❾

75006. **Map** 12 D4.
Ⓜ *St-Germain-des-Prés.*

THIS SHORT street, between the Boulevard St-Germain and the Carrefour de la Croix Rouge, dates back to the Middle Ages and still has houses from the 17th and 18th centuries. Notice their large doors, tall windows, and ironwork balconies. A group of Flemish painters lived at No. 37 before the Revolution. The novelist Victor Hugo rented a garret at No. 30 when a 19-year-old bachelor.

A plaque at No. 30 Rue du Dragon commemorating Victor Hugo's house

Le Procope

13 Rue de l'Ancienne-Comédie 75006.
Map 12 F4. **C** *01 40 46 79 00.* **M**
Odéon. **Open** *7am–1am daily. See*
The History of Paris *pp26–7.*

THIS CLAIMS to be the world's first coffeehouse, having been founded in 1686 by the Sicilian Francesco Procopio dei Coltelli. It quickly became fashionable with the city's political and literary elite and with the actors from the Comédie-Française company.

Its patrons have included the philosopher Voltaire – who supposedly drank 40 cups of his favorite mixture of coffee and chocolate every day. The young Napoleon would leave his hat as security while he went searching for the money to pay the bill. Now a restaurant, Le Procope was revamped in 1989 in the style of the 18th century.

The rear facade of Le Procope restaurant

The Théâtre de l'Odéon, former home of the Comédie-Française

Rue de l'Odéon ❶

75006. **Map** 12 F5. **M** *Odéon.*

SYLVIA BEACH'S bookshop Shakespeare & Company *(see pp320–21)* stood at No. 12 from 1921 to 1940. She befriended many struggling American and British writers, such as Ezra Pound, T. S. Eliot, Scott Fitzgerald and Ernest Hemingway. It was largely due to her support – as secretary, editor, agent and banker – that James Joyce's *Ulysses* was first published in English. Adrianne Monnier's French equivalent at No. 7 opposite, Les Amis des Livres, was frequented by André Gide and Paul Valéry.

Opened in 1779 to improve access to the Odéon theater, this was the first street in Paris to have pavements with gutters, and it still has many attractive houses and shops, most of them dating from the 18th century.

Théâtre National de l'Odéon ❷

1 Pl Paul-Claudel 75006.
Map 12 F5. **C** *01 44 41 36 00.*
M *Odéon, Luxembourg.*
Open *for performances only.*
See **Entertainment** *pp332–3.*

THIS NEO-CLASSICAL theater was built in 1779 by Marie-Josephe Peyre and Charles de Wailly in the grounds of the former Hôtel de Condé. The site had been purchased by the king and given to the city to house the Comédie Française. The premiere of *The Marriage of Figaro*, by Beaumarchais, took place here in 1784. With the arrival of a new company in 1797 the name of the theater was changed to Odéon. In 1807 the theater was consumed by fire. It was rebuilt in the same year by the achitect Jean-François Chalgrin.

Following World War II, the theater specialized in 20th-century drama and was the best attended in Paris. It was badly damaged during the 1968 student riots, a political rather than aesthetic gesture, but has since been restored.

A young Hemingway in the 1920s

Cour de Rohan ❸

75006. **Map** 12 F4. **M** *Odéon.*
Access *from the Rue du Jardinet until 8pm; 8pm–8am access from the Blvd St-Germain.*

The unusual middle courtyard in the Cour de Rohan

THIS PICTURESQUE series of three courtyards was originally part of the 15th-century pied-à-terre of the archbishops of Rouen (corrupted to "Rohan"). The middle courtyard is the most unusual. Its three-legged wrought-iron mounting block, known as a *pas-de-mule*, was used at one time by elderly women and overweight prelates to mount their mules. It is probably the last mounting block left in Paris. Overlooking the yard is the facade of a fine Renaissance building, dating from the beginning of the 17th century. One of its important former residents was Henri II's mistress, Diane de Poitiers.

The third courtyard opens on to the tiny Rue du Jardinet, where the composer Saint-Saëns was born in 1835.

Cour du Commerce St-André ⓮

75006. **Map** 12 F4. Ⓜ *Odéon.*

THE GRISLY specter of the guillotine hangs over No. 9, since it was here that Dr. Guillotin is supposed to have perfected his "philanthropic decapitating machine." In fact, although the idea was Guillotin's, it was Dr. Louis, a Parisian surgeon, who was responsible for putting the "humane" plan into action. When the guillotine was first used for execution in 1792 it was known as a *Louisette.*

A print of a Revolutionary mob at a guillotine execution

Musée de la Monnaie ⓯

11 Quai de Conti 75006. **Map** 12 F3.
🄲 01 40 46 55 35. Ⓜ *Pont-Neuf, Odéon.* **Open** *noon–5pm Sun.* 🄳 🄵 *groups, by appt (adm charge), for museum and workshop.* **Movies.**

WHEN LOUIS XV decided to rehouse the Mint in the late 18th century, he hit upon the idea of launching a design competition for the new building. The present Hôtel

des Monnaies is the result of this competition. It was completed in 1777, and the architect, Jacques Antoine, was so pleased with the building that he lived there until his death in 1801.

Coins were minted in the mansion until 1973, when the process was moved to Pessac in the Gironde. The minting and milling halls now contain the coin and medallion museum. The extensive collection is displayed in vertical glass stands so that both sides of the coins are visible, and everything is presented in the context of the history of the day. The final room of the museum shows a production cycle with late 19th-century and early 20th-century tools and machines on display.

Instead of minting coins, the building's workshops are now devoted to the creation of medallions, a selection of which are on sale.

Institut de France ⓰

23 Quai de Conti 75006.
Map 12 E3. 🄲 01 44 41 43 35.
Ⓜ *Pont-Neuf, St.-Germain-des-Prés.*
Open *Sat & Sun by appointment only.*
Adm charge. 🄵

NOW HOME TO the illustrious Académie Française, this Baroque building was built as a palace in 1688 and was given over to the Institut de France in 1805. Its distinctive cupola was designed by the palace's architect, Louis Le Vau, to harmonize with the Palais du Louvre.

The Académie Française is the most famous of the five academies within the institute. It was founded in 1635 by

A sign of the former Mint, which is now a museum

Cardinal Richelieu and charged with the compilation of an official dictionary of the French language. From the beginning, membership has been limited to 40, who are entrusted with working on the dictionary.

Ecole Nationale Supérieure des Beaux-Arts ⓱

14 Rue Bonaparte 75006. **Map** 12 E3.
🄲 01 47 03 50 00. Ⓜ *St-Germain-des-Prés.* 🄵 *only: 2pm, 2:30pm, 3pm Mon (call 01 47 03 52 15 to arrange).* 🄳 **Library.**

THE MAIN FRENCH school of fine arts occupies an enviable position at the corner of the Rue Bonaparte and the riverside Quai Malaquais. It is housed in several buildings, the most imposing being the 19th-century Palais des Etudes.

A host of budding French and foreign painters and architects have crossed the large courtyard to study in the ateliers of the school. Young American architects, in particular, have studied there over the past century.

The facade of the Ecole Nationale Supérieure des Beaux-Arts

THE CELEBRATED CAFÉS OF PARIS

O NE OF THE most enduring images of Paris is the café scene. For the visitor, it is the romantic vision of great artists, writers or eminent intellectuals consorting in one of the Left Bank's celebrated cafés. For the Parisian, the café is one of life's constants, an everyday experience, providing people with a place to tryst, drink and meet friends; or to conclude business deals; or simply to watch the world go by.

The first café anywhere can be traced back to 1686, when, Le Procope *(see p140)* was opened. In the following century cafés became a vital part of Paris's social life. And with the widening of the city's streets, particularly during the 19th century and the building of Haussmann's Grands Boulevards, the cafés spread out on to the pavements, evoking Emile Zola's comment as to the "great silent crowds watching the street live."

The nature of a café was sometimes determined by the interests of its patrons. Some were the gathering places for those interested in playing chess, dominoes or billiards. Literary gents gathered in Le Procope during Molière's time in the 17th century. In the 19th century, First Empire Imperial guards officers were drawn to the Café d'Orsay, and Second Empire financiers gathered in the cafés along the Rue de la Chaussée d'Antim. The social set patronized the Café de Paris and Café Tortini, and theatergoers met at the cafés around the Opéra, including the Café de la Paix *(see p213).*

Newspaper reading is still a typical café pastime

Ecole Nationale d'Administration 18

13 Rue de l'Université 75007.
Map 12 D3. 01 49 26 45 45.
M *Rue du Bac.* **Not open** to the public.

T HIS FINE 18th-century mansion was originally built as two houses in 1643 by Briçonnet. In 1713, they were replaced by a *hôtel* built by Thomas Gobert for the widow of Denis Feydeau de Brou. It was passed on to her son, Paul-Espirit Feydeau de Brou, until his death in 1767. The *hôtel* then became the residence of the Venetian ambassador. It was occupied by Belzunce in 1787 and became a munitions depot during the Revolution, until the restoration of the monarchy. Until recently it housed the Ecole Nationale d'Administration, where the elite in politics, economics and science, such as former French prime minister Jacques Chirac, once studied.

Plaque marking the house on Quai Voltaire where Voltaire died

Quai Voltaire 19

75006 and 75007. **Map** 12 D3.
M *Rue du Bac.*

F ORMERLY PART of the Quai Malaquais, then later known as the Quai des Théatins, the Quai Voltaire is now home to some of the most important antiques dealers in Paris. It is also noted for its attractive 18th-century houses and for the famous people who lived in many of them, making it an especially interesting and pleasant street to walk along.

The 18th-century Swedish ambassador Count Tessin lived at No. 1, as did the sculptor James Pradier, famed for his statues and for his wife, who swam naked across the Seine. Louise de Kéroualle, spy for Louis XIV and created Duchess of Portsmouth by the infatuated Charles II of England, lived at Nos. 3–5.

Famous residents of No. 19 included the composers Richard Wagner and Jean Sibelius, the novelist Charles Baudelaire and the disgraced exile Oscar Wilde.

The French philosopher Voltaire died at No. 27, the Hôtel de la Villette. St-Sulpice, the local church, refused to accept his corpse (because of his atheism), and his body was rushed into the country to avoid the indignity of a pauper's grave.

Entertainment in the Claude Alain café in the Rue de Seine during the 1950s

The most famous cafés are on the Left Bank, in St-Germain and Montparnasse, where the literati of old used to gather and where the glitterati of today love to be seen. Before World War I, Montparnasse was haunted by hordes of Russian revolutionaries, most eminently Lenin and Trotsky, who whiled away their days in the cafés, grappling with the problems of Russia and the world over a *petit café*. Cultural life flourished in the 1920s, when Surrealists, like Salvador Dalí and Jean Cocteau, dominated café life, and later when American writers led by Ernest Hemingway and F. Scott Fitzgerald talked, drank and wrote in various cafés, among them La Coupole (*see p178*), Le Sélect and La Closerie des Lilas (*see p179*).

After the end of World War II, the cultural scene shifted northward to St-Germain. Existentialism had become the dominant creed and Jean-Paul Sartre its tiny charismatic leader. Sartre and his intellectual peers and followers, among them the writers Simone de Beauvoir and Albert Camus, the poet Boris Vian and the enigmatic singer Juliette Greco, gathered to work and discuss their ideas in Les Deux Magots (*see p138*) and the nearby rival Café de Flore (*see p139*). The traditional habitué of these cafés is still to be seen, albeit mixing with the international jet-set and with self-publicizing intellectuals hunched over their notebooks.

Works by one of St-Germain's elite, Albert Camus (1913–60)

Musée d'Orsay ⑳

See pp144–7.

Musée Nationale de la Légion d'Honneur ㉑

2 Rue de Bellechasse 75007.
Map 11 C2. ☎ 01 40 62 84 00.
Ⓜ Solférino. 🆁 Musée d'Orsay.
Open 11am–5pm Tue–Sun. **Adm charge.** 🔲 🔲

Nᴇxᴛ ᴛᴏ ᴛʜᴇ Musée d'Orsay is the truly massive Hôtel de Salm. It was one of the last great mansions to be built in the area (1782). The first owner was a German count, Prince de Salm-Kyrbourg, who was guillotined in 1794.

Today the building contains a museum where one can learn all about the Legion of Honor, a decoration launched by Napoleon I and so cherished by the French (and foreigners). Those awarded the honor wear a small red rosette in their buttonhole. The impressive displays of medals and insignia are complemented by paintings. In one of the rooms, Napoleon's Legion of Honor is on display with his sword and breastplate.

The museum also covers decorations from most parts of the world, among them the British Victoria Cross and the American Purple Heart.

The Musée d'Orsay, converted from a railroad station into a museum

Napoleon III's Great Cross of the Legion of Honor

Musée d'Orsay ⑳

IN 1986, 47 YEARS AFTER it had closed as a mainline railroad station, Victor Laloux's superb turn-of-the-century building was reopened as the Musée d'Orsay. Originally commissioned by the Orléans railroad company to be its terminal in the heart of Paris, it narrowly avoided demolition in the 1970s following the outcry over the destruction of Baltard's pavilions at Les Halles food market. During the conversion much of the original architecture was retained. The new museum was set up to present each of the arts of the period from 1848 to 1914 in the context of the contemporary society and all the various forms of creative activity happening at the time.

The Museum, from the Right Bank
Victor Laloux designed the building for the Universal Exhibition in 1900.

Chair by Charles Rennie Mackintosh
The style developed by Mackintosh was an attempt to express ideas in a framework of vertical and horizontal forms, as in this tearoom chair (1900).

★ **The Gates of Hell** *(1880–1917)
Rodin included figures that he had already created, such as* The Thinker *and* The Kiss, *in this famous gateway.*

★ **Le Déjeuner sur l'Herbe** *(1863)
Manet's painting, first exhibited in Napoleon III's Salon des Refusés, is presently on display in the first area of the upper level.*

KEY TO FLOOR PLAN

- ☐ Architecture & Decorative Arts
- ☐ Sculpture
- ☐ Painting before 1870
- ☐ Impressionism
- ☐ Neo-Impressionism
- ☐ Naturalism and Symbolism
- ☐ Art Nouveau
- ☐ Temporary exhibitions
- ☐ Nonexhibition space

GALLERY GUIDE

The collection occupies three levels. On the ground floor there are works from the mid- to late-19th century. The middle level features Art Nouveau decorative art and a range of paintings and sculptures from the second half of the 19th century to the early 20th century. The upper level has an outstanding collection of Impressionist and Neo-Impressionist art.

The Dance *(1867–8)
Carpeaux's sculpture caused a scandal when first exhibited.*

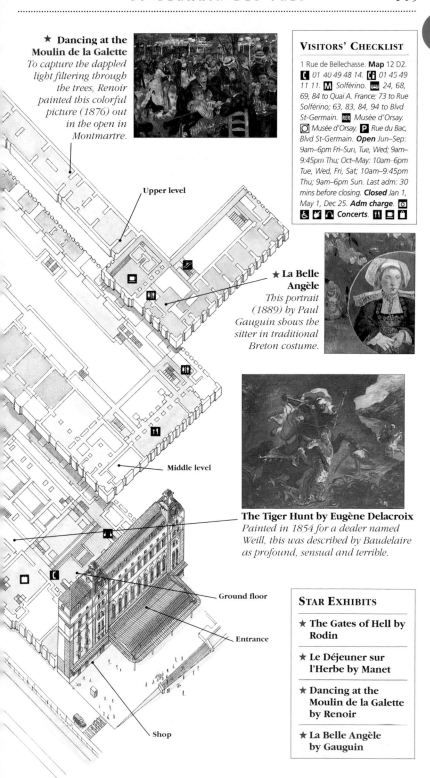

★ Dancing at the Moulin de la Galette
To capture the dappled light filtering through the trees, Renoir painted this colorful picture (1876) out in the open in Montmartre.

VISITORS' CHECKLIST

1 Rue de Bellechasse. **Map** 12 D2.
C 01 40 49 48 14. **F** 01 45 49 11 11. **M** Solférino. **Bus** 24, 68, 69, 84 to Quai A. France; 73 to Rue Solférino; 63, 83, 84, 94 to Blvd St-Germain. **RER** Musée d'Orsay. **Ⓞ** Musée d'Orsay. **P** Rue du Bac, Blvd St-Germain. **Open** Jun–Sep: 9am–6pm Fri–Sun, Tue, Wed; 9am–9:45pm Thu; Oct–May: 10am–6pm Tue, Wed, Fri, Sat; 10am–9:45pm Thu; 9am–6pm Sun. Last adm: 30 mins before closing. **Closed** Jan 1, May 1, Dec 25. **Adm charge.** **Ⓞ** **♿ 🎧 🎦** Concerts. **🍴 🛍 📷**

Upper level

★ La Belle Angèle
This portrait (1889) by Paul Gauguin shows the sitter in traditional Breton costume.

Middle level

The Tiger Hunt by Eugène Delacroix
Painted in 1854 for a dealer named Weill, this was described by Baudelaire as profound, sensual and terrible.

Ground floor

Entrance

STAR EXHIBITS

★ **The Gates of Hell by Rodin**

★ **Le Déjeuner sur l'Herbe by Manet**

★ **Dancing at the Moulin de la Galette by Renoir**

★ **La Belle Angèle by Gauguin**

Shop

Exploring the Orsay

Many of the exhibits now in the Musée d'Orsay originally came from the Louvre, and the superb collection of Impressionist art that was housed in the cramped Jeu de Paume until it closed in 1986 has been rehung here. In addition to the main exhibition, there are displays that explain the social, political and technological context in which the art was created, including exhibits on the newspaper industry and the history of cinematography.

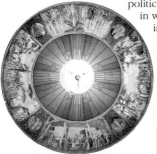

Ceiling design (1911) by the artist and designer Maurice Denis

Art Nouveau

The Belgian architect and designer Victor Horta was among the first to give free rein to the sinuous line that gave Art Nouveau its French sobriquet of *Style Nouille* (noodle style). Taking its name from a gallery of modern design that opened in Paris in 1895, Art Nouveau flourished throughout Europe until World War I.

In Vienna, Otto Wagner, Koloman Moser and Josef Hoffmann combined high craft with the new design, while the School of Glasgow, under the impetus of Charles Rennie Mackintosh, developed a more rectilinear approach that anticipated the work of Frank Lloyd Wright in the United States.

René Lalique introduced the aesthetics of Art Nouveau into jewelry and glassware, while Hector Guimard, inspired by Horta, is most famous today for his once-ubiquitous Art Nouveau entrances to the Paris metro.

One exhibit not to be missed is the carved wooden bookcase by Rupert Carabin (1890), with its proliferation of allegorical seated female nudes, bronze palm fronds and severed bearded heads.

Sculpture

The museum's central aisle overflows with an odd assortment of sculptures. These illustrate the eclectic mood around the middle of the 19th century, when the Classicism of Eugène Guillaume's *Cenotaph of the Gracchi* (1848–53) co-existed with the Romanticism of François Rude. Rude created the relief on the Arc de Triomphe (1836), often referred to as *La Marseillaise* (see p209).

There is a wonderful series of 36 busts of members of parliament (1832) – bloated, ugly, and self-important – by the satirist Honoré Daumier, and work by the short-lived genius Jean-Baptiste Carpeaux, whose first major bronze, *Count Ugolino* (1862), was a character from Dante. From 1867 to 1868 he produced his Dionysian delight, *The Dance*, which caused a storm of protest as "an insult to public morality." This contrasts with the derivative and mannered work of such sculptors as Alexandre Falguière and Hyppolyte Moulin.

Edgar Degas' famous *Young Dancer of Fourteen* (1881) was displayed during his lifetime, but the many bronzes on exhibit were made from wax sculptures found in his

studio after his death. In contrast, the sculpture of Auguste Rodin was very much in the public eye, and his sensuous and forceful work makes him preeminent among 19th-century sculptors. The museum contains many of his works, including the original plaster of *Balzac* (1897). Rodin's talented companion, Camille Claudel, who spent much of her life in an asylum, is represented by a grim allegory of mortality, *Maturity* (1899–1903).

The turn of the century is marked by the work of Emile-Antoine Bourdelle and Aristide Maillol.

Painting Before 1870

The surprising diversity of styles in 19th-century painting is emphasized by the close juxtaposition on the ground floor of all paintings prior to 1870 – the crucial year in which Impressionism first made a name for itself. The raging color and almost Expressionistic vigor of Eugène Delacroix's *Lion Hunt* (1854) stands next to Jean-Dominiques Ingres' cool Classical *The Spring* (1820–56). As a reminder of the academic manner that dominated the century up to that point, the uninspired waxwork style of Thomas Couture's monumental *The Romans in the Age of Decadence* (1847) dominates the central aisle. In a class of their own are Edouard Manet's provocative *Olympia* and *Le Déjeuner sur l'Herbe* (1863), while works painted around the same time by his friends, Claude Monet, Pierre-Auguste Renoir, Frédéric Bazille and Alfred Sisley, give a glimpse of the Impressionists before the Impressionist movement began.

Young Dancer of Fourteen (1881) by Edgar Degas

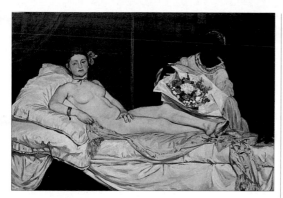

Olympia (1863) by Edouard Manet

IMPRESSIONISM

ROUEN CATHEDRAL caught at various moments of the day (1892–3) is one of the many works displayed by Claude Monet, the leading figure of the Impressionist movement. Pierre-Auguste Renoir's plump nudes and his young people *Dancing at the Moulin de la Galette* (1876) were painted at the high point of his Impressionist period. Other artists on display include Camille Pissarro, Alfred Sisley and Mary Cassatt.

Edgar Degas, Paul Cézanne and Vincent Van Gogh are included here although their techniques differed from those of the Impressionists. Degas often favored crisp Realism, though he was quite capable of using the sketchy manner of the Impressionists, as, for instance, in *L'Absinthe* (1876). Cézanne was more concerned with substance than light, as can be seen in his *Apples and*

Blue Waterlilies (1919) by Claude Monet

Oranges (1895–1900). Van Gogh was momentarily influenced by the movement but then went his own way, illustrated here by works from the collection of Dr. Gachet.

Breton Peasant Women (1894) by Paul Gauguin

NEO-IMPRESSIONISM

ALTHOUGH LABELED Neo-Impressionism, the work of Georges Seurat (which includes *The Circus* from 1891) was quite unrelated to the older movement. He, along with Maximilien Luce and Paul Signac, painted by applying small dots of color that blended together when viewed from a distance.

Jane Avril Dancing (1892) is just one of many pictures by Henri de Toulouse-Lautrec on display. The work Paul Gauguin did at Pont-Aven in Brittany is shown next to that of younger

artists who knew him at the time, such as Émile Bernard and the Nabis group. There are also a number of paintings from his Tahitian period.

The Nabis (which included Pierre Bonnard) tended to treat the canvas as a flat surface out of which a sense of depth emerged as the viewer gazed upon it.

The dreamlike visions of Odilon Redon are in the Symbolist vein, while the naïve art of Henri (Douanier) Rousseau is represented by *War* (1894) and *The Snake Charmer* (1907).

NATURALISM AND SYMBOLISM

THREE LARGE ROOMS are devoted to paintings that filled the Salons from 1880 to 1900. The work of the Naturalists was sanctioned by the Third Republic and widely reproduced at the time. Fernand Cormon's figure of *Cain* was highly acclaimed when it first appeared in the 1880 Salon. Jules Bastien-Lepage's interest lay in illustrating peasant life, and in 1877 he painted *Haymaking*, which established him as one of the leading Naturalists. His fairly free handling of paint was influenced by what he had learned from Manet and his friends. More somberly (and effectively) naturalistic is Lionel Walden's view of *The Docks of Cardiff* (1894).

Symbolism developed as a reaction against Realism and Impressionism and tended to be dominated by images of dreams and thoughts. This resulted in a wide variety of subjects and modes of expression. There is the oversweet vision of levitating harpists, *Serenity* by Henri Martin (1899), Edward Burne-Jones' monumental work *Wheel of Fortune* (1883) and Jean Delville's *School of Plato* (1898). One of the most evocative paintings in this section is Winslow Homer's lyrical *Summer Night* (1890).

LATIN QUARTER

15th-century stained glass in Musée de Cluny

STUDENT BOOK-STORES, cafés, movie theaters and jazz clubs fill this ancient riverside quarter between the Seine and the Luxembourg Gardens. Famous institutes of learning abound, among them the two most prestigious *lycées*, Henri IV and Louis le Grand, through which passes a large percentage of the future French elite.

As the leaders of the 1968 revolt *(see pp38–9)* disappeared into the mainstream of French life, so the Boulevard St-Michel, the area's spine, turned increasingly to commerce, not demonstrations. Today, there are inexpensive shops and fast-food outlets, and the maze of narrow cobbled streets off the boulevard are full of ethnic shops, quirky boutiques and avant-garde theaters and cinemas. But the area's 800 years of history are difficult to efface. The Sorbonne retains much of its old character, and the eastern half of the area has streets dating back to the 13th century. Also still remaining is Rue St-Jacques, the long Roman road stretching out of the city, and the forerunner of all the city's streets.

A young musician playing music under the Pont St-Michel is part of the Latin Quarter's long tradition as a focus for the young from all walks of life.

SIGHTS AT A GLANCE

Historic Buildings and Streets
Boulevard St-Michel ❷
La Sorbonne ❼
Collège de France ❽

Museums and Galleries
Musée de Cluny pp154–7 ❶
Musée de la Préfecture de la Police ❻

Churches and Temples
St-Séverin ❸
St-Julien-le-Pauvre ❹

Squares
Place Maubert ❺

Eglise de la Sorbonne ❾
St-Etienne-du-Mont ❿
Panthéon pp158–9 ⓫

GETTING THERE
Metro stations in the area include those at St-Michel and Cluny La Sorbonne. The Balabus and routes 24 and 87 travel along Boulevard St-Germain, and 38 travels along Boulevard St-Michel, passing the Sorbonne and the Musée de Cluny.

SEE ALSO
• *Street Finder*, maps 12, 13, 17
• *Where to Stay* pp278–9
• *Restaurants* pp296–8

0 meters   400
0 yards   400

KEY
▨	Street-by-Street map
Ⓜ	Metro station
▣	Batobus boarding point
RER	RER station
P	Parking

A peaceful spot along a Latin Quarter quay

Street-by-Street: Latin Quarter

SINCE THE MIDDLE AGES this riverside quarter has been dominated by the Sorbonne, and acquired its name from the early Latin-speaking students. It dates back to the Roman town across from the Ile de la Cité; at that time, the Rue St-Jacques was one of the main roads out of Paris. The area is generally associated with artists, intellectuals and the bohemian way of life; it also has a history of political unrest. In 1871, the Place St-Michel became the center of the Paris Commune, and in May 1968 it was the site of the student uprisings. Today the eastern half has become sufficiently chic, however, to contain the homes of some of the Establishment.

Place St-Michel contains a fountain by Davioud. The bronze statue by Duret shows St. Michael killing the dragon.

Metro St-Michel

Little Athens is a lively place in the evening, especially on weekends, when the Greek restaurants situated in the picturesque streets around St-Séverin are at their busiest.

Metro Cluny La Sorbonne

★ **Boulevard St-Michel**
The northern end of the Boul'Mich, as it is affectionately known, is a lively mélange of cafés, book and clothes stores, with nightclubs and experimental film houses nearby ❷

★ **Musée de Cluny**
One of the finest collections of medieval art in the world is kept here in a superb late-15th-century building, which includes the ruins of some Gallo-Roman baths ❶

No. 22 Rue St-Séverin is the narrowest house in Paris and used to be the residence of Abbé Prévost, author of *Manon Lescaut.*

★ St-Séverin
Begun in the 13th century, this beautiful church took three centuries to build and is a fine example of the flamboyant Gothic style ❸

Rue du Chat qui Pêche is a narrow pedestrianized street which has changed little in its 200-year history.

LOCATOR MAP
SEE CENTRAL PARIS MAP PP12-13

Shakespeare & Co
(see pp320 & 321) at No.37 Rue de la Bûcherie is a delightful, if chaotic, bookshop. Any books purchased here are stamped with *Shakespeare & Co Kilometre Zéro Paris.*

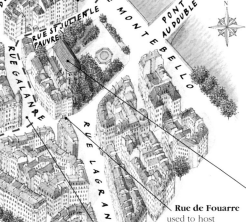

Metro
Maubert
Mutualité

Rue Galande was home to the rich and chic in the 17th century, but subsequently became notorious for its taverns.

Rue de Fouarre used to host lectures in the Middle Ages. The students sat on straw *(fouarre)* in the street.

★ St-Julien-le-Pauvre
Rebuilt in the 17th century, this church was used to store animal feed during the Revolution ❹

STAR SIGHTS

★ **Musée de Cluny**

★ **St-Séverin**

★ **St-Julien-le-Pauvre**

★ **Boulevard St-Michel**

KEY

— — — Suggested route

0 meters	100
0 yards	100

Musée de Cluny ●

See pp154–7.

Boulevard St-Michel ●

75005 & 75006. **Map** 12 F5 & 16 F2.
Ⓜ St-Michel, Cluny-La Sorbonne.
ⓇⒺⓇ Luxembourg.

CUT THROUGH the area in 1869, the boulevard gained fame initially from the literary cafés that have existed along it from its earliest days. Much of the boulevard is now lined with clothes shops, but the Café Cluny remains a cosmopolitan meeting place at the junction of Boulevard St-Germain. In the Place St-Michel, marble plaques commemorate the many students who died here in 1944 fighting the Nazis.

Gargoyles adorning St-Séverin

St-Séverin ●

1 Rue-des-Prêtres-St-Séverin 75005.
Map 13 A4. Ⓒ 01 42 34 93 50.
Ⓜ St-Michel. **Open** 11am–7:45pm
Mon–Fri; 11am–8pm Sat; 9am–9pm
Sun. 🎵 **Sacred music concerts.**

ONE OF THE most beautiful churches in Paris, St-Séverin is a perfect example of the Flamboyant Gothic style. It is named after a 6th-century hermit who lived in the area and persuaded the future St. Cloud, grandson of King Clovis, to take holy orders. Construction finished in the early 16th century and included a remarkable double ambulatory circling the

Inside St-Julien-le-Pauvre

chancel. In 1684 the Grande Mademoiselle, cousin to Louis XIV, adopted St-Séverin after breaking with her parish church of St-Sulpice and had the chancel modernized.

The burial ground, now a garden, was the site of the first operation for gall stones in 1474. An archer, condemned to death, was offered his freedom by Louis XI if he consented to the operation and lived. (It was a success, and the archer went free.) In the garden stands the church's medieval gable-roofed charnel house.

St-Julien-le-Pauvre ●

1 Rue St-Julien-le-Pauvre 75005.
Map 13 A4. Ⓒ 01 43 29 09 09.
Ⓜ St-Michel. ⓇⒺⓇ St-Michel. **Open**
10am–1:30pm, 3pm–7pm daily.
Concerts. See Entertainment p336.

AT LEAST THREE saints can claim to be patron of this church, but the most likely is St. Julian the Hospitaler. The church, together with St-Germain-des-Prés, is one of the oldest in Paris, dating from between 1165 and 1220. The university held its official meetings in the church until 1524, when a student protest created so much damage that university meetings were barred from the church by parliament. Since 1889 it has belonged to the Melchite sect of the Greek Orthodox Church, and it is now the setting for chamber and religious music concerts.

Place Maubert ●

75005. **Map** 13 A5.
Ⓜ Maubert-Mutualité.

FROM THE 12TH to the middle of the 13th century, "La Maub" was one of Paris's scholastic centers, with lectures given in the open air. After the scholars moved to the new colleges of the Montagne St-Geneviève, the square became a place of torture and execution, including that of the philosopher Etienne Dolet, who was burned alive at the stake as a heretic in 1546. So many Protestants were burnt here in the 16th century that it became a place of pilgrimage for the followers of the new faith. Today, its infamous reputation has been replaced by respectability and a notable street market.

Musée de la Préfecture de la Police ●

4 Rue de la Mountagne Ste-Geneviève
75005. **Map** 13 A5. Ⓒ 01 44 41 52
50. Ⓜ Maubert-Mutualité. **Open** 9am–
5pm Mon–Fri; 10am–5pm Sat (last
adm: 4:30pm). **Closed** public hols.

Weapons in the Police Museum

A DARKER SIDE to Paris's history is illustrated in this small museum. Created in 1909, the museum traces the development of the police in Paris from the Middle Ages to the 20th century. Curiosities displayed here include arrest warrants for figures such as the famous revolutionary Danton and a rather sobering display of weapons and tools used by famous criminals. There is also a section on the part the police played in the Resistance and subsequent liberation of Paris.

La Sorbonne ❼

47 Rue des Ecoles 75005.
Map 13 A5. **[** 01 40 46 22 11.
M Cluny-La Sorbonne, Maubert-Mutualité. **Open** 9am–5pm Mon–Fri.
Closed public hols. **[** only, by appt: write to Service des Visites.

THE SORBONNE, seat of the University of Paris, was established in 1253 by Robert de Sorbon, confessor to Louis IX, for 16 poor students to study theology. From these modest beginnings the college soon became the center of scholastic theology. In 1469, the rector had three printing machines brought over from Mainz, thereby founding the first printing house in France. The college's opposition to liberal 18th-century philosophy led to its suppression during the Revolution. It was re-established by Napoleon in 1806. The buildings built by Richelieu in the early 17th century were replaced by the ones seen today.

Statues outside the college

Collège de France ❽

11 Pl Marcelin-Berthelot 75005.
Map 13 A5. **[** 01 44 27 12 11.
M Maubert-Mutualité. **Open** Oct–Jun: 9am–6:30pm Mon–Fri.

ONE OF PARIS'S great institutes of research and learning, the college was established in 1530 by François I. Guided by the great humanist Guillaume Budé, the king aimed to counteract the intolerance and dogmatism of the Sorbonne. A statue of Budé stands in the west courtyard, and the unbiased approach to learning is reflected in the inscription on the entrance to the old college: *docet omnia* (all are taught here). Lectures are free and open to the public.

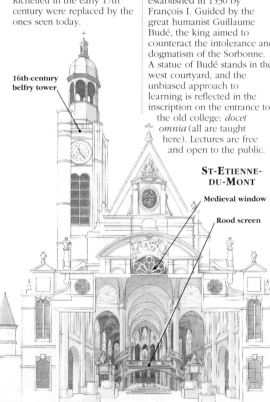

ST-ETIENNE-DU-MONT

16th-century belfry tower

Medieval window

Rood screen

Chapelle de la Sorbonne ❾

Pl de la Sorbonne 75005.
Map 13 A5. **[** 01 40 46 22 11.
M Cluny-La Sorbonne, Maubert-Mutualité. **RER** Luxembourg.
Open for temporary exhibitions only. **Adm charge.**

ERECTED BY Lemercier between 1635 and 1642, this chapel is, in effect, a monument to Richelieu, with his coat of arms on the dome supports and his white marble tomb, carved by Girardon in 1694, in the chancel. The chapel's attractive lateral facade looks on to the main courtyard of the Sorbonne.

Eglise de la Sorbonne clock

St-Etienne-du-Mont ❿

Pl Ste-Geneviève 75005. **Map** 17 A1.
[01 43 54 11 79. **M** Cardinal Lemoine. **Open** 8am–noon Mon–Sat, 9am–noon, 3pm–7pm Sun. **Closed** public hols, Mon during Jul–Aug.

THIS REMARKABLE church houses not only the shrine of Sainte Geneviève, patron saint of Paris, but also the remains of the great literary figures Racine and Pascal. Some parts are in the Gothic style, and others date from the Renaissance, including a magnificent rood screen. Also of note is the stained glass.

Panthéon ⓫

See pp158–9.

Musée de Cluny ❶

Head of St John
the Baptist

THE MUSEUM, now officially known as the Musée National du Moyen Age – Thermes de Cluny, offers a unique combination of Gallo-Roman ruins, incorporated into a medieval mansion, and one of the world's finest collections of medieval art and crafts. The museum's name came from the Abbot of Cluny in Burgundy, Pierre de Chalus, who bought the ruins in 1330.

Medieval Mansion
The museum building, completed in 1500, was erected by Jacques d'Amboise, Abbot of Cluny.

Medieval chapel

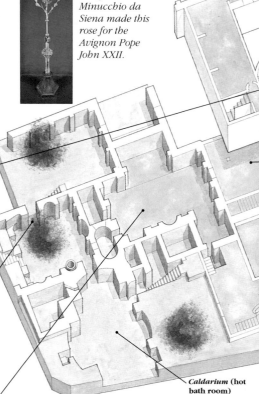

★ **Golden Rose of Basel** *(1330)*
The goldsmith Minucchio da Siena made this rose for the Avignon Pope John XXII.

★ **Lady with the Unicorn**
This outstanding series of tapestries is a fine example of the millefleurs *style, which was developed in the 15th and early 16th centuries. The style is noted for its graceful depiction of plants, animals and people.*

Gallo-Roman Baths
Built in AD 200, the baths lasted for about 100 years before being sacked by the barbarians.

Caldarium (hot bath room)

STAR EXHIBITS

★ **Gallery of the Kings**

★ **Lady with the Unicorn**

★ **Golden Rose of Basel**

Gallo-Roman Frigidarium
The arches of this cold bath room, dating from the late 2nd and early 3rd centuries, were once decorated with pairs of carved ship prows, the symbol of the association of Paris boatmen (nautes).

Books of Hours

The museum has two Books of Hours from the first half of the 15th century. The illuminated pages include scenes showing the Labors of the Months, each accompanied by the relevant sign of the zodiac.

★ Gallery of the Kings

In 1977, 21 of the 28 stone heads of the Kings of Judah (carved around 1220 in the reign of Philippe Auguste) were unearthed during excavations in the Rue de la Chaussée-d'Antin behind the Opéra.

GALLERY GUIDE

The collection is spread throughout the two floors of the building. It is mainly medieval and covers a wide range of items, including illuminated manuscripts, tapestries, textiles, precious metals, alabaster, ceramics, sculpture and church furnishings. A number of Gallo-Roman artifacts are displayed around the sides of the frigidarium, *and the small circular room nearby contains some capitals.*

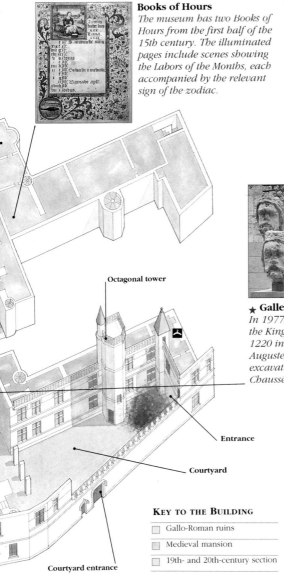

Octagonal tower

Entrance

Courtyard

Courtyard entrance

KEY TO THE BUILDING

- ☐ Gallo-Roman ruins
- ☐ Medieval mansion
- ☐ 19th- and 20th-century section

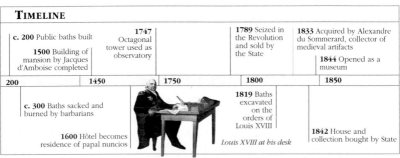

TIMELINE

c. 200 Public baths built	**1747** Octagonal tower used as observatory		**1789** Seized in the Revolution and sold by the State	**1833** Acquired by Alexandre du Sommerard, collector of medieval artifacts
1500 Building of mansion by Jacques d'Amboise completed				**1844** Opened as a museum

200	1450	1750	1800	1850

c. 300 Baths sacked and burned by barbarians			**1819** Baths excavated on the orders of Louis XVIII	
1600 Hôtel becomes residence of papal nuncios		*Louis XVIII at his desk*		**1842** House and collection bought by State

Exploring the Cluny's Collection

ALEXANDRE DU SOMMERARD took over the Hôtel de Cluny in 1833 and installed his art collection with great sensitivity to the surroundings and a strong sense of the dramatic. After his death, the Hôtel and its contents were sold to the state and turned into a museum.

The Grape Harvest tapestry

TAPESTRIES

THE MUSEUM's tapestries are remarkable for their quality, age and state of preservation. The images present a surprising mixture of the naive with more complex notions. One of the earliest, *The Offering of the Heart* (early 15th century), shows a man who is literally proffering his heart to a seated medieval beauty. More everyday scenes are shown in the magnificent series *The Noble Life* (about 1500). Upstairs is the mysterious *Lady with the Unicorn* series.

CARVINGS

THE DIVERSE techniques of medieval European woodcarvers are well represented. From the Nottingham workshops in England, there are wood as well as alabaster works that were widely used as altarpieces all over Europe. Smaller works include *The School*, which is touchingly realistic and dates from the early 16th century. Upstairs there are some fine Flemish and southern German woodcarvings. The multicolored figure of St. John is typical. Two notable altarpieces are the intricately carved and painted *Lamentation of Christ* (about 1485) from the Duchy of Clèves and the Averbode altarpiece, made in 1523 in Antwerp, which depicts three scenes, including the Last Supper. Not to be missed is the full-length figure of Mary Magdalene.

STAINED GLASS

MOST OF THE CLUNY'S glass from the 12th and 13th centuries is French. The oldest examples were originally installed in the Basilique St-Denis in 1144. There are also three fragments from the Troyes Cathedral, destroyed by fire, two of which illustrate the life of St. Nicholas while the third depicts that of Christ. Numerous panels came to the Cluny from Sainte-Chapelle (*see pp88–9*), during its mid-19th-century restoration, and were never returned, including five scenes from the story of Samson dating from 1248.

The technique of contrasting colored glass with surrounding grisaille (gray-and-white panels) developed in the latter half of the 13th century. Four panels from the royal château at Rouen illustrate this technique.

Stained-glass scenes from Brittany (1400)

The School woodcarving (English, early 16th century)

Head of a queen from St-Denis from before 1120

SCULPTURE

THE HIGHLIGHT HERE is the Gallery of the Kings, a display of heads and decapitated figures from Notre-Dame. There is also an very graceful statue of Adam, sculped in the 1260s.

In the vaulted room opposite are displays of fine Romanesque sculpture retrieved from French churches. Among the earliest are the 12 capitals from the nave of St-Germain-des-Prés, from the early 11th century. Retrieved from the portal of St-Denis is a boldly sculpted head of a queen (c.1140) which, though badly mutilated, is still compelling.

Other Romanesque and early Gothic capitals include six finely sculptured works from Catalonia and four of the museum's most famous statues, early 13th-century apostles made for Sainte-Chapelle.

EVERYDAY OBJECTS

HOUSEHOLD ITEMS show another side to medieval life, and this large collection is grouped in a sensitive way to illustrate their use – from wallhangings and caskets to kitchen tools and clothing. Children's toys bring a very human aspect to the display, while travel cases and religious emblems evoke journeys of exploration and pilgrimage.

PRECIOUS METALWORK

THE CLUNY HAS a fine collection of jewelry, coins, metal and enamelwork from Gallic times to the Middle Ages. The showcase of Gallic jewelry includes gold torques, bracelets and rings, all of a simple design. In between these is one of the Cluny's most precious exhibits, the Golden Rose of Basel, a delicately wrought piece from 1330 and the oldest known of its kind.

The earliest enamelwork on display are the late Roman and Byzantine *cloisonné* pieces, culminating in the remarkable Limoges enamels, which flourished in the late 12th century. There are also two exceptional altarpieces, the Golden Altar of Basel and the Stavelot altarpiece.

Cross from Italy (late 15th century)

The Pillar of the Nautes

GALLO-ROMAN RUINS

ONE OF THE MAIN reasons for visiting the Musée de Cluny is to see the scale and layout of its earliest function, the Gallo-Roman baths. The vaulted *frigidarium* (cold bath room) was the largest of its kind in France. Here there is another of the Cluny's highlights, the Pillar of the Nautes (boatmen), unearthed during excavations beneath Notre-Dame in 1711.

Composed of five carved stone blocks representing Gallic and Roman divinities, its crowning element is presumed to depict the Seine's boatmen. There are also the ruins of the *caldarium* and *tepidarium* (hot and tepid baths), and visitors can tour the underground vaults.

LADY WITH THE UNICORN TAPESTRIES

This series of six tapestries was woven in the late 15th century in the southern Netherlands. It is valued for its fresh harmonious colors and the poetic elegance of the central figure. Allegories of the senses are illustrated in the first five: sight (gazing into a mirror), hearing (playing a portable organ), taste (sampling sweets), smell (sniffing carnations) and touch (the lady holding the unicorn's horn). The enigmatic sixth tapestry (showing jewels being placed in a box) includes the words "to my only desire" and is now thought to represent the principle of free choice.

Unicorn on the sixth tapestry

Panthéon ⑪

WHEN LOUIS XV recovered from desperate illness in 1744, he was so grateful to be alive that he conceived a magnificent church to honor Sainte Geneviève. The design was entrusted to the French architect Jacques-Germain Soufflot, who planned the church in Neoclassical style. Work began in 1764 and was completed in 1790, ten years after Soufflot's death, under the control of Guillaume Rondelet. But with the Revolution underway, the church was soon turned into a pantheon – a location for the tombs of France's good and great. Napoleon returned it to the Church in 1806, but it was secularized and then desecularized once more before finally being made a civic building in 1885.

The Facade
Based on the Rome Pantheon, the temple portico has 22 Corinthian columns.

The arches of the dome show a renewed interest in the lightness of Gothic architecture and were designed by Rondelet. They link four pillars supporting the dome, which weighs 10,000 tons and is 272 ft (83 m) high.

Pediment Relief
David d'Angers' pediment bas-relief depicts the mother country (France) granting laurels to her great men.

The Panthéon Interior
The interior has four aisles arranged in the shape of a Greek cross, from the center of which the great dome rises.

Entrance

STAR FEATURES

★ **Iron-Framed Dome**

★ **Frescoes of Sainte Geneviève**

★ **Crypt**

★ **Frescoes of Sainte Geneviève**
Murals along the south wall of the nave depict the life of Sainte Geneviève. They are by Pierre Puvis de Chavannes, the 19th-century fresco painter.

The dome lantern
allows only a little light
to filter into the church's
center. Intense light was
thought inappropriate
for the place where
France's heroes rested.

★ **Iron-Framed Dome**
*The tall dome, with its stone
cupolas and three layers of
shells, was inspired by St.
Paul's in London and the
Dôme Church (see p188).*

The dome galleries afford a
magnificent panoramic view of
France's capital.

Colonnade
*The colonnade encircling the
dome is both decorative
and part of an ingenious
supporting system.*

Monument to Diderot
*This is Alphonse Terroir's
statue (1925) to the political
writer Denis Diderot.*

★ **Crypt**
*Covering the entire area under
the building, the crypt divides
into galleries flanked by Doric
columns. Many French notables
rest here.*

THE PANTHÉON'S ENSHRINED

The first of France's great men to be
entombed here was the popular orator
Honoré Mirabeau. (Later, under the
revolutionary leadership of Maximilien
Robespierre, he fell from grace and his
body was removed.) Voltaire followed.
He died in 1788 and was buried outside
Paris, so his remains were moved to the
city in a funerary procession. A statue of
Voltaire by Jean-Antoine Houdon stands
in front of his tomb. In the 1970s the
remains of the wartime Resistance leader
Jean Moulin were reburied here. Others
here include Jean-Jacques Rousseau,
Victor Hugo and Emile Zola.

JARDIN DES PLANTES QUARTER

THIS PARIS AREA has traditionally been one of the most tranquil corners of the city. It takes its character from the 17th-century botanical gardens where the kings of the *ancien régime* grew their medicinal herbs and where the National Natural History Institute stands today. The many hospitals in the area, notably Paris's largest, Pitié Salpêtrière, add to the atmosphere. Bustle is very much a feature of the colorful market that takes over much of Rue Mouffetard every day. And the streets off Mouffetard are truly evocative of life in medieval times.

SIGHTS AT A GLANCE

Museums and Galleries
Musée de la Sculpture en Plein Air ❷
Collection des Minéraux de l'Université ❹
Muséum National d'Histoire Naturelle ❿
La Manufacture des Gobelins ⓭

Modern Architecture
Institut du Monde Arabe ❶

Churches and Temples
St-Médard ❽
Mosquée de Paris/Institut Musulman ❾

Squares, Parks and Gardens
Ménagerie ❸
Place de la Contrescarpe ❻
Jardin des Plantes ⓫

Historic Buildings and Streets
Arène de Lutèce ❺
Rue Mouffetard ❼
Groupe Hospitalier Pitié-Salpêtrière ⓬

KEY

▨	Street-by-Street map
Ⓜ	Metro station
🚇RER	RER station
🚉	SNCF (train) station
🅿	Parking

0 meters 400
0 yards 400

GETTING THERE
There are metro stations at Cardinal Lemoine, Gare d'Austerlitz, St-Marcel and Place d'Italie, and RER and SNCF stations at Gare d'Austerlitz. The bus route 47 travels down Rue Monge, and 89 passes around the gardens.

SEE ALSO
• *Street Finder*, map 17–18
• *Where to Stay* pp278–9
• *Restaurants* pp296–8

Market scene on the Rue Mouffetard

Street by Street: Jardin des Plantes Quarter

Two physicians to Louis XIII, Jean Hérouard and Guy de la Brosse, obtained permission to establish the royal medicinal herb garden in the sparsely populated St-Victor suburb in 1626. The herb garden and gardens of various religious houses gave the region a rural character. In the 19th century the population and thus the area expanded, and it became more built up, until it gradually assumed the character it has today: a well-to-do residential patchwork of 19th- and early 20th-century buildings interspersed with much older and some more recent buildings.

Metro Cardinal Lemoine

Place de la Contrescarpe
This villagelike square filled with restaurants and cafés buzzes with students after dusk ❻

★ **Rue Mouffetard**
Locals flock to the daily open-air market here that is one of the oldest Paris street markets. A hoard of louis d'or *gold coins from the 18th century was found at No. 53 during its demolition in 1938* ❼

Pot de Fer fountain is one of 14 that Marie de Médicis had built on the Left Bank in 1624 as a source of water for her palace in the Jardin du Luxembourg. The fountain was rebuilt in 1671.

Metro Monge

Passage des Postes is an ancient alley that was opened in 1830. Its entrance is in the Rue Mouffetard.

St-Médard
This church was started in the mid-15th century and completed by 1655. In 1784 the choir was made Classical in style, and the nave's 16th-century windows were replaced with contemporary stained glass ❽

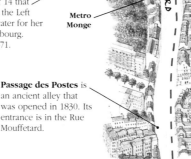

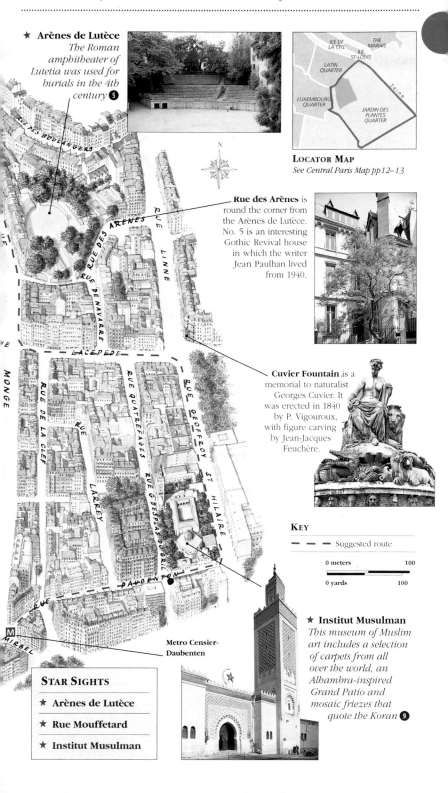

★ **Arènes de Lutèce**
*The Roman
amphitheater of
Lutetia was used for
burials in the 4th
century* 5

LOCATOR MAP
See Central Paris Map pp12–13

Rue des Arènes is
round the corner from
the Arènes de Lutèce.
No. 5 is an interesting
Gothic Revival house
in which the writer
Jean Paulhan lived
from 1940.

Cuvier Fountain is a
memorial to naturalist
Georges Cuvier. It
was erected in 1840
by P. Vigouroux,
with figure carving
by Jean-Jacques
Feuchère.

KEY

– – – Suggested route

| 0 meters | 100 |
| 0 yards | 100 |

**Metro Censier-
Daubenten**

★ **Institut Musulman**
*This museum of Muslim
art includes a selection
of carpets from all
over the world, an
Alhambra-inspired
Grand Patio and
mosaic friezes that
quote the Koran* 9

STAR SIGHTS

★ **Arènes de Lutèce**

★ **Rue Mouffetard**

★ **Institut Musulman**

Institut du Monde Arabe ❶

1 Rue des Fossées St-Bernard 75005.
Map 13 C5. 『 *01 40 51 38 38.*
Ⓜ *Jussieu, Cardinal-Lemoine.*
**Museum & temporary exhibitions
open** *10am–6pm Tue–Sun.* **Library
open** *1pm–8pm Tue–Sat.* **Adm
charge.** & 🄵 **Lectures.** 🍴 ▣

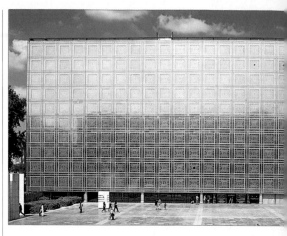

Tᴴɪs ᴄᴜʟᴛᴜʀᴀʟ ɪɴsᴛɪᴛᴜᴛᴇ was
founded in 1980 by France
and 20 Arab countries with
the intention of fostering
cultural links between the
Islamic world and the West. It
is housed in a magnificent
modern building, designed by
the French architect Jean
Nouvel, that combines
modern materials with the
spirit of traditional Arab
architecture. The white marble
book tower, which can be
seen through the glass of the
west wall, spirals upward,
bringing to mind the minaret
of a mosque. The emphasis
that is traditionally placed on
interior space in Arab architecture has been used here to
create an enclosed courtyard
reached by a narrow gap
splitting the building in two.
    On the seventh floor there
is a fascinating display of
Islamic works of art from the
9th to the 19th centuries,
including glassware, ceramics,
sculpture, carpets and a fine
collection of astrolabes, so
prized by ancient Arabic
astronomers. There is also a
library and media archive.

Pont de Sully and Quai St-Bernard ❷

75004/ 75005. **Map** 13 C5.
Ⓜ *Gare d'Austerlitz.*

Bᴜᴛᴛɪɴɢ ᴜᴘ to the left
hand corner of the
Institut du Monde Arabe, the
Pont de Sully links the Ile St
Louis with both banks of the
Seine. Opened in 1877 and
built of cast iron, the Pont
de Sully is not an especially
beautiful structure. Despite
this, it is well worth pausing
for a moment on the bridge
for a fabulous view of Notre-
Dame rising dramatically
behind the wonderfully
graceful Pont Marie.
Running along the river from
the Pont de Sully as far as
the Pont d'Austerlitz is the
peaceful Quai St-Bernard.
Not always so peaceful,
Quai St-Bernard was famous
during the 17th century as a
spot for nude bathing, until
scandalised public opinion
made it illegal. The grassy
slopes adjoining the quai
make a perfect spot to enjoy
a picnic. Opened in 1975
they are known as the Jardin
Tino Rossi in honour of the
celebrated Corsican singer.
Until recently the garden
played host to a display of
open-air sculpture of
variable quality known as
the Musée de la Sculpture
en Plein Air. Vandalism and
other problems have now
unfortunately forced the
removal of the exhibits.

Ménagerie ❸

57 Rue Cuvier 75005. **Map** 17 C1. 『
01 40 79 37 94. Ⓜ *Jussieu, Austerlitz.*
Open *Oct–Mar: 9am–5pm Mon–Sat
(5:30pm Sun & public hols); Apr–Sep:
9am–6pm Mon–Sat (6:30pm Sun &
public hols).* **Adm charge.** 🍴 ▣

Fʀᴀɴᴄᴇ's ᴏʟᴅᴇsᴛ public zoo
is situated in the lovely
surroundings of the Jardin des
Plantes. It was set up during
the Revolution to house
survivors from the Royal
menagerie at Versailles –
all four of them. The state
then rounded up animals
from circuses and
exotic creatures were
sent from abroad.
During the Prussian
siege of Paris
(1870–71) most of them were
slaughtered to feed the
hungry citizens *(see
pp224–5).* Today the zoo
specializes in small mammals,
insects, birds, primates and
reptiles, and it is a great
favorite with children as it is
possible for them to get quite
close to the animals. The lion
house contains a number of
large cats, including panthers
from China. Other attractions
include a large monkey house,
bear pits, a large waterfowl
aviary and wild sheep and goats.
    The displays in the vivarium
(enclosures of live animals in
natural habitat) are changed at
regular intervals throughout the
year and there is a permanent
exhibition of micro-arthropods

**Child playing
at the zoo**

Light Screens
The south elevation is made up of 1,600 high-tech metal screens that filter the light entering the building. Their design is based on moucharabiyahs *(carved wooden screens found on the outsides of buildings from Morocco to Southeast Asia).*

Each screen contains 21 irises that are controlled electronically, opening and closing in response to the amount of sunlight falling on photosensitive screens.

The central iris is made up of interlocking metal blades that move to adjust the size of the central opening.

The peripheral irises are linked to one another and to the central iris. They open and close in unison, forming a delicate pattern of light and shade inside the institute.

Collection des Minéraux de l'Université ❹

Université Pierre et Marie Curie, 34 Rue Jussieu 75005. **Map** 13 C5. ☎ *01 44 27 52 88.* Ⓜ *Jussieu.*
Open *1pm–6pm Wed–Mon.* **Closed** *Jan 1, Easter, May 1, Jul 14, Nov 1, Dec 25.* ⓧ ▯
Adm charge.

T HIS FASCINATING small museum is housed in the basement of the main university building, named after the distinguished scientists. The collection comprises cut and uncut gemstones and rock crystal from all over the world, shown to maximum advantage through the expert use of specialized lighting.

Topaz

Arènes de Lutèce ❺

Rue de Navarre 75005. **Map** 17 B1. Ⓜ *Jussieu. See p19.*

T HE REMAINS of this vast Roman arena (Lutetia was the Roman name for Paris) date from the late 2nd century. Its destruction began toward the end of the 3rd century at the hands of the Barbarians, and later, parts of it were used to build the walls of the Ile de la Cité. The arena was then gradually buried and its exact location preserved only in old documents and the local name Clos des Arènes. It was rediscovered in 1869 during the construc-tion of the Rue Monge and the allocation of building plots nearby. Action toward its restoration began with the campaigning of Victor Hugo (among others) in the 19th century, but work did not get really underway until 1918.

With a seating capacity of 15,000, arranged in 35 tiers, the original arena was used both for theatrical perfor-mances and as an amphitheater for the more gruesome spectacle of gladiator fights. This type of combined use was peculiar to Gaul (France), and the arena is similar to the other French ones in Nîmes and Arles.

The public park at the Arènes de Lutèce

BUFFON AND THE JARDIN DES PLANTES

At the age of 32 Georges Louis Leclerc, Comte de Buffon (1707–88), became the curator of the Jardin des Plantes, at a time when the study of natural history was at the forefront of contemporary thought – Charles Darwin's *The Origin of Species* was to be published 120 years later. Buffon masterminded the reorganization of the Jardin, propelling it to a preeminent position within the scientific world. He was elected to the Académie Française in 1752 following the publication of his two main works, *Natural History* and *The Epoques of Nature*. He died in his house in the Jardin.

Illustration of a primate from Buffon's *Natural History*

Place de la Contrescarpe ➏

75005. **Map** 17 A1. **M** *Place Monge*.

AT ONE TIME this site lay outside the city walls. It gets its name from the backfilling of the moat that ran along Philippe-Auguste's wall. The present square was laid out in 1852. At No. 1 there is a memorial plaque to the old "pine-cone club" immortalized in the writings of Rabelais; here a group of writers known as *La Pléiade* (named after the constellation of The Pleiades) used to meet in the 16th century.

The area has always been used for meetings and festivals. Today it is extremely lively at weekends, and on Bastille Day *(see pp64–5)* a delightful ball is held here.

Part of the medieval city wall

Cheese in the Mouffetard market

Rue Mouffetard ➐

75005. **Map** 17 B2. **M** *Censier-Daubenton, Place Monge*. **Market open** *8am–1pm Tue–Sun*. See **Shops and Markets** *p326*.

A MAJOR THOROUGHFARE since Roman times, when it ran between Lutetia (Paris) and Rome, this street is one of the oldest in the city. In the 17th and 18th centuries it was known as the Grande Rue du Faubourg St-Marcel, and many of its buildings date from this period. Some of the small shops still have ancient painted signs, and some of the houses have mansard roofs. No. 125 has an attractive, restored Louis XIII facade, and the entire front of No. 134 has beautiful decoration of wild beasts, flowers and plants.

The whole area is well known for its open-air markets, especially those in Place Maubert, Place Monge, and Rue Daubenton, a side street where a lively African market takes place.

St-Médard ➑

141 Rue Mouffetard 75005. **Map** 17 B2. **🄲** *01 44 08 87 00.* **M** *Censier-Daubenton.* **Open** *9am–noon daily, 2:30pm–7:30pm Mon–Sat.* 🄾 ♿

THE ORIGINS OF this charming church go back to the 9th century. St Médard, counselor to the Merovingian kings, was known for his custom of giving a wreath of white roses to young girls noted for their virtue. The churchyard, now a garden, became notorious in the 18th century as the center of the cult of the Convulsionnaires, whose hysterical fits were brought on by the contemplation of miracle cures. The interior has many fine paintings, including the 17th-century *St Joseph Walking with the Christ Child* by Francisco de Zurbarán.

Mosquée de Paris/Institut Musulman ➒

Pl du Puits de l'Ermite 75005. **Map** 17 C2. **🄲** *01 45 35 97 33.* **M** *Place Monge.* **Open** *9am–noon, 2pm–6pm Sat–Thu.* **Closed** *Muslim hols.* **Adm charge.** 🄾 🍴 🖵 📚 **Library**.

BUILT IN THE 1920s in the Hispano-Moorish style, this group of buildings is the spiritual center for Paris's Muslim community and the home of the Grand Imam. The complex comprises religious, educational and commercial sections; at its

Decoration inside the mosque

heart is a mosque. Each of the mosque's domes is decorated uniquely, and the minaret stands 100 ft (33 m) high. Inside is a grand patio inspired by the Alhambra, with mosaics on the walls and tracery on the arches.

Once used only by scholars, the mosque's place in Parisian life has grown over the years. The Turkish baths there can be enjoyed by both men and women but on alternate days.

Muséum National d'Histoire Naturelle ⑩

2 Rue Buffon 75005. **Map** 17 C2. **C** 01 40 79 30 00. **M** Jussieu, Austerlitz. **Open** 10am–5pm Wed–Mon (last adm: 4:30pm). **Adm charge**. ⊘ ⓖ restricted. ▯ ▯ **Library**.

Skull of the reptile dimetrodon

T HE NATURAL HISTORY Museum is organized into four departments: paleontology, featuring skeletons, casts of various animals and an exhibition showing the evolution of the vertebrate skeleton; paleobotany, devoted to plant fossils; mineralogy, including gemstones; and entomology, with some of the oldest fossilized insects on earth. A new evolution gallery is planned. The bookshop is in the house that was occupied by the naturalist Buffon, from 1772 until his death in 1788.

Jardin des Plantes ⑪

57 Rue Cuvier 75005. **Map** 17 C1. **M** Jussieu, Austerlitz. **Open** 9am–6pm (5pm winter) daily.

T HE BOTANICAL gardens were established in 1626 when Jean Hérouard and Guy de la Brosse, Louis XIII's physicians, obtained permission to found

a royal medicinal herb garden here and then a school of botany, natural history and pharmacy. The garden was opened to the public in 1640 and flourished under the inspired direction of Buffon. Now one of Paris's great parks, it includes a natural history museum, botanical school and zoo.

As well as beautiful vistas and walkways flanked by ancient trees and punctuated with statues, the park has a remarkable alpine garden with plants from Corsica, Morocco, the Alps and the Himalayas and an unrivaled display of herbaceous and wild plants. It also has the first Cedar of Lebanon to be planted in France, originally from Britain's Kew Gardens.

Groupe Hospitalier Pitié-Salpêtrière ⑫

47 Blvd de l'Hôpital 75013. **Map** 18 D3. **M** St-Marcel, Austerlitz. **RER** Gare d'Austerlitz. **Chapel open** 8:30am–6:30pm daily. ✝ 3:30pm.

T HE VAST Salpêtrière Hospital stands on the site of an old gunpowder factory and derives its name from the saltpeter used in the making of explosives. It was founded by Louis XIV in 1656 to help sick or socially disadvantaged women and children and later became renowned for its pioneering humane treatment of the insane. The main architectural feature is the domed chapel designed by Libéral Bruand in about 1670.

The Cedar of Lebanon in the Jardin

Outside the Hôpital Salpêtrière

La Manufacture des Gobelins ⑬

42 Ave des Gobelins 75013. **Map** 17 B3. **C** 01 44 61 21 69. **M** Gobelins. **Open for guided tours only** 2pm, 2:45pm Tue–Thu (arrive 15 mins earlier). **Adm charge**. **Closed** public hols.

Versailles tapestry by Le Brun

O RIGINALLY A dyeing workshop set up in about 1440 by the Gobelin brothers, this building became a tapestry factory early in the 17th century. Louis XIV took it over in 1662 and gathered together the greatest crafts-men of the day – carpet weavers, cabinet makers and silversmiths – to furnish his new palace at Versailles (see pp248–53). Working under the direction of court painter Charles Le Brun, 250 Flemish weavers laid the foundations for the factory's international reputation. Today weavers continue to work in the traditional way but with modern designs, including those of Picasso and Matisse.

LUXEMBOURG QUARTER

MANY A PARISIAN dreams of someday living in the vicinity of the Luxembourg Gardens, a quieter, greener and somehow more reflective place than its neighboring areas. Luxembourg is one of the most captivating places in the capital. Its charm is in its old gateways and streets, its bookshops and its sumptuous yet intimate gardens. Though writers of the eminence of Paul Verlaine and André Gide no longer stroll in its groves, the paths, lawns and avenues are still full of charm, drawing the numerous students from the nearby *grandes écoles* and *lycées*. And on warm days, old men meet under the chestnut trees to play chess or to pitch balls in a traditional game of *boules*.

To the west the buildings are public and official; on the east the houses are shaded by the tall chestnut trees lining the long Boulevard St. Michel.

Sailing boats can be rented for children and adults to sail in the *grand bassin* (ornamental pond) in the Luxembourg Gardens.

SIGHTS AT A GLANCE

Museums
Musée du Service de Santé des Armées **10**
Ecole Nationale Supérieure des Mines **11**

Historic Buildings
Palais du Luxembourg **3**
Institut Catholique de Paris **6**

Churches
St-Sulpice **2**
St-Joseph-des-Carmes **7**
Val-de-Grâce **9**

Squares and Gardens
Place St-Sulpice **1**
Jardin du Luxembourg **5**

Fountains
Fontaine de Médicis **4**
Fontaine de l'Observatoire **8**

GETTING THERE
The area is served by the metro, with stations at Mabillon and St-Sulpice, and by the RER, with a station at Luxembourg. Several bus routes pass through the area. Route 38 travels along Boulevard St-Michel on the east side of the Gardens, and 58 and 89 pass along the Rue de Rennes on the north side. Route 82 passes along the southern end.

SEE ALSO
• **Street Finder**, maps 12, 16
• **Where to Stay** pp278–9
• **Restaurants** pp296–8

KEY
▦	Street-by-Street map
M	Metro station
RER	RER station
P	Parking

0 meters 400
0 yards 400

Playing chess in the Jardin du Luxembourg

Street by Street: Luxembourg Quarter

Sᴵᴛᴜᴀᴛᴇᴅ ᴏɴʟʏ ᴀ ꜰᴇᴡ steps from the bustle of St-Germain-des-Prés, this graceful and historic area offers a peaceful haven in the heart of a modern city. The Jardin du Luxembourg and Palais du Luxembourg dominate the vicinity. The gardens fully opened to the public in the 19th century under the ownership of the Comte de Provence (later Louis XVIII): for a small fee visitors could come in and feast on fruit from the orchard. Today the gardens, palace and old houses on the streets to the north remain unspoiled and attract many visitors.

★ St-Sulpice
This Classical church took over 134 years to build to Daniel Gittard's plans. It has a facade by the Italian architect Giovanni Servandoni ❷

To St-Germain-des-Prés

RUE HENRI DE JOUVENEL
RUE SERVANDONI
RUE GARANCIERE
RUE GAROU
RUE DE VAUGIRARD

Place St-Sulpice
The Fontaine des Quatre Points Cardinaux depicts four church leaders at the cardinal points of the compass. Point also means "never": the leaders were never made cardinals ❶

The Monument to Delacroix
(1890) by Jules Dalou is situated near the private gardens of the French Senate. Beneath the bust of the leading Romantic painter Eugène Delacroix are the allegorical figures of Art, Time and Glory.

Sᴛᴀʀ Sɪɢʜᴛs
★ St-Sulpice
★ Jardin du Luxembourg
★ Palais du Luxembourg
★ Fontaine de Médicis

★ Jardin du Luxembourg
Many fine statues were erected in the Luxembourg gardens in the 19th century during the reign of Louis-Philippe ❺

The Rue de Tournon is full of elegant architecture, boutiques and old bookshops. At No. 12 is the Grand Hôtel d'Entragues, reconstructed by Neveu in the 18th century during Louis XVI's reign.

LOCATOR MAP
See Central Paris Map pp12–13

KEY

– – – Suggested route

0 meters 100

0 yards 100

★ **Palais du Luxembourg**
In 1794, during the Revolution, the painter Jacques-Louis David was imprisoned here and made sketches for the Intervention of the Sabine Women ❸

★ **Fontaine de Médicis**
This 17th-century fountain is in the style of an Italian grotto and is thought to have been designed by Salomon de Brosse ❹

Sainte Geneviève by Michel-Louis Victor (1845) pays homage to the patron saint of Paris, a wealthy 5th-century Gallo-Roman land-owner. When the Huns invaded Paris in AD 451, she prayed with women friends that their beloved city would be spared, and their prayers were answered.

The Octagonal Lake, (Grand Bassin), attributed to Jean-François Chalgrin, is surrounded by formal terraces where visitors to the gardens often sunbathe.

Place St-Sulpice ●

75006. **Map** 12 E4. M *St-Sulpice.*

THIS LARGE SQUARE, which is dominated on the east side by the enormous church from which it takes its name, was built in the last half of the 18th century.

Two main features of the square are the Fountain of the Four Bishops by Joachim Visconti (1844) and the pink-flowering chestnut trees. There is also the Café de la Mairie, a rendezvous of writers and students that often appears in French movies.

Stained-glass window of St-Sulpice

St-Sulpice ●

Pl St-Sulpice 75006. **Map** 12 E5.
C 01 46 33 21 78. M *St-Sulpice.*
Open 8:30am–7:30pm daily.
frequent.

IT TOOK more than a century, from 1646, for this huge and imposing church to be built. The result is a simple two-story west front with two tiers of elegant columns. The overall harmony of the

building is marred only by the towers, one at each end, which do not match.

Large arched windows fill the vast interior with light. By the front door are two enormous shells given to François I by the Venetian Republic – they rest on rocklike bases sculpted by Jean-Baptiste Pigalle.

In the side chapel to the right of the main door are some magnificent murals by Eugène Delacroix, including his famous *Jacob Wrestling with the Angel (see p137)* and *Heliodorus Driven from the Temple.* Visitors can often enjoy recitals, which are given on the splendid organ.

Palais du Luxembourg ●

15 Rue de Vaugirard 75006.
Map 12 E5. C 01 42 34 20 00.
M *Odéon.* RER *Luxembourg.* 1st
Sun of month, 10:30am–12:30pm.
Visits organized through the Caisse
Nationale de Monuments. C 01 44
61 20 89. Apply in advance. **Adm
charge.**

NOW THE HOME of the French Senate, this palace was built to remind Marie de Médicis, widow of Henri IV, of her native Florence. By the time it was finished (1631) she had been banished, but it remained a royal palace until the Revolution. Since then the palace has been used (briefly) as a prison, and in World War II it was the headquarters of the Luftwaffe.

It was designed by Salomon de Brosse, who decided to build it in the style of the Pitti Palace in Florence.

Figures on the Fontaine de Médicis

Fontaine de Médicis ●

15 Rue de Vaugirard 75006.
Map 12 F5. RER *Luxembourg.*

BUILT IN 1624 for Marie de Médici by an unknown architect, this vigorous Baroque fountain stands at the end of a long pond filled with goldfish and shaded by trees. The mythological figures were added much later by Auguste Ottin (1866).

Jardin du Luxembourg ●

Blvd St-Michel 75006. **Map** 12 E5.
C 01 42 34 20 00. RER *Luxembourg.*
Open Apr–Oct: 7:30am–9:30pm
daily; Nov–Mar: 8:15am–5pm
daily (times may vary slightly).

A GREEN OASIS covering 60 acres (25 ha) in the heart of the Left Bank, this is the most popular park in the whole of Paris. The layout of the gardens is centered around the Luxembourg Palace and is dominated by a splendid octagonal pool – usually full of toy sailboats.

Apart from the attraction of its formal terraces, broad avenues and many statues, the park also includes an open-air café, a puppet theater, numerous tennis courts, a bandstand and a bee-keeping school. There is also a riding school nearby.

Sculptures on Palais du Luxembourg

Institut Catholique de Paris ❻

21 Rue d'Assas 75006.
Map 12 D5. Ⓜ St-Placide, Rennes.
Not open to the public.

FOUNDED IN 1875, this is one of the most distinguished teaching institutions in France. It also houses two small museums, which unfortunately have recently been closed to the public for an indefinite period. One is devoted to the physicist Edouard Branly, inventor of the radio conductor (which made the wireless possible). The other shows objects excavated in the Holy Land.

Courtyard statue at the Institut Catholique

St-Joseph-des-Carmes ❼

70 Rue de Vaugirard 75006.
Map 12 D5. Ⓒ 01 44 39 52 00.
Ⓜ St-Placide. **Open** 7am–7pm Mon–Sat; 9am–7pm Sun. **Closed** Easter Mon, Pentecost. ♿ restricted. ⚑ 3pm Sat.

COMPLETED IN 1620, this church was built as the chapel for a Carmelite convent but was used as a prison during the Revolution. In 1792 a hundred priests met a grisly end in the church's courtyard as part of the September Massacres *(see pp28–9)*. Their remains are now kept in the crypt.

Carpeaux's fountain sculpture

Fontaine de l'Observatoire ❽

Pl Ernest Denis, in Ave de l'Observatoire. **Map** 16 E2.
RER Port Royal.

SITUATED AT THE southern tip of the Jardin du Luxembourg, this is one of the liveliest fountains in Paris. Made of bronze, it has four women holding aloft a globe representing four continents – the fifth, Oceania, was left out for reasons of symmetry. There are some subsidiary figures, including dolphins, horses and a turtle. The sculpture was erected in 1873 by Jean-Baptiste Carpeaux.

Val-de-Grâce ❾

1 Pl Alphonse-Laveran 75005. **Map** 16 F2. Ⓒ 01 40 51 51 92. Ⓜ Gobelins. RER Port Royal. **Open** noon–6pm Tue, Wed, Sat & Sun. **Adm charge** (except for nave). ✝ frequent, pm. ⚑

ONE OF THE MOST beautiful churches in France. It was built for Anne of Austria (wife of Louis XIII) in thanks for the birth of her son. Young Louis XIV himself laid the first stone in 1645. The design is in the style of the great François Mansart. The church is noted

for its beautiful lead-and-gilt dome. In the cupola, is Pierre Mignard's enormous fresco, with over 200 triple-life-size figures. The six huge, twisted marble columns that frame the altar are similar to those by Bernini for St. Peter's in Rome.

Musée du Service de Santé des Armées ❿

1 Pl Alphonse-Laveran 75005.
Map 16 F2. Ⓒ 01 40 51 51 92.
RER Port Royal. **Open** noon–6pm Tue, Wed, Sat & Sun. **Adm charge**. ⚑ groups only, call to arrange.

FOUNDED DURING World War I and run by the army medical corps, this museum is also known as the Musée du Val-de-Grâce. It is in the west wing of the Val-de-Grâce church, where it became a military hospital in 1795.

The exhibits cover the history of medicine with gruesome memorabilia such as artificial limbs and surgical instruments. There are even reconstructions of military hospital trains that took wounded soldiers to hospital.

Engraving of the interior of a hospital train from 1887

Ecole Nationale Supérieure des Mines ⓫

60 Blvd St-Michel. **Map** 16 F1. Ⓒ 01 40 51 91 45. RER Luxembourg. **Museum open** 10am–noon Sat, 1:30pm–6pm Tue–Sat. **Adm charge**. 📷 ⚑

LOUIS XIV set up the School of Mines in 1783 to train mining engineers. Today, it is one of the most prestigious *grandes écoles* – schools that provide the élite for the civil service and professions. It also houses the national collection of minerals – the Musée de Minéralogie.

Facade of St-Joseph-des-Carmes

MONTPARNASSE

IN THE FIRST three decades of this century, Montparnasse was a thriving artistic and literary center. Many modern painters and sculptors, novelists and poets, the great and the unknown, were drawn to this area. Its ateliers, conviviality and renowned Bohemian lifestyle made it a magnet for genius, some of it French, much of it foreign. The great epoch ended with World War II, and change continued with the destruction of many of the ateliers and the construction of the soaring Tour Montparnasse, Paris's tallest office tower, which heralded the more modern *quartier*. Yet the area has not lost its appeal. The great cafés remain very much in business and attract a lively international crowd. Small café-theaters have opened, and the area springs to life on the weekends with movie crowds.

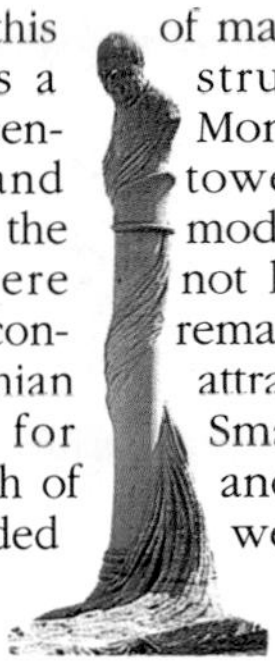

Monument to Charles Augustin Ste-Beuve in the Cimetière du Montparnasse

SIGHTS AT A GLANCE

Historic Buildings and Streets
Rue Campagne-Première 3
Catacombs 10
Observatoire de Paris 11

Cemeteries
Cimetière du Montparnasse pp180–1 4

Museums and Galleries
Musée Zadkine 2
Musée Antoine Bourdelle 6
Musée de la Poste 7
Musée Montparnasse 8
Fondation Cartier 9

Modern Architecture
Tour Montparnasse 5

Cafés and Restaurants
La Coupole 1
La Closerie des Lilas 12

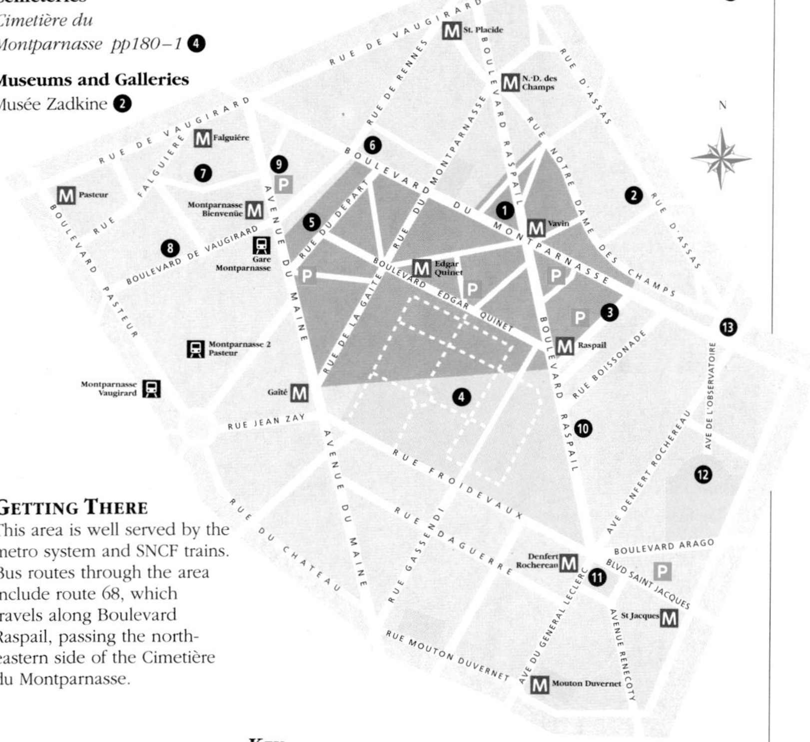

GETTING THERE

This area is well served by the metro system and SNCF trains. Bus routes through the area include route 68, which travels along Boulevard Raspail, passing the north-eastern side of the Cimetière du Montparnasse.

KEY

Street-by-Street map
Metro station
SNCF (train) station
Parking

0 meters 400
0 yards 400

SEE ALSO

• ***Street Finder***, map 15–16
• ***Where to Stay*** pp278–9
• ***Restaurants*** pp296–8

View of Montparnasse from the Eiffel Tower

Street by Street: Montparnasse

R ENOWNED FOR ITS MIX of art and high
living, Montparnasse continues to
live up to its name: Mount Parnassus
was the mountain dedicated by the
ancient Greeks to Apollo, god of poetry,
music and beauty. That mix was
especially potent in the 1920s and 1930s,
when such artists and writers as Picasso,
Hemingway, Cocteau, Giacometti,
Matisse and Modigliani were to be seen
in the local bars, cafés and cabarets.

★ La Coupole
*This traditional
brasserie-style café,
with its large
enclosed terrace,
opened in 1927 and
became a famous
meeting place for
artists and
writers* ❶

**★ Cimetière du
Montparnasse**
This fine sculpture, The
Separation of a Couple
*by de Max, stands in
the smallest of the city's
major cemeteries* ❹

The Théâtre Montparnasse
at No. 31 still has its original
decor from the 1880s.

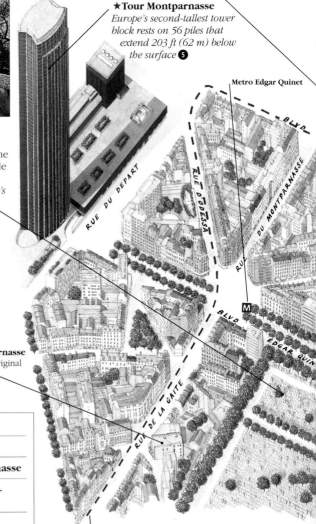

★Tour Montparnasse
*Europe's second-tallest tower
block rests on 56 piles that
extend 203 ft (62 m) below
the surface* ❺

Metro Edgar Quinet

RUE DU DEPART

RUE D'ODESSA

RUE DU MONTPARNASSE

BLVD

BLVD

EDGAR QUIN

RUE DE LA GAITE

To Metro Gaîté

STAR SIGHTS

★ La Coupole

★ Tour Montparnasse

★ Rue Campagne-
Première

★ Cimetière du
Montparnasse

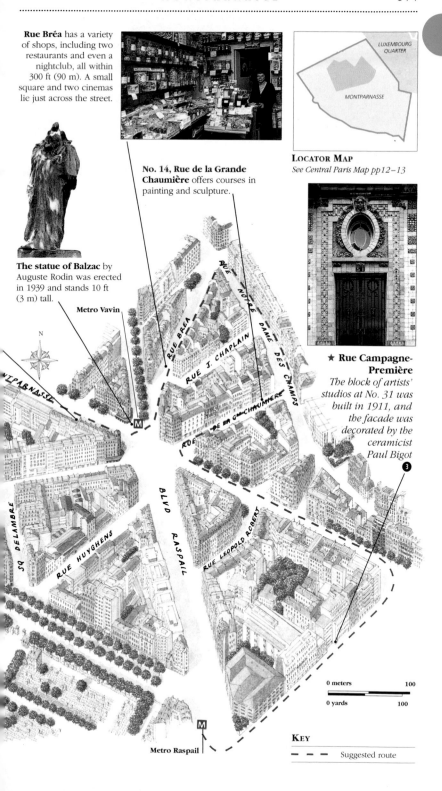

Rue Bréa has a variety of shops, including two restaurants and even a nightclub, all within 300 ft (90 m). A small square and two cinemas lie just across the street.

The statue of Balzac by Auguste Rodin was erected in 1939 and stands 10 ft (3 m) tall.

No. 14, Rue de la Grande Chaumière offers courses in painting and sculpture.

LOCATOR MAP
See Central Paris Map pp12–13

LUXEMBOURG QUARTER

MONTPARNASSE

★ **Rue Campagne-Première**
The block of artists' studios at No. 31 was built in 1911, and the facade was decorated by the ceramicist Paul Bigot

❸

Metro Vavin

N

RUE BRÉA

RUE J. CHAPLAIN

RUE NOTRE DAME DES CHAMPS

RUE DE LA G^de CHAUMIÈRE

Ⓜ

BLVD RASPAIL

RUE HUYGHENS

SQ DELAMBRE

NIPARNASSE

RUE LEOPOLD ROBERT

0 meters   100
0 yards   100

KEY

– – –   Suggested route

Ⓜ
Metro Raspail

The interior of La Coupole

La Coupole ❶

102 Blvd du Montparnasse 75014.
Map 16 D2. **[** 01 43 20 14 20. **M**
Vavin, Montparnasse. **Open** 7:30am–
2am daily. **Closed** Dec 24 evening.
See **Restaurants and Cafés** p303.

ESTABLISHED IN 1927, this
historic café-restaurant and
dance hall underwent a face-
lift in the late 1980s. Its red
velvet seats and famous
columns, decorated by various
local artists, have survived.
Among its clientele have been
Jean-Paul Sartre, Josephine
Baker, and Roman Polanski.

The museum's *Les Trois Belles*
(1950) by Ossip Zadkine

Musée Zadkine ❷

100 bis Rue d'Assas 75116. **Map** 16 E1.
[01 43 26 91 90. **M** Notre-Dame-Les
Champs. **Open** 10am–5:30pm Tue–Sun.
Closed public hols. **Adm charge**. 📷
🎥 👥 limited.

THE RUSSIAN-BORN sculptor
Ossip Zadkine lived here
from 1928 until his death in

1967. The small house, studio,
and daffodil-filled garden
contain his often tormented-
looking works. Here he
produced his great commemorative sculpture, *Ville Détruite*,
commissioned by Rotter-
dam after World War II,
and two monuments to
Vincent Van Gogh, one for
Holland and one for Auvers-
sur-Oise, where Van Gogh
died. The museum's works
span the development of
Zadkine's style, from his Cubist beginnings to Expressionism and Abstractionism.

Rue Campagne-Première ❸

75014. **Map** 16 E2. **M** Raspail.

THIS STREET HAS some
interesting Art Deco
buildings and a long artistic
tradition. Modigliani, ravaged
by opium and tuberculosis,
lived at No. 3. Between the
wars many artists resided
here, including Picasso, Joan
Miró, and Kandinsky.

Cimetière du Montparnasse ❹

See pp180–1.

Tour Montparnasse ❺

Pl Raoul Dautry 75014. **Map** 15 C2.
M Montparnasse-Bienvenüe. **[** 01
45 38 52 56. **Open** Apr–Sep: 9:30am–
11:30pm daily; Oct–Mar: 10am–10pm
daily. **Adm charge**. 🍴 💻 🎥 by appt.

THIS WAS EUROPE'S largest
office block when it was
built in 1973 as the focal
point of a new business
sector intended to
revitalize a run-down
inner-city area. It
stands 209 m (690 ft)
high, is made of
curved steel and
smoked glass, and
totally dominates the
quarter's skyline.
The bar, restaurant
and observatory on
the 56th floor offer
excellent panoramic
views of the city.

The Archer (1909) by Antoine
Bourdelle

Musée Antoine Bourdelle ❻

18 Rue Antoine Bourdelle 75015.
Map 15 B1. **[** 01 49 54 73 73.
M Montparnasse-Bienvenüe.
Open 10am–5:40pm Tue–Sun
(last adm 5:15pm). **Closed** public
hols. **Adm charge**. 📷 👥 limited.

THE PROLIFIC sculptor,
Antoine Bourdelle, lived
and worked in the studio
here from 1884 until his death
in 1929. The house, studio
and garden are now a
museum devoted to his life
and work. Among the 900
sculptures on display are the
original plaster casts of his
monumental works planned
for wide public squares. They
are housed in the Great Hall
in an extension and include
the group of sculptures for
the relief decoration of the
Théatre des Champs-Elysées.

Musée de la Poste ❼

34 Blvd de Vaugirard 75015.
Map 15 B2. **[** 01 42 79 23 45.
M Montparnasse-Bienvenüe. **Open**
10am–6pm Mon–Sat.
Closed public hols. **Adm**
charge 📷 👥 **Library**.

EVERY CONCEIVABLE
aspect of the
history of the
French postal
service and methods
of transportation is
covered in this well
laid out collection.
There is even a

A view of the tower   room devoted to

mail delivery in times of war – carrier pigeons were used during the Franco-Prussian War with postmarks stamped on their wings. Postage stamp art is displayed in the gallery.

A Miró-designed postage stamp

Musée du Montparnasse **8**

21 Ave du Maine 75015. **Map** 15 C1. **℃** 01 42 22 91 96. **M** Montparnasse Bienvenüe-Falguière. **Open** 1pm–7pm Wed–Sun.

DURING WORLD WAR I, this was a canteen for needy artists which, by its status as a private club, was not subject to curfew, and so the likes of Picasso, Braque, Modigliani, and Léger could eat for 65 centimes and then party until late at night. This symbolic place is now a museum that recalls, through paintings and photos, how at the Vavin crossroads Western art turned some of the most beautiful pages of its modern history.

Fondation Cartier **9**

261 Blvd Raspail 75014. **Map** 11 A2. **℃** 01 45 56 60 17. **M** Raspail. **Open** noon–8pm Tue–Sun (Thu 10pm). **Closed** Jan 1, Dec 25. **Adm charge**.

THIS FOUNDATION for contemporary art is housed in a building designed by architect Jean Nouvel. He has created an air of transparency and light, as well as incorporating a cedar of Lebanon planted in 1823 by François-René de Chateaubriand. The structure complements the nature of the exhibitions of progressive art, which showcase personal, group or thematic displays, often with works by young unknowns.

Catacombs **10**

1 Pl Denfert-Rochereau 75014. **Map** 16 E3. **℃** 01 43 22 47 63. **M** Denfert-Rochereau. **Open** 2pm–4pm Tue–Fri; 9am–11am, 2pm–4pm Sat, Sun. **Closed** public hols. **Adm charge**.

IN 1786 A MONUMENTAL project began here: the removal of the millions of skulls and bones from the unsanitary city cemetery in Les Halles to the ancient quarries formed by excavations at the base of the three "mountains": Montparnasse, Montrouge, and Montsouris. It took 15 months to transport the bones and rotting corpses at night across the city in huge carts to their new resting place.

Just before the Revolution, the Comte d'Artois (later Charles X) threw wild parties in the catacombs, and during World War II the French Resistance set up its headquarters here. Above the door outside are the words "Stop! This is the empire of death."

Observatoire de Paris **11**

61 Ave de l'Observatoire 75014. **Map** 16 E3. **℃** 01 40 51 22 21. **M** Denfert-Rochereau. **Open** 1st Sat of month, 2:30pm – reserve in advance by post except during exhibitions. **Closed** Aug. **Adm charge**.

IN 1667 Louis XIV was persuaded by his scientists and astronomers that France needed a royal observatory. Building began on June 21, the day of the summer solstice, and took five years to reach completion

Astronomical research undertaken here included the calculation of the exact dimensions of the solar system in 1672, calculations of the dimensions of longitude, the mapping of the moon in 1679, and the discovery of the planet Neptune in 1846.

The facade of the Observatoire

La Closerie des Lilas **12**

171 Blvd du Montparnasse 75014. **Map** 16 E2. **℃** 01 40 51 34 50. **M** Vavin. **RER** Port Royal. **Open** Bar: 11–2am, brasserie: noon–1am daily.

LENIN, TROTSKY, Hemingway, and Scott Fitzgerald all frequented the numerous bars and cafés of Montparnasse, but the Closerie was their favorite. Much of Hemingway's novel *The Sun Also Rises* takes place here. Hemingway wrote it on the terrace in just six weeks. Today the terrace is ringed with trees and the whole place is decidedly more elegant in appearance.

Skulls and bones stored in the catacombs

Cimetière du Montparnasse ❹

THE MONTPARNASSE CEMETERY was planned by Napoleon outside the city walls to replace the numerous congested small cemeteries within the old city, viewed as a health hazard at the turn of the 19th century. It was opened in 1824 and became the resting place of many illustrious Parisians, particularly Left Bank personalities. Like all French cemeteries, it is divided into rigidly aligned paths forming blocks or divisions. The Rue Emile Richard cuts it into two parts: the Grand Cimetière and the Petit Cimetière.

★ Charles Baudelaire Cenotaph
This is a monument to the great poet and critic (1821–67), author of The Flowers of Evil.

Samuel Beckett, the great Irish playwright renowned for *Waiting for Godot*, spent most of his life in Paris. He died in 1989.

The Pétain tomb contains the family of the marshal who collaborated with the Germans during World War II. Pétain himself is buried near Nantes, where he was imprisoned.

Guy de Maupassant was a 19th-century novelist.

Alfred Dreyfus was a Jewish army officer whose unjust trial for treason in 1894 provoked a political and social scandal.

Frédéric Auguste Bartholdi was the sculptor of the Statue of Liberty (1886) in New York.

André Citroën, an engineer and industrialist who died in 1935, founded the famous French car firm.

★ Charles Pigeon Family Tomb
This wonderfully pompous Belle Epoque tomb depicts the French industrialist and inventor in bed with his wife.

AVE DU MIDI

AVE THIERRY

RUE EMILE

AVE DE L'EST

RICHARD

The Kiss by Brancusi
This is the famous Primitivo-Cubist sculpture (a response to Rodin's Kiss*) by the great Romanian artist, who died in 1957 and is buried just off the Rue Emile Richard.*

Charles-Augustin Sainte-Beuve was a critic of the French Romantic generation and is generally described as the "father of modern criticism."

Camille Saint-Saëns, the pianist, organist and composer who died in 1921, was one of France's great post-Romantic musicians.

STAR FEATURES

- ★ Charles Baudelaire Cenotaph
- ★ Charles Pigeon Family Tomb
- ★ Jean-Paul Sartre and Simone de Beauvoir
- ★ Serge Gainsbourg

★ Serge Gainsbourg
The French singer, composer and pop icon of the 1970s and 1980s, is best known for his wistful and irreverent songs. He is married to the actress Jane Birkin.

The Tower is all that remains of a 17th-century windmill. It was part of the old property of the Brothers of Charity on which the cemetery was built.

Génie du Sommeil Eternel
H. Daillion's wistful bronze angel of Eternal Sleep is the cemetery's centerpiece.

Tristen Tzara, the Romanian writer, was leader of the literary and artistic Dada movement in Paris in the 1920s.

Henri Laurens
The French sculptor (1885–1954) was a leading figure in the Cubist movement.

ALLEE RAFFET

VE TRANSVERSALE

ALLEE LENOIR

AVE PRINCIPALE

AVE DE L'OUEST

E DU NORD

E DU BOULEVARD

Man Ray was an American photographer who immortalized the Montparnasse artistic and café scene in the 1920s and 1930s.

Charles Baudelaire, the 19th-century poet, is buried here in his detested stepfather's family tomb, along with his beloved mother.

Chaim Soutine, a poor Jewish Ukranian, was a Montparnasse Bohemian painter of the 1920s. He was adopted by the Italian artist Modigliani.

JEAN PAUL SARTRE
1905 – 1980
SIMONE DE BEAUVOIR
1908 – 1986

Jean Seberg
The Hollywood actress, adopted by the French New Wave film-makers of the 1960s, was the epitome of American blonde beauty, youth and candor.

★ Jean-Paul Sartre and Simone de Beauvoir
The famous existentialist couple, undisputed leaders of the post-war literary scene, lie here close to their Left Bank haunts.

INVALIDES AND EIFFEL TOWER QUARTER

Musée de l'Armée cannon

EVERYTHING in the area of Invalides is on a monumental scale. Starting from the sprawling 18th-century buildings of the Ecole Militaire on the corner of Avenue de la Motte Piquet, the Parc du Champs de Mars stretches down to the Eiffel Tower and the Seine. The avenues around the Tower are lined with luxurious buildings, some in the Art Nouveau style, and numerous embassies. The area was already highly prized between the world wars when the noted actor Sacha Guitry lived there. Even earlier, in the 18th century, wealthy residents of the Marais moved to this part of the city, building the wonderful aristocratic town houses that line the Rue de Varenne and Rue de Grenelle.

SIGHTS AT A GLANCE

Historic Buildings and Streets
Hôtel des Invalides **6**
Hôtel Matignon **8**
Assemblée Nationale Palais-Bourbon **11**
Rue Cler **13**
Les Egouts **14**
Champ-de-Mars **15**
No. 29 Avenue Rapp **17**
Ecole Militaire **19**

Museums and Galleries
Musée de l'Ordre de la Libération **3**
Musée de l'Armée **4**
Musée des Plans-Reliefs **5**

Musée Rodin **7**
Musée de la Seita **12**

Churches and Temples
Dôme Church pp188–9 **1**
St-Louis-des-Invalides **2**
Sainte-Clothilde **10**

Monuments and Fountains
Fontaine des Quatre Saisons **9**
Eiffel Tower pp192–3 **16**

Modern Architecture
Village Suisse **18**
UNESCO **20**

GETTING THERE
The metro system serves this area well, with stations at Invalides, Solferino, Sèvres Babylone, Varenne, Latour Maubourg and Ecole Militaire. There are also several bus routes through the area. Route 69 passes along Rue St-Dominique heading east and along Rue de Grenelle on the way back. Route 87 travels along the Avenue de Suffren and 28 along Avenue Motte Picquet.

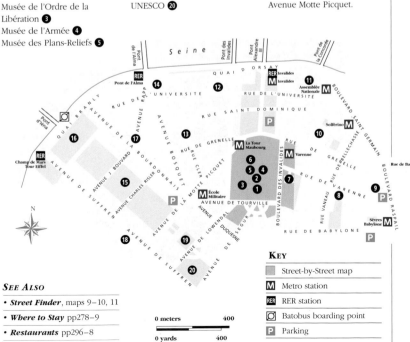

KEY

▦	Street-by-Street map
M	Metro station
RER	RER station
⊡	Batobus boarding point
P	Parking

View of the Eiffel Tower at night

Street by Street: Invalides

THE IMPOSING HOTEL DES INVALIDES, from which the area takes its name, was built from 1671 to 1676 by Louis XIV for his wounded and homeless veterans and as a monument to his own glory. At its center lies the glittering golden roof of the Sun King's Dôme Church, which marks the final resting place of Napoleon Bonaparte. The emperor's body was brought here from St Helena in 1840, 19 years after he died, and placed inside the majestic red sarcophagus, designed by Joachim Visconti, that lies at the center of the Dôme's circular glass-topped crypt. Just to the east of the Hôtel on the corner of the Boulevard des Invalides, the superb Musée Rodin offers artistic relief from the pomp and circumstance of the surrounding area.

Mounted military policeman

Metro La Tour Maubourg

The facade of the Hôtel is 645 ft (196 m) long and is topped by dormer windows, each decorated in the shape of a different trophy. A head of Hercules sits above the central entrance.

★ Musée de l'Armée
This museum covers military history from the Stone Age to World War II. It includes an exhibition on the development of the French flag, from the various standards of the ancien régime *to the Tricolor* ❹

STAR SIGHTS

★ **Dôme Church and Napoleon's Tomb**

★ **St-Louis-des-Invalides**

★ **Musée de l'Armée**

★ **Musée Rodin**

Musée de l'Ordre de la Libération
The Order was set up to honor feats of heroism during World War II ❸

KEY

– – –   Suggested route

0 meters	100
0 yards	100

AVE DE TOURVILLE

Musée des Plans-Reliefs
This museum contains military models of forts and towns, as well as a display on model-making ❺

General de Gaulle's Liberation Order and compass

Hôtel des Invalides
*After the two world wars,
Louis XIV's Hôtel was
returned to its
original use as a
hospital for
veterans* ❻

LOCATOR MAP
See Central Paris Map pp12–13

The Invalides gardens were
designed by de Cotte in 1704 and
are lined by bronze cannons from
the 17th and 18th centuries.

Metro Varenne

The Cour d'Honneur is still used for
military parades. Seurre's statue of
Napoleon, known as the Little
Corporal, stands above the south side.

★ **St-Louis-des-
Invalides**
*From St-Louis, the
soldier's chapel, it is
possible to see into
the Dôme, which
was built as Louis
XIV's private chapel* ❷

★ **Musée Rodin**
*By the time he died in 1917,
Auguste Rodin had revolutionized
the art of sculpture. All his key
works, including* The Thinker
(about 1880), are on display ❼

★ **Dôme Church and Napoleon's Tomb**
*The Dôme took 27 years to build. In the crypt
lies Napoleon, whose final wish was to have
his ashes "rest on the banks of the Seine"* ❶

Dôme Church ●

See pp188–9.

St-Louis-des-Invalides ●

Hôtel des Invalides 75007. **Map** 11 A3. **M** *Varenne Latour-Maubourg.* **℃** *01 44 42 37 65.* **Open** *Apr–Sep: 9:30am–6pm daily; Oct–Mar: 9:30am–4pm daily.*

A**LSO KNOWN AS** the "soldiers' church," this is the chapel of the Hôtel des Invalides. It was built from 1679 to 1708 by Jules Hardouin-Mansart from the original designs by Libéral Bruand, architect of the Hôtel des Invalides. The imposing, but stark, interior is decorated with banners seized in battle.

The fine 17th-century organ was built by Alexandre Thierry. The first performance of Berlioz's *Requiem* was given on it in 1837, with an orchestra accompanied by a battery of outside artillery.

Musée de l'Ordre de la Libération ●

51 bis Blvd de Latour-Maubourg 75007. **Map** 11 A4. **℃** *01 47 05 04 10.* **M** *Latour-Maubourg.* **Open** *10am–5pm daily.* **Closed** *public hols.* **Adm charge.** *by appt one month in advance.*

T**HIS MUSEUM** is devoted to the wartime Free French and their leader, General Charles de Gaulle. The Order

The altar of St-Louis-des-Invalides

The facade of the Musée de l'Ordre de la Libération

of Liberation was created by de Gaulle at Brazzaville in 1940 to honor those who made an outstanding contribution to the final victory of the Allies in World War II. It is France's highest honor. The *companions* who received the honor were French civilians and members of the armed forces, plus a handful of overseas leaders, including King George VI, Winston Churchill and General Dwight Eisenhower.

Cannons at the Musée de l'Armée

Musée de l'Armée ●

Hôtel des Invalides 75007. **Map** 11 A3. **℃** *01 44 42 37 72.* **M** *Latour-Maubourg, Varenne.* **RER** *Invalides.* **Open** *Apr–Sep: 10am–6pm (5pm winter) daily.* **Closed** *public hols.* **Adm charge.** *ground floor only.* **Film.**

T**HIS IS ONE** of the most comprehensive museums of military history in the world, with exhibits ranging from the Stone Age to the final days of World War II. The museum is housed in galleries occupying two of the former four refectories on either side of the magnificent courtyard of the 17th-century Hôtel des Invalides.

In the Turenne gallery on the east side there is an impressive array of banners dating from 1619 to 1945, including Napoleon's flag of farewell that was flown at Fontainebleau in 1814, after his first abdication. The Restoration gallery on the

second floor of the same wing recalls the emperor's imprisonment on Elba; the Hundred Days; Waterloo; and his final exile on St. Helena, movingly represented by the reconstruction of the room where Napoleon died in 1821.

On the west side, the Oriental gallery has a rich display of arms and armor from China, Japan, India and Turkey; the Pauillac gallery has Renaissance swords and daggers; and the Arsenal has suits of armor, 1,000 helmets and hundreds of spears, swords and firearms.

Musée des Plans-Reliefs ●

Hôtel des Invalides 75007. **Map** 11 B3. **℃** *01 44 42 30 11.* **M** *Latour-Maubourg, Varenne.* **RER** *Invalides.* **Open** *10am–6pm (5pm winter) daily.* **Closed** *Jan 1, May 1, Nov 1 & 11, Dec 25.* **Adm charge.**

A map of Alessandria, Italy (1813)

T**HE DETAILED** models of French forts and fortified towns, some dating back to Louis XIV's reign, were considered top secret until the 1950s, when they were put on public display. The oldest model is that of Perpignan, dating to 1686. It shows the fortifications drawn up by the legendary 17th-century military architect Vauban, who built the defenses around several French towns, including Briançon.

Hôtel des Invalides ❻

75007. **Map** 11 A3. [C] 01 44 42 37 70.
[M] Latour-Maubourg, Varenne. **Open**
10am–6pm daily (5pm winter).
Closed public
hols.

The Invalides main entrance

FOUNDED BY Louis XIV, this was the first military hospital and home for French war veterans and soldiers who had hitherto been reduced to begging. The decree for building this vast complex was signed in 1670, and construction, following the designs of Libéral Bruand, was finished five years later.

Today the harmonious classical facade is one of the most impressive sights in Paris, with its four stories, cannon in the forecourt, garden and tree-lined esplanade stretching to the Seine. The south side leads to St-Louis-des-Invalides, the soldiers' church, which is in front of the magnificent Dôme church of Jules Hardouin-Mansart. The dome was regilded in 1989 and now glitters anew.

Musée Rodin ❼

77 Rue de Varenne 75007.
Map 11 B3. [C] 01 47 05 01 34.
[M] Varenne. **Open** Apr–Sep:
9:30am–5:45pm Tue–Sun; Oct–Mar:
10am–4:45pm Tue–Sun. **Closed**
Jan 1, May 1, Dec 25. **Adm charge**.
[image icons] restricted. [icons]

AUGUSTE RODIN, widely regarded as the greatest 19th-century French sculptor, lived and worked in the Hôtel

Biron, an elegant 18th-century mansion, from 1908 until his death in 1917. In return for a state-owned flat and studio, Rodin left his work to the nation, and it is now exhibited here. Some of his most celebrated sculptures are on display in the garden: *The Burghers of Calais*, *The Thinker*, *The Gates of Hell* and *Balzac*. The garden has a stunning array of 2,000 rosebushes.

The indoor exhibits are arranged in chronological order, spanning the whole of Rodin's career, with such highlights as *The Kiss* and *Eve*.

Hôtel Matignon ❽

57 Rue de Varenne 75007.
Map 11 C4. [M] Solférino, Rue du
Bac. **Not open** to the public.

ONE OF THE MOST beautiful mansions in the Faubourg area, this was built by Jean Courtonne in 1721 and has been substantially remodeled since. Former owners include Talleyrand, the statesman and diplomat who held legendary parties and receptions here, and several members of the nobility. It has been the official residence of the French Prime Minister since 1958 and has the largest private garden in Paris.

Rodin's *The Kiss* (1886) at the Musée Rodin

Fontaine des Quatre Saisons ❾

57–59 Rue de Grenelle 75007.
Map 11 C4. [M] Rue du Bac.

IN 1739 THE EMINENT sculptor Edme Bouchardon was commissioned to design an attractive and practical fountain to supply water to the wealthy who lived around the Boulevard Raspail. He decorated it with large allegorical figures of the city of Paris and the four seasons.

In the house behind the fountain (No. 59) lived Alfred de Musset, the 19th-century French novelist. It has now been converted into a museum dedicated to the sculptor Aristide Maillol, with works donated by his former model, Dina Vierny.

Sculptured figures at Ste-Clothilde

Sainte-Clothilde ❿

12 Rue Martignac 75007.
Map 11 B3. [C] 01 44 18 62 64.
[M] Solférino, Varenne, Invalides.
Open 8am–7pm daily. **Closed** non-
religious public hols. [icons]

DESIGNED BY the German-born architect Christian Gau and the first of its kind to be built in Paris, this Neo-Gothic church was inspired by the mid-19th-century enthusiasm for the Middle Ages, made fashionable by such writers as Victor Hugo. The church is noted for its imposing twin towers, visible from across the Seine. The interior decoration includes wall paintings by James Pradier and stained-glass windows with scenes relating to the patron saint of the church. The composer César Franck was the church organist here for 32 years.

Dôme Church ❶

JULES HARDOUIN-MANSART was asked in 1676 by the Sun King, Louis XIV, to build the Dôme Church among the existing buildings of the Invalides military refuge. A soldiers' church had already been built, but the Dôme was to be reserved for the exclusive use of the Sun King and for the location of royal tombs. The resulting masterpiece complements the surrounding buildings and is one of the greatest examples of 17th-century French architecture.

After Louis XIV's death, plans to bury the royal family in the church were abandoned, and it became a monument to Bourbon glory. In 1841 Louis-Philippe decided to install Napoleon's remains in the crypt, and the addition of the tombs of Vauban, Marshal Foch and other figures of military prominence have since turned this church into a French military memorial.

Gilded Dome
The cupola was first gilded in 1715.

① Tomb of Joseph Bonaparte
The sarcophagus of Napoleon's older brother, the King of Naples and later of Spain, is in the side chapel to the right as visitors enter.

Main entrance

② Memorial to Vauban
Commissioned by Napoleon I in 1808, this contains an urn with Sébastien le Prestre de Vauban's heart. He was Louis XIV's great military architect and engineer who died in 1707. His long military career culminated in his appointment as Marshal of France in 1703. He revolutionized siege warfare when he introduced his ricochet batteries. His reclining figure by Antoine Etex lies on top of the memorial, mourned by Science and War.

⑥ Glass Gallery
Access to the glass-topped crypt containing Napoleon's tomb is by the curved stairs in front of the altar. The glass partition behind the altar separates the Dôme from the older Invalides chapel beyond.

⑤ St. Jérôme's Chapel
Passing across the center of the church, the side chapel to the right of the main entrance contains the tomb of Napoleon's younger brother, Jérôme, King of Westphalia.

Stairs to crypt

③

④ Dôme Ceiling
Charles de la Fosse's circular painting (1692) on the ceiling is called the Glory of Paradise, with Saint Louis presenting his sword to Christ.

③ Tomb of Marshal Foch
Ferdinand Foch's imposing bronze tomb was built by Paul Landowski in 1937.

NAPOLEON'S RETURN
King Louis-Philippe decided to bring the Emperor Napoleon's body back from St. Helena *(see pp30–31)* as a gesture of reconciliation to the Republican and Bonapartist parties contesting his regime. The Dôme Church, with its historical and military associations, was an obvious choice for Napoleon's final resting place. His body was encased in six coffins and finally placed in the crypt in 1861, in the culmination of a grand ceremony that was attended by Napoleon III.

Assemblée Nationale Palais-Bourbon ⑪

126 Rue de l'Université 75007.
Map 11 B2. 🎜 *01 40 63 60 00.*
Ⓜ *Assemblée-Nationale.* 🚇 *Invalides.*
Open *10am, 2pm, 3pm Sat. Enter at
33 Quai d'Orsay. ID necessary.* 📷
🎫 *for groups call 01 40 63 64 08.*

Bᵁᴵᴸᵀ ᴵᴺ 1722 for the
Duchesse de Bourbon,
daughter of Louis XIV, the
Palais-Bourbon was confiscated during the Revolution.
It has been home to the lower
house of the French Parliament since 1830.

The Assemblée Nationale

Musée de la Seita ⑫

12 Rue Surcouf 75007. **Map** 11 A2.
🎜 *01 45 56 60 17/61 48.*
Ⓜ *Invalides, Latour-Maubourg.*
Open *11am–7pm Tue–Sun.* **Closed**
public hols. 📷 ♿ 📷

Hᴼᵁˢᴱᴰ ᴵᴺ the administ-
ration building of an old
tobacco factory, this state-run
museum relates the history of

A 19th-century smoking pipe

tobacco since it was brought
to Europe from the New
World 500 years ago.
   The collection covers pipe
smoking, snuff taking,
tobacco chewing, and the
medical uses of tobacco and
displays an extensive range of
tobacco-related objects. This
museum provides fascinating
insight into the use and abuse
of the humble weed. Even
Napoleon III's 19th-century
cigar chest made by Diehl is
included in the collection.

Rue Cler ⑬

75007. **Map** 10 F3.
Ⓜ *Ecole-Militaire, Latour-Maubourg.*
Market open *Tue–Sat. See* **Shops
and Markets** *pp326–7.*

Tʜᴵˢ ᴵˢ ᴛʜᴱ ˢᴛʀᴱᴱᴛ market of
the seventh arrondisse-
ment, the richest in Paris, for
here live the bulk of senior
civil servants, captains of
industry and many diplomats.
The market area occupies a

pedestrian precinct stretching
south from the Rue de
Grenelle. It is an active and
colorful but very much exclusive market, with the best-
dressed shoppers in town. As
one would expect, the produce is excellent, the pâtisserie
and cheese shops in particular.
   Of architectural interest are
the Art Nouveau buildings at
No. 33 and No. 151.

Les Egouts ⑭

In front of 93 Quai d'Orsay 75007.
Map 10 F2. 🎜 *01 53 68 27 81 (in
English).* Ⓜ *Pont-de-l'Alma.* **Open**
11am–4pm Sat–Wed. **Adm charge.**
📷 🎫 *reserve in advance for groups.*

Oᴺᴱ ᴼꜰ Baron Haussmann's
finest achievements, the
majority of Paris's sewers
(égouts) date from the Second
Empire *(see pp32–3).* If laid
end to end, the 1,300 miles
(2,100 km) of sewers would
stretch from Paris to Istanbul.
In this century the sewers became a popular attraction with
tourists. All tours have been
limited to a small area around
the Quai d'Orsay entrance and
are now on foot. A museum
has now been established here,
where visitors can discover
the mysteries of underground
Paris. There are also displays
of machinery used in the past
and in the sewers of today.

The interior of a wine shop in the Rue Cler

Doorway at No. 29 Avenue Rapp

Champ-de-Mars ⓯

75007. **Map** 10 E3. Ⓜ *Ecole-Militaire.*
RER *Champ-de-Mars–Tour-Eiffel.*

THE GARDENS stretching from the Eiffel Tower to the Ecole Militaire were originally a parade ground for the officer cadets of the Ecole Militaire (Military School). The area has since been used for horse racing; balloon ascents; and the mass ceremonies to celebrate the anniversary of the Revolution on July 14. The first ceremony was held in 1790 in the presence of a glum, captive Louis XVI.

Mammoth exhibitions were held here in the late 19th century, among them the 1889 World Fair for which the Eiffel Tower was erected.

A Paris balloon ascent

Eiffel Tower ⓰

See pp192–3.

No. 29 Avenue Rapp ⓱

75007. **Map** 10 E2. Ⓜ *Pont-de-l'Alma.*

A PRIME EXAMPLE OF Art Nouveau architecture is No. 29 and it won its designer, Jules Lavirotte, first prize at the Concours des Facades de la Ville de Paris in 1901. Its ceramics and brickwork are decorated with animal and flower motifs intermingling with female figures. These are superimposed on a multicolored sandstone base to produce a facade that is deliberately erotic and was certainly subversive in its day. Also worth visiting is Lavirotte's building, complete with watchtower, which can be found in the Square Rapp.

Village Suisse ⓲

Ave de Suffren 75015. **Map** 10 E4.
Ⓜ *Dupleix.* **Open** *Thu–Mon.*

THE SWISS government built a mock-Alpine village for the 1900 Universal Exhibition held in the nearby Champ-de-Mars. It was later used as a center for dealing in secondhand goods, but the arrival of antiques dealers in the 1950s and 1960s made the area fashionable and the items more expensive. The village was renovated in the late 1960s.

Ecole Militaire ⓳

1 Pl Joffre 75007. **Map** 10 F4.
Ⓜ *Ecole-Militaire.* **Visits** *by special permission only – contact the Commandant in writing.* 📷

THE ROYAL MILITARY academy of Louis XV was founded in 1751 to educate 500 sons of impoverished officers. It was designed by architect Jacques-Ange Gabriel, and one of the features is the central pavilion. This is a magnificent example of the French classical style, with eight Corinthian pillars and a quadrangular dome. The interior is decorated in Louis XVI style; of main interest are the chapel and a superb Gabriel-designed wrought-iron banister on the main staircase.

An early cadet at the academy was Napoleon, whose passing-out report stated that "he could go far if the circumstances are right."

A 1751 engraving shows the planning of the Ecole Militaire

UNESCO ⓴

7 Pl de Fontenoy 75007. **Map** 10 F5.
📞 *01 45 68 10 00.* 📠 *01 45 68 10 60 (in English).* Ⓜ *Ségur, Cambronne.*
Open *9:30am–12:30pm, 2:30pm–6pm Mon–Fri (last adm: 5pm).* **Closed** *public hols & during conference sessions.*
📷 ♿ 🎬 🏨 🛈 *Exhibitions, movies.*

THIS IS THE headquarters of the United Nations Educational, Scientific and Cultural Organization (UNESCO). The organization's aim is to contribute to international peace and security through education, science and culture.

UNESCO is a treasure trove of modern art, notably an enormous mural by Pablo Picasso, ceramics designed by Joan Miró and sculptures by Henry Moore.

Moore's *Reclining Figure* at UNESCO (erected 1958)

Eiffel Tower ⓰

Eiffel Tower from the Trocadéro

Oʀɪɢɪɴᴀʟʟʏ ʙᴜɪʟᴛ to impress visitors to the Universal Exhibition of 1889, the Eiffel Tower (Tour Eiffel) was meant to be a temporary addition to the Paris skyline. Designed by the engineer Gustave Eiffel, it was fiercely decried by 19th-century aesthetes. The poet Paul Verlaine would take a detour to avoid seeing it. The world's tallest building until 1931, when New York's Empire State Building was completed, the tower is now the symbol of Paris. Since its recent renovation and installation of new lighting it has never looked better.

Ironwork Pattern
According to Eiffel, he chose the complex pattern of pig-iron girders to stabilize the tower in strong winds. But Eiffel's design also quickly won admirers for its pleasing symmetry.

Elevator Engine Room
Eiffel emphasized safety over speed in choosing elevators for the Tower.

Sᴛᴀʀ Fᴇᴀᴛᴜʀᴇꜱ

★ **Eiffel Bust**

★ **Cineiffel**

★ **Hydraulic Elevator Mechanism**

★ **Viewing Gallery**

★ **Cineiffel**
This small museum tells the history of the Tower through a short film. It includes footage of famous personalities who have visited the Tower, including Charlie Chaplin, Josephine Baker and Adolf Hitler.

Tʜᴇ Dᴀʀɪɴɢ ᴀɴᴅ ᴛʜᴇ Dᴇʟᴜᴅᴇᴅ

The Tower has inspired many crazy stunts. It has been climbed by mountaineers, cycled down by a journalist, and used as a launch pad by parachutists and as a setting by trapeze artists. In 1912 a Parisian tailor named Reisfeldt attempted to fly from the parapet with only a modified cape for wings. He plunged to his death in front of a large crowd. According to the autopsy, he died of a heart attack before even touching the ground.

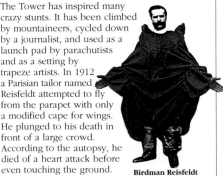

Birdman Reisfeldt

★ **Hydraulic Elevator Mechanism**
Still working, this 1889 mechanism helped lift the elevator from the second level to the top.

The third level, 899 ft (274 m) above the ground, can hold 400 people at a time.

★ **Viewing Gallery**
*On a clear day it is possible to see
for 45 miles (72 km), including a
distant view of Chartres Cathedral.*

Double-Decker Elevators
*During the tourist season, the
limited capacity of the elevators
means that it can take up to two
hours to reach the top. Taking the
elevators requires patience and a
good head for heights.*

THE TOWER IN FIGURES
• the top (including the antennae) is 1,046 ft (319 m) high
• the top is 6 in (15 cm) higher on hot days due to metal expansion
• 1,655 steps to the third level
• 2.5 million rivets hold tower together
• never sways more than 4 in (12 cm)
• 10,100 tons in weight
• 50 tons of paint are used every seven years

The second level is at 376 ft (115 m), separated from the first level by 359 steps, or a few minutes in the lift.

Jules Verne Restaurant is one of the best restaurants in Paris, offering superb food and panoramic views *(see p304).*

Workman building the Tower

The first level, at 187 ft (57 m) high, can be reached by elevator or by 360 steps. There is a post office here.

★ **Eiffel Bust**
*Eiffel's (1832–1923)
achievement was
crowned with the Légion
d'Honneur in 1889.
Another honor was the
bust by Antoine
Bourdelle, placed
beneath the Tower
in 1929.*

Gilded bronze
statues by a number
of sculptors
decorating the
central square of the
Palais de Chaillot

RER Avenue
Foche

11

BOULEVARD FLANDRIN

RUE DE LA FAISANDE

AVENUE

RER Avenue
Henri Martin

AVE HENRI MART

RUE

M La Muette

RUE D

RER Boulain
La Muet

RUE DES

RUE DE BOULAINVILLI

RUE

CHAILLOT QUARTER

HE VILLAGE of Chaillot was absorbed into Paris in the 19th century and transformed into an area rich in grand Second Empire avenues *(see pp32–3)*, opulent mansions and fascinating museums. Some of the avenues converge on the Place du Trocadéro, (renowned for its elegant cafés), which leads on to the Avenue du Président Wilson, with a greater concentration of museums

Sculptures at the base of the Chaillot pool

than any other street in Paris. Many of the sumptuous once-private mansions are occupied by embassies, including the imposing Vatican embassy, and by major company headquarters. Others are celebrated for their once-glittering gatherings of distinguished Parisians. To the west is the territory of the *haute bourgeoisie*, one of Paris's most exclusive, if staid, residential neighborhoods.

SIGHTS AT A GLANCE

Museums and Galleries
Cinémathèque Française ❷
Centre du Patrimoine et de l'Architecture ❸
Musée du Cinéma Henri Langlois ❹
Musée de l'Homme ❺
Musée de la Marine ❻
Musée du Vin ❽
Maison de Balzac ❾
Musée de Radio-France ❿
Musée de la Contrefaçon ⓫
Musée National d'Ennery ⓬
Musée Arménien ⓭
Musée National des Arts Asiatiques Guimet ⓮
Musée de la Mode et du Costume Palais Galliera ⓯
Musée d'Art Moderne de la Ville de Paris ⓰

Gardens
Jardins du Trocadéro ❼

Modern Architecture
Palais de Chaillot ❶

GETTING THERE
This area is served by the metro and RER system, with metro stations at Passy, Trocadéro and Iéna, and RER stations at Avenue Foch and Avenue Henri Martin. Among the bus routes through the area is No. 63, which travels along Avenue Georges Mandel and Avenue du Président Wilson.

SEE ALSO
- *Street Finder*, maps 3, 9–10
- *Where to Stay* pp278–9
- *Restaurants* pp296–8

KEY
	Street-by-Street map
M	Metro station
RER	RER station
P	Parking

Street by Street: Chaillot

THE CHAILLOT HILL, with its superb position overlooking the Seine, was the site chosen by Napoleon for "the biggest and most extraordinary" palace that was to be built for his son – but by the time of his downfall only a few ramparts had been completed. Today, the monumental Palais de Chaillot, with its two massive curved wings, stands on the site. From the terrace in front of the Palais there is a magnificent view over the Trocadéro gardens and the Seine to the Eiffel Tower in the distance.

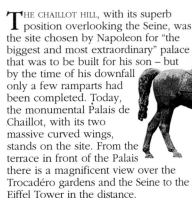

The statue of Marshal Ferdinand Foch, who led the Allies to victory in 1918, was unveiled on November 11, 1951. It was built by Robert Wlérick and Raymond Martin to commemorate the centenary of Foch's birth and the 33rd anniversary of the 1918 Armistice.

Metro Trocadéro

The Place du Trocadéro was created for the Universal Exhibition of 1878. Initially it was known as the Place du Roi-de-Rome, in honor of Napoleon's son.

★ **Musée de la Marine**
While concentrating on France's maritime history, this museum also has exhibits of navigational instruments ❻

Palais de Chaillot
This Neoclassical building was constructed for the World Fair of 1937. It replaced the Palais du Trocadéro, which was built in 1878 ❶

★ **Musée de l'Homme**
This chair from Benin is just one of the many artifacts from Africa that the museum possesses ❺

★ **Musée du Cinéma Henri Langlois**
Props from movies, including the mannequin for Mother Bates in Psycho, *are on display here* ❹

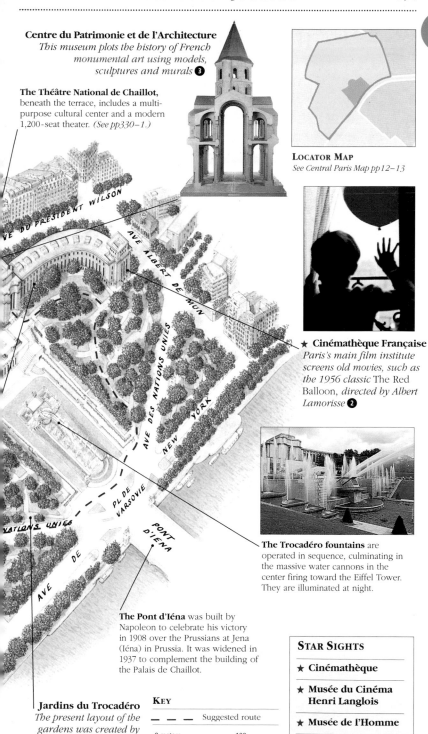

Centre du Patrimonie et de l'Architecture
This museum plots the history of French monumental art using models, sculptures and murals ❸

The Théâtre National de Chaillot, beneath the terrace, includes a multi-purpose cultural center and a modern 1,200-seat theater. *(See pp330–1.)*

LOCATOR MAP
See Central Paris Map pp12–13

★ **Cinémathèque Française**
Paris's main film institute screens old movies, such as the 1956 classic The Red Balloon, *directed by Albert Lamorisse* ❷

The Trocadéro fountains are operated in sequence, culminating in the massive water cannons in the center firing toward the Eiffel Tower. They are illuminated at night.

The Pont d'Iéna was built by Napoleon to celebrate his victory in 1908 over the Prussians at Jena (Iéna) in Prussia. It was widened in 1937 to complement the building of the Palais de Chaillot.

Jardins du Trocadéro
The present layout of the gardens was created by R. Lardat after the World's Fair of 1937 ❼

KEY

‒ ‒ ‒   Suggested route

0 meters   100

0 yards   100

STAR SIGHTS

★ **Cinémathèque**

★ **Musée du Cinéma Henri Langlois**

★ **Musée de l'Homme**

★ **Musée de la Marine**

Trocadéro fountains in front of the Palais de Chaillot

Palais de Chaillot ❶

17 Pl du Trocadéro 75016.
Map 9 C2. Ⓜ Trocadéro. **Open**
9:45am–5:15pm Wed–Mon.
🔢 🖼 🏛

THE PALAIS, with its huge, curved colonnaded wings each culminating in an immense pavilion, houses four museums, a theater and the Cinémathèque. Designed in Neoclassical style for the 1937 Paris Exhibition by Azéma, Louis-Auguste Boileau and Jacques Carlu, it is adorned with sculptures and bas-reliefs. On the walls of the pavilions there are gold inscriptions by the poet and essayist Paul Valéry.

The *parvis*, or square, situated between the two pavilions is decorated with large bronze sculptures and ornamental pools. On the terrace in front of the *parvis*

stand two bronzes, *Apollo* by Henri Bouchard and *Hercules* by Pommier. Stairways lead from the terrace to the Théâtre National de Chaillot *(see pp330–31)*, which, after World War II, enjoyed huge fame for its avant-garde productions.

Cinémathèque Française ❷

Palais de Chaillot, 7 Ave Albert de Mun
75016. **Map** 10 D2. 【 01 40 22 09
79. 🎬 01 56 26 01 01 for screenings.
Ⓜ Trocadéro, Iéna. **Adm charge**.
See **Entertainment** pp340–41.

DEVASTATED BY FIRE in 1997, this magnificent movie library has now been restored and reopened. Its archive contains the world's largest selection of movie classics. Frequent retrospectives offer an opportunity to catch some

of the all-time screen greats *(see p341* for the address of the *salle de cinéma)*. Both the Cinémathèque and the Musée du Cinéma Henri Langlois are due to move eventually to the nearby Palais de Tokyo.

Church model from the Paris suburb, Bagneux, in the Monuments Museum

Centre du Patrimonie et de l'Architecture ❸

Palais de Chaillot, Pl du Trocadéro
75016. **Map** 9 C2. 【 01 44 05 39 10.
Ⓜ Trocadéro. **Closed** until 2001 for renovation. **Adm charge**.
📷 🔢 🏛

OPENED IN 1789, this museum is devoted to French monumental art. It was the inspiration of Eugène Viollet-Le-Duc, who restored Notre-Dame in the 19th century. Here by means of copies, models and reproductions the visitor can follow the development of monumental sculpture, statuary and mural painting from the early Romanesque to the Gothic decoration of the great cathedrals such as St-Denis, Chartres and Notre-Dame.

Sequence from the movie *Journey to the Moon* directed by Méliés in 1902

Musée du Cinéma Henri Langlois ❹

Palais de Chaillot, 17 Pl du Trocadéro 75016. **Map** 9 C2. **[** 01 40 22 09 79. **M** Trocadéro. **Closed** for renovation until 2001. **Adm charge.** *compulsory. See **Entertainment** pp340–41.*

HENRI LANGLOIS was obsessed with the history of the cinema and put together this brilliantly eclectic collection, covering the evolution of moviemaking. It includes over 5,000 movie-related objects, with magic lanterns, shadow puppets, scripts, photographic stills, costumes worn by such stars as Rudolf Valentino and Marilyn Monroe. The museum has preserved many early movies and has several movie sets, notably a street scene from *Les Enfants du Paradis*, regularly voted France's greatest-ever movie, and a reconstruction of Georges Méliès' studios.

Robot in the Musée du Cinéma

Musée de la Marine ❻

Palais de Chaillot, 17 Pl du Trocadéro 75016. **Map** 9 C2. **[** 01 53 65 69 69. **M** Trocadéro. **Open** 10am– 6pm Wed–Mon (last adm: 5:30pm). **Closed** Jan 1, May 1, Dec 25. **Adm charge.** **Movies, videos. Reference library** by appointment only.

FRENCH MARITIME history from the days of the royal wooden warships to today's aircraft carriers and nuclear submarines is told through wonderfully exact scale models (most of them two centuries old), mementoes of naval heroes, paintings and navigational instruments. The museum was set up by Charles X in 1827 and was then moved to the Chaillot palace in 1943. The exhibits include Napoleon's barge, models of the fleet he assembled at Boulogne-sur-Mer in 1805 for his planned invasion of Britain, and displays on underwater exploration and fishing vessels.

Relief outside the Maritime Museum

Musée de l'Homme ❺

Palais de Chaillot, 17 Pl du Trocadéro 75016. **Map** 9 C2. **[** 01 44 05 72 72. **M** Trocadéro. **Open** 9:45am–5:15pm Wed–Mon. **Closed** public hols. **Adm charge.** **Exhibitions, movies.**

Gabon mask at Musée de l'Homme

SITUATED IN THE west wing of the Chaillot palace, this museum traces human evolution through a series of anthropological, archaeological and ethnologic displays. The anthropology section covers subjects as diverse as tattooing, mummification and head-shrinking.

The African exhibits are particularly striking, with frescoes from the Sahara, Central African sculpture, magical figures and musical instruments. Other highlights include Asian costumes, and a gigantic Easter Island head in the Oceania section.

Jardins du Trocadéro ❼

75016. **Map** 10 D2. **M** Trocadéro.

THESE LOVELY gardens cover 25 acres (10 ha). Their centerpiece is a long rectangular ornamental pool, bordered by stone and bronze-gilt statues that look spectacular at night when the fountains are illuminated. The statues include *Man* by P. Traverse and *Woman* by G. Braque, *Bull* by P. Jouve and *Horse* by G. Guyot. On either side of the pool, the slopes of the Chaillot hill gently lead down to the Seine and the Pont d'Iéna. There is a freshwater aquarium in the northeast corner of the gardens, which are richly laid out with trees, walkways, small streams and bridges – a romantic place for a quiet evening stroll.

Bridge in the Trocadéro gardens

Musée du Vin – Caveau des Echansons ❽

Rue des Eaux, 5 Sq Charles Dickens 75016. **Map** 9 C3. **[** 01 45 25 63 26. **M** Passy. **Open** 10am–6pm Tue–Sun. **Closed** Dec 25–Jan 1. **Adm charge.** *call to reserve.*

WAXWORK FIGURES illustrate the history of wine-making in these vaulted medieval cellars, once used by the monks of Passy. The exhibits include a collection of old wine bottles and glasses, as well as an array of scientific instruments that were used in the wine-making and bottling processes. There is also a wine bar, wine for sale and tours that include a wine-tasting session.

Plaque marking Balzac's house

Maison de Balzac ❾

47 Rue Raynouard 75016. **Map** 9 B3.
[01 42 24 56 38. **M** Passy, La
Muette. **Open** 10am–5.40pm
Tue–Sun (last adm: 5.30pm). **Closed**
public hols. **Adm charge.** 🔲 🔲 🔲

THE AUTHOR Honoré de
Balzac lived here from
1840 to 1847 under a false
name, Monsieur de Brugnol,
to avoid his numerous
creditors. During this time he
wrote many of his most
famous novels, among them
La Cousine Bette (1846).

The house now contains a
reference library, with some
of his original works, and a
museum with memorabilia
from his life. Many of the
rooms have drawings and
paintings portraying Balzac's
family and close friends. The
Madame Hanska room is
devoted to the memory of the
Russian woman who
corresponded with Balzac for
18 years and was his wife for
the five months before his
death in 1850.

The house has a back
entrance leading into the Rue
Berton, which was used to
evade unwelcome callers. Rue
Berton, with its ivy-covered
walls, has retained much of
its old, country-like charm.

Radio (1955) in radio museum

Musée de Radio-France ❿

116 Ave du Président-Kennedy
75016. **Map** 9 B4. **[** 01 42 30 21
80. **M** Ranelagh. **Open** for tours
only, Mon–Sat. **Closed** public hols.
Adm charge. ⊘ 🔲 🔲 10:30am,
11:30am, 2:30pm, 3:30pm, 4:30pm
(groups by reservation only).

RADIO-FRANCE HOUSE is an
impressive building de-
signed by Henri Bernard in
1963 as the headquarters of
the state-run Radio-France.
The largest single structure in
France, it is made up of
three incomplete
concentric circular
constructions with a
rectangular tower. The
building covers an area
of 5 acres (2 ha).

Here, in the 60
studios and main
auditorium, French
radio programs are
produced. Visitors
can get a fascinating
insight to how
programs are made while
visiting the museum, which
traces the history of commun-
ications from the first Chappe
telegraph of 1793 to the latest
electronic transistors.

Musée de la Contrefaçon ⓫

16 Rue de la Faisanderie 75016.
Map 3 A5. **[** 01 52 26 14 00. **M**
Porte Dauphine. **Open** 2pm–5pm Mon–
Thu, 9:30am–noon Fri, 2pm–6pm Sun.
Closed public hols. **Adm charge.** 🔲

FRENCH COGNAC and perfume
producers, and the luxury
trade in general, have been
plagued for years by counter-
feiters operating around the
world. This museum was set
up by the manufacturers'
union and illustrates the
history of this type of fraud,
which has been going on
since Roman times. Among
the impressive display of
forgeries are copies of Louis
Vuitton luggage, Cartier
watches and fake wine from
the Narbonne region. The
museum also has a display
on the fate awaiting anyone
who may be tempted to
imitate a product.

Musée National d'Ennery ⓬

59 Ave Foch 75016. **Map** 3 B5.
[01 45 53 57 96. **M** Porte
Dauphine. **Closed** for renovation until
further notice. 🔲

THIS MANSION, which dates
from the Second Empire
period, contains two highly
personal museums of
precious objets d'art. Both
have been recently
renovated. The first
museum contains a huge
collection of Chinese and
Japanese items
dating from the
17th to the 19th
centuries.
Assembled by
Adolphe d'Ennery,
the 19th-century
dramatist and
collector of Far
Eastern art, this
display includes
human and
animal figures,
furniture,

**Musée d'Ennery Chinese
vase (about 18th century)**

Japanese ceramic boxes, and
hundreds of *netsuke* – small,
carved belt ornaments made
of bone, wood or ivory.

Armenian crown (19th century)

Musée Arménien ⓭

59 Ave Foch 75016. **Map** 3 B5.
[01 45 53 57 96. **M** Porte
Dauphine. **Open** 2pm–6pm Thu &
Sun. **Closed** public hols and Aug.

THE GROUND FLOOR of No. 59
Avenue Foch houses the
Armenian Museum, founded
after World War II. Despite its
small size the collection has
many fascinating treasures,
including church plates,
miniatures, silverware,
ceramics, carpets and
contemporary paintings.

Entrance to the Guimet Museum

Musée National des Arts Asiatiques Guimet ⑭

6 Pl d'Iéna 75116. **Map** 10 D1.
【 01 45 05 00 98. M Iéna. **Closed**
for restoration until 2000. **Adm
charge**. 📷 ♿ 🎫 🛍 Additional
galleries at 19 Ave d'Iéna (call to
check opening hours).

ONE OF THE world's leading
museums of Asian art, the
Guimet has the finest
collection of Cambodian
(Khmer) art in the West. It
was originally set up in Lyon
in 1879 by the industrialist
and orientalist Emile Guimet
and moved to Paris in 1884. It
includes an Asian research
center. On display are several
rare, large Khmer temple
sculptures and many statues
of Buddha from Japan, India,
Vietnam and Indonesia. Other
highlights include Chinese
bronzes and lacquerware.

Musée de la Mode et du Costume Palais Galliera ⑮

10 Ave Pierre 1er de Serbie 75116.
Map 10 E1. 【 01 47 20 85 23.
M Iéna, Alma, Marceau. **Open** for
exhibitions only, 10am–6pm Tue–Sun.
Adm charge. **Children's room**.

DEVOTED TO THE evolution
of fashion, this museum
is housed in the Renaissance-
style palace built for the
Duchesse Maria de Ferrari
Galliera in 1892. The
collection has more than
100,000 outfits, from the 18th
century to the present day.
Some, from more recent
times, have been donated by
such fashionable women as
Baronne Hélène de Roths-
child and the late Princess
Grace of Monaco. Eminent
couturiers such as Balmain
and Balenciaga have donated
their designs to the museum.
Owing to the fragility of the
fashions, the exhibits are
displayed in rotation in two
major exhibitions per year.
These highlight a particular
couturier's career or explore a
single theme.

Musée d'Art Moderne de la Ville de Paris ⑯

11 Ave du Président-Wilson 75016.
Map 10 E1. 【 01 53 67 40 00.
M Iéna. **Open** 10am–5:30pm
Tue–Fri; 10am–6:45pm Sat & Sun.
Adm charge. ♿ 🎫 for certain
exhibitions. 🛍 🍴 **Movies**.

Sculptures by Gabriel Forestier on the doorway of the museum

THIS lively museum covers
the significant trends in
20th-century art and is located
in the east wing of the Palais
de Tokyo. Highlights include
Raoul Dufy's gigantic mural,
The Spirit of Electricity
(created for the 1937 World
Fair) and Matisse's *The Dance*
(1932). The Fauves are
particularly well represented,
with many paintings by
Georges Rouault.

Garden and rear facade of the Palais Galliera

CHAMPS-ELYSÉES

TWO GREAT STREETS dominate this area: the Avenue des Champs-Elysées and the Rue St-Honoré. The former is the capital's most famous thoroughfare. Its breadth is spectacular. The pavements are wide and cafés, movie theaters and shops attract throngs of people, who come to eat and shop but also to see and to be seen. Rond Point des Champs-Elysées is the pretty end, with shady chestnut trees and pavements colorfully bordered by flower beds. The avenue is a place of great parades as well as stunning street fashion and a hedonistic lifestyle. Luxury and political power are nearby. Five-star hotels, fine restaurants plus upscale shops line the streets and avenues radiating off the Champs-Elysées. And along the Rue St-Honoré are the impressive, heavily guarded Palais de l'Elysée, the sumptuous town mansions of business executives, and the many embassies and consulates.

Ornate lamp-post on Pont Alexandre III

SIGHTS AT A GLANCE

Historic Buildings and Streets
Palais de l'Elysée ⑤

Avenue Montaigne ⑥
Avenue des Champs-Elysées ⑧
Place Charles de Gaulle (l'Etoile) ⑨

Monuments
Arc de Triomphe pp208–9 ⑩

Bridges
Pont Alexandre III ①

Museums and Galleries
Grand Palais ②
Palais de la Découverte ③
Petit Palais ④
Musée Jacquemart-André ⑦

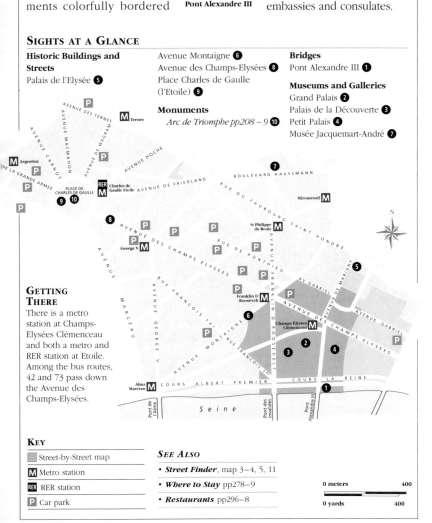

GETTING THERE
There is a metro station at Champs-Elysées Clémenceau and both a metro and RER station at Etoile. Among the bus routes, 42 and 73 pass down the Avenue des Champs-Elysées.

KEY

▦	Street-by-Street map
Ⓜ	Metro station
RER	RER station
Ⓟ	Car park

SEE ALSO

0 meters   400
0 yards   400

View of the Arc de Triomphe at night

Street by Street: Champs-Elysées

THE FORMAL GARDENS that line the Champs-Elysées from the Place de la Concorde to the Rond-Point have changed little since they were laid out by the architect Jacques Hittorff in 1838. They were used as the setting for the World Fair of 1855, which included the Palais de l'Industrie, Paris's response to London's Crystal Palace. The Palais was later replaced by the Grand Palais and Petit Palais, which were created as a showpiece of the Third Republic for the Universal Exhibition of 1900. They sit on either side of an impressive vista stretching from the Place Clémenceau across the elegant curve of the Pont Alexandre III to the Invalides.

The Théâtre du Rond-Point is the home of the Renaud-Barrault Company. There are plaques on the back door of the theater representing Napoleon's campaigns.

Metro Franklin D. Roosevelt Ⓜ

Avenue Montaigne
Christian Dior and other haute couture houses are based in this chic avenue ❻

★ Grand Palais
Designed by Charles Girault, this grand 19th-century exhibition hall is still used for major displays ❷

The Lasserre restaurant is decorated in the style of a luxurious ocean liner from the 1930s.

ROOSEVELT

AVE G⁺ EISENHOWER

RUE JEAN GOUJON

FRANKLIN

RUE FRANÇOIS PREMIER

AVE

PL DU CANADA

COURS   L.

PONT DES INVALIDES

STAR SIGHTS

- ★ **Avenue des Champs-Elysées**
- ★ **Grand Palais**
- ★ **Petit Palais**
- ★ **Pont Alexandre III**

Palais de la Découverte
Outside this museum of scientific discoveries is a pair of equestrian statues ❸

KEY

– – – Suggested route

| 0 meters | 100 |
| 0 yards | 100 |

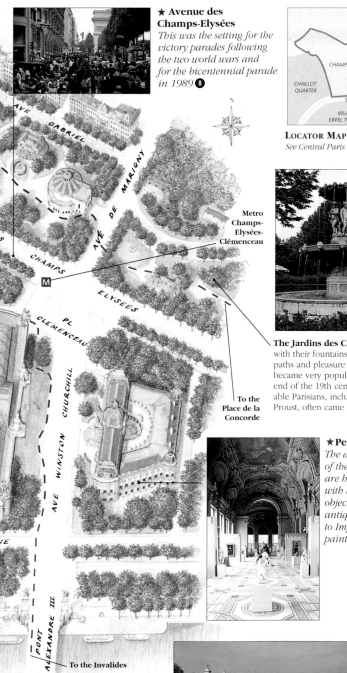

★ **Avenue des Champs-Elysées**
This was the setting for the victory parades following the two world wars and for the bicentennial parade in 1989 ❽

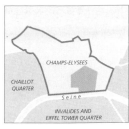

LOCATOR MAP
See Central Paris Map pp12–13

Metro Champs-Elysées-Clémenceau

To the Place de la Concorde

The Jardins des Champs-Elysées, with their fountains, flower beds, paths and pleasure pavilions, became very popular toward the end of the 19th century. Fashionable Parisians, including Marcel Proust, often came here.

★ **Petit Palais**
The art collections of the city of Paris are housed here, with a range of objects – from antique sculptures to Impressionist paintings ❹

To the Invalides

★ **Pont Alexandre III**
This bridge's four columns help anchor the piers that absorb the immense forces generated by such a large single-span structure ❶

Pont Alexandre III ❶

75008. **Map** 11 A1. Ⓜ *Champs-Elysées-Clémenceau.*

T HIS IS PARIS'S prettiest bridge, with exuberant Art Nouveau decoration of lamps, cherubs, nymphs and winged horses at either end. It was built between 1896 and 1900, in time for the Universal Exhibition, and it was named after Tsar Alexander III (father of Nicholas II), who laid the foundation stone in October 1896.

The style of the bridge reflects that of the Grand Palais, to which it leads on the Right Bank. The construction of the bridge is a marvel of 19th-century engineering, consisting of a single-span steel arch that is 18 ft (6 m) high. The design was subject to strict controls that prevented the bridge from obscuring the view of the Champs-Elysées or the Invalides. So, today, you can still enjoy magnificent views from here.

Pont Alexandre III

Grand Palais ❷

Porte A, Ave Eisenhower 75008. **Map** 11 A1. 📞 *01 44 13 17 30.* Ⓜ *Champs-Elysées-Clémenceau.* **Open** *10am–8pm Thu–Mon, 10am–10pm Wed.* **Adm charge.** 🚫 ♿ 📷 *Wed pm & Sat pm.* 🎧 🖥 🚪

B UILT AT THE SAME time as the Petit Palais and the Pont Alexandre III, the exterior of this massive palace combines an imposing Classical stone facade with a riot of Art Nouveau ironwork. It has a splendid glass roof,

with Récipon's colossal bronze statues of flying horses and chariots at its four corners. The building looks best at night, when the glass roof glows with the lights from inside and the statues are silhouetted against the sky. The great hall and its glass dome can be seen from inside during temporary exhibitions (including art exhibitions), which are held in the Galeries Nationales du Grand Palais.

The palace has a major police station in the basement which helps protect the exhibits on show.

Palais de la Découverte

Palais de la Découverte ❸

Ave Franklin D Roosevelt 75008. **Map** 11 A1. 📞 *01 40 74 80 00.* Ⓜ *Franklin D Roosevelt.* **Open** *9:30am–6pm Tue–Sat; 10am–7pm Sun.* **Closed** *Jan 1, May 1, Jul 14, Aug 15, Dec 25.* **Adm charge.** 📷 *by permission.* 🚪 🖥

O PENED IN A WING of the Grand Palais for the World Fair of 1937, this museum of scientific discoveries was an immediate success and has continued to be popular ever since. The displays explain the basics of all the sciences.

Entrance to the Petit Palais

Petit Palais ❹

Ave Winston Churchill 75008. **Map** 11 B1. 📞 *01 42 65 12 73.* Ⓜ *Champs-Elysées-Clémenceau.* **Open** *10am–5:40pm Tue–Sun.* **Closed** *public hols.* **Adm charge.** 📷 🎞 *for exhibitions.*

B UILT FOR the Universal Exhibition in 1900, to stage a major display of French art, this jewel of a building now houses the Musée des Beaux-Arts de la Ville de Paris. Arranged around a pretty semicircular courtyard and garden, the palace is similar in style to the Grand Palais and has Ionic columns, a grand porch and a dome echoing that of the Invalides across the river.

The exhibits are divided into sections: the Dutuit Collection of medieval and Renaissance objets d'art, paintings and drawings; the Tuck Collection of 18th-century furniture and objets d'art; and the City of Paris collections of works by the French artists Jean Ingres, Eugène Delacroix and Gustave Courbet, as well as those by the landscape painters of the Barbizon School and the Impressionists.

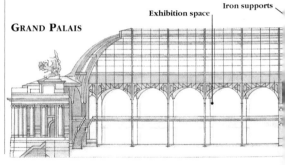

GRAND PALAIS

Exhibition space

Iron supports

Palais de l'Elysée ⑤

55 Rue du Faubourg-St-Honoré
75008. **Map** 5 B5. **M** *St-Philippe-du-Roule.* **Not open** to the public.

S ET AMID SPLENDID English-
style gardens, the Elysée
Palace was built in 1718 and
has been the official
residence of the president of
the Republic since 1873.
    In the 19th century it
was occupied by
Napoleon's sister,
Caroline, and her
husband, Murat. Two
charming rooms
have been preserved
from this period: the
Salon Murat and the
Salon d'Argent.
General de Gaulle
used to give press
conferences in the
Hall of Mirrors.
Today, the
president's
modernized
apartments can be found on
the first floor opposite the
Rue de l'Elysée.

Elysée guard

Avenue Montaigne ⑥

75008. **Map** 10 F1. **M** *Franklin D. Roosevelt.*

I N THE 19TH century this
avenue was famous for its
dance halls and its Winter
Garden, where Parisians went
to hear Adolphe Sax play his
newly invented saxophone.
Today it is still one of Paris's
most fashionable
streets, bustling with
restaurants, cafés,
hotels and smart
boutiques.

Inside the Musée Jacquemart-André

Musée Jacquemart-André ⑦

158 Blvd Haussmann 75008. **Map** 5
A4. **C** 01 45 62 39 94. **M** *Miromesnil,
St-Philippe-du-Roule.* **Open** 10am–
6pm daily. 🚫 🅿 🔊

T HIS MUSEUM is known for
its fine collection of Italian
Renaissance and French 18th-
century works of art. It
includes Tiepolo frescoes of
great beauty; works by
Andrea Mantegna; Paolo
Uccello's masterpiece *St.
George and the Dragon*
(about 1435); 18th-century
tapestries and furniture; and
paintings by François Boucher
and Jean Honoré Fragonard.

Avenue des Champs-Elysées ⑧

75008. **Map** 5 A5. **M** *Franklin D.
Roosevelt, George V.*

P ARIS'S MOST famous and
popular thoroughfare had
its beginnings in about 1667,
when the landscape garden

designer, André Le Nôtre,
extended the royal view from
the Tuileries by creating a
tree-lined avenue that
eventually became known as
the Champs-Elysées (Elysian
Fields). It has been the
"triumphal way" (as the
French call it) ever since the
homecoming of Napoleon's
body from St. Helena in 1840.
With the addition of cafés and
restaurants in the second half
of the 19th century, the
Champs-Elysées became the
place in which to be seen.

Place Charles de Gaulle (l'Etoile) ⑨

75008. **Map** 4 D4. **M** *Charles de
Gaulle-Etoile.*

K NOWN AS the Place de
l'Etoile until the death of
Charles de Gaulle in 1969, the
area is still referred to simply
as l'Etoile, the star. The
present *place* was laid out in
accordance with Baron
Haussmann's plans of 1854
(see pp32–3). For motorists, it
is the ultimate challenge.

Arc de Triomphe from the west

Arc de Triomphe ⑩

See pp208–9.

Quadriga (chariot
and four horses)
by Récipon

Glass cupola

Arc de Triomphe ⓾

The east facade of the Arc de Triomphe

AFTER HIS greatest victory, the Battle of Austerlitz in 1805, Napoleon promised his men, "You shall go home beneath triumphal arches." The first stone of what was to become the world's most famous triumphal arch was laid the following year. But disruptions to architect Jean Chalgrin's plans and the demise of Napoleonic power delayed the completion of this monumental building until 1836. Standing 164 ft (50 m) high, the arch is now the customary starting point for victory celebrations and parades.

The Battle of Aboukir, a bas-relief by Seurre the Elder, depicts a scene of Napoleon's victory over the Turkish army in 1799.

Triumph of Napoleon
J.P. Cortot's high-relief celebrates the Treaty of Vienna peace agreement of 1810.

Thirty shields just below the Arc's roof each bear the name of a victorious Napoleonic battle fought in either Europe or Africa.

East facade

The frieze was executed by Rude, Brun, Jacquet, Laitié, Caillouette and Seurre the Elder. This east facade shows the departure of the French armies for new campaigns. The west side shows their return.

STAR FEATURES

★ **Departure of the Volunteers in 1792**

★ **Tomb of the Unknown Soldier**

★ **Tomb of the Unknown Soldier**
An unknown French soldier from World War I is buried here.

TIMELINE

1806 Napoleon commissions Chalgrin to build triumphal Arc

1836 Louis Philippe completes the Arc

1885 Victor Hugo's body lies in state under the Arc

1944 Liberation of Paris. De Gaulle leads the crowd from the Arc

1800	1850	1900	1950

1815 Downfall of Napoleon. Work on Arc ceases

1840 Napoleon's cortège passes under the Arc

1919 Victory parade of Allied armies through the Arc

NAPOLEON'S NUPTIAL PARADE

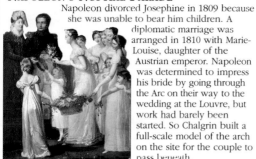

Napoleon divorced Josephine in 1809 because she was unable to bear him children. A diplomatic marriage was arranged in 1810 with Marie-Louise, daughter of the Austrian emperor. Napoleon was determined to impress his bride by going through the Arc on their way to the wedding at the Louvre, but work had barely been started. So Chalgrin built a full-scale model of the arch on the site for the couple to pass beneath.

VISITORS' CHECKLIST

Pl Charles de Gaulle. **Map** 4 D4.
[C] 01 55 37 73 77. [M] Charles
de Gaulle–Étoile. 22, 30, 31,
73, 92 to Pl C de Gaulle. [P] off
Pl C de Gaulle. **Museum open**
Apr–Sep: 9:30am–11pm daily;
Oct–Mar:10am–10:30pm daily
(last adm 30 mins earlier). **Closed**
Jan 1, May 1, Jul 14, Nov 11, Dec
25. **Adm charge.**

The viewing platform affords one of the best views in Paris, overlooking the grand Champs-Elysées on one side. Beyond the other side is La Défense.

General Marceau's Funeral
Marceau defeated the Austrians in 1795, only to be killed in fighting them the next year.

The Battle of Austerlitz by Gechter shows Napoleon's army breaking up the ice on the Satschan lake in Austria to drown thousands of enemy troops.

Officers of the Imperial Army are listed on the walls of the smaller arches.

Entrance to museum

★ **Departure of the Volunteers in 1792**
François Rude's work shows citizens leaving to defend the nation.

Place Charles de Gaulle
Twelve avenues radiate from the Arc at the center. Some bear the names of important French military leaders, such as avenues Marceau and Foch.
(See pp32–3.)

OPÉRA QUARTER

THE OPERA QUARTER bustles with bankers and stockbrokers, newspaper workers and shoppers, theatergoers and sightseers. Much of its 19th-century grandeur survives in the Grands Boulevards of Baron Haussmann's urban design. These are still a favorite with thousands of both Parisian and foreign promenaders, drawn by the profusion of shops and department stores, which range from the exclusively expensive to the popular.

Much more of the area's older character can be found in the many *passages*, delightful narrow shopping arcades with steel-and-glass roofs, remnants of another age. Fashion's bad boy, Jean-Paul Gaultier, has a shop in the smartest one, Galerie Vivienne. But more authentically old-style Parisian are the Passage des Panoramas and the Passage Jouffroy; the Passage Verdeau, with its old cameras and comics; and the tiny Passage des Princes, a pipe smoker's dream. Two of the city's finest food shops are in this area: Fauchon and Hédiard are noted for their mouthwatering displays of costly mustards, jams, spices, pâtés and sauces. The area still has a reputation as an important press center, although *Le Monde* has recently moved out, and it has a history of movies and theater. It was here in 1895 that the Lumière brothers held the world's first public film show and that the Opéra de Paris Garnier provided the setting for grand theatrical events.

Les Coulisses de l'Opéra (1889) by J Beraud

SIGHTS AT A GLANCE

Historic Buildings and Streets
Place de la Madeleine **2**
Les Grands Boulevards **3**
Palais de la Bourse **9**
Avenue de l'Opéra **12**

Churches
La Madeleine **1**

Opera Houses
Opéra de Paris Garnier **4**

Museums and Galleries
Musée de l'Opéra **5**
Musée Grévin **7**

Musée du Cabinet des Médailles et des Antiques **10**
Bibliothèque Nationale **11**

Shops
Drouot (Hôtel des Ventes) **6**
Les Galeries **8**

GETTING THERE
This area is served by the metro and RER systems. Metro lines 3, 7 and 8 serve the station at the Opéra, and the RER Line A stops at Auber. Among the bus routes passing through the area, 42 and 52 travel along Boulevard Madeleine, and 21, 27 and 29 along Avenue de l'Opéra.

KEY

▨	Street-by-Street map
M	Metro station
RER	RER station
P	Parking

SEE ALSO
• *Street Finder*, map 5–6
• *Where to Stay* pp278–9
• *Restaurants* pp296–8

0 meters   400
0 yards   400

Lamppost statues of the Vestal Virgins outside the Opéra de Paris Garnier

Street by Street: Opéra Quarter

I T HAS BEEN SAID that if you sit for long enough at the Café de la Paix (opposite the Opéra de Paris Garnier) the whole world will pass by. During the day, the area is a mixture of commerce – France's top three banks are based here – and tourism. The shops range from the chic, in the elegant Place de l'Opéra, to the more popular, such as the Marks & Spencer store just off Place Diaghilev. In the

Statue by Gurnery on the Opéra

evening, the theaters and movie houses attract a totally different crowd, and the cafés along the Boulevard des Capucines throb with life.

Place de la Madeleine
On the north side of the square, the windows of the Fauchon shop are filled with food from around the world ❷

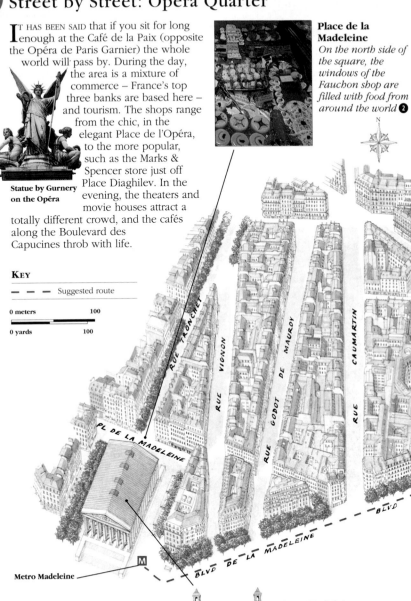

KEY

– – – Suggested route

| 0 meters | 100 |
| 0 yards | 100 |

Metro Madeleine

PL DE LA MADELEINE

RUE TRONCHET

RUE VIGNON

RUE GODOT DE MAUROY

RUE CAUMARTIN

BLVD DE LA MADELEINE

M

★ **La Madeleine**
The final design of this church, which is dedicated to Mary Magdalene, differs from this original model, now in the Musée Carnavalet (see pp96–7) ❶

STAR SIGHTS

★ **La Madeleine**

★ **Boulevard des Capucines**

★ **Opéra de Paris Garnier**

★ **Opéra de Paris Garnier**
With a mixture of styles ranging from Classical to Baroque, this building from 1875 has come to symbolize the opulence of the Second Empire ❹

Metro Chaussée d'Antin

Musée de l'Opéra
Famous artists' work is often shown in temporary exhibition rooms ❺

The Place de l'Opéra
was designed by Baron Haussmann and is one of Paris's busiest intersections.

Metro Opéra

The Café de la Paix maintains its old-fashioned ways and still has its 19th-century decor, designed by Garnier. *(See p311.)*

Harry's Bar was named after Harry MacElhone, a bartender who bought the bar in 1913. Past regulars have included F. Scott Fitzgerald and Ernest Hemingway.

★ **Boulevard des Capucines**
At No. 14 a plaque tells of the world's first public screening of a movie, by the Lumière brothers in 1895; it took place in the Salon Indien, a room in the Grand Café ❸

Charles Marochetti's *Mary Magdalene Ascending to Heaven* (1837) behind the high altar of La Madeleine

La Madeleine ❶

Pl de la Madeleine 75008. **Map** 5 C5.
☎ 01 44 51 69 00. Ⓜ *Madeleine*.
Open 7:30am–7pm Mon–Sat;
7:45am–7pm Sun. ✝ *frequent*.
Concerts. 📷 🎫 *See*
Entertainment pp333–4.

THIS CHURCH, which is dedicated to Mary Magdalene, is one of the best-known buildings in Paris because of its prominent location and great size. It stands at one end of the curve of the Grands Boulevards and is the architectural counterpoint of the Palais-Bourbon (home of the Assemblée Nationale, the French parliament) across the river. It was started in 1764 but not consecrated until 1845. There were proposals to convert it into a parliament, a bank and a Temple of Glory to Napoleon's army.

The building that stands today is based on Barthélemy Vignon's design for Napoleon's Temple of Glory, commissioned in 1806 after the Battle of Jena (Iéna). A colonnade of Corinthian columns encircles the building and supports a sculptured frieze. The bas-reliefs on the bronze doors are by Henri de Triqueti and show the Ten Commandments.

Fauchon tin

The inside is lavishly decorated with marble and gilt and has some fine sculpture, notably François Rude's *Baptism of Christ*.

Place de la Madeleine ❷

75008. **Map** 5 C5.
Ⓜ *Madeleine*. **Flower market open** 8am–7:30pm Tue–Sat.

THE PLACE de la Madeleine was created at the same time as the Madeleine church. It is a food lover's paradise, with many shops specializing in luxuries such as truffles, champagne, caviar and handmade chocolates. Fauchon, the millionaires' supermarket, is situated at No. 26 and stocks more than 20,000 items (see pp322–3). The large house at No. 9 is where Marcel Proust spent his childhood. To the east of La Madeleine is a small flower market (see p326).

Scenery backdrop operated by pulley

OPÉRA DE PARIS GARNIER

Backstage area | **Stage**

Les Grands Boulevards ❸

75002 & 75009. **Map** 6 D5–7C5.
Ⓜ Madeleine, Opéra, Richelieu-Drouot, Montmartre.

EIGHT BROAD boulevards – Madeleine, Capucines, Italiens, Montmartre, Poissonnière, Bonne Nouvelle, St-Denis and St-Martin – run from La Madeleine to the Place de la République. They were constructed in the 17th century to turn obsolete city fortifications into fashionable promenades – *boulevard* came from the Middle Dutch *bulwerc*, which means "bulwark" or "rampart." The boulevards became so famous in the 19th century that the name *boulevardier* was coined for one who cuts a figure on the boulevards.

Around the Madeleine church and the Opéra it is still possible to gain an impression of what the Grands Boulevards looked like in their heyday, lined with cafés and chic shops. Elsewhere, most of the cafés and restaurants have long since gone, and the old facades are now hidden by neon advertising.

However, the Grands Boulevards and the nearby department stores on the Boulevard Haussmann continue to attract large crowds.

Boulevard des Italiens

Opéra de Paris Garnier ❹

Pl de l'Opéra 75009. **Map** 6 E4.
Ⓒ 01 40 01 22 63. Ⓜ Opéra.
Open 10am–5pm daily. **Closed** public hols. **Adm charge.** ⬚
See **Entertainment** pp334–6.

SOMETIMES COMPARED to a giant wedding cake, this sumptuous building was designed by Charles Garnier for Napoleon III; construction started in 1862. Its unique appearance is due to a mixture of materials (including stone, marble and bronze) and styles, ranging from Classical to Baroque, with a multitude of columns, friezes and sculptures on the exterior. The building took 13 years to complete, with interruptions during the Prussian War and the uprising of 1871, finally opening in 1875.

In 1858 Orsini had attempted to assassinate the emperor outside the old opera house. This prompted Garnier to include a pavilion on the east side of the new building, with a curved ramp leading up to it so that the sovereign could safely step out of his carriage into the suite of rooms adjoining the royal box.

The functions performed by each part of the building are reflected in the structure. Behind the flat-topped foyer, the cupola sits above the auditorium, while the triangular pediment that rises up behind the cupola marks the front of the stage. Underneath the building is a small lake, which provided inspiration for the phantom's hiding place in Paul Leroux's *Phantom of the Opera*.

Inside, don't miss the magnificent Grand Staircase, made of white marble with a balustrade of red and green marble, and the Grand Foyer, with its domed ceiling covered with mosaics. The five-tiered auditorium is a riot of red velvet, plaster cherubs and gold leaf, which contrast with the false ceiling painted by Marc Chagall in 1964.

Most operas are now performed in the new Opéra Bastille *(see p98)*, but the ballet remains here.

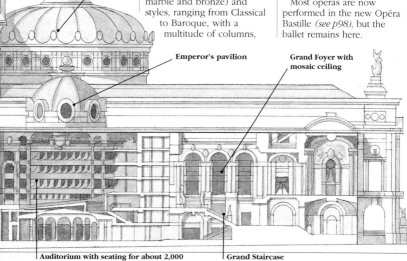

Statue by Millet

Copper-green roofed cupola

Emperor's pavilion

Grand Foyer with mosaic ceiling

Auditorium with seating for about 2,000

Grand Staircase

Sign outside the Musée Grévin

Musée de l'Opéra ❺

Pl de l'Opéra 75009. **Map** 6 E5. **C** 01
40 01 17 89. **M** Opéra. **Open** 10am–
5pm daily (Jul–Aug: 10am–6pm).
Closed Jan 1, May 1, and during
performances. 01 40 01 22 63.

The entrance to this small,
charming museum was ori-
ginally the emperor's private
entrance to the Opéra. The
museum relates the history
of opera through a large
collection of musical scores,
manuscripts, photographs and
artists' memorabilia, such as
the Russian dancer Vaslav
Nijinsky's ballet slippers and
tarot cards. Other exhibits
include models of stage sets
and busts of major composers.
The museum also houses a
superb library, containing
books and manuscripts on
theater, dance and music, as
well as more memorabilia.

Drouot (Hôtel des Ventes) ❻

9 Rue Drouot 75009. **Map** 6 F4.
C 01 48 00 20 20. **M** Richelieu Drouot.
Open 11am–6pm Mon–Sat.
See **Shops and Markets** pp324–5.

This is the leading French
auction house (Hôtel des
Ventes), and it takes its name
from the Comte de Drouot,
who was Napoleon's aide-de-
camp. There has been an
auction house on the site
since 1858, and in 1860
Napoleon III visited the Hôtel
to purchase some earthen-
ware pots. It has been known
as the Nouveau Drouot since
the 1970s, when the existing
building was demolished and
replaced with the present less
inspiring structure.
Although overshadowed
internationally by those at
Christie's and Sotheby's,
auctions at the Nouveau
Drouot nevertheless provide
a lively spectacle and involve
a fascinating range of rare
objects. Its presence in the
area has attracted many
antiques and stamp shops,
located in the nearby Galeries.

Musée Grévin ❼

10 Blvd Montmartre 75009.
Map 6 F4. **C** 01 47 70 85 05.
M Rue Montmartre. **Open** 1pm–
7pm daily, 10am–7pm school hols
(last adm: 6pm). **Adm charge.**

This waxwork museum was
founded in 1882 and is
now a Paris landmark, on a
par with Madame Tussaud's in

London. It contains tableaux
of vivid historical scenes (such
as Louis XIV at Versailles and
the arrest of Louis XVI),
distorting mirrors and the
Cabinet Fantastique, which
includes regular conjuring
shows given by a live
magician. Famous figures
from the worlds of art, sports
and politics are also on
display, with new celebrities
replacing faded stars.

Galerie Vivienne

Les Galeries ❽

75002. **Map** 6 F5. **M** Bourse.

The early 19th-century
Parisian shopping arcades
(known as galeries or
passages) are located between
the Boulevard Montmartre
and the Rue St-Marc (the
extensive Passage des
Panoramas). Other arcades
are found between the Rue
du Quatre Septembre and the
Rue des Petits Champs.
At the time of their
construction, the Galeries
represented a new traffic-free
area for commerce, work-
shops and apartments. They
fell into disuse but were
dramatically revamped in the
1970s and now house an
eclectic mixture of small
shops selling anything from
designer jewelry to rare
books. They have high,
vaulted roofs of iron and
glass. One of the most
charming is the Galerie
Vivienne (off the Rue
Vivienne or the Rue des Petits
Champs), with its mosaic floor
and excellent tearoom.

Model of a set for Les Huguenots (1875) in the Musée de l'Opéra

The colonnaded Neoclassical facade of the Palais de la Bourse

Palais de la Bourse ❾

(Bourse des Valeurs) 4 Pl de la Bourse 75002. **Map** 6 F5. [*01 40 41 62 20 (tours).* **M** *Bourse.* **Open** *1:15pm–5pm Mon–Fri (last adm 4pm).* ✗ **Adm charge.** ✔ *compulsory.* **Movies.**

THIS NEOCLASSICAL temple of commerce was commissioned by Napoleon and was home to the French Stock Exchange from 1826 to 1987. Today the French stock market is fully computerized. The hectic floor trading of the Palais de la Bourse has been considerably reduced and is limited to the Matif (the futures market) and the Monep (the traded options market).

Sainte-Chapelle cameo in Musée du Cabinet

Musée du Cabinet des Médailles et des Antiques ❿

58 Rue de Richelieu 75002. **Map** 6 F5. [*01 47 03 83 32.* **M** *Bourse.* **Open** *1pm–5:45pm Mon–Fri, 1pm–4:45pm Sat, noon–6pm Sun.* **Closed** *public hols.* **Adm charge.** ✗ ▯

THIS VALUABLE collection of coins, medals, jewels and Classical objects is part of the Bibliothèque Nationale.

Exhibits include the Berthouville Treasure (1st-century Gallo-Roman silverware) and the Grand Camée (cameo) from Sainte-Chapelle.

Bibliothèque Nationale ⓫

58 Rue de Richelieu 75002. **Map** 6 F5. [*01 47 03 81 26.* **M** *Bourse.* **Not open** to the public.

THE BIBLIOTHEQUE Nationale (National Library) originated with the manuscript collections of medieval kings, to which a copy of every French book printed since 1537 has, by law, been added. The collection, which includes two Gutenberg bibles, is partially housed in this complex, created in the 17th century by Cardinal Mazarin. Despite the recent removal of the printed books, periodicals, and CD Roms to the newly-built Bibliothèque Nationale de France *(see p246)* at Tolbiac, the rue Richelieu buildings still contain a huge variety of items, including original manuscripts by Victor Hugo and Marcel Proust, among others. The library has the richest collection of engravings and photographs in the world, and departments for maps and plans, theatrical arts, and musical scores. Sadly, the 19th-century reading room is not open to the public.

Bibliothèque Nationale

Avenue de l'Opéra ⓬

75001 & 75002. **Map** 6 E5. **M** *Opéra, Pyramides.*

THIS BROAD avenue is a notable example of Baron Haussmann's dramatic modernization of Paris in the 1860s and 1870s *(see pp32–3)*. Much of the medieval city was swept away to make way for the wide thoroughfares of today. The Avenue de l'Opéra, which runs from the Louvre to the Opéra de Paris Garnier, was completed in 1876. The imposing uniformity of the five-story buildings that line it contrast with those found in nearby streets, which date from the 17th and 18th centuries. Just off the avenue, in the Place Gaillon, is the Café and Restaurant Drouant, where the prestigious Goncourt Prize for literature is decided each year. Today, the avenue is dominated by the travel industry and luxurious shops. At No. 27 is the National Center for the Visual Arts, which has a false entrance.

Avenue de l'Opéra

MONTMARTRE

ONTMARTRE AND ART are insep-
arable. By the end of the
19th century, the area
was a mecca for artists, writers,
poets and their disciples, who
gathered to sample the bor-
dellos, cabarets, revues and
other exotica that contributed
to Montmartre's reputation as
a place of depravity, in the
eyes of the city's more up-
standing citizens. Many of the
artists and writers have long
since left the area, and the lively night
life no longer has the same charm.

Street theater in
Montmartre

But the hill of Montmartre (the
Butte) still has its physical charms,
and the village atmosphere remains
remarkably intact. Mobs of eager
tourists ascend the hill, most of them

gathering in the most spacious parts,
alive with talented quick portrait
artists and souvenir sellers, as
in the old village square, the
Place du Tertre. Elsewhere there
are charming and exquisite
squares, winding streets,
small terraces and long stairways, plus the Butte's famous
vineyard, where the few
grapes are harvested in an
atmosphere of revelry in early
autumn. And there are spectacular views of the city from various
points, most especially from the
monumental Sacré-Coeur. The Butte
has long been a place to have fun,
and this tradition continues with lat-
ter-day, would-be Edith Piafs singing
in the restaurants and cafés.

SIGHTS AT A GLANCE

Historic Buildings and Streets
Bateau-Lavoir 11
Moulin de la Galette 14
Avenue Junot 15

Churches
Sacré-Coeur pp224–5 1
St-Pierre de Montmartre 2

Chapelle du Martyre 8
St-Jean l'Evangéliste de Montmartre 10

Museums and Galleries
Espace Montmartre 4
Musée de Montmartre 5
Musée d'Art Naïf Max Fourny 7
Placard d'Erik Satie 16

Squares
Place du Tertre 3
Place des Abbesses 9

Cemeteries
Cimetière de Montmartre 13

Theaters and Nightclubs
Au Lapin Agile 6
Moulin Rouge 12

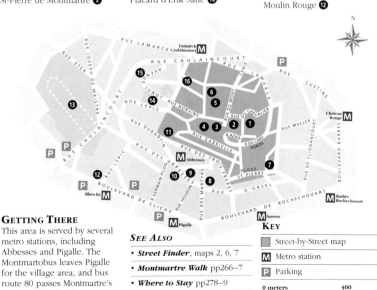

GETTING THERE
This area is served by several
metro stations, including
Abbesses and Pigalle. The
Montmartrobus leaves Pigalle
for the village area, and bus
route 80 passes Montmartre's
cemetery. Route 85 passes
along Rue de Clignancourt.

SEE ALSO
• **Street Finder**, maps 2, 6, 7
• **Montmartre Walk** pp266–7
• **Where to Stay** pp278–9
• **Restaurants** pp296–8

KEY
Street-by-Street map
M Metro station
P Parking

0 meters 400
0 yards 400

The narrow Rue St-Rustique winding up the hill to Sacré-Coeur

Street by Street: Montmartre

THE STEEP *butte* (hill) of Montmartre has been associated with artists for 200 years. Théodore Géricault and Camille Corot came here at the start of the 19th century, and in the 20th century Maurice Utrillo immortalized the streets in his works. Today street painters thrive on a lively tourist trade, as travelers flock to this picturesque district, which in places still preserves the atmosphere of prewar Paris. The name of the area is ascribed to local martyrs tortured in Paris around AD 250, hence *mons martyrium*.

Streetside painter

Montmartre vineyard is the the last surviving vineyard in Paris. On the first Saturday in October the start of the grape harvest is celebrated.

Metro Lamarck Caulaincourt

RUE DES SAULES
RUE DE L'ABREUVOIR
RUE C
RUE ST-L
RUE
NORVINS
RUE LEPI
B X B CLEMENT
RUE POULBO
RUE D'
RAVIGNAN
PL E GOUDEAU
RUE
RUE
RUE DES TROIS FRERES
RUE

★ **Au Lapin Agile**
Literary meetings have been held in this rustic nightclub ("The Agile Rabbit") since 1910 ❻

Placard d'Erik Satie
The composer's tiny studio is now open as the smallest museum in the world. ⓰

A La Mère Catherine was a favorite eating place of Russian Cossacks in 1814. They would bang on the table and shout *"Bistro!"* (Russian for "quick") – hence the bistro was named.

Espace Montmartre Salvador Dali
The exhibition pays homage to the eclectic artist Dali. Some of the works are on public display for the first time in France ❹

★ **Place du Tertre**
This square is the tourist center of Montmartre and is full of portraitists. Number 3 commemorates local children, as popularized in the artist Poulbot's drawings ❸

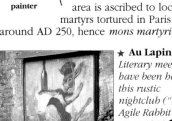

STAR SIGHTS

★ **Sacré-Coeur**

★ **Place du Tertre**

★ **Musée de Montmartre**

★ **Au Lapin Agile**

KEY

‒ ‒ ‒ Suggested route

0 meters   100

0 yards   100

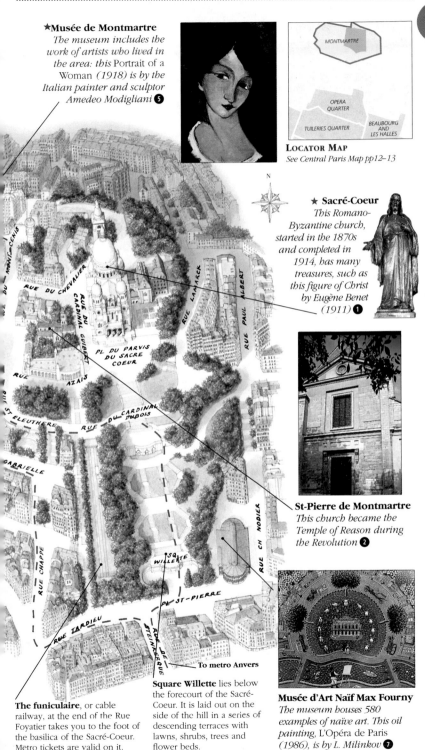

★Musée de Montmartre
The museum includes the work of artists who lived in the area: this Portrait of a Woman (1918) is by the Italian painter and sculptor Amedeo Modigliani **5**

LOCATOR MAP
See Central Paris Map pp12–13

★ Sacré-Coeur
This Romano-Byzantine church, started in the 1870s and completed in 1914, has many treasures, such as this figure of Christ by Eugène Benet (1911) **1**

St-Pierre de Montmartre
This church became the Temple of Reason during the Revolution **2**

Musée d'Art Naïf Max Fourny
The museum houses 580 examples of naïve art. This oil painting, L'Opéra de Paris (1986), is by L. Milinkov **7**

The funiculaire, or cable railway, at the end of the Rue Foyatier takes you to the foot of the basilica of the Sacré-Coeur. Metro tickets are valid on it.

Square Willette lies below the forecourt of the Sacré-Coeur. It is laid out on the side of the hill in a series of descending terraces with lawns, shrubs, trees and flower beds.

To metro Anvers

Montmartre streetside paintings

Sacré-Coeur ❶

See pp224–5.

St-Pierre de Montmartre ❷

2 Rue du Mont-Cenis 75018. **Map** 6 F1.
📞 *01 46 06 57 63.* Ⓜ *Abbesses.*
Open *8:30am–7pm daily.* ✝
frequent. 📷 ♿ **Concerts.**

Sᴵᵀᵁᴬᵀᴱᴰ ᴵɴ the shadow of Sacré-Coeur, St-Pierre de Montmartre is one of the oldest churches in Paris. It is all that remains of the great Benedictine Abbey of Montmartre, founded in 1133 by Louis VI and his wife, Adelaide of Savoy, who, as its first abbess, is buried here.

Inside are four marble columns supposedly from a Roman temple that originally stood on the site. The vaulted choir dates from the 12th century; the nave was remodeled in the 15th century and the west front in the 18th. During the Revolution the abbess was guillotined, and the church fell into disuse. It was reconsecrated in 1908. Gothic-style stained-glass windows replaced those destroyed by a stray bomb in World War II. The church also has a tiny cemetery, which is open to the public only on November 1.

Place du Tertre ❸

75018. **Map** 6 F1. Ⓜ *Abbesses.*

Tᴱᴿᴛᴿᴇ ᴍᴇᴀɴs "hillock," or "mound," and this picturesque square is the highest point in Paris at some 430 ft (130 m). It was once the site of the abbey gallows but is associated with artists, who began exhibiting paintings here in the 19th century. It is lined with colorful restaurants – La Mère Catherine dates back to 1793. No. 21 was formerly the home of the irreverent "Free Commune," founded in 1920 to perpetuate the Bohemian spirit of the area and now the site of the Old Montmartre information office.

The Spanish artist Salvador Dali

Espace Montmartre Salvador Dali ❹

11 Rue Poulbot 75018.
Map 6 F1. 📞 *01 42 64 40 10.* Ⓜ *Abbesses.*
Open *10am–6pm daily.*
Adm charge.
📷 *groups by appt.*

Aᴾᴱᴿᴹᴬɴᴇɴᴛ exhibition of 330 works of the painter and sculptor Salvador Dali is on display here in Montmartre's center. Inside, the vast, dark setting reflects the dramatic character of this 20th-century genius as

Doors to St-Pierre church

moving lights grace first one, then another Surrealist work. This in turn is counterpointed with the regular rhythm of Dali's voice. There is an additional art gallery as well as a library housed in this original museum.

Musée de Montmartre ❺

12 Rue Cortot 75018. **Map** 2 F5.
📞 *01 46 06 61 11.* Ⓜ *Lamarck-Caulaincourt.* **Open** *11am–5:30pm Tue–Sun.* **Adm charge.**
🚫 📷

Dᴜᴿᴵɴɢ ᴛʜᴇ 17th century this charming home belonged to the actor Roze de Rosimond (Claude de la Rose), a member of Molière's theater company who, like his mentor Molière, died during a performance of Molière's play *Le Malade Imaginaire.* From 1875 the big white house, undoubtedly the finest in Montmartre, provided living and studio space for numerous artists, including Maurice Utrillo and his mother, Suzanne Valadon, a former acrobat and model who became a talented painter.

The museum recounts the history of Montmartre from the days of the abbesses to the present, through artifacts, documents, drawings and photographs. It is particularly rich in memorabilia of Bohemian life and even has a reconstruction of the Café de l'Abreuvoir, Utrillo's favorite watering hole.

Café de l'Abreuvoir reconstructed

The deceptively rustic exterior of Au Lapin Agile, one of the best-known nightspots in Paris

Au Lapin Agile 6

26 Rue des Saules 75018.
Map 2 F5. 01 46 06 85 87.
Lamarck-Caulaincourt.
Open 9pm–2am Tue–Sun.
See **Entertainment** pp330–31.

THE FORMER Cabaret des Assassins derived its current name from a sign painted by the humorist André Gill. His picture of a rabbit escaping from a pot (*Le Lapin à Gill*) became known as the nimble rabbit (*Lapin Agile*). The club enjoyed popularity with intellectuals and artists at the turn of the century. Here in 1911 the novelist Roland Dorgelès' hatred for modern art, as practiced by Picasso and the other painters at the "Bâteau-Lavoir" (No. 13 Place Emile-Goudeau), led him to play a practical joke on one of the customers, Guillaume Apollinaire – poet, art critic and champion of Cubism. He tied a paintbrush to the tail of the café owner's donkey, and the resulting "artwork" was shown at a Salon des Indépendents exhibition under the enlightening title *Sunset over the Adriatic*.

In 1903 the premises were bought by the cabaret entrepreneur Aristide Bruand (painted in a series of posters by Toulouse-Lautrec). Today it manages to retain much of its original atmosphere.

Musée d'Art Naïf Max Fourny 7

Halle St-Pierre, 2 Rue Ronsard 75018.
Map 7 A1. 01 42 58 72 89.
Anvers. **Open** 10am–6pm (last adm: 5:30pm) daily. **Adm charge**.

NAIVE ART is usually characterized by simple themes, bright, flat colors and a disregard for perspective. Max Fourny's publishing activities brought him into contact with many naïve-style painters, and this unusual museum, located in the Halle St-Pierre, contains his collection of paintings and sculptures from more than 30 countries

The Wall by F. Tremblot (1944)

and rotates exhibitions on selected themes. Many of the paintings are rarely seen in museums.

The Halle St-Pierre also houses the Musée en Herbe, a children's museum designed to introduce conservation issues through exhibitions and workshops. The building is a 19th-century iron-and-glass structure that was once part of the St-Pierre fabrics market.

Chapelle du Martyre 8

9 Rue Yvonne-Le-Tac 75018.
Map 6 F1. Pigalle.
Open 10am–noon, 3pm–5pm Fri–Wed.

THIS 19TH-CENTURY chapel stands on the site of a medieval convent's chapel, which was said to mark the place where the early Christian martyr and first bishop of Paris, Saint Denis, was beheaded by the Romans in AD 250. In the crypt of the original chapel in 1534 Ignatius de Loyola, founder of the Society of Jesus (the mighty Jesuit order designed to save the Catholic Church from the onslaught of the Protestant Reformation), took his Jesuit vows with six companions.

Sacré-Coeur ❶

Southeast rose window (1960)

A T THE OUTBREAK of the Franco Prussian War in 1870, two Catholic businessmen made a private religious vow. It was to build a church dedicated to the Sacred Heart of Christ should France be spared the impending Prussian onslaught. The two men, Alexandre Legentil and Rohault de Fleury, lived to see Paris saved from invasion despite the war and a lengthy siege – and the start of what is the Sacré-Coeur basilica. The project was taken up by Archbishop Guibert of Paris. Work began in 1875 to Paul Abadie's designs. They were inspired by the Romano-Byzantine church of St-Front in Périgueux. The basilica was completed in 1914, but the German invasion forestalled its consecration until 1919, when France was victorious.

The Facade
The best view of the domed and turreted Sacré-Coeur is from the gardens below.

The bell tower (1895) is 252 ft (83 m) high and contains one of the heaviest bells in the world. The bell itself weighs 18.5 ton, and the clapper is 1,900 lb (850 kg).

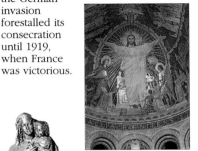

★ **Great Mosaic of Christ**
The colossal Byzantine mosaic of Christ (1912–22) dominating the chancel vault is by Luc Olivier Merson.

Virgin Mary and Child *(1896)*
This Renaissance-style silver statue is one of two in the ambulatory by P. Brunet.

THE SIEGE OF PARIS

Prussia invaded France in 1870. During the four-month siege of Paris, instigated by the Prusso-German statesman Otto von Bismarck, Parisians became so hungry that they ate all the animals in the city.

★ **Crypt Vaults**
A chapel in the basilica's crypt contains Legentil's heart in a stone urn.

★ **Ovoid Dome**
This is the second-highest point in Paris, after the Eiffel Tower.

Spiral staircase

The inner structure supporting the dome is made from stone.

The stained-glass gallery affords a view of the whole of the interior.

Statue of Christ
The basilica's most important statue is symbolically placed above the two bronze saints.

Equestrian Statues
The statue of Joan of Arc is one of a pair by H. Lefèbvre. The other is of Saint Louis.

★ **Bronze Doors**
Relief sculptures on the doors in the portico entrance illustrate scenes from the life of Christ, such as the Last Supper.

Main entrance

The famous silhouette of the Moulin Rouge nightclub

Place des Abbesses **9**

75018. **Map** 6 F1. **M** *Abbesses*.

THIS IS ONE OF PARIS'S most picturesque squares. It is sandwiched between the rather dubious attractions of the Place Pigalle with its strip clubs and the Place du Tertre, which is always mobbed with hundreds of tourists. Be sure not to miss the Abbesses metro station with its unusual green wrought-iron arches and amber lights. Designed by the architect Hector Guimard, it is one of the few original Art Nouveau stations.

St-Jean l'Evangéliste de Montmartre **10**

19 Rue des Abbesses 75018. **Map** 6 F1. **[** *01 46 06 43 96.* **M** *Abbesses.* **Open** *9am– noon, 3pm–7pm Mon–Sat; 2pm–7pm Sun.* **†** *frequent.* **◙ ☑** *second and fourth Sunday of each month.*

DESIGNED BY Anatole de Baudot and completed in 1904, this church was the first to be built from reinforced concrete. The flower motifs on the interior are typical of Art Nouveau, while its interlocking arches suggest Islamic architecture. The red-brick facing has earned it the nickname St-Jean-des-Briques.

Entrance to the Abbesses metro

Detail of St-Jean l'Evangéliste facade

Bateau-Lavoir **11**

13 Pl Emile-Goudeau 75018. **Map** 6 F1. **M** *Abbesses.* **Not open** *to public.*

THIS ARTISTIC and literary mecca was an old piano factory. Its name comes from its resemblance to the laundry boats that used to travel along the River Seine. Between 1890 and 1920 it was home to some of the most talented artists and poets of the day. They lived in squalid conditions with only cold water and took turns sleeping in the beds. The artists Picasso, Van Dongen, Marie Laurencin, Juan Gris and Modigliani were just a few of the residents. It was here that Picasso painted *Les Demoiselles d'Avignon* in 1907, usually regarded as the painting that inspired Cubism. The shabby building burned down in 1970, but a concrete replica has been built – with studio space for up-and-coming artists.

Moulin Rouge **12**

82 Blvd de Clichy 75018. **Map** 6 E1. **[** *01 53 09 82 82.* **M** *Blanche.* **Open** *Dinner: 7pm; 1st show: 9pm; 2nd show: 11pm daily.* **Adm charge**. *See* **Entertainment** *p339.*

BUILT IN 1885 and turned into a dance hall in 1900, only the red sails outside date from the original nightclub. The cancan originated in the polka gardens of the Rue de la Grande-Chaumière in Montparnasse but it will always be associated with the Moulin Rouge where the wild and colorful dance shows were immortalized in the posters and drawings of Henri de Toulouse-Lautrec. The high-kicking routines of famous dancers such as Jane Avril and Yvette Guilbert continue today in a glittering, Las Vegas-style revue that includes computerized lights and displays of magic.

Waslaw Nijinsky lies in Montmartre

Cimetière de Montmartre **⑬**

20 Ave Rachel 75018.
Map 2 D5. **[** 01 43 87 64 24.
M Place de Clichy. **Open** 8am–6pm
Mon–Sat; 9am–6pm Sun (last adm:
5:45pm). **[&**

THIS HAS been the resting place for many artistic luminaries since the beginning of the 19th century. Composers Hector Berlioz and Jacques Offenbach (who wrote the can-can tune), German poet Heinrich Heine, Russian dancer Vaslav Nijinsky and film director François Truffaut are just a few of the notable celebrities buried here.

There is also a Montmartre cemetery near Square Roland-Dorgelès – the St-Vincent cemetery – where the French painter Maurice Utrillo lies.

Moulin de la Galette **⑭**

T-junction at Rue Tholoze and Rue
Lepic 75018. **Map** 2 E5. **M** Lamarck-
Caulaincourt. **Not open** to public.

ONCE MORE THAN 30 windmills dotted the Montmartre skyline and were used for grinding wheat and pressing grapes. Now only two remain: the Moulin du Radet, which stands farther along the Rue Lepic, and the rebuilt Moulin de la Galette.

The latter was built in 1622 and is also known as the Blute-fin; one of the mill owners, Debray, was supposedly crucified on the windmill's sails during the 1814 Siege of Paris. He had been trying to repulse the invading Cossacks. At the turn of the century the mill became a famous dance hall and provided inspiration for many artists, notably Auguste Renoir and Vincent Van Gogh.

The steep Rue Lepic is a busy shopping area with a good market (see p327). The Impressionist industrial and seascape painter Armand Guillaumin once lived on the first floor of No. 54, and Van Gogh inhabited its third floor.

Moulin de la Galette

Avenue Junot **⑮**

75018. **Map** 2 E5. **M** Lamarck-
Caulaincourt.

OPENED IN 1910, this broad, peaceful street includes many painters' studios and family houses. No. 13 has mosaics designed by its former illustrator resident, Francisque Poulbot, famous for his drawings of urchins. He is credited with having invented a bar billiards game. At No. 15 is Maison Tristan Tzara, named after its previous owner, the Romanian Dadaist poet. It was eccentrically designed by the Austrian architect Adolf Loos to complement the poet's character.

Just off the Avenue Junot up the steps of the Allée des Brouillards is an 18th-century architectural folly, the Château des Brouillards. In the 19th century it was the home of the mad French symbolist writer Gérard de Nerval, who committed suicide in 1855.

Le Placard d'Erik Satie **⑯**

6 Rue Cortot 75018. **Map** 6 F1.
[01 42 78 15 18. **M** Lamarck-
Caulaincourt. **Open** by appointment
only. **[**

THE TINY STUDIO in which the composer lived from 1890 to 1898 is just 3 sq m (10 sq ft), and so it is no wonder that he used to refer to it as his "cupboard" (placard). Today, this cubbyhole can lay claim to the title of "smallest museum in the world."

Paintings, drawings, manuscripts, and other documents are displayed here, where Erik Satie composed six *Gnossiennes* and the *Messe des Pauvres* (Paupers' Mass). The only problem is that the items in the Satie Foundation cannot all be shown at the same time in the limited space, and so temporary exhibitions focus on a single work accompanied by the relevant documents.

However, this enterprising museum manages to put on concerts of previously unknown works of a length not exceeding a few minutes – some last only a few seconds – for audiences limited to just seven people. This miniature treasure-house can only be seen by appointment and individual visits are advised.

Innovative composer Erik Satie (1866–1925)

FARTHER AFIELD

MANY OF THE GREAT châteaux outside Paris originally built as country retreats for the aristocracy and post-revolutionary bourgeoisie are now preserved as museums. Versailles is one of the finest, but if your tastes are Modernist, there's also Le Corbusier architecture to see. There are two theme parks – Disneyland Paris and Parc de la Villette – to amuse adults and children alike, and excellent parks to relax in when the bustle of the city gets too much.

SIGHTS AT A GLANCE

Museums and Galleries
Musée Nissim de Camondo ❸
Musée Cernuschi ❹
Musée Gustave Moreau ❺
Musée de Cristal de Baccarat ❽
Centre Internationale d'Automobile ❽
Musée Edith Piaf ⓮
Musée National des Arts Africains et Océaniens ⓲
Musée Marmottan ❸⓿
Espace Landowski ❸❷

Churches
St-Alexandre-Nevsky Cathédral ❶
Basilique Saint-Denis ❼
Notre-Dame du Travail ㉔

Historic Buildings and Streets
Bercy ⓴
Bibliotheque Nationale de France ㉑
Cité Universitaire ㉓
Institut Pasteur ㉕
Versailles pp248–53 ㉗
Rue de la Fontaine ㉘
Fondation Le Corbusier ㉙
La Défense ㉝
Château de Malmaison ㉞

Markets
Marché aux Puces de St-Ouen ❻
Portes St-Denis et St-Martin ❾
Marché d'Aligre ⓱

Parks, Gardens, and Canals
Parc Monceau ❷
Canal St-Martin ❿
Parc des Buttes-Chaumont ⓫
Château et Bois de Vincennes ⓳
Parc Montsouris ㉒
Parc André Citroën ㉖
Bois de Boulogne ㉛

Cemeteries
Cimetière du Père Lachaise pp240–41 ⓯

Theme Parks
Parc de la Villette pp234–9 ⓬
Disneyland Paris pp242–5 ⓰

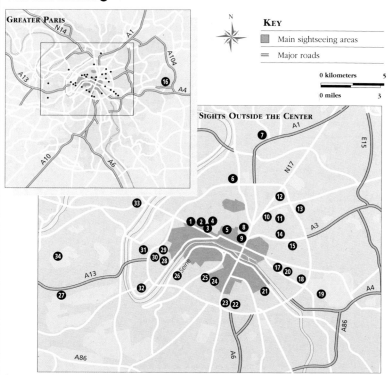

GREATER PARIS

KEY
- Main sightseeing areas
- Major roads

0 kilometers 5
0 miles 3

SIGHTS OUTSIDE THE CENTER

A landscaped island in the Bois de Boulogne

North of the City

St-Alexandre-Nevsky Cathédral

St-Alexandre-Nevsky Cathédral ❶

12 Rue Daru 75008. **Map** 4 F3.
【 01 42 27 37 34. 🄼 Courcelle.
Open 3pm–5pm Tue, Fri, Sun.
✝ 6pm Sat, 10:30am Sun. 🞸 🖼

THIS IMPOSING Russian Orthodox cathedral with its five golden-copper domes signals the presence of a large Russian community in Paris. Designed by members of the St. Petersburg Fine Arts Academy and financed jointly by Tzar Alexander II and the local Russian community, the cathedral was completed in 1861. Inside, a wall of icons divides the church in two. The Greek-cross plan and the rich interior mosaics and frescoes are Neo-Byzantine in style, while the exterior and gilt domes are traditional Russian Orthodox in design.

The Russian population in the city increased dramatically following the Bolshevik Revolution of 1917, when thousands of Russians fled to Paris for safety. The Rue Daru, in which the cathedral stands, and the surrounding area form "Little Russia," with its Russian schools and the many dance academies and delightful tea shops and bookshops where visitors can browse around.

Parc Monceau ❷

Blvd de Courcelles 75017.**Map** 5 A3.
【 01 42 27 08 64. 🄼 Monceau.
Open 7am–9pm daily (10pm summer).
See **Five Guided Walks** pp258–9.

THIS GREEN HAVEN dates back to 1778 when the Duc de Chartres (later Duc d'Orléans) commissioned the painter-writer and amateur landscape designer Louis Carmontelle to create a magnificent garden. Also a theater designer, Carmontelle created a "garden of dreams," an exotic landscape full of architectural follies in imitation of English and German fashion of the time. In 1783 the Scottish landscape gardener Thomas Blaikie laid out an area of the garden in English style. The park was the scene of the first recorded parachute landing, made by André-Jacques Garnerin on October 22, 1797.

Over the years it changed hands and in 1852 was acquired by the state and half the land sold off for property development. The remaining 9 ha (22 acres) were made into public gardens. These were restored and new buildings were erected by Adolphe Alphand, architect of the Bois de Boulogne and the Bois de Vincennes.

Today the park remains one of the most chic in the capital but has lost many of its early features. A *naumachia* basin flanked by Corinthian columns remains. This is an ornamental version of a Roman pool used for simulating naval battles. There are also a Renaissance arcade, pyramids, a river and the Pavillon de Chartres, a charming rotunda that was once used as a tollhouse.

Musée Nissim de Camondo

Musée Nissim de Camondo ❸

63 Rue de Monceau 75008.
Map 5 A3. 🄵 01 53 89 06 40.
🄼 Monceau, Villiers.
Open 10am–5pm Wed–Sun
(last adm: 4:30pm). **Closed** public
hols. **Adm charge.** 🞸 🖼

COMTE MOISE de Camondo, a leading Jewish financier, commissioned this mansion in 1914 in the style of the Petit Trianon, at Versailles (see pp248–9) to house a rare collection of 18th-century furniture, tapestries, paintings and other precious objects. The museum has been faithfully restored to recreate an aristocratic town house of the Louis XV and XVI eras. In the museum are Savonnerie carpets, Beauvais tapestries, and the Buffon service (the Sèvres porcelain table service with bird decoration).

De Camondo left his mansion to the nation in 1935 in memory of his son, Nissim, killed during World War I.

Colonnade beside the *naumachia* basin in Parc Monceau

Musée Cernuschi ④

7 Ave Vélasquez 75008. **Map** 5 A3.
C 01 45 63 50 75. **M** *Villiers,
Monceau.* **Open** *10am–5:40pm
Tue–Sun.* **Closed** *public hols.* **Adm
charge.** ∅ ⓖ *groups, by appt.* ⓗ

THIS MANSION near Parc
Monceau contains an
intriguing private collection
of late East Asian art that was
amassed by the politician and
banker Enrico Cernuschi
(1821–96). The wide-ranging
collection includes such treats
as the 5th-century seated
Bodhisattva (Buddhist divine
being) from Yunkang; *La
Tigresse*, a 12th-century BC
bronze vase; and *Horses and
Grooms*, an 8th-century T'ang
painting on silk attributed to
the era's greatest horse painter,
the court artist Han Kan.

Bodhisattva in the Musée Cernuschi

Musée Gustave Moreau ⑤

14 Rue de la Rochefoucauld 75009.
Map 6 E3. **C** 01 48 74 38 50.
M *Trinité.* **Open** *11am–5:15pm, Mon
& Wed; 10am–12:45pm, 2pm–5:15pm
Thu–Sun.* **Closed** *Jan 1, May 1, Dec 25
(call to check).* **Adm charge.** ⓞ ⓗ

THE SYMBOLIST painter
Gustave Moreau (1826–
98), known for his vivid,
imaginative works depicting
biblical and mythological
fantasies, left to the state a
vast collection of more than
1,000 oils, watercolors and
some 7,000 drawings in
his town house. One of
Moreau's best-known and
most outstanding works,
Jupiter and Semele, can be
seen here.

**Angel Traveler by Gustave Moreau,
in the Musée Gustave Moreau**

Marché aux Puces de St-Ouen ⑥

Rue des Rosiers, St-Ouen 75018.
Map 2 F2. **M** *Porte-de-
Clignancourt.* **Open** *7am–6pm
Sat–Mon. See* **Markets** *p327.*

THIS IS THE OLDEST and largest
of the Paris flea markets,
covering 15 acres (6 ha). In
the 19th century, rag merchants
and tramps would gather
outside the city limits and offer
their wares for sale. By the
1920s, there was a proper
market here, where masterpieces could sometimes be
purchased cheaply from the
then-unknowing sellers.
    Today it is divided into
specialist markets. It is known
especially for its profusion of
furniture and ornaments from
the Second Empire (1852–
70). Few bargains are to be
found these days, yet some
150,000 weekend bargain
hunters, tourists, and dealers
still flock here to browse
among the more than 2,000
open or covered market stalls.

Basilique Saint-Denis ⑦

2 Rue de Strasbourg, 93200 St-Denis.
C 01 48 09 83 54. **M** *St-Denis-Bas-
ilique.* RER *St-Denis.* **Open** *Apr–Sep:
10am–6:30pm Mon–Sat, noon–6:30pm
Sun; Oct–Mar: 10am–4:30pm Mon–
Sat, noon–4:30pm Sun.* ⓣ *8:30am,
10am Sun.* **Adm charge.** ⓞ ⓖ ⓗ

CONSTRUCTED BETWEEN 1137
and 1281, the basilica is
on the site of the tomb of St.
Denis, the first bishop of Paris,
who was beheaded in Mont-
martre in AD 250. The building
was the original influence for
Gothic art in Europe. From
Merovingian times, it was a
burial place for rulers of France.
During the Revolution, many
tombs were desecrated and
scattered, but the best were
stored and now represent a
fine collection of funerary art.
Memorials include those of
Dagobert (died 638), François I
(died 1547), Henri II (died
1559), Catherine de'Medici
(died 1589) and Louis XVI and
Marie-Antoinette (died 1793).

**Le Vase d'Abyssinie, made of
Baccarat crystal and bronze**

Musée de Cristal de Baccarat ⑧

30 bis Rue de Paradis 75010.
Map 7 B4. **C** 01 47 70 64 30.
M *Château d'Eau.* **Open** *10am–
6pm Mon–Sat.* **Adm charge.** ⓞ ⓖ
by appointment (01 40 22 11 32). ⓗ

THE RUE DE PARADIS is home
to many glass and ceramics
retailers, including the Baccarat
company, founded in 1764 in
Lorraine. The Musée de Cristal,
also known as the Musée
Baccarat, is beside the Baccarat
showroom and has on display
over 1,200 articles made by
the company. These include
services created for the royal
and imperial courts of Europe
and the finest pieces created
in the workshops.

Western arch of the Porte St-Denis, once the entrance to the city

Portes St-Denis et St-Martin **9**

Blvds St-Denis & St-Martin 75010.
Map 7 B5. **M** *St-Martin, Strasbourg-St-Denis.*

THESE GATES give access to the two ancient and important north–south thoroughfares whose names they bear. They once marked the entrance to the city. The Porte St-Denis is 76 ft (23m) high and was built in 1672 by François Blondel. It is decorated with figures by Louis XIV's sculptor, François Girardon. They commemorate victories of the king's armies in Flanders and the Rhine that year. Porte St-Martin is 56 ft (17 m) tall and was built in 1674 by Pierre Bullet. It celebrates Besançon's capture and the defeat of the Triple Alliance of Spain, Holland and Germany.

Boats berthed at Port de l'Arsenal

East of the City

Canal St-Martin **10**

Map 8 E2. **M** *Jaurès, J Bonsergent, Goncourt. See* **Five Guided Walks** *pp260–61.*

THE 3-MILE (5 kilometer) canal, opened in 1825, provides a shortcut for river traffic between loops of the Seine. It has long been loved by novelists, film directors and tourists alike. It is dotted with barges and pleasure boats that leave from the Arsenal. At the north end of the canal is the Bassin de la Villette waterway and the elegant Neoclassical Rotonde de la Villette, spectacularly floodlit at night.

Parc des Buttes-Chaumont **11**

Rue Manin 75019 (main access from Rue Armand Carrel). **C** *01 53 35 89 35.* **M** *Botzaris, Buttes-Chaumont.* **Open** *Oct–Apr: 6:45am–9pm daily; May–Sep: 6:45am–11pm daily.* **11**

FOR MANY THIS is the most pleasant and unexpected park in Paris. The panoramic hilly site was converted in the 1860s by Baron Haussmann

from a rubbish dump and quarry with a gallows below. Haussmann worked with the landscape architect/designer Adolphe Alphand, who organized a vast program to furnish the new sidewalk-lined avenues with benches and lampposts. Others involved in the creation of what was then a highly praised park were the engineer Darcel and the landscape gardener Barillet-Deschamps. They created a lake, made an island with real and artificial rocks, gave it a Roman-style temple and added a waterfall, streams, footbridges leading to the island, and beaches and firs. Today visitors will also find boating facilities and donkey rides.

Island, rocks and temple in the Parc des Buttes-Chaumont

Parc de la Villette **12**

See pp234–9.

Renault racing car, Centre Internationale d'Automobile

Centre Internationale d'Automobile **13**

25 Rue d'Estienne d'Orves, 93500 Pantin. **f** *01 48 10 80 00.* **M** *Hoche.* **Open** *for groups only, by appt.* **Adm** *charge.* **&** *Movies, videos. Library.* **f** *by appt only.* **11**

BASED IN A FORMER factory, this conference center makes superb use of the vast, light space of 100,000 sq m (over 1 million sq ft) in order to display its well-chosen collection of over 120 cars and motorcycles. In addition to classic models from the past, visitors can also see examples of the latest prototypes in both early and advance stages, and get an idea of transportation styles and methods of the future. Exhibitions change frequently and regular events are held in the Discovery Area.

Sadly, the center is currently open only to visitors attending conferences and exhibitions, which are held in the various halls of the complex, and not to the general public until further notice.

Musée Edith Piaf 🄸

5 Rue Crespin du Gast 75011. 📞 01 43 55 52 72. Ⓜ Ménilmontant. **Open** 1pm–6pm Mon–Thu (last adm: 5:30pm). **Visits** by appointment only. **Closed** public hols. **Adm charge**. 🚫 📷 📱

BORN EDITH GASSION in the working-class east end of Paris in 1915, Edith Piaf took her stage name from her nickname meaning "the little sparrow." She started her career as a torch singer in local cafés and bars before becoming an international star in the late 1930s.

She never lived at the address of this museum, which was founded in 1967 by an association of fans, Les Amis d'Edith Piaf. They have since collected a host of memorabilia and squeezed it into this small apartment. It

Edith Piaf – "the little sparrow" (1915–63)

contains many photographs and portraits, intimate letters, clothes, lithographs by Charles Kiffer, and books – gifts from Piaf's parents-in-law or bequests from other singers. Records by the singer, who died in 1963 and lies in Père Lachaise cemetery *(see pp240–41)*, are played in the museum on request.

Cimetière du Père Lachaise 🄵

See pp240–41.

Minnie and Mickey Mouse

Disneyland Paris 🄶

See pp242–5.

Marché d'Aligre 🄷

Place d'Aligre 75012. **Map** 14 F5. Ⓜ Ledru-Rollin. **Open** 9:30am–1pm daily.

ON SUNDAY mornings this lively market offers one of the most colorful sights in Paris. French, Arab, and African traders hawk fruit, vegetables, flowers, and clothing on the streets, while the adjoining covered market, the Beauveau St-Antoine, offers meats, cheeses, pâtés, and many intriguing international delicacies.

Aligre is where old and new Paris meet. Here the established community of this old artisan quarter coexists with a more recently established group of up-and-coming young people. They

have been lured here to live and work by the recent transformation of the nearby Bastille area *(see p98)*.

Exterior relief on Musée National des Arts Africains et Océaniens

Musée National des Arts Africains et Océaniens 🄸

293 Ave Daumesnil 75012. 📞 01 44 74 84 80. Ⓜ Porte Dorée. **Open** 10am–5:30pm Wed–Mon (last adm: 4:50pm). **Aquarium open** 10am–5:30pm Wed–Mon. **Closed** May 1. **Adm charge**. 🚫 ♿ restricted. 📱

THIS MUSEUM IS housed in a beautiful Art Deco building which was designed by the architects Albett Laprade and Léon Jaussely especially for the 1931 Colonial Exhibition. The impressive facade has a vast frieze by A Janniot, depicting the contributions of France's overseas territories.

Inside is a remarkable display of primitive and tribal art covering West, Central, and North Africa, as well as Oceania and Australasia. The exhibits include antelope masks from Mali; finely carved ivory tusks from Benin; Moroccan jewelry; Aboriginal bark paintings; plus West and Central African masks and carved wooden and copper figures.

In the basement there is a tropical aquarium filled with vivid fish, as well as terrariums containing tortoises and crocodiles.

Parc de la Villette ⓬

THE OLD SLAUGHTERHOUSES and livestock market of Paris have been transformed into this massive urban park, designed by Bernard Tschumi. Its vast and ambitious facilities stretch across 55 ha (136 acres) of a previously run-down part of the city. The great plan is to revive the tradition of parks for meetings and activities and to stimulate interest in the arts and sciences. Work began in 1984 and the park has grown to include a huge science museum, a pop concert hall, an exhibition pavilion, a spherical theater and a music center. Linking them all is the park itself, with its follies, walkways, gardens and playgrounds.

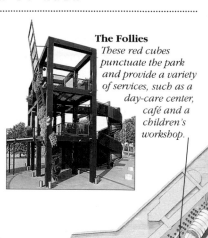

The Follies
These red cubes punctuate the park and provide a variety of services, such as a day-care center, café and a children's workshop.

Children's Playground
A dragon slide, sand pits and colorful play equipment in a maze-like setting make the playground a paradise for young children.

★ **Grande Halle**
The old cattle hall has been transformed into a flexible exhibition space with mobile floors and auditorium.

Entrance

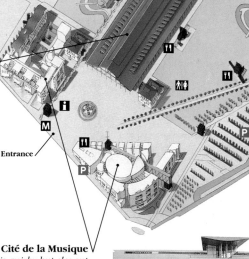

★ **Cité de la Musique**
This quirky but elegant all-white complex holds the music conservatory, a concert hall, library, studios and a museum.

STAR BUILDINGS

★ **Cité des Sciences**

★ **Grande Halle**

★ **Cité de la Musique**

★ **Zénith Theatre**

Maison de la Villette is a history center with documents and displays on the history of the site and area.

Entrance

★ **Cité des Sciences**
This huge science museum boasts the latest in futurist equipment and has dazzling hands-on displays.

VISITORS' CHECKLIST

30 Ave Corentin-Cariou 75019. 01 40 05 80 00. M Porte de la Villette. 150, 152, 250A to Porte de la Villette. P on site. **Open** 10am–6pm Tue–Sun (last adm: 5:30pm). **Adm charge** (free for buses). **Concerts. Movies, videos. Conference center. Library.**

La Géode
The theater's gigantic 360° movie screen combines visual and sound effects to create fantastic experiences, such as the sense of traveling in space.

★ **Zénith Theatre**
This vast polyester tent was built as a venue for pop concerts, with a capacity to seat more than 6,000 spectators.

Musicians from Guadeloupe performing outside the Museum

LE MUSÉE DE LA MUSIQUE

This museum brings together a collection of over 4,500 instruments, objects, tools, and works of art covering the history of music since the Renaissance. The permanent collection of over 900 items is displayed chronologically and can be traced using infrared audio headphones.

L'Argonaute
The exhibit consists of a 1950s submarine and a nearby navigation museum.

La Villette: Cité des Sciences

Statue of Atlas

THIS IMMENSE science and technology museum occupies the largest of the old Villette slaughterhouses. The building soars 40 m (133 ft) high and stretches over 3 ha (7 acres). Architect Adrien Fainsilber has created an imaginative interplay between the building and three natural themes: water surrounds the structure; vegetation penetrates through the greenhouses; and light flows in through the cupolas. The museum is on five levels. Its heart is the Explora exhibits on levels 1 and 2, where lively and entertaining displays of equipment and activities promote an interest in science and technology. Visitors can actively engage in computerized games on space, computers and sound. On other levels are movie theaters, a science newsroom, a conference center, a library and shops.

Cupolas
The two glass domes, 17 m (56 ft) in diameter, filter the flow of natural light into the main hall.

★ Planetarium
In this 260-seat auditorium, special-effects projectors and the latest sound systems create exciting images of the stars and planets.

Main Hall
A soaring network of shafts, bridges, escalators and balconies creates a cathedral-like atmosphere here.

Entrance from the west

STAR EXHIBITS

★ Planetarium

★ Ariane Rocket

★ La Géode

★ Ariane Rocket
The fascinating displays of rockets explain how astronauts are launched into outer space, and include an example of the European rocket Ariane.

The moat was designed by Fainsilber at 13 m (43 ft) below the level of the park, so that natural light could penetrate into the lower levels of the building. The sense of the building's massiveness is enhanced by reflections in the water.

Mirage Aircraft
A full-scale model of the French-built jet fighter plane is just one of the exhibits illustrating dramatic advances in technology.

Children's Science City
In this lively, extensive area, children can experiment and play with interactive machines that show them how scientific principles work.

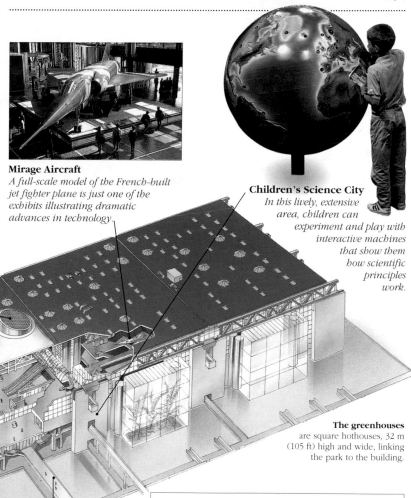

The greenhouses
are square hothouses, 32 m (105 ft) high and wide, linking the park to the building.

To the Géode

370-seat auditorium

Hemispheric screen

Main lobby

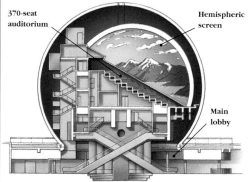

Walkways
The walkways cross the encircling moat to link the various floors of the museum to the Géode and the park.

LA GÉODE
This giant entertainment sphere, 36 m (116 ft) in diameter, has a "skin" composed of 6,500 stainless-steel triangles, which reflect the surroundings and the sky. Inside, a huge hemispheric movie screen, 1,000 sq m (11,000 sq ft), shows films on nature, travel and space.

Cité des Sciences: Explora

THE EXPLORA exhibits on levels 1 and 2 of the Cité are a fascinating guide to the worlds of science and technology. Our understanding of computers, space, ocean, earth, sound and movies is heightened by bold, imaginative presentations of multimedia displays, interactive computer exhibits and informative models. Children and adults can learn while playing with light, space and sound. Young children can walk through the sound sponge, experience optical illusions, see how astronauts live in outer space, whisper to one another through the parabolic sound screen, and listen to talking walls. Older children can learn more about how man lives and works under water, how special effects are made in movies, listen to the story of a star, and see the birth of a mountain.

Sound Dishes
These parabolic sound screens transmit a conversation between people standing 48 ft (15 m) apart.

Monory's frescoes are Jacques Monory's painted aluminium plates, linked by neon tubes, which decorate the Planetarium's external walls.

★ **Star Display**
Ten thousand stars are projected on to the dome of the Planetarium by the astronomic simulator. The visual and sound effects simulate breathtaking voyages through space.

Level 2

Starball
The Planetarium's 10,000-lens sphere reproduces images of what the sky looks like to astronauts traveling beyond the earth's atmosphere.

Level 1

Tele-X is a full-scale model of a satellite with interactive exhibits.

Sounds
A wealth of interactive exhibits, such as this instrument demonstating resonance, help visitors to explore the amazing world of sound and hearing.

KEY TO FLOOR PLAN

☐	Permanent exhibitions
☐	Temporary exhibitions
☐	Planetarium
☐	Future exhibition space
☐	Nonexhibition space

The Flight Simulator *re-creates a hands-on experience of an aircraft flight with feed in and feed-back computer data.*

The Double Perspective Room creates an optical illusion: people in the room appear to be much larger or smaller than they really are.

Interactive Robot
This captivating remote-controlled robot wanders around the Explora exhibitions, communicating with the visitors.

Odorama
The fun of this display is in guessing the smell associated with the picture projected on the screen.

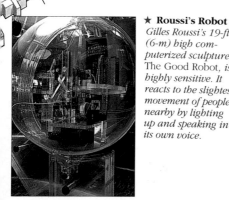

★ **Roussi's Robot**
Gilles Roussi's 19-ft (6-m) high computerized sculpture, The Good Robot, *is highly sensitive. It reacts to the slightest movement of people nearby by lighting up and speaking in its own voice.*

Meteovision
Weather forecasting is demonstrated with maps and satellite pictures. Constantly updated weather reports are provided for 240 cities around the world.

Cimetière du Père Lachaise ⓯

PARIS'S MOST PRESTIGIOUS cemetery is set on a wooded hill overlooking the city. The land was once owned by Père de la Chaise, Louis XIV's confessor, but in 1803 Napoleon ordered it bought and laid out as a new cemetery. The cemetery became so popular with the bourgeoisie that it was expanded six times during the century. Here were buried such celebrities as the writer Honoré de Balzac and the composer Frédéric Chopin and, more recently, the singer Jim Morrison and the actor Yves Montand. Famous graves and striking funerary sculpture make this a pleasant place for a leisurely, nostalgic stroll.

The Columbarium was built at the end of the 19th century. The American dancer Isadora Duncan is one of the many celebrities whose ashes are housed here.

Marcel Proust
Proust brilliantly chronicled the Belle Epoque in his novel Remembrance of Things Past.

★ Simone Signoret and Yves Montand
France's most famous post-war film couple were renowned for their left-wing views and long turbulent relationship.

Allan Kardec was the founder of a 19th-century spiritual cult that still has a strong following. His tomb is forever covered in pilgrims' flowers.

Sarah Bernhardt
The great French tragedienne, who died in 1923 at age 78, was famous for her portrayal of Racine heroines.

Monument aux Morts
by Paul Albert Bartholmé is one of the best monumental sculptures in the cemetery. It dominates the central avenue.

Entrance

Frédéric Chopin, the great Polish composer, belonged to the French Romantic generation.

Théodore Géricault
This French Romantic painter's masterpiece, The Raft of the Medusa *(see p124), is depicted on his tomb.*

STAR FEATURES

- ★ Oscar Wilde
- ★ Jim Morrison
- ★ Edith Piaf
- ★ Simone Signoret and Yves Montand

★ Oscar Wilde
The Irish dramatist, aesthete and great wit, was cast away from virtuous Britain to die of drink and dissipation in Paris in 1900. Jacob Epstein sculpted the monument.

The remains of Molière, the great 17th-century actor and dramatist, were transferred here in 1817 to add historic glamour to the new cemetery.

VISITORS' CHECKLIST

16 Rue du Repos. **(** 01 43 70 70 33. **M** Père Lachaise, Alexandre Dumas. **🚌** 62, 69, 26 to Pl Gambetta. **P** Pl Gambetta. **Open** 8am–5:30pm daily.
📷 ✂ ℹ

Mur des Fédérés is the wall against which the last Communard rebels were shot by government forces in 1871. It is now a place of pilgrimage for left-wing sympathizers.

★ Edith Piaf
Known as "the little sparrow" because of her size, Piaf was this century's greatest French popular singer. In her tragic voice she sang of the sorrows and love woes of the Paris working class.

Victor Noir
The life-size statue of this 19th-century journalist shot by Pierre Bonaparte, a cousin of Napoleon III, is said to have fertility powers.

George Rodenbach, the 19th-century poet, is depicted as rising out of his tomb with a rose in the hand of his outstretched arm.

Elizabeth Demidoff, a Russian princess who died in 1818, is honored by a three-story Classical temple by Quaglia.

★ Jim Morrison
The death of The Doors' lead singer in Paris in 1971 is still a mystery.

François Raspail
The tomb of this much-imprisoned partisan of the 1830 and 1840 revolutions is in the form of a prison.

Disneyland Paris ⑯

THIS THEME PARK is part of the vast Disneyland Paris Resort, which is spread across 1,500 acres (600 ha) of Marne-la-Vallée, 20 miles (32 km) east of Paris. Inspired by California's Magic Kingdom, the five-themed park has a European touch in the form of attractions based on such children's fictional characters as Peter Pan and Sleeping Beauty. However, it is predominantly American in character and spirit, through its style of presentation and in the major sections on small-town America and the Wild West. The resort opened in 1992, complete with the theme park, hotels and facilities for sports and camping.

Minnie Mouse

Alice's Curious Labyrinth
Peopled by Alice in Wonderland characters, this garden maze is dominated by the Queen of Hearts' castle.

Pirates of the Caribbean has animated pirates besieging a massive fortress.

Adventure Isle is the site of Captain Hook's Pirate Ship and Ben Gunn's cave.

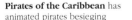

La Cabane des Robinson is a hideaway high among the branches of an artificial, giant banyan tree.

Cottonwood Creek Ranch is a model working ranch with stables and corrals, Native American crafts and a railroad depot.

★ Big Thunder Mountain
A runaway mine train speeds around this mountain, which was inspired by the landscapes of the American West.

Disneyland Paris railroad has four 1890s-style steam trains circling the theme park via the Grand Canyon Diorama.

Phantom Manor creates a ghostly realm with its animated characters and special effects.

Entrance

KEY TO THEME PARK

- ☐ Main Street, USA
- ☐ Frontierland
- ☐ Adventureland
- ☐ Fantasyland
- ☐ Discoveryland

★ Main Street Station
The Victorian-style station is the gateway to the theme park and a departure point for steam trains.

★ Château de la Belle au Bois Dormant

Sleeping Beauty's Castle is the park's centerpiece, mixing the styles of a medieval palace and a French château.

It's a Small World is a musical voyage through landscapes peopled with children in native costumes.

STAR FEATURES

★ **Big Thunder Mountain**

★ **Château de la Belle au Bois Dormant**

★ **Main Street Station**

Le Visionarium's film is an interplay between animated images, live actors and computerized special effects.

Videopolis is a venue for live shows. A massive airship hovers over the entrance.

Star Tours, inspired by the *Star Wars* film, takes you on a high-speed journey through space in a Starspeeder 3000 craft.

Orbitron

This is a kind of futuristic merry-go-round, in which visitors fly high over the theme park in rockets inspired by Leonardo da Vinci's drawings of flying machines.

Autopia

Here visitors can speed around a twisting utopian landscape in futuristic racing cars.

WALT DISNEY'S LEGACY

Disney's passion for animation led him to Hollywood in the 1920s and to the creation of great classic cartoon characters, such as Mickey Mouse and Pluto. His sophisticated animation techniques and shrewd business sense, in the service of childhood nostalgia and escapist fantasy, proved to be a recipe for success in the years of the Depression and World War II. In 1954 his ultimate fantasy, the cartoon brought to life in three dimensions, was realized with the inauguration of the first Disneyland near Los Angeles. Walt Disney died in 1966, but his creations and legacy continue to be enjoyed by millions.

Exploring Disneyland Paris

T HE THEME PARK'S 56 ha (138 acres) are divided into five themes: Main Street USA, Frontierland, Adventureland, Fantasyland and Discoveryland. Each theme is a nostalgic evocation of a legendary past or a place strongly colored by Hollywood folklore. The entire concept, with its imitation exotic buildings, train rides and technological wonders, owes much to the great 19th-century world's fairs.

MAIN STREET, USA

A view down Main Street, USA

M AIN STREET is an evocation of small-town America at the turn of the century. The Victorian building fronts have been designed for color, variety, and authentic detail. Street traffic includes horse-drawn rail cars, old double-decker buses, an antique fire engine, and a Keystone-cop style paddy wagon, all of which transport visitors up to the main hub of the park near Sleeping Beauty's Castle. This is the Central Plaza, the point from which paths radiate to the other four theme lands.

From the Main Street rail-road station, at the entrance to the park, old-fashioned steam trains leave for a circular tour of the park, taking visitors past the Grand Canyon Diorama, with stops at Discoveryland, Frontierland, and Fantasyland.

The street's many delightful attractions include a tradition-al barbershop. At the Main Street Motors car dealer there are authentic antique cars. Among them is a superb 1907 Reliable Dayton High Wheeler Model C.

The 19th-century Emporium department store abounds in authentic features of the period, one of which is an overhead cable-driven money-exchange system. The Emporium is packed full of goods that make delightful gifts. Back outside on Main Street, a variety of musicians such as the Dixieland ragtime band provide exuberant street performances throughout the day.

But the event not to be missed on Main Street is the extravagantly illuminated Electrical Parade, a grand nightly display of richly ornate floats, life-size Disney characters, and dozens of performers.

FRONTIERLAND

T HE WILD WEST of 19th-century America inspired the theme of Frontierland, which visitors enter through

Big Thunder Mountain train

Pluto on Main Street

the log gates of Fort Comstock. Here begins one of the great roller-coaster rides that are among the chief Disneyland attractions. A runaway mining train thrillingly speeds around Big Thunder Mountain, through a canyon landscape of dry boulders, animal bones, mine shafts and shaky bridges.

In Rivers of the Far West, *Mark Twain* and *Molly Brown* paddlewheel steamboats and Indian canoes provide a leisurely journey past other outstanding features of Frontierland.

Phantom Manor is a gingerbread mansion amusingly haunted by mischievous ghosts in dark and eerie rooms, and the Lucky Nugget Saloon features a boisterous music-hall revue with French cancan dancers.

As the Disneyland train circles the theme park, it passes through the Grand Canyon Diorama at the southern tip of Frontierland, where the landscape is dramatized by mountain crags, mountain lions and an assortment of other replica wildlife in the dry wilderness.

More sprightly forms of animal life inhabit Cottonwood Creek Ranch, where children can mix with freely roaming farm animals. Stroll along the wooden sidewalks of the bustling western mining town of Thunder Mesa and visit the railroad station with its period furnishings to see what a traditional telegraph key and pot-bellied stove look like.

ADVENTURELAND

T HE THEME of this land was inspired by characters and tales from adventure fiction. One of the star attractions is the Pirates of the Caribbean. Here an 18th-century Spanish colonial fortress is plundered by life-size animated robot pirates in a crescendo of terrifying explosions and sound effects. Even more impressive is Indiana Jones ™ and the Temple of Doom, a wild trip through an abandoned archeological site, based on the movies of Steven Spielberg. Johann David Wyss' story of *Swiss Family Robinson*, an immigrant family ship-wrecked on a South Seas desert island, inspired the family treehouse, La Cabane des Robinson, which has been constructed on Adventure Isle in a replica of a 27-m (88-ft) high banyan tree. A twisting, creaky stairway runs to the various levels of living space and to the summit, where there are panoramic views of the park.

At Cannonball Cove, the gigantic Skull Rock and Captain Hook's 18th-century pirate ship are used by children as playgrounds. On the north side of the Isle, a treasure hunt delves deep into the cave of Ben Gunn, one of the characters in RL Stevenson's *Treasure Island,* through a maze of stalactites and stalagmites in an eerie atmosphere created by special effects of bat sounds and pirate ghosts singing sea shanties.

The exotically styled bazaar, with its decorative entrance, sandstone towers, and colorful onion domes, sells trinkets, jewelry, and carved masks.

Captain Hook's red and gold galleon

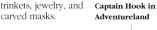

Captain Hook in Adventureland

FANTASYLAND

THIS IS THE theme land with most appeal to younger children. Here the most

Mad Hatter's spinning Tea Cups

famous children's tales come to life in a style inspired by classic Disney movies.

The center of the park is dominated by the Disney emblem, Sleeping Beauty's Castle, fittingly known here as *Le Château de la Belle au Bois Dormant.* The picturesque medley of soaring slender towers of the Euro version is in part inspired by the medieval Louvre *(see pp122–3)* and the Loire Valley châteaus. The village itself is an engaging mixture of medieval French, German and Swiss architecture.

You can walk or ride through the different sections, each devoted to various Disney characters and tales.

In the Snow White and the Seven Dwarfs section, visitors can ride in the Seven Dwarfs' mine train and witness Snow White in danger from the evil witch lurking in the haunted forest. Pinocchio's travels are enacted by puppets and human performers, with favorite characters such as Geppetto and Jiminy Cricket.

Visitors can also fly over London and Never Land with the flying boy Peter Pan, whirl on an aerial merry-go-round with Dumbo the Flying Elephant, spin in the Mad Hatter's Tea Cups and search a way through the Alice in Wonderland maze to the Queen of Heart's Castle.

DISCOVERYLAND

DEVOTED TO the future and to man's great inventions, this is the most modernistic of the theme lands, with futurist architecture and the latest sophisticated technology.

The newest attraction – "Honey, I Shrunk the Audience" – is here, in which over 600 people at a time are miniaturized to the size of mice by hapless inventor Wayne Szalinksi (Rick Moranis).

The Visionarium is an extraordinary movie theater with a vast wrap-around screen showing a voyage through time.

Through the use of stunning special effects, the Star Tours attraction realistically simulates a thrilling space journey based on the *Star Wars* movies. At the Videopolis show, a dancing and concert venue, the massive Hyperion airship towers over the entrance.

Hyperion at Videopolis entrance

Château et Bois de Vincennes ⑲

M *Château de Vincennes.* RER *Vincennes.* **Château** *Ave de Paris 94300 Vincennes.* C *01 48 08 31 20.* **Open** *10am–6pm (5pm winter) daily.* **Adm charge.** ⊙ ✦ *compulsory in keep & chapel.* ⬛ **Bois de Vincennes** *Open dusk to dawn daily.* **Zoological Park** Cf *01 44 75 20 10.* **Open** *9am–6pm (5pm winter) daily (last adm 30 minutes earlier).* **Adm charge.** ⬛ ⬛

The CHATEAU de Vincennes, enclosed by a defensive wall and a moat, was once a royal residence. It was here that Henry V of England died painfully of dysentery in 1422. His body was boiled in the château's kitchen to prepare it for shipping back to England. Abandoned when Versailles was completed, the château was converted into an arsenal by Napoleon and in 1840 became a fortress.

The 14th-century keep is a fine example of medieval military architecture and houses the château's museum. The Gothic chapel was finished around 1550, with beautiful stone rose windows and a magnificent single aisle. Two 17th-century pavilions house a museum of army insignia.

Once a royal hunting ground, the forest of Vincennes was given to the City of Paris by Napoleon III in 1860 as a public park. Baron Haussman's landscape architect, added ornamental lakes and cascades. Among its main attractions are the zoo and the largest carnival in France (held from Palm Sunday to the end of May).

Bibliothèque Nationale de France

Bercy ⑳

75012. **Map** *18 F3.* M *Cour St-Emilion.*

This OLD WINE VILLAGE, with its pavillions and warehouses, is undergoing a major transformation. With the wine merchants gone, Paris is revitalizing and modernizing this eastern district. New housing has been built around a 70-ha (173-acre) park, a business zone developed around Bercy-Expo, and the Bercy sports center plays host to some of the city's biggest events. Of the old wine village, the pavilions have been restored and now house a museum of carnival art, music fairs, and the Paris School of Bakery Patisserie. Wine warehouses in St-Emilion Court are to become a leisure and cultural center called Bercy-Village, and architect Frank Gehry's new American Cultural Center will house the future Masion du Cinéma.

Bibliothèque Nationale de France ㉑

Quai François-Mauriac 75013. **Map** *18 F4.* Cf *01 53 79 59 59.* M *Quai de la Gare.* **Open** *10am–8pm Tue–Sat; noon–7pm Sun.* **Closed** *public hols & 2 wks mid-Sep.* **Adm charge.** ⬛ ⬛ ⬛

The NATIONAL LIBRARY of France at Tolbiac was opened in 1995 to allow the library to expand from its site on rue Richelieu *(see p217).* Four great towers house over 12 million volumes. Reference and research libraries are in the central podium, offering access to over 400,000 titles. Other resources include over 50,000 digitized illustrations, sound archives and CD-ROMs.

South of the City

Parc Montsouris ㉒

Blvd Jourdan 75014. C *01 45 88 28 60.* M *Porte d'Orléans.* RER *Cité Universitaire.* **Open** *summer: 7:30am–7pm daily; winter: 7:30am–5:30pm daily.* ⬛

This ENGLISH-STYLE park was laid out by the landscape architect Adophe Alphand, between 1865 and 1878. It has a pleasant restaurant, lawns, slopes, elegant tall trees and a lake that is home to many different species of birds. This park is the second largest in central Paris and is also the site of the municipal meteorological weather station.

The imposing Château de Vincennes

Cité Universitaire ㉓

19–21 Blvd Jourdan 75014. ☎ 01 44 16 64 00. 🚉 Cité Universitaire.

THIS IS AN INTERNATIONAL city in miniature for more than 5,000 foreign students attending the University of Paris. Created orginally in the 1920s by benefactors from all over the world, it now contains 37 houses, each in a different architectural style linked to different countries. The Swiss House and the Franco-Brazilian House were designed by the Modernist architect Le Corbusier. The International House, donated by John D Rockefeller in 1936, has a library, restaurant, swimming pool and theater. The student community makes this a lively and stimulating area of the city.

Japan House at Cité Universitaire

Notre-Dame du Travail ㉔

59 Rue Vercingetorix 75014. **Map** 15 B3. ☎ 01 44 10 72 92. 🚇 Pernety. **Open** 10am–noon Mon–Fri, 2:30pm–6:30pm Mon–Sat. ✝ 6:30pm Sat, 9am, 11am Sun.

THIS CHURCH DATES from 1902 and is made of an unusual mix of materials: stone, rubble and bricks over a riveted steel and iron framework. It was the creation of Father Soulange-Boudin, a priest who organized cooperatives and sought to reconcile labor and capitalism. Local parishioners

The Sebastopol Bell in Notre-Dame du Travail

raised the money for its construction, but lack of funds meant that many features, such as the bell towers, were never built. On the façade hangs the Sebastopol Bell, a trophy from the Crimean War given to the people of the Plaisance district by Napoleon III. The Art Nouveau interior has recently been restored and features paintings of patron saints.

Institut Pasteur ㉕

25 Rue du Docteur Roux 75015. **Map** 15 A2. ☎ 01 45 68 82 83. 🚇 Pasteur. **Open** 2–5:30pm Mon–Fri (last adm: 5pm). **Closed** Aug, public hols. **Adm charge**. 📷 **Movies, videos**. 🎥 compulsory. 📷

THE INSTITUT PASTEUR is France's leading medical research center and was founded by the world-renowned scientist Louis Pasteur in 1888–9. He discovered the process of milk pasteurization as well as vaccines against rabies and anthrax. The research center houses a museum that includes a recon-struction of Pasteur's apartment and laboratory. It was designed by his grand-children (also scientists) and is faithful to the original down to the last detail. Pasteur's tomb is in a basement crypt built in the style of a small Byzantine chapel. The tomb of Dr Emile Roux, the inventor

Louis Pasteur

of the treatment of diphtheria by serum injection, lies in the garden. The institute has laboratories for pure and applied research, lecture rooms, a reference section and a hospital founded to apply Pasteur's theories.

There is also a library – the institute's original building from 1888 – where research into AIDS is carried out, led by pioneering Professor Luc Montagnier, who discovered the HIV virus in 1983.

Garden in the Parc André Citroën

Parc André Citroën ㉖

Rue Balard 75015. 🚇 Javel, Balard. **Open** 7:30am–dusk Mon–Fri, 9am–dusk Sat, Sun & public hols.

OPENED IN 1992, this park is the third large-scale vista on the Seine, along with Les Invalides and the Champ-de-Mars. Designed by both landscapers and architects, it is a fascinating blend of styles, ranging from a wildflower meadow in the north to the sophisticated mono-chrome mineral and sculpture gardens of the southern section. Numerous modern water sculptures dot the park, and huge greenhouses nurture a range of environments from a Mediterranean garden and a Southern Hemisphere zone to an orangery that is used for horticultural shows in summer.

Versailles ㉗

See pp248–53.

The Palace and Gardens of Versailles ㉘

VISITORS passing through the rich interior of this colossal palace, or those strolling in its vast gardens, will understand why it was the glory of the Sun King's reign. Starting in 1668 with his father's modest hunting lodge, Louis XIV built the largest palace in Europe, housing 20,000 people at a time. Architects Louis Le Vau and Jules Hardouin-Mansart designed the buildings; Charles Le Brun did the interiors; and André Le Nôtre, the great landscaper, redesigned the gardens, which are formally styled into paths and groves, hedges and flower beds, water pools and fountains.

Garden statue of a flautist

★ Formal Gardens
Geometric paths and shrubberies are features of the formal gardens.

The Orangerie was built beneath the Parterre du Midi to house exotic plants in winter.

The South Parterre's shrubbery and ornate flower beds overlook the Swiss pond.

★ The Château
Louis XIV made the château into the center of political power in France.

The Water Parterre's vast pools are decorated with superb bronze statues.

Fountain of Latona
Marble basins rise to Balthazar Marsy's statue of the goddess Latona.

Dragon Fountain
The fountain's centerpiece is a winged monster.

The King's Garden with Mirror Pool is a 19th-century English garden and pool created by Louis XVIII.

Colonnade
Mansart designed this circle of marble arches in 1685.

VISITORS' CHECKLIST

Versailles. 01 30 84 74 00.
01 30 84 76 76. 1/1 to
Versailles. RER Versailles Rive
Gauche. **Château open** Oct–
Apr: 9am–5:30pm Tue–Sun; May–
Sep: 9am–6:30pm Tue–Sun. **Adm
charge. Grand Trianon & Petit
Trianon open** Oct–Apr: 10am–
12:30pm, 2pm–5:30pm Tue–Fri;
10am–5:30pm Sat & Sun; May–
Sep: 10am–6:30pm Tue–Sun
(last adm: 30 mins before closing).
Adm charge.

The Grand Canal was the setting for Louis XIV's many boating parties.

Petit Trianon
Built in 1762 as a retreat for Louis XV, this small château became a favorite of Marie-Antoinette.

Fountain of Neptune
Groups of sculptures spray spectacular jets of water in Le Nôtre and Mansart's 17th-century fountain.

★ **Grand Trianon**
Louis XIV built this small palace of stone and pink marble in 1687 to escape the rigors of court life and to enjoy the company of his mistress, Madame de Maintenon.

STAR SIGHTS

★ **The Château**

★ **Formal Gardens**

★ **Grand Trianon**

The Main Palace Buildings of Versailles

Gold crest from the Petit Trianon

THE PRESENT palace grew as a series of envelopes enfolding the original hunting lodge, whose low brick front is still visible in the center. In the 1660s, Louis Le Vau built the first envelope, a series of wings that expanded into an enlarged courtyard. It was decorated with marble busts, antique trophies and gilded roofs. On the garden side, columns were added to the west facade, and a great terrace was created on the first floor. Mansart took over in 1678 and added the two immense north and south wings and filled Le Vau's terrace to form the Hall of Mirrors. He designed the chapel, which was finished in 1710. The Opera House *(L'Opéra)* was added by Louis XV in 1770.

South Wing
The wing's original apartments for great nobles were replaced by Louis-Philippe's museum of French history.

The Royal Courtyard was separated from the Ministers' Courtyard by elaborate grillwork during Louis XIV's reign. It was accessible only to royal carriages.

Louis XIV's statue, erected by Louis Philippe in 1837, stands where a gilded gateway once marked the beginning of the Royal Courtyard.

STAR SIGHTS

★ **Marble Courtyard**

★ **L'Opéra**

★ **Chapelle Royale**

Ministers' Courtyard

Main Gate
Mansart's original gateway grille, surmounted by the royal arms, is the entrance to the Ministers' Courtyard.

TIMELINE

1650	1700	1750	1800	1850

1667 Grand Canal begun

1668 Construction of new château by Le Vau

Louis XV

1722 12-year-old Louis XV occupies Versailles

1793 Louis XVI and Marie Antoinette executed

1833 Louis Philippe turns the château into a museum

1671 Interior decoration by Le Brun begun

1715 Death of Louis XIV. Versailles abandoned by court

1789 King and queen forced to leave Versailles for Paris

1661 Louis XIV enlarges château

1682 Louis XIV and Marie-Thérèse move to Versailles

1774 Louis XVI and Marie Antoinette live at Versailles

1919 Treaty of Versailles signed on June 28

The Clock
Hercules and Mars flank the clock overlooking the Marble Courtyard.

★ **Marble Courtyard**
The courtyard is decorated with marble paving, urns, busts and a gilded balcony.

North Wing
The chapel, Opéra and picture galleries occupy this wing, which originally housed royal apartments.

★ **L'Opéra**
The Opéra was completed in 1770, in time for the marriage of the future Louis XVI and Marie Antoinette.

★ **Chapelle Royale**
Mansart's last great work, this two-story Baroque chapel, was Louis XIV's last addition to Versailles.

Inside the Château of Versailles

THE SUMPTUOUS main apartments are on the first floor of the vast château complex. Around the Marble Courtyard are the private apartments of the king and the queen. On the garden side are the state apartments where official Court life took place. These were richly decorated by Charles Le Brun with colored marbles, stone and wood carvings, murals, velvet, silver and gilded furniture. Beginning with the Salon d'Hercule, each state room is dedicated to an Olympian deity. The climax is the Hall of Mirrors, where 17 great mirrors face tall arched windows.

★ Queen's Bedroom
In this room the queens of France gave birth to the royal children in full public view.

STAR SIGHTS

★ **Chapelle Royale**

★ **Salon de Venus**

★ **Hall of Mirrors**

★ **Queen's Bedroom**

KEY

- South wing
- Coronation room
- Madame de Maintenon's apartments
- Queen's apartments and private suite
- State apartments
- King's apartments and private suite
- North wing
- Non-exhibition space

Entrance

Louis XVI's library
features Neoclassical paneling and the king's terrestrial globe.

The Salon du Sacre   **Entrance**
is adorned with huge paintings of Napoleon by Jacques-Louis David.

★ Salon de Venus
A Louis XIV statue stands amidst the rich marble decor of this room.

★ Chapelle Royale
The chapel's first floor was reserved for the royal family and the ground floor for the Court. The interior is richly decorated in white marble, gilding and Baroque murals.

★ **Hall of Mirrors**
Great state occasions were held in this multimirrored room stretching 233 ft (70 m) along the west facade. Here in 1919 the Treaty of Versailles was ratified, ending World War I.

Oeil-de-Boeuf

The King's Bedroom
is where Louis XIV died in 1715, aged 77.

Salon de la Guerre
The room's theme of war is dramatically reinforced by Antoine Coysevox's stuccoed relief of Louis XIV riding to victory.

The Cabinet du Conseil is where the king received his ministers and his family.

Salon d'Apollon
Designed by Le Brun and dedicated to the god Apollo, this was Louis XIV's throne room. A copy of Hyacinthe Rigaud's famous portrait of the king (1701) hangs here.

Salon d'Hercule

Stairs to ground-floor reception area

PURSUIT OF THE QUEEN
On October 6, 1789, a Parisian mob invaded the palace seeking the despised Marie Antoinette. The queen, roused in alarm from her bed, fled toward the king's rooms through the anteroom known as the Oeil-de-Boeuf. As the mob tried to break into the room, the queen beat on the door of the king's bedroom. Once admitted she was safe, at least until morning, when she and the king were removed to Paris by the cheering and triumphant mob.

West of the City

An Art Nouveau window in the Rue la Fontaine

Rue la Fontaine ㉘

75016. **Map** 9 A4. Ⓜ *Jasmin, Michel-Ange Auteuil.*

T HE RUE LA FONTAINE and surrounding streets act as a showcase for some of the most exciting architecture of the early 20th century. At No. 14 stands the Castel Béranger, a stunning apartment house made from cheap building materials to keep costs low, yet featuring stained glass, convoluted ironwork, balconies and mosaics. It established the reputation of Art Nouveau architect Hector Guimard, who went on to design the entrances for the Paris metro. Several more examples of his work can be seen farther along the street, such as the Hôtel Mezzara at No. 60.

Fondation Le Corbusier ㉙

8–10 Square du Docteur Blanche 75016. Ⓒ *01 42 88 41 53.* Ⓜ *Jasmin.* **Open** *10am–12:30pm, 1:30pm–6pm Mon–Fri.* **Closed** *public hols, Aug, Dec 24–Jan 2.* **Adm charge.** 🎥 **Movies, videos.** 📖 *See* **History of Paris** *pp36–7.*

I N A QUIET CORNER of Auteuil stand the villas La Roche (*see p265*) and Jeanneret, the first two Parisian houses built by the brilliant and influential 20th-century architect Charles-Edouard Jeanneret, known as Le Corbusier. Built at the start of the 1920s, they demonstrate his revolutionary use of white concrete in Cubist forms. Rooms flow into one another allowing maximum light and volume, and the houses stand on stilts with windows along their entire length.

Villa La Roche was owned by the art patron Raoul La Roche. Today both villas serve as a documentation center on Le Corbusier where lectures on his work are given.

Musée Marmottan ㉚

2 Rue Louis Boilly 75016. 📷 *01 44 96 50 33.* Ⓜ *Muette.* **Open** *10am–5pm Tue–Sun (last adm: 4:30pm).* **Closed** *Jan 1, May 1, Dec 25.* **Adm charge.** 📷

T HE MUSEUM WAS created in the 19th-century mansion of the art historian Paul Marmottan in 1932, when he bequeathed his house and his Renaissance, Consular and First Empire collections of paintings and furniture to the Institut de France. The focus of the museum changed in 1971 after the bequest by Michel Monet of 65 paintings by his father, the Impressionist painter Claude Monet. Some of Monet's most famous paintings are here, including *Impression – Sunrise* (from which the term "Impressionist" was derived), a painting of Rouen Cathedral and several *Water Lilies*.

Part of Monet's personal art collection also passed to the museum, including paintings by Camille Pissarro and the Impressionists Pierre Auguste Renoir and Alfred Sisley. The museum also displays medieval illuminated manuscripts.

La Barque (1887) by Claude Monet, in the Musée Marmottan

Bois de Boulogne ㉛

75016. Ⓜ *Porte Maillot, Porte Dauphine, Porte d'Auteuil, Sablons.* **Open** *24 hrs daily.* **Adm charge** *to specialist gardens and museum.* ♿ **Shakespeare garden** 🎭 **Open-air theater** Ⓒ *01 40 19 95 33/01 42 76 55 06.* **Open** *May–Sep.* **Bagatelle & Rose gardens** Ⓒ *01 40 67 97 00.* **Open** *8:30am. Closing times vary from 4:30pm to 8pm according to season.* **Jardin d'Acclimatation** Ⓒ *01 40 67 90 82.* **Open** *10am–7pm daily (Oct–May: to 6pm daily).* 📷 🍴 **Musée en Herbe** Ⓒ *01 40 67 97 66.* **Open** *10am–6pm Mon–Fri, 2pm–6pm Sat.* **Adm charge.** ♿ **Musée des Arts et Traditions Populaires** Ⓒ *01 44 17 60 00.* **Open** *9:30am–5pm Wed–Mon.* **Adm charge.** ♿ 📷 *by appt, 1 month in advance.*

B ETWEEN THE western edges of Paris and the River Seine this 865-ha (2,137-acre) park offers a vast belt of greenery for strolling, cycling, riding, boating, picnicking, or

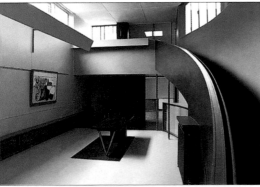

Villa La Roche, home of the Fondation Le Corbusier

Kiosque de l'Empereur, on an island in the Grand Lac, Bois de Boulogne

spending a day at the races. The Bois de Boulogne is all that remains of the vast Forêt du Rouvre. In the mid-19th century Napoleon III had it redesigned and landscaped by Haussmann along the lines of London's Hyde Park.

There are many beautiful areas within the Bois. The Pré Catelan is a self-contained park with the widest beech tree in Paris, and the charming Bagatelle gardens feature architectural follies and an 18th-century villa famous for its rose garden, where an international rose competition is held on June 21. The villa was built in 64 days as a bet between the Comte d'Artois and Marie-Antoinette. The Bois has a reputation as a seedy area after dark so is best avoided at night.

Espace Landowski 🔞

28 Ave André Morizet, Boulogne-Billancourt 92104. **C** *01 44 96 50 33.* **M** *Marcel Sembat.* **Open** *10am–6pm Wed, Sat, 2–8pm Thu, 2–6pm Fri, 1–6pm Sun.* 👌 ✉ *by appt.* 📷

La Grande Arche in La Défense

INAUGURATED IN 1998, this arts complex brings together a museum of the 1930s, a library, a gallery of video directors, a movie theater, and a multimedia center.

The complex is named for Paul Landowski, a sculptor who lived in Boulogne-Billancourt from 1905 until his death in 1961, and his musician brother, Marcel. Several of Paul's works are on show in the museum. Through paintings, drawings, sculpture, and artifacts, the museum gives a vivid impression of the aesthetic mood of the era. The museum also organizes temporary thematic exhibitions relating to the period, while the multimedia center has creative studios for contemporary artists to use. Themed tours of the architectural and industrial heritage of Boulogne-Billancourt are also run by the center.

La Défense 🔞

La Grande Arche. **C** *01 49 07 27 57.* **RER** *La Défense.* **Open** *10am–7pm daily (last adm: 1 hr before closing).* **Adm charge.** 📷 ℹ *See History of Paris pp38–9.*

THIS SKYSCRAPER business city on the western edge of Paris is the largest new office development in Europe and covers 80 ha (198 acres). It was launched

in the 1960s to create a new home for leading French and multinational companies A major artistic scheme has transformed many of the squares into fascinating open-air museums.

In 1989 La Grande Arche was added to the complex, an enormous hollow cube large enough to contain Notre-Dame cathedral. This was designed by Danish architect Otto von Spreckelsen as part of major construction works, or *Grands Travaux*, which were initiated by (and are now a memorial to) President François Mitterrand.

The arch now houses an exhibition gallery and a conference center, and commands a superb view over the city of Paris.

Château de Malmaison 🔞

Ave du Château 92500 Rueil-Malmaison. **C** *01 41 29 05 55.* **RER** *La Défense then bus 258.* **Open** *10 am daily; closing times vary according to season; call for details.* **Adm charge.** 📷 *See History of Paris pp30–31.*

The Empress Josephine's bed in the Château de Malmaison

THIS 17TH-CENTURY château was bought in 1799 by Josephine de Beauharnais, wife of Napoleon I. A magnificent veranda, Classical statues and a small theater were added. After his campaigns, Napoleon and his entourage would come here to relax. The château became Josephine's main residence after their divorce. Today, it is an important Napoleonic museum, together with the nearby Château de Bois-Préau.

Furniture, portraits, artifacts, and mementoes of the imperial family are displayed in rooms reconstructed in the style of the First Empire.

Part of the original grounds still exists, including Josephine's famous rose garden.

FIVE GUIDED WALKS

ARIS IS A CITY for walking. It is more compact and easier to get around than many other great capitals. Most of its magnificent sights are within walking distance of one another, and they are close to the central heart of the city, the Ile de la Cité.

Fourteen classic tourist areas are described in the *Area by Area* section of this book, each with a short walk marked on its *Street-by-Street* map, taking you past many of the most interesting sights. Paris also offers a wealth of lesser-known but equally remarkable sections whose special history, architecture and local customs reveal to the visitor other facets of the city.

The five walks around the following neighborhoods not only take in their main sights but also introduce visitors to the subtle details and contrasts that contribute to the special character of each district. These include cafés, street markets, quirky churches, canals, gardens, old village

Parc Monceau statue

streets and bridges, all rich in literary, artistic and historical associations. Everywhere, past and present blend, in the changing and vibrant life of the modern city.

The walks contrast the smart areas of Auteuil, Monceau and Ile St-Louis with the old working-class areas of Montmartre and St-Martin. Auteuil is renowned for its luxury modern residential architecture; Monceau for its sumptuous Second Empire mansions; and Ile St-Louis for its *ancien régime* town houses, tree-lined river quays, narrow streets and film-star and literati residents. Village streets that were once home to famous artists and bohemians still enrich Montmartre, and the old-fashioned charm of the iron footbridges survives along the old industrial Canal St-Martin.

All the walk areas are readily accessible by public transportation, and the nearest metro stations and bus routes are listed in the *Tips for Walkers* boxes. There are suggestions on resting points such as cafés, restaurants, gardens and squares, along each route.

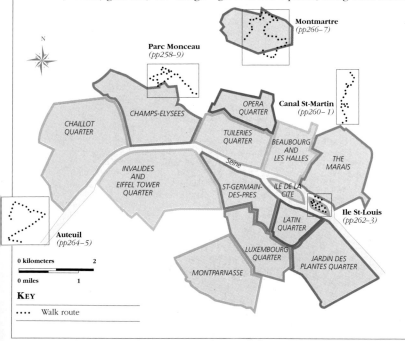

Montmartre
(pp266–7)

Parc Monceau
(pp258–9)

N

Canal St-Martin
(pp260–1)

CHAILLOT QUARTER

CHAMPS-ELYSEES

OPERA QUARTER

TUILERIES QUARTER

BEAUBOURG AND LES HALLES

THE MARAIS

INVALIDES AND EIFFEL TOWER QUARTER

Seine

ST-GERMAIN-DES-PRES

ILE DE LA CITE

Ile St-Louis
(pp262–3)

Auteuil
(pp264–5)

LATIN QUARTER

LUXEMBOURG QUARTER

JARDIN DES PLANTES QUARTER

MONTPARNASSE

0 kilometers 2

0 miles 1

KEY

•••• Walk route

Autumnal scene along a Seine quayside

A 90-Minute Walk around Parc Monceau

THIS LEISURELY WALK passes through the exquisite late 18th-century Parc Monceau, the centerpiece of an elegant Second Empire district. It then follows a route along surrounding streets, where groups of opulent mansions stunningly convey the magnificence in which some Parisians live, before ending at Place St-Augustin. For details on Monceau sights, see pages 230 to 231.

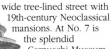

Ruysdaël gate

Parc Monceau to Avenue Velasquez

The walk starts at the Monceau metro station ① on the Boulevard de Courcelles. Enter the park where Nicolas Ledoux's 18th-century toll house ② stands. On either side are sumptuously gilded 19th-century wrought-iron gates which support ornate lampposts.

Take the second path on the left, past the monument to Guy de Maupassant ③ (1897). This is only one of a series of six Belle Epoque monuments of prominent French writers and musicians which are picturesquely scattered throughout the park. Most of them feature a solemn bust of a great man who is accompanied by a swooning muse.

Straight ahead is the most important remaining folly, a moss-covered Corinthian colonnade ④ running around the edge of a charming tiny lake with the requisite island in the center. Walk around the colonnade and under a 16th-century arch ⑤ transplanted from the old Paris Hôtel de Ville (see p102), which burned down in 1871.

Turn left on the Allée de la Comtesse de Ségur and go onto Avenue Velasquez, a

wide tree-lined street with 19th-century Neoclassical mansions. At No. 7 is the splendid Cernuschi Museum ⑥, which houses a collection of Far Eastern art.

Parc Monceau's toll house ②

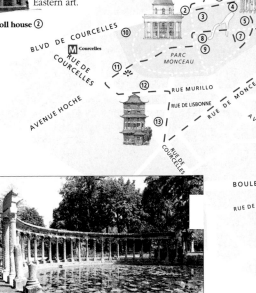

Ambroise Thomas statue ⑧

Avenue Velasquez to Avenue Van Dyck

Reenter the park and turn left into the second small winding path, which is bordered by an 18th-century mossy pyramid ⑦, antique tombs, a stone arcade, an obelisk and a small Chinese stone pagoda. The romantically melancholy tone of these false ruins suits the spirit of the late 18th century.

Turn right on the first path past the pyramid and walk back to the central avenue. Straight ahead, a Renaissance bridge fords the little stream running from the lake. Turn left and walk past the

Colonnade in Parc Monceau ④

monument (1902) to the musician Ambroise Thomas ⑧. Immediately behind there is a lovely artificial mountain with a cascade. Turn left on the next avenue and approach the monument (1897) to the composer Charles Gounod ⑨ on the left. From here, follow the first winding path toward the Avenue Van Dyck exit on the left. Ahead to the right, in the corner of the park, is the Chopin monument ⑩ (1906), and along the Allée de la Comtesse de Ségur is the monument to the 19th-century French poet Alfred de Musset.

Avenue Van Dyck to Rue de Monceau

Leave the park and pass onto Avenue Van Dyck. No. 5 on the right is a most impressive Parc Monceau mansion ⑪, a Neo-Baroque structure built by chocolate manufacturer Emile Menier; No. 6 is in the French Renaissance style that came back into favor in the 1860s. Straight ahead, beyond the ornate grille, there is a fine view of Avenue Hoche and in the distance the Arc de Triomphe. Walk past the

The mountain cascade ⑧

gate and turn left onto Rue de Courcelles and left again onto Rue Murillo, bordered by more elaborate town houses in 18th-century and French Renaissance styles ⑫. At the crossing of Rue Rembrandt, which is on the left, is another gate into the park; on the right are a massive apartment building dating from 1900 (No. 7) and an elegant French Renaissance house with an elaborately carved wooden door (No. 1). At the corner of the Rue Rembrandt and the Rue de Courcelles stands the oddest of all the neighborhood buildings, a striking five-story red Chinese pagoda ⑬. It is an exclusive emporium of Chinese art.

Turn left on to the Rue de Monceau, walk past Avenue Ruysdaël and continue to the Musée Nissim de Camondo at No. 63 Rue de Monceau ⑭. Some nearby buildings worth having a look at are Nos. 52, 60 and 61 ⑮.

Boulevard Malesherbes

At the junction of Rue de Monceau and Boulevard Malesherbes turn right. This long boulevard with dignified six-story apartment buildings is typical of the great avenues cut through Paris by Baron Haussmann, Prefect of the Seine during the Second Empire *(see pp32–3)*. They

greatly pleased the Industrial Age bourgeoisie but horrified sensitive souls and writers, who compared them with the buildings of New York.

No. 75 is the posh marble front of Benneton, the most fashionable Paris card and stationery engraver ⑯. On the left, near the Boulevard Haussmann, looms the greatest 19th-century Paris church, St-Augustin ⑰, built by Victor-Louis Baltard. Enter the church through the back door on Rue de la Bien-faisance. Walk through the church and leave by the main door. On the left is the massive stone building of the French Officers' club, the Cercle Militaire ⑱. Straight ahead is a bronze statue of Joan of Arc ⑲. Continue on to Place St-Augustin to St-Augustin metro station.

Joan of Arc statue ⑲

KEY

— Walk route
⚜ Good viewing point
Ⓜ Metro station

| 0 meters | 250 |
| 0 yards | 250 |

Chinese pagoda emporium ⑬

TIPS FOR WALKERS

Starting point: *Blvd de Courcelles.*
Length: *2 miles (3 km).*
Getting there: *The nearest metro is Monceau; buses that take you there are Nos. 30, 84 and 94.*
St-Augustin church: *Open 7am–7pm daily.*
Stopping-off points: *Near the Renaissance bridge in the Parc Monceau is a kiosk serving coffee and sandwiches. There are two cafés at Place de Rio de Janeiro servicing the office-workers in the surrounding area, and there is a brasserie opposite St-Augustin church. The Square M. Pagnol is a pleasant place to relax and take in the beauty of the park at the end of the walk.*

A 90-Minute Walk along the Canal St-Martin

THE WALK ALONG the quays on either side of the Canal St-Martin is a very different experience of Paris than what one finds in the more elegant districts. Here, the older surviving landmarks of the neighborhood – the factories, warehouses, dwellings, taverns and cafés – hint at life in a thriving 19th-century industrial, working-class world. Here there are the softer charms of the old iron footbridges, the tree-lined quays, the inevitable fishermen, the river barges and the still waters of the broad canal basins. A walk along the canal, which connects the Bassin de la Villette with the Seine, will evoke images of the Pernod-drinking working-class Paris of Jean Gabin and Edith Piaf.

The 18th-century
Barrière de la Villette ②

Bassin de la Villette looking north ③

Place de Stalingrad to Avenue Jean-Jaurès

From the Stalingrad metro station ①, follow Boulevard de la Villette to the new square in front of the Barrière de la Villette ②. This is one of the few remaining 18th-century toll houses in Paris, designed by the celebrated Neoclassical architect Nicolas Ledoux in the 1780s. The fountains, square and terraces were designed in the 1980s to provide an attractive setting and fine views of the Bassin de la Villette ③ to the north.

Walk toward Avenue Jean-Jaurès. On the left is the first lock ④ leading down to the canal.

Quai de Valmy to Rue Bichat

Cross over to the Quai de Jemmapes, which runs the whole length of the east side

View from Rue E. Varlin bridge ⑦

KEY

— Walk route

☆ Good viewing point

Ⓜ Metro station

| 0 meters | 500 |
| 0 yards | 500 |

Courtyard garden of Hôpital St-Louis ⑭

Iron footbridges over the canal ⑤

French Communist Party headquarters ⑨, on Place du Colonel Fabien. The building can be recognized by its curving glazed tower.

Return to the Quai de Jemmapes, where at No. 134 ⑩ stands one of the few surviving brick-and-iron industrial buildings that used to line the canal in the 19th century. At No. 126 ⑪ is another notable modern building, a residence for the aged, with monumental concrete arches and glazed bay windows. Farther along, at No. 112 ⑫, is an Art Deco apartment building with bay windows, decorative iron balconies and tiles. On the ground floor is a typical 1930s proletarian café. Here the canal curves gracefully into the third lock, spanned by a charming transparent iron footbridge ⑬.

Hôpital St-Louis to Rue Léon Jouhaux

Turn left into Rue Bichat, which leads to the remarkable 17th-century Hôpital St-Louis ⑭. Enter through the hospital's old main gate with its high-pitched roof and massive stone arch. Pass into the courtyard. The hospital was founded in 1607 by Henri IV, the first Bourbon king, to care for the victims of the plague. Leave the courtyard from the central gate on the wing on your left. Here you pass by the 17th-century hospital chapel ⑮ and out into the Rue de la Grange aux Belles.

Turn left and walk back to the canal. At the junction of

Rue de la Grange and the Quai de Jemmapes stood, until 1627, the notorious Montfaucon gallows ⑯, one of the chief public execution spots of medieval Paris. Turn onto the Quai de Jemmapes. At No. 101 ⑰ is the original front of the Hôtel du Nord, which was made famous in the 1930s film of the same name. In front is another iron footbridge and a drawbridge ⑱ for traffic, providing a charming setting with views of the canal on either side. Cross over and continue down the Quai de Valmy until reaching the last footbridge ⑲ at the corner of the Rue Léon Jouhaux. From here you'll see the canal disappearing under the surface of Paris, to continue its journey, through a great stone arch.

Entrance to Hôpital St-Louis ⑭

Square Frédéric Lemaître to Place de la République

Walk along Square Frédéric Lemaître ⑳ to the start of Boulevard Jules Ferry, which has a public garden stretching down its center. The garden was built over the canal in the 1860s. At its head stands a charmingly nostalgic statue of a flower girl of the 1830s, *La Grisette* ㉑. On the left is a busy working-class street, Rue du Faubourg du Temple ㉒, with flourishing ethnic shops and restaurants. Follow the street to the right and walk on to the metro station in the Place de la République.

of the canal and down to the first bridge on Rue Louis Blanc ⑤. Cross the bridge to the Quai de Valmy. From the corner you'll get a glimpse of the oblique granite-and-glass front of the new Paris Industrial Tribunal ⑥ on the Rue Louis Blanc.

Continue along Quai de Valmy. At Rue E. Varlin cross the bridge ⑦, from where there is an attractive view of the second canal lock, lock-keeper's house, public gardens and old lampposts. At the other side of the bridge, at the corner of Quai de Jemmapes and along the pedestrianized street Rue Haendel, there is a good view of the towering, terraced buildings of a social housing estate ⑧. Nearby is the

A shop front in Rue du Temple ㉒

A 90-Minute Walk around the Ile St-Louis

THE WALK AROUND this charming tiny island passes along the enchanting, picturesque tree-lined quays from Pont Louis-Philippe to Quai d'Anjou, taking in the sumptuous 17th-century *hôtels* that infuse the area with such a powerful sense of period. It then penetrates into the heart of the island along the main street, Rue St-Louis-en-l'Ile – enlivened by chic restaurants, cafés, art galleries and boutiques – before returning to the north side of the island and to Pont Marie. For more information on the main sights, see pages 77 and 87.

Left Bank view of the Ile St-Louis

Fishing on a St-Louis quayside

Metro Pont Marie to Rue Jean du Bellay

From the Pont Marie metro station ① walk down Quai des Celestins and take the nearest available exit to Voie Georges Pompidou. Continue down Voie Georges Pompidou to Pont Louis-Philippe ②. Cross the bridge and immediately to the right take the steps down to the lower quay. Walk around the tree-shaded west point of the island ③, then up the other

side to the Pont St-Louis ④. Opposite the bridge, on the corner of Rue Jean du Bellay, is the Flore en l'Ile ⑤, the smartest café on the island. Next to it is one of the Berthillon shops, famous for its fruit ices.

Quai d'Orléans

From the corner of Rue Jean du Bellay and Quai d'Orléans there are fine views of the Panthéon's dome and Notre-Dame. Along the quay, No. 12 ⑥ is one of several stately 17th-century houses with fine wrought-iron balconies. At Nos. 18–20 the Hôtel Rolland has unusual Hispano-Moorish windows.

KEY

— Walk route

☆ Good viewing point

Ⓜ Metro station

0 meters	250
0 yards	250

At No. 6, the Polish library, founded in 1838, has a small museum devoted to the Polish poet Adam Mickiewicz ⑦; it also contains some Chopin scores and autographs by George Sand and Victor Hugo. On the right, the Pont de la Tournelle ⑧ links the island to the Left Bank.

Seine barge passing a St-Louis quay

Quai de Béthune to Pont Marie

Continue beyond the bridge and onto Quai de Béthune, where the Nobel laureate Marie Curie lived at No. 36 ⑨ and where beautiful wrought-iron balconies gracefully decorate Nos. 34 and 30. The Hôtel Richelieu ⑩ at No. 18 is one of the island's most beautiful houses.

St-Louis church door ⑰

It features a fine garden where the original Classical blind arcades have been retained.

Turn left down Rue Bretonvilliers, where there is an imposing 17th-century house ⑪ with a high-pitched roof resting on a great Classical arch spanning the street. Return to the Quai de Béthune and proceed to the Pont de Sully ⑫, a late 19th-century bridge joining the river banks. Ahead is the charming 19th-century Square Barye ⑬, a shady public garden at the east point of the island, from where there are fine river views. From here travel towards the Quai d'Anjou as far as the corner of Rue St-Louis-en-l'Ile to see the most

small, chic bistro-style restaurants with pleasantly old-fashioned decors. No. 31 is the original Berthillon shop ⑱; No. 60 is a charming antiques shop ⑲ with an original 19th-century window front; and at No. 51 is one of the few 18th-century *hôtels* on the island, Hôtel Chernizot ⑳, with a superb Rococo balcony that rests on leering gargoyles.

Gargoyle at No. 51 Rue St-Louis-l'Ile ⑳

Turn right onto Rue Jean du Bellay and walk to Pont Louis Philippe. Turn right again onto the Quai de Bourbon, which is lined by one of the island's finest rows of *hôtels*, the most notable being Hôtel Jassaud at No. 19 ㉑. Continue to the 17th-century Pont Marie ㉒ and cross it to the Pont Marie metro on the other side.

The 17th-century Pont Marie ㉒

famous house on the island, the Hôtel Lambert ⑭ *(see pp24–5)*. Continue onto the Quai d'Anjou, where Hôtel de Lauzun ⑮ has a severe Classical front and beautiful gilded balcony and drainpipes. Turn left onto Rue Poulletier and note the convent of the Daughters of Charity ⑯ at No. 5 bis. Farther on, at the corner of Rue Poulletier and Rue St-Louis-en-l'Ile, is the island church St-Louis ⑰, with its unusual tower, projecting clock and carved main door.

Proceed along Rue St-Louis-en-l'Ile, which abounds in

Windows of the Hôtel Rolland

TIPS FOR WALKERS

Starting point: St-Paul metro.
Length: 1.6 miles (2.6 km).
Getting there: The walk starts from the St-Paul metro. However, bus route 67 takes you to Rue du Pont Louis Philippe and also crosses the island along Rue des Deux Ponts and Boulevard Pont de Sully; routes 86 and 87 also cross the island along Blvd Pont de Sully.
Stopping-off points: There are cafés, such as Flore en l'Ile (see p311) and the Berthillon shops for ice cream (p311). Restaurants on the Rue St-Louis-en-l'Ile include Auberge de la Reine Blanche and Au Gourmet de l'Ile, as well as a pâtisserie and a cheese shop. Places to rest include the tree-shaded quays and Square Barye at the eastern end of the island.

A 90-Minute Walk in Auteuil

P ART OF THE FASCINATION of the walk around this bastion of bourgeois life in westernmost Paris lies in the contrasting nature of the area's streets. The walk begins with the old village provincialism of Rue d'Auteuil, then leads to the masterpieces of luxurious modern architecture along Rue La Fontaine and Rue du Docteur Blanche. The walk ends at the Jasmin metro station. For more on the sights of Auteuil, see page 254.

Obelisk, Place d'Auteuil ①

Rue d'Auteuil
The walk begins at Place d'Auteuil ①, a leafy village square with a striking Guimard-designed metro station entrance, an 18th-century funerary obelisk and the 19th-century Neo-Romanesque Notre Dame d'Auteuil. Walk down Rue d'Auteuil, the main street of the old village, and take in the sense of a past provincial world. The Batifol brasserie ② now occupies the premises of the area's oldest tavern, favored by Molière and his actors in the 17th century. The house at Nos. 45–47 ③ was the residence of American presidents John Adams and his son, John Quincy Adams. Move on to the pleasantly shaded Place Jean Lorrain ④, the site of the local market. Here there is a Wallace drinking fountain, donated by

Wallace fountain ④

the English millionaire Richard Wallace in the 19th century. On the right, go down Rue Donizetti to the Villa Montmorency ⑤, a private enclave of luxury villas, built on the former country estate of the Comtesse de Boufflers.

Rue La Fontaine
Continue the walk along Rue La Fontaine, renowned for its many Hector Guimard buildings. Henri Sauvage's ensemble of artists' studios at No. 65 ⑥ is one of the most original Art Deco buildings in Paris. No. 60 is a Guimard Art Nouveau house ⑦ with medieval turret and elegant cast-iron balconies. Farther along there is a small Neo-Gothic chapel at No. 40 ⑧, with Art Nouveau apartment buildings at Nos. 19 and 21 ⑨. No. 14 is Guimard's most spectacular building, the Castel Béranger ⑩, with a superb iron gate.

Doorway of No. 28 Rue d'Auteuil

RUE DU DOCTEUR BLANCHE

RUE DE L'YVET

RUE RAFFET

Villa Montmorency

RUE DE LA SOURCE

RUE POUSSIN

RUE LA FONTA

RUE D'AUTEUIL

RUE MICHEL ANGE

RUE BOILEAU

Michel Ange Auteuil

D'AUTE

AVENUE M

KEY

— Walk route

Good viewing point

M Metro station

0 meters	250
0 yards	250

Rue de l'Assomption to Rue Mallet Stevens

At the corner of Rue de l'Assomption there is a view of the massive Maison de Radio-France ⑪, built in 1963 to house French radio and television studios (see p200). It was one of the first modern postwar buildings in the city. Turn left onto Rue de l'Assomption and walk to the fine 1920s apartment building at No. 18 ⑫. Turn left onto Rue du Général Dubail and follow it to Place Rodin, where the great sculptor's bronze nude, The

Shuttered bay window at No. 3 Square Jasmin ⑲

Age of Bronze (1877) ⑬, occupies the center of the traffic circle.

Take the Avenue Théodore Rousseau back to Rue de l'Assomption and turn left

toward Avenue Mozart. Cut through in the 1880s, this is the principal artery of the 16th arrondissement, linking north and south and lined with typical bourgeois apartment buildings of the late 19th century. Cross the avenue and continue to the Avenue des Chalets, where there is a typical collection of weekend villas ⑭ recalling the quieter suburban Auteuil of the mid-19th century. Farther along Rue de l'Assomption, Notre-Dame de l'Assomption ⑮ is a Neo-Renaissance 19th-century church. Turn left onto Rue du Docteur Blanche. At No. 9 and down the adjoining Rue Mallet Stevens ⑯ there is a row of celebrated houses in the International Modern style by the architect Mallet Stevens. In this expensive, once avant-garde enclave lived architects, designers, artists and their modern-minded clients. The original proportions, however, were

altered dramatically by the addition of an extra three stories in the 1960s.

Continue on Rue du Docteur Blanche until coming to Villa du Docteur Blanche on the left. At the end of this small cul-de-sac is the most celebrated modern house in Auteuil, Le Corbusier's Villa Roche ⑰. Together with the adjoining Villa Jeanneret, it is now part of the Corbusier Foundation (see pp36–7). Built for an art collector in 1924 using the new technique of reinforced concrete, the house, with its geometric forms and lack of ornamentation, is a model of early Modernism.

No. 18 Rue de l'Assomption, detail ⑫

Rue du Docteur Blanche to Rue Jasmin

Walk back to Rue du Docteur Blanche and turn right onto Rue Henri Heine. No. 18 bis ⑱ is a very elegant Neo-classical 1920s apartment building offering a good contrast to one of Guimard's last creations (from 1926) next door – an Art Nouveau facade much tamer than that at Castel Béranger but still employing brick, and featuring projecting bay windows and a terraced roof. Turn left on Rue Jasmin. In the second cul-de-sac on the left there is another Guimard house at No. 3 Square Jasmin ⑲. Toward the end of Rue Jasmin is the metro station.

The Age of Bronze ⑬

Courtyard of No. 14 Rue La Fontaine

A 90-Minute Walk in Montmartre

THE WALK BEGINS at the base of the sand-stone *butte* (hill), where old theaters and dance halls, once frequented and depicted by painters from Renoir to Picasso, have now been taken over by rock clubs. It continues steeply uphill to the original village, along streets that still retain the atmosphere caught by artists like Van Gogh, before winding downhill to end at Place Blanche. For more on the main sights of Montmartre and the Sacré-Coeur, see pages 218 to 227.

Montmartre seen from a distance

Place Pigalle to Rue Ravignan

The walk starts at the lively Place Pigalle ① and follows Rue Frochot to the Rue Victor Massé. At the corner is the ornate entrance to an exclusive private street bordered by turn-of-the-century chalets ②. Opposite, at No. 27 Rue Victor Massé, is an ornate mid-19th century apartment building, and No. 25 is where Vincent Van Gogh and his brother, Theo, lived in 1886 ③. The famous Chat Noir ④, Montmartre's most renowned artistic cabaret in the 1890s, flourished at No. 12. At the end of the street begins the wide tree-lined Avenue Trudaine. Take Rue Lallier on the left to Boulevard de Rochechouart. Continue east. No. 84 is the first address of the Chat Noir, and No. 82 is the Grand Trianon ⑤, the oldest surviving movie

Entrance gate to Avenue Frochot

theater, from the early 1890s. Farther along, No. 74 is the original front of Montmartre's first great cancan dance hall, the Elysée-Montmartre ⑥.

Turn left onto Rue Steinkerque, which leads to Sacré-Coeur gardens, and then left onto Rue d'Orsel, which leads to the leafy Place Charles Dullin, where the small early 19th-century Théâtre de l'Atelier ⑦ stands. Continue up the hill on Rue des Trois Frères and turn left on Rue Yvonne le Tac, which leads to Place des Abbesses ⑧. This is one of the most pleasant and liveliest squares in the area. It has conserved its entire canopied Art Nouveau metro entrance by Hector Guimard. Opposite is St-Jean l'Evangéliste ⑨, an unusual brick-and-mosaic Art

Tips for Walkers

Starting point: *Place Pigalle.*
Length: *1.4 miles (2.3 km). The walk goes up some very steep streets to the top; if you do not feel like the climb, consider taking the Montmartrobus, which covers most of the walk and starts at Place Pigalle.*
Getting there: *The nearest metro is Pigalle; buses that take you there are Nos. 30, 54 and 67.*
Stopping-off points: *There are many cafés and shops on Rue Lepic, and Rue des Abbesses. Rayons de la Santé, in Place Dullin, is one of the city's best vegetarian restaurants. For shade and a rest, Place Jean-Baptiste Clément and Square S. Busson at Avenue Junot are charming public squares.*

Rue André Antoine ⑩

Nouveau church. To the right of the church, a flight of steep steps leads to the tiny Rue André Antoine, where the pointillist painter Georges Seurat lived at No. 39 ⑩. Continue along Rue des Abbesses and turn right at Rue Ravignan.

Rue Ravignan
From here there is a sweeping view of Paris. Climb the steps straight ahead to the deeply shaded Place Emile Goudeau ⑪. To the left, at No. 13, is the original entrance to the Bateau-Lavoir, the most important cluster of artists' studios

Artist selling his work at Place du Tertre ⑮

St-Jean l'Evangéliste, detail ⑨

in Montmartre. Here Picasso lived and worked in the early 1900s. Farther up, at the corner of Rue Orchampt and Rue Ravignan, there is a row of picturesque 19th-century artists' studios ⑫.

Rue Ravignan to Rue Lepic
Continue up the hill along the small public garden, Place Jean-Baptiste Clément ⑬. At the top, cross Rue Norvins. Opposite is an old Monmartois restaurant, A la Bonne Franquette ⑭, which, as Aux Billards en Bois, used to be a favorite gathering place for 19th-century artists. Continue along the narrow Rue St-Rustique, from where Sacré-Coeur can be seen. At the end and to the right is Place du Tertre ⑮, the main village square. From here go north on Rue du Mont Cenis and turn left to Rue Cortot. Erik Satie, the eccentric composer, lived in No. 6 ⑯, and at No. 12 is the Musée de Montmartre ⑰. Turn right on Rue des Saules and walk past the very pretty Montmartre vineyard ⑱ to the Au Lapin Agile ⑲, at the corner

of Rue St-Vincent. Return along Rue des Saules and turn right on Rue de l'Abreuvoir, an attractive street of turn-of-the-century villas and gardens. Continue into l'Allée des Brouillards, a leafy pedestrian alley. No. 6 ⑳ was Renoir's last house in Montmartre. Take the steps down into the Rue Simon Dereure and immediately turn left into a small park, which can be crossed to reach Avenue Junot. Here, No. 15 ㉑ was the house of Dadaist Tristan Tzara in the early 1920s. Continue up Avenue Junot, then turn right on Rue Girardon and right again on Rue Lepic.

Au Lapin Agile nightclub ⑲

Rue Lepic to Place Blanche
At the corner is one of Montmartre's few surviving windmills, the Moulin du Radet ㉒. Continue along Rue Lepic: to the right at the top of a slope is another windmill survivor, the Moulin de la Galette ㉓. Turn left on Rue de l'Armée d'Orient, with its picturesque artists' studios ㉔, and left again into Rue Lepic. Van Gogh lived at No. 54 ㉕ in June 1886. Continue to Place Blanche. On Boulevard de Clichy to the right is one of the area's great landmarks, the Moulin Rouge ㉖.

KEY
— Walk route
✵ Good viewing point
Ⓜ Metro station
0 meters 250
0 yards 250

Moulin Rouge nightclub near the Place Blanche ㉖

TRAVELERS' NEEDS

WHERE TO STAY

Paris boasts more guest accommodations than any other city in Europe. Hotels vary from magnificent luxurious places like the Ritz (the French call them *palaces*) and exclusive establishments like L'Hôtel to much simpler hotels – *hôtels de charme* – in charming older parts of Paris.

We have inspected hotels in all price brackets and selected a broad range, all of which will give you good value for your money. The chart on pages 278 to 279 will help narrow down your choice of hotels; for more details on each, turn to the catalog on pages 280 to 285. Both the catalog and the chart are organized by area according to hotel price. Information on other types of accommodations can be found on pages 272 to 274.

One should note that *hôtel* does not always mean "hotel." It can also mean a city hall (*hôtel de ville*), hospital (*Hôtel-Dieu*) or mansion.

WHERE TO LOOK

Hotels in Paris tend to be clustered by type in particular areas, with the river separating the business and tourist districts. Luxury hotels tend to be on the north side, with *hôtels de charme* on the south side.

In the fashionable districts near the Champs-Elysées lie many of the grandest hotels in Paris, including the Royal Monceau, the Bristol, the George V, the Meurice and the Plaza Athénée. Several less well-known but elegant hotels can be found in the residential and ambassadorial quarter near the Palais de Chaillot.

To the east, in the regenerated Marais on the Right Bank, a number of the old mansions and palaces have been converted into exceptionally attractive small hotels at reasonable prices. The nearby areas around Les Halles and the Rue St-Denis, however, attract prostitutes and drug addicts. Just south of the Marais, across the Seine, the Ile St-Louis and Ile de la Cité have several delightful hotels.

The Left Bank covers some of the most popular tourist areas and has an excellent range of small hotels of great character. The atmosphere subtly changes from the bohemian Latin Quarter to the chic and arty St-Germain-des-Prés to the more staid institutional area toward Les Invalides and the Eiffel Tower. The hotels reflect the character of their areas.

Farther from the center, Montparnasse has several large business hotels in high-rise blocks. The station areas around Gare du Nord and Gare de Lyon offer a number of basic hotels (some are positively sleazy, so choose carefully). Montmartre has one or two pleasant hotels,

Hôtel de Crillon *(see p280)*

if you don't mind the hilly location, but beware of hotels allegedly in Montmartre but actually in the red-light sex-show district of Pigalle. If you're looking for a hotel in person, the best times for inspecting are late morning (after checkout and cleaning time) or mid-afternoon. If the hotels are full, try again after 6pm, when unclaimed reservations become free. Don't rely on the impression of a hotel given by someone at the desk: ask to see the room yourself, and if it isn't acceptable, ask to be shown another.

Information about airport hotels is in the Getting to Paris section (*see pp360–65*).

HOTEL PRICES

Hotel prices aren't always cheaper in low season (mid-November to March or July and August) because fashion shows and other major

The Hôtel du Louvre *(see p281)*, between the Louvre and the Palais Royal

events throughout the year can fill hotels, raising prices. However, in the older hotels differences in room size and position can have a marked effect on cost. Small rooms tend to be the cheapest.

Twin rooms are slightly more expensive than doubles; single occupancy rates as high or nearly as high as for two people sharing (rates are nearly always quoted per room, not per person). Single rooms are rare, and many are extremely tiny or poorly equipped. Rooms without a bath tend to be about 20% cheaper than those with. You might find a room with a meal unnecessary with such a wide choice of good restaurants around.

It's always worth asking for a discount: you may get a corporate rate, for instance. In some hotels special deals are offered for students, families or senior citizens.

HIDDEN EXTRAS

BY LAW, TAX and service must be included in the price quoted or displayed at the reception desk or in the rooms. Tips are unnecessary other than for exceptional service – if the concierge reserves show tickets, for instance, or if the maid sees to laundry for you. However, before you make a reservation you should always establish whether breakfast is included in the price. Beware of extras such as drinks or snacks from an

The Hôtel Meurice *(see p281)* in the Tuileries Quarter

in-room minibar, which will probably be expensive, as will laundry services, garage parking or telephone calls from your room – especially calls made through the switchboard.

Exchange rates in hotels invariably tend to be lower than those in banks, so make sure you have enough cash to pay your bill – unless you are paying by credit card or traveler's checks.

HOTEL RATINGS

FRENCH HOTELS are classified by the tourist authorities into five broad categories: one to four stars, plus a four-star deluxe rating. Some very simple places are unclassified. Star ratings indicate something about the level of facilities you can expect (for example, any hotel with more than three stars should have an elevator). But the rating system is no reliable guide to friendliness, cleanliness or tastefulness of decor.

FACILITIES

FEW PARISIAN hotels below a four-star rating have a restaurant, although there is nearly always a breakfast room. Quite a few hotel restaurants close in August. Many of the older hotels also lack a public lounge area. More modern or expensive hotels have correspondingly better facilities and generally some kind of bar. Inexpensive hotels may not have an elevator – significant when you are dragging suitcases upstairs. Usually only the more expensive hotels have parking facilities. For exceptions to this rule, consult the listings on pages 280 to 285. If you are driving you may prefer to stay in one of the peripheral motel-style chain hotels *(see pp273–4)*. All but the very simplest of city hotels will have a telephone in the bedroom. Many hotels also have televisions, though they rarely have radios. Double beds *(grands lits)* are common, but you must specify that you want one.

The Hôtel George V *(see pp284–5)*

Statue in the Hôtel Relais Christine *(see p282)*

The Plaza Athénée *(see p285)* in Champs-Elysées

WHAT TO EXPECT

MANY HOTEL beds still stick to the time-honored French bolster, a sausage-shaped headrest that can be uncomfortable if you are unused to it. If you prefer pillows, ask for *oreillers*. If you want to make sure you get a toilet, specify a *WC*, and if you want a bath, ask for a *bain*. Otherwise, you will get a *cabinet de toilette*, just a basin and bidet, or *eau courant*, which means simply a basin with hot and cold running water. A duplex room is a two-floor suite.

The traditional French hotel breakfast of fresh coffee, croissants, jam and orange juice is in Paris gradually changing into an elaborate buffet breakfast with cold meats and cheeses. Whatever the type, insist on an *orange pressée* (freshly-squeezed orange juice) and not a *jus d'orange*, which will usually be from a can. Some of the luxury hotels are now such popular venues for breakfast that it is worth reserving a

place in the breakfast area if you don't want to eat in your room. A pleasant alternative is to head for the nearest café, where French workers will be enjoying breakfast over a newspaper.

Checkout time is usually noon, and if you stay longer you will pay for an extra day.

SPECIAL BREAKS

SINCE PARIS IS such a popular destination with leisure as well as business travelers, weekend packages are rare. Providing there are no major events taking place, you can reduce costs by visiting in low season and negotiating a discount or by seeking an all-inclusive package.

TRAVELING WITH CHILDREN

FAMILIES with young children will often find they can share a room at no or very little extra cost, and some operators offer packages with this in mind. Few hotels refuse to accept children, though facilities specifically for children are not universal.

DISABLED TRAVELERS

OUR INFORMATION about wheelchair access to hotels was gathered by questionnaire and therefore relies on each hotel's own assessment of its suitability. Not many are well-geared for use by disabled visitors. The **Association des Paralysés de France** and the **Comité Nationale Française de Liaison pour la Réadaptation des Handicapés** both publish useful leaflets. *(For addresses see Directory p274.)*

EFFICIENCY ACCOMMODATION

AN AGENCY called **Résidences de Tourisme** provides apartments, some with kitchens in specially run apartment hotels. Some hotel-type facilities are also available through them, but these cost more. Prices vary from around F400 per night for a small studio to over F2,000 per night

The quiet Hôtel des Grands Hommes *(see p282)*

for an apartment for several people. Either contact **Paris-Séjour-Réservation** or get in touch with each *résidence* directly. The Paris **Office du Tourisme** provides a full list of *résidences*.

Other companies specialising in efficiency accommodation include **At Home In Paris**, **Paris Appartements Services** and **Allo Logement Temporaire**. All provide high-quality furnished apartments for stays from one week to six months, sometimes in the apartment of a Parisian who is abroad. Prices are comparable to those of the Résidences de Tourisme, sometimes slightly cheaper for the larger apartments. **France-Lodge** and **Bed and Breakfast 1 Connection**, which are primarily bed and breakfast agencies *(see below)*, will also arrange efficiency apartments. *(For addresses see* Directory *p274.)*

STAYING IN PRIVATE HOMES

BED-AND-BREAKFAST, popular in the US and Britain, is becoming increasingly popular in France under the name *café-couette* ("coffee and a quilt"); B&B accommodation is now available at moderate prices usually between F100 and F250 for a double room per night. **France-Lodge** are both agencies which will find you a room including breakfast in a private house.

CHAIN HOTELS

ON THE OUTSKIRTS of Paris, a burgeoning crop of motel-style establishments belonging to chains such as Campanile, Formule 1, **Mercure**, Ibis and Primèvere now take large numbers of both business and leisure visitors. These places are practical, relatively inexpensive and useful if you have a car; but lack any real Parisian atmosphere or character. Many are in charmless locations on busy roads and may suffer from traffic noise. The newer motels of these chains are better equipped and more smartly decorated than the older ones. Several

The Hôtel Atala terrace *(see p284)*

The garden of the Relais Christine *(see p282)*

chains (**Sofitel, Novotel, Frantour** and **Mercure**) are especially geared to business travelers, providing better facilities at higher rates; reductions can make these hotels good value at week-ends. Many of the hotels have restaurants attached. Most of the chains produce

The Hôtel Prince de Galles Sheraton *(see p285)*

their own brochures, often with useful maps detailing the motel's precise location. *(See* Directory *p275.)*

HOSTELS AND DORMITORY ACCOMMODATIONS

A SAME-DAY hostel reservation service is offered by **Office de Tourisme de l' Université (O. T. U.)**, which also offers an advance phone-booking service for credit card holders. You may book single or double rooms, or a simple bed in a dormitory. Rates are between F110 and F220 per

night, and there is no upper age limit for hostelers.

There are several networks of hostels in Paris. **Maisons Internationales de la Jeunesse et des Etudiants** (MIJE) provides dormitory accommodations for the18–30s in three splendid mansions in the Marais. You cannot reserve in advance (except for groups) – you have to call at the central offices on the day.

La Maison de l'UCRIF (Union des Centres de Rencontres Internationales de France) has nine centers around Paris with individual, shared and dormitory rooms. No age limit is imposed. Cultural and sporting activities are available at some centers.

Fédération Unie des Auberges de Jeunesse (FUAJ) is a member of the International Youth Hostels Federation. There is no age limit at their two Paris hostels. *(For addresses see* Directory *p274.)*

CAMPING

THE ONLY campsite in Paris itself is the **Camping du Bois de Boulogne/Ile de France** (around F60–150 per night). This well-equipped site next to the Seine is usually fully booked during the summer. There are many more campsites in the surrounding region, however, some of which are close to an RER line. Details can be obtained from the Paris Office du Tourisme or from a booklet produced by the **Fédération Française de Camping-Caravaning**. *(See* Directory *p274.)*

DIRECTORY

AGENCIES

Ely 12 12
9 Rue d'Artois 75008.
☎ 01 43 59 12 12.
FAX 01 42 56 24 31.

Paris-Séjour-Réservation
90 Ave des Champs-Elysées 75008.
☎ 01 53 89 10 50.
FAX 01 53 89 10 59.

OFFICE DU TOURISME ET DES CONGRES

Main office:
127 Ave des Champs-Elysées 75008.
📞 08 36 68 31 12.
Branches at airports, stations and the Eiffel Tower.

DISABLED TRAVELERS

Association des Paralysés de France
17 Blvd August Blanqui 75013.
☎ 01 53 62 84 00.
FAX 01 45 89 08 54.

CNFLRH
236 bis rue Tolbias 75013.
☎ 01 53 80 66 66.
FAX 01 53 80 66 67.

EFFICIENCY APARTMENTS

Allo Logement Temporaire
64 rue du Temple 75003.
☎ 01 42 72 00 06.
FAX 01 42 72 03 11.

At Home in Paris
16 Rue Médéric 75017.
☎ 01 42 12 40 40.
FAX 01 42 12 40 48.

Paris Appartements Services
69 Rue d'Argout 75002.
☎ 01 40 28 01 28.
FAX 01 40 28 92 01.

RÉSIDENCES DE TOURISME

Beverly Hills
35 Rue de Berri 75008.
☎ 01 53 77 56 00.
FAX 01 42 56 52 75.

Les Citadines
27 Rue Esquirol 75013.
☎ 01 44 23 51 51.
FAX 01 45 86 59 76.

Flatotel
14 Rue du Théâtre 75015.
☎ 01 45 75 62 20.
FAX 01 45 79 73 30.

Pierre et Vacances
10 Pl Charles-Dullin 75018.
☎ 01 42 57 14 55.
FAX 01 42 54 48 87.

Résidence Orion
18 Pl d'Italie 75013.
☎ 01 40 78 15 00.
FAX 01 40 78 16 99.

Résidence du Roy
8 Rue François-1er 75008.
☎ 01 42 89 59 59.
FAX 01 40 74 07 92.

STAYING IN PRIVATE HOMES

France-Lodge
41 Rue La Fayette 75009.
☎ 01 53 20 09 09.
FAX 01 53 20 01 25.

CHAIN HOTELS

Frantour Suffren
20 Rue Jean Rey 75015.
☎ 01 45 78 50 00.
FAX 01 45 78 91 42.

Golden Tulip St-Honoré
218 Rue du Faubourg St-Honoré 75008.
☎ 01 49 53 03 03.
FAX 01 40 75 02 00.

Hilton
18 Ave de Suffren 75015.
☎ 01 44 38 56 00.
FAX 01 44 38 56 10.

Holiday Inn
92 Rue de Vaugirard 75006.
☎ 01 42 22 00 56.
FAX 01 42 22 05 39.

Holiday Inn République
10 Pl de la République 75011. ☎ 01 43 55 44 34.
FAX 01 47 00 32 34.

Mercure Paris Bercy
77 Rue de Bercy 75012.
☎ 01 53 46 50 50.
FAX 01 53 46 50 99.

Mercure Pont Bercy
6 Blvd Vincent Auriol 75013.
☎ 01 45 82 48 00.
FAX 01 45 82 19 16.

Mercure Paris Montparnasse
20 Rue de la Gaîté 75014.
☎ 01 43 35 28 28.
FAX 01 43 27 98 64.

Mercure Paris Porte de Versailles
69 Blvd Victor 75015.
☎ 01 44 19 03 03.
FAX 01 48 28 22 11.

Méridien Montparnasse
19 Rue du Commandant René Mouchotte 75014.
☎ 01 44 36 44 36.
FAX 01 44 36 47 00.

Nikko
61 Quai de Grenelle 75015.
☎ 01 40 58 20 00.
FAX 01 40 58 24 44.

Novotel Paris Bercy
85 Rue de Bercy 75012.
☎ 01 43 42 30 00.
FAX 01 43 45 30 60.

Novotel Paris Les Halles
8 Pl Marguerite de Navarre 75001.
☎ 01 42 21 31 31.
FAX 01 42 21 05 79.

Sofitel Paris Forum Rive Gauche
17 Blvd St-Jacques 75014.
☎ 01 40 78 79 80.
FAX 01 45 88 43 93.

Sofitel Paris
8 Rue Louis Armand 75015.
☎ 01 40 60 30 30.
FAX 01 45 57 04 22.

Sofitel Paris CNIT
2 Pl de la Défense, BP 210 92053.
☎ 01 46 92 10 10.
FAX 01 46 92 10 50.

Sofitel Paris La Défense Centre 4 Etoiles
34 Cours Michelet 92800 Puteaux.
☎ 01 47 76 44 43.
FAX 01 47 73 72 74.

Sofitel Paris Arc de Triomphe
14 Rue Beaujon 75008.
☎ 01 53 89 50 50.
FAX 01 53 89 50 51.

Warwick
5 Rue de Berri 75008.
☎ 01 45 63 14 11.
FAX 01 43 59 00 98.

HOSTELS AND DORMITORY ACCOMMODATION

Fédération Unie des Auberges de Jeunesse – Centre National
27 Rue Pajol 75018.
☎ 01 44 89 87 27.
FAX 01 44 89 87 10.

Maison Internationale de la Jeunesse et des Etudiants
Head Office: 11 Rue du Fauconnier 75004.
☎ 01 42 74 23 45.
FAX 01 40 27 81 64.

La Maison de l'UCRIF
27 rue de Turbigo 75002.
☎ 01 40 26 57 64.
FAX 01 40 26 58 20.

O. T. U.
151 Avenue Ledru-Rollin 75011.
☎ 01 43 79 53 86.
FAX 01 43 79 35 63.

CAMPING

Camping du Bois de Boulogne/Ile de France
Allée du Bord de l'Eau 75016.
☎ 01 45 24 30 00.
FAX 01 42 24 42 95.

Fédération Française de Camping-Caravaning
78 Rue de Rivoli 75004.
☎ 01 42 72 84 08.
FAX 01 42 72 70 21.

RESERVATIONS

THE BUSIEST Paris tourist seasons are May, June, September and October, but special events – such as fashion shows, trade fairs and major exhibitions – can fill most rooms in Paris throughout the year. Disneyland Paris has further increased the pressure to find accommodations, as many visitors choose to stay in the capital and commute to the park on the RER. July and August are quieter, as many Parisians are on their annual holiday. But the August shutdown of old is no longer the case – around half the hotels, restaurants and shops remain open.

If you have decided on a hotel, it is vital to reserve ahead by at least a month, because Paris is a popular destination. The hotels in the listings are among the best in their category and will fill particularly fast. Make a reservation six weeks in advance between May and October. The best way is to call the hotel directly. If you make your initial inquiry by telephone, call during the day if possible – you are more likely to find staff who are authorized to take reservations. During busy periods you will usually have to send written confirmation of your reservation by fax or letter.

If you prefer to use an agency, **Ely 12 12** and **Paris-Séjour-Réservation** can reserve hotels and other accommodations, sometimes even a barge along the Seine.

If you aren't too fussy about where you stay, or if all the hotels are reportedly full, you can reserve via the Paris **Office du Tourisme**, which has an on-the-spot reservation service for a reasonable fee.

DEPOSITS

IF YOU MAKE a reservation by telephone, you will be asked for either your credit card number (from which any cancellation fee may be deducted) or a deposit, termed the *arrhes*. These *arrhes* can be as much as the price of a night's stay but usually cost

Tourist information desk, Charles de Gaulle airport

only about 15% of this. Pay your deposit by credit card or by sending a Eurocheque or an international money order. You can sometimes send an ordinary check for an amount equivalent to the deposit as evidence of your intention to keep the booking. Usually the hotel will simply keep your foreign check as security until you arrive, then return it to you and give you one total bill when you leave. But do check with the hotel before sending an ordinary check. It's also quite acceptable in France to specify your choice of room when you reserve.

Try to arrive at your hotel by 6pm on the day you have reserved, or at least call to say you will be late; otherwise you may lose the room. A hotel that does not honor a confirmed, prepaid reservation is breaking a contract, and the client is entitled to compensation of at least twice any deposit paid. If you have any problems, consult the Office du Tourisme.

TOURIST INFORMATION DESKS

YOU CAN BOOK hotels at airport information desks but only in person and for the same day. Gare du Nord, Gare de Lyon, Gare d'Auster-litz and Gare Montparnasse all have information desks which provide a similar booking service. Many Paris information desks also keep a complete list of city hotels and some are able to book entertainment tickets (see Practical Information p350).

USING THE LISTINGS

The hotels on pages 280 to 285 are organized according to area and price. All are centrally situated. The symbols after the hotel's address summarize the facilities offered.

🛏 all rooms with bath and/or shower, unless otherwise stated
1 single-rate rooms available
🛌 rooms for more than two people available, or an extra bed can be put in a double room
24 24-hour room service
TV television in all rooms
Y minibar in all rooms
🚭 no-smoking rooms available
🏔 good views from hotel
☰ air conditioning in all rooms
Y gym/fitness facilities
🏊 swimming pool in hotel
🗂 business facilities: message-taking service, fax machine for guests, desk and telephone in each room and a meeting room within the hotel
🧒 children's facilities: cribs and baby-sitting service
♿ wheelchair access
🛗 elevator
🐕 pets allowed in the bedrooms (confirm that you are bringing a pet). Most hotels will allow guide dogs.
P hotel parking available
🌳 garden/terrace
Y bar
🍴 restaurant
ℹ tourist information desk
💳 credit cards accepted:
AE American Express
DC Diners Club
MC MasterCard/Access
V VISA
JCB Japanese Credit Bureau

Price categories for a double room, including breakfast, tax and service:
Ⓕ under F600
ⒻⒻ F600–900
ⒻⒻⒻ F901–1,300
ⒻⒻⒻⒻ F1,301–1,700
ⒻⒻⒻⒻⒻ over F1,700

Paris's Best: Hotels

PARIS IS FAMOUS FOR its hotels. It excels in all categories – from the glittering opulent *palaces* (the top luxury hotels) to the *hôtels de charme*, full of character and romantic appeal, to the simpler affordable family hotels in quiet back streets. As a center of culture and fashion, the city has long been a mecca for the rich and famous as well as travelers from all walks of life. Not surprisingly, it boasts some of the most magnificent hotels in the world and has more than a thousand hotels in the inner city alone. Whatever their price level, however, the hotels in our listings *(see pp280–85)* all show that inimitable style and taste that Parisians bring to everything they do. These are a selection of the very best.

Bristol
In the chic heart of Paris, this epitomizes luxury. (See p284.)

Champs-Elysées

Chaillot Quarter

Invalides and Eiffel Tower Quarter

Balzac
Small but stylish, this hotel exudes period charm. The restaurant Bice is highly rated. (See p284.)

Hôtel de Crillon
One of the great palace *hotels, this was built for Louis XV.* (See p280.)

Plaza Athénée
In the heart of haute couture Paris, this is the favorite haunt of the fashion world. Magnificent decor and a superb restaurant are the main attractions. (See p285.)

Duc de St-Simon
Bedrooms overlook a lovely garden in this comfortable and peaceful hôtel de charme, *situated in an 18th-century mansion south of the Seine.* (See p283.)

Le Grand Hôtel
Built for Napoleon III in 1862, this historic hotel has been patronized by the rich and famous from Mata Hari to Winston Churchill. (See p285.)

L'Hôtel
Best known as the last home of Oscar Wilde, this stylish hotel boasts rooms both impressive and slightly bizarre. One room was furnished and occupied by the music-hall star Mistinguett.
(See p281.)

Opéra Quarter

eries Quarter

Beaubourg and Les Halles

Relais Christine
An oasis of calm in the hub of the city, this charming hotel offers traditional comforts such as a welcoming open fire in the drawing room. (See p282.)

Germain-des-Prés

The Marais

Ile de la Cité

Ile St-Louis

Luxembourg Quarter

Latin Quarter

Jardin des Plantes Quarter

Hôtel du Jeu de Paume
This cleverly converted hotel was once a court for playing real tennis – jeu de paume. (See p280.)

0 kilometers 1

0 miles 0.5

L'Abbaye St-Germain
A pleasant garden and courtyard and attractive rooms are features of this small secluded hotel near the Jardins du Luxembourg. (See p282.)

Lutétia
This was decorated by top designer Sonia Rykiel. (See p282.)

Choosing a Hotel

THE HOTELS LISTED on the following pages have all been individually inspected and assessed especially for this guide. This chart includes various factors that may influence your choice. For more information on each hotel, see the listings on pages 280 to 285.

Hotel	Price	Number of Rooms	Large Rooms	Business Facilities	Children's Facilities	Recommended Restaurant	Close to Shops and Restaurants	Quiet Location	24-Hour Room Service
ILE ST-LOUIS, THE MARAIS (see p280)									
Hôtel de la Bretonnerie	ⓕⓕ	30			●		●		
Hôtel des Deux-Iles	ⓕⓕ	17						■	
St-Merry	ⓕⓕ	11					●		
St-Paul-le-Marais	ⓕⓕ	27		■			●		
Hôtel du Jeu de Paume	ⓕⓕⓕ	32			●			■	
Pavillon de la Reine	ⓕⓕⓕⓕ	55			●		●	■	
TUILERIES QUARTER (see pp280–81)									
Brighton	ⓕⓕ	70			●		●		
St-James et Albany	ⓕⓕⓕ	208		■	●		●		
Hôtel du Louvre	ⓕⓕⓕⓕ	199		■	●		●		●
Regina	ⓕⓕⓕⓕ	130	●	■	●		●		●
Hôtel de Crillon	ⓕⓕⓕⓕⓕ	163	●	■	●	■	●		●
Intercontinental	ⓕⓕⓕⓕⓕ	450		■	●	■	●		●
Lotti	ⓕⓕⓕⓕⓕ	133		■			●		
Meurice	ⓕⓕⓕⓕⓕ	180	●	■		■	●		●
Ritz	ⓕⓕⓕⓕⓕ	187	●	■	●	■	●		●
ST-GERMAIN-DES-PRÉS (see pp281–2)									
Lenox St-Germain	ⓕⓕ	34					●	■	
Hôtel d'Angleterre	ⓕⓕ	27					●	■	
Hôtel de Lille	ⓕⓕ	20					●		
Hôtel des Marronniers	ⓕⓕ	37					●	■	
Hôtel des Sts-Pères	ⓕⓕ	39					●	■	
Hôtel du Quai Voltaire	ⓕⓕ	33			●				●
Senateur	ⓕⓕ	43		■	●		●		
La Villa	ⓕⓕⓕ	32			●		●	■	●
L'Hôtel	ⓕⓕⓕⓕ	27			●	■	●		
Lutétia	ⓕⓕⓕⓕ	250	●	■	●	■	●		●
Montalembert	ⓕⓕⓕⓕⓕ	56		■		■	●	■	●
Relais Christine	ⓕⓕⓕⓕⓕ	51		■	●		●	■	●
LATIN QUARTER (see p282)									
Esmeralda	ⓕ	19						■	●
Hôtel des Grandes Ecoles	ⓕ	51			●			■	
Hôtel des Grands Hommes	ⓕⓕ	32			●			■	
Hôtel de Notre-Dame	ⓕⓕ	34					●	■	
Hôtel du Panthéon	ⓕⓕ	34			●			■	
LUXEMBOURG QUARTER (see p282)									
Perreyve	ⓕ	30						■	●
Récamier	ⓕⓕ	30					●	■	
Hôtel de l'Abbaye St-Germain	ⓕⓕⓕ	46			●		●	■	
MONTPARNASSE (see pp282–3)									
L'Atelier Montparnasse	ⓕ	17			●			■	

Price categories for a standard double room per night, including breakfast and necessary charges:
ⓕ under F600
ⓕⓕ F600–900
ⓕⓕⓕ F901–1,300
ⓕⓕⓕⓕ F1,301–1,700
ⓕⓕⓕⓕⓕ over F1,700

CLOSE TO SHOPS AND RESTAURANTS
Within a 5-minute walk of a good center for shops and restaurants.

CHILDREN'S FACILITIES
Indicates child cribs and a baby-sitting service available. A few hotels also provide children's portions and highchairs in the dining areas.

BUSINESS FACILITIES
Message-taking service, fax machine for guests, desk and telephone in each room and a meeting room within the hotel.

	Price	Number of Rooms	Large Rooms	Business Facilities	Children's Facilities	Recommended Restaurant	Close to Shops and Restaurants	Quiet Location	24-Hour Room Service
Lenox Montparnasse	ⓕ	52			●			●	
Ferrandi	ⓕⓕ	42						●	
Le St-Grégoire	ⓕⓕ	20			●		●	●	
Ste-Beuve	ⓕⓕ	22			●			●	
Villa des Artistes	ⓕⓕ	59			●			●	
INVALIDES *(see p283)*									
Hôtel de Suède	ⓕⓕ	39			●			●	
Hôtel de Varenne	ⓕⓕ	24			●				
Hôtel Bourgogne et Montana	ⓕⓕⓕ	33						●	
Duc de St-Simon	ⓕⓕⓕⓕ	34					●	●	
CHAILLOT QUARTER, PORTE MAILLOT *(see pp283–4)*									
Hôtel de Banville	ⓕⓕ	38			●				●
Alexander	ⓕⓕⓕⓕ	62	●		●		●		●
Concorde La Fayette	ⓕⓕⓕⓕ	968				●			●
Le Méridien	ⓕⓕⓕⓕ	1,025	●		●	●			●
Villa Maillot	ⓕⓕⓕⓕ	42	●						
Zébra Square	ⓕⓕⓕⓕ	22	●						
Raphaël	ⓕⓕⓕⓕⓕ	90	●	●			●	●	●
St-James	ⓕⓕⓕⓕⓕ	48		●		●		●	●
CHAMPS-ELYSÉES *(see pp284–5)*									
Résidence Lord Byron	ⓕⓕ	31					●	●	
Atala	ⓕⓕⓕⓕ	48			●	●	●	●	
Claridge-Bellman	ⓕⓕⓕⓕ	42	●				●		
Balzac	ⓕⓕⓕⓕⓕ	70	●			●		●	●
Bristol	ⓕⓕⓕⓕⓕ	192	●	●	●	●	●		●
George V	ⓕⓕⓕⓕⓕ	298	●	●	●	●	●		●
Plaza Athénée	ⓕⓕⓕⓕⓕ	204	●	●	●	●	●		●
Prince de Galles Sheraton	ⓕⓕⓕⓕⓕ	168	●	●	●	●	●		●
Royal Monceau	ⓕⓕⓕⓕⓕ	219		●		●			●
San Regis	ⓕⓕⓕⓕⓕ	44			●		●	●	●
Sofitel Paris Arc de Triomphe	ⓕⓕⓕⓕⓕ	135	●	●	●	●	●		●
Hôtel de la Trémoille	ⓕⓕⓕⓕⓕ	107	●	●	●	●	●	●	
Vernet	ⓕⓕⓕⓕⓕ	57			●		●		●
OPÉRA QUARTER *(see p285)*									
Ambassador	ⓕⓕⓕⓕ	288	●	●	●	●	●		●
Le Grand Hôtel	ⓕⓕⓕⓕ	514		●	●	●	●		●
Westminster	ⓕⓕⓕⓕ	101		●	●		●		
MONTMARTRE *(see p285)*									
Terrass' Hôtel	ⓕⓕⓕ	101		●	●				

ILE ST-LOUIS
THE MARAIS

Hôtel de la Bretonnerie

22 Rue Ste-Croix de la Bretonnerie 75004. **Map** 13 C3. **(** 01 48 87 77 63. **FAX** 01 42 77 26 78. **Closed** Aug. **Rooms:** 30. 🛏 📺 🍸 🏋 🔁 🗧 MC, V. **FF**

The 17th-century Hôtel de la Bretonnerie, situated on the charming Rue Ste-Croix de la Bretonnerie, is one of the most comfortable hotels in the Marais. The spacious bedrooms have wooden ceiling beams, antique furniture and standard bathrooms. The kind welcome is especially notable.

Hôtel des Deux-Iles

59 Rue St-Louis-en-l'Ile 75004. **Map** 13 C4. **(** 01 43 26 13 35. **FAX** 01 43 29 60 25. **Rooms:** 17. 🛏 1 📺 🔁 🛉 🗧 AE, MC, V. **FF**

It's a privilege to be able to stay on the Ile St-Louis, and the Hôtel des Deux-Iles, a converted 17th-century mansion, offers small rooms at a reasonable price. The atmosphere is peaceful; the small bedrooms are attractive and well insulated; and the lounge in the vaulted cellar has a real fire.

St-Merry

78 Rue de la Verrerie 75004. **Map** 13 B3. **(** 01 42 78 14 15. **FAX** 01 40 29 06 82. **Rooms:** 11. 🛏 🚻 🛉 🗧 AE, MC, V. **FF**

The Hôtel St-Merry, close to the Pompidou Center, was the 17th-century presbytery of the adjoining St-Merry church. Furnished in appropriately Gothic style, this hotel is worth a visit if only to glance at room 9, built into the side of the church, with the church's flying buttresses crossing the room.

St-Paul-le-Marais

8 Rue de Sévigné 75004. **Map** 14 D3. **(** 01 48 04 97 27. **FAX** 01 48 87 37 04. **Rooms:** 27. 🛏 1 🚻 📺 🛉 🗧 AE, DC, MC, V, JCB. **FF**

Close to the Place des Vosges, in the heart of the Marais, this hotel with its wooden beams and old stone will suit those who like a rustic environment; the furnishings are simple, yet stylish and modern. Ask for bedrooms facing the courtyard to avoid the noise of traffic coming from the narrow Rue de Sévigné. Guests are welcomed with a smile and made to feel immediately at ease.

Hôtel du Jeu de Paume

54 Rue St-Louis-en-l'Ile 75004. **Map** 13 C4. **(** 01 43 26 14 18. **FAX** 01 40 46 02 76. **Rooms:** 32. 🛏 1 📺 🍸 🔁 🛅 🛉 🛉 🗧 AE, DC, MC, V, JCB. **FFF**

Standing on the site of a former real tennis court on the Ile St-Louis, this hotel has been skillfully converted into an exemplary family hotel. Features include a glass-walled elevator, wooden beams, old terra-cotta paving, a sauna and several charming duplex rooms. You will receive a warm welcome here.

Pavillon de la Reine

28 Pl des Vosges 75003. **Map** 14 D3. **(** 01 40 29 19 19. **FAX** 01 40 29 19 20. **Rooms:** 55. 🛏 📺 🍸 🗄 🛉 🛅 🔁 🗓 🛉 🗧 AE, DC, MC, V, JCB. **FFFF**

This hotel, set back from the marvelous Place des Vosges, is *the* luxury hotel of the Marais. The courtyard is a haven of peace, and the bedrooms have been sumptuously renovated and furnished with excellent reproduction antiques.

TUILERIES QUARTER

Brighton

218 Rue de Rivoli 75001. **Map** 12 D1. **(** 01 47 03 61 61. **FAX** 01 42 60 41 78. **Rooms:** 70. 🛏 🚻 📺 🛉 🌂 🔁 🛉 🗧 AE, DC, MC, V, JCB. **FF**

The Hôtel Brighton, once the glory of the Rue de Rivoli, has been rescued from decline by a Japanese company. The bedrooms have high molded ceilings and large windows looking either on to the Jardin des Tuileries or the courtyard. Courtyard rooms are quieter but less attractive. Some rooms have balconies.

St-James et Albany

202 Rue de Rivoli 75001. **Map** 12 E1. **(** 01 44 58 43 21. **FAX** 01 44 58 43 11. **Rooms:** 208. 🛏 🚻 📺 🍸 🛉 🛉 🛅 🔁 🗓 🛉 🗧 AE, DC, MC, V, JCB. **FFF**

The St-James et Albany is an ill-matched group of buildings that includes the Hôtel Noailles with its fine historic facade. The hotel is quiet and tidy but in need of restoration. It is perfectly situated opposite the Jardin des Tuileries. Given the noise from traffic on the Rue de Rivoli, it's probably best to ask for a room overlooking the courtyard.

Hôtel du Louvre

Pl André Malraux 75001. **Map** 12 E1. **(** 01 44 58 38 38. **FAX** 01 44 58 38 01. **Rooms:** 199. 🛏 1 🚻 24 📺 🍸 🌂 🛉 🛅 🔁 🗓 🛉 🗓 🛉 🗧 AE, DC, MC, V, JCB. **FFFF**

The Hôtel du Louvre is an enigma. In a prime location between the Louvre and the Palais Royal, it has never been appreciated by locals, and its brasserie tends to be rather empty. Reserve the Pissarro Suite, where the artist painted *Place du Théâtre Français*.

Regina

2 Pl des Pyramides 75001. **Map** 12 E1. **(** 01 42 60 31 10. **FAX** 01 40 15 95 16. **TX** 670834. **Rooms:** 130. 🛏 🚻 24 📺 🍸 🌂 🛉 🛅 🔁 🗓 🛉 🗓 🛉 🗧 AE, DC, MC, V, JCB. **FFFF**

Surprisingly, the Hôtel Regina is not known to many tourists. The wood detail in the lounge is stunning Art Nouveau, and many movies have been shot here. Superb views can be enjoyed from rooms on the Rue de Rivoli; these are furnished with antiques.

Hôtel de Crillon

10 Pl de la Concorde 75008. **Map** 11 C1. **(** 01 44 71 15 00. **FAX** 01 44 71 15 02. **TX** 290204. **Rooms:** 163. 🛏 24 📺 🍸 🌂 🗄 🛉 🛅 🔁 🗓 🗧 AE, DC, MC, V, JCB. **FFFFF**

Occupying an unrivaled position on the Place de la Concorde, the Hôtel de Crillon offers elegance. Features include the marble lounge, gilded oak gallery and magnificent dining room in the Ambassadors Salon. The hotel is used by foreign statesmen during official visits. Bedrooms overlooking the Place de la Concorde are best. The hotel has a magnificent Royal Suite and terrace.

Intercontinental

3 Rue de Castiglione 75001. **Map** 12 D1. **(** 01 44 77 11 11. **FAX** 01 44 77 14 60. **Rooms:** 450. 🛏 1 24 📺 🍸 🌂 🗄 🛉 🛅 🔁 🗓 🛉 🛉 🗧 AE, DC, MC, V, JCB. **FFFFF**

This elegant late 19th-century hotel is ideally situated between the Jardin des Tuileries and the Place Vendôme. It was designed by Charles Garnier, architect of the Paris Opéra, and its historic salons are often used for haute couture fashion shows. Breakfast is served in the sunny courtyard in summer. Bedrooms are quiet – the best overlook one of the courtyards.

Lotti

7 Rue de Castiglione 75001.
Map 12 D1. ☎ *01 42 60 37 34.*
FAX *01 40 15 93 56.* **Rooms:** *133.*
🛏 1 TV Y 🔁 🗏 🔆 & 🔾
Y 🍴 🗏 *AE, DC, MC, V, JCB.*
ⒻⒻⒻⒻ

A subdued atmosphere of quiet
decay surrounds this once-
celebrated hotel, creating something of a feeling of *temps perdu.*
However, some of the bedrooms
are quite large, and the attic rooms
on the sixth floor are charming.

Meurice

228 Rue de Rivoli 75001. **Map** 12 D1.
☎ *01 44 58 10 10.* **FAX** *01 44 58 10 17.*
Rooms: *180.* 🛏 1 24 TV Y 🔆
🗏 🗏 & 🔾 🍴 Y 🍴 🗏 *AE,
DC, MC, V, JCB.* ⒻⒻⒻⒻⒻ

The Hôtel Meurice is a perfect
example of successful restoration,
with excellent replicas of the
original plasterwork and
furnishings. The dining room is in
the Grand Salon on the ground
floor. Delightful musical afternoons are held in the Pompadour
Salon, where a roaring fire is often
lit during the winter months.
Luxurious and spacious bedrooms
on the first and second floors
overlook the Jardin des Tuileries
so be sure to reserve these rooms
well in advance.

Ritz

15 Pl Vendôme 75001. **Map** 6 D5.
☎ *01 43 16 30 30.* **FAX** *01 43 16 36
69.* **TX** *670112.* **Rooms:** *187.* 🛏 1
🏋 24 TV Y 🗏 🗏 & 🗏 🔆
🛏 🍴 Y 🍴 🗏 *AE, DC, MC, V,
JCB.* ⒻⒻⒻⒻⒻ

After a century, the discreet Ritz
still lives up to its high reputation
for elegance and comfort. The
Louis XVI furniture, marble
fireplaces and chandeliers are all
the originals. The Duke of Windsor
was a guest in the Windsor Suite.
Hemingway regularly frequented
the Hemingway Bar (now used
only for special occasions).
Autographed photographs testify
to his visits. The Ritz still equates
to glamour, so don't be surprised
if you end up breakfasting next to
the likes of Kissinger or Madonna.

ST-GERMAIN-DES-PRÉS

Lenox St-Germain

9 Rue de l'Université 75007.
Map 12 D3. ☎ *01 42 96 10 95.*
FAX *01 42 61 52 83.* **Rooms:** *34.*
🛏 TV 🔾 Y 🗏 *AE, DC, MC, JCB,
V.* ⒻⒻ

Located in the heart of Faubourg
St-Germain, this hotel is blessed
with the charm of simplicity. The
welcome is often casual. The
rooms are impeccably decorated;
duplex rooms have balconies with
plants, corner fireplaces and
wooden beams.

Hôtel d'Angleterre

44 Rue Jacob 75006. **Map** 12 E3.
☎ *01 42 60 34 72.* **FAX** *01 42 60 16
93.* **Rooms:** *27.* 🛏 1 🏋 TV 🔾
🔆 Y 🗏 *AE, DC, MC, V, JCB.*
ⒻⒻ

Once the British Embassy, the
Hôtel d'Angleterre has retained
many of the original features,
including the fine old staircase,
the exquisite garden and the salon
mantelpiece. Similarly impressive
mantelpieces can be seen in the
stylish bedrooms, all of which are
uniquely decorated, and many of
which have beams and four-
poster beds. This is a charming,
utterly civilized hotel.

Hôtel de Lille

40 Rue de Lille 75007. **Map** 12 D2.
☎ *01 42 61 29 09.* **FAX** *01 42 61 53
97.* **Rooms:** *20.* 🛏 TV 🔾 Y
🗏 *AE, DC, MC, V.* ⒻⒻ

The Hôtel de Lille is situated near
the Orsay and Louvre museums
in the heart of the aristocratic
Faubourg St-Germain. The
modern, standard bedrooms are
small, and the bar is minute. A
few bathrooms have showers
only. There is a small, charming
lounge in the arched basement.

Hôtel des Marronniers

21 Rue Jacob 75006. **Map** 12 E3.
☎ *01 43 25 30 60.* **FAX** *01 40 46 83
56.* **Rooms:** *37.* 🛏 1 🏋 🔆 🔾
🗏 ⒻⒻ

Situated between a courtyard and
a garden, this hotel provides total
quiet. The decor is unremarkable,
but the fourth-floor bedrooms, on
the garden side, overlook the
roofs of Paris and the St-Germain-
des-Prés church steeple. Reserve
well in advance since the hotel
has many regular customers.

Hôtel des Sts-Pères

65 Rue des Sts-Pères 75006.
Map 12 E3. ☎ *01 45 44 50 00.*
FAX *01 45 44 90 83.* **Rooms:** *39.*
🛏 🏋 TV Y 🔾 🗏 Y 🗏 *MC, V,
AE.* ⒻⒻ

The Hôtel des Sts-Pères occupies
one of the old aristocratic
mansions of St-Germain-des-Prés.
It has kept its inner galeries and
original staircase with a 17th-
century wooden banister.

The lounge may seem cold, but
the bedrooms are quiet and roomy
the best has a ceiling fresco and
a bathroom that is separated only
by a screen.

Hôtel du Quai Voltaire

19 Quai Voltaire 75007. **Map** 12 D2.
☎ *01 42 61 50 91.* **FAX** *01 42 61 62
26.* **Rooms:** *33.* 🛏 30. 1 🏋 24
TV *on request.* 🔆 🔾 Y 🍴
🗏 *AE, DC, MC, V, JCB.* ⒻⒻ

Overlooking the river, this hotel
was once the favorite of Blondin,
Baudelaire and Pissarro. There is
no soundproofing, so bedrooms
on the quay suffer from traffic
noise. However the views are
superb; the rooms are charmingly
decorated; and the place has soul.

Senateur

10 Rue de Vaugirard 75006.
Map 12 F5. ☎ *01 43 26 08 83.*
FAX *01 46 34 04 66.* **Rooms:** *43.* 🛏
1 🏋 TV Y 🗏 🔆 🔾 & 🗏
🍴 🗏 *AE, DC, MC, V, JCB.* ⒻⒻ

The prime appeal of the Senateur
is its geographical location, near
the Senate and the Jardins du
Luxembourg. Most of the rooms
are decorated in a Classical and
functional style, although the
lounge has tropical wallpaper. The
bathrooms are gleaming.

La Villa

29 Rue Jacob 75006. **Map** 12 E3.
☎ *01 43 26 60 00.* **FAX** *01 46 34 63
63.* **Rooms:** *32.* 🛏 🏋 TV Y 🗏
🔆 & 🔾 Y 🗏 *AE, DC, MC, V, JCB.*
ⒻⒻ

Close to St-Germain-des-Prés, La
Villa is a striking modern hotel
with its own Jazz club. Although
its stark, stylized simplicity may
not appeal to everyone, the ground-
floor lounge is distinctly elegant.
The service could be improved.

L'Hôtel

13 Rue des Beaux-Arts 75006.
Map 12 E3. ☎ *01 43 25 27 22.*
FAX *01 43 25 64 81.* **Rooms:** *27.*
🛏 TV Y 🗏 🗏 & 🗏 ⒻⒻⒻⒻ
🗏 *AE, DC, MC, V.* ⒻⒻⒻⒻ

Nowhere else will you find a domed
stairwell, a basement with vaulted
ceilings in the style of a harem, a
tree trunk across the dining room,
a golden-fleeced metallic lamb, and
a parrot in a gigantic cage. Here it
is possible to stay in the room
where Oscar Wilde died insolvent,
sleep in Mistinguett's bed or
occupy the Cardinal's Chamber.
Apart from such novelties, L'Hôtel
is impressive for its quality and
style and is an oasis of calm in the
heart of St-Germain-des-Prés.

For key to symbols see p275.

Lutétia

45 Blvd Raspail 75006. **Map** 12 D4.
(01 49 54 46 46. **FAX** 01 49 54 46
00. **TX** 270424. **Rooms:** 250. 🛏 🎫
🕓 📺 ☎ ⛵ 🍴 🔋 🔷 🔽 🐕
🍴 🎿 🅸 🍴 *AE, DC, MC, V, JCB.*
🅕🅕🅕🅕

The Lutétia, the only *palace hôtel*
(luxury hotel) on the south side of
the river, has long been visited by
regular provincial customers. An
ambitious renovation program has
spruced up the building, which is
partly Art Nouveau and partly Art
Deco. Publishers in the
neighborhood are regular
customers of its restaurant and its
literary bar. The Lutétia is a
fashionable place to be, and the
French sculptor César Baldiaccini
lives here permanently.

Montalembert

3 Rue de Montalembert 75007.
Map 12 D3. **(** 01 45 49 68 68.
FAX 01 45 49 69 49. **Rooms:** 56.
🛏 🕓 📺 ☎ ⛵ 🍴 🔽 🔋 🐕
🍴 🅸 *AE, DC, MC, V.*
🅕🅕🅕🅕🅕

Situated in the heart of the
publishing district, the Hôtel
Montalembert has been
sumptuously restored. The bar
has become an increasingly
fashionable meeting place, and the
bedrooms boast fine wood and
designer fabrics and are equipped
with video recorders. The eighth-
floor suites (under the roof) have
good views.

Relais Christine

3 Rue Christine 75006. **Map** 12 F4.
(01 40 51 60 80. **FAX** 01 40 51 60
81. **Rooms:** 51. 🛏 🕓 📺 ☎ ⛵
🔋 🐕 🔽 🐕 🅿 🍴 🅸 *AE,*
DC, MC, V, JCB. 🅕🅕🅕🅕🅕

Always full, the Relais Christine
is the epitome of the *hôtel de
charme.* It is part of the cloister
of a 16th-century abbey and is a
romantic haven of peace in the
heart of St-Germain-des-Prés.
Breakfast is served in an old
chapel. The bedrooms are bright
and spacious, especially the
duplex rooms.

Esmeralda

4 Rue St-Julien-le-Pauvre 75005.
Map 13 A4. **(** 01 43 54 19 20.
FAX 01 40 51 00 68. **Rooms:** 19. 🛏
16. 🅸 🎫 🕓 ⛵ 🐕 🅕

The bohemian Esmeralda lies in
the heart of the Latin Quarter. The
decor reflects contrasting ages and

styles behind old stone walls and
under beamed ceilings. Its
irresistible charm has, in the past,
seduced the likes of Chet Baker,
Terence Stamp and Serge
Gainsbourg into staying here. The
best rooms overlook Notre-Dame.

Hôtel des Grandes Ecoles

75 Rue Cardinal Lemoine 75005.
Map 13 B5. **(** 01 43 26 79 23.
FAX 01 43 25 28 15. **Rooms:** 51. 🛏
🎫 🐕 🔽 🐕 🎙 🅸 *MC, V.* 🅕

Situated between the Panthéon
and the Place de la Contrescarpe,
the Hôtel des Grandes Ecoles is an
astonishing cluster of three small
houses with a garden. Although
the university has moved, the
hotel still remains on the
Montagne Ste-Geneviève site.
The main building has been
competently renovated, but the
other two houses have retained
their old-fashioned charm.

Hôtel des Grands Hommes

17 Pl du Panthéon 75005. **Map** 17
A1. **(** 01 46 34 19 60. **FAX** 01 43 26
67 32. **Rooms:** 32. 🛏 🅸 🎫 📺
☎ ⛵ 🔽 🅸 *AE, DC, MC,*
V, JCB. 🅕🅕

Teachers at the Sorbonne frequent
this quiet family hotel in the heart
of the Latin Quarter, close to the
Jardins du Luxembourg. It boasts
an unrivaled view of the Panthéon
from the attic rooms on the upper
floor. The bedrooms are comfortable,
with pleasant bathrooms, but are
otherwise unexceptional.

Hôtel de Notre-Dame

19 Rue Maître Albert 75006.
Map 13 B5. **(** 01 43 26 79 00.
FAX 01 46 33 50 11. **Rooms:** 34. 🛏
📺 ☎ 🅸 *AE, DC, MC, V.* 🅕🅕

The Hôtel de Notre-Dame, not to
be mistaken for the hotel of the
same name on the Quai St-Michel,
overlooks Notre-Dame cathedral
on one side and the Panthéon on
the other. It is the ideal base from
which to discover old Paris.

Hôtel du Panthéon

19 Pl du Panthéon 75005.
Map 17 A1. **(** 01 43 54 32 95.
FAX 01 43 26 64 65. **Rooms:** 34. 🛏
📺 ☎ 🐕 🔽 🅸 *AE, DC, MC, V.*
🅕🅕

This hotel is managed by the same
family as the Hôtel des Grands
Hommes: the welcome is equally
warm and the decor similarly
Classical. There is a four-poster
bed in room 33.

Perreyve

63 Rue Madame 75006.
Map 12 E5. **(** 01 45 48 35 01.
FAX 01 42 84 03 30. **Rooms:** 30. 🛏
🅸 🎫 📺 🔽 🐕 🅸 *AE, DC, MC, V.*
🅕

The Hôtel Perreyve is situated
on a quiet street between
Montparnasse and St-Germain-
des-Prés. It has 30 simple, clean
bedrooms and is frequented by
many doctors and university
members, who are welcomed as
friends. The corner bedrooms or
sixth-floor attic rooms are best.

Récamier

3 bis Pl St-Sulpice 75006.
Map 12 E4. **(** 01 43 26 04 89.
FAX 01 46 33 27 73. **Rooms:** 30.
🛏 23. 🎫 🔽 🅸 *MC, V.* 🅕🅕

The Hôtel Récamier, situated on the
Place St-Sulpice, within walking
distance of St-Germain-des-Prés, is
a family hotel with no television
sets or restaurant. With its air of old-
fashioned charm, it is well known
to writers and Left Bank tourists.
Try to get a bedroom that looks
on to the square, for the view.

Hôtel de l'Abbaye St-Germain

10 Rue Cassette 75006. **Map** 12 D5.
(01 45 44 38 11. **FAX** 01 45 48 07
86. **Rooms:** 46. 🛏 🅸 📺 ☎
🔽 🎙 🐕 🅸 *AE, MC, V, JCB.*
🅕🅕🅕

Once an abbey, this is an elegant
hotel with a tranquil atmosphere.
The bedrooms are small but are
impeccably furnished, and some
retain their original beams. The
pretty courtyard and real fire in
the salon encourage visitors to
relax. The ground-floor bedrooms
overlooking the garden, and the
comfortable duplex rooms, are
recommended.

Lenox Montparnasse

15 Rue Delambre 75014.
Map 16 D2. **(** 01 43 35 34 50.
FAX 01 43 20 46 64. **Rooms:** 52. 🛏
📺 🐕 🔽 🐕 🅸 *AE, DC, MC, V,*
JCB. 🅕

With less style than the Lenox St-
Germain, the Montparnasse hotel
is nevertheless centrally located in
a district that has few hotels of
charm. The bar is decorated in Art
Deco style, and the overall

atmosphere is one of restrained elegance. Each of the six large suites on the upper floor has a fireplace. You can order light meals in your room until 2am – unusual for a hotel of this size.

L'Atelier Montparnasse

49 Rue Vavin 75006. **Map** 16 D1.
☎ 01 46 33 60 00. FAX 01 40 51 04 21. **Rooms:** 17. ⬛ 1 TV ☒ ⬛ ☒ ⬛ ⬛ ☲ AE, DC, MC, V, JCB. Ⓕ

The Atelier Montparnasse features a floral-patterned mosaic on the lobby floor made by the family that runs the hotel. The bedrooms are simply decorated in pastel hues, while the bathrooms have mosaic reproductions of works by painters such as Gauguin, Picasso and Chagall. This is a comfortable, very original hotel where visitors receive a gracious family welcome.

Ferrandi

92 Rue du Cherche-Midi 75006.
Map 15 C1. ☎ 01 42 22 97 40.
FAX 01 45 44 89 97. **Rooms:** 42. ⬛ TV ⬛ ⬛ ☲ AE, DC, MC, V, JCB. ⒻⒻ

The Rue du Cherche-Midi is known to lovers of antiques and bistros. The Hôtel Ferrandi is a quiet hotel with a fireplace in the lounge and with comfortable bedrooms, many with four-poster or canopied beds.

Le St-Grégoire

43 Rue de l'Abbé Grégoire 75006.
Map 11 C5. ☎ 01 45 48 23 23.
FAX 01 45 48 33 95. **Rooms:** 20. ⬛ 1 TV ⬛ ⬛ 🛈 ☲ AE, DC, MC, V, JCB. ⒻⒻ

The Le St-Grégoire is a fashionable town-house hotel featuring immaculately-decorated bedrooms with 19th-century furnishings. At the center of the drawing room is a charming fireplace with a real fire. The excellent breakfast is served in the vaulted cellar. Some of the rooms have their own private terrace.

Villa des Artistes

9 Rue de la Grande Chaumière 75006.
Map 16 D2. ☎ 01 43 26 60 86.
FAX 01 43 54 73 70. **Rooms:** 59. ⬛ ⬛ TV ☒ ⬛ ⬛ ☲ AE, DC, MC, V, JCB. ⒻⒻ

The Villa des Artistes aims to re-create the Belle Epoque era to which the Montparnasse painters were so attached. The bedrooms are clean, with good bathrooms, but the main charm of the hotel is its large patio garden and fountain, where you can breakfast in peace. Some rooms overlook the courtyard. Children over 5 are welcome.

Ste-Beuve

9 Rue Ste Beuve 75006.
Map 16 D1. ☎ 01 45 48 20 07.
FAX 01 45 48 67 52. **Rooms:** 22. ⬛ ⬛ TV ☒ ⬛ ⬛ ⬛ ☲ AE, MC, V, JCB. ⒻⒻ

The Ste-Beuve is a small carefully restored hotel for aesthetes and habitués of the Rive Gauche galleries. Here you will receive an attentive welcome in charming surroundings (the decor was conceived by the British interior designer David Hicks). There is a fireplace in the hall; the rooms are pleasantly decorated in pastel shades; and there are a number of classic contemporary paintings. For breakfast, croissants and specialty teas are bought in from top suppliers and served at bridge tables or at sofas in the salon. The atmosphere is warm and cozy.

INVALIDES

Hôtel de Suède

31 Rue Vaneau 75007.
Map 11 B4. ☎ 01 47 05 00 08.
FAX 01 47 05 69 27. **Rooms:** 39. ⬛ 1 ⬛ ⬛ ⬛ TV ☲ AE, MC, V.

The Hôtel de Suède looks directly over the park of the Hôtel Matignon, home of the Prime Minister. The elegant rooms are decorated in late 18th-century styles in pale tones and the welcome is of rare warmth. Rooms on the topmost floors have park views.

Hôtel de Varenne

44 Rue de Bourgogne 75007.
Map 11 B2. ☎ 01 45 51 45 55.
FAX 01 45 51 86 63. **Rooms:** 24. ⬛ ⬛ TV ⬛ ☒ ⬛ ☲ AE, MC, V. ⒻⒻ

Beyond its severe facade, this hotel conceals a narrow courtyard garden where guests breakfast in the summer. Double glazing in the bedrooms minimizes street noise, but rooms overlooking the courtyard are the most quiet and cheerful.

Hôtel Bourgogne et Montana

3 Rue de Bourgogne 75007.
Map 11 B2. ☎ 01 45 51 20 22.
FAX 01 45 56 11 98. **Rooms:** 33. ⬛ TV ☒ ⬛ ⬛ ☲ AE, DC, MC, V, JCB. ⒻⒻⒻ

Situated in front of the Assemblée Nationale, the Hôtel de Bourgogne et Montana has an air of sobriety. Features include a mahogany bar,

an old elevator and a circular hall with pink marble columns. The bedrooms seem ordinary by comparison, except for those on the fourth floor, which allow a glimpse of the Place de la Concorde. This is a relaxing, intimate hotel.

Duc de St-Simon

14 Rue de St-Simon 75007.
Map 11 C3. ☎ 01 45 48 35 66.
FAX 01 45 48 68 25. **Rooms:** 34. ⬛ TV ☒ ⒻⒻⒻⒻ

The Hôtel Duc de St-Simon, among the most sought after hotels on the south side of the river, is popular with Americans. A charming 18th-century mansion furnished with antiques, it lives up to its aristocratic pretensions and is a match for the most famous houses in the Faubourg St-Germain. The bedrooms overlooking the large terrace are a rare treat.

CHAILLOT QUARTER
PORTE MAILLOT

Hôtel de Banville

166 Blvd Berthier 75017. **Map** 4 D1.
☎ 01 42 67 70 16. FAX 01 44 40 42 77. **Rooms:** 38. ⬛ 1 24 TV ☒ ⬛ ⬛ ☒ ⬛ 🛈 ☲ AE, DC, MC, V. ⒻⒻ

This 1930s hotel was a family house and has retained the original iron gate, stone staircase and elevator. The salons are opulent and the bedrooms comfortable, with good views from the eighth floor.

Alexander

102 Ave Victor Hugo 75116.
Map 3 B5. ☎ 01 45 53 64 65.
FAX 01 45 53 12 51. **Rooms:** 62. ⬛ 1 ⬛ TV ☒ ⬛ ⬛ 🛈 ☲ AE, DC, MC, V, JCB. ⒻⒻⒻⒻ

This comfortable, traditional hotel reflects the bourgeois self-confidence of the Avenue Victor Hugo. The small, quiet public rooms convey a sense of warmth and intimacy and are perfect for meeting with friends. The well-equipped bedrooms are large, with spacious bathrooms. Ask for a room on the courtyard.

Concorde La Fayette

3 Pl du Général Koenig 75017.
Map 3 C2. ☎ 01 40 68 50 68.
FAX 01 40 68 50 43. **Rooms:** 968. ⬛ ⬛ 24 TV ☒ ⬛ ⬛ ⬛ ⬛ 1 11 ☲ AE, DC, MC, V, JCB. ⒻⒻⒻⒻ

The formulaic Concorde La Fayette, with its egg-shaped tower, overlooks the Palais des Congrès on the Porte Maillot and is absolutely high-tech. It has many facilities – a fitness club, an amazing bar on the 33rd floor, several restaurants, a shopping gallery, and identical bedrooms with splendid views – the higher you are, the better the views.

Le Méridien

81 Blvd Gouvion St-Cyr 75017. **Map** 3 C2. 01 40 68 34 34. FAX 01 40 68 31 31. **Rooms:** 1,025.
AE, DC, MC, V, JCB. ⒻⒻⒻⒻ

Despite its lack of charm, the Hôtel Le Méridien is one of the most popular hotels in Paris. It is conveniently located opposite the Palais des Congrès and the Air France terminal for Roissy, and its restaurant is one of the best in Parisian hotels. Its Lionel Hampton Club has built a reliable reputation in the world of jazz and hosts a jazz brunch in the lounge, with a big band on winter Sundays.

Villa Maillot

143 Ave de Malakoff 75116. **Map** 3 C4. 01 53 64 52 52. FAX 01 45 00 60 61. **Rooms:** 42.
AE, DC, MC, V, JCB. ⒻⒻⒻⒻ

Conveniently situated for Porte Maillot and La Défense, the Villa Maillot is a modern creation that harks back to the 1930s with its Art Deco–inspired furnishings. The rooms have large beds, concealed kitchenettes and marble bathrooms. On the eighth floor are suites, each one devoted to a different painter.

Zébra Square

3 Rue de Boulainvilliers 75016. **Map** 9 4A. 01 44 14 91 90. FAX 01 44 14 91 99. **Rooms:** 22.
AE, DC, MC, V. ⒻⒻⒻⒻ

Close to the Seine and with some great views over the river to the Eiffel Tower, this is a hotel which manages to be both stylishly modern and luxuriously welcoming. The 22 rooms and suites, some of which are designed for use by disabled guests, are furnished with sumptuous fabrics and exotic woods and each has its own marble bathroom. There are direct lines and faxes in all rooms. Exhibitions of work by leading contemporary artists are mounted in the atrium.

Raphaël

17 Ave Kléber 75116. **Map** 4 D4. 01 44 28 00 28. FAX 01 45 01 21 50. **Rooms:** 90.
AE, DC, MC, V, JCB.

Many movies are shot in the Neo-Gothic bar of this timeless hotel. Here no one asks questions, Italian movie stars are sheltered from the paparazzi, and the Turner hanging in the hall doesn't even attract a passing glance.

St-James

43 Ave Bugeaud 75116. **Map** 3 B5. 01 44 05 81 81. FAX 01 44 05 81 82. **Rooms:** 48.
AE, DC, MC, V, JCB. ⒻⒻⒻⒻⒻ

The St-James occupies a mansion with a small park near the Avenue Foch and the Bois de Boulogne. Visitors are entitled "temporary members" (of the hotel club), and a token fee is included in the room price. The hotel has a princely atmosphere, with English-style salons, wood-paneled libraries, billiards rooms and large bedrooms opening on to the park.

CHAMPS-ELYSÉES

Résidence Lord Byron

5 Rue Chateaubriand 75008. **Map** 4 E4. 01 43 59 89 98. FAX 01 42 89 46 04. **Rooms:** 31.
AE, DC, MC, V, JCB. ⒻⒻ

Close to the Etoile, the Résidence Lord Byron is a discreet, small hotel with a courtyard garden where you can take breakfast during the summer. Its bright bedrooms are relatively quiet but not large, and the sixth-floor rooms have good views. If you want more space, ask for one of the few salon bedrooms or for a ground-floor room in the pavilion between the two gardens.

Atala

10 Rue Chateaubriand 75008. **Map** 4 E4. 01 45 62 01 62. FAX 01 42 25 66 38. **Rooms:** 48.
AE, DC, MC, V, JCB. ⒻⒻⒻⒻ

Situated in a quiet street yet within a few minutes' walk to the busy Champs-Elysées, the Atala's rooms overlook a tranquil garden with tall trees. The terrace restaurant is surrounded by hydrangeas, and the eighth-floor bedroom views of the Eiffel Tower are spectacular. However, the bedroom decor is unimaginative, and the reception and restaurant are ordinary.

Claridge-Bellman

37 Rue François-1er 75008. **Map** 4 F5. 01 47 23 54 42. FAX 01 47 23 08 84. **Rooms:** 42.
AE, DC, MC, V. ⒻⒻⒻⒻ

The Claridge-Bellman is a miniature version of the old Claridge Hotel and is managed by its former directors. The hotel has a truly traditional feel. It is quiet, sober, and efficiently run, and is furnished throughout with tapestries and antiques. The sixth-floor attic rooms are charming.

Balzac

6 Rue Balzac 75008. **Map** 4 F4. 01 45 61 97 22. FAX 01 44 35 18 05. **Rooms:** 70.
AE, DC, MC, V, JCB. ⒻⒻⒻⒻⒻ

Situated near the Etoile, the Balzac is known mainly for its fashionable restaurant, the Bice. But this small luxury hotel deserves to be visited for its own sake. Behind the fin-de-siècle facade is an impressive lounge with columns.

Bristol

112 Rue du Faubourg-St-Honoré 75008. **Map** 5 A4. 01 53 43 43 00. FAX 01 53 43 43 26. **Rooms:** 192.
AE, DC, MC, V, JCB. ⒻⒻⒻⒻⒻ

One of Paris's finest hotels, the Bristol is ideally located for those attending meetings at the Elysée Palace or visiting the chic shops of the Faubourg St-Honoré. The large rooms are sumptuously decorated with antiques and have magnificent marble bathrooms. The period dining room is decorated with Flemish tapestries and glittering crystal chandeliers. In summer, lunch is served under an awning.

George V

31 Ave George V 75008. **Map** 4 E5. 01 47 23 54 00. FAX 01 47 20 06 49. **Rooms:** 298.
AE, DC, MC, V, JCB. ⒻⒻⒻⒻⒻ

The luxurious George V has an elegant Les Princes restaurant with a patio. This legendary hotel, dotted with secret salons, old furniture, and art, has lost a little of its charm during renovation. The breakfast lounge is frequented by media people. There is a wide range of facilities, and the service is excellent.

Plaza Athénée

25 Ave Montaigne 75008.
Map 10 F1. **[** 01 53 67 66 65.
FAX 01 53 67 66 66. **Rooms:** 204.
① ⚙ 24 TV ☎ 🖥 🔒 🕭 🐾 🛏
🕭 ❚❚ 🕯 🍴 *AE, DC, MC, V, JCB.*
€€€€€

The legendary Plaza Athénée has stood on the glamorous Avenue Montaigne for more than 80 years. It is a hotel for honeymooners, old aristocracy and for haute couture. Its Gobelins tapestries are superb. Of the restaurants, Le Régence is wonderfully romantic, especially in summer on the ivy-decked terrace, while Le Relais has a reputation as the most snobbish grill in Paris. The hotel's recently refurbished bedrooms conform to the very highest contemporary standards of luxury, as well as to the timeless dictates of comfort.

Prince de Galles Sheraton

33 Ave George V 75008.
Map 4 E5. **[** 01 53 23 77 77.
FAX 01 53 23 78 78. **Rooms:** 168.
🛏 ① 24 TV ☎ 🖥 🔒 🕭 🐾
🕯 ❚❚ 🍴 *AE, DC, MC, V, JCB.*
€€€€€

The Prince de Galles Sheraton suffers from being a second choice after its neighbor, the George V. The hotel is less prestigious and the bedrooms overdue for restoration. Only the comfortably British bar and the restaurant bear comparison. The hotel is conveniently situated near the Champs-Elysées.

Royal Monceau

37 Ave Hoche 75008.
Map 4 F3. **[** 01 42 99 88 00.
FAX 01 42 99 89 91. **Rooms:** 219.
24 TV ☎ 🖥 🔒 🕭 🐾 🛏 P
🕯 ❚❚ 🍴 *AE, DC, MC, V, JCB.*
€€€€€

Lying majestically between the Place de l'Etoile and the Parc Monceau, the Royal Monceau has been splendidly restored to its former glory. Its health club is now one of the most luxurious in Paris, and its Le Carpaccio restaurant is one of the city's best Italian eateries. Judicious use of the former might even undo some of the damage incurred through over-indulgence at the latter. The breakfast room is unusual in its design – a striking glass gazebo with curved walls. The bedrooms are elegant – pamper yourself and pick a room overlooking the courtyard if possible or one of the prestigious suites.

San Regis

12 Rue Jean Goujon 75008.
Map 11 A1. **[** 01 43 59 41 90.
FAX 01 45 61 05 48. **Rooms:** 44.
🛏 ① ⚙ 24 TV ☎ 🖥 🔒 🕭
🕯 ❚❚ 🍴 *AE, DC, MC, V, JCB.*
€€€€€

Since it opened in 1923, the San Regis has been the haunt of masters of haute couture and movie actors, who enjoy its quiet but central location near the Champs-Elysées. This particularly welcoming, intimate luxury hotel is undeniably British in style – this is especially true of the famous bar. The suites on the upperfloors overlook a pleasant terrace.

Sofitel Arc de Triomphe

14 Rue Beaujon 75008. **Map** 4 E4.
[01 45 63 04 04. FAX 01 42 25 36 81. **Rooms:** 135. 🛏 ① ⚙ 24 TV
☎ 🖥 🖥 🔒 🕭 🐾 🛏 🕯 ❚❚
🍴 *AE, DC, MC, V, JCB.*
€€€€€

The Sofitel Arc de Triomphe, situated in the business area near the Etoile, is a quiet hotel. The bedrooms have been restored in Pullman style and Neo-Art Deco furniture. The Clovis restaurant is astonishingly good, and the junior suites are particularly comfortable. The Parc Monceau is nearby.

Hôtel de la Trémoille

14 Rue de la Trémoille 75008.
Map 10 F1. **[** 01 47 23 34 20.
FAX 01 40 70 01 08. **Rooms:** 107.
🛏 ① TV ☎ 🖥 🔒 🕭 🐾 🛏
🕯 ❚❚ 🍴 *AE, DC, MC, V.*
€€€€€

The Hôtel de la Trémoille is impressive but at the same time relaxed. Housemaids customarily cast a ray of sunshine through residents' days by responding with a smile to the first ring; a fire burns in the restaurant fireplace; rooms are furnished with comfortable antiques; and the bathrooms are divine in their luxury.

Vernet

25 Rue Vernet 75008. **Map** 4 E4.
[01 44 31 98 00. FAX 01 44 31 85 69. **Rooms:** 57. 🛏 ① ⚙ 24 TV
☎ 🖥 🔒 🕭 🐾 🛏 🕯 ❚❚ 🍴 *AE, DC, MC, V, JCB.* €€€€€

The Hôtel Vernet is still relatively unknown to the general public. Gustave Eiffel, architect of the Eiffel Tower, created the dazzling glass roof of the dining room. The large, quiet bedrooms are pleasantly furnished, and guests have free use of the Royal Monceau's fitness club.

Ambassador

16 Blvd Haussmann 75009.
Map 6 E4. **[** 01 42 46 92 63.
FAX 01 40 22 08 74. **Rooms:** 288. 🛏
① ⚙ 24 TV ☎ 🖥 🔒 🕭 🐾 🛏
🛏 🕯 ❚❚ 🍴 *AE, DC, MC, V, JCB.* €€€€

One of the best of Paris's Art Deco hotels, the Ambassador has been restored to its former glory and has deep carpeting and antique furniture. The ground floor has pink marble columns, Baccarat crystal chandeliers and Aubusson tapestries. The food is outstanding – the chef formerly managed the kitchen at the Grand Véfour restaurant *(see p301).*

Le Grand Hôtel

2 Rue Scribe 75009. **Map** 6 D5.
[01 40 07 32 32. FAX 01 42 66 12 51. **Rooms:** 514. 🛏 ① 24 TV ☎
🐾 🖥 🕭 🔒 🕭 🐾 🛏 👁 🕯
❚❚ 🍴 *AE, DC, MC, V, JCB.*
€€€€€

The Intercontinental chain has invested many millions of francs in Le Grand Hôtel. A top-floor health club has been installed, and the bedrooms are now equipped with the utmost in contemporary comfort. The hotel has a sumptuous Opera Salon beneath an Art Deco cupola.

Westminster

13 Rue de la Paix 75002. **Map** 6 D5.
[01 42 61 57 46. FAX 01 42 60 30 66.
Rooms: 101. 🛏 TV ☎ 🖥 🔒 🕭
🛏 🐾 🕭 🕯 ❚❚ 🍴 *AE, DC, MC, V, JCB.* €€€€€

The Westminster is between the Ritz and the Jardin des Tuileries. Although the restaurant isn't popular, the bedrooms are pleasantly furnished, some in period style with marble mantelpieces, chandeliers and 18th-century clocks.

Terrass' Hôtel

12 Rue Joseph-de-Maistre 75018.
Map 6 E1. **[** 01 46 06 72 85.
FAX 01 42 52 29 11. **Rooms:** 101.
🛏 ① ⚙ TV ☎ 🖥 🔒 🕭 🐾 🛏
P 👁 🕯 ❚❚ 🕯 🍴 *AE, DC, MC, V, JCB.* €€€

The Terrass Hôtel has a panoramic view over the rooftops of Paris from the upper floors and from the breakfast terrace. All the rooms are comfortably, if unremarkably, furnished. A few bedrooms retain the original Art Deco woodwork.

For key to symbols *see p275.*

RESTAURANTS, CAFÉS AND BARS

THE FRENCH NATIONAL passion for excellent cuisine makes eating out one of the greatest pleasures of a visit to Paris. Everywhere in the city you see people eating – in restaurants, bistros, tea salons, cafés and wine bars.

Most restaurants serve French food, but in many areas there is a range of Chinese, Vietnamese and North African eateries, as well as Italian, Greek, Lebanese and Indian places. The restaurants in the listings (see

pp299–309) have been selected from the best that Paris can offer across all the price ranges. The listings and Choosing a Restaurant on pages 296 to 298 are organized by area and price. Most places will serve lunch from noon until around 2pm, and the menu often includes fixed-price meals. Parisians usually start to fill restaurants for dinner around 8:30pm, and most places serve from around 7:30pm until 11pm. (See also Light Meals and Snacks pp310–11.)

WHAT TO EAT

A TREMENDOUS RANGE of food is available in Paris from the rich meat dishes and perfect pâtisserie for which France is most famous to simpler French regional cuisines (see pp290–91). The latter are available in brasseries and bistros – the type usually depends on the birthplace of the chef. At any time of day simple, tasty meals can be had in cafés, wine and beer bars, and brasseries, bistros and cake shops – or pâtisseries – are found in abundance. Some cafés, like the Bar de la Croix Rouge (see p311) in St-Germain-des-Prés, are known for their cold food and don't offer hot meals at lunchtime.

The best ethnic food comes from France's former colonies: Vietnam or North Africa. North African places are known as couscous restaurants and serve filling, somewhat spicy, inexpensive

food that varies in quality. Vietnamese restaurants are also good value and provide a light alternative to rich French food. Paris also has a number of good Japanese restaurants, notably on the Rue St-Roch.

WHERE TO FIND GOOD RESTAURANTS AND CAFÉS

YOU CAN EAT well in almost any part of Paris. Wherever you are, as a rule of thumb you will find that the most outstanding restaurants and cafés are those that cater predominantly to a French clientele.

The Left Bank probably has the greatest concentration of restaurants, especially in tourist areas like St-Germain-des-Prés and the Latin Quarter. The quality of food varies, but there are some commendable bistros, outdoor cafés and wine bars. (For bistros, brasseries and restaurants with outdoor

Beauvilliers restaurant (see p307)

tables, see Choosing a Restaurant on pages 296 to 298.) The Latin Quarter also has a high concentration of Chinese and Vietnamese restaurants, centered chiefly around Maubert-Mutualité and the Rue des Ecoles.

In the trendy Marais and Bastille areas, small bistros, tea salons and cafés are plentiful, some new and fashionable. There are also many good, traditional long-established bistros and brasseries.

In the Champs-Elysées and Madeleine area, it is difficult to find inexpensive good food. It is overrun with fast-food joints and pricey but not very good cafés. There are, however, some very good expensive restaurants here.

Some great cafés of the 1920s are in Montparnasse on the Boulevard Montparnasse, including Le Sélect and La Rotonde (see p311). Sensitive renovation has recaptured

The prim Mariage Frères shop and tea room (see p311)

much of their old splendor. There are excellent bistros in this area as well.

There are many noteworthy restaurants, bistros and cafés in the Louvre-Rivoli area, competing with overpriced tourist-oriented cafés. Just to the east, Les Halles is filled with fast-food joints and mediocre restaurants, but there are few places of note.

Good Japanese food and some fine brasseries can be found near the Opéra, but otherwise the area around the Opéra and Grands Boulevards is not the best for restaurants. Near the Bourse is a number of reputable restaurants and bistros frequented by stockbrokers.

Montmartre has a predictable number of tourist restaurants, but it also has a few very pleasant small bistros. More expensive are the luxurious Beauvilliers (see p307) and the Italian-influenced La Table d'Anvers (see p307) near the Butte Montmartre.

Quiet neighborhoods in the evening, the Invalides, Eiffel Tower and Palais de Chaillot tend to have less noisy, more serious restaurants than areas with lively nightlife. Prices can be quite high.

Two Chinatowns, one in the area south of the Place d'Italie, the other in the traditionally working-class hilltop area of Belleville, have concentrations of ethnic food but few French restaurants of note. There is a number of Vietnamese eating places as well as large, inexpensive Chinese ones, and Belleville is packed with small North African restaurants.

Le Grand Véfour in the Tuileries (see p301)

TYPES OF RESTAURANTS AND CAFÉS

ONE OF THE MOST enjoyable aspects of eating in Paris is the diversity of places to eat. Bistros are small, often moderately priced restaurants with a limited selection of dishes. Those from the Belle Epoque era are particularly beautiful, with zinc bars, mirrors and attractive tiles. The food is generally, but not always, regional and traditional. Many chefs from the most elegant restaurants have now also opened bistros, and these can be excellent choices.

Brasseries are generally large, fun, bustling eateries, many with an Alsatian character serving carafes of Alsatian wine and platters of sauerkraut and sausage. They have immense menus, and most serve food throughout the day and are open late. Outside, you may well see impressive pavement displays of shellfish, with apron-clad oyster shuckers working late into the night.

Cafés (and some wine bars) open early in the morning, and apart from the large tourist cafés, the majority close by around 9pm. They serve drinks and food all day long from a short menu of salads, sandwiches and eggs.

Menu at Le Bistrot du Dôme

At lunch, most also offer a small choice of hot daily specials. Café prices vary from area to area, in direct proportion to the number of tourists. Upscale cafés, like Café de Flore and Les Deux Magots, serve food until late at night. Those cafés specializing in beer almost always include onion tarts, french fries and hearty bowls of steamed mussels on the menu.

Wine bars are informal. They usually have moderately priced, simple lunch menus and serve wine by the glass. They serve snacks at any time of day – such as marvelous open sandwiches (tartines) made with sourdough Poilâne bread topped with cheese, sausage or pâté – until around 9pm, but a few stay open for dinner.

Tea salons open for breakfast or at mid-morning and close in the early evening. Many offer lunch, as well as a selection of sweet pastries for afternoon tea. They are at their best in the middle of the afternoon and offer coffee, hot chocolate and fine teas. Some, like Le Loir dans la Théière, are casual, with sofas and big tables, while Mariage Frères is more formal. Angélina on the Rue de Rivoli is famous for its hot chocolate, and Ladurée has excellent chocolate macaroons. (For addresses see p311.)

Tour d'Argent decoration (see p302)

VEGETARIAN FOOD

VEGETARIAN RESTAURANTS in Paris are few, and non-vegetarian restaurant menus are usually firmly oriented toward meat and fish. However, you can get a good salad almost anywhere, and you can often fare well by ordering two dishes from the list of entrées (first courses). The North African restaurants will serve you *couscous nature* – which doesn't have meat.

Never be timid about asking for a change in a dish. If you see a salad with ham, bacon or foie gras, ask the waiter for it without the meat. If you are going to a better restaurant, telephone in advance and ask the manager if it would be possible for them to prepare a special meal for you. Most restaurants will be happy to oblige.

HOW MUCH TO PAY

PRICES FOR MEALS in Paris range from extremely economic to astronomical. You can still enjoy a hearty restaurant or café lunch for F80, but a typical good bistro, brasserie or restaurant meal in central Paris will average F200 to F250 with wine. (Remember that the better French wines will increase the size of your bill significantly.) More expensive restaurants begin at about F300 with wine and go up to F1,000 for the top places. Many places offer a *formule* or *prix-fixe* (fixed-price) menu, especially at lunch, and this will almost

Le Carré des Feuillants *(see p301)*

always offer the best value. Some restaurants feature menus for under F100 – a few at this price include wine. Coffee usually carries an extra charge.

All French restaurants are obliged by law to display their menu outside. The posted rates include service but a tip for particularly good service will always be appreciated (any amount from a few francs to 5% of the total).

The most widely accepted credit card is VISA. Few restaurants accept American Express, and some bistros do not accept credit cards at all, so inquire when you make a reservation. Traveler's checks and Eurocheques are not widely accepted either; cafés almost always require cash.

MAKING RESERVATIONS

IT IS BEST TO reserve a table in all restaurants, brasseries and bistros. Although you can usually get into a brasserie without a reservation, you may have to wait for a table.

DRESS CODE

EXCEPT FOR SOME three-star restaurants, which can be rather formal, you can dress up or down in Parisian restaurants – within reason. The restaurant listings *(see pp299–309)* indicate which places require formal dress.

READING THE MENU AND ORDERING

MENUS IN SMALL restaurants and bistros, and even in big brasseries, are often handwritten and can be difficult to decipher, so ask for help if necessary.

The waiter usually takes first your choice of *entrée* (first course), then the *plat* (main course). Dessert is ordered after you have finished your main course, unless you wish a hot dessert that has to be ordered at the start of the

The Angélina restaurant, also known for its tea room *(see p311)*

meal. The waiter will explain this, or the dessert section of the menu will be marked *à commander avant le repas*.

The first course generally includes a choice of seasonal salads or vegetables, pâté and small hot or cold vegetable dishes or tarts. Small fish dishes like smoked salmon, grilled sardines, herring, fish salads and tartares are also offered. Brasseries have such shellfish as oysters, which can also be eaten as a main course. Main dishes usually include a selection of meat, poultry and fish, and upscale restaurants offer game in autumn. Most restaurants also offer daily specials *(plats du jour)*.

Le Pavillon Montsouris near the Parc Montsouris *(see p309)*

Le Train Bleu station restaurant in the Gare de Lyon *(see p309)*

These dishes will incorporate seasonal fresh produce and are reasonably priced.

If you choose to have it, cheese is eaten either as a dessert or as a predessert course. Some people have a green salad with their cheese. Coffee is served after, not with, dessert. You will need to specify whether you want it *au lait* (with milk). Herbal teas *(tisanes)* are also popular after-dinner beverages.

In most restaurants you will be asked if you would like a drink before ordering food. A typical apéritif is *kir* (white wine with a drop of crème de cassis, a blackcurrant liqueur) or *kir royale* (champagne with crème de cassis). Spirits, however, aren't generally drunk before a meal in France *(see* What to Drink in Paris *pp292–3)*.

Lucas Carton restaurant *(see p307)*

Bistros and brasseries usually include the wine list with the menu. The more expensive restaurants have separate wine lists, which are generally brought to the table by the wine steward after you have had a look at the meal menu.

SERVICE

Eating is a leisurely pastime in France, although the general standard of service in Paris restaurants is high, it is not always fast. In small restaurants in particular, don't expect rapid attention: there may be only one waiter, and dishes are cooked to order.

CHILDREN

Children are usually very welcome, but there may be little room in a busy restaurant for strollers or carriages. Nor are special facilities like highchairs or baby seats commonly provided in eating places.

SMOKING

France has passed strict legislation forcing restaurants to provide no-smoking sections, but it remains to be seen how strictly the law will be observed. Eating places, especially cafés, tend to be very smoky.

WHEELCHAIR ACCESS

Wheelchair access may be restricted. A word when you are reserving should ensure that you are given a conveniently situated table and help when you arrive.

USING THE LISTINGS
Key to symbols in the listings on pages 299 to 309.

🍽 fixed-price menu
V vegetarian specialties
⑂ children's portions provided
♿ wheelchair access
👔 jacket and tie required
♫ live music
⌂ outdoor tables
♟ particularly good wine list
★ highly recommended
💳 credit cards accepted:
AE American Express
DC Diners Club
MC MasterCard/Access
V   VISA
JCB Japanese Credit Bureau

Price categories for a three-course meal, including a half-bottle of house wine, tax and service:
Ⓕ under F150
ⒻⒻ F150–250
ⒻⒻⒻ F251–350
ⒻⒻⒻⒻ F351–500
ⒻⒻⒻⒻⒻ over F500

What to Eat in Paris

FRENCH CUISINE is a still-evolving art. Classical French cooking is butter-based and centers on meat, poultry and fish. However, it is no longer all super-rich, nor is it the "nouvelle cuisine" of the 1980s. Today the chefs of many Parisian restaurants are interested in regional food and in simple homestyle cooking. This relies on seasonal fresh ingredients, as in the shellfish dishes *coquilles Saint-Jacques* and *moules marinières* shown here. French cooking tends not to be highly spiced, although fresh herbs like chives, parsley and tarragon are essential ingredients in the sauces and stocks. The most popular regional cooking in Paris is from Lyon, Burgundy and the southwest. Provençal traditions with scents of garlic and olive oil are also gaining in popularity. Lyonnais cooking is characterized by copious salads and hearty meat-based main dishes like *andouillettes.* Burgundian and southwestern food is rich; typical dishes are *foie gras* (fattened liver), *jambon* or *homard persillé* (ham or lobster with parsley) and *cassoulet,* (a hearty main course with pork and beans).

Goat's cheese

Croissants
These flaky pastry crescents are eaten for breakfast.

Pains au Chocolat
These chocolate-filled pastries are an alternative to croissants.

Brioches
Doughy buns, they are torn and dipped in coffee.

Baguette
This characteristic long crusty loaf is wonderful as a sandwich or simply buttered fresh from a bakery.

Piped potato   **Scallops**
Coquilles Saint-Jacques
Scallops can be prepared and garnished in many ways but are classically cooked with sliced mushrooms in white wine, lemon juice and butter and then served on one half of the scallop shell. A piping of mashed potato is often used to keep the scallops and their sauce in the shell.

Foie Gras
This is the liver of specially fattened geese or ducks.

Moules Marinières
Mussels are steamed in garlicky wine stock.

Escargots à la Bourguignonne
Cooked snails are replaced in their shells and garnished.

Homard Persillé
This lobster terrine is cooked in a flavored stock with parsley, shallots and herbs.

Oeufs en Cocotte à l'Estragon
A tarragon-flavored sauce is poured over baked eggs.

Andouillettes à la Lyonnaise
These sausages made from pork intestines are grilled or fried and served with onions.

Noisettes d'Agneau
Small, tender lamb cutlets are fried in butter and served with a variety of garnishes.

Chèvre Tiede sur un Lit de Salade
Grilled goat's cheese sits on a classic mixed-leaf salad.

Slice of Brie de Meaux   **Crottins de Chavignol**

Cheeses *(Fromages)*
Cheese is one of the glories of France. Many varieties are made – from cow's, sheep's and goat's milk. The soft and semisoft mild cheeses, such as Brie and Camembert, are available in all Parisian restaurants.

Slice of Pont l'Evêque

Whole Camembert

Crêpes Suzettes
Crêpes are served with tangerine-and-Curaçao sauce.

Tarte Tatin
This upside-down apple tart is a Parisian specialty.

Tarte Alsacienne
Classic Alsatian tarts contain confectioner's custard and fruit.

What to Drink in Paris

PARIS IS THE BEST place in France to
sample a wide range of the country's
many different wines. It's cheapest to order
wine by the carafe, normally referred to by
size – 25 cl *(quart)*, 50 cl *(demi)* or 75 cl
(pichet, equivalent to a bottle*)*. Cafés and
wine bars always offer wine by the glass:
un petit blanc is a small glass of white; a
larger glass of red, *un ballon rouge*. House
wine is nearly always a reliable choice.

Paris's last vineyard, near Sacré-Coeur *(see p220)*

RED WINE

SOME OF THE world's finest
and most expensive red
wines come from the Bordeaux
and Burgundy regions, but
for everyday drinking
choose from the enormous
range of basic Bordeaux or
Côtes du Rhône wines.
Alternatively, try Beaujolais,
which comes from the
southern end of Burgundy
and is light enough to
serve chilled.

**Distinctive bottle shapes for
Bordeaux and Burgundy**

Bordeaux châteaus
include Margaux,
which makes some of
the world's most
elegant red wines.

Burgundy includes
some big, strong red
wines from the village
of Gevrey-Chambertin
in the Côte de Nuits.

Beaujolais Nouveau,
the fruity first taste of
the year's new wine, is
released on the third
Thursday of November.

The Loire has very
good red wines from
the area around Chinon.
They are usually quite
light and very dry.

Southern Rhône is
famous for its dark,
rich red wines from
Châteauneuf-du-Pape,
north of Avignon.

Northern Rhône has
some dark, fragrant red
wines, best aged for at
least 10 years, from
Côte-Rôtie near Vienne.

FINE WINE VINTAGE CHART

	1997	1996	1995	1994	1993	1992	1991	1990	1989
BORDEAUX									
Margaux, St-Julien, Pauillac, St-Estèphe	7	8	8	7	5	6	5	7	8
Graves, Pessac-Léognan (red)	7	7	7	7	7	5	5	7	8
Graves, Pessac-Léognan (white)	8	7	6	7	7	6	6	8	8
St-Emilion, Pomerol	8	8	8	6	6	5	3	8	8
BURGUNDY									
Chablis	8	8	9	7	6	7	5	7	9
Côte de Nuits (red)	8	8	8	5	6	7	6	9	8
Côte de Beaune (white)	8	8	8	6	6	5	8	8	9
LOIRE									
Bourgueil, Chinon	9	9	8	6	6	5	5	9	9
Sancerre (white)	9	8	8	7	6	6	6	8	8
RHONE									
Hermitage (red)	7	9	8	7	5	6	6	8	8
Hermitage (white)	8	8	7	7	5	6	7	9	8
Côte-Rôtie	7	9	8	7	5	6	9	7	8
Châteauneuf-du-Pape	7	8	8	7	6	5	4	9	10

The quality scale from 1 to 10 represents an overall rating for the year and is only a guideline.

WHITE WINE

THE FINEST white Bordeaux and Burgundy are best with food, but for everyday drinking try a light dry wine such as Entre-Deux-Mers from Bordeaux, or Anjou Blanc or Sauvignon de Touraine from the Loire. Alsace makes some reliable white wines. Dessert wines such as Sauternes, Barsac or Coteaux du Layon are delicious with fruit.

Alsace Riesling and Burgundy

SPARKLING WINE

IN FRANCE champagne is the first choice for a celebration drink, and styles range from nonvintage to deluxe. Many other wine regions make sparkling wines by the champagne method, which tend to be a lot cheaper. Look for Crémant de Loire, Crémant de Bourgogne, Vouvray Mousseux, Saumur Mousseux and Blanquette de Limoux.

Champagne

Alsace wines are usually labeled by grape variety. Gewürztraminer is one of the most distinctive.

Burgundy wines include Chablis, a fresh, full-flavored dry wine from the northernmost vineyards.

Champagne vineyards east of Paris produce the famous sparkling wine. Billecart-Salmon is a light, pink Champagne.

Loire wines include Pouilly-Fumé, from the east of the region. It is very dry, often with a slightly smoky perfume.

The Loire has the perfect partner to seafood dishes in Muscadet, a dry white wine from the Atlantic Coast.

Sweet Bordeaux are luscious, golden-colored dessert wines, the most famous being Barsac and Sauternes.

APÉRITIFS AND DIGESTIFS

KIR, WHITE WINE mixed with a small amount of blackcurrant liqueur or *crème de cassis*, is the ubiquitous apéritif. Also common is anise-flavored *pastis*, which is served with ice and a pitcher of water and can be very refreshing. Vermouths, especially Noilly-Prat, are also common apéritifs. *Digestifs*, or after-dinner drinks, are often ordered with coffee and include *eaux-de-vie*, the strong colorless spirits infused with fruit, and brandies such as Cognac, Armagnac and Calvados.

Kir: white wine with *cassis*

BEERS

BEER IN FRANCE is sold either by the bottle or, more cheaply, on tap by the glass – *un demi*. The cheapest is lager-style *bière française*, and the best brands are Meteor and Mutzig, followed by "33" and Kronenbourg. A maltier beer is Leffe, which comes as *blonde* (lager) or *brune* (darker, more fully flavored). Pelforth makes very good dark beer and lager. Some bars and cafés specialize in foreign beers, especially from Belgium, and these are very malty and strong. (For beer bars see *Light Meals and Snacks* on pages 310–11.)

OTHER DRINKS

THE BRIGHTLY-COLORED drinks consumed in cafés all over Paris are mixtures of flavored syrups and mineral waters, called *sirops à l'eau*. The emerald-green drinks use mint syrup, the red ones grenadine. Fruit juices, like tomato juice, are sold in bottles unless you specify *citron pressé* (freshly squeezed lemon) or *orange pressée* (freshly squeezed orange). The squeezed fruit juice is served with a pitcher of water and with sugar or sugar syrup for you to dilute and sweeten to taste. Tap water is perfectly drinkable, and sparkling or still mineral waters *(l'eau gazeuse* or *l'eau naturelle)* are available everywhere.

Fresh lemon juice is served with water and sugar syrup.

Paris's Best: Restaurants

PARIS POSSESSES A GREATER WEALTH of eating places than any other city of comparable size. From the simplest of bars to the grandest of elegant restaurants, it has something for everybody. Even in the humblest bistro the bread and pastries will be fresh from the bakery, and the cheese will be perfectly ripe. The restaurants here are just a few of Paris's most memorable, chosen from the listings on pages 299 to 309 as much for the beauty of their decor as the excellence of their authentic food.

Le Grand Colbert
This pretty brasserie is in a historic building and serves classic fare until late.
(See p306.)

Champs-Elysées

Opéra Quarter

Chaillot Quarter

Tuileries
Quarter

RIVER SEINE

Invalides
and
Eiffel Tower Quarter

St-Germain-
des-Prés

Chiberta
Superbly presented modern French food at its best is the star feature of this stylish restaurant.
(See p305.)

Luxemb
Qua

Montparnasse

Taillevent
The discreetly luxurious surroundings, exquisite modern classic cuisine, extraordinary wine list and impeccable service make this a top restaurant. (See p306.)

0 kilometers   1

0 miles   0.5

L'Arpège
This starkly modern restaurant near the Musée Rodin offers wonderfully elegant haute cuisine. (See p304.)

Chartier
The bustling atmosphere and inexpensive basic French food make this turn-of-the-century soup kitchen with historic decor a popular choice. (See p306.)

Brasserie Flo
It's worth the trip to this brasserie for the authentic Alsatian cuisine. Sauerkraut platters, seafood and excellent regional wines and beers draw customers. (See p308.)

Au Pied de Cochon
This colorfully restored landmark of old Les Halles serves authentic brasserie fare. (See p300.)

Beaubourg and Les Halles

The Marais

Benoît
Classic French cuisine is served in this archetypal bistro with its 1912 mirrored interior. (See p300.)

Ile de la Cité
Ile St-Louis

atin Quarter

Brasserie Bofinger
Dating from 1864, the oldest and one of the most popular brasseries in Paris is known for its marvelous decor, excellent shellfish and reliable menu. (See p299.)

Jardin des Plantes Quarter

Pharamond
Mosaics and colored tiles make this old bistro an Art Nouveau gem. (See p300.)

La Tour d'Argent
This famous restaurant with a panoramic view is the ultimate in luxury – and expense. (See p302.)

Choosing a Restaurant

THE RESTAURANTS LISTED on the following pages have been selected for their good value or exceptional food. This choosing chart highlights some of the main factors which may influence your choice. For more information on each restaurant see pages 299–309. Details of snack and sandwich bars are in Light Meals and Snacks on pages 310–11.

Restaurant	Price	Seafood Restaurant	Fixed-Price Menu	Late Opening (after 11:30pm)	Children's Facilities	Outdoor Eating	Quiet Restaurant	Vegetarian Specialties
ÎLE DE LA CITÉ (see p299)								
Vieux Bistrot	₣₣₣		■			●		
THE MARAIS (see pp299–300)								
Le Trumilou	₣		■		■	●		●
L'Alisier	₣₣		■		■			
Le Baracane	₣₣		■					
Brasserie Bofinger	₣₣			●				
Chez Jenny	₣₣		■	●		●		●
La Guirlande de Julie	₣₣		■	●		●		
Le Passage	₣₣				■		■	
Le Bar à Huîtres	₣₣₣	●	■	●		●		
Au Bourguignon du Marais	₣₣₣						■	
Miravile	₣₣₣		■			●		●
L'Ambroisie ★	₣₣₣₣₣						■	
BEAUBOURG AND LES HALLES (see p300)								
Chez Elle	₣₣		■			●		
Le Grizzli	₣₣		■			●		
Saudade	₣₣							
Bleu Marine	₣₣	●	■			●	■	
Au Pied de Cochon	₣₣₣		■	●		●		
Pharamond	₣₣₣		■			●		
Benoît ★	₣₣₣₣₣							
TUILERIES QUARTER (see pp300–1)								
Gaya	₣₣	●						
Le Grand Louvre	₣₣		■		■			
Armand au Palais Royal	₣₣₣		■					
Les Ambassadeurs ★	₣₣₣₣₣		■					
Le Carré des Feuillants ★	₣₣₣₣₣		■					
L'Espadon ★	₣₣₣₣₣		■		■	●		
Goumard	₣₣₣₣₣	●						
Le Grand Véfour ★	₣₣₣₣₣		■					
ST-GERMAIN-DES-PRÉS (see pp301–2)								
Le Petit St-Benoît	₣₣							●
Aux Charpentiers	₣₣					●		
Le Muniche	₣₣		■	●		●		
Aux Fins Gourmets	₣₣₣							
Brasserie Lipp	₣₣₣			●		●		
Le Procope	₣₣₣		■	●	■			
Rôtisserie d'en Face	₣₣₣		■					
Yugaraj	₣₣₣		■					●
Tan Dinh	₣₣₣₣						■	
Lapérouse	₣₣₣₣₣		■					
Restaurant Jacques Cagna ★	₣₣₣₣₣		■					
LATIN QUARTER (see p302)								
Chez Pento	₣₣		■					
Loubnane	₣₣		■	●	■			

Price categories per person for a three-course meal with a half-bottle of house wine, including tax and service:
(F) under F150
(F)(F) F150–250
(F)(F)(F) F250–350
(F)(F)(F)(F) F350–500
(F)(F)(F)(F)(F) over F500

★ Means highly recommended.

FIXED-PRICE MENU
Fixed-price menu available at lunch, dinner or both.

CHILDREN'S FACILITIES
Children's portions provided. (Children are welcome in most restaurants in Paris even if special arrangements are not made for them.)

QUIET RESTAURANT
Restaurant has a quiet, intimate atmosphere. No piped music.

	Price	Seafood Restaurant	Fixed-Price Menu	Late Opening (after 11:30pm)	Children's Facilities	Outdoor Eating	Quiet Restaurant	Vegetarian Specialties
Brasserie Balzar	(F)(F)(F)			●		●		
Campagne et Provence	(F)(F)(F)							
Restaurant Moissonnier	(F)(F)(F)							
Rôtisserie du Beaujolais	(F)(F)(F)		■				●	
La Tour d'Argent ★	(F)(F)(F)(F)(F)		■		■		■	
JARDIN DES PLANTES QUARTER (see p302)								
Au Petit Marguéry	(F)(F)(F)		■			●		
MONTPARNASSE (see p303)								
La Coupole	(F)(F)		■	●				
Le Bistrot du Dôme	(F)(F)(F)	●				●		
La Cagouille ★	(F)(F)(F)	●	■		■	●		
Contre-Allée	(F)(F)(F)		■	●		●		
L'Assiette	(F)(F)(F)							
INVALIDES AND EIFFEL TOWER QUARTER (see pp303–4)								
Le Bistrot de Breteuil	(F)(F)		■		■			
L'Oeillade	(F)(F)		■					●
La Serre	(F)(F)		■		■			
Thoumieux	(F)(F)							
Morot-Gaudry	(F)(F)(F)		■			●		
Vin sur Vin	(F)(F)(F)(F)							
L'Arpège ★	(F)(F)(F)(F)(F)		■					
Le Jules Verne	(F)(F)(F)(F)(F)		■					
CHAILLOT QUARTER, PORTE MAILLOT (see p304)								
La Butte Chaillot	(F)(F)(F)			●	■	●		
Chez Géraud	(F)(F)(F)		■					
L'Huîtrier	(F)(F)(F)	●						
Oum El Banine	(F)(F)(F)						■	
Le Timgad	(F)(F)(F)		■		■			
Le Port-Alma	(F)(F)(F)(F)	●	■					
Alain Ducasse	(F)(F)(F)(F)(F)		■		■			
Amphyclès ★	(F)(F)(F)(F)(F)		■		■			
Le Vivarois ★	(F)(F)(F)(F)(F)		■					
CHAMPS-ELYSÉES (see pp305–6)								
L'Avenue	(F)(F)		■	●	■			
Casa de Delfo	(F)(F)		■	●		●		
La Fermette Marbeuf 1900	(F)(F)		■			●		
Savy	(F)(F)						■	
Sébillon	(F)(F)			●				
Le Cercle Ledoyen	(F)(F)		■			●		
Au Petit Colombier	(F)(F)(F)(F)		■					
Chiberta ★	(F)(F)(F)(F)		■					
Guy Savoy ★	(F)(F)(F)(F)(F)							
Lasserre	(F)(F)(F)(F)(F)							
Laurent ★	(F)(F)(F)(F)(F)		■			●		
La Maison Blanche/15 Avenue Montaigne	(F)(F)(F)(F)(F)					●		
Taillevent ★	(F)(F)(F)(F)(F)							

Price categories per person for a three-course meal with a half-bottle of house wine, including tax and service:
Ⓕ under F150
ⒻⒻ F150–250
ⒻⒻⒻ F250–350
ⒻⒻⒻⒻ F350–500
ⒻⒻⒻⒻⒻ over F500

★ Means highly recommended.

FIXED-PRICE MENU
Fixed-price menu available at lunch, dinner or both.

CHILDREN'S FACILITIES
Children's portions provided. (Children are welcome in most restaurants in Paris even if special arrangements are not made for them.)

QUIET RESTAURANT
Restaurant has a quiet, intimate atmosphere. No piped music.

	SEAFOOD RESTAURANT	FIXED-PRICE MENU	LATE OPENING (AFTER 11:30PM)	CHILDREN'S FACILITIES	OUTDOOR EATING	QUIET RESTAURANT	VEGETARIAN SPECIALTIES
OPÉRA QUARTER (see pp306–7)							
Chartier Ⓕ		■					
Au Petit Riche ⒻⒻ		■	●				
Chez Clément ⒻⒻ			●	■			
Café Runtz ⒻⒻ		■	●				
La Ferme St-Hubert ⒻⒻ						■	●
Le Grand Colbert ⒻⒻ		■	●	■			
Les Noces de Jeannette ⒻⒻ		■		■		■	
A.G. Le Poète ⒻⒻ		■					
Le Vaudeville ⒻⒻ		■	●	■	●		
Chez Georges ⒻⒻⒻ							
Café Drouant ⒻⒻⒻⒻ		■	●				
Le Trente ⒻⒻⒻⒻ		■			●		
Lucas Carton ★ ⒻⒻⒻⒻⒻ		■					
MONTMARTRE (see p307)							
La Table d'Anvers ⒻⒻⒻ		■					
Beauvilliers ⒻⒻⒻⒻⒻ		■				●	
FARTHER AFIELD (see pp307–9)							
Dao Vien (75013) Ⓕ		■					
Les Allobroges (75020) ⒻⒻ		■					
L'Armoise (75015) ⒻⒻ		■					
Astier (75011) ⒻⒻ		■		■			
L'Auberge du Bonheur (75016) ⒻⒻ		■		■	●		
Aux Senteurs de Provence (75015) ⒻⒻ		■			●		
La Maison du Cantal (75015) ⒻⒻ		■					
Le Bistro des Deux Théâtres (75009) ⒻⒻ		■	●	■			
Chez Fernand (75011) ⒻⒻ		■					
La Perle des Antilles (75014) Ⓕ		■			●		
Les Amognes (75011) ⒻⒻⒻ		■		·		●	
Le Bistrot d'à Côté Flaubert (75017) ⒻⒻⒻ						●	
Brasserie Flo (75010) ⒻⒻⒻ		■	●	■			
Le Chardenoux (75011) ⒻⒻⒻ				■			
Le Clos Morillons (75015) ⒻⒻⒻ		■				■	
Julien (75010) ⒻⒻⒻ			●				
L'Oulette (75012) ⒻⒻⒻ					●		
Le Pavillon Montsouris (75014) ⒻⒻⒻ		■		■	●		
La Table de Pierre (75017) ⒻⒻⒻ				■	●		
Le Train Bleu (75012) ⒻⒻⒻ							
Au Trou Gascon (75012) ⒻⒻⒻ		■					
Augusta (75017) ⒻⒻⒻⒻ	●			■		■	
Au Pressoir (75012) ⒻⒻⒻⒻ		■		■			
Faucher (75017) ⒻⒻⒻⒻ		■		■	●		
Pavillon Puebla (75019) ⒻⒻⒻⒻ		■		■	●		●
Apicius (75017) ★ ⒻⒻⒻⒻⒻ							
Le Pré Catelan (75016) ⒻⒻⒻⒻⒻ		■		■	●		

ILE DE LA CITÉ

Vieux Bistrot

14 Rue du Cloître-Notre-Dame 75004.
Map 13 B4. **[** 01 43 54 18 95.
Open noon–2pm, 7pm–10:30pm
daily. **Closed** Dec 24–25. 🍴 🍷 MC,
V. **F** **F** **F**

Despite the obvious name and
touristy location next to Notre-
Dame, this is an authentic, honest
bistro, popular with many Paris
restaurateurs and entertainment
stars. The slightly rundown decor
suits the place and the rendition
of favorites like beef filet with
marrow, *boeuf bourguignon*,
gratin dauphinois (sliced potatoes
baked in cream), *tarte tatin*
(upside-down apple tart) and
profiteroles is very good.

THE MARAIS

Le Trumilou

84 Quai de l'Hotel de Ville 75004.
Map 13 B3. **[** 01 42 77 63 98.
Open noon–2pm, 7pm–11pm daily.
🍴 🍷 MC, V. **F**

Despite the unremarkable decor in
this large restaurant on the banks
of the River Seine, it appeals to
students and people on a budget.
Prices are low, service is friendly;
and you really know you are in
Paris. The food is straightforward
and old-fashioned, and includes
terrines, hard-boiled eggs with
mayonnaise, leg of lamb, duck
with prunes and a tasty apple tart.

L'Alisier

26 Rue de Montmorency 75003.
Map 13 B2. **[** 01 42 72 31 04.
Open noon–2pm, 8pm–10pm Mon–
Fri. **Closed** Aug. 🍴 🍷 MC, V.
F **F**

Chef/owner Jean-Luc Dodeman
produces interesting and carefully-
prepared food, such as a *croustillant*
of snails (snails wrapped in pastry
and oven baked) with ratatouille,
smoked salmon and duck breast
salad, escalopines of tuna, as well
as chicken with rosemary and
ginger. Though the restaurant is
small, you can choose between the
bistrolike ground floor or the more
elegant Louis XV-style first floor.
The lunch and dinner set menus
offer remarkable value.

Le Baracane

38 Rue des Tournelles 75004.
Map 14 E3. **[** 01 42 71 43 33.
Open noon–2:30pm, 7pm–midnight
Mon–Fri; 7pm–midnight Sat. 🍴
🍷 MC, V. **F** **F**

In the tourist-intensive, pricey
Marais district, this tiny restaurant
has very good quality food at
reasonable prices. It is the original
premises of l'Oulette (now in La
Nation district) and, still under the
same owner, continues to serve
the same excellent southwestern
cuisine which includes a delicious
rabbit *confit* (cooked and potted),
braised oxtail, pears poached in
Madeira and cassis (blackcurrant
liqueur), and superb homemade
chestnut bread.

Brasserie Bofinger

5 Rue de la Bastille 75004.
Map 14 E4. **[** 01 42 72 87 82.
Open noon–3pm, 6:30pm–1am
Mon–Fri, noon–1am, Sat & Sun. 🍴
🍷 AE, DC, MC, V. **F** **F**

Bofinger claims to be the oldest
brasserie in Paris, established in
1864. It is certainly one of the
prettiest, with turn-of-the-century
stained glass, leather banquettes,
brass decorations and murals by
the Alsatian artist Hansi. Excellent
shellfish is served, as well as
respectable *choucroute* (sauerkraut),
grilled meats. This is a very
popular place, situated just across
the Place de la Bastille from the
new opera house. You may have
to wait for a table (even with a
reservation) before or after
performances.

Chez Jenny

39 Blvd du Temple 75003.
Map 14 D1. **[** 01 42 74 75 75.
Open 11:30am–1am daily. 🍴 **V**
🍷 AE, DC, MC, V. **F** **F**

This huge brasserie on the Place
de la République has been a
bastion of Alsatian cooking since
it was founded over 60 years ago.
Service by women in Alsatian
dress adds to the convivial
atmosphere. The basic *choucroute*
(sauerkraut) *spéciale Jenny* makes
a hearty meal with a fruit tart or
sorbet served with a corresponding fruit liqueur for dessert.

La Guirlande de Julie

25 Pl des Vosges 75003. **Map** 14 D3.
[01 48 87 94 07. **Open** noon–
2:30pm, 7pm–10:30pm Tue–Sun.
🍴 🍷 MC, V. **F** **F**

This is a fine restaurant on the
fabulous 17th-century Place des
Vosges. Consummate restaurant
professional Claude Terrail of the
Tour d'Argent *(see p302)* has
employed a good chef at the
Guirlande de Julie, and the decor
is feminine, fresh and appealing.
The best views are from the
window in the first dining room.
In good weather, meals are served
under the vaulted stone arcades.

Le Passage

18 Passage de la Bonne Graine 75011.
Map 14 F4. **[** 01 47 00 73 30.
Open noon–2:30pm, 7:30pm–
11:30pm Mon–Fri, 7.30pm–11:30pm
Sat. 🍴 🍷 AE, MC, V. **F** **F**

This friendly restaurant is hidden
in the Passage de la Bonne Graine,
a short walk from the Place de la
Bastille. Although it calls itself a
wine bar (and the selection of
wines by the glass and bottle is
excellent), it offers a full menu,
including five styles of *andouillette*
(tripe sausage) and a varied selection of daily specials, frequently
served with a delicious potato
gratin. The cheeses are excellent,
and desserts include a monumental
chocolate éclair.

Le Bar à Huîtres

33 Blvd Beaumarchais 75003. **Map** 14
E3. **[** 01 48 87 98 92. **Open** noon–
1am Sun–Thu, noon– 2am Fri & Sat.
🍴 🍷 AE, MC, V. **F** **F** **F**

Oysters and other shellfish
predominate in Paris's two Bars à
Huîtres (the other bar is in Montparnasse). You can compose your
own appetizer platter, then follow
with a choice of hot fish dishes,
but meat is available for the hope-
less carnivore. This is an upbeat
place convenient for both the
Place de la Bastille and the Marais.

Au Bourguignon du Marais

52 Rue François Miron 75004. **Map**
13 3C. **[** 01 48 87 15 40. **Open**
10:30am–10:30pm Mon–Sat. **Closed**
Public hols, mid-Jul–mid-Aug. 🍴
🍷 AE, DC, MC, V. **F** **F** **F**

A policy of minimal mark-ups here
means that you can sip a superior
wine with your meal at little more
than a shop price. And you can be
sure the dishes you choose will do
it justice. Media types flock here
for classic bourgeoise cuisine and
excellent cheeses as well as the air
of bistro-informality.

Miravile

72 Quai de l'Hôtel de Ville 75004.
Map 13 B3. **[** 01 42 74 72 22.
Open noon–1:30pm Tue–Fri, 8pm–
11:30pm Mon–Sat. 🍴 🍷
🍷 AE, MC, V. **F** **F** **F**

This is the third location for young
chef Gilles Epié's Miravile, and the
restaurant seems to improve with
each move. Monsieur Epié's
cuisine continues to be inventive
and exciting with *foie gras* with
celeriac *rémoulade* (piquant
mayonnaise sauce), lobster with
potatoes, rabbit with olives and
chocolate *millefeuille*.

L'Ambroisie

9 Pl des Vosges 75004.
Map 14 D3. **[** 01 42 78 51 45.
Open noon–1:30pm, 8pm–10pm
Tue–Sat. **&** **☂** **★** **☲** AE, MC, V.
ⒻⒻⒻⒻⒻ

This discreet, romantic spot is one
of only five Michelin three-star
restaurants in Paris. Reservations
for the 40 seats are accepted one
month ahead (not a day earlier or
later). The chef Monsieur Pacaud
has restored this former jewelry
shop, giving it a handsome stone
floor and subtle lighting. The
cuisine includes a mousse of
sweet red peppers, truffle *feuilleté*
(layered pastry), langoustines with
sesame and *croustillant* of lamb.

BEAUBOURG AND LES HALLES

Bleu Marine

28 Rue Léopold Bellan 75002.
Map 13 A1. **[** 01 42 36 92 44.
Open noon–2:30pm, 8pm–10:30pm
Mon–Fri, 8pm–10:30pm Sat. **☲** **⭑❶**
☲ MC, V. **ⒻⒻ**

The limited menu of this
welcoming neighborhood
restaurant is seasonal, with such
dishes as marinated sardines,
salmon profiteroles and sea trout
with basil. The varnished ivory-
colored ash wood decor with
abundant flowers is refreshing.

Chez Elle

7 Rue des Prouvaires 75001.
Map 13 A2. **[** 01 45 08 04 10.
Open noon–2:15pm, 7:45pm–
10:30pm Mon–Fri. **⭑❶** **☲**
☲ AE, MC, V. **ⒻⒻ**

This pleasant bistro decorated in
shades of yellow has one of the
few upscale addresses in the
touristy Les Halles area. The menu
is classic bistro and includes warm
lentil salad with bacon, steak
tartare, grilled meats and such
desserts as *oeufs à la neige* (a melt-
in-the-mouth meringue in vanilla
custard) and crème caramel.

Le Grizzli

7 Rue St-Martin 75004. **Map** 13 B3.
[01 48 87 77 56. **Open** noon–
2:30pm, 7:30pm–11pm Mon–Sat.
⭑❶ **☲** **☲** AE, MC, V, JCB. **ⒻⒻ**

A change of ownership has
breathed new life into the Grizzli –
founded in 1903, when it was one
of the last Parisian places to have
dancing bears. The owner orders
much produce from his native
southwest including raw ham,

cheeses, and wines made by his
family. The decor is warm, and there
is a dumbwaiter in frequent use.

Saudade

34 Rue des Bourdonnais 75001.
Map 13 A2. **[** 01 42 36 30 71.
Open noon–2pm Mon–Sat, 7:30pm–
10:30pm Mon–Fri, 7:30–11pm Sat.
☲ AE, MC, V. **ⒻⒻ**

This is probably the finest Portuguese restaurant in Paris, and with
all the pretty tiles you'd expect to
find the Tajo and not the Seine
nearby. The Portuguese staple salt
cod is prepared in various ways:
in fritters, with tomato and onion
or with potatoes and eggs. Roast
suckling pig and *cozido* (Portugal's
national stew) are other typical,
flavorful dishes. There is a good
selection of Portuguese wine and
hearty port.

Au Pied de Cochon

6 Rue Coquillière 75001. **Map** 12 F1.
[01 40 13 77 00. **Open** 24 hrs daily.
⭑❶ **&** **☲** **☲** AE, DC, MC, V.
ⒻⒻⒻ

This colorfully restored brasserie
was once popular with high
society, who in the small hours
came to pass a few bourgeois
minutes observing the workers
toiling in the old market of Les
Halles and to relish the onion
soup, while discussing matters of
pith and moment. Although
touristy, this gigantic place is fun
and has a menu with something
for everyone.

Pharamond

24 Rue de la Grande-Truanderie 75001.
Map 13 B2. **[** 01 42 33 06 72.
Open noon–2:30pm Tue–Sat, 7:30pm–
10:30pm Mon. **⭑❶** **☲**
☲ AE, DC, MC, V. **ⒻⒻⒻ**

Founded in 1870, this solid bistro
has survived the transfer of the Les
Halles market out of the city and
remains a charming remnant of
the 19th century – with colored
tiles and mosaics, handsome woodwork and mirrors. Specialties
include *tripes à la mode de Caen*
(tripe cooked with onions, leeks,
cider and Calvados) and *boeuf en
daube* (beef stew). Try the
excellent Normandy cider.

Benoît

20 Rue St-Martin 75004. **Map** 13 B2.
[01 42 72 25 76. **Open** noon–2pm,
7:45pm–10pm daily. **⭑❶** **☂** **★**
☲ AE, MC, V. **ⒻⒻⒻⒻⒻ**

This is a gem of a Parisian bistro,
combining classic dependability
with a non-prohibitive price tag.
The owner has retained the *faux-*

marbre, polished brass and lace-
curtain decor created by his
grandfather in 1912. The excellent
bistro cuisine includes *saladiers*
(assorted cold salads), house *foie
gras, boeuf à la mode* and *cassoulet*
(white bean and meat stew). The
wine list is outstanding.

TUILERIES QUARTER

Gaya

17 Rue Duphot 75001. **Map** 5 C5.
[01 42 60 43 03. **Open** noon–
2:30pm, 7pm–11pm Mon–Sat. **⭑❶**
☲ AE, MC, V. **ⒻⒻ**

Monsieur Goumard's *bistrot de la
mer* (seafood bistro) was once his
upscale fish restaurant before he
restored the 19th-century Goumard
Prunier. The menu consists of
simply prepared fish dishes; the
ground-floor dining area is
particularly eye-catching, on
account of its very pretty
Portuguese tiles.

Le Grand Louvre

Le Louvre 75001. **Map** 12 F2.
[01 40 20 53 41. **Open** noon–3pm,
7pm–10pm Wed–Mon. **☂** **&** **⭑❶**
☲ AE, DC, MC, V, JCB. **ⒻⒻ**

It is rare to find such a good
restaurant in a museum, and that
is only part of the attraction of this
establishment. It is situated under
the Louvre's glass pyramid
entrance, and the sober wood-
and-metal decor complements the
controversial glass structure. The
menu is influenced by the
southwest – stuffed goose neck,
foie gras, boeuf en daube (beef
stew), prune ice cream with
Armagnac – and was originally
developed by André Daguin, one
of the region's gastronomic stars.

Armand au Palais Royal

6 Rue de Beaujolais 75001. **Map** 12 F1.
[01 42 60 05 11. **Open** noon–2pm,
8pm–10:30pm Mon–Fri, 8pm–10:30pm
Sat. **⭑❶** **☲** AE, MC, V, JCB.
ⒻⒻⒻ

This charming restaurant behind
the Palais Royal was once a stable,
but this is absolutely no reflection
on the food: the chef, Monsieur
Perron, has worked with some of
the best. Lunches are quiet;
dinners are romantic and very
Parisian under stone and brick
arches. The tempting à la carte
menu includes oysters with curry,
filet of John Dory with orange,
and pigeon *estouffade* (slowly
stewed in fine wine).

Les Ambassadeurs

10 Pl de la Concorde 75008. **Map** 11 C1. 01 44 71 16 16. **Open** 7am–10:30am, noon–2:30pm, 7pm–10:30pm daily. ★ AE, DC, MC, V, JCB. € € € € €

Part of the Hôtel de Crillon (see p280), this is one of only two hotel restaurants in Paris with two Michelin stars. Chef Dominique Bouchet has recently taken over the kitchens from the famous Christian Constant, maintaining the latter's high standards of creative cooking while introducing his own particular brand of classical French food with a modern touch and a meticulous attention to detail. Bouchet changes his menus with the seasons, but look out for such delights as bacon-wrapped scallops with basil and tomato and crisp potato pancakes with whipped cream, smoked salmon and caviar. The service is superb, and the all-marble dining room, overlooking the Place de la Concorde, is quite stunning.

Le Carré des Feuillants

14 Rue de Castiglione 75001. **Map** 12 D1. 01 42 86 82 82. **Open** Sep–Jul: noon–2:30pm, 7:30pm–10:30pm Mon–Fri, 7:30pm–10:30pm Sat. ★ AE, DC, MC, V, JCB. € € € € €

This is the showcase for star chef Alain Dutournier and the best products of his native southwest, including specially ordered lamb, beef, foie gras and poultry. The Venetian glass and illusionistic painted ceilings gives the restaurant a rural touch. The wine list is exceptional.

L'Espadon

15 Pl Vendôme 75001. **Map** 6 D5. 01 43 16 30 80. **Open** 7am–11am, noon–3pm, 7:30pm–11pm daily. ★ AE, DC, MC, V, JCB. € € € € €

Part of the Ritz (see p281), this is the second of the two Michelin-starred hotel restaurants in Paris and is well-worth the expense of the meal: its many merits include handsome decor, an idyllic garden, perfectly executed service and modern classic cuisine from the chef Guy Legay.

Goumard

9 Rue Duphot 75001. **Map** 5 C5. 01 42 60 36 07. **Open** noon–2:30pm, 7pm–10:30pm Tue–Sat. AE, DC, MC, V, JCB. € € € € €

Formerly Prunier – a name still almost synonymous with seafood. This 19th-century restaurant was restored in lavish good taste by Monsieur Goumard. No expense has been spared with the handsome kitchen, fabulous Lalique light fixtures and sculptures, which harmonize well with the remaining original 1900s and 1930s elements. The fish is always fresh and there is a selection of excellent desserts.

Le Grand Véfour

17 Rue de Beaujolais 75001. **Map** 12 F1. 01 42 96 56 27. **Open** 12:30pm–2pm, 7:30pm–10pm Mon–Fri. **Closed** Aug. ★ AE, DC, MC, V, JCB. € € € € €

This 18th-century restaurant with its ornate listed decor is considered by many to be the most attractive in Paris. The chef Guy Martin has apparently effortlessly kept his two Michelin stars with dishes such as scallops with Beaufort cheese, cabbage ravioli with a truffle cream and endive galette (pancake). Ask to be seated at Colette's favorite table (or Victor Hugo's or Napoleon's). This is very much a place for celebrations.

ST-GERMAIN-DES-PRÉS

Aux Charpentiers

10 Rue Mabillon 75006. **Map** 12 E4. 01 43 26 30 05. **Open** noon–3pm, 7pm–11:30pm daily. AE, DC, MC, V. € €

There are no culinary surprises at this old-established bistro, eternally popular with students and St-Germain-des-Prés locals. Count on well-prepared bistro standbys such as veal marengo, boeuf à la mode and homely pastries, served at reasonable prices in the big, noisy Aux Charpentiers dining room.

Le Muniche

7 Rue St Benoit 75006. **Map** 12 E4. 01 42 61 12 70. **Open** noon–2am daily. AE, DC, MC, V. € €

This and its sister restaurant next door, Le Petit Zinc, are almost institutions for regular St-Germain-des-Prés customers. The classic brasserie menu is straightforward and includes shellfish, choucroute (sauerkraut) and grilled fish and meats. The friendly waiters add to the buoyant atmosphere.

Le Petit St-Benoît

4 Rue St-Benoît 75006. **Map** 12 E3. 01 42 60 27 92. **Open** noon–2:30pm, 7pm–10:30pm Mon–Sat. € €

This is the place for anyone who's on a budget or just wants to mix with the locals; the waitresses speak their mind, and you might be seated at a table with others. Not much has been done to the decor over the years, but the good-value food is simple and tasty.

Rôtisserie d'en Face

2 Rue Christine 75006. **Map** 12 F4. 01 43 26 40 98. **Open** 2:15pm, 7pm–10:45pm (11:15pm Fri) Mon–Fri, 7pm–11:15pm Sat. AE, DC, MC, V, JCB. € € €

This elegant, bistro-style second restaurant of two-star chef Jacques Cagna was an overnight sensation. Even the wealthy appreciate a bargain and a smart crowd comes here for the very reasonable fixed-price formula where the best ingredients are used. Farm chicken from the rôtisserie with mashed potatoes, grilled salmon with fresh spinach, and profiteroles with chocolate sauce are among the dishes served here.

Aux Fins Gourmets

213 Blvd St-Germain 75007. **Map** 11 C3. 01 42 22 06 57. **Open** noon–2:30pm, 7:30pm–10pm Tue–Sat, 7:30pm–10pm Mon. € € €

Situated for many years at the far end of the Boulevard St-Germain near the Assemblée Nationale, this friendly neighborhood place offers hearty, unpretentious cuisine. This features specialties from the southwest, including a good cassoulet (stew of white beans and meat). Pastries come from the excellent pâtisserie Peltier.

Brasserie Lipp

151 Blvd St Germain 75006. **Map** 12 E4. 01 45 48 53 91. **Open** noon–1am daily. AE, DC, MC, V. € € €

This is the brasserie that everyone loves to hate. However, its clientele of entertainment personalities and politicians keeps returning for the straightforward brasserie food. The dishes include good herring in cream and a monumental millefeuille pastry. Ask to be seated downstairs if you want to be with the "in" crowd: the first floor is referred to as Siberia.

Le Procope

13 Rue de l'Ancienne Comédie 75006. **Map** 12 F4. 01 40 46 79 00. **Open** 11am–1am daily. AE, MC, V. € € €

While the cuisine here may be sound but unexceptional, this is nonetheless a place you will want to visit if you like the idea of having some of the great names of Parisian history as your ghostly dining companions. Since its founding in 1686 (making it the longest surviving brasserie in the city) it has been the gathering place of choice for writers, artists, politicians and philosophers, from Diderot to Danton, Beaumarchais to Balzac. It still cherishes its role as an artists' and writers' café and its 3-course menu for about F110 (served until 8pm) seems made for impoverished intellectuals.

Yugaraj

14 Rue Dauphine 75006. **Map** 12 F3. **{** 01 43 26 44 91. **Open** noon–2:15pm Tue–Sun, 7pm–11pm daily. **¶☺ Ⅴ ☜** AE, DC, MC, V. **FFF**

Recently redecorated, this is considered by many to be the best Indian restaurant in Paris. The chef emphasizes dishes from his native northern India, and key spices are brought in directly from the sub-continent. The wine list is good too.

Tan Dinh

60 Rue de Verneuil 75007. **Map** 12 D3. **{** 01 45 44 04 84. **Open** noon–2pm, 7:30pm–11pm Mon–Sat. **Closed** Aug. **☒ FFFF**

The relatively high prices in this Franco-Vietnamese restaurant run by the discreet Vifian family are due to a combination of the very good quality cuisine and an outstanding wine list with one of the biggest collections of Pomerols in the city. There are no Oriental lanterns here – the interior decor is suitably sober and does not need to rely on flamboyance to create a pleasant atmosphere for eating.

Lapérouse

51 Quai des Grands Augustins 75006. **Map** 12 F4. **{** 01 43 26 68 04. **Open** noon–2:30pm Mon–Fri, 6pm–10pm Mon–Sat. **¶☺ ☝ 🛈 ☒ 🛈** AE, DC, MC, V. **FFFFF**

This famous establishment from the 19th century was once one of the glories of Paris. Now restored and with a good chef, it is on the way up again. The series of salons have kept their 1850s decor. The best tables are by the window.

Restaurant Jacques Cagna

14 Rue des Grands Augustins 75006. **Map** 12 F4. **{** 01 43 26 49 39. **Open** noon–2pm, 7:30pm–10:30pm Tue–Fri, 7:30pm–10:30pm Sat. **¶☺ 🛈 ★ ☜** AE, DC, MC, V, JCB. **FFFFF**

This elegant 17th-century townhouse in the heart of old Paris is a showcase for the expensive trinkets and excellent classic-cum-contemporary cuisine of chef/owner Jacques Cagna. Occasional Oriental touches to the food show his love of the East. Possible dishes are red mullet salad with *foie gras*, pigeon *confit* (cooked and potted) with turnips, and a classic Paris-Brest (choux pastry filled with praline-flavored cream). The wine list is admirable.

LATIN QUARTER

Chez Pento

9 Rue Cujas 75005. **Map** 13 A5. **{** 01 43 26 81 54. **Open** noon–2pm, 7:15pm–11pm Mon–Fri, 7pm–11pm Mon–Sat. **¶☺ ☜** AE, MC, V. **FF**

This fashionable bistro offers a set menu with many tempting choices. Don't expect to linger – the rapid service keeps prices down. Good house *foie gras*, brioche with marrow, oysters with curry sauce, *petit salé* of duck, or steak of the day are among the possibilities.

Loubnane

29 Rue Galande 75005. **Map** 9 A4. **{** 01 43 26 70 60. **Open** noon–3pm, 7pm–midnight daily. **¶☺ ♿ 🎵 🛈 ☜** AE, DC, MC, V. **FF**

A Lebanese restaurant whose specialties include delicious and generous *mezzes*, served under the watchful eye of a *patron* whose main aim in life seems to be the happiness of his customers. Live Lebanese music is often performed in the basement.

Brasserie Balzar

49 Rue des Ecoles 75005. **Map** 13 A5. **{** 01 43 54 13 67. **Open** noon–midnight daily. **🛈 ☜** AE, MC, V. **FFF**

There's a fair choice of brasserie food at this venue, but the main attraction is the ambience. It is typically Left Bank in atmosphere and is frequented by Sorbonne professors and students.

Campagne et Provence

25 Quai de la Tournelle 75005. **Map** 13 B5. **{** 01 43 54 05 17. **Open** 12:30pm–2pm Tue–Fri, 7pm–11pm Mon–Sat. **¶☺ ☜** MC, V. **FFF**

This little place on a quay facing Notre-Dame provides outstanding cooking for the price. Renowned chef Gilles Epié, of Miravile (*see p300*), has put together a tempting

menu full of Provençale flavor and color: vegetables stuffed with cod *brandade* (salt cod and garlic purée), and ratatouille omelette *anchoyade* (flavored with anchovies). The regional wine list is varied and quite reasonably priced.

Restaurant Moissonnier

28 Rue des Fossés St-Bernard 75005. **Map** 13 B5. **{** 01 43 29 87 65. **Open** noon–2pm Tue–Sun, 7:30pm–10:30pm Tue–Sat. **Closed** Aug. **¶☺ ☜** MC, V. **FF**

This family-run bistro gives a taste of the provinces in Paris. It serves standard favorites which have Lyonnais overtones, such as *saladiers* (assorted salads), *grasdouble* (tripe), quenelles, and chocolate cake. The wine list features Beaujolais wines. Ask to be seated downstairs.

Rôtisserie du Beaujolais

19 Quai de la Tournelle 75005. **Map** 13 B5. **{** 01 43 54 17 47. **Open** noon–2:30pm, 7:30pm–11pm Tue–Sun. **♿ ☜** MC, V. **FFF**

Facing the Seine and owned by Claude Terrail of the Tour d'Argent next door, the restaurant has a large rôtisserie for roasting poultry and meats. Many of the meats and cheeses are specially ordered from the best suppliers in Lyon. A Beaujolais is, of course, the wine to order here.

La Tour d'Argent

15–17 Quai de la Tournelle 75005. **Map** 13 B5. **{** 01 43 54 23 31. **Open** noon–1:30pm, 7:30pm–9:30pm Tue–Sun. **¶☺ ♿ 🛈 🛈 ★ ☜** AE, MC, V. **FFFFF**

Established in 1582, the Tour appears to be eternal, but it is not moribund. Patrician owner Claude Terrail has hired a series of young chefs who have rejuvenated the classic menu. The ground-floor bar is also a gastronomic museum; from here there is a lift to the panoramic restaurant and its unbridled luxury. The wine cellar must be one of the finest on earth.

JARDIN DES PLANTES QUARTER

Au Petit Marguéry

9 Blvd de Port-Royal 75013. **Map** 17 B3. **{** 01 43 31 58 59. **Open** noon–2:15pm, 7:30pm–10:15pm Tue–Sat. **¶☺ ♿ 🖶 ☜** AE, MC, V. **FFF**

This comfortable, reliable bistro is run by three brothers who create many dishes not found on classic bistro menus: cold lobster consommé with caviar, mushroom salad with *foie gras*, cod with spices and chocolate cake with a mocha sabayon sauce.

MONTPARNASSE

La Coupole

102 Blvd du Montparnasse 75014. **Map** 16 D2. **01 43 20 14 20. Open** 7:30am–2am daily. **Closed** Dec 24 eve. AE, DC, MC, V, JCB.

This famous brasserie has been popular with the fashion crowd and with artists and thinkers since its creation in 1927. Under the same ownership as Brasserie Flo, La Coupole has a similar menu: good shellfish, smoked salmon, *choucroute* (sauerkraut) and many good desserts. Lamb curry is a specialty. The remarkable semi-monumental decor has been restored; this is a boisterous and lively place all through the day, from breakfast to 2am. *(See also catalog entry p178.)*

Le Bistrot du Dôme

1 Rue Delambre 75014. **Map** 16 D2. **01 43 35 32 00. Open** 12:30pm–3pm, 7:30pm–11pm daily. AE, MC, V.

This is the sister restaurant of the famous Montparnasse brasserie Le Dôme. Customers come here for the fish (including seafood) – it is very fresh here – from humble sardines to more upmarket turbot. Preparations are simple, and the fish speaks for itself. The decor is pretty on a yellow and blue theme, with colorful tiles and festive Venetian glass fixtures. This is a restaurant with no pretense and a lot of fun.

La Cagouille

10–12 Pl Constantin Brancusi 75014. **Map** 15 C3. **01 43 22 09 01. Open** noon–2pm, 7:30pm–10:30pm daily. ★ AE, MC, V.

Situated on the stark new Place Brancusi in the rebuilt Montparnasse district, this large modern venue has a nautical atmosphere and is one of the best fish restaurants in Paris. Big fish are served simply with few sauces or adornments, and you might also find unusual seasonal ingredients like black bay scallops and *vendangeurs* – tiny red mullet. The shellfish platter is one of the finest in Paris, as is the collection of Cognacs.

Contre-Allée

83 Ave Denfert-Rochereau 75014. **Map** 16 E3. **01 43 54 99 86. Open** noon–2pm Mon–Fri, 8pm–10pm Mon–Sat. AE, MC, V.

This restaurant off the Place Denfert-Rochereau is popular with professors from the Sorbonne as well as with the iconoclastic locals. The cuisine is a mix of good pasta dishes, cod with Parmesan, *hachis parmentier* (a kind of shepherd's pie) with *foie gras* and duck, delicious calves' liver and orange gratin. The decor is minimalist with striking black-and-white photographs; and the service is young and energetic.

L'Assiette

181 Rue du Château 75014. **Map** 15 C4. **01 43 22 64 86. Open** noon–2:30pm, 8pm–10:30pm Wed–Sun. AE, MC, V.

What began as a simple neighborhood *charcuterie*-turned-restaurant run by its eccentric owner, Lulu, is now an upscale fashionable address popular with politicians and stars. Prices have soared but the food is very good with a flavor of the southwest. The food includes *foie gras*, breast of duck, good game in season and tasty desserts. Service can be less than attentive.

INVALIDES AND EIFFEL TOWER QUARTER

Le Bistrot de Breteuil

3 Pl de Breteuil 75007. **Map** 11 A5. **01 45 67 07 27. Open** noon–2:30pm, 7:15pm–10:30pm daily. AE, MC, V.

On the agreeable Place de Breteuil this bistro attracts the well-off locals for its reasonable prices more than the quality of its food. Dishes include snails with hazelnuts, salmon and spinach, and steak *marchand de vin* (in red wine sauce). There is a pleasant terrace.

L'Oeillade

10 Rue de St-Simon 75007. **Map** 11 C3. **01 42 22 01 60. Open** 12:30pm–2pm, 7:30pm–11pm Mon–Sat. MC, V.

Abroad major articles featuring this welcoming restaurant have turned it into a place for tourists. But it has a good-value, varied set menu that includes deep-fried smelt, *pipérade* (stewed sweet peppers, tomatoes and garlic) with poached egg, sole

meunière, cod *brandade* (salt cod and garlic purée), roast lamb with cumin and *oeufs à la neige* (meringue in vanilla custard).

La Serre

29 Rue de l'Exposition 75007. **Map** 10 F3. **01 45 55 20 96. Open** noon–3pm Tue–Sat, 7pm–11pm Tue–Sun. MC, V.

This small, cozy restaurant on a quiet street near the Eiffel Tower has a warm atmosphere. Owners Mary-Alice and Philippe Beraud offer good home cooking, using the freshest ingredients, at reasonable prices. The cooking is tasty, with specialties from the southwest such as *gésiers confit* (preserved gizzards) *sur salade, cuisse de canard confite* (preserved leg of duck) with sauteed potatoes, and a cooked-to-perfection pot-roasted calves' liver served with a *confiture d'onions*.

Thoumieux

79 Rue St-Dominique 75007. **Map** 11 A2. **01 47 05 49 75. Open** noon–3:30pm, 6:30pm–midnight daily. AE, MC, V.

This well-run restaurant is excellent value for money. Ingredients are fresh and almost everything is made on the premises, including *foie gras*, duck *rillettes* (similar to pâté), *cassoulet* (white bean and meat stew) and chocolate mousse.

Morot-Gaudry

8 Rue de la Cavalerie 75015. **Map** 10 E5. **01 45 67 06 85. Open** noon–2:30pm, 7:30pm–10:30pm Mon–Fri. AE, DC, MC, V, JCB.

Friendly chef Jean-Pierre Morot-Gaudry enjoys combining lowly ingredients with expensive ones, and many of the dishes are subtly enlivened with herbs and spices. The pretty, bright dining room is at the top of a building with views of the Eiffel Tower. It is supervised by Madame Morot-Gaudry.

Vin sur Vin

20 Rue de Monttessuy 75007. **Map** 10 E2. **01 47 05 14 20. Open** noon–2pm Tue–Fri, 8pm–10pm Mon–Sat. MC, V.

Owner Patrice Vidal is justly proud of his eight-table restaurant close to the Eiffel Tower. The menu is seasonal and original, the wine list fabulous with interesting wines at reasonable prices. Dishes might include *galette* (pancake) of squid, snail turnover, *blanquette* of whiting (with white sauce) and duck with peaches.

For key to symbols *see p289*

L'Arpège

84 Rue de Varenne 75007. **Map** 11 B3.
[01 45 51 47 33. **Open** 12:30pm–
2:30pm, 7:30pm–10:30pm Mon–Fri.
¶●¶ ☐ ★ ☑ AE, DC, MC, V.
ⒻⒻⒻⒻⒻ

Chef/owner Alain Passard's
restaurant near the Musée Rodin is
one of the most highly thought of
in Paris. It has striking pale-wood
decor and sprightly young service
as well as good food. Passard's
lobster and turnip vinaigrette and
duck Louise Passard are classics.
Dishes are completed in the dining
room. Don't miss the apple tart.

Le Jules Verne

2nd platform, Eiffel Tower 75007.
Map 10 D3. **[** 01 45 55 61 44.
Open 12:30pm–2pm, 7:30pm–10pm
daily. **¶●¶ ☒ ♫ ☑ ☑** AE, DC,
MC, V. **ⒻⒻⒻⒻⒻ**

This is no tourist trap: the Jules
Verne on the second platform of
the Eiffel Tower is now one of the
hardest dinner reservations to obtain
in Paris. The sleek, all-black decor
suits the monument perfectly and
the pretty, flavorful cuisine is very
good indeed. Ask for the dining
room facing east or west.

CHAILLOT QUARTER
PORTE MAILLOT

La Butte Chaillot

110 bis Ave Kléber 75116. **Map** 4 D5.
[01 47 27 88 88. **Open** noon–
2:30pm, 7pm–midnight daily. **▦**
☑ AE, MC, V, JCB. **ⒻⒻⒻ**

This is the most recent boutique
restaurant of the renowned chef Guy
Savoy. It is also the most modern
with polished wood floors, glazed
ochre and beige walls, and a massive steel and glass-sided staircase
leading to tables on a lower floor.
The sophisticated country/bistro
cuisine includes snail salad, oysters
with a cream mousse, roast breast
of veal with rosemary and apple
tart. It attracts a very stylish crowd.

Chez Géraud

31 Rue Vital 75016. **Map** 9 B3.
[01 45 20 33 00. **Open** noon–
2pm, 7:30pm–10pm Mon–Fri. **Closed**
Aug. **¶●¶ ☑** AE, MC, V. **ⒻⒻⒻ**

Géraud Rongier, this bistro's jovial,
cherubic owner, welcomes you like
a friend and obviously wants you to
enjoy your meal. His is a scrupulous
cuisine du marché using what's best
at the market that day to create
dishes like duck gizzard salad,
sabodet sausage in red wine sauce,

skate with mustard, roast pigeon
with port sauce and bitter chocolate
cake. The pretty tile mural was
created specially for the restaurant.

L'Huîtrier

16 Rue Saussier Leroy 75017. **Map** 4 E2.
[01 40 54 83 44. **Open** noon–
2:30pm, 7pm–10:30pm Tue–Sat, noon–
2:30pm Sun. **☑** AE, MC, V. **ⒻⒻⒻ**

This freshly decorated restaurant
specializes in shellfish, especially
oysters which you order by the
half-dozen or dozen. It also serves
several hot fish dishes and makes
a good restorative stop before or
after visiting the animated market
in the nearby Rue Poncelet.

Oum El Banine

16 bis Rue Dufrenoy 75016. **Map** 9 A1.
[01 45 04 91 22. **Open** noon–
2pm, 8pm–10:30pm Mon–Fri, 8pm–
10:30pm Sat. **☑** AE, MC, V. **ⒻⒻⒻ**

The owner of this small restaurant
in the chic residential quarter
learned her art from her mother in
Morocco and here prepares her
favorite dishes. There is good
harira soup (a thick, spicy soup),
pastilla (a savory puff-pastry tart)
and *brik* (stuffed pastry triangle).
The couscous served with the five
choices of ragoût is exemplary. The
tagines (braised stews) are very
flavorful. This is a low-key,
authentic restaurant.

Le Timgad

21 Rue Brunel 75017. **Map** 3 C3.
[01 45 74 23 70. **Open** 12:15pm–
2:30pm, 7:15pm–11pm daily. **☑** AE,
DC, MC, V. **ⒻⒻⒻⒻ**

This has been Paris's best-known,
most elegant Maghrebian restaurant
for years. The menu is extensive
with many different *briks* (stuffed
pastry triangles), *tagines* (braised
stews) and couscous dishes, as well
as specialties like grilled pigeon,
pastilla (a savory puff-pastry tart)
and *méchoui* (whole roast lamb) if
ordered in advance. Waiters in
dinner jackets, the rich and
elaborate, lacy stuccoed interior
and an international clientele add
to the atmosphere of opulence.

Le Port-Alma

10 Ave de New-York 75116. **Map** 10 E1.
[01 47 23 75 11. **Open** 12:30pm–
2:30pm, 7:30pm–10:30pm Mon–Sat.
☒ ☑ AE, DC, MC, V. **ⒻⒻⒻ**

With its nautical blue and pastel
festive decor, the delightful welcome
of Madame Canal and the excellent
cuisine of Monsieur Canal, this is one
of the finest fish restaurants in Paris.
Many dishes are influenced by the
chef's native Southwest France, such

as the *bourride* soup of turbot
with garlic, sea bass in a salt crust
with a fennel gratin and crab
gazpacho. There is also a good, hot
chocolate soufflé and raspberry
millefeuille.

Alain Ducasse

59 Ave Raymond Poincaré 75116.
Map 9 C1. **[** 01 47 27 12 27. **Open**
noon–2pm, 7:45pm–10pm Mon–Fri,
Closed public hols, mid-Jul–mid-Aug,
25 Dec–1st week Jan. **¶●¶ ☒ ☒ ☒**
☑ AE, DC, MC, V, JCB. **ⒻⒻⒻⒻⒻ**

In this historic town house with its
'Belle Époque' façade, Alain
Ducasse creates the great 'classic'
dishes of France with exceptional
devotion to the quality of the
ingredients. The menu features
meticulously chosen produce from
every culinary region of France,
with particular influences from his
native southwest. The stylish dining
room, decorated with *trompe l'oeil*
and sculptures, is the perfect setting
for this wonderfully elegant cuisine.
Dishes include *turbot de Bretagne,
chevreuil* (venison) *d'Alsace*, lamb
in Pauillac wine and *fois gras de
canard des Landes*. There is an
enviable wine list with some great
treasures from Bordeaux.

Amphyclès

78 Ave des Ternes 75017. **Map** 3 C2.
[01 40 68 01 01. **Open** noon–
2:30pm, 8pm–10:30pm Mon–Sat
(May–Sep: Tue–Sat). **¶●¶ ☒ ☒**
★ ☑ AE, DC, MC, V, JCB.
ⒻⒻⒻⒻⒻ

This small place with a fresh,
gardenlike feel is the showcase for
Philippe Groult, who made it one
of the finest restaurants in Paris
within months of the opening
night. House classics include a
soup of morel mushrooms, lobster
risotto with girolle mushrooms,
and duckling with orange and
coriander. Other creations include
steamed *foie gras* with beans, filet
of sea bass with sesame and pigeon
in a seaweed crust. Desserts are
served from a well-stocked trolley.

Le Vivarois

192–194 Ave Victor Hugo 75016.
Map 9 A1. **[** 01 45 04 04 31.
Open noon–1:30pm, 8pm–9:30pm
Mon–Fri. **Closed** Aug. **¶●¶ ☒ ★**
☑ AE, DC, MC, V. **ⒻⒻⒻⒻⒻ**

Claude Peyrot, the erratic genius
chef of this starkly modern restaurant, is one of the greatest of his
generation. Few could make puff
pastry better or improve on his
fish. His red-pepper mousse and
hot curried oysters are modern
classics. Sometimes he will
prepare a special menu for you –
it could be wonderful.

CHAMPS-ELYSÉES

L'Avenue

41 Ave Montaigne 75008.
Map 10 F1. **C** 01 40 70 14 91.
Open 8am–midnight daily. **TGT**
AE, DC, MC, V. FF

Located at the intersection of the
Avenues Montaigne and François-
1er – the hub of couture fashion –
L'Avenue attracts an expectedly
elegant crowd. The unusual Neo-
1950s decor is fresh and full of
color. Service can get somewhat
hectic at peak lunch and dinner
times, but then L'Avenue is a
brasserie. The cuisine is good,
there is something for all tastes
and appetites and late-night
supper is served.

Casa de Delfo

10 Rue de la Trémoille 75008.
Map 10 F1. **C** 01 47 23 53 53.
Open noon–3pm, 7pm–midnight
daily. **AE, DC, MC, V.**
FF

Situated conveniently near the
Champs-Elysées this former
Catalan bistro now offers French
and Italian standards. In a neigh-
bourhood known for its inflated
prices this bistro is an exception –
handy for travelers on a budget.

La Fermette Marbeuf 1900

5 Rue Marbeuf 75008. **Map** 4 F5.
C 01 53 23 08 00. **Open** noon–3pm
daily, 7:30pm–11:30pm Sun–Wed,
7:30pm–12:30am Thu–Sat. **TGT**
AE, DC, MC, V. FF

Fabulous Belle Époque mosaics,
tiles and ironwork were discovered
beneath the formica walls of this
Champs-Elysées bistro, putting it
on the map. Aside from the
beautiful surroundings, La
Fermette Marbeuf serves good
brasserie-style food, including a
commendable set menu with many
wines of appellation contrôlée
status – a measure of their quality.
It is very Parisian and very noisy
late in the evening.

Savy

23 Rue Bayard 75008. **Map** 10 F1.
C 01 47 23 46 98. **Open** noon–3pm,
7pm–11pm Mon–Fri. **Closed** Aug.
TGT AE, MC, V. FF

Although just up the street from
Dior and other such renowned
addresses, Savy has somehow
remained an unpretentious local
bistro. The Art Deco interior is
rustic, and the hearty cuisine
inspired by Monsieur Savy's native

Auvergne is very flavorful, with
dishes such as stuffed cabbage, cod
fishcakes, roast shoulder of lamb,
roast guinea fowl and prune tart.

Sébillon

66 Rue Pierre Charron 75008.
Map 4 F5. **C** 01 43 59 28 15.
Open noon–3pm, 6:45pm–midnight
daily. **TGT AE, DC, MC, V. FF**

Recently opened just off the
Champs-Elysées, this is an
offshoot of the original Sébillon
which has been nurturing
residents of the bourgeois suburb
of Neuilly since 1913. The menu is
the same, with lots of shellfish,
lobster salad, scallops à la
provençale, rib roast of beef and
gigantic éclairs. The great specialty
here is leg of lamb – as much as
you want, sliced in the pretty
polished dining room.

Le Cercle Ledoyen

1 Ave Dutuit 75001. **Map** 11 B1.
C 01 53 05 10 02. **Open** noon–
2pm, 7pm–11pm Mon–Sat. **TGT**
AE, DC, MC, V, JCB.
FFF

The cuisine is rather more refined
with grilled brill and wild
mushrooms and pheasant with
quince, or a more simple dish of
smoked salmon (prepared by the
owners) and scrambled eggs.
There is a wonderful selection of
chocolate desserts. The handsome
curved dining room creates the
atmosphere of a 1950's grill room
with ceiling and wall panels
decorated with scenes of Paris.
Alternatively, have a heavenly meal
outside on the stunning terrace.

Au Petit Colombier

42 Rue des Acacias 75017. **Map** 4
D3. **C** 01 43 80 28 54. **Open**
12:30pm–2:30pm Mon–Fri, 7:30pm–
10:30pm daily. **Closed** Aug 1–15.
TGT AE, MC, V.
FFFF

The rustic air in this comfortable
restaurant recalls the provinces.
The chef Monsieur Fournier
champions traditional French
cuisine – pike mousse, milk-fed
veal en cocotte (casseroled) or with
cider vinegar, guinea fowl fricassée
with mushrooms, and game in
season. The wine list is good.

Chiberta

3 Rue Arsène-Houssaye 75008.
Map 4 E4. **C** 01 53 53 42 00.
Open noon–2:30pm Mon–Fri,
7pm–10pm Mon–Sat. **TGT**
★ AE, DC, MC, V, JCB.
FFFF

The decor at Chiberta is starkly
modern, but the warm welcome
of Monsieur Richard, the owner
and the masses of flowers on
display make up for it. The cuisine
itself is excellent and wonderfully
presented. It includes special
raviolis, John Dory with ginger,
cod with wild mushroom sauce
and endive, calves' kidneys with
horseradish and capers. For
dessert, miniature babas. Service
is stylish, and this is also a very
festive place.

Guy Savoy

18 Rue Troyon 75017. **Map** 4 D3.
C 01 43 80 40 61. **Open** 12:30pm–
2:30pm Mon–Fri, 7:30pm–10:30pm
Mon–Sat. **Closed** 3 weeks Aug. **T**
★ AE, MC, V, JCB.
FFFFF

Guy Savoy has the best of
everything. It provides a large,
handsome dining room and
professional service, and the
remarkable cuisine of Guy Savoy
himself looks as good as it tastes.
Choose between dishes such as
cold oysters in aspic, mussels with
mushrooms, Bresse chicken with a
sherry vinegar-glaze and poached
or grilled pigeon with lentils; then
from the extraordinary desserts.

Lasserre

17 Ave Franklin D Roosevelt 75008.
Map 11 A1. **C** 01 43 59 53 43, 01
43 59 67 45 **Open** 12:30pm–2:30pm
Tue–Sat, 7:30pm–10:30pm Mon–Sat.
T AE, MC, V. FFFFF

This discreet restaurant opposite
the Grand Palais is one of the
finest in Paris. Charismatic owner
René Lasserre has for over 50
years continued to create an
opulent yet friendly ambience. The
menu rests with the classic and
fine. Chef Bernard Joinville offers
cuisine of irreproachable quality
such as canard (duck) de Chaillans
à l'orange, which is reputably the
best of its kind. Other favorites
include Mesclagne Landais Mère
Irma (a dish of foie gras and
chicken named after Lasserre's
mother), pigeon André Malraux
and sole rôtie aux Crustacés, sauce
Noilly. The beautifully sculpted
desserts are sublime; the wine list
is exceptional. Enjoy watching the
stars in the summer when the
rooftop opens up to reveal the
night sky.

Laurent

41 Ave Gabriel 75008. **Map** 5 B5.
C 01 42 25 00 39. **Open** 12:30pm–
2:30pm, 7:30pm–11pm Mon–Fri,
7:30pm–11pm Sat. **Closed** public
hols. **TGT ★ AE,
DC, MC, V. FFFFF**

For key to symbols see p289

This pretty, slightly pink-colored 19th-century building is situated in the gardens of the Champs-Elysées. Laurent is where the rich and powerful eat out. The dining room is opulently decorated, and outside a marvelous terrace is screened by high hedges. The hors d'oeuvres arrive on a trolley, and the lobster salad is prepared at the table. Dishes such as cannelloni of vegetables with squid, an excellent rack of lamb and a selection of wonderful pastries are typical.

La Maison Blanche/ 15 Avenue Montaigne

15 Ave Montaigne 75008. **Map** 10 F1. 01 47 23 55 99. **Open** noon–2pm, 8pm–11pm Mon–Sat. **Closed** Aug. AE, MC, V, JCB. FFFFF

The popular Maison Blanche restaurant affixed 15 Avenue Montaigne to its name when it moved here, on top of the Théâtre des Champs-Elysées. Although the decor is severely modern, the restaurant is almost opulently vast. The cuisine, with its Provençale and Southwestern influences, is full of flavor and color and is the main attraction for the worldly clientele that flocks here.

Taillevent

15 Rue Lamennais 75008. **Map** 4 F4. 01 45 61 12 90. **Open** noon–2pm, 7pm–10:30pm Mon–Fri. ★ AE, DC, MC, V, JCB. FFFFF

Taillevent is the most elegant and patrician of Paris's three-star restaurants. The quiet, dignified ambience doesn't suit everyone, but the sincere welcome of owner Jean-Claude Vrinat, impeccable service, extraordinary wine list and tempered neo-classic cuisine of the young chef Philippe Legendre make for memorable meals. Other dishes on the Taillevent menu include celeriac turnover with morels and truffles, Pyrenees lamb with cabbage and a *moelleux* (cream) of lobster with bell pepper. The pastry chef is one of the finest in Paris. Not surprisingly, you need to book months ahead for dinner.

OPÉRA QUARTER

Chartier

7 Rue du Faubourg Montmartre 75009. **Map** 6 F4. 01 47 70 86 29. **Open** 11:30am–3pm, 6pm–10pm daily. MC, V. F

Despite the impressive, listed 1900s decor of this cavernous restaurant, it caters today, as it always has, to people on a budget. These are now mostly students and tourists, but some of the old *habitués* still come here for the basic cuisine (hard-boiled eggs with mayonnaise, house pâté, roast chicken and pepper steak).

Au Petit Riche

25 Rue le Peletier 75009. **Map** 6 F4. 01 47 70 68 68. **Open** noon–2:15pm, 7pm–midnight Mon–Sat. AE, DC, MC, V, JCB. FF

This bistro has tremendous atmosphere. The small rooms, resplendent in polished copper, mirrors and woodwork, are popular at lunch with the Drouot auction house crowd and at dinner with a Parisian clientele. The Loire region is reflected in the Vouvray-style *rillettes* (meat paste, similar to pâté), *boudin* (black or white pudding), *andouillette* (tripe sausage) and regional wines.

Chez Clément

17 blvd des Capucines 75002. **Map** 6 E5. 01 53 43 82 00. **Open** 7am–1am daily. MC, V. FF

Just two minutes' walk from the Opéra, this comfortable bistro serves its signature dishes of roast meats until well after midnight every day of the year. The dish of the day is always of particularly good value, and is available at both lunch and dinner.

Café Runtz

16 Rue Favart 75002. **Map** 6 F5. 01 42 96 69 86. **Open** 10am–11pm Mon–Fri. **Closed** public hols. AE, MC, V, DC. FF

One of the few genuine Alsatian brasseries in Paris, Café Runtz has been doing business since the turn of the century. Photos of entertainment stars remind you that the Salle Favart (the former Opéra Comique) is next door. Regional specialties include Gruyère salad, onion tart, *choucroute* (sauerkraut) and fruit tarts. The service is friendly.

La Ferme St-Hubert

21 Rue Vignon 75008. **Map** 6 D5. 01 47 42 79 20. **Open** noon–3:30pm, 7pm–11pm Mon–Sat. V AE, MC, V. FF

This, the simple restaurant of the well-known *fromagerie* (cheese delicatessen) of the same name next door, is mobbed at lunch and busy at dinner. The cheese-based cuisine is good and makes a pleasant change from the usual French fare: the restaurant boasts

the best *croque-monsieur* in Paris, *raclette* (all you can eat of this Swiss cheese dish), two styles of cheese fondue, salads with cheese and just plain cheese. Happily situated for all gourmets, it is very convenient for the fine food shops on the Place de la Madeleine.

Le Grand Colbert

2 Rue Vivienne 75002. **Map** 6 F5. 01 42 86 87 88. **Open** noon–3:30pm, 7pm–1am daily. **Closed** mid-Jul–Aug. AE, DC, MC, V. FF

Situated in the restored Galérie Colbert owned by the Bibliothèque Nationale, Le Grand Colbert must be one of the prettiest brasseries in Paris. Its one long dining area is divided by frosted-glass panels and decorated with paintings and mirrors. The menu offers classic brasserie fare – herring filets with potatoes or cream, snails, onion soup, classic whiting Colbert (in breadcrumbs) and grilled meats.

Les Noces de Jeannette

14 Rue Favart 75002. **Map** 6 F5. 01 42 96 36 89. **Open** noon–2pm, 7pm–9:30pm daily. AE, DC, MC, V. FF

This is a typical Parisian bistro, named for the one-act curtain-raising opera which is performed at the Opera Comique just across the street. A rather ornate interior belies the cozy, welcoming atmosphere. The fixed-price menu is good value, offering a wide choice of classic bistro dishes. Try the Vichyssoise or *terrine de crustacés à la crème d'Oseille.*

A.G. Le Poète

27 Rue Pasquier 75008. **Map** 5 C4. 01 47 42 00 64. **Open** noon–3pm, 7pm–10:30pm Mon–Fri, 7pm–10:30pm Sat. **Closed** 3 weeks Aug. AE, MC, V, JCB. FF

Situated near to the Place de la Madeleine, this romantically styled restaurant with its red velvet decor and soft lighting offers some interesting dishes on its menu. Poet and chef Antoine Gayet provides a menu that is not only a delight to read but also to choose from. A.G.'s passion for cooking is evident, with dishes that include red mullet and baby scallops served with creamed wild nettles and roast langoustines with fried pig's trotters.

Chez Georges

1 Rue du Mail 75002. **Map** 12 F1. 01 42 60 07 11. **Open** noon–2:30pm, 7:15pm–9:45pm Mon–Sat. **Closed** public hols, 3 weeks Aug. AE, MC, V. FFF

Most of the authentic local restaurants around the Place des Victoires have been turned into trendy clothes boutiques, but Chez Georges is one of the few that has resisted. With its eclectic decor and no-nonsense waitresses it attracts Parisians who enjoy the bistro cuisine of chicken liver terrine, sole *meunière* (coated with flour, sautéed and served in hot melted butter with sliced lemon) and rum babas.

Le Vaudeville

29 Rue Vivienne 75002. **Map** 6 F5.
01 40 20 04 62. **Open** noon–2:30pm, 7pm–2am daily. 🍴 V 🚶
🔁 🍷 AE, DC, MC, V, JCB. Ⓕ Ⓕ

This is one of seven brasseries belonging to Paris's brasserie king, Jean-Paul Bucher. The bright, attractive Art Deco interior provides an appealing backdrop to the food: good shellfish, Bucher's famous smoked salmon, many different fish dishes as well as classic brasserie standbys like pig's trotters and *andouillette* (tripe sausage). The speedy, friendly service and noisy atmosphere make it lots of fun, and it's always full.

Café Drouant

18 Rue Gaillon 75002. **Map** 6 E5.
01 42 65 15 16. **Open** noon–2:30pm, 7pm–midnight daily.
Closed Aug. 🍴 ♿ 🍷 AE, DC, MC, V. Ⓕ Ⓕ Ⓕ

Founded in the 19th century, Drouant is one of Paris's most historic restaurants. The café, not to be confused with the much more expensive restaurant, is a fashionable spot which serves excellent food until late and has an extremely good value menu at dinner. The interior includes a famous shellfish-motif ceiling.

Le Trente

30 Pl de la Madeleine 75008.
Map 5 C5. 01 47 42 56 58. **Open** 12:15pm–2:30pm, 7:30pm–10:30pm Mon–Sat. 🍴 ♿ 🍷 🍷 AE, DC, MC, V, JCB. Ⓕ Ⓕ Ⓕ Ⓕ

The expansion of Fauchon – the luxury food shop on the Place de la Madeleine – included the setting up of Le Trente. This is a very good restaurant with Neo-Roman decor and a gloriously lush garden. Young chef Bruno Deligne's menu has many tempting dishes: *foie gras* prepared two ways, fricassée of *petits gris* snails, lemon sole with fennel purée, and veal medallions with a delicious macaroni gratin to name a few. Desserts, prepared by Fauchon's pastry chef, are superb. Ask for a table near a window overlooking the Place de la Madeleine.

Lucas Carton

9 Pl de la Madeleine 75008. **Map** 5 C5.
01 42 65 22 90. **Open** noon–2:30pm, 7:45pm–10:30pm Mon–Fri, 7:45pm–10:30pm Sat. **Closed** Aug.
🍴 🍷 ★ 🔁 AE, DC, MC, V.
Ⓕ Ⓕ Ⓕ Ⓕ

The audacious three-Michelin-starred cuisine of super-chef Alain Senderens is something you will either love or hate. His legendary creations include *foie gras* with cabbage, spicy duck Apicius and a mango *tarte tatin*. The restaurant's Belle Époque decor is stunning, the service crisp and efficient and the crowd glamorous.

MONTMARTRE

La Table d'Anvers

2 Pl d'Anvers 75009. **Map** 7 A2.
01 48 78 35 21. **Open** noon–2pm Mon–Fri, 7pm–11pm Mon–Sat. 🍴 ♿ 🍷 🔁 AE, MC, V, JCB.
Ⓕ Ⓕ Ⓕ

Near the Butte Montmartre, this serious restaurant is run by a father and two sons. The menu has many Italian and Provençale touches such as gnocchi of langoustines and wild mushrooms, rabbit with polenta, and sea bass with thyme and lemon. The pastries and other desserts are among the best in Paris.

Beauvilliers

52 Rue Lamarck 75018. **Map** 2 E5.
01 42 54 54 42. **Open** 12:30pm–2pm, 7:30pm–10:30pm Tue–Sat, 7:30pm–10:30pm Mon. 🍴 🍷
🔁 🔁 AE, DC, MC, V, JCB.
Ⓕ Ⓕ Ⓕ Ⓕ

This joyful place is the best in Montmartre and one of the most festive in Paris. Flower-filled rooms are animated by the effusive chef Edouard Carlier. The renowned chef Paul Bocuse dines here, and the restaurant is also popular with entertainment stars. Carlier delves into old cookbooks for ideas and his menu is always exciting and different: *escabèche* of red mullet (the fish is cooked and marinated), veal *rognonnade* (part of a loin of veal with the kidney included), stuffed beef filet and a very lemony lemon tart are among the choices. There is a delightful covered terrace.

FARTHER AFIELD

Dao Vien

82 Rue Baudricourt 75013.
01 45 85 20 70. **Open** noon–3pm, 7pm–11pm daily. 🍴 ♿ Ⓕ

There are many Oriental restaurants in the original Paris Chinatown, but this friendly Vietnamese joint is especially pleasant. *Soupe Saïgonnaise* is a specialty, along with egg-stuffed crêpes, chicken with ginger, and jasmine tea.

Les Allobroges

17 Rue des Grands-Champs 75020.
01 43 73 40 00. **Open** noon–2pm, 8pm–10pm Tue–Sat.
🔁 AE, MC, V. Ⓕ Ⓕ

It's worth the trip out into the 20th *arrondissement* to taste the fresh and innovative cooking of chef Olivier Pateyron. Especially good is the lobster soup which arrives as a complimentary *amuse-gueule*, and the lightly cooked tuna steak wrapped in bacon and served with a delicately flavored, emerald green cabbage coulis. Both service and ambience are rather lack-luster – this is not the venue to impress a hot date – but for delicious food which won't break the bank, this is a great place to choose.

L'Armoise

67 Rue des Entrepreneurs 75015.
01 45 79 03 31. **Open** 12:15–2pm, 7:30pm–10pm Mon–Fri, 7:30pm–10:30pm Sat. **Closed** Aug. 🍴
🔁 MC, V. Ⓕ Ⓕ

The talented chef owner of this neighborhood restaurant deserves more attention. His *foie gras* with celeriac *rémoulade*, calves' liver, or duck breast with honey are as good as they come and prices are reasonable. This is a pleasant place with a family atmosphere.

Astier

44 Rue Jean-Pierre Timbaud 75011.
Map 14 E1. 01 43 57 16 35.
Open noon–2pm, 8pm–11pm Mon–Fri. **Closed** Aug & public hols.
🍴 🔁 MC, V. Ⓕ Ⓕ

Quality here is among the best for the price in Paris, and the dining rooms are always full. The food is very good, including mussel soup with saffron, rabbit in mustard sauce, duck breast with honey, and good cheeses and wines.

Aux Senteurs de Provence

295 Rue Lecourbe 75015. 01 45 57 11 98. **Open** 12:15pm–2pm, 7:30pm–10:30pm Mon–Fri, 7:30pm–10:30pm Sat. **Closed** Aug 1–21. 🍴 ♿ 🔁
🔁 AE, DC, MC, V. Ⓕ Ⓕ

Tuscany meets Provence in the cuisine of this neutral-grey and wine-red quiet restaurant owned by an Italian. Tuna ravioli, cod with sorrel, *daube* (stew) of lamb, *bouillabaisse*, and *bourride* (garlicky fish soup) are among the better dishes. The *assiette de gourmandise* is a tasty plate of different desserts.

L'Auberge du Bonheur

Allée de Longchamps, Bois de Boulogne 75016. **Map** 3 A3.
〖 *01 42 24 10 17*. **Open** *Mar–Aug: noon–3pm, 7:30pm–10:30pm daily; Sep–Jan: noon–3pm Sun–Fri.* **Closed** *Feb.* 🍴🚹🔥♿🍽 ☰ AE, MC, V, JCB. ⒻⒻ

This is probably the only affordable restaurant in the Bois de Boulogne. In summer, you can sit on the gravel terrace at tables under chestnut and plane trees, surrounded by wisteria and bamboo. It is also delightful in cool weather inside the cozy chalet. The unpretentious service complements cuisine that emphasizes grilled meats.

Le Bistro des Deux Théâtres

18 Rue Blanche 75009. **Map** 6 D3.
〖 *01 45 26 41 43.* **Open** *noon–2:30pm, 7pm–12:30am daily.* 🍴
☰ MC, V. ⒻⒻ

If you are on a strict budget, this formula restaurant in the theater district is a real find, and even if you have a good few francs left to invest in an enjoyable meal, it is still very much worth considering. The reasonable set menu includes apéritif, a choice of first and main courses, cheese or dessert and a half-bottle of wine. The food is good, including duck *foie gras* and smoked salmon with *blinis* (small savory pancakes).

Chez Fernand

7–19 Rue de la Fontaine au Roi 75011. **Map** 8 E5. 〖 *01 43 57 46 25.*
Open *noon–2:30pm, 7:30pm–11:30pm Tue–Sat.* **Closed** *Aug.*
🍴 ☰ MC, V. ⒻⒻ

The banal decor of this small restaurant near the Place de la République is no reflection of the good Normandy-based cuisine with a touch of creativity: mackerel *rillettes* (similar to pâté), skate with Camembert, duck, *tarte Normande* (apple tart) flambéed with Calvados. Prices are excellent, and the chef's smaller Fernandises next door is even less expensive.

La Maison Du Cantal

1 Pl Falguière 75015. **Map** 15 A3.
〖 *01 47 34 12 24.* **Open** *noon–2pm Mon–Sat, 7pm–10:30pm Tue–Sat.* 🍴 ☰ AE, MC, V. ⒻⒻ

This is the place to come on a chilly evening for the hearty country dishes of the Auvergne. Fresh trout fried in butter with crispy *lardons* makes a delicious first course, followed perhaps by a tender rump steak with *blue d'Auvergne* cheese sauce.

La Perle des Antilles

36 Ave Jean-Moulin 75014.
Map 16 D5. 〖 *01 45 42 91 25.*
Open *noon–2:30pm, 7:45pm–11pm Mon–Sat.* 🍴🚹♿🎵🍽 MC, V. ⒻⒻ

This pretty white restaurant with green-and-yellow speckled walls is like a bit of the Antilles in Paris. Haïtian specialties are lovingly prepared by a winning Haïtian couple: vegetable *acras* (savory fritters), gratin of mirliton (a kind of squash), various crab dishes and chicken creole. Spices are used with discretion and all the ingredients are fresh. Come here on a weekend evening for some uptempo live music, order a punch, knock it back, relax and pretend you are in the islands.

Les Amognes

243 Rue du Faubourg St-Antoine 75011. 〖 *01 43 72 73 05.* **Open** *noon–2pm Tue–Fri, 7:30pm–11pm Mon–Sat.* **Closed** *Aug.* 🍴🍽 MC, V. ⒻⒻⒻ

Chef Thierry Coué has worked under Alain Senderens of Lucas Carton (see page 307), quite a recommendation, and an indication of the fare on offer. His small restaurant between the Bastille and Nation is not pretty, but the food is very good and original. It includes sardine tart, cod fritters with tomatoes and basil, tuna with artichokes and bell pepper, sea bream with a chilli-oil and pineapple soup with Pina Colada. It's worth the trip.

Le Bistrot d'à Côté Flaubert

10 Rue Gustave Flaubert 75017.
Map 4 E2. 〖 *01 42 67 05 81.*
Open *12:30pm–2:30pm, 7:30pm–11pm daily.* 🔥🍽 ☰ AE, MC, V. ⒻⒻⒻ

This was the first and remains the most appealing of star-chef Michel Rostang's boutique bistros. The tiny dining room with *de rigueur* mole-skin banquettes gives the appearance of having been furnished from grandmother's attic. Many Lyonnais dishes are served including lentil salad, *cervelas* or *sabodet* sausage, *andouillette* (tripe sausage), and macaroni gratin. It is popular at lunch with local executives and in the evening with the bourgeoisie.

Brasserie Flo

7 Cour des Petites-Ecuries 75010.
Map 7 B4. 〖 *01 47 70 13 59.* **Open** *noon–3pm, 7pm–1am daily.* 🍴♿ ☰ AE, DC, MC, V. ⒻⒻⒻ

This authentic Alsatian brasserie is situated in a passageway in a slightly unsavory neighborhood. But it is worth the effort to find it: the rich wood and stained-glass decor is unique and very pretty and the straightforward brasserie menu includes good shellfish and *choucroute* (sauerkraut). Alsatian wine is sold by the jug.

Le Chardenoux

1 Rue Jules Vallés 75011. 〖 *01 43 71 49 52.* **Open** *noon–2:30pm, 8pm–10:30pm Mon–Fri, 8pm–10:30pm Sat.* **Closed** *Public hols, Aug.* 🍽 AE, MC, V. ⒻⒻⒻ

This classic bistro needs sprucing up but is still one of the prettiest in Paris with its wood paneling, frosted cut glass and impressive marble bar with 17 varieties of stone. There is a wide choice of salads and egg dishes, charcuteries and some uncommon regional dishes like *aligot* (a cheese and potato mixture) and *gigot brayaude* (leg of lamb pierced with cloves of garlic and braised in white wine with potatoes). Loire Valley and Bordeaux wines are emphasized. The atmosphere is pleasant and relaxed.

Le Clos Morillons

50 Rue des Morillons 75015. 〖 *01 48 28 04 37.* **Open** *noon–2pm, 8pm–10pm Mon–Fri, 8pm–10pm Sat.* 🍴🍽 ☰ AE, MC, V. ⒻⒻⒻ

This discreet family-run restaurant has a constantly evolving menu. The chef's trips to the Far East are evident in specialties such as pigeon with sesame and monkfish and lobster with ginger. Other dishes on the menu are more typically French, and of these the terrine of potatoes and *foie gras* is especially delicious. Many good Loire wines are included in the good-value set menu.

Julien

16 Rue du Faubourg St-Denis 75010.
Map 7 B5. 〖 *01 47 70 12 06.*
Open *noon–3pm, 7pm–1:30am daily.* 🍽 AE, DC, MC, V. ⒻⒻⒻ

With its superb 1880s decor, Julien sets an upmarket scene at reasonable prices. Under the same ownership as Brasserie Flo, it has the same friendly service and wide variety of desserts. The brasserie cuisine shows imagination and includes hot *foie gras* with lentils, breaded pig's trotter, grilled sole and Julien's version of *cassoulet* (white bean and meat stew).

L'Oulette

15 Pl Lachambeaudie 75012.
📞 01 40 02 02 12. **Open** noon–
2:30pm, 8pm–10:15pm Mon–Fri,
8pm–10:15pm Sat. 🍴 ⛔ 🛗 🎫
🍷 AE, DC, MC, V. ⒻⒻⒻ

The success of L'Oulette allowed it
to move to much larger quarters in
the new Bercy district. Its current
large, very modern decor lacks the
intimacy of the former restaurant.
However, the cuisine of chef
Marcel Baudis, reflecting his native
Quercy, remains excellent – it is
pretty visually and rich in flavors.
Dishes include *croustillant* of
cèpes (wild mushrooms wrapped
in a pastry parcel and baked in
the oven), salmon in bacon,
braised ox-tail, and *pain d'épices*
(a kind of spice cake).

Le Pavillon Montsouris

20 Rue Gazan 75014. 📞 01 45 88
38 52. **Open** noon–2:30pm, 7:30pm–
10:30pm daily. 🍴 🚸 🛗 🍷 MC,
V. ⒻⒻⒻ

This restored building on the edge
of the pretty Parc Montsouris has
had a long history and once
counted Trotsky, Mata Hari and
Lenin among its customers. Today
the attractive pastel interior and
terrace under the trees make
beguiling surroundings for a set
menu that is excellent value for
money. Dishes include mussel
soup, duck *carpaccio* (in thin raw,
cured slices), *galette* (pancake) of
pigeon and mango *clafoutis* (a type
of batter pudding). Service can be
slow when the restaurant is full.

La Table de Pierre

116 Blvd Pereire 75017. **Map** 4 E1.
📞 01 43 80 88 68. **Open** noon–
2:30pm, 8pm–10:30pm Mon–Fri,
8pm–10:30pm Sat. 🚸 ⛔ 🛗 🍷 AE,
MC, V. ⒻⒻⒻ

The Louis XVI decor inherited
from the previous restaurant does
not suit this Basque establishment,
but is more than made up for by
the jovial owner and interesting
menu. A smart crowd enjoys
regional specialties like *pipérade*
(stewed sweet peppers, tomatoes
and garlic), sweet peppers stuffed
with cod *brandade* (salt cod and
garlic purée), cod filet with green
sauce, stuffed duck's leg and *gâteau
Basque* (sponge cake, crème
pâtissière and cherries).

Au Trou Gascon

40 Rue Taine 75012. 📞 01 43 44 34
26. **Open** noon–2pm, 7:30pm–10pm
Mon–Fri, 7:30pm–10pm Sat. **Closed**
Aug, Xmas–New Year. 🍴 🟥
🍷 AE, DC, MC, V, JCB. ⒻⒻⒻ

This authentic 1900s bistro owned
by star-chef Alain Dutournier (of
Carré des Feuillants) is consistently
one of the most popular places in
Paris. The delicious Gascon food
includes ham from the Chalosse
region, top *foie gras*, lamb from
the Pyrenees and local poultry.
Dutournier's white-chocolate
mousse is now a classic.

Le Train Bleu

20 Blvd Diderot 75012. **Map** 18 E1.
📞 01 43 43 09 06. **Open** 11:30pm–
3pm, 7pm–11pm daily. 🍴 ⛔ 🎫
🍷 AE, DC, MC, V. ⒻⒻⒻ

Train station restaurants were
once grand places for a meal.
Today, only the Train Bleu (named
after the fast train that once took
the élite down to the Riviera) in
the Gare de Lyon remains so.
The food is upmarket brasserie
cuisine such as hot Lyonnais
sausage, with excellent pastries.
The fabulous Belle Époque decor
makes the place a landmark.

Augusta

98 Rue de Tocqueville 75017.
Map 5 A1. 📞 01 47 63 39 97.
Open noon–2pm, 7:30pm–10pm
Mon–Fri, 7:30pm–10pm Sat. **Closed**
Sat & Sun in summer. ⛔ 🟥 🍷 MC, V.
ⒻⒻⒻⒻ

This reliable restaurant serves excellent fish and a few meat dishes.
The *salade Augusta* is generously
garnished with shellfish and the
house specialty of *bouillabaisse*
with potatoes must be one of the
best in Paris. An unusual dish is
lobster lasagne with Parmesan.
The wine list is popular with well-
off local regulars.

Au Pressoir

257 Ave Daumesnil 75012.
📞 01 43 44 38 21. **Open** noon–
2:30pm, 7:30pm–10:30pm Mon–Fri.
Closed Aug. 🍴 🚸 🟥 🍷 AE,
MC, V. ⒻⒻⒻ

Chef Séguin and his wife are
passionate about quality. Dishes
are often unusual, such as
monkfish with bacon and split
peas, *foie gras* with Jerusalem
artichokes, pigeon with eggplant
blinis (small savory pancakes)
and chocolate soup with brioche.
The service is excellent, as is the
wine list, and the surroundings
are very comfortable.

Faucher

123 Ave de Wagram 75017.
Map 4 E2. 📞 01 42 27 61 50.
Open noon–2pm, 8pm–10pm
Mon–Fri, 8pm–10pm Sat. 🍴 🟥
🍷 🍷 AE, MC, V, JCB. ⒻⒻⒻⒻ

Monsieur and Mme Faucher take a
great interest in their restaurant
and guests. The big beige dining
room with large windows is very
pretty and the terrace is a delight
in fine weather. The food has
original touches and includes
millefeuille of spinach and sliced
raw beef, truffle-stuffed egg, turbot
with caviar cream and a very good
selection of desserts.

Pavillon Puebla

Parc des Buttes-Chaumont 75019.
📞 01 42 08 92 62.
Open noon–2pm, 7:30pm–10pm
Tue–Sat. 🍴 Ⓥ 🟥 ⛔ 🎫 🍷 AE,
V. ⒻⒻⒻⒻ

This elegant, floral building, built
under Napoleon III as an
adornment for his new Parc des
Buttes-Chaumont, is a delight both
inside and outside on the terrace
in fine weather. Chef Vergès
prepares flavorful cuisine with a
Catalan influence, which includes
oyster ravioli with curry, squid in
its ink with spices, veal tournedos
with truffle juice and *crème
Catalane* (crème brûlée). The
entrance is on Rue Botzaris.

Apicius

122 Ave de Villiers 75017.
Map 4 D1. 📞 01 43 80 19 66. **Open**
noon–2pm, 8pm–10pm Mon–Fri. 🟥
🍷 ★ 🍷 AE, DC, MC, V, JCB.
ⒻⒻⒻⒻ

Chef/owner Jean-Pierre Vigato
looks more like a model than a
chef. His cuisine has its hearty
side – he enjoys preparing offal
and treating fish almost like meat.
Dishes include pig's trotters roasted
en crépinette (with small sausages),
roast turbot with bacon, roast
sweetbreads, all-caramel or all-
chocolate desserts. Service in two
airy dining rooms is professionally
and personally supervised by
Madame Vigato.

Le Pré Catelan

Route de Suresnes, Bois de Boulogne
75016. 📞 01 45 24 55 58. **Open**
noon–2:30pm Tue–Sun,
7pm–10:30pm Tue– Sat. 🚸 🎫
🍴 🍷 AE, DC, MC, V.
ⒻⒻⒻⒻⒻ

This very elegant Belle Époque
restaurant in the Bois de Boulogne
is a delight, either in midsummer,
when you can dine on the idyllic
terrace, or midwinter, when the
lights and decoration inside are
magical. The menu is luxurious,
with huge langoustines, special
Duclair duck with spices and sea
urchin soufflé. Desserts are
fabulous – the restaurant is
managed by Madame Lenôtre,
wife of the king of French pastry.

For key to symbols *see p289*

Light Meals and Snacks

GOOD FOOD AND DRINK are so much a part of everyday life in Paris that you can eat and drink well without ever going to a restaurant. Whether you want to enjoy a meal or casual drink at a café, wine bar or tea room, buy a crêpe, quiche, pizza or a snack from a street stand or bakery, or put together a picnic from cheeses, breads, salads and pâtés, informal eating is one of the great gastronomic strengths of the city.

Paris is also wonderful simply for drinking. Wine bars in every quarter offer many different wines by the glass. Beer bars have astounding selections, and Paris's Irish pubs serve Guinness in a relaxed, sometimes rowdy, atmosphere. Hotel bars or late-night bars are also options. *(See also* What to Drink in Paris *pp292–3.)*

CAFÉS

YOU CAN'T WALK far in Paris without passing a café. They range in size from tiny to huge, some with pinball machines, some with elegant Belle Epoque decorations. Most will serve you food and drink at any time of day.

Breakfast is one of the busiest times, and fresh croissants and *pains au chocolat* (chocolate-filled pastries) sell fast. The French often eat these dipped in a bowl or large cup of coffee or hot chocolate.

The café lunch usually includes *plats du jour* (daily specials) and in the smaller cafés is one of the great Parisian bargains, rarely costing more than F80 for two courses with wine. The specials are often substantial meat dishes, such as *sauté d'agneau* (sautéed lamb) or *blanquette de veau* (veal with a white sauce), with fruit tarts for dessert. For a simpler lunch, salads, sandwiches and omelettes are usually available at any time of day. One of the best places for this kind of food is the **Bar de la Croix Rouge** in St-Germain-des-Prés.

Most museums have reliable cafés, but those at the Pompidou Center *(see pp110–11)* and the Musée d'Orsay *(see pp144–5)* are especially good. Should you find yourself in the department store La Samaritaine *(see p313)*, it's worth going to the café for the view over Paris.

Cafés in the main tourist and nightlife areas (Boulevard St-Germain, Avenue des Champs-Elysées, Boulevard Montparnasse, Opéra and Bastille) generally stay open late – some until 3am.

WINE BARS

MOST PARISIAN wine bars are small, convivial neighborhood places. They open early, many doubling as cafés for breakfast, and offer a small, good-quality lunch menu. It's best to get there early or after 1:30pm if you want to avoid the crowd. Most wine bars close by 9pm.

Wine-bar owners tend to be passionate about wine, most of them buying directly from producers. Young Bordeaux wines and those from the Loire, Rhône and the Jura can be surprisingly good, and wine-bar owners have a knack for finding good ones. The **L'Ecluse** chain specializes in Bordeaux, but for the most part you will find delicious lesser-known wines at very reasonable prices.

BEER BARS AND PUBS

PARIS HAS BOTH pubs and beer bars. Whereas pubs are simply for drinking, beer bars also serve a particular style of food and are larger. *Moules-frites* (a generous bowl of steamed mussels served with french fries), *tarte aux poireaux* (leek tart) and *tarte aux oignons* (onion tart) are classic examples of the food they serve. The chief reason for going to a beer bar, however, is for the beer.

The lists are often vast: some specialize in Belgian *gueuze* (heavy, malty, very alcoholic beer); others have beers from all around the world.

Some beer bars are open from noon, whereas pubs open later in the afternoon. Pubs are usually open every day, often until 1 or 2am.

BARS

PARIS HAS ITS share of cocktail and smoky late-night bars, too. Some pretty Paris brasseries, such as **La Coupole** and **Le Boeuf sur le Toit**, have long wooden or zinc bars and accomplished bartenders. The most elegant hotel bar in Paris (and possibly the most expensive) is the main bar at the **Hôtel Ritz** *(see p281)*. The **Hemingway Bar** at the Ritz is darker and less elegant, but full of nostalgia. It's open only for special occasions.

Equally chic, and not in a hotel, is the bar at **Le Fouquet's** restaurant on the Champs-Elysées. One of the most fun late-night bars in Paris, complete with a piano player, is **Le Closerie des Lilas**, while **Le Rosebud** and the **China Club** are young and trendy. Funkier still is **Le Piano Vache**, and **Birdland** has a great jazz jukebox.

TAKE-OUT FOOD

CREPES ARE THE traditional Parisian street food. Although there are fewer good crêpe stands than there used to be, they still exist. Sandwich bars provide baguettes with a wide range of fillings, but the best fast food in Paris is a new invention: freshly baked flat focaccia bread sprinkled with savory flavorings. It is sold fresh from a wood-burning oven and filled with one or more fillings of your choice. You can buy it at **Cosi**.

Ice cream stands tend to open just before noon and close late in summer or around 7pm in winter. It's still worth lining up around the block at **Maison Berthillon** for the city's best ice cream.

DIRECTORY

ILE DE LA CITÉ AND ILE ST-LOUIS

Wine Bars
Au Franc Pinot
1 Quai de Bourbon
75004. **Map** 13 C4.

Taverne Henri IV
13 Pl du Pont-Neuf
75001. **Map** 12 F3.

Tea Salons
Le Flore en l'Ile
42 Quai d'Orléans
75004. **Map** 13 B4.

Ice Cream Parlors
Maison Berthillon
31 Rue St-Louis-en-l'Ile
75004. **Map** 13 C4.

THE MARAIS

Cafés
Ma Bourgogne
19 Pl des Vosges 75004.
Map 14 D3.

Wine Bars
Le Passage
18 Passage de la Bonne-
Graine 75011. **Map** 14 F4.

La Tartine
24 Rue de Rivoli 75004.
Map 13 C3.

Tea Salons
Le Loir dans la Théière
3 Rue des Rosiers 75004.
Map 13 C3.

Mariage Frères
30–32 Rue du Bourg-
Tibourg 75004.
Map 13 C3.

Bars
China Club
50 Rue de Charenton
75012. **Map** 14 F5.

La Mousson
9 Rue de la Bastille
75004. **Map** 14 E4.

Beer Bars
Café des Musées
49 Rue de Turenne
75003. **Map** 14 D3.

BEAUBOURG AND LES HALLES

Cafés
Bistrot D'Eustache
(See p109.)

Café Beaubourg
43 Rue St-Mérri 75004.
Map 13 B3.

Pubs
Flann O'Brien
6 Rue Bailleul 75001.
Map 12 F2.

TUILERIES QUARTER

Wine Bars
Blue Fox Bar
25 Rue Royale 75008.
Map 5 C5.

La Cloche des Halles
28 Rue Coquillière 75001.
Map 12 F1.

Juvenile's
47 Rue de Richelieu 75001.
Map 12 E1.

Tea Salons
Angélina
226 Rue de Rivoli 75001.
Map 12 D1.

Ladurée
16 Rue Royale 75008.
Map 5 C5.

Bars
Bars du Ritz
15 Pl Vendôme 75001.
Map 6 D5.

ST-GERMAIN-DES-PRÉS

Cafés
Bar de la Croix Rouge
2 Carrefour de la Croix
Rouge 75006. **Map** 12 D4.

Café de Flore
(See p139.)

Les Deux Magots
(See p138.)

Sandwich Bars
Cosi
54 Rue de Seine 75006.
Map 12 E4.

Wine Bars
Bistro des Augustins
39 Quai des Grands-
Augustins 75006.
Map 12 F4.

Au Sauvignon
80 Rue des Sts-Pères
75007. **Map** 12 D4.

Bars
Birdland
8 Rue Guisarde 75006.
Map 12 E4.

Le Lenox
9 Rue de l'Université
75007. **Map** 11 B2.

La Villa à l'Hôtel
La Villa 29 Rue Jacob
75006. **Map** 12 E3.

LATIN QUARTER

Wine Bars
Les Pipos
2 Rue de l'Ecole
Polytechnique 75005.
Map 13 A5.

Bars
Le Piano-Vache
8 Rue Laplace 75005.
Map 13 A5.

Beer Bars
La Gueuze
19 Rue Soufflot 75005.
Map 12 F5.

JARDIN DES PLANTES

Cafés
Le Moule à Gâteau
111 Rue Mouffetard
75005. **Map** 17 B2.

Pubs
Finnegan's Wake
9 Rue des Boulangers
75005. **Map** 17 B1.

Ice Cream Parlors
Häagen-Dazs
3 Pl de la Contrescarpe
75005. **Map** 17 A1.

LUXEMBOURG QUARTER

Cafés
Le Rostand
6 Pl Edmond Rostand
75006. **Map** 12 F5.

Beer Bars
L'Académie de la Bière
88 Blvd de Port-Royal
75005. **Map** 17 B3.

MONTPARNASSE

Bars
La Closerie des Lilas
171 Blvd du Montparnasse
75006. **Map** 16 E2.

Cafés
Café de la Place
23 Rue d'Odessa 75014.
Map 15 C2.

La Rotonde
7 Place 25 Août 1944,
75014.

Le Sélect
99 Blvd du Montparnasse
75006. **Map** 16 D2.

Wine Bars
Le Rallye Peret
6 Rue Daguerre 75014.
Map 16 D4.

Tea Salons
Max Poilâne
29 Rue de l'Ouest
75014. **Map** 15 C3.

Bars
La Coupole (café bar)
102 Blvd du
Montparnasse 75014.
Map 16 D2.
(See also p178.)

Le Rosebud
11 bis Rue Delambre
75014. **Map** 16 D2.

CHAMPS-ELYSÉES

Wine Bars
L'Ecluse
64 Rue François-1er
75008. **Map** 4 F5.

Ma Bourgogne
133 Blvd Haussmann
75008. **Map** 5 B4.

Bars
Le Boeuf sur le Toit
34 Rue du Colisée
75008. **Map** 5 A5.

Le Fouquet's (café bar)
99 Ave des Champs-
Elysées 75008. **Map** 4 F5.

OPÉRA QUARTER

Cafés
Café de la Paix
12 Blvd des Capucines
75009. **Map** 6 E5.
(See also p213.)

Wine Bars
Bistro du Sommelier
97 Blvd Haussmann
75008. **Map** 5 C4.

SHOPS AND MARKETS

Paris seems to be the very definition of luxury and good living. Beautifully dressed men and women sip wine by the banks of the Seine against a backdrop of splendid French architecture or shop at small specialist stores. The least expensive way of joining the chic set is to create French style with accessories or costume jewelry. But here you can also buy world-famous fashion or treat yourself to wonderful food and related items.

Remember, too, that Parisian shops and markets are the ideal places to indulge in the French custom of seeing and being seen. For high fashion, the Rue du Faubourg St-Honoré has many exquisite couture-house window displays, or you can browse around the the bookstalls along the Seine. A survey of some of the best and most famous places to shop follows.

OPENING HOURS

Shops are usually open from 9:30am to 7pm on Monday to Saturday, but hours can vary considerably. Boutiques may shut for an hour or two at midday, and markets and local neighborhood shops close on Mondays. Some places shut down for the summer, usually in August, but those selling essentials may leave a note on the door with the name of an open equivalent nearby.

HOW TO PAY

Besides cash, traveler's checks are common currency. VISA is the most widely accepted credit card in Paris, but some shops may accept others. In theory, Eurocheques can be used in France, but some banks try to avoid them, and Crédit Agricole insists you cash a minimum of £200. Only the bigger stores are likely to accept them.

VAT EXEMPTION

A sales tax (value-added tax, known here as TVA) from 5% to 25% is imposed on most goods and services in EC countries. Non-EC residents shopping in France are entitled to a refund if they spend a minimum of F2,000 in one shop. You must have been in France for less than six months and either carry the goods with you out of the country or get the shop to forward them. If you're with a group, you can usually buy goods together to reach the minimum.

Larger shops will generally supply a form *(bordereau de détaxe* or *bordereau de vente)* and help you to fill it in. When you leave France or the EC, you present the form at Customs, who forward your claim to the place where you bought the goods; the shop eventually sends you a refund in French francs. If you know

Shopping in Avenue Montaigne

someone in Paris it may be quicker if they can pick up the refund for you at the shop. Alternatively, at large airports like Orly and Roissy some banks may have the facilities to refund you on the spot. Though the process involves a lot of paperwork, it can be worth it. There is no refund on food, wine and tobacco.

SALES

The best sales *(soldes)* are in January and July, although you can sometimes find sale items before Christmas – a treat that used to be unheard of. If you see goods labeled *Stock,* it means that they are stock items. *Dégriffé* means designer labels marked down, frequently from the previous year's collections. *Fripes* means that the clothes are second-hand. The sales tend to occupy prime floor space for the first month and are then relegated to the back of the store.

La Samaritaine department store in Beaubourg and Les Halles

DEPARTMENT STORES

MUCH OF THE pleasure of shopping in Paris is derived from going to the specialty shops. But if time is short and you want to get all your purchases under one roof, then try the *grands magasins* (department stores).

Most department stores still operate a ticket system for selling goods. The shop assistant writes up a ticket for goods from their own boutique, then you take the ticket to a cashier. You then return with your validated ticket to pick up your purchase. This can be frustrating and time-consuming, so go early in the morning and don't shop on Saturdays. The French don't pay much attention to lines, so be assertive!

Though the city's department store are generally stocked with similar merchandise, they have different emphases. All have somewhere to eat. **Au Printemps** is noted for its exciting and innovative household goods, and there is a building each for menswear, household goods, and women's and children's clothes. Fashion shows are on Tuesdays and Fridays at 10am. The beauty department

Snails from the *charcuterie*

Lionel Poilâne's bread bearing his trademark – a square *(see pp322–3)*

Kenzo designerwear in the Place des Victoires *(see pp316–17)*

has one of the world's largest perfume selections, and the domed restaurant in a cupola is one of the best in such stores.

BHV (Le Bazar de l'Hôtel de Ville) is a do-it-yourself paradise. Shop here for household basics and visit the restaurant for views of the Seine.

Designed by Gustave Eiffel, the Left Bank **Au Bon Marché** was the first department store in Paris and is the most chic, with a good food hall. **Galeries Lafayette** has a wide range of clothes at all price levels. Fashion shows are held at 11am on Wednesdays (and Fridays in summer). Open late on Wednesdays, **La Samaritaine** is one of the oldest shops in Paris. It is full of bargains and often carries the same merchandise as Galeries Lafayette, at lower prices. It includes a shop devoted to sportswear and equipment, and there are good sales on household goods and furnishings. There is a panoramic view of the Seine from the restaurant (closed from the end of October until the beginning of April). **Virgin Megastore** is open until late and has a wide selection of old and new recordings and an extremely good book section. **FNAC** specializes in recordings, books (foreign editions at Les Halles) and also electronic equipment. **FNAC Microinformatique** sells computer-related material.

ADDRESSES

Au Printemps
64 Blvd Haussman 01 75009.
Map 6 D4. 01 42 82 50 00.

BHV
52–64 Rue de Rivoli 75004.
Map 13 B3. 01 42 74 90 00.

Bon Marché
22 Rue de Sèvres 75007.
Map 11 C5. 01 44 39 80 00.

Bookstall, Vanves market *(see p327)*

FNAC
Forum Les Halles, 1 Rue Pierre Lescot
75001. **Map** 13 A2. 01 40 41 40 00.
One of five branches.

FNAC Microinformatique
71 Blvd St-Germain 75005.
Map 13 A5. 01 44 41 31 50.

Galeries Lafayette
40 Blvd Haussmann 75009.
Map 6 E4. 01 42 82 34 56.
One of two branches.

La Samaritaine
19 Rue de la Monnaie 75001.
Map 2 F2. 01 40 41 20 20.

Virgin Megastore
52–60 Ave des Champs-Elysées
75008. **Map** 4 F5. 01 49 53 50 00.

Paris's Best: Shops and Markets

Old-fashioned and conservative yet full of surprises, Paris is a treasure trove of quality shops and boutiques. Time-honored emporia mix with modern precincts in a city that buzzes with life in its inner quarters, and especially in the markets. Here you can buy everything from exotic fruit and vegetables to fine china and antiques. Whether you're shopping for handmade shoes, perfectly cut clothes or traditionally made cheeses – or simply looking for atmosphere – you won't be disappointed.

Place de la Madeleine
Top-grade groceries and delicacies are sold on the north side of this square. (See p214.)

THE CENTER OF PARIS COUTURE

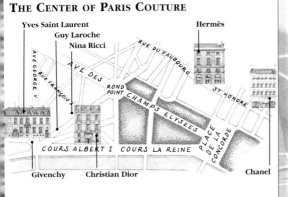

Yves Saint Laurent
Guy Laroche
Nina Ricci
Hermès
AVE GEORGE V
RUE FRANÇOIS I
AVE DES
RUE DU FAUBOURG
ROND POINT
CHAMPS ELYSEES
ST HONORE
COURS ALBERT I COURS LA REINE
PLACE DE LA CONCORDE
Givenchy
Christian Dior
Chanel

See inset map

Champs-Elysées

R I V E R

Chanel
Coco Chanel (1883–1971) reigned over the fashion world from No. 31 Rue Cambon. The main boutique is in the Avenue Montaigne. (See p317.)

Invalides and Eiffel Tower Quarter

Rue de Rivoli
Inexpensive mementos like this Paris snow globe can be found in the shops on the Rue de Rivoli. (See p130.)

Marché de la Porte de Vanves
This charming and relaxed market sells old books, linen, postcards, china and musical instruments. (See p327.)

Kenzo
The Japanese designer has colorful apparel for men, women and children in his clothes shops. (See p317.)

Cartier
The early Cartier jewelry designs with their beautifully cut stones are still highly sought after. This shop in the Rue de la Paix sells all the Cartier lines. (See p319.)

Rue de Paradis
You can buy porcelain and crystal at reduced prices at the company showrooms on this street. Watch for Porcelainor, Baccarat and Lumicristal. (See pp320–21.)

Passage des Panoramas
This once-prosperous arcade at Les Galeries has an old engraving house. (See p216.)

Opéra Quarter

```
0 kilometers        1
0 miles        0.5
```

N

Tuileries Quarter

Beaubourg and Les Halles

The Marais

St-Germain-des-Prés

Ile de la Cité

Ile St-Louis

Latin Quarter

Luxembourg Quarter

Jardin des Plantes Quarter

Montparnasse

Rue des Francs-Bourgeois
A L'Image du Grenier sur L'Eau sells old postcards, posters and prints. (See pp324–5.)

Rue Mouffetard
The market sells cheeses and other quality foods. (See p327.)

Forum des Halles
This modern glass arcade has many shops. (See p109.)

Clothes and Accessories

FOR MANY PEOPLE, PARIS is synonymous with fashion, and Parisian style is the ultimate in chic. More than anywhere else in the world, women in Paris seem to be in tune with current trends, and when a new season arrives they seem to don the look as one. Though less trend-conscious generally, Parisian men are also aware of style and mix and match patterns and colors with élan.

Finding the right clothes at the right price means knowing where to shop. For every luxury boutique on the Avenue Montaigne, there are ten shops of young designers waiting to become the next Christian Lacroix – and hundreds more selling imitations.

HAUTE COUTURE

PARIS IS THE home of haute couture. The original haute couture garments, as opposed to the imitations and adaptations, are one-of-a-kind creations, designed by one of the 23 couture houses listed with the Fédération Française de la Couture. The rules for being classified haute couture are fairly strict, and many of the best designers, such as Claude Montana and Karl Lagerfeld, are not included. Astronomical prices put haute couture beyond the reach of most pockets, but it's still the lifeblood of the fashion industry, providing inspiration for the mass market.

The fashion seasons are launched with the haute couture shows in January and July. Most shows are held in the Cour Carrée du Louvre (see p123). If you want to see a show, you stand a better chance of getting a seat at the private couture shows (the main shows are for buyers and the press). Call the press office of the haute couture houses a month in advance. You can be sure you have a place only when you receive the ticket. For the private shows, telephone the house or, if you're in Paris, try going to the boutique and asking if there's a show – and remember to dress the part.

Most couture houses make prêt-à-porter clothes as well – ready-to-wear clothes fitted on a standard model. They're still not cheap but give you some of the designer elegance and creativity at a fraction of the haute couture cost.

WOMEN'S CLOTHES

THE HIGHEST concentration of couture houses is on the Right Bank. Most are on or near the Rue du Faubourg-St-Honoré and the classier Avenue Montaigne: **Chanel**, **Ungaro**, **Christian Lacroix**, **Nina Ricci**, **Louis Féraud**, **Yves Saint Laurent**, **Pierre Cardin**, **Gianni Versace**, **Christian Dior**, **Guy Laroche**, **Jean-Louis Scherrer**; the list is almost endless. This is where you will rub shoulders with the rich and famous.

Hermès has classic country chic. **MaxMara's** Italian elegance is quite popular in France, and no one can resist a **Giorgio Armani** suit. **Karl Lagerfeld**, despite designing for Chanel, has also created his own sleek line.

The theatrical **Paco Rabanne** is the only official haute couturier on the Left Bank, but it is surrounded by many fine fashion houses. Try **Sonia Rykiel** for knitwear, **Junko Shimada** for sporty casuals and **Barbara Bui** for soft, feminine clothes.

Many designers have a Left Bank branch in addition to their Right Bank bastions. For sheer quality there's **Georges Rech**, but don't forget **Yves Saint Laurent's** sophisticated tailoring and **Myrène de Prémonville** for power dressing. They all have ready-to-wear shops here. **Diaposi-tive's** body-hugging clothes are popular. Go to **Irié** for reasonably priced clothes with just enough touches to be trendy but that will also stand the test of time.

Ready-to-wear shops blanket Paris, and in the beautiful Place des Victoires they thrive on shoppers visiting the Rue du Faubourg St-Honoré. The **Victoire** boutique offers one of the best collections of current designer labels, with Michael Klein, Helmut Lang and Thierry Mugler among many others. If your wardrobe lacks color, then the Place des Victoires also includes **Kenzo**; or try **Thierry Mugler** for that 1940s *film noir* look. Just down the street, **Ventilo** has a charming tea room, and **Equipment** is known for classic silk shirts in a vast range of colors. **Comme des Garçons** has avant-garde, quirky fashion for both sexes. The nearby Rue Jean-Jacques-Rousseau has recently become one of the city's prime shopping stops: **Kashiyama** encourages a cult following with some imaginative clothes.

Eccentric designer **Jean-Paul Gaultier** has his shop at Les Halles shopping center. His "senior" and "junior" collections reflect price and attitude rather than age, while **Claudie Pierlot** and **Agnès B.**'s clothes have timeless elegance. There are also shops selling inexpensive copies of new designs in the center.

The Marais is a haven for up-and-coming designers and is always busy on Saturdays. Don't miss Rue des Rosiers, with **Lolita Lempicka**, **L'Eclaireur**, and a branch of **Tehen** for clothes. **Nina Jacob** is on the neighboring Rue des Francs-Bourgeois, along with **Le Garage**, an imaginative unisex shirt shop. Daring designer **Azzedine Alaïa's** fascinating shop is just around the corner.

The Bastille area has many trendy boutiques, while the swimsuit store is **Eres**. For leather, there's **Mac Douglas**.

For young dressing, **Kookaï** has little dresses and tiny tops. **Bruce Field**, **Chipie**, and **Chevignon** offer 1950s-style Americana. Try **Rag Time** for fabulous, if pricey, clothes from the 1920s to the 1950s, and **Réciproque** for some of the best nearly-new designer garb in Paris.

DIRECTORY

WOMEN'S CLOTHES

Agnès B
6 Rue du Jour 75001.
Map 13 A1.
📞 01 45 08 56 56.
One of several branches.

Azzedine Alaïa
7 Rue de Moussy 75004.
Map 13 C3.
📞 01 40 27 85 58.

Barbara Bui
23 Rue Etienne-Marcel
75001. **Map** 13 A1.
📞 01 40 26 43 65.
One of two branches.

Chanel
42 Ave Montaigne 75008.
Map 5 A5.
📞 01 47 20 84 45.
One of several branches.

Chevignon
49 Rue Etienne Marcel
75001. **Map** 12 F1.
📞 01 40 28 05 77.

Chipie
129 Rue Pompe
75116.
📞 01 47 04 34 03.

Christian Dior
30 Avenue Montaigne
75008. **Map** 10 F1.
📞 01 40 73 54 44.

Christian Lacroix
73 Rue du Faubourg-St-
Honoré 75008. **Map** 5 B5.
📞 01 42 68 79 00.

Claudie Pierlot
1 Rue Montmartre
75001.
Map 13 A1.
📞 01 42 21 38 38.
One of two branches.

**Comme des
Garçons**
40–42 Rue Etienne-Marcel
75002. **Map** 13 A1.
📞 01 42 33 05 21.

Diapositive
12 Rue du Jour 75001.
Map 13 A1.
📞 01 42 21 34 41.
One of several branches.

L'Eclaireur
3 ter Rue des Rosiers
75004.
Map 13 C3.
📞 01 48 87 10 22.

Elsa Field
25 Rue Rambuteau
75004.
Map 13 B2.
📞 01 42 72 74 17.

Equipment
46 Rue Etienne-Marcel
75002.
Map 13 A1.
📞 01 40 26 17 84.

Eres
2 Rue Tronchet
75008. **Map** 5 C5.
📞 01 47 42 24 55.
One of two branches.

Georges Rech
273 Rue St-Honoré
75008. **Map** 12 D1.
📞 01 42 61 41 14.
One of several branches.

Gianni Versace
62 Rue du Faubourg-St-
Honoré 75008.
Map 5 C5.
📞 01 47 42 88 02.
One of two branches.

Giorgio Armani
6 Pl Vendôme 75001.
Map 6 D5.
📞 01 42 61 55 09.

Guy Laroche
30 Rue du Faubourg-St-
Honoré 75008.
Map 5 C5.
📞 01 40 06 01 70.
One of several branches.

Hermès
24 Rue du Faubourg-St-
Honoré 75008.
Map 5 C5.
📞 01 40 17 47 17.

Irié
8 Rue du Pré-aux-Clercs
75007. **Map** 12 D3.
📞 01 42 61 18 28.

Jean-Louis Scherrer
51 Ave Montaigne
75008. **Map** 5 A5.
📞 01 56 59 98 41.

Jean-Paul Gaultier
6 Rue Vivienne
75002. **Map** 12 F1.
📞 01 42 86 05 05.

Junko Shimada
54 Rue Etienne-Marcel
75002. **Map** 12 F1.
📞 01 42 36 36 97.
One of two branches.

Kashiyama
147 Blvd St-Germain
75006. **Map** 12 E4.
📞 01 55 42 77 55.
One of two branches.

Kenzo
3 Pl des Victoires
75001.
Map 12 F1.
📞 01 40 39 72 03.

Kookaï
46 Rue St-Denis, Pl des
Innocents 75001.
Map 13 A2.
📞 01 40 26 40 30.
One of several branches.

Lolita Lempicka
2 bis Rue des Rosiers
75004.
Map 13 C3.
📞 01 48 87 09 67.

Louis Féraud
88 Rue du Faubourg-St-
Honoré 75008.
Map 5 B5.
📞 01 42 65 27 29.
One of several branches.

Mac Douglas
9 Rue de Sèvres
75006.
Map 12 D4.
📞 01 45 48 14 09.
One of several branches.

MaxMara
37 Rue du Four
75006.
Map 12 D4.
📞 01 43 29 91 10.
One of two branches.

**Myrène de
Prémonville**
24 Rue Boissy d'Anglas
75008. **Map** 5 C5.
📞 01 42 65 00 60.

Nina Jacob
23 Rue des Francs-
Bourgeouis 75004
Map 14 D3.
📞 01 42 77 41 20.

Nina Ricci
39 Avenue Montaigne
75008.
Map 10 F1.
📞 01 49 52 56 00.

Paco Rabanne
83 Rue des Sts Pères
75006. **Map** 12 D4.
📞 01 45 48 82 26.

Pierre Cardin
27 Ave de Marigny 75008.
Map 5 B5.
📞 01 42 66 68 98.
One of two branches.

Rag Time
23 Rue du Roule 75001.
Map 12 F3.
📞 01 42 36 89 36.

Réciproque
95 Rue de la Pompe
75016. **Map** 9 A1.
📞 01 47 04 30 28.

Sonia Rykiel
175 Blvd St-Germain
75006. **Map** 12 D4.
📞 01 49 54 60 60.
One of two branches.

Tehen
5 bis Rue des Rosiers
75004. **Map** 13 C3.
📞 01 40 27 97 37.
One of several branches.

Thierry Mugler
49 Ave Montaigne 75008.
Map 10 F1.
📞 01 47 23 37 62.
One of two branches.

Ungaro
2 Ave Montaigne 75008.
Map 10 F1.
📞 01 53 57 00 00.

Ventilo
27 bis Rue du Louvre
75002. **Map** 12 F2.
📞 01 42 33 18 67.

Victoire
12 Pl des Victoires 75002.
Map 12 F1.
📞 01 42 61 09 02.
One of several branches.

Yves Saint Laurent
38 Rue de Faubourg-St-
Honoré 75008.
Map 5 C5.
📞 01 42 65 23 16.
One of several branches.

CHILDREN'S CLOTHES

O PTIONS FOR children exist in all styles and price ranges. Many designers of adult clothes have boutiques for children, including **Kenzo**, **Baby Dior**, **Sonia Rykiel**, **Agnès B.** and **Caddie**. The latter carries a range of designers' children's lines.

Ready-to-wear chains like **Benetton** and **Bonpoint** (which sell chic, expensive, well-made clothes) offer good quality selections; and **Tartine et Chocolat**'s best-sellers are colorful overalls.

For little feet, **Froment-Leroyer** probably offers the best allround classics. **Six Pieds Trois Pouces** has a vast choice of styles.

MEN'S CLOTHES

M EN DON'T HAVE the luxury of haute couture dressing: their choice is limited to ready-to-wear. Some men's clothes, mostly by womenswear designers, are very expensive.

On the Right Bank, there's **Giorgio Armani**, **Karl Lagerfeld**, **Pierre Cardin**, **Kenzo**, **Lanvin** (also good for accessories) and **Yves Saint Laurent**. On the Left Bank, **Michel Axael** is known for his ties, and **Francesco Smalto**'s elegant creations are worn by Jean-Paul Belmondo. **Yohji Yamamoto**'s clothes are for those who want to make a serious fashion statement, while **Gianni Versace** is classic Italian in style, and the **Olivier Strelli** look is always chic without being overtly trendy.

JEWELRY

T HE COUTURE houses probably sell some of the best jewelry and scarves. **Chanel**'s jewels are classics, and **Christian Lacroix**'s are fun. **Boutique YSL** is for accessories, and **Kalinger** is one of the biggest names in costume jewelry. **Isabel Canovas** has outrageous earrings, hats and gloves.

Among the main expensive Paris jewelry outlets are **Boucheron** and **Mauboussin**. They are for the serious

jewelry buyer. Two other top retailers are **Harry Winston** (where Elizabeth Taylor shops) and **Cartier**.

Trends and imitations can be found around the Marais, the Bastille and Les Halles, in that order for quality. Those of note include **Fugit Amor** for its large selection of jewelry, **Scooter** where chic young Parisians shop and **Agatha** for copies of Chanel designs and basics.

SHOES, BAGS AND BELTS

F OR SHEER LUXURY, **Harel** has a wide range of exotic leather footwear. Go to **Charles Jourdan** for a big selection of colors or to **Sidonie Larizzi**, who will make up shoes from one of numerous leather swatches. **Carel** stocks smart basics.

Bowen has a selection of traditional men's shoes, and **Fenestrier** makes chic versions of classics. **Christian Lacroix** and **Paloma Picasso** make wonderful handbags.

Leather goods can also be found at **Longchamp**, **Gucci** and **Hermès**. Designer imitations are available in Les Halles shopping center, from streetside stalls and in metro station kiosks. **Zandoli** has the widest selection of belts.

HATS

W ITH SHOPS on the Right and Left Banks, **Marie Mercié** is one of Paris's favorite milliners, known for big, bold and beautiful boaters. **Chéri-Bibi** is affordable and frivolous, and **Philippe Model** is one of Paris's most creative and stylish hatmakers.

LINGERIE

F OR FLATTERING, sophisticated and expensive lingerie go to **Capucine Puerari** whose tiny shop is filled with beautiful underwear. **La Boite à Bas** sells fine French stockings, while **Bas et Haut** offers a selection of stylish and serviceable items.

SIZE CHART
For Australian sizes follow the British and American conversions.

Children's clothing

French	2-3	4-5	6-7	8-9	10-11	12	14	14+ (years)
British	2-3	4-5	6-7	8-9	10-11	12	14	14+ (years)
American	2-3	4-5	6-6x	7-8	10		12	14	16 (size)

Children's shoes

French	24	25½	27	28	29	30	32	33	34
British	7	8	9	10	11	12	13	1	2
American	7½	8½	9½	10½	11½	12½	13½	1½	2½

Women's dresses coats and skirts

French	34	36	38	40	42	44	46
British	8	10	12	14	16	18	20
American	6	8	10	12	14	16	18

Women's blouses and sweaters

French	81	84	87	90	93	96	99 (cm)
British	31	32	34	36	38	40	42 (inches)
American	6	8	10	12	14	16	18 (size)

Women's shoes

French	36	37	38	39	40	41
British	3	4	5	6	7	8
American	5	6	7	8	9	10

Men's suits

French	44	46	48	50	52	54	56	58
British	34	36	38	40	42	44	46	48
American	34	36	38	40	42	44	46	48

Men's shirts

French	36	38	39	41	42	43	44	45
British	14	15	15½	16	16½	17	17½	18
American	14	15	15½	16	16½	17	17½	18

Men's shoes

French	39	40	41	42	43	44	45	46
British	6	7	7½	8	9	10	11	12
American	7	7½	8	8½	9½	10½	11	11½

DIRECTORY

CHILDREN'S CLOTHES

Agnès B
(See p317.)

Baby Dior
30 Ave Montaigne 75008.
Map 10 F1.
01 40 73 54 44.

Benetton
63 Rue de Rennes 75006.
Map 12 E4.
01 45 48 80 92.
One of several branches.

Bonpoint
15 Rue Royale 75008.
Map 5 C5.
01 47 42 52 63.
One of several branches.

Caddie
38 Rue François-1er
75008. **Map** 10 F1.
01 47 20 79 79.

Froment-Leroyer
7 Rue Vavin 75006.
Map 16 E1.
01 43 54 33 15.
One of several branches.

Kenzo
(See p317.)

Six Pieds Trois Pouces
78 Ave de Wagram
75017. **Map** 4 E2.
01 46 22 81 64.
One of several branches.

Sonia Rykiel
(See p317.)

Tartine et Chocolat
105 Rue du Faubourg-St-
Honoré 75008. **Map** 5 B5.
01 45 62 44 04.
One of several branches.

MEN'S CLOTHES

Francesco Smalto
44 Rue François-1er
75008. **Map** 4 F5.
01 47 20 70 63.

Gianni Versace
(See p317.)

Giorgio Armani
(See p317.)

Kenzo
(See p317.)

Lanvin
32 Rue Marbeuf
75008. **Map** 4 F5.
01 53 75 02 20.
One of two branches.

Michel Axael
121 Blvd St-Germain
75006. **Map** 12 E4.
01 43 26 01 96.

Olivier Strelli
7 Blvd Raspail 75007.
Map 12 D4.
01 45 44 77 17.
One of two branches.

Pierre Cardin
27 Ave de Marigny
75008. **Map** 5 B5.
01 42 66 92 25.

Yohji Yamamoto
69 Rue des Sts-Pères
75006. **Map** 12 E4.
01 45 48 22 56.

Yves Saint Laurent
12 Pl St-Sulpice
75006.
Map 12 E4.
01 43 26 84 40.

JEWELERY

Agatha
97 Rue de Rennes 75006.
Map 12 D5.
01 45 48 81 30.
One of several branches.

Boucheron
26 Pl Vendôme 75001.
Map 6 D5.
01 42 61 58 16.

Boutique YSL
32 Rue du Faubourg-St-
Honoré 75008.
Map 5 C5.
01 42 65 01 15.

Cartier
13 Rue de la Paix
75002.
Map 6 D5.
01 42 61 58 56.
One of several branches.

Chanel
(See p317.)

Christian Lacroix
(See p317.)

Daniel Swarovski Boutique
7 Rue Royale 75008.
Map 5 C5.
01 40 17 07 40.

Fugit Amor
11 Rue des Francs-
Bourgeois 75004.
Map 14 D3.
01 42 74 52 37.

Harry Winston
29 Ave Montaigne 75008.
Map 10 F1.
01 47 20 03 09.

Mauboussin
20 Pl Vendôme 75001.
Map 6 D5.
01 44 55 10 00.

Scooter
10 Rue de Turbigo 75001.
Map 13 A1.
01 45 08 50 54.
One of several branches.

SHOES, BAGS, AND BELTS

Bowen
5 Pl des Ternes 75017.
Map 4 E3.
01 42 27 09 23.
One of several branches.

Carel
4 Rue Tronchet 75008.
Map 6 D4.
01 42 66 21 58.
One of several branches.

Charles Jourdan
86 Ave de Champs-Elysées
75008. **Map** 4 F5.
01 45 62 29 28.
One of several branches.

Fenestrier
23 Rue du Cherche-Midi
75006. **Map** 12 D5.
01 42 22 66 02.

Gucci
350 Rue St-Honoré
75001. **Map** 5 C5.
01 42 96 83 27.
One of two branches.

Harel
8 Ave Montaigne 75008.
Map 10 F1.
01 47 23 83 03.
One of two branches.

Hermès
(See p317.)

Jet-Set
85 Rue de Passy
75016.
Map 9 B3.
01 42 88 21 59.
One of two branches.

Longchamp
390 Rue St-Honoré
75001. **Map** 5 C5.
01 42 60 00 00.

Sepcoeur
3 Rue Chambiges
75008.
Map 10 F1.
01 47 20 98 24.

Sidonie Larizzi
8 Rue de Marignan
75008.
Map 4 F5.
01 43 59 38 87.

Zandoli
2 Rue du Parc-Royal
75003. **Map** 14 D3.
01 42 71 90 39.

HATS

Chéri-Bibi
82 Rue de Charonne
75011. **Map** 14 F4.
01 43 70 51 72.

Marie Mercié
56 Rue Tiquetonne
75002. **Map** 13 A1.
01 40 26 60 68.
One of two branches.

Philippe Model
33 Pl du Marché St-
Honoré 75001.
Map 12 D1.
01 42 96 89 02.

LINGERIE

Bas et Haut
182 Blvd St-Germain
75006.
Map 11 C3.
01 45 48 15 88.

La Boîte à Bas
27 Rue Boissy-d'Anglas
75008. **Map** 5 C5.
01 42 66 26 85.
One of several branches.

Capucine Puerari
63 bis Rue des Sts-Pères
75006.
Map 12 D4.
01 42 22 14 09.

Gifts and Souvenirs

Paris offers a wealth of stylish gifts and predictable souvenirs, from designer accessories and perfume to French delicacies and Eiffel Tower paperweights. Shops on the Rue de Rivoli offer a range of inexpensive tourist paraphernalia, or you can go to some of the souvenir shops, such as **Les Drapeaux de France**. Mementos can often be found in museum shops, including reproductions and creations by young designers. Try **Le Musée** or **Le Musée du Louvre**, **Musée d'Orsay** or **Musée Carnavalet**.

PERFUME

Many shops advertise discounted perfume and cosmetics. Some even offer duty-free perfume to shoppers outside the EC, with discounts on the marked prices when you show your passport. They include **Eiffel Shopping** near the Eiffel Tower. The **Sephora** chain has a big selection, or try the department stores for a range of designers' perfumes.

Among the traditional perfumeries is the old-fashioned store **Détaille**. **Parfums Caron** has many scents created at the turn of the century that are unavailable elsewhere, while beautifully packaged perfumes made from natural essences are available at **Annick Goutal**. **Guerlain** has the ultimate in beauty care, and **L'Artisan Parfumeur** specializes in making scents that evoke specific memories and has reissued favorites from the past, including perfume worn at the court of Versailles.

HOUSEHOLD GOODS

France produces some very elegant tableware, though it's rather delicate to carry home. Many shops will arrange to ship crockery overseas. Luxury household goods can be found on the Rue Royale, where many of the best shops are located. They sell such items as rustic china and reproduction and modern silverware. **Lalique**'s Art Nouveau and Art Deco glass sculptures are collected all over the world.

Many of the brand names have showrooms on the Rue de Paradis, and here you may make significant savings on porcelain and crystal. Try **Lumicristal**, which stocks Baccarat, Daum and Limoges crystal, or go to **Baccarat** itself. Baccarat also has a boutique on the Place de la Madeleine. For a unique knife, go to **Peter** and choose a handle made from wood or precious stones. And set the atmosphere for dinner with candles from **Point à la Ligne**'s huge selection.

For fabrics, try **Agnès Comar**. Alternatively, the interior designers **Pierre et Patrick Frey** have an upstairs showroom displaying fabulous fabrics that have been made into cushions, bedspreads and tablecloths.

La Chaise Longue has a selection of well-designed objets for the home, along with fun gift ideas. **Axis** specializes in designer gadgets, while **La Tuile à Loup** carries more traditional French handicrafts.

BOOKS, MAGAZINES AND NEWSPAPERS

Many english and American publications can be found at large magazine stands or at some of the bookshops listed. If French is no obstacle, the weeklies *Pariscope*, *L'Officiel des Spectacles* and *7 à Paris* have the most comprehensive listings of what's going on around town.

Two English-language newspapers exist in France: the *International Herald Tribune*, a daily, and *The European*, a weekly. Two periodicals, the monthly *Boulevard* and the biweekly *France–US Contacts*, are published in English.

Some of the large department stores have a book section *(see* Department Stores *p313)*. There is a large and helpful branch of **WH Smith** on the Rue de Rivoli, or try **Brentano**'s. A small, somewhat disorganized but cozy and convivial bookshop is **Shakespeare and Co**. The American-influenced **Village Voice** has a good literary and intellectual selection of new books, and **The Abbey Bookshop** does the same for secondhand books. **Tea and Tattered Pages** is a British secondhand bookshop.

French-language bookshops include **La Hune**, specializing in art, design, architecture, literature, photography, fashion, theater and movies; **Gibert Joseph**, selling general and educational books; and **Le Divan**, which has strong social science, psychology, literature and poetry sections.

FLOWERS

Some parisian florists, such as **Christian Tortu**, have become very well known, competing for headlines with politicians and fashion designers. **Aquarelle** offers a good selection at reasonable prices; and **Mille Feuilles** is the place to go to in the Marais. *(See also* Specialist Markets *p326.)*

SPECIALTY SHOPS

For cigars, **A La Civette** is perhaps the most beautiful tobacconist in all of Paris and even has humidified shop windows to preserve the merchandise perfectly.

Go to **A l'Olivier** for a selection of exotic oils and vinegar. Or if honey is your favorite condiment, try **La Maison du Miel**, where you can buy all sorts of fine honeys including those made from the flowers of lavender and acacia. You can also buy beeswax soap and candles. **Mariage Frères** has become a cult favorite for its 350 varieties of tea and also its choice of teapots.

Couture fabrics can be purchased from a selection at **Wolff et Descourtis**, and at **Vassilev** you can buy violins old and new, cheap and expensive. For an unusual gift of traditional French card games or tarot cards, go to **Jeux Descartes**.

One of the world's most famous toy shops is **Au Nain Bleu**, while the name **Cassegrain** is synonymous with high-quality stationery and paper products. **Calligrane**

sells a range of designer desk accessories and paper products. If you're looking for a fountain pen, browse through the selection at **Les Crayons de Julie**.

DIRECTORY

SOUVENIR AND MUSEUM SHOPS

Les Drapeaux de France
34 Galerie Montpensier 75001. **Map** 12 E1.
📞 01 40 20 00 11.

Le Musée
(Official National Museum reproductions.) Niveau 2, Forum des Halles, Porte Berger 75001. **Map** 13 A2.
📞 01 40 39 97 91.

Musée Carnavalet
(See p97.)

Musée du Louvre
(See p123.)

Musée d'Orsay
(See p145.)

PERFUME

Annick Goutal
16 Rue de Bellechasse 75007. **Map** 11 C3.
📞 01 45 51 36 13.
One of several branches.

L'Artisan Parfumeur
24 Blvd Raspail 75007.
Map 16 D1.
📞 01 42 22 23 32.
One of several branches.

Détaille
10 Rue St-Lazare 75009.
Map 6 D3.
📞 01 48 78 68 50.

Eiffel Shopping
9 Ave de Suffren 75007.
Map 10 D3.
📞 01 45 66 55 30.

Guerlain
68 Ave des Champs-Elysées 75008. **Map** 4 F5.
📞 01 45 62 11 21.
One of several branches.

Parfums Caron
34 Ave Montaigne 75008.
Map 10 F1.
📞 01 47 23 40 82.

Sephora
50 Rue de Passy 75016.
Map 9 B3.
📞 01 45 20 93 41.
One of several branches.

HOUSEHOLD GOODS

Agnès Comar
7 Ave George V 75008.
Map 10 E1.
📞 01 47 23 33 85.

Axis
14 Rue Lobineau 75006.
Map 12 E4.
📞 01 43 29 66 23.
One of two branches.

Baccarat
11 Pl de la Madeleine 75008. **Map** 5 C5.
📞 01 42 65 36 26.
(See also p231.)

La Chaise Longue
30 Rue Croix-des-Petits-Champs 75001. **Map** 12 F1.
📞 01 42 96 32 14.
One of several branches.

Lalique
11 Rue Royale 75008.
Map 5 C5.
📞 01 53 05 12 12.

Lumicristal
22 bis Rue de Paradis 75010. **Map** 7 B4.
📞 01 47 70 27 97.

Peter
at: Ercuis Raynaud, 9 Rue Royale 75008. **Map** 5 C5.
📞 01 40 07 05 28.

Pierre et Patrick Frey
7 Rue Jacob 75116. **Map** 12 E3.
📞 01 43 26 82 61.

Point à la Ligne
67 Ave Victor Hugo 75116. **Map** 3 B5.
📞 01 45 00 87 01.

La Tuile à Loup
35 Rue Daubenton 75005.
Map 17 B2.
📞 01 47 07 28 90.

BOOKS, MAGAZINES AND NEWSPAPERS

Abbey Bookshop
29 Rue de la Parcheminerie 75005. **Map** 13 A4.
📞 01 46 33 16 24.

Brentano
37 Ave de l'Opéra 75002.
Map 6 E5.
📞 01 42 61 52 50.

Le Divan
203 Rue de la Convention 75015.
Map 12 E3.
📞 01 53 68 90 68.

Gibert Joseph
26 Blvd St-Michel 75006.
Map 12 F5.
📞 01 44 41 88 88.

La Hune
170 Blvd St-Germain 75006. **Map** 12 D4.
📞 01 45 48 35 85.

Shakespeare & Co.
37 Rue de la Bûcherie 75005. **Map** 13 A4.
📞 01 43 26 96 50.

Tea and Tattered Pages
24 Rue Mayet 75006.
Map 15 B1.
📞 01 40 65 94 35.

Village Voice
6 Rue Princesse 75006.
Map 12 E4.
📞 01 46 33 36 47.

WH Smith
248 Rue de Rivoli 75001.
Map 13 A4.
📞 01 44 77 88 99.

FLOWERS

Aquarelle
15 Rue de Rivoli 75004.
Map 13 C3.
📞 01 40 27 91 21.

Christian Tortu
6 Carrefour de l'Odéon 75006. **Map** 12 F4.
📞 01 43 26 02 56.
One of two branches.

Mille Feuilles
2 Rue Rambuteau 75003.
Map 13 C2.
📞 01 42 78 32 93.

SPECIALTY SHOPS

A La Civette
157 Rue St-Honoré 75001. **Map** 12 F2.
📞 01 42 96 04 99.

A L'Olivier
23 Rue de Rivoli 75004.
Map 13 C3.
📞 01 48 04 86 59.

Au Nain Bleu
408 Rue St-Honoré 75008.
Map 5 C5.
📞 01 42 60 39 01.

Calligrane
4–6 Rue du Pont-Louis-Philippe 75004.
Map 13 B4.
📞 01 48 04 31 89.

Cassegrain
422 Rue St-Honoré 75008.
Map 5 C5.
📞 01 42 60 20 08.
One of two branches.

Les Crayons de Julie
17 Rue de Longchamps 75116. **Map** 10 D1.
📞 01 44 05 02 01.

Jeux Descartes
52 Rue des Écoles 75005.
Map 13 A5.
📞 01 43 26 79 83.
One of three branches.

La Maison du Miel
24 Rue Vignon 75009.
Map 6 D5.
📞 01 47 42 26 70.

Mariage Frères
(See p286.)

Vassilev
45 Rue de Rome 75008.
Map 5 C3.
📞 01 45 22 69 03.

Wolff et Descourtis
18 Galerie Vivienne 75002. **Map** 12 F1.
📞 01 42 61 80 84.

Food and Drink

Paris is as famous for food as it is for fashion. Gastronomic treats include foie gras, cold meats from the *charcuterie*, cheese and wine. Certain streets are so overflowing with food shops that you can create a picnic for 20 in no time: try Rue Montorgueil *(see p327)*. Rue Rambuteau, running on either side of the Pompidou Center, has a marvelous row of fish stores, cheese delicatessens and shops selling prepared foods. *(See also* What to Eat and Drink in Paris *pp290–93 and* Light Meals and Snacks *pp310–11.)*

BREAD AND CAKES

There is a vast range of breads and pastries in France's capital. The *baguette* is often translated "French bread"; a *bâtard* is similar but thicker, while a *ficelle* is thinner. A *fougasse* is a crusty flat loaf made from *baguette* dough, often filled with onions, herbs or spices. Since most French bread contains no fat it goes stale quickly: the sooner you eat it, the better.

The croissant can be bought *ordinaire* or *au beurre* – the latter is flakier and more buttery. *Pain au chocolat* is a chocolate-filled pastry eaten for breakfast, and *chausson aux pommes* is filled with apples. There are also pear, plum and rhubarb variations.

L'établissement Poilâne sells perhaps the only bread in Paris known by the name of its baker, and his excellent, hearty whole-wheat loaves are tremendously popular. There are long lines on the weekend and around 4pm, when a fresh batch comes out of the oven.

Many think **Ganachaud** bakes the best bread in Paris. Thirty different kinds, including ingredients such as walnuts and fruit, are made in the old-fashioned ovens.

Although **Les Panetons** is part of a larger chain, it is one of the best of its kind, with a broad range of breads. Favorites include five-grain bread, sesame rolls, and *mouchoir aux pommes*, a variation on the traditional *chausson*.

Many of the Jewish delicatessens have the best ryes and the only pumpernickels in town. **Jo Goldenberg's** is the best known. **Stohrer** was founded by the pastry makers to Louis XV in 1730 and still makes some of the capital's best croissants.

Le Moulin de la Vierge uses a wood fire to make organic breads and rich pound cakes. **Maison Meli** is second only to **Max Poilâne** in the Montparnasse area with *baguettes*, *fougasses*, cakes and pastries. **J. L. Poujauran** is known for his black-olive bread and nut-and-raisin wholegrain breads.

CHOCOLATE

Like all food in France, chocolate is to be savored. **Christian Constant's** low-sugar creations are made with pure cocoa and are known to connoisseurs. **Dalloyau** makes all types of chocolate and is not too expensive (it's also known for its pâtisserie and cold meats). **Fauchon** is world famous for its luxury food products. Its chocolates are excellent, as is the pâtisserie. **Lenôtre** makes classic truffles and pralines. Robert Linxe at **La Maison du Chocolat** is constantly inventing fresh, rich chocolates with mouthwatering exotic ingredients. **Richart** boasts beautifully presented and hugely expensive chocolates, which are usually coated with dark chocolate or filled with delicious liqueur.

CHARCUTERIE AND FOIE GRAS

Charcuteries often sell cheese, snails, truffles, smoked salmon, caviar and wine as well as cold meats. **Fauchon** has a good grocery, as does the basement of the department store **Au Bon Marché**. **Hédiard** is a luxury shop similar to Fauchon, and **Maison de la Truffe** sells foie gras and sausages as well as truffles. For Beluga caviar, Georgian tea and Russian vodka, go to **Petrossian**.

The Lyon and Auvergne regions of France are the best known for their *charcuterie*. Examples can be bought from **Terrier. Aux Vrais Produits d'Auvergne** has a number of outlets where you can stock up on dried and fresh sausages and delicious Cantal cheese (rather like Cheddar). **Pou** is a sparklingly clean and popular shop selling *pâté en croute* (pâté baked in pastry), *boudins* (black and white puddings), Lyonnais sausages, ham and foie gras. Just off the Champs-Elysées, **Vignon** has superb foie gras and Lyonnais sausages as well as popular prepared foods.

Together with truffles and caviar, foie gras is the ultimate in gourmet food. The quality (and price) depends upon the percentage of liver used. Though most specialist food shops sell foie gras, you can be sure of quality at **Comtesse du Barry** which has six outlets in Paris. **Divay** is relatively inexpensive and will ship overseas. **Labeyrie** has a range of beautifully packaged foie gras suitable for giving as presents.

CHEESE

Although Camembert is undoubtedly a favorite, there is an overwhelming range of cheeses available. A friendly *fromager* will help you choose. **Marie-Anne Cantin** is one of the leading figures in the fight to protect traditional production methods, and her fine cheeses are available from the shop that she inherited from her father. Some say that **Alléosse** is the best cheese delicatessen in Paris: the facade may be in need of renovation, but all the cheeses are made using traditional methods. **Maison du Fromage** sells farm-made cheeses, many of which are in danger of becoming extinct, including a rare and delicious truffle Brie (when in season). **Boursault** is one of the best stores in Paris for all types of cheese: the *chèvre* (goat's cheese) is particularly good, and outside on the pavement the daily specials are offered at remarkably reasonable prices. **Barthelemy** in the Rue de Grenelle has exceptional Roquefort.

WINE

THE CHAIN store that has practically cornered the market is **Nicolas**: there's a branch in every neighborhood with a range of wine for all pockets. As a rule, the salespeople are knowledgeable and helpful. The stars shop at **L'Arbre à Vin**, **Caves Retrou**, or try the charming **Legrand** for a carefully chosen

selection. **Caves Taillevent** is worth a sightseeing tour. It is an enormous, overwhelming cellar with some of the most expensive wine. **Bernard Péret** has a vast selection and can advise you on all of it. The beautiful **Ryst-Dupeyron** displays ports, whiskies, wines and Monsieur Ryst's own Armagnac. He will even personalize a bottle for that very special occasion.

DIRECTORY

BREAD AND CAKES

Ganachaud
150–4 Rue de Ménilmontant 75020.
[01 46 36 13 82.

J L Poujauran
20 Rue Jean-Nicot 75007.
Map 10 F2.
[01 47 05 80 88.

Jo Goldenberg
7 Rue des Rosiers 75004.
Map 13 C3.
[01 48 87 20 16.

L'établissement Poilâne
8 Rue du Cherche-Midi 75006. **Map** 12 D4.
[01 45 48 42 59.

Maison Meli
4 Pl Constantin Brancusi 75014. **Map** 15 C3.
[01 43 21 76 18.

Max Poilâne
29 Rue de l'Ouest 75014.
Map 15 B3.
[01 43 27 24 91.

Le Moulin de la Vierge
105 Rue Vercingétorix 75014. **Map** 15 A4.
[01 45 43 09 84.

Les Panetons
113 Rue Mouffetard 75005. **Map** 17 B2.
[01 47 07 12 08.

Stohrer
51 Rue Montorgueil 75002. **Map** 13 A1.
[01 42 33 38 20.

CHOCOLATE

Christian Constant
37 Rue d'Assas 75006.
Map 16 E1.
[01 53 63 15 15.

Dalloyau
99–101 Rue du Faubourg-St-Honoré 75008.
Map 5 B5.
[01 42 99 90 00.

Fauchon
26 Pl de la Madeleine 75008.
Map 5 C5.
[01 47 42 60 11.

Lenôtre
15 Blvd de Courcelles 75008.
Map 5 B2.
[01 45 63 87 63.

La Maison du Chocolat
225 Rue du Faubourg-St-Honoré 75008.
Map 4 E3.
[01 42 27 39 44.

Richart
258 Blvd St-Germain 75007.
Map 11 C2.
[01 45 55 66 00.

CHARCUTERIE AND FOIE GRAS

Au Bon Marché
(See p313.)

Aux Vrais Produits d'Auvergne
98 Rue Montorgueil 75002. **Map** 13 A1.
[01 42 36 28 99.

Comtesse du Barry
1 Rue de Sèvres 75006.
Map 12 D4.
[01 45 48 32 04.

Divay
4 rue Bayen 75017.
Map 4 D2.
[01 43 80 16 97.

Fauchon
26 Pl Madeleine 75008.
Map 5 C5.
[01 47 42 60 11.

Hédiard
21 Pl de la Madeleine 75008.
Map 5 C5.
[01 43 12 88 75.

Labeyrie
6 Rue Montmartre 75001.
Map 13 A1.
[01 45 08 95 26.

Maison de la Truffe
19 Pl de la Madeleine 75008.
Map 5 C5.
[01 42 65 53 22.

Petrossian
18 Blvd Latour-Maubourg 75007. **Map** 11 A2.
[01 44 11 32 22.

Pou
16 Ave des Ternes 75017.
Map 4 D3.
[01 43 80 19 24.

Terrier
58 Rue des Martyrs 75009.
Map 6 F2.
[01 48 78 96 45.

Vignon
14 Rue Marbeuf 75008.
Map 4 F5.
[01 47 20 24 26.

CHEESE

Alléosse
13 Rue Poncelet 75017. **Map** 4 E3.
[01 46 22 50 45.

Barthelemy
51 Rue de Grenelle 75007.
Map 12 D4.
[01 45 48 56 75.

Boursault
71 Ave du Général-Leclerc 75014. **Map** 16 D5.
[01 43 27 93 30.

Maison du Fromage
62 Rue de Sèvres 75007.
Map 11 C5.
[01 47 34 33 45.

Marie-Anne Cantin
12 Rue du Champ-de-Mars 75007.
Map 10 F3.
[01 45 50 43 94.

WINE

L'Arbre à Vin, Caves Retrou
2 Rue du Rendez-Vous 75012.
[01 43 46 81 10.

Bernard Péret
6 Rue Daguerre 75014.
Map 16 D4.
[01 43 22 08 64.

Caves Taillevent
199 Rue du Faubourg-St-Honoré 75008.
Map 4 F3.
[01 45 61 14 09.

Legrand
1 Rue de la Banque 75002.
Map 12 F1.
[01 42 60 07 12.

Nicolas
31 Pl de la Madeleine 75008. **Map** 5 C5.
[01 42 68 00 16.

Ryst-Dupeyron
79 Rue du Bac 75007.
Map 12 D3.
[01 45 48 80 93.

Art and Antiques

IN PARIS YOU CAN BUY art and antiques either from shops and galleries with established reputations or from flea markets and avant-garde galleries. Many of the prestigious antiques shops and galleries are located around the Rue du Faubourg St-Honoré and are worth a visit even if you can't afford to buy. On the Left Bank is the Carré Rive Gauche, an organization of 30 antiques dealers. You will need a certificate of authenticity to export designated objets d'art over 20 years old, and any goods over a century old worth more than F1,000,000, in order to avoid paying duty. Seek professional advice from one of the large antiques shops and declare the item at Customs if you are in any doubt.

EXPORTING

THE MINISTRY of Culture designates objets d'art. Export licenses are available from the **Centre Français du Commerce Extérieur**. Full information appears in the *Bulletin Officiel des Douanes*, available from the **Service des Commandes**.

MODERN CRAFTS AND FURNITURE

ONE IF THE BEST places for furniture and objetsd'art by up-and-coming designers is **Avant-Scène** in the Latin Qyarter. If you enjoy beautifully designed modern furniture for the office, then **Havvorth** is well worth a visit. **Le Viaduc des Arts** is a railway viaduct, each arch of which has been transformed into a shop front and workshop space. Stroll along this street for a great show of contemporary metal-work, tapestry, sculpture, ceramics and more.

ANTIQUES AND OBJETS D'ART

IF YOU WISH to buy antiques, you will enjoy a stroll around the areas that boast many galleries: in Le Carré Rive Gauche around Quai Malaquais, try **L'Arc en Seine** and **Anne-Sophie Duval** for Art Nouveau and Art Deco.

Close to the Louvre, the Louvre des Antiquaires *(see p120)* sells expensive, quality furniture. On the Rue due Faubourg-St-Honoré you will find **Didier Aaran**, expert on furniture of the 17th and 18th centuries. **Village St-Paul** is the most charming group of antiques shops and is open on Sundays.

For antique silverware, **Jean-Pierre de Castro**, is definately worth a visit. **La Calinière** has an excellent range of objets d'art and old lighting fixtures. European glassware from the 19th century to the 1960s is sold at **Verreglass**.

REPRODUCTIONS, POSTERS AND PRINTS

A BEAUTIFUL contemporary art gallery called **Artcurial** has one of the best selections of international art periodicals, books and prints. On the Boulevard St-Germain, **La Hune** is a popular book store, particularly for art publications. The museum book stores, especially those in the Musée d'Art Moderne *(see p201)*, Louvre *(see p123)*, Musée d'Orsay *(see p145)* and Pompidou Center *(see p111)* are good places for recent art books and posters.

Galerie Documents sells original antique posters of all sorts. **A L'Image du Grenier sur L'Eau** is a place where you can easily take an entire afternoon browsing through a vast number of old postcards as well as posters and prints. Alternatively, walk along the Seine and leaf through the secondhand books sold at the stalls along its banks.

ART GALLERIES

ESTABLISHED art galleries are located on or around the Avenue Montaigne. The **Louise Leiris** gallery was founded by D. H. Kahnweiler, the dealer who "discovered" both Pablo Picasso and Georges Braque. The gallery still shows Cubist masterpieces.

Artcurial holds many exhibitions and has an impressive permanent collection of 20th-century works, including works by Joan Miró, Max Ernst, Picasso and Alberto Giacometti. **Lelong** is devoted to contemporary artists.

On the Left Bank, **Adrian Maeght** has a tremendous stock of paintings; he also publishes fine art books. **Galerie 1900–2000** organizes very good retrospective exhibitions, and **Daniel Gervis** has a wide selection of abstract prints, engravings and lithographs. **Dina Vierny** is a bastion of Modernism, founded by one of the sculptor Aristide Maillol's models.

Some of the newest additions to the art gallery world are in the Marais and the Bastille and display mainly avant-garde, contemporary works. In the Marais try **Yvon Lambert**, **Daniel Templon** (specializing in American art), **Zabriskie** and **Alain Blondel**, and in the Bastille, **Levignes-Bastille** and **L. et M. Durand-Dessert**, also a fashionable place to buy catalogs on new artists.

AUCTIONS AND AUCTION HOUSES

THE GREAT Paris auction center, in operation since 1858, is **Drouot-Richelieu** *(see p216)*. Bidding can be intimidating since most of it is done by dealers. If your French is not fluent then take a French friend – the high-speed auctioneer's patter is not easy to decipher in a foreign language. *La Gazette de L'Hôtel Drouot* tells you what auctions are coming up and when. Drouot-Richelieu has its own auction catalog available as well.

The house accepts only cash and French checks but there is an exchange desk in house. A 10% to 15% commission to the house is charged, so add it on to any price you hear. You may view from 11am to 6pm on the day before the sale, and from 11am to noon on the morning of the sale. Items considered not good enough for the main house are sold at **Drouot-Nord**. Here auctions take place from 9am to noon, and viewing is just 5 minutes before the sales begin. The most prestigious auctions are held at **Drouot-Montaigne**.

The **Crédit Municipal** holds around 12 auctions a month, and almost all the items on sale are small objects and furs donated by rich Parisians. The rules follow those at Drouot. Information about these auctions can also be found in *La Gazette de L'Hôtel Drouot*.

Service des Domaines sells all sorts of odds and ends, and here you can still find bargains. Many of the wares come from bailiffs and from Customs and Excise confiscations. Viewing is from 10am to 11:30am on the day of the sale.

DIRECTORY

EXPORTING

Centre Français du Commerce Extérieur
10 Ave d'Iéna 75016. **Map** 10 D1. 01 40 73 30 00.

Service des Commandes
SEDEC, 10 Ave Iéna, BP 2010-16, 75761 Paris Cedex 16.
01 40 73 39 25.

MODERN CRAFTS AND FURNITURE

Avant-Scène
4 Pl de l'Odéon 75006.
Map 12 F5.
01 46 33 12 40.

Havvorth
166 Rue du Faubourg-St-Honoré 75008.
Map 5 A4.
01 44 95 00 40.

Le Viaduc des Arts
9–129 Ave Daumesnil 750012.
Map 14 F5.
Headquarters 29–37 Ave Daumesnil 750012.
01 46 28 11 11.

ANTIQUES AND OBJETS D'ART

Anne-Sophie Duval
5 Quai Malaquais 75006.
Map 12 E3.
01 43 54 51 16.

L'Arc en Seine
31 Rue de Seine 75006.
Map 12 E3.
01 43 29 11 02.

Didier Aaron
118 Rue du Faubourg-St-Honoré 75008.
Map 5 C5.
01 47 42 47 34.

Village St-Paul
Between the Quai des Célestins, the Rue St-Paul and the Rue Charlemagne 75004.
Map 13 C4.

La Calinière
68 Rue Vieille-du-Temple 75003.
Map 13 C3.
01 42 77 40 46.

Jean-Pierre de Castro
17 Rue des Francs-Bourgeois 75004.
Map 14 D3.
01 42 72 04 00.

Verreglass
32 Rue de Charonne 75011. **Map** 14 F4.
01 48 05 78 43.

REPRODUCTIONS, POSTERS, PRINTS

A L'Image du Grenier sur L'Eau
45 Rue des Francs-Bourgeois 75004.
Map 13 C3.
01 42 71 02 31.

Artcurial
9 Ave Matignon 75008.
Map 5 A5.
01 42 99 16 16.

Galerie Documents
53 Rue de Seine 75006.
Map 12 E4.
01 43 54 50 68.

La Hune
(See p321.)

L. et M. Durand-Dessert
28 Rue de Lappe 75011.
Map 14 F4.
01 48 06 92 23.

ART GALLERIES

Adrian Maeght
42 Rue du Bac 75007.
Map 12 D3.
01 45 48 45 15.

Alain Blondel
4 Rue Aubry-Le-Boucher 75004.
Map 13 B2.
01 42 78 66 67.
One of two galleries.

Daniel Gervis
14 Rue de Grenelle 75007.
Map 12 D4.
01 45 44 41 90.

Daniel Templon
30 Rue Beaubourg 75003.
Map 13 B1.
01 42 72 14 10.
One of two galleries.

Dina Vierny
36 Rue Jacob 75006.
Map 12 E3.
01 42 60 23 18.

Galerie 1900–2000
8 Rue Bonaparte 75006.
Map 12 E3.
01 43 25 84 20.

Lelong
13–14 Rue de Téhéran 75008.
Map 5 A3.
01 45 63 13 19.

Levignes-Bastille
27 Rue de Charonne 75011.
Map 14 F4.
01 47 00 88 18.

Louise Leiris
47 Rue de Monceau 75008.
Map 5 A3.
01 45 63 28 85.

Yvon Lambert
108 Rue Vieille-du-Temple 75003.
Map 14 D2.
01 42 71 09 33.

Zabriskie
37 Rue Quincampoix 75004. **Map** 13 B2.
01 42 72 35 47.

AUCTION HOUSES

Crédit Municipal
55 Rue des Francs-Bourgeois 75004. **Map** 13 C3.
01 44 61 64 00.

Drouot-Montaigne
15 Ave Montaigne 75008.
Map 10 F1.
01 48 00 20 80.

Drouot-Nord
64 Rue Doudeauville 75018.
01 48 00 20 99.

Drouot-Richelieu
9 Rue Drouot 75009.
Map 6 F4.
01 48 00 20 20.

Service des Domaines
15–17 Rue Scribe 75009.
Map 6 D4.
01 44 94 78 78.

Markets

FOR EYE-CATCHING displays of wonderful food or a lively shopping atmosphere, there is no better place than a Paris market. There are large covered food markets; markets where stalls change regularly; and permanent street markets with a mixture of shops and stalls that are open on a daily basis. Each has its own personality reflecting the area in which it is located. Following is a list of some of the more famous markets, with approximate opening times. For a complete list of markets, contact the Paris Office du Tourisme (see p274). And while you're enjoying browsing around the stalls, remember to keep an eye on your money – and be prepared to bargain to get just the right price.

FRUIT-AND-VEGETABLE MARKETS

THE FRENCH treat food with the kind of reverence usually reserved for religion. Most still shop on a daily basis to be sure of buying the freshest produce possible, so food markets tend to be busy. The majority of fruit-and-vegetable markets are open from around 8am to 1pm and from 4 to 7pm on Tuesday to Saturday and from 9am to 1pm on Sunday.

Watch what you buy in the food markets or you may find you purchase a kilo of fruit or vegetables from a marvelous display only to discover later that all the produce hidden underneath is rotten. To avoid this, try to buy produce loose rather than in boxes. Most outdoor stalls prefer to serve you rather than allow you to help yourself, but you can point to the individual fruit and vegetables of your choice. A little language is useful for specifying *pas trop mûr* (not too ripe) or *pour manger ce soir* (to be eaten tonight). If you go to the same market every day, you'll become familiar to the stall holders and are far less likely to be cheated. You will also get to know the stalls worth buying from and the produce worth buying. Seasonal fruit and vegetables are, of course, usually a good buy, tending to be fresher and cheaper than at other times of the year. Finally, it's best to go early in the day, when the food is freshest and the lines are shortest.

FLEA MARKETS

IT'S OFTEN SAID that you can no longer find bargains at the Paris flea markets. Though for the most part this is true, it's still worth going to flea markets for the sheer fun of browsing. And bear in mind that the price quoted is probably not the price that you are expected to pay – it's generally assumed that you will bargain. Most flea markets are located on the boundaries of the city. Whether you pick up any real bargains probably has as much to do with luck as with judgment. Often the sellers themselves have little or no idea of the true value of the goods they are selling – which can work either for or against you. The biggest and most famous Paris flea market, incorporating a number of smaller markets, is the Marché aux Puces de St-Ouen.

SPECIALTY MARKETS

Try the Marché aux Fleurs Madeleine in the Opéra, the Marché aux Fleurs on the Ile de la Cité (see p81) or the Marché aux Fleurs Ternes in the Champs-Elysées district for fresh flowers. On the Ile de la Cité on Sundays, the Marché aux Oiseaux bird market replaces the flower market. Stamp collectors will enjoy the permanent Marché aux Timbres, where you can also buy old postcards. In Montmartre, the Marché St-Pierre, famous for cheap fabrics, is patronized by professional designers.

Marché d'Aligre

(See p233.)

Reminiscent of a Moroccan bazaar, this must be the cheapest and liveliest market in the city. Here traders hawk such ingredients as North African olives, groundnuts and hot peppers, and there are even a few halal – traditional Muslim butchers. The noise reaches a crescendo on weekends, when the cries of the market boys mingle with those of militants of all political persuasions in the Place d'Aligre. The stalls on the square sell mostly secondhand clothes and bric-à-brac. This is a less affluent area of town, with few tourists and many Parisians. There is also a covered market with a good cheese delicatessen, Maison du Fromage-Radenac (see pp322–3).

Rue Cler

(See p190.)

This high-class pedestrianized food market is patronized mainly by the politicians and business people who live and work in the vicinity. The produce is excellent: there's a Breton delicatessen and some good cheese delicatessens.

Marché Enfant Rouges

39 Rue de Bretagne 75003. **Map** 14 D2. **M** Temple, Filles-du-Calvaire. **Open** 8am–1pm & 4–7pm Tue–Sat, 9am–1pm Sun.

This long-established charming fruit-and-vegetable market on the Rue de Bretagne is part-covered, part-outdoors and dates from 1620. On Sunday mornings, street singers and accordionists sometimes enliven the proceedings.

Marché aux Fleurs Madeleine

Pl de la Madeleine 75008. **Map** 5 C5. **M** Madeleine. **Open** 8am–7:30pm Tue–Sun.

Marché aux Fleurs Ternes

Pl des Ternes 75008. **Map** 4 E3. **M** Ternes. **Open** 8am–1pm & 2–7:30pm Tue–Sat, 8am–1pm Sun.

Marché St-Pierre

Pl St-Pierre 75018. **Map** 6 F1. **M** Anvers. **Open** 9am–6pm Mon–Sat.

Marché aux Timbres

Cour Marigny 75008. **Map** 5 B5. **M** Champs-Elysées. **Open** 10am–sunset Thu, Sun & public hols.

Marché St-Germain

Rue Mabillon and Rue Lobineau
75005. **Map** 12 E4. **M** *Mabillon.*
Open *8am–1pm & 4–7pm Tue–Sat,
9am–1pm Sun.*

St-Germain is one of the few covered markets left in Paris and has been enhanced by renovation. Here you can buy Italian, Mexican, Greek, Asian and organic produce and goods.

Rue Lepic

75018. **Map** 6 F1. **M** *Blanche,
Lamarck-Caulaincourt.* **Open**
8am–1pm Tue–Sun.

The Rue Lepic fruit-and-vegetable market is situated conveniently close to the sights of Montmartre in this refreshingly unspoiled winding old quarry road. The market is at its liveliest on weekends.

Rue de Lévis

Blvd des Batignolles 75017. **Map** 5 B2.
M *Villiers.* **Open** *8am–1pm & 4–7pm
Tue–Sat, 9am–1pm Sun.*

Rue de Lévis is a bustling popular food market near the Parc Monceau, with a number of good pâtisseries, an excellent cheese delicatessen and a charcuterie that is known for its savory pies. The part of the street that leads to the Rue Cardinet has vendors selling haberdashery and fabrics.

Rue Montorgueil

75001 & 75002. **Map** 13 A1.
M *Les Halles.* **Open** *8am–1pm &
4–7pm Tue–Sat, 9am–1pm Sun.*

The Rue Montorgueil is what remains of the old Les Halles market. The street has now been repaved and restored to its former glory. Here you can buy exotic fruit and vegetables, like green bananas and yams from the market gardeners' stalls, or sample offerings from the delicatessens or from the Stohrer pastry shop *(see pp322–3).* Alternatively, pick up some of the pretty Moroccan pottery for sale.

Rue Mouffetard

(See p166.)

Rue Mouffetard is one of the oldest market streets in Paris. Although it has become touristy and somewhat overpriced, it's still a charming winding street full of quality food products. It's worth lining up for the freshly made bread at Les Panetons bakery at No. 113 *(see pp322–3).* There is also a lively African market down the nearby side street of Rue Daubenton.

Rue Poncelet

75017. **Map** 4 E3. **M** *Ternes.*
Open *8am–12:30pm & 4–7:30pm
Tue–Sat, 8am–12:30pm Sun.*

The Rue Poncelet food market is situated away from the main tourist areas of Paris but is worth visiting for its authentic French atmosphere. Choose from the many bakeries, pâtisseries and charcuteries, or enjoy authentic Auvergne specialties from Aux Fermes d'Auvergnes.

Marché de la Porte de Vanves

Ave Georges-Lafenestre & Ave Marc-Sangnier 75014. **M** *Porte-de-Vanves.*
Open *8am– 6:30pm Sat & Sun.*

Porte de Vanves is a small market selling good-quality bric-à-brac and junk, as well as some second-hand furniture. It's best to get to the market early on Saturday morning for the best choice of wares. Artists exhibit nearby in the Place des Artistes.

Marché Président-Wilson

Situated in Ave du Président-Wilson, between Pl d'Iéna & Rue Debrousse 75016. **Map** 10 D1. **M** *Alma-Marceau.*
Open *7am–1pm Wed & Sat.*

This very chic food market on Avenue Président-Wilson is close to the Musée d'Art Moderne and the Palais Galliera fashion museum. It has become important because there are no other food shops nearby. It is best for meat.

Marché aux Puces de Montreuil

Porte de Montreuil, 93 Montreuil 75020. **M** *Porte-de-Montreuil.*
Open *8am–6pm Sat, Sun & Mon.*

Go early to the Porte de Montreuil flea market, where the substantial secondhand clothes section attracts many young people. Much of the market is given over to African salespeople hawking hardware, and there's also a variety of bric-à-brac and an exotic spices stand.

Marché aux Puces de St-Ouen

(See p231.)

This is the most well known, the most crowded and the most expensive of all the flea markets, situated on the northern outskirts of the city. Here you'll find a range of markets, locals dealing from their car trunks and a number of extremely large buildings packed

with stalls. Some of them are very upscale; others sell junk. The flea market is a 10- to 15-minute walk from Clignancourt metro – don't be put off by the somewhat run-down Marché Malik that you have to pass through on your way from the metro. A *Guide des Puces* (guide to the flea markets) can be obtained from the information kiosk in the Marché Biron on the Rue des Rosiers. The more exclusive markets will take credit cards and arrange for goods to be shipped. New stock arrives on Friday, when professionals come from all over the world to sweep up the best buys.

Among the markets here, the Marché Jules Vallès is good for turn-of-the-century objets d'art. Marché Paul-Bert is more expensive, but charming. Items on sale include furniture, books and prints. Both markets deal in second-hand goods rather than antiques.

In a different league, Marché Biron sells elegant, expensive antique furniture of very high quality. Marché Vernaison is the oldest and biggest market, good for such collectibles as jewelry, as well as lamps and clothes. No information about the Marché aux Puces is complete without mentioning Chez Louisette in the Vernaison market. This café is always full of locals enjoying the home cooking and the well-intentioned renditions of Edith Piaf songs. Marché Cambo is a fairly small market with beautifully displayed antique furniture. Marché Serpette is popular with the dealers: everything sold here is in mint condition.

Marché Raspail

Situated on Blvd Raspail between Rue du Cherche-Midi & Rue de Rennes 75006. **Map** 12 D5. **M** *Rennes.*
Open *7am–1pm Tue, Fri & Sun.*

The Raspail market sells typical French groceries as well as Portuguese produce on Tuesdays and Fridays. But Sunday is the day for which it's famous, when health-conscious Parisians turn up in droves for the organically grown produce. Marché Raspail is not a cheap market, but it is very good.

Rue de Seine and Rue de Buci

75006. **Map** 12 E4. **M** *Odéon.*
Open *8am–1pm & 4–7pm Tue–Sat,
9am–1pm Sun.*

The stalls set along the Rue de Seine and the Rue de Buci are expensive and crowded but sell quality fruit and vegetables. There is also a large florist's and two excellent pâtisseries.

ENTERTAINMENT IN PARIS

W HETHER YOUR preference is for classical drama or cabaret, a nightclub show or a ballet, opera or jazz, watching a movie or dancing the night away, Paris has it all. There is plenty of free entertainment as well, from street performers outside the Pompidou Center to street musicians in the metros and all over town.

Parisians themselves like nothing better than strolling along the boulevards or sitting at pavement café tables and nursing a drink as they watch the world go by. If, however, you're looking for the ultimate "Gay Paree" experience, there are always the showgirls at the celebrated nightclubs.

For fans of spectator sports there is tennis, the Tour de France or horse racing. Recreation centers and gyms cater to the more active. And for those disposed either way, there's always the popular type of ball played in Paris: *pétanque*.

PRACTICAL INFORMATION

F OR THE VISITOR in Paris there is no shortage of information about what's being offered in the city. The **Office du Tourisme et des Congrés de Paris** is the city's main tourism data distribution center for leaflets and schedules of events. There are branches in the main railroad terminals and at the Eiffel Tower.

The office runs a recorded telephone information service giving details of free concerts and exhibitions plus information on transportation and events. Your hotel reception desk or concierge should also be able to help. They usually keep a supply of free brochures and leaflets and may even make reservations for you.

BOOKING TICKETS

D EPENDING ON the event, tickets can often be bought at the door, but for blockbuster concerts it is wiser, and often necessary, to get advance tickets. For most major events, including some classical music concerts and museum shows, tickets can be purchased at the **FNAC** chain or **Virgin Megastore**.

For dance, opera and theater performances, very inexpensive tickets are often available up to the last minute. If they are marked *sans visibilité*, you will be able to see the stage only partially, perhaps not at all. Often, obliging ushers will put you in a better seat, depending on their

Ballerina of the Ballet de l'Opéra

Nightclubbing in Paris

availability, but don't forget to tip them a few francs.

Theater box offices are open daily from approximately 11am to 7pm (times vary). Most box offices accept credit card reservations by telephone or in person. But you may have to arrive early to pick up your tickets if you reserved by telephone, or they may be sold to someone else at the last minute.

LISTINGS MAGAZINES

Paris has several good listings magazines. Among them are *Pariscope,* the simplest to use; *L'Officiel des Spectacles;* and *Sept à Paris.* They are published every Wednesday and are available at all newsstands. *Le Figaro* also has a good listings section on Wednesdays. *Boulevard Europe* is published every three months in English and is available at newsstands or **W.H. Smith** *(see p329).*

A concert at the Opéra de Paris Garnier *(see p335)*

Buying tickets at the box office of a comedy club

You can always turn up at the box office just before the performance in case there are unclaimed or returned tickets.

LAST-MINUTE TICKETS

IF YOU MUST HAVE a ticket to a sold-out performance, do as the French do: stand at the entrance with a sign that says *cherche une place* (or *deux*, etc.). Many people have an extra ticket to sell. However, make sure you don't buy a counterfeit or overpriced one.

DISCOUNT TICKETS

HALF-PRICE TICKETS to current plays are sold on the day of performance at Kiosque Théâtre. Credit cards are not accepted, and there is a small handling charge per ticket.

Pétanque players *(see p342)*

There is a booth on the Place de la Madeleine *(see p214)*, open from 12:30 to 8pm, on Tuesday to Sunday, and in the RER station at Châtelet-Les Halles *(see p105)*, open from 12:30 to 6pm on Tuesday to Saturday.

DISABLED VISITORS' FACILITIES

WHERE FACILITIES do exist, they are either very good or dreadful. Many venues have wheelchair space, but always phone in advance to make sure it is properly equipped. As for as public transportation, the metro, with its long stairways, is completely inaccessible to wheelchairs, as are the buses.

NIGHT TRANSPORTATION

THE PARIS METRO *(see pp 368– 9)* stops running at 1am. The last train leaves the end station at 12:45am, but to be sure of making any connections, be at the station by 12:30am at the latest.

After that time, the only choices are to take night buses, which run only once an hour and do not cover the whole city, or to take a taxi.

Taxis can be hailed on the street or found at a taxi rank, but at peak hours (and at 2am, when many bars close), they can be difficult to find.

USEFUL ADDRESSES

FNAC
Forum des Halles, 1 Rue Pierre-Lescot
75001. **Map** 13 A2. (*01 40 41 40 00*.

The Grand Rex theater *(see p340)*

FNAC
26 Ave des Ternes 75017.
Map 4 D3. (*01 44 09 18 00*.
Plus other branches.

Office du Tourisme et des Congrès de Paris
127 Ave des Champs-Elysées 75008.
Map 4 E4.
(*08 36 68 31 12*.

Virgin Megastore
52–60 Ave des Champs-Elysées
75008. **Map** 4 F5.
(*01 49 53 50 00*.

W H Smith
248 Rue de Rivoli 75001.
Map 11 C1.
(*01 44 77 88 99*.

Theater

FROM THE GRANDEUR OF the Comédie Française to slap-stick farce and avant-garde drama, theater is flourishing in Paris. The city also has a long tradition of playing host to visiting companies, and today it attracts many foreign productions, often in their original languages.

Theaters are scattered at a multiplicity of locations throughout the city, and the theater season runs from September to July; national theaters close during August, but many commercial ones stay open. For complete listings of what's playing during your stay, read *Pariscope* or *L'Officiel des Spectacles* (see p328).

NATIONAL THEATERS

FOUNDED IN 1680 by royal decree, the **Comédie-Française** (see p120), with its strict conventions regarding the style of acting and interpretation, is the bastion of French theater. Its aim is to keep classical drama in the public eye and also to perform works by the best modern playwrights.

The Comédie-Française is the oldest national theater in the world and one of the few institutions of *ancien-régime* France to have survived the Revolution. It settled into its present home after players occupied the Palais-Royal next door during the Revolution. It was completely refurbished in the 1970s, and now the traditionally styled red velvet auditorium has a vast stage equipped with the latest technology.

The majority of the repertoire is classical, dominated by Corneille, Racine and Molière, followed by second strings Marivaux, Alfred de Musset and Victor Hugo. The company also performs modern plays by French and foreign playwrights.

The **Odéon Théâtre de l'Europe**, also known as the Théâtre National de l'Odéon (see p140), was at one time the second theater of the Comédie-Française. It now specializes in performing plays from other countries in their original languages.

Next door, the **Petit Odéon** features new plays and those in foreign languages.

The **Théâtre National de Chaillot** is a huge underground auditorium in the Art Deco Palais de Chaillot (see p198). It stages lively productions of mainstream European classics and, occasionally, musical revues. The theater also contains a studio, the **Salle Gémier,** for more experimental work.

The **Théâtre National de la Colline** has two performance spaces and specializes in contemporary dramas.

FARTHER AFIELD

A THRIVING multitheater complex in the Bois de Vincennes, the **Cartoucherie** (see p246), houses five avant-garde theaters, including the internationally famous **Théâtre du Soleil.**

INDEPENDENT THEATERS

AMONG THE most important of the serious independents are the **Comédie des Champs-Elysées**; the **Hébertot**; and the **Atelier**, which aims to be experimental. Other notable theaters include the **Oeuvre**, for excellent modern French drama; the **Montparnasse**; and the **Antoine-Simone Berriau**, which pioneered the use of realism on stage. The **Madeleine** maintains consistently high standards, and the **Huchette** specializes in Ionesco plays. The avant-garde producer/director Peter Brook has a loyal following at the **Bouffes-du-Nord.**

For over a hundred years, the **Palais Royal** has been the temple of risqué farce. With fewer French Feydeau-style farce writers these days, translations of English and American sex comedies are filling the gap. The **Bouffes-Parisiens**, **La Bruyère,** the **Michel** and the **St-Georges** also mount productions, and the **Gymnase-Marie Bell** presents popular one-person comedy shows.

CAFÉ-THEATERS AND CHANSONNIERS

THERE IS A LONG tradition of entertainment in cafés, but the café-theaters of today have nothing in common with the "café-concerts" of the turn of the century. These modern entertainments originally developed because young actors and new playwrights could not find work, while drama students were unable to pay to rent established theaters. Café-theaters rose to prominence during the 1960s and 1970s, when unknowns such as Coluche, Gérard Depardieu and Miou-Miou made their debuts at the **Café de la Gare** before going on to success in the movies.

Good places for seeing new talent include the **Café d'Edgar** and **Au Bec Fin**, while the **Lucernaire** stages more conventional fare. Traditional *chansonniers* – cabarets where ballads, folk songs and humor abound – include **Au Lapin Agile** (see p233). Political satire is featured at the **Caveau de la République** and the **Deux Anes** in Montmartre.

CHILDREN'S THEATER

SOME PARIS THEATERS, such as the **Gymnase-Marie Bell**, the **Porte St-Martin** and the **Café d'Edgar**, have children's matinees on Saturdays, Sundays and Wednesdays. In the city parks there are tiny puppet (marionette) theaters that are sure to delight children and adults alike. *(See Independent Theaters p331.)*

OPEN-AIR THEATER

DURING THE summer, weather permitting, open-air performances of Shakespeare in French and classic French plays are given in the beautiful Shakespeare Garden in the Bois de Boulogne (see p254).

ENGLISH-LANGUAGE THEATER IN PARIS

OCCASIONALLY English and American plays are performed in their original language. The **Marie Stuart** has performances in English on Sundays and Mondays.

STREET THEATER

STREET THEATER thrives during the summer. Jugglers, mime artists, fire-eaters and musicians can be seen mainly in tourist areas, such as the Pompidou Center (see pp110–11), St-Germain-des-Prés and Les Halles.

BUYING TICKETS

TICKETS CAN BE bought at the box office, by telephone or through theater agencies. Box offices are open daily from about 11am to 7pm; some accept credit card reservations by telephone or in person.

TICKET PRICES

TICKET PRICES range from F45 to F195 for the national theaters and F50 to F250 for the independents. Discount tickets and student stand-bys are available in some theaters just before curtain.

The Kiosque Théâtre offers half-price tickets on the day of performance: credit cards are not accepted, and there is a small handling charge for each ticket sold. There is a ticket booth in the Place de la Madeleine and one in the RER station at Châtelet – Les Halles (see p105).

DRESS

EVENING CLOTHES are now worn only to gala events at the Opéra de Paris Garnier, the Comédie-Française or the grand premiere of an important play.

DIRECTORY

NATIONAL THEATERS

Comédie Française
2 Rue de Richelieu 75001. **Map** 12 E1.
[01 44 81 15 15.

Odéon Théâtre de l'Europe
Pl de l'Odéon 75006. **Map** 12 F5.
[01 44 41 36 36.

Petit Odéon
See Odéon Théâtre de l'Europe.

Salle Gémier
See Théâtre National de Chaillot.

Théâtre National de Chaillot
Pl du Trocadéro 75016. **Map** 9 C2.
[01 53 65 30 00.

Théâtre National de la Colline
15 Rue Malte-Brun 75020.
[01 44 62 52 52.

FARTHER AFIELD

Cartoucherie
See Théâtre du Soleil.

Théâtre du Soleil
(Cartoucherie) Route du Champ-des-Manoeuvres 75012.
[01 43 74 24 08.

INDEPENDENT THEATERS

Antoine-Simone Berriau
14 Blvd de Strasbourg 75010. **Map** 7 B5.
[01 42 08 77 71 & 01 42 08 76 58.

Atelier
Pl Charles Dullin 75018. **Map** 6 F2.
[01 46 06 49 24.

Bouffes-du-Nord
37 bis Blvd de la Chapelle 75010. **Map** 7 C1.
[01 46 07 34 50.

Bouffes-Parisiens
4 Rue Monsigny 75002. **Map** 6 E5.
[01 42 96 92 42.

La Bruyère
5 Rue La Bruyère 75009. **Map** 6 E3.
[01 48 74 76 99.

Comédie des Champs-Elysées
15 Ave Montaigne 75008. **Map** 10 F1.
[01 53 23 99 19.

Gymnase-Marie Bell
38 Blvd Bonne-Nouvelle 75010. **Map** 7 A5.
[01 42 46 79 79.

Hébertot
78 bis Rue des Batignolles 75017. **Map** 5 B2.
[01 43 87 23 23.

Huchette
23 Rue de la Huchette 75005. **Map** 13 A4.
[01 43 26 38 99.

Madeleine
19 Rue de Surène 75008. **Map** 5 C5.
[01 42 65 07 09.

Marie Stuart
4 Rue Marie-Stuart 75002. **Map** 13 A1.

Michel
38 Rue des Mathurins 75008. **Map** 5 C4.
[01 42 65 35 02.

Montparnasse
31 Rue de la Gaîté 75014. **Map** 15 C2.
[01 43 22 77 74.

Oeuvre
55 Rue de Clichy 75009. **Map** 6 D2.
[01 44 53 88 88.

Palais Royal
38 Rue Montpensier 75001. **Map** 12 E1.
[01 42 97 59 81 & 01 42 97 59 85.

Porte St-Martin
16 Blvd St-Martin 75010. **Map** 7 C5.
[01 42 08 00 32.

St-Georges
51 Rue St-Georges 75009. Map 6 E3.
[01 48 78 63 47.

CAFÉ-THEATERS AND CHANSONNIERS

Au Bec Fin
6 Rue Thérèse 75001. **Map** 12 E1.
[01 42 96 29 35.

Au Lapin Agile
22 Rue des Saules 75018. **Map** 2 F5.
[01 46 06 85 87.

Café d'Edgar
58 Blvd Edgar-Quinet 75014. **Map** 16 D2.
[01 42 79 97 97.

Café de la Gare
41 Rue du Temple 75004. **Map** 13 B2.
[01 42 78 52 51.

Caveau de la République
1 Blvd St-Martin 75003. **Map** 8 D5.
[01 42 78 44 45.

Deux Anes
100 Blvd de Clichy 75018. **Map** 6 D1.
[01 46 06 10 26.

Lucernaire
53 Rue Notre-Dame-des-Champs 75006. **Map** 16 D1.
[01 45 44 57 34.

Classical Music

THE MUSIC SCENE in Paris has never been so busy. Government spending has ensured that there are many first-class concert halls with an excellent range of opera as well as classical and contemporary music productions. There are also numerous concerts in churches and many music festivals.

Information about what's being offered is listed in *Pariscope*, *7 à Paris* and *L'Officiel des Spectacles*. A free monthly listing of musical events is given out at most concert halls. Also, try the Office du Tourisme et des Congrès de Paris *(see pp328–9)* for details of many free and open-air classical music performances.

OPERA

OPERA LOVERS will find themselves with many choices, including productions at the Bastille and the Opéra Comique. Opera is also an important part of the programming at the Théâtre du Châtelet and the Théâtre des Champs-Elysées. It is produced intermittently by a variety of small organizations, and sometimes there are performances by superstars, such as Luciano Pavarotti, in the sports stadiums.

The Opéra de Paris's ultra-modern home at the **Opéra de Paris Bastille** *(see p98)* opened officially in 1989, and performances have finally begun to make full use of the house's mind-boggling array of high-tech stage mechanisms. There are 2,700 seats, all with a good view of the stage.

Productions feature classic and modern operas, but the interpretations may be avant-garde. One production of *The Magic Flute* was done in the style of Japanese Noh, with some of the cast delivering their lines while balancing on one leg; Messiaen's *St. Francis of Assisi* had video screens and neon added to bring the story up-to-date.

There are also occasional dance performances, when the Bastille plays host to the ballet company from the Opéra de Paris Garnier *(see p215)*, plus film festivals. The house includes two smaller spaces, the **Auditorium** (500 seats) and the **Studio** (200 seats), for smaller-scale events ranging from chamber music and recitals to operas and plays.

The **Opéra Comique** (also known as the Salle Favart) is now used as the Paris showcase for productions that have originated elsewhere. Though it specializes in staging operettas, it also mounts some very fine productions of well-known fullscale operas.

CONCERTS

PARIS IS THE HOME of three major symphony orchestras and a good half-dozen other orchestras; it is also a major locale for European and American orchestras on tour. Chamber music is also flourishing, either as part of the programming of the major sites or in smaller halls and churches.

The **Salle Pleyel** is Paris's principal concert hall, with 2,300 seats, and is the home of the Orchestre de Paris. Its season runs from October to June, with an average of two concerts a week. The Salle Pleyel is also the main base of the Ensemble Orchestral de Paris and such reputable orchestral associations as the Lamoureux, the Pasdeloup and the Colonne, which organize concert seasons from October to Easter. The building also includes two smaller halls for chamber music: the Salle Chopin (470 seats) and the Salle Debussy (120 seats).

Over the last few years the **Théâtre du Châtelet** has become one of the city's principal places for all kinds of concerts, opera and dance. The high-quality program includes opera classics from Mozart's *Così fan tutte* to

Verdi's *La Traviata*, as well as more modern works, such as Berg's *Wozzeck*, plus occasional concerts by international opera stars. There is an annual cycle of 20th-century music, and the Philharmonia Orchestra of London is in residence during February. Throughout the season there are also lunchtime concerts and recitals held in the foyer.

The theater uses the **Auditorium du Châtelet** for its smaller-scale productions. Also known as the Auditorium des Halles, it is a relatively new, medium-size hall almost lost in the vast RER station.

The **Théâtre des Champs-Elysées** is a celebrated classical music venue that also produces some opera and dance. Radio-France is part-owner of the theater, and its Orchestre National de France gives several concerts here, as do many touring orchestras and soloists. There are also several concerts – ranging from Baroque to 20th-century music. The Concerts du Dimanche Matin organization stages excellent concerts – mostly chamber music – on Sundays at 11am.

Radio-France is the biggest single concert organizer in Paris, with a musical force that includes two major symphony orchestras: the Orchestre National de France and the Orchestre Philharmonique. Many of its concerts are given in Paris's other concert halls, but the **Maison de Radio-France** has a large hall and several smaller studios that are used for concerts and broadcasts open to the public *(see p200, Musée de Radio France)*.

The **Salle Gaveau** is a medium-size concert hall with a busy schedule of chamber music and recitals. Radio-France puts on a series of "brunch" concerts on Sundays at 11am during the season.

The **Auditorium du Louvre** is a new auditorium, built as part of the ongoing expansion of the Louvre *(see pp122–9)*; it is used mostly for chamber music recitals. The **Auditorium du Musée d'Orsay** is a medium-size auditorium, with an active concert program, at the Musée d'Orsay *(see pp144–7)*. Lunchtime concerts are free with the purchase of museum tickets; evening concerts have varying prices.

Other museums often stage concerts as part of an exhibition theme – such as troubadours at the Musée de Cluny *(see p154–7)* – so check the listings magazines.

The Musique à la Sorbonne organization puts on a concert series in the **Grand Amphithéâtre de la Sorbonne** and the **Amphi-théâtre Richelieu de la Sorbonne**. Productions have included the Slavonic Music Festival, featuring the works of East European composers.

Occasionally concerts are given in the **Conservatoire d'Art Dramatique**, where Ludwig van Beethoven was introduced to Paris audiences in 1828 and where some of Hector Berlioz's works were first performed. Otherwise, it is not usually open to the general public.

For something slightly different, the new **Opus Café** is a stylish cocktail bar where string quartets play classical music – see *Pariscope* for details of its current schedule.

CONTEMPORARY MUSIC

CONTEMPORARY music in Paris has a high profile and is definitely alive and kicking. One world-renowned Paris-based leader of the contemporary music scene is Pierre Boulez who heads the ground-breaking Ensemble InterContemporain. Lavishly supported by the French state, the Ensemble InterContemporain has recently moved from **IRCAM**, the vast laboratory of "digital signal processing" underneath the Pompidou Center, into a new home as the **Cité de la Musique** *(see pp234–5)*. Other bright stars among the host of talented composers include Paul Mefano, director of the ensemble 2E2M, Pascal Dusapin and George

Benjamin. Look out too for younger talents such as Georges Aperghis who specialises in musical theater.

The newly completed and fabulously designed Cité de la Musique complex at Parc de la Villette includes both a spectacularly domed *salle de concerts* surrounded by a glass-roofed arcade, and the **Conservatoire National de Musique** with its opera theater and two concert halls. Both venues are used for regular performances of all sorts of music, including contemporary, jazz, *chansons* and early music.

For concert details, either call the venue concerned or consult the usual listings magazines. For those with a serious interest in contemporary music, the quarterly magazine *Résonance* is published by IRCAM at the Pompidou Center.

FESTIVALS

SOME OF THE MOST important music festivals come about as a result of the work of the **Festival d'Automne à Paris**, which is not so much a series of performances as a behind the scenes stimulator: commissioning new works, subsidizing others and in general enlivening the Parisian musical, dance and theatrical scene from September to December.

The **Festival St-Denis** running throughout June and July holds concerts, with an emphasis on large-scale choral works. Most performances are given in the Basilique St-Denis.

The **Musique Baroque au Château de Versailles** begins around the middle of September and runs through to the middle of October. It is an offshoot of the Baroque Music Center, founded in Versailles in 1988. Operas, concerts, recitals, chamber music, dance and theater are performed in the fabulous surroundings of Versailles *(see pp248–53)*.

For tickets it is usually necessary to go to the box office of the theater or venue concerned, though

for some festivals you may be able to write ahead for tickets.

CHURCHES

MUSIC IS everywhere in Paris's churches, in the form of classical concerts, organ recitals or religious services. Among the most outstanding of all the churches that hold regular concerts are **La Madeleine** *(see p214)*, **St-Germain-des-Prés** *(see p138)*, **St-Julien-le-Pauvre** *(see p152)* and **St-Roch** *(see p121)*. Music is also performed in the **Eglise des Billettes**, **St-Sulpice** *(see p172)*, **St-Gervais–St-Protais** *(see p99)*, **Notre-Dame** *(see pp82–5)*, **St-Louis-en-l'Ile** *(see p87)* and **Sainte-Chapelle** *(see pp88–9)*.

Some, but not all, of these concerts are free. If you have difficulty contacting the church in question, try the Office du Tourisme et des Congrès de Paris for information *(see pp328–9)*.

EARLY MUSIC

A NUMBER OF early-music ensembles have taken up residence in Paris. The Chapelle Royale gives a concert series at the **Théâtre des Champs-Elysées**, with programs ranging from Renaissance vocal music to Mozart. Their sacred music concerts (watch for Bach cantatas) take place in the **Notre-Dame des Blancs Manteaux** *(see p102)*.

Baroque opera is more the domain of Les Arts Florissants, who sometimes appear at the **Théâtre du Châtelet**, performing French and Italian operas from Rossi to Rameau, although they also appear at the Salle Favart (**Opéra Comique**), where they put on Lully's famous musical, *Atys*.

The **Théâtre de la Ville** is the main venue for chamber music. For a uniquely French experience, there is the Ensemble Clément Janequin, masters of the bawdy 16th-century *chanson parisienne*, who perform at the **Théâtre du Musée Grévin** *(see p216)*.

RESERVING TICKETS

FOR TICKETS, dealing directly with the relevant box office is almost always the best bet. Reserving tickets at the main venues is possible by mail up to two months before the performance and by telephone two weeks to one month in advance. If you want to be assured of a good seat, it is always best to reserve in advance since tickets tend to sell quickly.

Last-minute tickets may also be available at the box office; also certain places, such as the Opéra de Paris Bastille, keep a certain number of tickets for the cheaper seats aside for the purpose.

Ticket agents, notably in the FNAC stores *(see p329)*, and a good hotel concierge may be able to help. These agencies will accept credit card reservations – a useful service since some places do not accept credit cards.

Half-price tickets on the day of performance can be bought at the Kiosque Théâtre *(see p329)*, which is found in the Place de la Madeleine, and also at the RER station at Châtelet–Les Halles. However, these agencies usually have tickets only for performances taking place at private theaters.

Note, however, that many theaters and concert halls may be closed during the holiday season in August, so inquire first to avoid disappointment.

TICKET PRICES

TICKET PRICES CAN range from F50 to F550 for the Opéra de Paris Bastille and the principal classical music venues, and from F30 to F150 for the smaller halls and concerts in churches, such as Sainte-Chapelle.

CLASSICAL MUSIC VENUES

Amphithéâtre Richelieu de la Sorbonne
17 Rue de la Sorbonne 75005. **Map** 12 F5.
☎ 01 42 62 71 71.

Auditorium
See Opéra de Paris Bastille.

Auditorium du Châtelet
(Auditorium des Halles)
Forum des Halles, Porte St-Eustache. **Map** 13 A2.
☎ 01 40 28 28 40.

Auditorium du Louvre
Musée du Louvre, Rue de Rivoli 75001. **Map** 12 E2.
☎ 01 40 20 52 29.

Auditorium du Musée d'Orsay
102 Rue de Lille 75007. **Map** 12 D2.
☎ 01 40 49 48 14.

Cité de la Musique
Parc de La Villette, 221 Ave Jean-Jaurès 75019. ☎ 01 44 84 44 84.

Conservatoire d'Art Dramatique
2 bis Rue du Conservatoire 75009. **Map** 7 A4.
☎ 01 42 46 12 91.

Conservatoire National de Musique
See Cité de la Musique.

Eglise des Billettes
24 Rue des Archives 75004. **Map** 13 C2.
☎ 01 42 72 38 79.

Festival d'Automne à Paris
156 Rue de Rivoli 75001. **Map** 12 F2.5
☎ 01 42 96 12 27.

Festival St-Denis
6 Pl Legion d'Honneur 93200 St-Denis.
Map 15 C3.
☎ 01 48 13 06 07.

Grand Amphithéâtre de la Sorbonne
47 Rue des Ecoles 75005.
Map 13 A5.
☎ 01 42 62 71 71.

IRCAM
1 Pl Igor Stravinsky 75004.
Map 13 B2.
☎ 01 44 78 48 43.

La Madeleine
Pl de la Madeleine 75008.
Map 5 C5.
☎ 01 44 51 69 00.

Maison de Radio-France
116 Ave du Président-Kennedy 75016. **Map** 9 B4.
☎ 01 42 30 15 16.

Musique Baroque au Château de Versailles
Château de Versailles, Chapelle Royal, 78000 Versailles ☎ 01 30 84 74 00.

Notre-Dame
Pl du Parvis-Notre-Dame.
Map 13 A4.
☎ 01 42 34 56 10.

Notre-Dame-des-Blancs-Manteaux
12 Rue des Blanc-Manteaux 75004.
Map 13 A4.
☎ 01 42 72 09 37.

Opéra Comique
(Salle Favart)
5 Rue Favart 75002.
Map 6 F5.
☎ 01 42 44 45 46.

Opéra de Paris Bastille
120 Rue de Lyon 75012.
Map 14 E4.
☎ 01 44 73 13 99.

New Opus Café
167 Quai de Valmy 75010. **Map** 8 D3.
☎ 01 40 34 70 00

Pompidou Centre
Plateau Beaubourg 75004.
Map 13 B2.
Closed until Jan 1, 2000.

Sainte-Chapelle
4 Blvd du Palais.
Map 13 A3.
☎ 01 53 73 78 50.

St-Germain-des-Prés
Pl St-Germain-des-Prés 75006. **Map** 12 E4.
☎ 01 43 25 41 71.

St-Gervais–St-Protais
Pl St-Gervais 75004.
Map 13 B3.
☎ 01 48 87 32 02.

St-Julien-le-Pauvre
1 Rue St-Julien-le-Pauvre 75005. **Map** 13 A4.
☎ 01 43 29 09 09.

St-Louis-en-l'Ile
19 bis Rue St-Louis-en-l'Ile 75004. **Map** 13 C5.
☎ 01 46 34 11 60.

St-Roch
296 Rue St-Honoré 75001.
Map 12 D1.
☎ 01 42 44 13 20.

St-Sulpice
Pl St-Sulpice 75006.
Map 12 E4.
☎ 01 46 33 21 78.

Salle Gaveau
45 Rue La Boétie 75008.
Map 5 B4.
☎ 01 49 53 05 07.

Salle Pleyel
252 Rue du Faubourg St-Honoré 75008. **Map** 4 E3.
☎ 01 45 61 53 00.

Studio
See Opéra de Paris Bastille.

Théâtre de la Ville
2 Pl du Châtelet 75001.
Map 13 A3.
☎ 01 42 74 22 77.

Théâtre des Champs-Élysées
15 Ave Montaigne 75008.
Map 10 F1.
☎ 01 49 52 50 50.
🎫 08 36 69 78 68.

Théâtre du Châtelet
Pl du Châtelet 75001.
Map 13 A3.
☎ 01 40 28 28 40.

Théâtre du Musée Grévin
10 Blvd Montmartre 75009. **Map** 6 F4.
☎ 01 42 46 84 47.

Dance

WHEN IT COMES to dance, Paris is more a cultural crossroads than a cultural center. Because of a deliberate government policy of decentralization, many of the top French dance companies are based in the provinces, but they frequently visit the capital. In addition, the greatest dance companies from all over the world perform in Paris. The French are very vocal in their appreciation or dislike of dance performances, and those who fail to please are subjected to boos, hisses and mass walk-outs in mid-performance.

CLASSICAL BALLET

THE OPULENT **Opéra de Paris Garnier** *(see p215)* is the home of the Ballet de l'Opéra de Paris, which is earning a reputation as one of the world's best classical dance companies.

Since the Opéra de Paris Bastille opened in 1989, the Opéra de Paris Garnier has been used almost exclusively for dance. It is one of the largest theaters in Europe, with performance space for 450 artists and a seating capacity of 2,200.

Modern dance companies such as the Martha Graham, Paul Taylor, Merce Cunningham, and Alvin Ailey, and Jerome Robbins and Roland Petit's Ballet de Marseille also regularly perform here.

In March 1996, the Opéra de Paris Garnier re-opened after renovation. It now shares operatic productions with the **Opera de Paris Bastille**.

MODERN DANCE

GOVERNMENT SUPPORT has helped the **Théâtre de la Ville** (once run by Sarah Bernhardt) to become Paris's most important venue for modern dance, with subsidies keeping ticket costs relatively low. Through performances at the Théâtre de la Ville, such modern choreographers as Jean-Claude Gallotta, Regine Chopinot, Maguy Marin and Anne Teresa de Keersmaeker have gained international recognition. Here you may also see such troupes as Pina Bausch's Wuppertal Dance Theatre, whose tormented, existential choreography may not be

to everyone's taste but is always popular with Parisian audiences.

Music performances also run throughout the season and include chamber music, recitals, world music and jazz.

The **Maison des Arts de Créteil** presents some of the most interesting dance works in Paris. It is located in the Paris suburb of Créteil, where the local council gives strong support to dance. Créteil's company choreographer, Maguy Marin, has won consistent praise for her darkly expressive work.

The Maison des Arts also brings in such innovative companies as the Sydney Ballet, plus the Kirov from St. Petersburg, which is more inclined toward the classical.

Set amid the opulent couture shops and embassies, the **Théâtre des Champs-Élysées** is an elegant place with 1,900 seats. It is frequented by an upscale audience who watch major international companies perform here. It was in this theater that Nijinsky first danced Stravinsky's iconoclastic *The Rite of Spring*, which led to rioting among the audience.

The theater is more famous for its classical music programs, but recent visitors have included the American Harlem Dance Company and London's Royal Ballet, and it is here that Mikhail Baryshnikov and American choreographer Mark Morris perform when they are in Paris. It also sponsors the *Géants de la Danse* series, an evening-length sampling of international ballet, a must-see for choreography connoisseurs.

The lovely old **Théâtre du Châtelet** is a renowned opera and classical music venue, but it is also host to choreographer William Forsythe's popular Frankfurt Ballet. New dance companies perform in the **Théâtre de la Bastille**, where innovative theater is also staged. Many directors and companies start here, and then go on to achieve international fame.

New companies not to miss include La P'tit Cie and L'Esquisse, neither based in any one place.

EVENTS LISTINGS

TO FIND OUT what your choices are, read the weekly entertainment guides *Pariscope* and *L'Officiel des Spectacles*. Posters advertising dance performances are in the metros and on the streets, especially on the green advertisement columns, the *colonnes Morris*.

TICKET PRICES

EXPECT TO PAY F60 to F650 for tickets to a opera at the Opéra de Paris Garnier (F30–F400 for a ballet), F40–F500 for the Théâtre des Champs-Élysées and anything from F60 to F180 for other venues.

DANCE VENUES

Maison des Arts et de la Culture de Créteil
Pl Salvador Allende 94000 Créteil.
℃ *01 45 13 19 19.*

Opéra de Paris Palais Garnier
See pp214–5.

Opéra de Paris Bastille
See pp98.

Théâtre de la Bastille
76 Rue de la Roquette 75011.
Map 14 F3. ℃ *01 43 57 42 14.*

Théâtre de la Ville
See p334.

Théâtre des Champs-Elysées
See p334.

Théâtre du Châtelet
See p334.

Rock, Jazz, and World Music

MUSIC LOVERS WILL FIND every imaginable form of music in Paris and the surrounding areas, from international pop stars in major arenas to talented street performers in the metro. There's a huge variety of styles on offer, with reggae, hip-hop, world music, blues, folk, rock, and jazz – Paris is said to be second only to New York in the number of jazz clubs and jazz recordings, and there is always an excellent selection of bands and solo performers.

On the summer solstice (June 21) each year, the *Fête de la Musique* takes place. This is the one day of the year when anyone can play any form of music, anywhere in Paris, without a license. Ears may be assailed by a heavy metal rock band or lulled by an accordionist playing traditional French songs.

For complete listings of what's happening during your visit, buy *Pariscope* (published every Wednesday) at any kiosk. Jazz aficionados should read the monthly *Jazz* magazine for lists of schedules and in-depth reviews.

MAJOR VENUES

THE TOP INTERNATIONAL events usually take place in the enormous arenas at the **Palais d'Omnisports** at Bercy or the **Zénith**. Smaller venues like the legendary *chanson* center of the universe, the **Olympia**, or the **Grand Rex** (also a movie theater) have assigned seating, a more intimate atmosphere and good acoustics. They host everyone from bewigged and cosmetically enhanced iconic first ladies of country to acid jazz stars.

ROCK AND POP

PARIS'S INDIGENOUS rock groups like Les Negresses Vertes, Noir Désir, and Mano Negra have enjoyed some international popularity. They play raucous French pop, a cross between rock and street music. Multi-ethnic youngsters from the *banlieue* (suburbs) are forming French-language rap groups, including Alliance Ethnique, NTM, and MC Solaar. Although they strive for hard-edged rebelliousness, few have emerged from a ghetto and they seem very innocent when compared with their authentic American counterparts.

Some of the best French pop singers are Françis Cabrel, Michel Jonasz, the beautiful and gifted Vanessa Paradis, Julien Clerc, and blues man Paul Personne. Local duo Les Rita Mitsouko are beginning to gather acclaim with their curious musical hybrid of rock, electro, *chanson*, Latin and scratch. Visitors might want to catch the many foreign groups passing through town. The young frequent the converted movie theatre of **La Cigale**, **Elysée-Montmartre**.

For rock, rhythm and blues, go to **Caf' Conc'**. The pagoda-fronted **Bataclan** and the **Rex Club** are the best places for hearing an eclectic selection of acts. Ever since the Beatles blew the roof off the **Olympia** in 1964, the major names on both the British and the American pop scenes have customarily regarded Paris as a must-play city, so it is always worth checking out who's in town.

Many Paris nightclubs also double up as live music spots (*see pp338–9*).

JAZZ

JAZZ-CRAZY Paris has innumerable packed clubs where the best talent can be heard any evening. Many American musicians have made the French capital their home because of the receptive atmosphere here. All styles, from free-form to Dixieland and swing, and even hiphop-jazz crossover, are on offer. Clubs range from quasi-concert halls to piano bars and pub-like venues. One of the most popular places, though more for the quality of the talent it attracts than for its comfortable ambience, is the **New Morning**. It's hot and smokey, and the table service is dreadful, but all the great jazz musicians have performed here. Arrive early to ensure a good seat. **Le Duc des Lombards** is a lively jazz club in Les Halles which also features salsa.

Many jazz clubs are also cafés, bars or restaurants. The latter includes the intimate **Bilboquet**, with its Belle Epoque interior. This is a stylish place favored by movie stars; downstairs is the disco **Club St-Germain**. Dining might not be a requirement, but call first.

Other jazz hotspots are **Le Petit Journal Montparnasse** for modern jazz, **Le Petit Journal St-Michel** for Dixieland and the **Sunset**. **Le Petit Opportun** is a tiny club (only 60 seats) with an excellent reputation. The **Café de la Plage** in the Bastille plays a variety of music to a trendy crowd. **Caveau de la Huchette** looks like the archetypal jazz joint but is no longer the leader of the jazz scene. Nowadays it favors swing and big-band music, and is popular with students.

For a change from smoke-filled basement clubs, try the local talent at small, friendly bars like the **Eustache**, which is less expensive than most, or the trendy **China Club**, with its 1940s *film noir* decor. The **Jazz-Club Lionel Hampton** in the Méridien hotel is a well-respected venue which features Sunday jazz brunch.

If you're in Paris in July, don't miss the annual JVC Halle That Jazz festival at the **Grande Halle de la Villette** where international jazz stars, such as Grover Washington Jr., Fats Domino, and B. B. King play. There are also movies on jazz and *boeufs* (jam sessions) with all the top musicians taking part. October sees the annual Paris Jazz Festival, with top swinging international musicians.

The **Slow Club**, with its rocking-couple neon sign, features swinging jazz and a dance-happy crowd showing off their talents.

WORLD MUSIC

Paris, with its large populations from West Africa and the countries of the Maghreb, the Antilles and Latin America, is a center for world music. The excellent **Chapelle des**

Lombards has played host to top acts; it also has jazz, salsa and Brazilian music with dancing until dawn. **Aux Trois Mailletz** is a medieval cellar with everything from blues to tango and rock and roll covers.

Many jazz clubs also intersperse their programs with ethnic music. **New Morning** has African, Brazilian and other sounds, **Café de la Plage** mixes reggae and salsa and **Baiser Salé** has everything from blues to Brazilian music. Popular acts to catch include Makossa, Kassav, Malavoi, and Manu Dibango.

TICKET PRICES

Prices at paris jazz clubs can be steep, and there may be a cover charge of over F100 at the door, which usually pays for the first drink. If there is no cover charge, it is likely that drinks will be expensive and at least one must be bought.

BUYING TICKETS

Tickets to most events can be bought from FNAC outlets and Virgin Megastore *(see p329)*, or directly from box offices at the location and at the door at clubs.

Discothèques and Nightclubs

Music in Paris clubs tends to follow trends set in the United States and Britain. In Paris the locals dance *le rock*, a well-studied version of the classic 1950s rock-and-roll dance. Only a few clubs, such as **Balajo** and **Folies Pigalle**, are up-to-the-minute. Clubs in Paris tend to be fairly well established: places like **Les Bains** have been around for years, riding the roller coaster of popularity but managing to keep a faithful clientele.

Le Figaro's weekly entertainment supplement; *7 à Paris;* and *Pariscope* list current information, with opening times and brief descriptions of club nights. Alternatively, read the posters at the Bastille metro station or listen to Radio NOVA 101.5 FM, which gives details of the night's best club dance scene or "rave."

Other popular nighttime options include ballroom dancing and piano bars. If you're wondering about what to wear, remember that most Parisians tend to dress up when going out on the town.

Mainstream

Le Bataclan is a vast yet convivial showcase for current bands. But, after the show on Saturday nights, it becomes the trendiest nightclub in Paris, legendary for its mouth-watering choice of funk, soul and new jack swing.

Club 79 is lively and a "retro"-orientated disco; the inexpensive **La Scala** attracts a large young crowd, while adventurous whirling hedonists roller-skate to rap and rock at **La Main Jaune**.

Les Bains, one-time Turkish bath, is the "glamma" nightspot for fashion and show-business people; its upstairs restaurant, now serving Thai food, is the current "in" for private dinner parties. The dance floor is tiny and music is mainly house, with 70s and 80s disco on Mondays, and R&B on Wednesdays. Gay night is *Café con Leche* on Sundays.

Advertising executives and filmmakers frequent the **Rex Club**. Music on different nights ranges from glam rock and house to "exotique": funk, reggae and world music. Sounds are mainly rock and roll at the smart and non-ageist **Zed Club.** The vast **La Locomotive** caters to mainstream tastes most nights, with rock, house, groove and dance music each occupying a different floor.

Exclusive

Being rich, beautiful and famous may not be enough to get you into **Castel's**, but it could help. It is a private club in the strictest sense, and the happy few who make it, dine in one of two very good restaurants before heading down to the dance floor.

Regine's is mostly full of be-suited executives and wealthy foreigners who dine and dance to the easy-listening music.

The wood-paneled, cozy **Ritz Club** in the legendary Ritz hotel is open only to members and hotel guests, though the chic and elegant are welcome. The ambience is upscale and the music is easy listening.

Trendy

Once a working-class music hall frequented by famous Parisians Edith Piaf and Jean Gabin, **Balajo** has now gone upmarket but is still one of the best clubs in Paris for dancing and one of the few open on Mondays. It also holds ballroom dancing nights.

An ultrahip young crowd flock to the small and cozy **Folies Pigalle**, one-time strip joint and present-day venue for live music. Its original theme nights make for some of the best fun clubbing around. For a top dancing night out try the fortnightly *Bal* with live big band at the **Elysée Montmartre**. Here too look out for the *Return to the Source*, Goa-trance nights all the way from London's Fridge.

World Music

A stylish and expensive African-Antillean club, **Keur Samba** is popular with the African jet-set. Things get going after 2am and last long into the night. **Le Casbah** is exclusive, jazzy and one of the best established spots on the Paris club scene. Its African–Middle Eastern decor has always been a magnet for models and trendies who, in between dances, do a little night shopping in the club's downstairs boutique. Le Casbah is currently enjoying something of a renaissance of its chicest of the chic reputation.

If your nervous system responds favorably to the heaving rhythms and throbbing beat of authentic Latin music, you should head for **La Java** which combines glorious sounds with the quaint appeal of a Belleville dance hall.

Other lively world music nights are held at **Trottoirs de Buenos-Aires**, **Chapelle des Lombards** and the cellar bar at **Aux Trois Mailletz** (*see* Rock, Jazz and World Music *pp336–7*).

Gay and Lesbian

A huge gay club, **La Queen** has a great line-up of house DJs. Monday is disco night and Friday and Saturday are garage and soul. Some of the raunchier events are men only. Girls should go with pretty boys. Sunday nights at **La Locomotive** are the *Gay Tea Dance* which has moved from the now bankrupt Le Palace. Wednesday is *Respect*, formally of Le Queen. Lesbian club **Christhom** is a re-named, glammed-up version of what used to be L'Entreacte. *Lounge* on Wednesdays is cocktails, armchairs, easy-listening and cabaret, while Thursday is house and disco. *Scream* is the hot new gay night at the popular **Elysée Montmartre**.

CABARET

THE MUSIC HALL revue is the entertainment form most associated with turn-of-the-century Paris. It evokes images of bohemian artists and champagne-induced debauchery. Nowadays, most of the girls are likely to be American, and the audience is made up mainly of foreign businessmen and tour groups.

When it comes to picking a cabaret the rule of thumb is simple: the better-known places are the best. Lesser-known cabaret shows resemble nothing so much as Grade-B strip shows. All of the cabarets listed here guarantee topless women sporting outrageous feather- and sequin-encrusted head-pieces; an assortment of vaudeville acts; and, depending on your point of view, a spectacularly entertaining evening or an exercise in comedic high kitsch. The **Lido** is the most Las Vegas–like of the cabarets and stars the legendary Bluebell Girls. The **Folies-Bergères** is renowned for lively entertainment. It is the oldest music hall in Paris and probably the most famous in the world.

The **Crazy Horse Saloon** features some of the more risqué costumes and performances, and dancers with such names as Betty Buttocks, Fila Volcana and Nouka Bazooka. It has been transformed from its Wild West barroom into a jewel-box theater with a champagne bucket fastened to each seat. Here the lowly striptease of burlesque shows has been refined into a vehicle for comedy sketches and international beauties.

Paradis Latin is the most "French" of all the city's cabaret shows. It has variety acts with remarkable special effects and scenery in a beautiful old Left Bank theater, partially designed by Gustave Eiffel.

The **Don Camillo Rive Guache** has more elegant, less touristy shows, with excellent *chanson* singers, comedians and other variety acts. The **Moulin Rouge** (*see p226*), once the haunt of Toulouse-Lautrec, is the birthplace of the cancan. Outrageously camp transvestite parodies of these showgirl reviews can be seen at **Chez Madame Arthur**.

ADMISSION CHARGES

SOME CLUBS are strictly private, others have a more generous admission policy. Prices can range from about F75 to F100 or F200 or more, and may be higher after midnight and on weekends. But quite often there are discounts for women.

You can have dinner with the show or just a drink – but neither is cheap. Expect to pay from F150 to F400 for a ticket; and F450 to F700 including dinner. In general, one drink (*la consommation*) is included in the entry price; thereafter it can become an extremely expensive evening.

DISCO AND CLUB VENUES

Les Bains
7 Rue du Bourg-L'Abbé
75003. **Map 13 B1.**
[01 48 87 01 80.

Balajo
9 Rue de Lappe 75011.
Map 14 E4.
[01 47 00 07 87.

Le Bataclan
50 blvd Voltaire 75011.
Map 13 E1.
[01 443 14 33 35.

La Casbah
18-20 Rue de la Forge-Royale 75011.
[01 43 71 04 39.

Castel's
15 Rue Princesse 75006.
Map 12 E4.
[01 40 51 52 80.

Chez Madame Arthur
75 bis Rue des Martyrs
75018. **Map 6 F2.**
[01 42 54 40 21.

Christhom
25 Blvd Poissonnière
75002. **Map 7 A5.**
[01 40 26 01 50.

Club 79
79 Ave des Champs-Elysées 75008.
Map 4 F5.
[01 47 23 68 75.

Crazy Horse Saloon
12 Ave George V 75008.
Map 10 E1.
[01 47 23 32 32.

Don Camillo Rive Gauche
10 Rue des Sts-Pères
75007.
Map 12 E3.
[01 42 60 82 84.

Elysée Montmartre
72 Blvd Rochechouart
75018. **Map 6 F2.**
[01 42 52 76 84.

Folies-Bergères
32 Rue Richer 75009.
Map 7 A4.
[01 44 79 98 98.

Folies Pigalle
11 Pl Pigalle 75009.
Map 6 E2.
[01 48 78 25 26.

La Java
105 Rue du Faubourg du Temple 75011. **Map 8 E5.**
[01 42 02 20 52.

Keur Samba
79 Rue de la Boétie 75008.
Map 5 A4.
[01 43 59 03 10.

Lido
116 bis Ave des Champs-Elysées 75008. **Map 4 E4.**
[01 40 76 56 10.

La Locomotive
90 Blvd de Clichy 75018.
Map 4 E4.
[01 53 41 88 88.

La Main Jaune
Pl de la Porte-Champerret
75017. **Map 3 C1.**
[01 47 63 26 47.

Moulin Rouge
82 Blvd de Clichy 75018.
Map 6 E1.
[01 46 06 00 19.

Paradis Latin
28 Rue du Cardinal-Lemoine
75005. **Map 13 B5.**
[01 43 25 28 28.

Le Queen
102 Ave des Champs-Elysées 75008. **Map 4 E4.**
[01 53 89 08 90.

Regine's
49-51 Rue Ponthieu
75008. **Map 5 A5.**
[01 43 59 21 60.

Rex Club
5 Blvd Poissonnière 75002.
Map 7 A5.
[01 42 36 83 98.

Ritz Club
Hôtel Ritz, 15 Pl Vendôme 75001.
Map 6 D5.
[01 43 16 30 30.

La Scala
188 bis Rue de Rivoli
75001.
Map 12 E2.
[01 42 60 45 64.

Zed Club
2 Rue des Anglais 75005.
Map 13 A5.
[01 43 54 93 78.

Movies

Paris is the world's capital of movie appreciation. It was the cradle of the cinematograph nearly 100 years ago, as well as the incubator of that very Parisian vanguard movement, the New Wave, when in the late 1950s and early 1960s such movie directors as Claude Chabrol, François Truffaut, Jean-Luc Godard and Eric Rohmer revolutionized the way movies were made and perceived.

There are more than 300 screens within the city limits, distributed among 100 theaters and multiplexes, showing a fabulous cornucopia of movies, both brand-new and classic. Although American movies dominate the market more than ever, virtually every movie-making industry in the world has found a niche in the city's art houses.

Movie theaters generally change their programs on Wednesdays. The cheapest practical guides to what's playing are *Pariscope* and *L'Officiel des Spectacles (see p328)*, with complete listings and timetables for some 300 movies. For more substantial reviews and articles, there are the larger-format weeklies, such as *Télérama* and *7 à Paris*, and, for the serious-minded movie-goer, the monthly magazines *Les Cahiers du Cinéma* and *Positif*.

Movies shown in subtitled original language versions are coded "VO" *(version originale)*, while dubbed movies are coded "VF" *(version française)*.

The Fête du Cinéma is held one day in June. You pay full price for one movie and then every movie seen subsequently in any theater on that day costs F1. Movie buffs have been known to watch six screenings in one day.

Movie Zones

Most Paris movie theaters are concentrated in several areas, which enjoy the added appeal of nearby restaurants and shops.

The Champs-Elysées remains the densest movie strip in town, where you can see the latest Hollywood smash or French *auteur* triumph, as well as some classic reissues in subtitled original-language versions. Theaters in the Grands Boulevards, in the vicinity of the Opéra de Paris Garnier, show movies in both subtitled and dubbed versions. The Place de Clichy is the last Parisian stronghold of Pathé, which operates no less than 13 screens there, all showing dubbed versions. The newest hub of Right Bank movie activity is in the Forum des Halles shopping mall.

The Left Bank, historically associated with the city's intellectual life, remains the center of the art and repertory theaters, yet has equally theaters showing the latest blockbusters. Over the past decade, many theaters in the Latin Quarter have closed, and the main area for Left Bank theaters is now the Odéon-St-Germain-des-Prés area. The Rue Champollion is an exception. It has enjoyed a revival as a minidistrict for both art and repertory movies.

Farther to the south, the area of Montparnasse remains a lively district for new movies, shown in both dubbed and subtitled versions.

Big Screens and Picture Palaces

Among surviving landmark theaters are two Grands Boulevards venues: the 2,800-seat **Le Grand Rex**, with its Baroque decor, and the **Max Linder Panorama**, which was completely refurbished by a group of independent movie buffs in the 1980s for both popular and art movie programming.

Another popular site is the **Gaumont Kinopanorama**, with its wide curved screen. Despite its far-flung location in Grenelle, it is one of the best-attended houses in town. The latest newcomer, with the largest screen in France, is the new **Gaumont** flagship in the Place d'Italie district.

In the Cité des Sciences et de l'Industrie at La Villette, scientific movies are shown at **La Géode** *(see p235)*. This has the largest screen in the world and an "omnimax" projector that uses 70-mm movie shot horizontally to project an image nine times larger than that of the standard 35-mm print.

Revival and Repertory Houses

Each week, more than 150 titles representing the best of world movies can be seen. For old Hollywood movies, the independent **Grand Action** minichain can't be beat. Other active repertory and re-issue venues include the **Reflets Médicis Logos** screens in the Rue Champollion and the newly renovated **Diagonal Europa** near the Jardin du Luxembourg, operated by distributor/exhibitor Acacias-Cinéaudience.

Cinémathèque Française

The private "school" of the New Wave generation, this famous movie archive and repertory theater was created by Henri Langlois in 1936 *(see p199)*. It has lost its monopoly on classic movie screenings, but it is still a must for buffs in search of that rare movie no longer in theatrical circulation or recently restored. The Cinémathèque now operates three cinemas, one at the **Cinémathèque Française Palais de Chaillot** *(see p198)*, and two others at the nearby **Cinémathèque Française Palais de Tokyo**, which also houses France's movie and television school, FEMIS. Tickets are priced at about F22, and there are subscriptions and special rates as well.

NONTHEATRICAL VENUES

IN ADDITION TO the Cinémathèque Française, movie programs and festivals are integral parts of two highly popular Paris cultural institutions, the Musée d'Orsay *(see pp144–5)* and the Pompidou Center *(see pp110–11)* with its **Salle Garance**. The Musée d'Orsay regularly schedules movie programs to complement current art exhibitions and is usually restricted to silent movies. The Pompidou Center organizes month-long comprehensive retrospectives, devoted to national movie industries and on occasion to some of the major movie companies.

Finally, the **Vidéothèque de Paris** *(see p109)* in the heart of Les Halles is a high-tech movie and video library, with a vast selection of movies and documentaries featuring the city of Paris from the late 19th century to the present day. The Vidéothèque has three theaters, all of which run daily screenings of feature movies, beginning at 2:30pm. One ticket allows the visitor access to both the video library and to the cinema screenings.

TICKET PRICES

EXPECT TO pay up to F45 for first-run movies or even more for movies of unusual length or special media attention. However, exhibitors practice a wide array of collective discount incentives, including cut-rate admissions for students, the unemployed, the elderly, old soldiers and large families. Wednesday is discount day for everybody at all the city's theaters – prices are slashed to as low as F28.

France's three exhibition giants – Gaumont, UGC and Pathé – also sell special discount cards and accept credit card reservations for their flagship houses, while repertory houses issue "fidelity" cards, offering a sixth admission free.

The traditional *pourboire*, or tip, given to the usherettes, or *ouvreuses*, has now been abolished by the major theaters, though independent ones still continue the practice: it is considered polite to tip around F2.

Shows usually begin at 2pm and the last *séance*, or program, starts between 9 and 10pm. There are midnight screenings on Fridays and Saturdays at most theaters showing first-run movies.

Some complexes, notably those in the Forum des Halles *(see p109)*, offer low-price late-morning screenings. A complete program is supposed to include a short movie before the main feature, but most exhibitors have dropped this in order to increase revenue with more advertising time. If you don't want to sit through 20 minutes of commercials, check the exact starting time for the feature. However, for particularly popular movies, you'll have to turn up early to line up for tickets if you want to be sure of getting a seat.

MOVIES WITH STRONG IMAGES OF PARIS

Historical Paris (studio-made)
An Italian Straw Hat
(René Clair, 1927)
Sous les Toits de Paris
(René Clair, 1930)
Les Misérables
(Raymond Bernard, 1934)
Hôtel du Nord
(Marcel Carné, 1937)
Les Enfants du Paradis
(Marcel Carné, 1945)
Casque d'Or
(Jacques Becker, 1952)
La Traversée de Paris
(Claude Autant-Lara, 1956)
Playtime
(Jacques Tati, 1967)

New Wave Paris (made on location)
Breathless
(Jean-Luc Godard, 1959)
Les 400 Coups
(François Truffaut, 1959)

Documentary Paris
Paris 1900
(Nicole Vedrès, 1948)
La Seine a Rencontré Paris
(Joris Ivans, 1957)

Paris as seen by Hollywood
Seventh Heaven
(Frank Borzage, 1927)
Camille
(George Cukor, 1936)
An American in Paris
(Vincente Minnelli, 1951)
Gigi
(Vincente Minnelli, 1958)
Irma La Douce
(Billy Wilder, 1963)

MOVIE THEATERS

Cinémathèque Française Palais de Chaillot
42 Blvd de Bonne Nouvelle 75010. **Map** 7 A5.
01 56 26 01 01.

Diagonal Europa
13 Rue Victor-Cousin 75005. **Map** 12 F5.
01 43 54 15 04.

Gaumont Gobelins
58 & 73 Ave des Gobelins 75013. **Map** 17 B4.

08 36 68 75 55.
Reservations 01 40 30 30 31.

La Géode
26 Ave Corentin-Cariou 75019.
01 40 05 12 12.

Grand Action
Action Rive Gauche, 5 Rue des Ecoles 75005.
Map 13 B5.
01 43 29 44 40.

Le Grand Rex
1 Blvd Poissonnière

75002. **Map** 7 A5.
01 42 36 83 93.

Gaumont Kinopanorama
60 Ave de la Motte-Picquet 75015.
Map 10 E5.
01 43 06 50 50.
Reservations 01 40 30 30 31.

Max Linder Panorama
24 Blvd Poissonnière 75009. **Map** 7 A5.
01 48 24 88 88.

Reflets Médicis Logos
3 Rue Champollion 75005.
Map 12 F5.
01 43 54 42 34.

Salle Garance
Centre Georges Pompidou, 19 Rue Beaubourg 75004.
Map 13 B2.
Closed until Jan 1, 2000.

Vidéothèque de Paris
2 Grande Galérie, Forum des Halles 75001. **Map** 13 A2.
01 44 76 62 20.

Sports and Fitness

There is no end of sporting activities in Paris. Certain events – such as the Roland Garros tennis tournament and the Tour de France bicycle race – are national institutions. The only drawback is that many sports facilities are on the outskirts of the city.

For details regarding all sporting events in and around Paris, contact **Allô Sports**, which runs a free information service (Monday to Friday, daytime only). The weekly entertainment guides *L'Officiel des Spectacles* and *Pariscope* and the Wednesday edition of *Le Figaro* also have good listings of the week's sporting events *(see p328)*. For in-depth sports coverage, there is the daily paper *L'Equipe*. See also *Children's Paris* on page 346.

OUTDOOR SPORTS

The annual Tour de France bicycle race finishes in July in Paris to citywide frenzy, when the French president awards the coveted *maillot jaune* (yellow jersey) to the winner.

For those brave enough to tackle just cycling through the city traffic, bikes may be rented from **Paris Vélo** *(see p367)*; or you can rent one from the parks. The French state railroad, SNCF, offers day trips with a bicycle as part of a package. The **Fédération Française de Cyclotourisme** will give you information on over 300 cycling clubs in and around Paris.

Parisians enjoy Sunday afternoon boating in the Bois de Vincennes *(see p246)*, the Bois de Boulogne *(see p254)* and the Parc des Buttes-Chaumont *(see p232)*. Just line up to rent a boat.

On weekends, amateur *pétanque* players stake out almost any available piece of gravel or earth to play the game that, in poll after poll, Parisians claim is their favorite sport. It is a game similar to bowls. Contact the **Fédération Française de Pétanque et de Jeux Provençales** for information.

All the golf courses are outside Paris. Many are private clubs, but some will admit nonmembers – for further information, contact the **Fédération Française du Golf**. Otherwise, try the **Golf de Chevry**, **Golf de St-Pierre du Perray**, **Golf de St-Quentin en Yvesline** or the **Golf de Villennes**. Expect to pay at least F160 each time you want to play. You can go riding in the Bois de Boulogne and the Bois de Vincennes. Contact the **Ligue Equestre de Paris** for further information.

Tennis can be played at municipal courts, such as the **Tennis Luxembourg** in the Jardin du Luxembourg. Courts are available daily on a first-come first-served basis. **Tennis de la Faluère** in the Bois de Vincennes is one of the better courts but must be reserved 24 hours in advance.

INDOOR SPORTS

There are plenty of Paris gyms that you can use with a day pass. Expect to pay F120 or more, depending on the facilities.

Espace Vit'halles was one of the first fitness clubs to open in Paris. **Gymnase Club** is a well-equipped, popular chain of gyms. **Jean de Beauvais** is a state-of-the-art gym with personalized fitness programs. **Club Quartier Gym** offers boxing and martial arts along with standard facilities.

In theory, the **Ritz Gym**, with probably the finest indoor swimming pool in Paris, is for guests or members only, but if the hotel is not too full you can buy a day pass.

Skating is a cheap pastime and can be enjoyed year-round at **Patinoire d'Asnières-sur-Seine** and from September to May at the **Patinoire des Buttes-Chaumont**.

Squash can be played at **Squash Club Quartier Latin**, where options also include billiards, gym and a sauna. Other good clubs include the **Squash Montmartre**, **Squash Rennes-Raspail** and the **Squash Front de Seine**.

SPECTATOR SPORTS

A day out at the races is a chance to see the rich in all their finery. The world-famous Prix de l'Arc de Triomphe is held at the **Hippodrome de Longchamp** on the first Sunday in October. More flat racing takes place at the **Hippodrome de St-Cloud** and **Maison Lafitte**, which are a short drive west of Paris. For steeplechasing, go to the **Hippodrome d'Auteuil**. The **Hippodrome de Vincennes** hosts the trotting races. For information, telephone the **Fédération des Sociétés des Courses de France**.

The 24-hour car race at Le Mans, 115 miles (185 km) southwest of Paris, is one of the best-known road races in the world. It takes place every year in mid-June. Contact the **Fédération Française de Sport Automobile** for details.

The **Palais d'Omnisports de Paris-Bercy** sports stadium hosts a vast range of major events, including the Paris tennis open, the six-day cycling race, show-jumping, world-class martial arts demonstrations and also rock concerts.

Parc des Princes can hold 50,000 people. It is home to the main Paris football team, Paris St-Germain, and hosts the rugby internationals.

The Roland Garros international tennis championship takes place at the **Stade Roland Garros** from late May to mid-June. During this period, everyone lives and breathes tennis. Business meetings are transferred from the office conference room to the stadium. Write for tickets several months in advance, because once the tournament begins, it is virtually impossible to obtain seats.

SWIMMING

THERE IS a massive aquatic fun park, known as **Aquaboulevard**, in south Paris *(see p346)*. Besides an exotic artificial beach, swimming pools, water toboggans and rapids, there are tennis and squash courts, golf, bowling, table tennis, billiards, a gym, bars and shops.

Of the many municipal swimming pools, one of the best is the **Piscine Nouveau Forum des Halles**, an Olympic-size swimming pool in the underground shopping complex.

For a lovely 1930s mosaic decor with two levels of private changing cabins, a whirlpool, sauna and water jets, go to the **Piscine Pontoise-Quartier Latin**.

The **Piscine Henry de Montherlant** is part of a municipal sports complex that includes tennis courts and a gym.

MISCELLANEOUS

BASEBALL, FENCING, jogging in the parks, volleyball, windsurfing at La Villette *(see pp234–9)* and bowling are just some of the other sporting activities that can be enjoyed during your stay.

Fishing on the Seine is fast becoming a popular pastime with Parisiens. Due to a cleaning up operation the Seine is now home to a variety of freshwater fish.

DIRECTORY

Allô Sports
25 Blvd Bourdon 75004.
Map 14 D5.
01 42 76 54 54.

Aquaboulevard
4 Rue Louis-Armand 75015.
01 40 60 10 00.

Club Quartier Gym
19 Rue de Pontoise 75005.
Map 13 B5.
01 43 25 31 99.

Espace Vit'halles
48 Rue Rambuteau 75003.
Map 13 B2.
01 42 77 21 71.

Fédération Française du Golf
68 Rue Anatole France, 923000 Levallois Perret.
01 41 49 77 00.

Fédération Française de Cylcotourisme
8 Rue Jean-Marie Jégo 75013. **Map** 17 B5.
01 44 16 88 88.

Fédération Française de Pétanque et Jeu Provençale
9 Rue Duperré 75009.
Map 6 E2.
01 48 74 61 63.

Française de Sport Automobile
17 Ave Général Mangin 75016. **Map** 9 B4.
01 44 30 24 00.

Fédération des Sociétés des Courses de France
10 Blvd Malesherbes 75008. **Map** 5 C5.
01 42 68 87 87.

Fédération Golf de Chevry
91190 Gif-sur-Yvette.
01 60 12 40 33.

Golf de St-Pierre du Perray
91380 St-Pierre du Perray.
01 60 75 17 47.

Golf de St-Quentin en Yvelines
78190 Trappes.
01 30 50 86 40.

Golf de Villennes
Route d'Orgeval, 78670 Villennes-sur-Seine.
01 39 08 18 18.

Gymnase Club
26 Rue Berri 75008.
Map 4 F4.
01 43 59 04 58.

Hippodrome d'Auteuil
Bois de Boulogne 75016.
01 40 71 47 47.

Hippodrome de Longchamp
Bois de Boulogne 75016.
01 44 30 75 00.

Hippodrome Maison Lafitte
1 Ave de la Pelouze, 78600 Maison Lafitte. **Map** 5 B2.
01 39 62 06 77.

Hippodrome de St-Cloud
1 Rue de Camp Canadien, 92210 St-Cloud.
01 47 71 69 26.

Hippodrome de Vincennes
2 Route de la Ferme, 75012 Vincennes.
01 49 77 17 17.

Jean de Beauvais
5 Rue Jean de Beauvais 75005.
Map 13 A5.
01 46 33 16 80.

Ligue Equestre de Paris
69 Rue Laugier 75017.
01 42 12 03 43.

Palais d'Omnisports de Paris-Bercy
8 Blvd Bercy 75012.
Map 18 F2.
01 44 68 44 68.

Parc des Princes
24 Rue du Commandant-Guilbaud 75016.
01 42 88 02 76.

Paris Vélo
2 Rue du Fer-à-Moulin 75005. **Map** 17 C2.
01 43 37 59 22.

Patinoire d'Asnières-sur-Seine
Blvd Pierre de Coubertin, 92600 Asnières.
01 47 99 96 06.

Piscine Deligny
25 Quai Anatole-France 75007. **Map** 11 C2.
01 45 56 96 21.

Piscine Henry de Montherlant
32 Blvd de Lannes 75016.
01 40 72 28 30.

Piscine Pontoise-Quartier Latin
19 Rue de Pontoise 75005.
Map 13 B5.
01 55 42 77 88.

Piscine Nouveau Forum des Halles
10 Pl de la Rotonde, Entrance Porte St Eustache, Les Halles 75001.
Map 13 A2.
01 42 36 98 44.

Ritz Gym
Ritz Hotel, Pl Vendôme 75001. **Map** 6 D5.
01 43 16 30 30.

Stade Roland Garros
2 Ave Gordon-Bennett 75016.
01 47 43 48 00.

Squash Club Quartier Latin
19 Rue de Pontoise 75005. **Map** 13 B5.
01 55 42 77 88.

Squash Front de Seine
21 Rue Gaston-de-Caillavet 75015. **Map** 9 B5.
01 45 75 35 37.

Squash Montmartre
14 Rue Achille-Martinet 75018. **Map** 2 E4.
01 42 55 38 30.

Squash Rennes-Raspail
149 Rue des Rennes 75006.
Map 16 D1.
01 44 39 03 30.

Tennis de la Faluère
Route de la Pyramide Bois de Vincennes 75012.
01 43 74 40 93.

Tennis Luxembourg Jardins du Luxembourg Blvd St-Michel 75006.
Map 12 E5.
01 43 25 79 18.

CHILDREN'S PARIS

IT'S NEVER TOO EARLY to instill in your children a lifelong taste for this magical city. A trip to Disneyland Paris *(see pp242–5)* or down the Seine *(see pp72–3)*, a ride up the dizzy heights of the Eiffel Tower *(see pp192–3)* or a visit to Notre-Dame *(see pp82–5)* is fun at any age, and with children in tow you will see old haunts through new eyes. The orderly and historic parks are probably best appreciated by older children and adults, but everyone loves the technological wizardry of the Euro Disney theme park. During the summer, fun fairs, circuses and all sorts of impromptu events are staged in gardens and parks, notably in the Bois de Boulogne *(see p254)*. Or, take children to an entertainment center, a museum, an adventure playground or a show at a cafe-theater.

La Cité des Enfants at La Villette

PRACTICAL ADVICE

PARIS WELCOMES young families in hotels *(see p272)* and most restaurants *(see p289)*. Many sights and attractions offer children's rates while infants under three or four enter free. The upper age limit for reductions is usually about 12 but can vary considerably. Many museums are free on Sundays; others allow children under 18 in free at any time. Ask at the Office du Tourisme *(see p274)* for full details of children's rates, or check in the weekly entertainment guides, such as *Pariscope*. *Paris Selection* (free from the Office du Tourisme) has a list of events and attractions.

A lot of the children's activities are geared to end-of-school times, including Wednesday afternoons when French children have time off. For information on museum workshops, contact the **Ministère de la Culture**. The **Centre d'Information et de Documentation Jeunesse** has a list of activities for children under 15.

Cribs and baby carriages can be rented from major baby-sitting agencies like **Home Service**. **Ababa** is another specialist baby-sitting organization.

MUSEUMS

TOP OF THE museum list for children is undoubtedly the Cité des Sciences et de l'Industrie *(see pp234–9)* at Parc de la Villette. Hands-on activities and changing exhibitions illuminate many aspects of science and modern technology in this immense complex. Highlights include the sound-and-light shows, the Odorama, the Flight Simulator and the high-tech La Géode movie screen *(see p235)*. There is also a new section for young children called La Cité des Enfants. In central Paris, the Palais de la Découverte *(see p206)* is an old-fashioned but lively science museum where staff members adopt the role of mad inventors.

Other enjoyable museums for children include the Musée de la Marine *(see p199)* and the Musée de la Poupée *(see p114)*. The Musée de la Marine covers the history of the French maritime tradition and includes scale models. The Musée de la Poupée displays handmade dolls dating from the mid-19th century. It also offers doll-making classes for both adults and children.

USEFUL CONTACTS

Ababa
[C] *01 45 49 46 46.*

Centre d'Information et de Documentation Jeunesse
101 Quai Branly 75015.
Map 10 D3.
[C] *01 44 49 12 00.*
[FAX] *01 44 65 02 61.*

Home Service
[C] *01 42 82 05 04.*

Ministère de la Culture
3 Rue de Valois 75001.
Map 12 F1.
[C] *01 40 15 80 00.*

The Café d'Edgar theater

The Guignol marionettes

PARKS, ZOOS AND ADVENTURE PLAYGROUNDS

THE BEST CHILDREN's park within Paris is the Jardin d'Acclimatation (see p254) in the Bois de Boulogne. It is, however, quite expensive. During school terms it's best to go on Wednesday afternoon or on the weekend, or you may find some attractions are not open.

The Musée en Herbe (see p254) offers educational, entertaining activities; you can leave children with supervisors in the Jardin des Halles in the Forum des Halles (see p109). In the Bois de Vincennes, the inexpensive

Pony rides, Jardin d'Acclimatation

Parc Floral (see p246) has simple amusements for children. The Bois de Vincennes also houses Paris's largest zoo (see p246). Perhaps the most appealing zoo is the small Ménagerie (see p164).

ENTERTAINMENT CENTERS

THERE ARE MANY supervised children's activity centers in Paris. The Atelier des Enfants in the Pompidou Center (see pp 110–11) has a workshop on Wednesdays and Saturdays from 2:30 to 4pm. The medium of instruction is French, but the circuses, mime-shows, marionettes and craft or museum workshops focus on actions rather than words.

Several café-theaters, including Café d'Edgar (see p331) and Au Bec Fin (see p331), offer children's shows where mime, dance or music form a large part of the content. Children's television programs are generally shown from 7 to 8am and 5 to 6pm. The most spectacular cinematic experience is in La Géode at the Cité des Sciences et de l'Industrie (see p235). The **Le Saint Lambert** movie theater specializes in French

Lion in the Bois de Vincennes zoo

children's movies and comic strips. Tickets are generally cheaper on Wednesdays, with no children's reductions on weekends.

A more unusual outing is a day at the circus. The **Cirque de Paris** offers children a day's entertainment when they can meet the animals, put on clown make-up or practice tightrope walking. Shows are held in the afternoon following lunch with the *artistes*.

The Guignol marionette puppet shows are a summer tradition in Paris. The themes are similar to the traditional English Punch and Judy shows, with a dominant wife battering a husband with the intervention of a policeman. Most of the main parks hold Guignol shows during the summer on Wednesday afternoons and at weekends. One or two shows are free. Consult the entertainment guides such as *L'Officiel des Spectacles* and *Pariscope*.

ADDRESSES

Cirque de Paris
115 Blvd Charles de Gaulle, 92390 Villeneuve la Garenne. ☎ 01 47 99 40 40.

Le Saint Lambert
6 Rue Peclet 75015. ☎ 01 45 32 91 68.

Circus acrobats training at the Cirque de Paris

Fireworks over Sleeping Beauty's Castle, Disneyland Paris

THEME PARKS

THE FIVE-THEMED park of Disneyland Paris at the Disneyland Paris Resort *(see pp242–5)* is the biggest and most spectacular of the Paris theme parks. Six imaginative hotels and a campsite provide onsite accommodations. The complex also includes a golf course, shops and restaurants.

Parc Asterix is a French theme park centering around the legendary world of Asterix the Gaul. Here six-themed "worlds" feature gladiators, slave auctions and rides among the many attractions. The park is situated 24 miles (38 km) northeast of Paris. Take the RER line B to Charles de Gaulle Airport, then take the shuttle bus to Parc Asterix.

SPORTS AND RECREATION

THE GIANT waterpark **Aquaboulevard** is one of the best places to take energetic youngsters. Another good swimming pool in Paris is the indoor pool at **Nouveau Forum**. The weekly entertainment guide *Pariscope* provides information about other swimming pools in and around Paris.

Accomplished roller skaters and skateboarders practice outside the Palais de Chaillot *(see p198)*.

Donald Duck

There is an official roller-skating rink in the Parc Monceau *(see pp258–9)*, and the Parc des Buttes-Chaumont *(see p232)* and Disneyland Paris Resort *(see pp242–5)* have ice-skating rinks. Disneyland Paris has a wide range of sports facilities.

Old-fashioned fairground carousels are situated near Sacré-Coeur *(see pp224–5)* and Forum Les Halles *(see p109)*. Great fun too is a boat trip. Several companies compete. The oldest is **Bateaux Mouches** *(see pp72–3)*, whose crafts depart from the Pont de l'Alma and pass a host of waterfront sites, including Notre-Dame, the Louvre, and the Musée d'Orsay.

Boats departing from La Villette travel along the Paris canal system. Radio-controlled model boats are popular on the ponds of the Jardin du Luxembourg *(see p172)*. Or, take the family boating on the lakes of the Bois de Boulogne *(see p254)* or the Bois de Vincennes *(see p246)*. Riding is also popular in these parks.

ADDRESSES

Aquaboulevard
4 Rue Louis Armand 75015.
【 *01 40 60 10 00.* **Open** *9am–11pm Mon–Thu, 9am–midnight Fri, 8am–midnight Sat, 8am–11pm Sun.*

Bateaux Mouches
Pont d'Alma. **Map** 10 F1.
【 *01 42 25 96 10.*
For departures, see p73.

Nouveau Forum
10 Pl de la Rotonde, Les Halles 75001.
Map 12 F2. 【 *01 42 36 98 44.* **Open** *11:30am–7:30pm Mon, 11:30am–10pm Wed–Fri, 9am–5pm Sat & Sun.*

Parc Asterix
Plailly 60128. 【 *08 36 68 30 10.*
Open *second week Apr–mid-Oct: 10am–6pm Mon–Fri, 10am–7pm Sat & Sun.*

CHILDREN'S SHOPS

There is no shortage of chic children's fashion in Paris. A good place to start is the Rue du Jour in Beaubourg and Les Halles, which has a number of children's boutiques, such as Un Après-Midi de Chien at No. 10 and Claude Vell at No. 8. The city has many appealing toy shops but, like the clothes shops, they can be prohibitively expensive. *(See also Children's Clothes p318.)*

Characters from the book *Tintin*, in Au Nain Bleu toy shop *(see p321)*

Roller skaters near the Eiffel Tower

Carousel near Sacré-Coeur

STREET LIFE AND MARKETS

OUTSIDE THE Pompidou Center (see pp110–11), street entertainers draw the crowds on sunny afternoons. Musicians, magicians, fire eaters and artists of all kinds perform here. In Montmartre there is a tradition of street-painting, predominantly in the Place du Tertre (see

Model boats for rent in the Jardin du Luxembourg

p222), where someone will always be willing to draw your child's portrait. It's also fun to take the funicular up the hill to Sacré-Coeur (see pp224–5), then walk down through the pretty streets.

Parisian markets are colorful and animated. Try taking children to the Marché aux Fleurs on the Ile de la Cité (see p81) or to the food markets on the Rue Mouffetard, in the Jardin des Plantes Quarter (see p166 and p327), or the Rue de Buci in St-Germain-des-Prés. The biggest flea market, Marché aux Puces de St-Ouen is on weekends in Place Clignancourt (see p231 and p327).

You can also take children to the quiet Ile de la Cité or Ile St-Louis on the Seine.

VIEWPOINTS AND SIGHTSEEING

TOP OF THE sightseeing list for children is a trip up the Eiffel Tower (see pp192–3). On a clear day, spectacular views over Paris will enable you to point out a number of sights, and at night the city is magically lit up. Elevators run until 11pm, and lines are much shorter in the evenings. If you are pushing a baby carriage bear in mind that the ascent is in three stages, using two separate elevators.

Other interesting sights for children include Sacré-Coeur (see pp224–5) with its ovoid dome – the second-highest point in Paris after the Eiffel Tower – and Notre-Dame cathedral (see pp82–3) on the Ile de la Cité. Children will enjoy feeding the pigeons in the cathedral square, counting the 28 kings of Judah on the west front and listening to you recount the story of the hunchback of Notre-Dame. There are incomparable views from the towers. Children and adults alike will appreciate the enchanting Sainte-Chapelle (see pp88–9), also on the Ile de la Cité. There are reductions for children under the age of 17.

Contrast ancient and modern Paris with a visit to the Pompidou Center (see pp110–11) and enjoy a ride on the caterpillar like escalators outside or go to the café on the roof terrace for the views. There is also the 56-story Montparnasse Tower (see p178) with some spectacular telescopic views from the top terrace; and there is the huge arch at La Défense (see p255), which has elevators to platforms where visitors can overlook the whole complex.

OTHER INTERESTS

CHILDREN are quick to see the funny side of unusual spectacles. Les Egouts, Paris's sewers, now welcome apprehensive visitors for a

Escalators at the Pompidou Center

short tour of the city's sewerage system (see p190). Display boards in several languages explain the processes.

The Catacombs (see p179) are a long series of quarry tunnels built in Roman times, now lined with ancient skulls.

On the Ile de la Cité is the Conciergerie (see p81), a turreted prison where many hapless aristocrats spent their final days. The Musée Grévin waxworks are in Boulevard Montmartre (see p216). The museum's Revolution rooms will especially appeal to older children, with gruesome scenes and grisly sound effects, demonstrating the reality of social upheaval.

EMERGENCIES

THE FREE 24-hour child helpline is Enfance et Partage, which can also be for adults. One of the largest children's hospitals in Paris is Hôpital Necker.

Enfance et Partage
☎ 01 53 36 53 53.

Hôpital Necker 149 Rue de Sèvres 75015. **Map** 15 B1. ☎ 01 44 49 40 00.

A young visitor to Paris

SURVIVAL
GUIDE

PRACTICAL INFORMATION

As IN MOST LARGE cities, it's easy to waste your limited sightseeing time in Paris traveling and then waiting in lines. A little advance planning can minimize this. Call in advance to confirm that each sight is open and not closed for refurbishment or holidays – a phonecard, or *télécarte,* is a wise investment *(see p356).* Purchase a *carnet,* or travel pass, to economize and simplify transportation on the buses and metro *(see pp368–71).* A *Paris Carte-Musée* will give unlimited access to museums and monuments and limit waiting in line. Beware the Paris lunch break (around 1–3pm), when many essential services shut down and some museums close. Guided tours are often the best way to see the major sights while you get your bearings. If you're on a tight budget, you should bear in mind that admission is sometimes lower at certain times or on Sundays; card-carrying students can obtain discounts on some tickets and admissions *(see p358).*

MUSEUMS AND MONUMENTS

THERE ARE 150 museums and monuments open to the public in Paris. Most are open Monday (or Tuesday) to Sunday, and from 10am to 5.40pm. Some offer evening visits. The national museums are closed on Tuesdays, except Versailles and the Musée d'Orsay, which are closed on Mondays. The municipal museums, such as those run by the city of Paris (Ville de Paris) are usually closed on Mondays.

An admission fee is usually charged, or a donation is expected. The entrance fee to national museums is reduced by half on Sundays. Those under 18 are admitted free and those 18 – 25 and over 60 pay half-price. The municipal museums, and some other museums, do not charge a fee to see their permanent collections on Sundays. Those under 7 and over 60 are admitted free at all times. To obtain the discounts you will have to provide absolute proof of who you are, what you do and how old you are.

Train station sign for information services

It is worth buying the pass known as *Paris Carte-Musée* (also known as the *Carte Inter-Musée).* This gives the bearer access to more than 63 museums and monuments. The user is also entitled to an unlimited number of visits and does not have to get in a line, a significant advantage in the Paris high season, when crowds can become a highly frustrating problem. The pass can be purchased at any of the city's museums and monuments, main metro and RER stations and also at the headquarters of the **Paris Convention and Visitors Bureau**.

Tourist Office emblem

OPENING HOURS

THIS GUIDE LISTS opening times for each sight individually. Most Paris businesses are open from 9–10am to 7–8pm, Mon–Sat, but may stay open longer in summer, with late closing on Saturday and early closing on Sunday, and before public holidays. Food shops open at about 7am and close about noon for lunch, then re-open at 4–5pm, and close at 8pm. Some restaurants close at least one day a week. Banks are open from around 9am to 4.30–5.15pm Mon–Fri, and 9am–2pm. Some close noon–2pm. The day before a public holiday they close at noon.

TOURIST INFORMATION

THERE ARE FOUR tourist offices in Paris, one at the Gare de Lyon, one at the Eiffel Tower, one on the Champs-Elysées *(see p351)* and one, for Paris and the Ile de France, is by the Louvre. All provide maps, information and brochures. They also offer last-minute hotel reservation services. At the Gare de Lyon office, which is particularly useful for incoming travelers, the service is slow in summer, when backpackers arrive in droves. Expect to wait.

ENTERTAINMENT

THE MAIN listings magazines in Paris, available at all newsstands, are *Pariscope* and *L'Officiel des Spectacles (see p328).* Each Wednesday they present full, up-to-date information on the week's current theater, movies, and exhibits, as well as on

Paris museum passes, for saving time and money

Paris sightseeing tour bus

cabarets, dinner clubs, and some restaurants.

Alpha-FNAC agencies have tickets for all the major entertainment attractions, including temporary museum shows. There are Alpha-FNAC branches throughout Paris. For more information, call the main central office (see p329).

For theater tickets only, the Kiosque Théâtre sells same-day tickets at 50% discount. The two locations are Place de la Madeleine and the Châtelet–Les Halles RER station (see p329).

Visitors should be aware that smoking is not allowed in theaters, movie houses, or other public places.

Kiosque Théâtre ticket kiosk

GUIDED TOURS

THERE ARE double-decker bus tours with commentaries in English, Italian, Japanese and German. These are operated by major companies – **Cityrama** and **Paris Vision**. The tours begin from the city center and take about two hours. They pass the main sights but do not stop at all of them. Because departure times vary, visitors should phone the bus operators for details. Another operator, **Parisbus**, runs tours on British double-decker buses stopping at many of Paris's great sights. These tours allow you to leave the bus at any of the stops and to rejoin the tour later.

The Caisse Nationale des Monuments Historiques (see p95) offers guided walking tours.

BUS TOUR OPERATORS

Cityrama
147 Rue St-Honoré 75001.
Map 12 E1. (01 44 55 61 00.

Paribus
3–5 Rue Talma 75016. **Map** 9 A3.
(01 42 88 92 88.

Paris Vision
214 Rue de Rivoli 75001.
Map 12 D1. (01 42 60 30 01.

DISABLED ACCESS

SERVICES FOR disabled persons are limited. Most pavements have been contoured to allow wheelchair passage, but many restaurants, hotels, and even museums and monuments are poorly equipped. However, better facilities are being incorporated into all renovated and new buildings. For information on public facilities for the disabled, call the **Paris Convention and Visitors Bureau** and ask for a copy of the (French language) pamphlet Touristes Quand Même.

DISABILITY INFORMATION

Association pour la Mobilité des Handicapées à Paris
65 rue de la Victoire 75009. **Map** 6 E4. (01 42 80 40 20. **Open** 9:30am–noon, 1pm–6pm Mon–Fri. Information, advice, assistance.

Les Compagnons du Voyage
17 Quai D'Austerlitz 75013.
Map 18 E2. (01 45 83 67 77.
Open 8:30am– noon, 2pm–5pm Mon–Fri. Seven-day escort services on all transportation. Costs vary.

Personal Security and Health

Paris is as safe or as dangerous as you make it – using common sense will usually keep you out of trouble. If, on the other hand, you fall sick during your visit, pharmacists are an excellent source of advice. In France pharmacists can diagnose many health problems and suggest appropriate treatment. For more serious medical help, someone at the emergency numbers below will be able to deal with most inquiries. There are many specialist services available, including a general advice line for English-speakers in crisis, an English-speaking Alcoholics Anonymous group and a phone line for psychiatric help.

French pharmacy sign

Emergency button at metro stations

Emergency Numbers

SAMU (ambulance)
15.

Police
17.

**Pompiers
(fire department)**
18.

**SOS Medecin
(doctor, house calls)**
01 47 07 77 77.

SOS Dentaire (dentist)
01 43 37 51 00.

Burn Specialists
01 42 34 17 58
or 01 42 34 12 12.

**SOS Help (English
language crisis line)**
01 47 23 80 80.
Open 3pm–11pm daily.

**SOS Dépression
(for psychiatric help)**
01 45 22 44 44.

Sexual Disease Center
01 40 78 26 00.

Family Planning Center
01 48 88 07 28.
Open 9am–5:30pm Mon–Fri.

Personal Security

For a city of 2–3 million people, Paris is surprisingly safe. The center of the city in particular has little violent crime. Muggings and fights do occur, but they are rare compared to what occurs in many other world capitals. However, do avoid poorly lit or isolated places. Beware of pickpockets, especially on the metro during the rush hour. Keep all valuables securely concealed, and if you carry a handbag or briefcase, never let it out of your sight.

When traveling late at night, it is a good idea, for women especially, to avoid long transfers in such metro stations as Montparnasse and Châtelet–Les Halles. Generally, areas around RER train stations attract groups of youths from outlying areas who come to Paris for entertainment and may become unruly. The last runs each night of RER trains to and from outlying areas should also be avoided. In an emergency in the metro, call the station agent by using the yellow telephone marked *Chef de Station* on all metro and RER platforms or go to the ticket booth at the entrance. Most metro stations do have emergency buttons. The metro cars also have alarm pulls. If there is a problem outside stations, or at bus stops, call the police by dialing 17.

Personal Property

Take great care with your personal property at all times. Make sure you insure your possessions before arrival. On sightseeing or pleasure trips, do not carry valuables with you. Also, take only as much cash as you think you will need. Traveler's checks are the

Paris fireman

Policewoman

Policeman

Typical Paris police car

Paris fire engine

Paris ambulance

safest method of carrying large sums of money. You should never leave your luggage unattended in metro or train stations – it may be stolen. For missing persons, or in the case of robbery or assault, call the police or go to the nearest police station (*Commissariat de Police*). For lost or stolen passports, call your consulate (*see p359*).

MEDICAL TREATMENT

ALL EUROPEAN community nationals are entitled to French Social Security coverage. However, treatment must be paid for, and hospital rates vary widely. Reimbursements may be obtained but the process is long and involved. All travelers should consider purchasing travel insurance and should also contact their doctors or insurance carriers before leaving home if they require ongoing prescriptions or medical care.

In the case of a medical emergency, call **SAMU** (*see box on facing page*) or the **Pompiers** (fire department). Fire department ambulances are often the quickest to arrive at an emergency. First-aid and emergency treatment is provided at all fire stations.

Hospitals with emergency departments are shown on the Street Finder (*see p374*). For English-language visitors, there are two hospitals with English-speaking staff and doctors: the **American Hospital** and the **British Hospital**.

There are many pharmacies throughout the city, and a short list is provided here. Pharmacies are recognized by the green crosses on the shop front. At night and on Sundays, closed pharmacies hang in their doorway the address of the nearest one that is open.

Banking and Local Currency

VISITORS TO PARIS will find that the banks usually offer them the best rates of exchange. Privately owned bureaux de change, on the other hand, have variable rates, and care should be taken to check small-print details relating to commission and minimum charges before any transaction is completed.

BANKING

THERE IS NO restriction on the amount of money or currency you may bring into France. It is wise to carry money in the form of traveler's checks. To change traveler's checks or cash, bureaux de change are located at airports, large railroad stations and some hotels and shops.

Many bank branches in central Paris have their own bureaux de change. They generally offer the best exchange rates but also charge a commission for doing the exchange.

Many independent, non-bank exchange offices do not charge commission but offer poorer rates of exchange. Central Paris non-bank exchanges are usually open 9am to 6pm on Monday to Saturday and are found along the Champs-Elysées, around the Opéra and Madeleine and near some tourist attractions and monuments. They are also found at all main railroad stations, open from 8am to 9pm daily. Note that the bureaux located at Gare St-Lazare and Gare d'Austerlitz are closed on Sunday. Airport offices are open from 7am to 11pm daily.

CHANGE
CAMBIO-WECHSEL

Sign at bureau de change

TRAVELER'S CHECKS AND CREDIT CARDS

THESE CAN be obtained from **American Express**, **Thomas Cook** or your bank.

American Express traveler's checks are widely accepted in France. You should look for the AmEx logo. If checks are exchanged at an AmEx office, no commission is charged. In the case of theft, checks are replaced immediately. Traveler's checks can be issued in francs by overseas branches of Crédit Lyonnais. They usually offer the best foreign exchange rate.

Due to the high commissions charged, many French businesses do not accept the AmEx card. The most widely used credit card is **VISA**.

Credit card cash dispenser

Restaurants and service stations generally accept payment by French check, traveler's check or credit cards.

Automatic tellers (ATMs) are found at banks and large supermarkets. Many ATMs give instructions in several European languages and accept foreign credit and debit cards with PIN codes. The cards that are accepted are shown. Credit card companies charge interest on cash withdrawals. To retrieve cards seized by ATM, ask in the branch concerned, or telephone the issuing bank.

THE EURO

THE EURO BECAME legal tender in 11 European Union countries including France on Jan 1, 1999. Only paper or electronic transactions can be made in Euros until Jan 1, 2002, when bills and coins come into circulation. From then on the Euro will be the single currency of all 11 states.

DIRECTORY

AFTER-HOURS BUREAUX DE CHANGE

Ancienne Comédie
5 Rue Ancienne-Comédie 75006.
Map 12 F4.
[01 43 26 33 30.
Open 9am–11pm daily.

CCF
115 Ave des Champs-Elysées 75008. **Map** 4 E4.
[01 40 70 27 22.
Open 8:45am–8pm Mon–Sat.

Europullman
10 Rue Alger 75001.
Map 12 D1.
[01 42 60 55 58.
Open 9am–7pm Mon–Sat.

Multichange
161 Rue de Rennes 75006.
Map 16 D1.
[01 42 22 09 63.
Open 9:30am–7pm Mon–Sat.

FOREIGN BANKS

American Express
11 Rue Scribe 75009.
Map 6 D5.
[01 47 14 50 00.

Barclays
45 Blvd Haussman 75009.
Map 6 F4.
[01 55 27 55 27.

Midland
20 bis Avenue Rapp 75007.
Map 3 C4.
[01 44 42 70 00.

Thomas Cook
8 Place de l'Opéra
75009. [01 47 42 46 52.

LOST CARDS AND TRAVELER'S CHECKS

American Express
Cards [01 47 77 72 00.
Checks [0800 90 86 00.

Mastercard
Cards [01 45 67 53 53.

VISA/Carte Bleue
Cards [08 36 69 08 80.

CURRENCY

THE OUTGOING FRENCH UNIT OF currency is the franc, which is indicated by the letter *F* before or, more usually, after the amount. It is distinguished from the Swiss or Belgian franc by the use of the letters *FF*. There are 100 centimes to the franc, but their value is now so small that 1 centime coins are no longer in circulation.

Bank Notes
French bills come in the denominations F20, F50, F100, F200 and F500. They increase in size progressively according to value and are different colors.

F500 bill

F200 bill

F100 bill

F50 bill

F20 bill

Coins
Coins (shown here actual size) come in the following denominations: 5, 10, 20 and 50 centimes; F1, F2, F5, F10 and F20. The 5, 10 and 20-centime coins are brass. The 50-centime, F1, F2 and F5 coins are silver alloy. The F10 and F20 coins are bimetal.

F20

F10

F5

F2

F1

50 centimes

20 centimes

10 centimes

5 centimes

Telephone and Postal Service

THE FRENCH TELECOMMUNICATIONS agency is called France Télécom; the postal service is La Poste. Both work efficiently, though the customer services of the post offices may not. So be prepared to wait in lines. There are many *bureaux des postes* scattered throughout the city. These are identified by the blue-on-

yellow La Poste sign *(see p357)*. Public telephones are located in most public places, including on the streets and in railroad and metro stations. If you are dialing abroad from Paris, the best way is to purchase a telephone card *(télécarte)*, then find a quiet location to call from.

Telephone Booths
Coin-operated telephone booths are now quite rare because of vandalism. The newer card-operated telephones are cheap and easy to use, but you must buy a télécarte *first.*

Modern, card-operated booth

Older-style booth

USING A PHONECARD (TÉLÉCARTE) TELEPHONE

1 Lift the receiver and wait for a dial tone.

2 Holding the *télécarte* with the arrow side up, insert it into the slot in the direction that the arrow is pointing.

3 Wait for the display screen to indicate how many units are stored on the card. The screen will then tell you to dial.

4 Dial the number and wait to be connected.

5 If you want to make another call, do not replace the receiver; simply press the green follow-on call button.

6 When you have finished the call, replace the receiver. The card will emerge from the slot. Remove it.

FRANCE TELECOM
600 AGENCES
PARTOUT
EN FRANCE
TELECARTE 50

Télécarte

USING THE TELEPHONE

MOST FRENCH telephones have push-buttons, but some older dial telephones are still found in cafés and restaurants. Telephone directories *(annuaires)* are found in post offices, cafés and restaurants, but not in telephone booths.

Telephones take either coins (F1, F2, F5 and F10) or plastic telephone cards *(télécartes)*. Cards are worth either 50 or 120 telephone units (one unit currently costs less than a franc). They can be bought at all post offices and *tabacs* (tobacconists). Cards tend to be cheaper and more convenient to use than coins. Coin telephones have virtually disappeared from the streets of Paris. They can still be found in cafés, but they are reserved for the use of customers. Collect calls are known as *PCV* in France. Most telephone booths can be called from anywhere. The telephone booth number is displayed above the telephone unit.

Since October 1996, all French telephone numbers have had ten digits. For calls to and within Paris and the Ile de France, add the prefix 01 to the old, eight-digit number; add 02 for northwestern regions; 03 for the northeast; 04 for the southeast; and 05 for the southwest.

To telephone Paris from the US, dial 011 33 and then the number. From the UK, dial 00 33. From Australia, dial 00 11 33. From New Zealand, dial 00 33. From the Republic of Ireland, dial 16 33. Omit the first zero of the Paris code.

The main post office *(see p357)* is open all day, and is cheaper than hotels for international calls.

REACHING THE RIGHT NUMBER

• Internal (French) directory inquiries, dial 12.
• International telegrams, dial (0800) 33 44 11.
• International information, dial 00, wait for the tone, then 33 12, then country code.
• USA Direct operator, dial 00, wait for the tone, then 00 11, then the number.
• British Telecom operator, dial 00, wait for the tone, then 00 44, then the number.

• To call the **US** and Canada, dial 00, wait for the tone, then 1, then the number (leave off the 0 from the area code).
• To call the **UK**, dial 00, wait for the tone, then 44, then the number.

• To call **Australia**, dial 00, wait for the tone, then 61, then the number.
• To call **New Zealand**, dial 00, wait for the tone, then 64, then the number.
• To call the **Irish Republic**, dial 00, wait for the tone, then 353, then the number.

The telephone yellow pages lists codes for every country under "Communication: Etranger." A full list of low rate periods to call abroad is under "Etranger–Tarification."
• **UK, Ireland, Australia,** and **New Zealand low-rate period**: 9:30pm–8am Mon–Fri; all day Sun and public hols.

In case of emergencies, dial 17.

Mail and Postal Services – Using La Poste

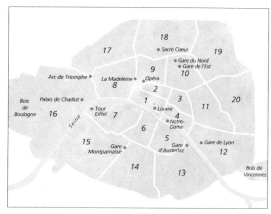

Post office sign

IN ADDITION TO ALL NORMAL services – telegrams, postage stamps, registered letters, special delivery, delivery of packages and books – the post office sells collectors' stamps and will cash or send international postal checks and money orders. Fax and telex services, as well as coin and card-operated telephones, are available in all main offices.

Paris-Champs Elysées
71 Ave des Champs Elysées 75008.
Map 4 F5.
☎ 01 53 89 05 80.
FAX 01 42 56 13 71.
Open 8am–7:30pm Mon–Fri,
10am–7pm Sat.

SENDING A LETTER

COMMON postage stamps *(timbres)* **are** sold singly or in *carnets* of ten. These are valid for letters and

A *carnet* (small book) of stamps

postcards up to 20 g (approx. half an ounce) to most EC countries. Stamps are also sold in *tabacs.*

Paris post office hours are 8am–7pm Mon–Fri, 8am–noon Sat. At the post offices you can consult the phone book *(annuaire)*, buy

phonecards, send or receive money orders *(mandats)* and call anywhere in the world.

Letters are dropped into yellow mailboxes.

For poste restante (mail holding), the sender should write the recipient's name in block letters, then "Poste Restante," then the address of the Paris-Louvre post office.

MAIN POST OFFICES

Paris-Louvre
52 Rue de Louvre 75001. **Map** 12 F1.
☎ 01 40 28 20 00. **FAX** 01 45 08 12 82. *Open* 24 hours daily.

Destinations

Paris mailbox

Paris Arrondissements
The districts, or arrondissements, *of Paris are numbered from 1 to 20 (see p374). The first three numbers of the postal code – 750 (sometimes 751) – indicate Paris; the last two give the* arrondissement *number. The first* arrondissement's *postal code is 75001.*

18
17
Sacré Coeur
19
Gare du Nord
Gare de l'Est
Arc de Triomphe
9
La Madeleine
Opéra
10
8
2
Palais de Chaillot
1
3
20
Bois de Boulogne
16
Tour Eiffel
7
Louvre
4
Notre-Dame
11
Seine
6
5
Gare d'Austerlitz
Gare de Lyon
15
Gare Montparnasse
12
14
13
Bois de Vincennes

CUSTOMS AND IMMIGRATION

CURRENTLY THERE are no visa requirements for EU nationals or tourists from the United States or New Zealand staying in France for under three months. After three months, a *carte de séjour* is required. Visitors from Canada, Australia and other countries should request information from the French consulate in their own country before leaving.

TAX-FREE GOODS

VISITORS RESIDENT outside the European Union can reclaim the sales tax (TVA, or VAT; *see p312*) they pay on French goods if they spend more than F2,000 and take the goods out of France.

Détaxe receipts can be issued on purchase to reclaim the tax paid, and reimbursements are collected when exiting the country, within three months of purchase. There are some goods you cannot claim a rebate on, namely food and drink, medicines, tobacco, cars and motorcycles, though tax can be reimbursed for bicycles.

Bottle of scent

DUTY-PAID LIMITS AND DUTY FREE GOODS

SINCE JANUARY 1, 1993, there are no longer restrictions on the quantities of duty-paid and VAT-paid goods you can take from one EU country to another, as long as they are for your own use and not for resale. You may be asked to prove the goods are for your own use if they exceed the EU suggested quantities. If you cannot do so, the entire amount of the goods (not just the deemed excess) may be confiscated and destroyed. The suggested limits are: 10 liters of spirits (i.e. drinks over 22° proof), 90 liters of wine, 110 liters of beer and 800 cigarettes. Some dangerous goods are illegal. Visitors under the age of 17 are not allowed to import duty-paid tobacco or alcohol.

On June 30, 1999, despite a strongly fought campaign by the ferry, airline and Eurotunnel services, and considerable public support, the European Union abolished the long-standing "duty free" limits. Whether this will result in higher fares remains to be seen, but it is likely that carriers will decide to recoup lost profits this way.

IMPORTING OTHER GOODS

IN GENERAL, personal goods (e.g., car or bicycle) may be imported to France duty-free and without paperwork if they are obviously for personal use and not for sale. The brochure *Bon Voyages* clarifies this and is available from the **Centre** below. The Centre can also give advice on import regulations, but this is usually in French.

CUSTOMS INFORMATION

Centre des Renseignements des Douanes
23 Rue de L'Université, 75007.
▪ 01 55 04 65 01.
Open 9am–5pm Mon–Fri.

ELECTRICAL ADAPTERS

THE VOLTAGE in France is 220 volts. Plugs have two small round pins; heavier-duty ones have two large round pins. Better hotels offer built-in voltage adapters for shavers only. Adapters can be bought at department stores, such as BHV *(see p313)*.

French two-pin electrical plug

STUDENT INFORMATION

STUDENTS WITH VALID ID cards benefit from discounts of 25% to 50% at theaters, museums, movie theaters and many public monuments. Students may purchase *Cartes Jeunes*, the French equivalent of the International Student ID card. This can be obtained from **CIDJ** (Centre d'Infor-mation et de Documentation Jeunesse; *see p359*). CIDJ provides information on student life in Paris and can furnish a list of inexpensive accommodations. It does not provide a hotel or hostel service, but three **AJF** youth hostels and information centers in Paris provide 8,000 beds for students and young people *(see p359)*.

PUBLIC TOILETS IN PARIS

Most old-fashioned urinals and toilets have been replaced by modern pay toilets. They are found on pavements all over the city. In some units, classical music is played. It is crucial that children under 10 are not allowed into these toilets on their own. They have an automatic cleaning function that can be a danger to small children.

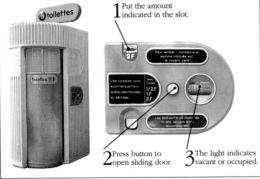

1 Put the amount indicated in the slot.

2 Press button to open sliding door.

3 The light indicates vacant or occupied.

TV, RADIO, NEWSPAPERS

THERE ARE ONLY a few French TV stations, all of them transmitting in French only: TF1, FR2, FR3, M6 and Arte. For English-speakers there is the French cable channel Canal +. On this you can get the American CBS "evening" news live at 7am daily. For other cable channels (such as Skynews or CNN), check hotel information services – some hotels receive satellite and cable TV. Radio France Internationale (89MHz FM and 738MW) broadcasts international news in English from 4 to 5pm daily (MW only). The *International Herald*

Foreign newspapers from kiosks

Tribune is published in Paris and contains good American news coverage. Major British daily, weekly and Sunday papers are sold from kiosks in the central tourist areas of Paris. They include *The Times*, *Sunday Times*, *Guardian International*, *Daily Mail*, *Financial Times* and *The Economist*. The major US, German, Swiss, Italian and Spanish newspapers are usually found at the same newsstands.

BRITISH RADIO NEWS

BBC World Service Information
United Kingdom
(*0171-240 3456.*

INTERNATIONAL BOOKSHOPS

Brentano's
37 Ave de l'Opéra 75002.
Map 6 E5. (*01 42 61 52 50.*
Open 10am–7pm Mon–Sat.

Gibert Jeune
27 Quai St-Michel 75005.
Map 13 A4. (*01 43 54 57 32.*
Open 10am–7pm Mon–Sat.

W. H. Smith
248 Rue de Rivoli 75001.
Map 11 C1. (*01 44 77 88 99.*
Open 9:30am–7pm Mon–Sat.

PARIS TIME

PARIS IS ONE hour ahead of Greenwich Mean Time (GMT). The French use the 24-hour or military clock (am and pm are not used). Therefore, 9am is 09:00, 9pm is 21:00 (add 12 to give the 24-hour clock time). Here are some standard time differences with other cities (these can vary with local summer changes to the time): London: -1 hour; New York -6 hours; Dallas: -7 hours; Los Angeles: -9 hours; Sydney: +9 hours; Tokyo: +8 hours; Auckland: +11 hours.

CONVERSION CHART

Imperial to metric
1 inch = 2.54 centimeters
1 foot = 30 centimeters
1 mile = 1.6 kilometers
1 ounce = 28 grams
1 pound = 454 grams
1 US pint = 0.5 liter
1 US gallon = 3.8 liters

Metric to imperial
1 millimeter = 0.04 inch
1 centimeter = 0.4 inch
1 meter = 3 feet 3 inches
1 kilometer = 0.6 mile
1 gram = 0.04 ounce
1 kilogram = 2.2 pounds
1 liter = 2 US pints

DIRECTORY

OTU OFFICES

Beaubourg
119 Rue St-Martin 75004.
Map 13 B2.
(*01 40 29 12 12.*

Quartier Latin
2 Rue Malus 75005.
Map 17 B1.
(*01 43 63 80 27.*

Bois de Boulogne
Ave de Pologne 75016.
Map 3 A5.
(*01 47 55 03 01.*

STUDENT INFO

CIDJ
101 Quai Branly 75015.
Map 10 E2.
(*01 44 49 12 00.*
Open 9:30am–6pm Mon–Fri, 9.30am–1pm Sat.

EMBASSIES

Australia
4 Rue Jean Rey 75015.
Map 10 D3.
(*01 40 59 33 00.*

Canada
35 Ave Montaigne 75008.
Map 10 F1.
(*01 44 43 29 00.*

Great Britain
35 Rue du Faubourg St-Honoré 75008.
Map 5 C5. **Consulate**
(visas) 16 Rue d'Anjou
75008. (*01 44 51 31 00.*

Ireland (Eire)
4 Rue Rude 75116. **Map**
4 D4. (*01 44 17 67 00.*

New Zealand
7 ter, Rue Léonard de
Vinci 75116. **Map** 3 C5.
(*01 45 00 24 11.*

USA
2 Ave Gabriel 75008.
Map 5 B5.
(*01 43 12 22 22.*

RELIGIOUS SERVICES

PROTESTANT
American Church
65 Quai d'Orsay 75007.
Map 10 F2.
(*01 40 62 05 00.*

Church of Scotland
17 Rue Bayard 75008.
Map 10 F1.
(*01 47 20 90 49.*

St George's Anglican Church
7 Rue Auguste Vacquerie
75116.
Map 4 E5.
(*01 47 20 22 51.*

CATHOLIC
Basilique du Sacré-Coeur
35 Rue du Chevalier de la
Barre 75018.
Map 6 F1.
(*01 53 41 89 00.*

Cathédrale de Notre-Dame
Pl du Parvis Notre-Dame
75004. **Map** 13 A4.
(*01 42 34 56 10.*

JEWISH
Synagogue Nazareth
15 Rue Notre Dame de
Nazareth 75003. **Map**
7 C5. (*01 42 78 00 30.*

MOSLEM
Grande Mosquée de Paris
Place du Puits de l'Ermite
75005. **Map** 17 B2.
(*01 45 35 97 33.*

GETTING TO PARIS

PARIS IS AN AIRLINE and railroad hub. All European capitals, and many main cities on the Continent, in Scandinavia and in the United Kingdom, offer direct flights, trains or ferry-train links to Paris. There are also direct flights from North America, Africa and Japan. However, none of the routes from

Boeing 737 passenger jet

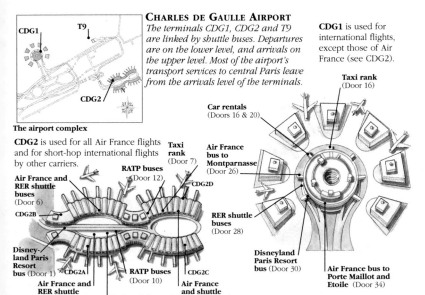

Australia or New Zealand goes directly to Paris. These travelers must change planes for a connecting flight to Paris. For land travelers, many national and international motorways converge on Paris, and the city is easily accessible for those traveling either by car or by long-distance coach.

ARRIVING BY AIR

FROM THE United States, there are regular flights through **American Airlines**, **Delta** and other major lines. **Air Canada** runs flights from Canada, and **Qantas** provides connecting flights from Australia and New Zealand. The main British airlines with regular flights to Paris are **British Airways** and **British Midland**, and the main French airline is **Air France**. For airline offices in Paris, see page 363.

The peak summer season in Paris is from July to September. Airline fares are at their highest during this time. Different airlines, however, may have slightly different high summer season periods,

so check with the airlines or an agent as to which months are covered by these fares.

With fierce competition between the airlines for business, some very attractive discount deals are available. APEX (advance purchase excursion) fares can be a good buy. However, the flight has to be booked some time in advance, in some cases as much as a month, in others 7 to 14 days. These fares have restrictions and cannot be changed or cancelled without penalty. There are also minimum and maximum stay requirements.

If you look around for the best deals, you can find very good ones from reputable discount agents. If you reserve a cheap deal with a

discount agent, check whether you will get a refund if the agent or operator goes out of business, and don't part with the full fare until you actually see the ticket.

Addresses of reputable discount agencies with offices in Paris are listed on page 363. These offer charters and regular scheduled flights at competitive prices. Many of them have representatives in other countries. Note that children can travel more cheaply than adults.

Flight Times

Here are flight times to Paris from different world cities – London: 1 hour; New York: 8 hours; Dublin: 90 minutes; Montreal: 7.5 hours; Los Angeles: 12 hours.

CHARLES DE GAULLE AIRPORT

The terminals CDG1, CDG2 and T9 are linked by shuttle buses. Departures are on the lower level, and arrivals on the upper level. Most of the airport's transport services to central Paris leave from the arrivals level of the terminals.

CDG1 is used for international flights, except those of Air France (see CDG2).

The airport complex

CDG1   T9

CDG2

Taxi rank (Door 16)

Car rentals (Doors 16 & 20)

CDG2 is used for all Air France flights and for short-hop international flights by other carriers.

Taxi rank (Door 7)

Air France bus to Montparnasse (Door 26)

RATP buses (Door 12)

Air France and RER shuttle buses (Door 6)

CDG2D

CDG2B

RER shuttle buses (Door 28)

Disney-land Paris Resort bus (Door 1)

CDG2A

RATP buses (Door 10)

CDG2C

Disneyland Paris Resort bus (Door 30)

Air France bus to Porte Maillot and Etoile (Door 34)

Air France and RER shuttle buses (Door 5)

Taxi rank (Door 7)

Air France and shuttle buses (Door 5)

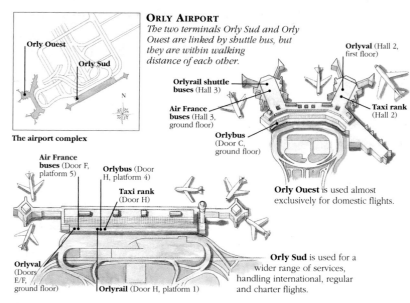

The airport complex

ORLY AIRPORT
The two terminals Orly Sud and Orly Ouest are linked by shuttle bus, but they are within walking distance of each other.

Orlyval (Hall 2, first floor)

Orlyrail shuttle buses (Hall 3)

Air France buses (Hall 3, ground floor)

Orlybus (Door C, ground floor)

Taxi rank (Hall 2)

Air France buses (Door F, platform 5)

Orlybus (Door H, platform 4)

Taxi rank (Door H)

Orlyval (Doors E/F, ground floor)

Orlyrail (Door H, platform 1)

Orly Ouest is used almost exclusively for domestic flights.

Orly Sud is used for a wider range of services, handling international, regular and charter flights.

CHARLES DE GAULLE (CDG) AIRPORT

THIS IS PARIS'S main airport, lying 19 miles (30 km) north of the city. It has two main terminals, CDG1 and CDG2, and a charter flight terminal, T9. CDG2 comprises two linked buildings in four sections, referred to as CDG2A, CDG2B, CDG2C and CDG2D.

Getting into Town
Travelers arriving at CDG can choose between a taxi, bus or train to reach central Paris. The bus services are provided by Air France and the RATP. Air France buses travel to the western side of the city, and the RATP buses to the north and east. The Air France service stops only twice: at Porte Maillot and Charles de Gaulle-Etoile. There you will find city-center bus stops and metro and RER stations. The journey takes about 40 minutes. There is also an Air France bus service to Montparnasse TGV train station, leaving every 30 minutes. The Roissybus service takes travelers to Opéra. This journey takes about 60 minutes and buses leave every 15–20 minutes. The bus termini are served by the metro and RER system.

A Disneyland Paris bus service operates every 25 minutes.

The nearby Roissy Rail RER train service is linked by shuttle bus service from the terminals. Trains leave every 15 minutes and take about 35 minutes to reach the city center, at the Gare du Nord, where there is a link to the metro and to other RER lines.

Taxis can be a good option for late-night arrivals and small groups, but lines can be long. Fares to the center run between F250 and F300.

ORLY AIRPORT (ORY)

THIS IS PARIS'S second airport, located 9 miles (15 km) south of the capital. It has two terminals, Orly Sud and Orly Ouest.

Getting into Town
Transportation services take travelers to the southern part of the city, and a special bus links the airport with the Disneyland Paris Resort, leaving every 45 minutes.

Travelers arriving at Orly can take a taxi, bus or train to central Paris. The bus services are run by Air France and RATP (Orlybus). Air France buses take about 30 minutes to reach the city center, stopping at Les Invalides and Montparnasse. The Orlybus leaves every 12 minutes and takes about 25 minutes to reach the city center at Denfert-Rochereau. The recent Jet Bus service takes travelers from the airport to Villejuif-Louis Aragon metro station every 15 minutes.

Shuttle buses link the airport with the RER Orlyrail services at nearby Rungis. Trains leave every 15 minutes (every 30 minutes after 9pm), taking 35 minutes to reach the Gare d'Austerlitz. A train service, Orlyval, links up with the Roissy Rail RER line B at Antony station nearby, with trains conveniently leaving every 4–8 minutes.

Taxis are readily available. They take 25 to 45 minutes to reach the city center depending on how heavy the traffic is, and cost F150 to F200.

Orlyval train leaving Orly Airport

CROSSING THE CHANNEL

TRAVELLERS FROM the UK making the journey to Paris can cross the Channel by ferry, hovercraft, or tunnel. **P&O-Stena Sealink** have frequent crossings from Dover to Calais, taking 75–90 minutes, and a 6-hour crossing from Portsmouth to Le Havre. They also operate a 6-hour service from Portsmouth to Cherbourg. **Brittany Ferries** runs a 9-hour service from Portsmouth to St-Malo.

Fast hovercraft services between Dover and Calais or Boulogne are operated by **Hoverspeed**. The high-speed catamaran is run by **Seacat** and carries both cars and passengers between Folkestone and Boulogne, and between Dover and Calais. Ferry tickets can also be purchased with coach and railroad connections.

The Channel Tunnel car-carrying railroad shuttle service is run by **Eurotunnel** between Folkestone and Calais. The journey time is 35 minutes (slightly longer at night). Trains depart at an average of three per hour and can be fully booked at peak times.

The tunnel's railroad service is run by **Eurostar**. Trains depart from Waterloo station in London and Ashford in Kent. The journey time from London to Paris (Gare du Nord) is 3 hours.

Driving times from Calais, Dunkirk and Boulogne to Paris are about 3 hours on the Autoroute A16, or 4–5 hours travelling on the N1 *route nationale*. From Dieppe and Le Havre it takes an average 2½–3 hours on the A13. Driving from Cherbourg (N13, then A13) and St Malo (N175, A84 then A13) to Paris can take 5–6 hours.

ARRIVING BY COACH

ONE OF THE MAIN coach stations is the Gare Routière at Porte de la Villette in northeastern Paris. It is served by the metro and many city bus lines. For some buses to Spain, Portugal and Holland the terminus is Porte de Charenton in the southeastern part of the city.

The main coach operator is **Eurolines**, based at the Gare Internationale in eastern Paris. Its coaches travel to Belgium, Holland, Ireland, Germany, Scandinavia, United Kingdom, Italy and Portugal.

The terminus for coaches in London is Victoria Coach Station. There are two buses each weekday, leaving at noon and 9pm, and three buses on Saturdays. The journey from London to Paris takes about 10 hours. For further information telephone the Victoria Coach Station.

A long-distance coach

USEFUL ADDRESSES AND PHONE NUMBERS

Coach Operators
Eurolines
Ave de Général de Gaulle, Bagnolet.
(01 49 72 51 51.

Victoria Coach Station, London SW1.
(0990-808 080.

Eurostar
London Waterloo International.
(0345 881 881.

Eurotunnel
(0990 353 535.

Ferry Information
Brittany Ferries
(02 33 88 44 88.

Hoverspeed/Seacat
(03 21 30 27 26.

P&O-Stena Ferries
(03 21 46 10 10.

ARRIVING BY RAILROAD

AS THE RAILROAD hub of France and the Continent, Paris boasts six major international train stations operated by the French state railroads, known as SNCF *(see p372)*. The Gare de Lyon in eastern Paris is

---

THE TGV

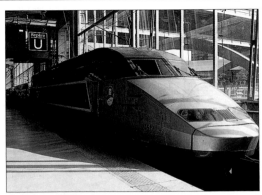

Trains à Grande Vitesse, or TGV high-speed trains, travel at speeds up to 300 km/h (185 mph). Trains for northern France leave from the Gare du Nord, for the Atlantic Coast and Brittany from Gare Montparnasse, and for Provence and the southeast from Gare de Lyon. The network serves a large number of stations on routes to these destinations, and the number of stations served is growing all the time, making this an ever-more convenient form of transportation *(see pp364–5)*.

The high-speed TGV train

the city's main station, serving the south of France, the Alps, Italy, Switzerland, and Greece. The Gare de l'Est serves eastern France, Austria, Switzerland and Germany.

Eurostar trains from the UK arrive at the Gare du Nord, as do trains from Holland, Belgium and Scandinavia. Trains from some Channel ports arrive at the Gare St-Lazare. The terminus for trains from Spain, as well as from the Brittany ports, is the Gare Montparnasse on the Left Bank. The other main stations are Massy-Palaiseau to the southwest of the city, Marne-la-Vallée for Disneyland Paris, and Aéroport Charles-de-Gaulle.

Journey times to Paris can be significantly cut by using the high-speed TGV service. Seats must be reserved in advance, and reservations can be booked at all the railroad stations and by phone, as well as in some countries before departure.

There is a tourist office at the Gare de Lyon where arriving travelers can seek advice (see p351). They can also book accommodations – useful if arriving at night.

All the railroad stations are served by city buses, the metro and RER trains. The stations have directional signs showing where to make connections to the city transit system.

ARRIVING BY CAR

PARIS IS AN oval-shaped city. It is surrounded by an outer ring road called the Boulevard Périphérique. All highways leading to the capital link in to the Périphérique, which separates the city from the suburbs. Each former city gate, called a porte, now corresponds to an exit from (or entrance to) the Périphérique. Arriving drivers should check their destination address and consult a map of central Paris to find the closest corresponding porte. For example, a driver who wants to get to the Arc de Triomphe should exit via Porte Maillot.

DIRECTORY

MAIN AIR CARRIERS SERVING PARIS

Aer Lingus
52–4 Rue Belle Feuille 92100.
[01 55 38 38 55.

Air Canada
10 Rue de la Paix 75002. Map 6 D5.
[01 44 50 20 20.

Air France
119 Ave des Champs-Elysées 75008. Map 4 E4.
[08 02 80 28 02.

American Airlines
109 Rue du Faubourg-St-Honoré 75008. Map 5 B5.
[08 01 87 28 72.

British Airways
13–15 Blvd de la Madeleine 75001. Map 6 D5. [08 02 80 29 02.

British Midland
4 Place de Londres, Roissy-en-France 95700.
[01 48 62 55 65.

Delta Airlines
4 Rue Scribe 75009. Map 6 D5.
[01 47 68 92 92.

Qantas Airways
13–15 Blvd de la Madeleine 75001. Map 6 D5. [01 44 55 52 05.

DISCOUNT TRAVEL AGENCIES

Access Voyages
6 Rue Pierre Lescot 75001. Map 13 A2.
[01 53 00 91 30.

Council Travel Services
16 Rue Vaugirard 75006.
[01 44 41 89 89.
London office:
28A Poland Street
London W1V 3DB.
[0171-437 7767.

Forum Voyages
1 Rue Cassette 75006. Map 12 D5.
[01 45 44 38 61.

Jet Tours
19 Ave de Tourville 75007. Map 11 A4.
[01 47 05 01 95.

Nouvelles Frontières
87 Blvd de Grenelle 75015. Map 10 D4.
[01 41 41 58 58.

USIT Voyages
6 Rue Vaugirard 75006.
[01 42 34 56 90.
London office:
Campus Travel
52 Grosvenor Gardens
London SW1W OAG.
[0171-730 3402.

CDG AIRPORT INFORMATION

Air France Bus
[01 41 56 89 00.

Customs
[01 48 62 62 85.

Disabled Assistance
[01 48 62 28 24 (CDG 1)
& 01 48 62 59 00 (CDG 2).

Emergency Medical
[01 48 62 28 00 (CDG 1)
& 01 48 62 53 32 (CDG 2).

Paging Travelers
[01 49 75 15 15 (Orly).
[01 48 62 22 80 (Roissy).

Travel Information
[01 48 62 22 80 (24 hrs).

RATP Bus
[08 36 68 77 14 and
numbers for RER (below).

RER Train
[Ile de France: 01 53 70
20 20 (6am–10pm); TGV:
08 36 35 35 35.

Lost property enqs to Service
Official des Objets Trouvés,
36 rue des Morillons, 75732.

ORLY AIRPORT INFORMATION

Air France Bus
[01 41 56 89 00.

Travel Information
[01 49 75 15 15.

RATP Bus/RER Train
[as listed under CDG.

Orlyrail Shuttle
[01 43 90 20 20.

CDG AIRPORT HOTELS

IBIS
Aéroport Charles de Gaulle 95701.
[01 49 19 19 19.

Eliance Cocoon
Aéroport Charles de Gaulle 95713.
[01 48 62 06 16.

Holiday Inn
1 Allée de Verger, 95700 Roissy-en-France.
[01 34 29 30 00.

Ibis
2 Ave Raperie, 95700 Roissy-en-France.
[01 34 29 34 34.

Novotel
Aéroport Charles de Gaulle 95705.
[01 49 19 27 27.

Sofitel
Aéroport Charles de Gaulle 95713.
[01 49 19 29 29.

ORLY SUD AIRPORT HOTELS

IBIS
[01 46 87 33 50.

Hilton Hotel
[01 45 12 45 12.

Mercure
[01 46 87 23 37.

Arriving in Paris

THIS MAP DEPICTS the bus and rail services between the two main airports and the city. It shows the ferry-rail links from the UK, the main railroad links from other parts of France and Europe, and the long-distance coach services from other European countries. It also shows the main city railroad and coach terminals, the airport shuttle connections and the airport bus and rail stops. The frequency of services and journey times from the airport are provided, as are the approximate times of rail journeys from other cities. Metro and RER line connections to other parts of Paris are indicated at the terminals and route stops.

CALAIS
Ferry links with Dover and Folkestone.
Le Shuttle link with Folkestone.
SNCF train to Gare du Nord (3 hrs).

BOULOGNE
Ferry links with Folkestone.
SNCF train to Gare du Nord (3 hrs 20 mins).

LE HAVRE
Ferry links with Portsmouth.
SNCF train to Gare St-Lazare (2 hrs).

DIEPPE
Ferry links with Newhaven.
SNCF train to Gare St-Lazare (2 hrs 20 mins).

CAEN
Ferry links with Portsmouth.
SNCF train to Gare St-Lazare (3 hrs 20 mins).

CHERBOURG
Ferry links with Portsmouth and Southampton.
SNCF train to Gare St-Lazare (4 hrs).

GARE MONTPARNASSE
Bordeaux (3 hrs)
Brest (4 hrs)
Lisbon (24 hrs)
Madrid (11 hrs)
Nantes (2 hrs)
Rennes (2 hrs)

Porte Maillot M(1) RER(A)(C)

Charles de Gaulle-Etoile M(1)(2)(6) RER(A)

Champs-Elysées

Chaillot Quarter

Gare St-La M(3)(12)

Invalides M(8)(13) RER(C)

Invalides and Eiffel Tower Quarter

Montparnasse

Gare Montparnasse M(4)(6)(12)(13)

Porte de Orléans M(4)

KEY
— SNCF *see pp362–3*
— Coaches *see p362*
— RATP bus *see p361*
— Air France bus *see p361*
— RER B-Roissy Rail *see p361*
— Orlyrail *see p361*
— Orlyval *see p361*
— Orlybus *see p361*
— Jet Bus *see p361*
M Metro station
RER RER station

GARE TGV DE MASSY-PALAISEAU
Bordeaux (3 hrs)
Lille (2 hrs)
Lyon (2 hrs)
Nantes (2 hrs)
Rennes (2 hrs)
Rouen (1 hr 30 mins)

Antony

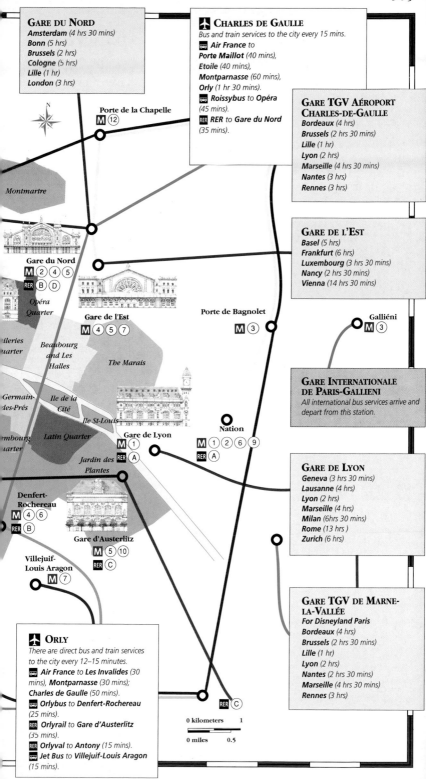

GARE DU NORD
Amsterdam (4 hrs 30 mins)
Bonn (5 hrs)
Brussels (2 hrs)
Cologne (5 hrs)
Lille (1 hr)
London (3 hrs)

✈ **CHARLES DE GAULLE**
Bus and train services to the city every 15 mins.
🚌 *Air France to*
Porte Maillot (40 mins),
Etoile (40 mins),
Montparnasse (60 mins),
Orly (1 hr 30 mins).
🚌 *Roissybus to Opéra*
(45 mins).
RER *RER to Gare du Nord*
(35 mins).

Porte de la Chapelle
M ⑫

GARE TGV AÉROPORT CHARLES-DE-GAULLE
Bordeaux (4 hrs)
Brussels (2 hrs 30 mins)
Lille (1 hr)
Lyon (2 hrs)
Marseille (4 hrs 30 mins)
Nantes (3 hrs)
Rennes (3 hrs)

N

Montmartre

Gare du Nord
M ② ④ ⑤
RER Ⓑ Ⓓ

Opéra Quarter

Gare de l'Est
M ④ ⑤ ⑦

Porte de Bagnolet
M ③

Galliéni
M ③

GARE DE L'EST
Basel (5 hrs)
Frankfurt (6 hrs)
Luxembourg (3 hrs 30 mins)
Nancy (2 hrs 30 mins)
Vienna (14 hrs 30 mins)

ileries quarter

Beaubourg and Les Halles

The Marais

Germain-des-Prés

Ile de la Cité

Ile St-Louis

Latin Quarter

mbourg uarter

Nation
M ① ② ⑥ ⑨
RER Ⓐ

GARE INTERNATIONALE DE PARIS-GALLIENI
All international bus services arrive and depart from this station.

Jardin des Plantes

Gare de Lyon
M ①
RER Ⓐ

Denfert-Rochereau
M ④ ⑥
RER Ⓑ

Gare d'Austerlitz
M ⑤ ⑩
RER Ⓒ

Villejuif-Louis Aragon
M ⑦

GARE DE LYON
Geneva (3 hrs 30 mins)
Lausanne (4 hrs)
Lyon (2 hrs)
Marseille (4 hrs)
Milan (6hrs 30 mins)
Rome (13 hrs)
Zurich (6 hrs)

GARE TGV DE MARNE-LA-VALLÉE
For Disneyland Paris
Bordeaux (4 hrs)
Brussels (2 hrs 30 mins)
Lille (1 hr)
Lyon (2 hrs)
Nantes (2 hrs 30 mins)
Marseille (4 hrs 30 mins)
Rennes (3 hrs)

✈ **ORLY**
There are direct bus and train services to the city every 12–15 minutes.
🚌 *Air France to Les Invalides* (30 mins), *Montparnasse* (30 mins); *Charles de Gaulle* (50 mins).
🚌 *Orlybus to Denfert-Rochereau* (25 mins).
RER *Orlyrail to Gare d'Austerlitz* (35 mins).
RER *Orlyval to Antony* (15 mins).
🚌 *Jet Bus to Villejuif-Louis Aragon* (15 mins).

RER Ⓒ

0 kilometers   1

0 miles   0.5

GETTING AROUND PARIS

Central Paris is compact. The best way to get around is to walk. However, visitors unfamiliar with the driving rules and undisciplined French driving need to take care. Cycling, too, can be dangerous, due to traffic conditions and aggressive drivers. Bike lanes are often not respected. Driving a car in the city center is not recommended. Traffic is often heavy, there are many one-way streets, and parking is difficult and expensive. However, a bus, metro and RER train system, operated by the RATP, makes getting around cheap and easy. The city is divided into five travel zones: zones 1 and 2 corresponding to the center and zones 3, 4 and 5 to the suburbs and the airport. The city is also divided into 20 arrondissements, which will help visitors in their search for addresses (see p357).

Parisian drivers do not always respect pedestrian crossings.

Stop sign   **Walk sign**

WALKING IN PARIS

As in the United States, cars drive on the right-hand side of the street. There are many two-stage street crossings where pedestrians wait on an island in the center of the road before proceeding. These are marked *piétons traversez en deux temps*. Exercise caution when crossing.

CYCLING IN PARIS

Though mostly flat, Paris is not a city of bicycles. Car traffic is heavy and there are few bike lanes. Where they exist they are rarely respected by motorists. Cyclists should wear protective helmets and reflective clothing and carry a light at night. Cyclists will find Paris easier in August, when most Parisians take their annual vacation.

SNCF train passengers are allowed to take bicycles on trains, and some suburban train stations rent bicycles. In summer, the RATP rents bicycles at several metro and RER stations at the weekends. They also rent bicycles on weekends at RATP bus stations outside the Parc Floral in the Bois de Vincennes, near the Château de Vincennes, and every day at the Bagatelle in the Bois de Boulogne.

A Parisian cyclist

TICKETS AND TRAVEL PASSES

A wide variety of tickets and passes can be purchased at all main metro and RER stations, at the airports, and several tourist offices. Among the most useful for tourists are: individual tickets, or a block of ten (*carnet*) at a discount; a one-day *Mobilis* card for selected zones; *Carte Orange*, giving unlimited travel for a week or month for selected zones, a Monday–Sunday (*hebdomaire*) ticket for two zones; and the *Paris Visite* pass for one, two, three, or five days, which includes discounted entry to some sights but is comparatively expensive.

Carte Paris Visite card

RER 2nd classs ticket

Carte Orange

Carte Orange one-month travel ticket fro zones 1 and 2

Mobilis card

Paris Visite ticket for 3 days

Tickets for use on metro, RER, or bus

An Hebdomadaire ticket

DRIVING IN PARIS

THOUGH DRIVING a car in central Paris is not recommended, a rental car can be useful for visiting outlying areas. To rent a car, a valid driving license and passport are required (most firms also require one major credit card). For payment by check or cash, additional ID may be required (including air tickets and credit cards). International driving licenses are not needed for drivers from EC countries, Scandinavia, North America, Australia and New Zealand.

Cars drive on the right-hand side of the road and must yield to traffic merging from the right, even on thoroughfares, unless marked by a *priorité* sign, which indicates right of way. Cars on traffic circles now have right of way throughout France, except at the Arc de Triomphe where cars yield to traffic from the right.

PARKING

PARKING IN Paris is difficult and expensive. Park only in areas with a large "P" or a *Parking Payant* sign on the pavement or on the road. Use the *horodateur* machines to pay for parking. For some machines, you will have to buy a parking payment card,

No entry sign

INTERDIT SUR TOUTE LA LONGUEUR DE LA VOIE

Parking Interdit (no parking)

30

ARRÊT GÊNANT
ARTICLE A 371 DU CODE DE LA ROUTE

Tow-away zone

Speed limit sign in km/h

available from tobacconists. In some residential neighborhoods, parking is allowed in unmarked areas.

Never park where *Parking Interdit* or *Stationnement Interdit* signs are present.

For towed or clamped cars, phone or go to the nearest police station (*Commissariat de Police*). For towing away there is a fine, plus a fee for each day the car is held. There are seven car pounds (*perfourrières*) in Paris. Cars are taken to them according to the *arrondissement* from which they were towed. Cars are kept at the pound for 48 hours, then sent to outlying long-term garages (*fouriéres*).

BICYCLE RENTAL AND REPAIR SERVICES

Bicloune
7 Rue Froment 75011.
Map 14 E3. 01 48 05 47 75.
Bicycle sales and repairs only.

Paris Vélo
2 Rue du Fer-à-Moulin 75005.
Map 17 C2.
01 43 37 59 22.
Bicycle rental.

Peugeot
72 Ave de la Grande Armée 75017. **Map** 3 C3.
01 45 74 27 38.
Bicycle sales and repairs only.

RATP Information
08 36 68 77 14.

SNCF Information
08 36 35 35 35.

CAR RENTAL AGENCIES

CAR RENTAL AGENCIES abound in Paris. Here is a list of major firms with agencies at Charles de Gaulle and Orly airports, main railroad stations and city-center locations. Telephone for reservations and pick-up and drop-off information.

ADA
01 49 58 44 44.

Avis
01 46 10 60 60.

Budget
01 47 55 61 00.

Europcar
01 45 00 08 06.

Hertz
01 39 38 38 38.

EMERGENCY NUMBERS

IN THE CASE OF AN accident or an emergency, telephone the police by dialing 17. The main number at the Prefecture of Police is 01 53 71 53 71. Other police numbers are in the telephone directory.

USING AN HORODATEUR MACHINE

Horodateurs (*parking meters*) *operate from 9am–7pm Mon–Fri. Unless otherwise indicated, parking is free Sat–Sun, public holidays and in August.*

Card-only machine

1 If using coins, insert according to the tariff shown. If using a card, see step 2.

MARIE DE PARIS PARIS CARTE 1

Parking card

2 If using a card, insert and press blue button for each 15 minutes required.

3 Press green button for ticket.

4 Remove ticket and place inside car windshield.

Traveling by Metro

Art Nouveau metro sign

Modern metro sign

THE RATP (Paris transport company) operates 15 metro lines, referred to by their number and terminus names, criss-crossing Paris and its suburbs. This is often the fastest and cheapest way to get across the capital, for there are dozens of stations scattered around the city. Metro stations are easily identified by their logo, a large circled *M*, and sometimes their elegant Art Nouveau entrances. Neighborhood maps are found in all stations, near the exits. The metro and RER (Paris rail network) systems operate in much the same way, though RER cars are slightly larger. The first trains leave their termini at 5:30am and the last return at 1:15am.

RATP logo

Reading the Metro Map

Metro and RER lines are shown in various colors on the metro map. Metro lines are identified by a number, which is located on the map at either end of a line. Some metro stations serve only one line; others serve more than one. There are stations sharing both metro and RER lines, and some are linked to one another by interconnecting passages.

Metro and RER stations with inter-connecting passage

RER and metro station serving the same lines

Metro line

Metro station serving two lines

Metro station serving one line

RER line

Metro line identification number

USING THE RER

THE RER is a system of commuter trains traveling underground in central Paris and above ground in outlying areas. Both metro tickets and passes are valid on it. There are four lines, known by their letters: A, B, C and D. Each line forks. For example, Line C has six forks, labeled C1, C2 etc. All RER trains bear names (for example, ALEX or VERA) to make it easier to read RER timetables in the station halls and on platforms. Digital panels on all RER platforms indicate train name, direction of travel (terminus) and upcoming stations.

RER stations are identified by a large circled logo. The main city stations are Charles de Gaulle-Etoile, Châtelet-Les-Halles, Gare de Lyon, Nation, St-Michel-Notre-Dame, Auber, and the Gare du Nord.

The RER and metro systems overlap in central Paris. It is often quicker to take an RER

train to a station served by both, as in the case of La Défense and Nation. However, getting into the RER stations, which are often linked to the metro by a maze of corridors, can be very time consuming.

The RER is particularly useful for getting to Paris airports and to many of the outlying towns and tourist attractions. Line B3 serves Charles de Gaulle Airport; Lines B4 and C2 serve Orly Airport; Line A4 goes to the Disneyland Paris Resort; and Line C5 runs to Versailles.

RER logo

BUYING A TICKET

TRAIN TICKETS are sold in the entrance halls of all metro and RER stations. Some metro and all RER stations have coin-operated machines selling individual tickets or packs of ten *(carnets)*. Station agents and ticket sellers also provide information and direct travelers to their destinations. All tickets on the metro are second class, but for the RER you can buy first- or second-class tickets.

One metro ticket "section urbaine" entitles you to travel anywhere on the metro, and on RER trains in central Paris. RER trips outside the city center (such as to airports) require special tickets. Fares to sub-urbs and nearby towns vary. Consult the fare charts posted in all stations. Passengers on city transportation must retain their tickets during the trip; regular inspections are made and fines can be imposed for not having a ticket.

MAKING A JOURNEY BY METRO

1 To determine which metro line to take, travelers should first find their destination on a metro map. (Maps can be found inside stations and also on the inside back cover of this book.) Trace the metro line by following the color coding and the number of the line. At the end of the line you will see the number of the terminus – remember this, for it will help you to find the correct train.

Insert the train ticket in the first barrier.

Remove the ticket from the second barrier.

2 Metro tickets are sold at all stations. Some stations are equipped with coin-operated automatic machines. All metro tickets are second class. One ticket allows the bearer travel for one journey and any transfers on the metro system.

3 To enter the platform area, insert the metro ticket, with the magnetic strip facing down, into the first barrier slot. Remove the ticket from the second slot, then push through the turnstile or step through the barrier if automatic.

← DIRECTION
Ⓜ ① CHÂTEAU DE VINCENNES

CORRESPONDANCES

GARE DE LYON
REUILLY-DIDEROT
NATION
PORTE DE VINCENNES
SAINT-MANDÉ-TOURELLE
BÉRAULT
CHÂTEAU DE VINCENNES

4 At the entrance to each station platform, or in the station corridors, there is a list of upcoming stations corresponding to a given terminus. Terminus names are also indicated on the platform and should be checked before boarding the train.

DIRECTION
Ⓜ ①
CHÂTEAU DE VINCENNES

5 To change lines, get off at the appropriate transfer station and follow the *correspondance* (connections) signs on the platform indicating the appropriate direction.

6 On older trains there are door handles that have to be lifted to open the door. On more modern trains there is a release button that you press to open the door. Before the doors open and close, a single tone will sound.

7 Inside the trains are charts of the line being served by the train. The station stops are plotted on the chart, so travelers can track their journeys.

← **SORTIE**

8 The "Sortie" sign indicates the way out. At all metro exits there are neighborhood maps.

Traveling by Bus

THE BUS IS AN EXCELLENT way to see the great sights of Paris. The bus system is run by the RATP, as is the metro, so you can use the same tickets for both. There are 60 bus lines in Paris and over 2,000 buses in daily circulation. This is often the fastest way to travel short distances. However, buses can get caught up in heavy traffic and are often crowded during peak hours. Visitors should check the times for the first and last buses as they vary widely, depending on the line. Most buses run from Monday to Saturday, from early morning to mid-evening (6am–8:30pm).

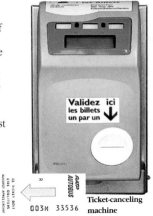

Validez ici
les billets
un par un ↓

56

Château
de Vincennes
Ⓜ

Bus terminus sign

Bus Stop Signs
Signs at bus stops display route numbers. A white background indicates a service every day all year; a black one means no service on Sundays or public holidays.

Ticket-canceling machine

003M 33536

Bus ticket

Canceling a Bus Ticket
Insert the ticket into the machine in the direction of the arrow, then withdraw it.

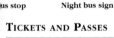

us stop   **Night bus sign**

TICKETS AND PASSES

TRAVELING ACROSS town by bus costs twice as much as a similar trip on the metro. Each bus route is divided into various sections. Formerly, a ticket entitled you to travel only two sections, but now

one ticket entitles the bearer to travel through all sections, but only in a single journey, on a single line. You can purchase a *carnet* of 10 tickets, each of them valid for a single journey. A *carnet* must be obtained at the metro stations, not on the buses. Children under four are allowed to travel for free, and those aged between four and 10 may travel at half price. Metro tickets may be used for bus travel. Bus-only tickets are purchased on board the bus, from the driver, and they must be canceled to be valid. To do this, insert the ticket into the canceling machine inside the

Red exit button

main doors of the bus. Be sure to keep your ticket until the end of the journey. Inspectors do make random checks and are empowered to levy on-the-spot fines if you cannot produce a valid, canceled ticket for your journey. Travel passes are a useful and economical idea if you want the freedom of unlimited travel on Paris buses. Never cancel these, as it will render them invalid. They should be shown to the bus driver whenever you board a bus, and to a ticket inspector on request.

Paris's Buses
Passengers can identify the route and destination of a bus from the information on the panels at the front. Some buses have open rear platforms; however, they are becoming more rare.

Bus route number

Bus destination

Bus route number on rear of bus

Passengers enter the bus at the front door

Bus front displaying information

Open rear platform

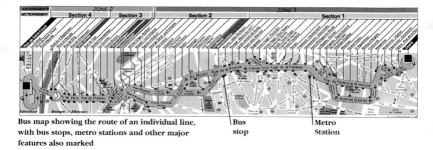

Bus map showing the route of an individual line, with bus stops, metro stations and other major features also marked | Bus stop | Metro Station

USING THE BUSES

BUS STOPS and shelters are identified by the number shields of the buses that stop at them, and by the distinctive RATP logo. Route maps at bus stops indicate transfers and nearby metro and RER stops. Bus stops also display timetables, and show first and last buses. Neighborhood maps are also displayed at most bus shelters.

Most buses must be flagged down. Some new models have multiple doors that must be opened by pressing a red button inside the bus to exit or outside the bus to enter. All buses have buttons and bells to signal for a stop. Some buses do not go all the way to their terminus; in that case, there will be a slash through the name of the destination on the front panel.

Buses do not have special facilities for the handicapped, but some seats are reserved for disabled and elderly persons, war veterans and pregnant women. These seats are identified by a sign and must be given up on request.

NIGHT AND SUMMER BUSES

THERE ARE 10 night bus lines operating throughout Paris, called Noctambuses. The terminus for all night bus lines is Châtelet, at Avenue Victoria or Rue St-Martin. Noctambus stops are clearly identified by a shield bearing an owl and a yellow moon. Noctambuses must be flagged down. Travel passes are valid, but the normal metro tickets are not. Fares vary according to destination. Travelers may buy tickets on board the bus.

The RATP also operates buses in the Bois de Vincennes and Bois de Boulogne during the summer. Call the **RATP** for information on these services. You can also find out the best ways to get around the city, and about tickets and passes in general.

RATP Information
53 Quai des Grands Augustins 75006. 01 43 46 14 14/08 36 68 77 14/08 00 15 24 24 (24 hrs).

USEFUL BUS ROUTES

Here is a selection of the best sightseeing bus routes around the center of Paris, taking in some of the great sights of the city. The routes show the major bus stops, the nearest metro stations and locations of some of the notable sights.

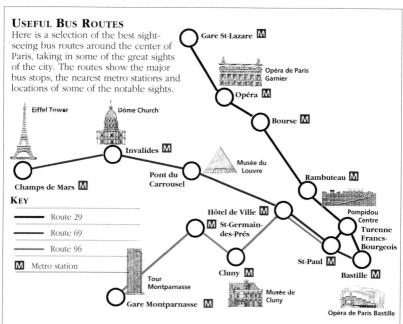

Using the SNCF Trains

THE FRENCH STATE railroad, Société Nationale des Chemins de Fer (**SNCF**), has two kinds of service in Paris: the Banlieue suburban service and the Grandes Lignes, or long-distance service. The suburban services all operate within the five-zone network *(see p366)*. The long-distance services operate throughout France. These services allow visitors to visit parts of France close to Paris in a day's round trip. The TGV high-speed service is particularly useful for such journeys, since it is capable of traveling about twice as fast as the normal trains *(see pp362–3)*.

**Gare de l'Est railway
station in 1920**

RAILROAD STATIONS

AS THE RAILWAY hub of France and the Continent, Paris boasts six major international railroad stations operated by the SNCF. The railroad stations are the Gare du Nord, Gare de l'Est, Gare de Lyon, Gare d'Austerlitz, Gare St-Lazare and Gare Montparnasse.

All the main train stations have long-distance and suburban destinations. Some of the main suburban locations, such as Versailles and Chantilly, are served by both long-distance and suburban trains.

**Rail traveler with
luggage trolley**

The stations have departures and arrivals boards showing the train number, departure and arrival time, delay, platform number or letter, origin and main stops along the route. For those with heavy luggage,

there are trolleys, requiring a F10 coin that is refunded when the trolley is returned.

TICKETS

TICKETS TO suburban destinations can often be purchased at coin-operated automatic machines located inside station halls, so carry F10 coins. The machines give change. Always ask for details at information centers or ticket booths before purchasing tickets.

Before boarding a train, travelers must time-punch *(composter)* their tickets and reservations in a *composteur* machine. Inspectors do check travelers' tickets, and anyone who fails to time-punch their ticket can be fined.

Ticket booths are usually marked with panels indicating the kind of tickets *(billets)* sold: Banlieue for suburban tickets, Grandes Lignes for main-line tickets, and Internationale for international tickets.

There are discounts for children, senior citizens,

Composteur Machine

The composteur *machines are located in station halls and at the head of each platform. Tickets and reservations must be inserted face up.*

A time-punched ticket

married couples, families with small children, and for round trips of 620 miles (1,000 km) or more. These tickets can be bought directly from SNCF stations and from agencies displaying a SNCF.logo.

STUDENT AND YOUTH DISCOUNT TICKETS

Nouvelles Frontières
87 Bld de Grenelle 75015.
Map 10 D4. ☎ *01 41 41 58 58.*

Wasteels
12 Rue La Fayette 75009. **Map** 6 E4.
☎ *01 42 47 09 77.*

SUBURBAN TRAINS

SUBURBAN LINES are found at all main Paris train stations and are clearly marked Banlieue. Tickets for city transportation cannot be used

A double-decker Banlieue train

on Banlieue trains, with the exception of some RER tickets to stations with both SNCF and RER lines.

Some favorite tourist destinations are served by the Banlieue trains. Among the most notable are Chantilly, Chartres, Fontainebleau, Giverny and Versailles *(see pp248–53)*. Telephone the SNCF for information about suburban trains.

Traveling by Taxi

Taxis are more expensive than trains or buses, but they are an advantage after 1am, when the metro has stopped running. There are taxi ranks (stands) throughout the city; a list of some of these is provided below.

A Paris taxi rank sign

Catching a Taxi

There are nearly 10,000 taxis operating in central Paris. Yet there never seem to be enough of them to meet demand, particularly during rush hours and on Friday and Saturday nights.

Taxis can be hailed in the street, but not within 165 ft (50 m) of a taxi rank. Since ranks always take priority over street stops, the easiest way to get a cab is to find a rank and join the line. Ranks are found at many busy crossroads; at main metro and RER stations, and at all hospitals, train stations; and airports. An illuminated white

light on the roof shows that the taxi is available. A small light lit below means that the taxi is occupied. If the white light is covered, the taxi is off duty. Taxis on their last run can refuse to take passengers.

The meter should have a specified initial amount showing on it when you first enter the taxi. Initial charges on radio taxis vary widely, depending on the distance

the taxi covers to arrive at the pick-up point. No checks or credit cards are accepted as payment.

The rates vary with the part of the city and the time of day. Rate A is the center-city rate and is measured by the kilometer traveled. The higher rate B applies to the city center, Sundays, holidays and night (7pm–7am), or daytime in the suburbs or airports. Rate C applies to the suburbs and airports at night. Again, this rate is higher. Taxis will charge extra for each piece of luggage carried.

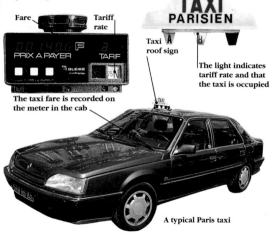

Fare   **Tariff rate**

The taxi fare is recorded on the meter in the cab

TAXI PARISIEN

Taxi roof sign

The light indicates tariff rate and that the taxi is occupied

A typical Paris taxi

DIRECTORY

Taxi Ranks

Charles de Gaulle-Etoile
1 Ave Wagram 75017.
Map 4 D4.
01 43 80 01 99.

Eiffel Tower
Quai Branly 75007.
Map 10 D3.
01 45 55 85 41.

Metro Concorde
252 Rue de Rivoli 75001.
Map 11 C1.
01 42 61 67 60.

Place de Clichy
Pl de Clichy 75009.
Map 6 D1.
01 42 85 00 00.

Place Denfert-Rochereau
297 Blvd Raspail 75014.
Map 16 E3.
01 43 35 00 00.

Place de la Madeleine
8 Blvd Malesherbes 75008.
Map 5 C5.
01 42 65 00 00.

Place de la République
1 Ave de la République 75011.
Map 14 D1.
01 43 55 92 64.

Place St-Michel
29 Quai St-Michel 75005.
Map 13 A4.
01 43 29 63 66.

Place du Trocadéro
1 Ave D'Eylau 75016.
Map 9 C1.
01 47 27 00 00.

Rond Point des Champs-Elysées
7 Ave Matignon 75008.
Map 5 A5.
01 42 56 29 00.

St-Paul
M St-Paul.
Map 13 C3.
01 48 87 49 39.

Calling for a Taxi

Alpha
01 45 85 85 85.

Artaxi
01 42 41 50 50 & 01 42 08 64 59 (to reserve).

G7
01 47 39 47 39 and 01 47 39 32 51 (to reserve ahead).

Les Taxis Bleus
01 49 36 10 10.

SNCF Information

General Information and Ticket Reservations
08 36 35 35 35.

TAA (Car trains)
01 40 19 60 11.

STREET FINDER

THE MAP REFERENCES given for all sights, hotels, restaurants, shops and entertainment venues described in this book refer to the maps in this section (*see* How the Map References Work, *opposite*). A complete index of street names and places of interest marked on the maps can be found on the following pages. The key map here shows the area of Paris covered by the *Street Finder*, with the arrondissement numbers for the various districts. The maps cover not only the *Street Finder* sightseeing areas (which are color-coded) but also the whole of central Paris with all the districts important for hotels, restaurants, shops and entertainment. The symbols used to represent sights and features on the *Street Finder* maps are listed opposite.

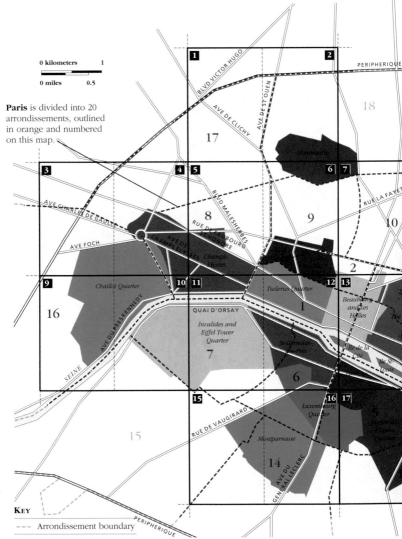

0 kilometers   1

0 miles   0.5

Paris is divided into 20 arrondissements, outlined in orange and numbered on this map.

KEY

--- Arrondissement boundary

HOW THE MAP REFERENCES WORK

The first figure tells you which *Street Finder* map to turn to.

Hôtel de Ville ⓳

4 Pl de l'Hôtel-de-Ville 75004.
Map 13 B3. ☎ *01 42 76 50 49*.
Ⓜ *Hôtel de Ville.* **Open** *10:30am Mon for tour, call to check.*
Closed *public hols & official functions* ♿ ✔

The letter and figure give the grid reference. Letters go across the map's top and bottom; figures on its sides.

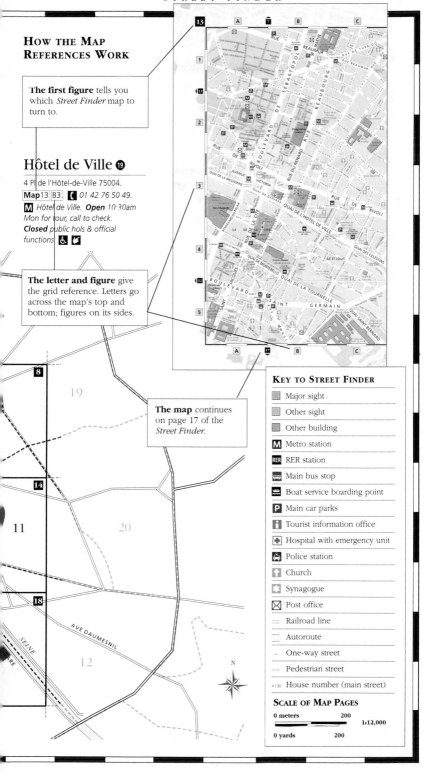

The map continues on page 17 of the *Street Finder.*

KEY TO STREET FINDER

▢	Major sight
▢	Other sight
▢	Other building
Ⓜ	Metro station
RER	RER station
🚌	Main bus stop
⛴	Boat service boarding point
P	Main car parks
🛈	Tourist information office
✚	Hospital with emergency unit
🚓	Police station
✝	Church
✡	Synagogue
⊠	Post office
═	Railroad line
─	Autoroute
⟶	One-way street
─	Pedestrian street
◄130	House number (main street)

SCALE OF MAP PAGES

0 meters   200
                              1:12,000
0 yards   200

Street Finder Index

Each place name is followed by its arrondissement number and then by its Street Finder reference.

Each place name is followed by its arrondissement number and then by its Street Finder reference.

Each place name is followed by its arrondissement number and then by its Street Finder reference.

Each place name is followed by its arrondissement number and then by its Street Finder reference.

Each place name is followed by its arrondissement number and then by its Street Finder reference.

Each place name is followed by its arrondissement number and then by its Street Finder reference.

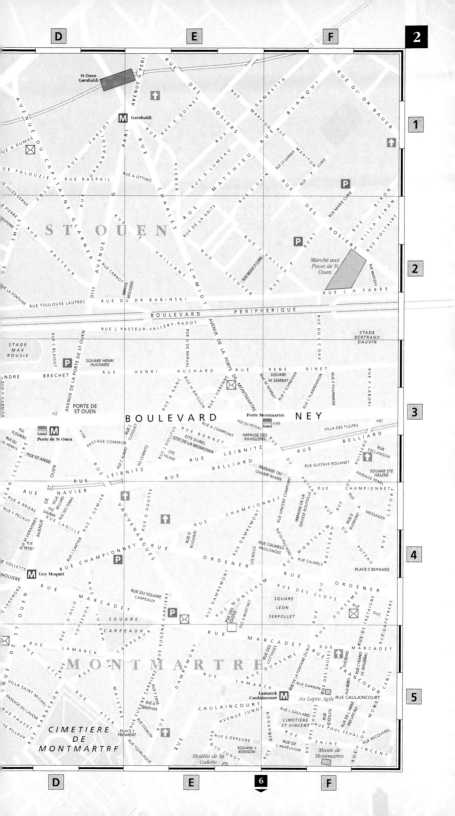

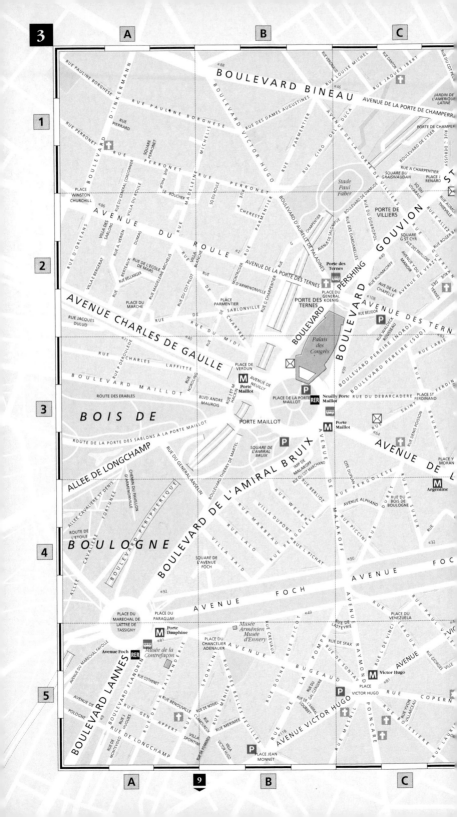

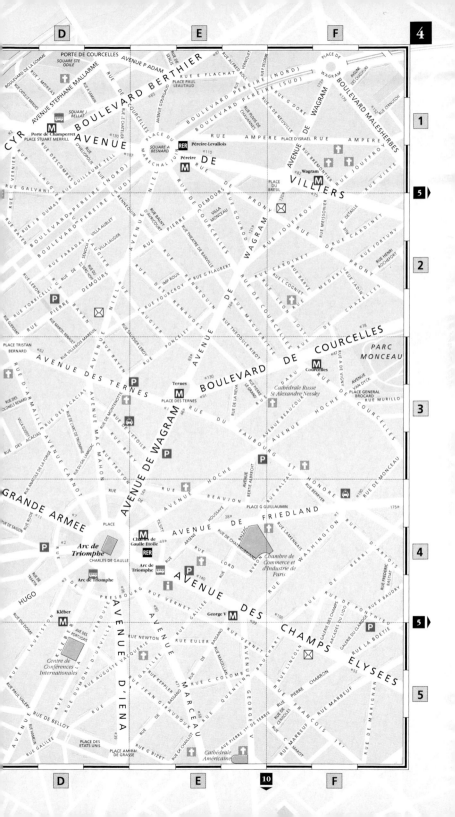

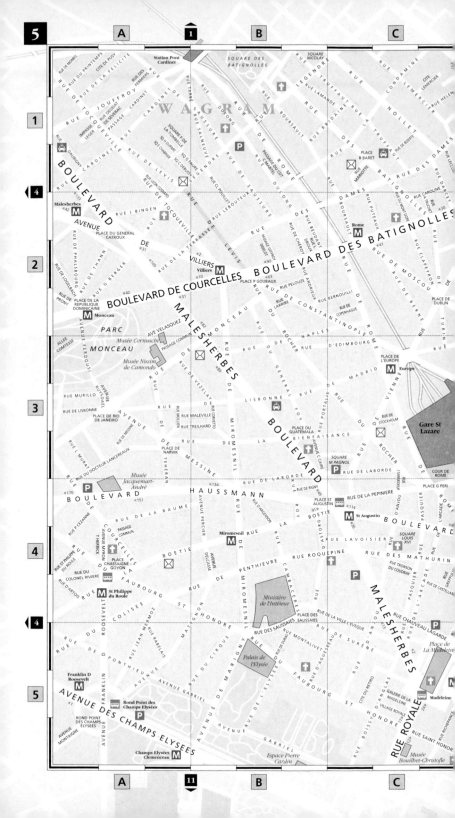

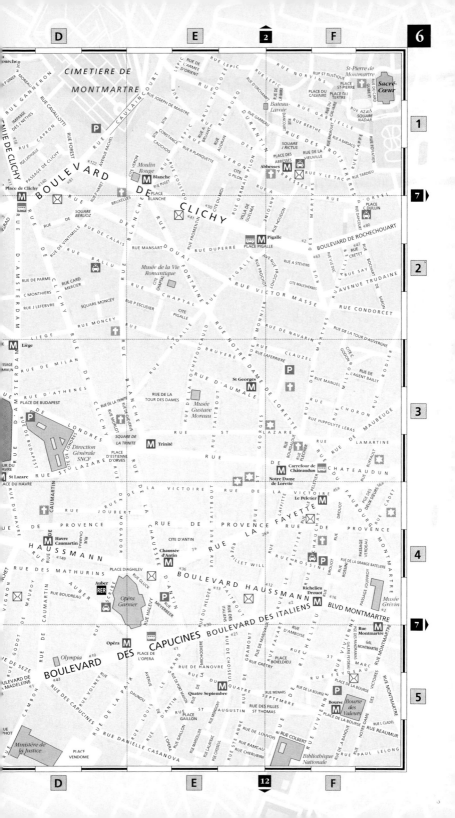

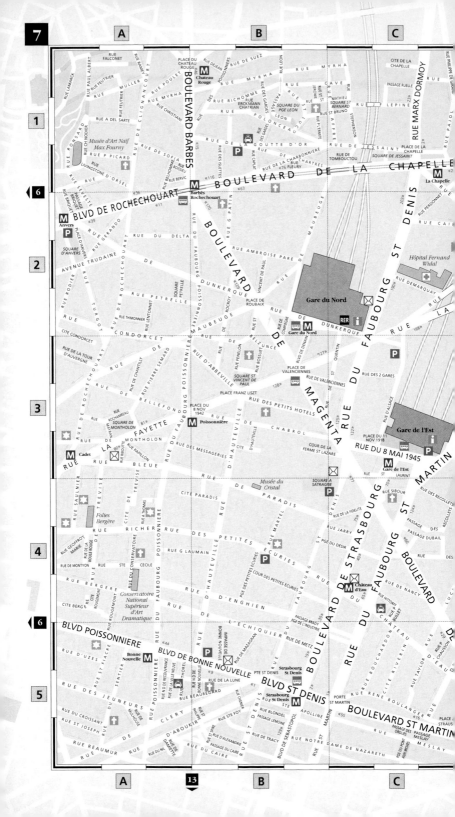

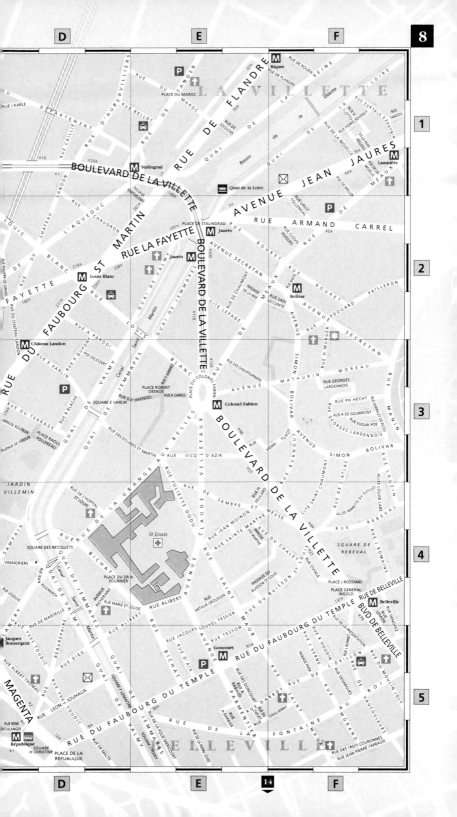

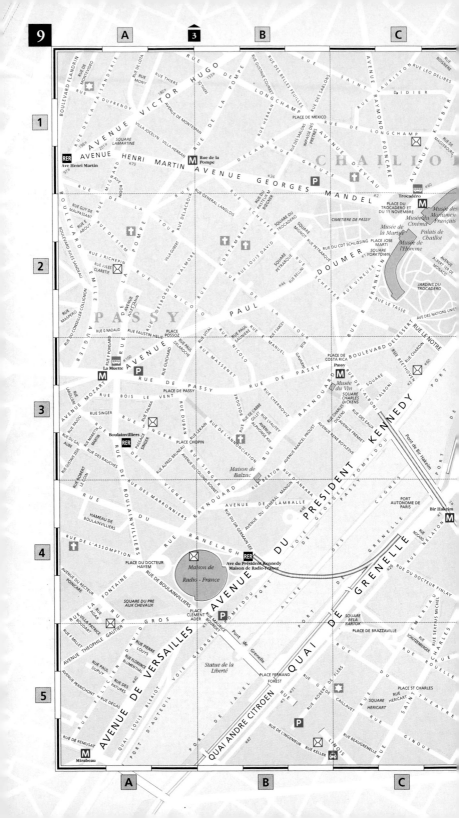

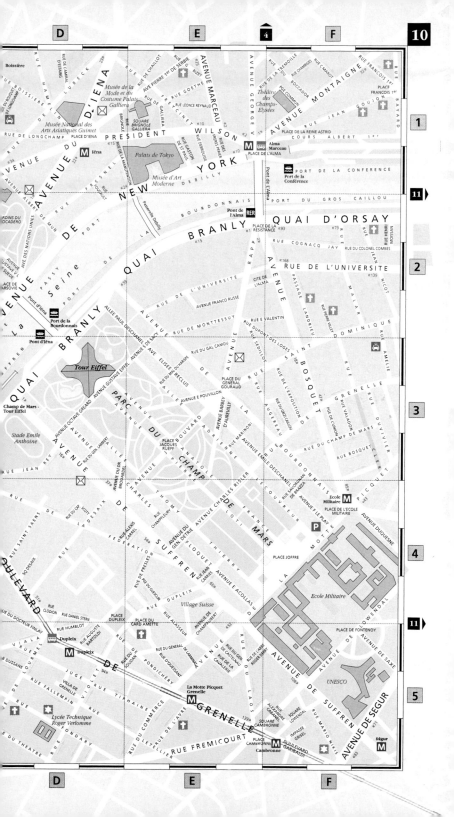

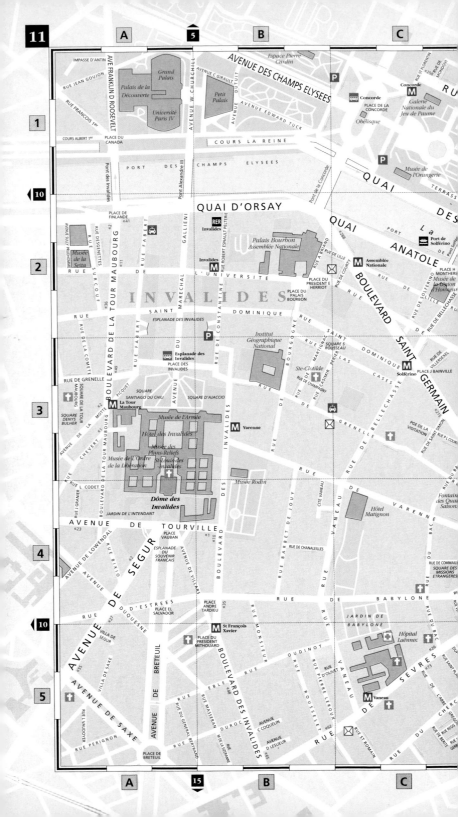

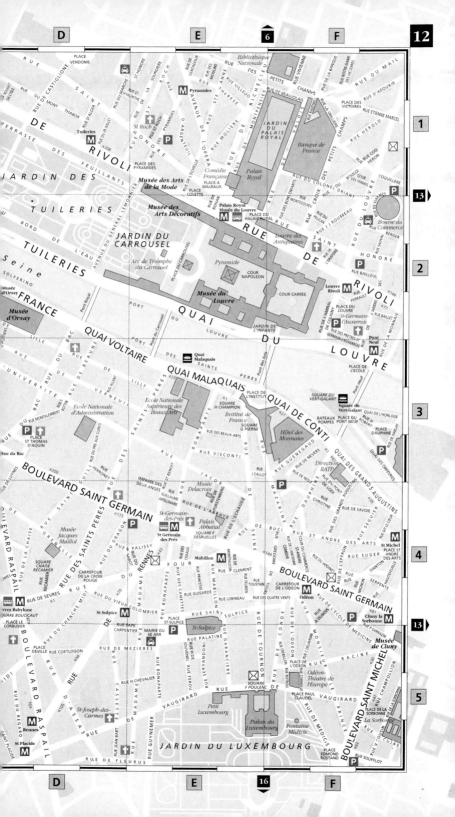

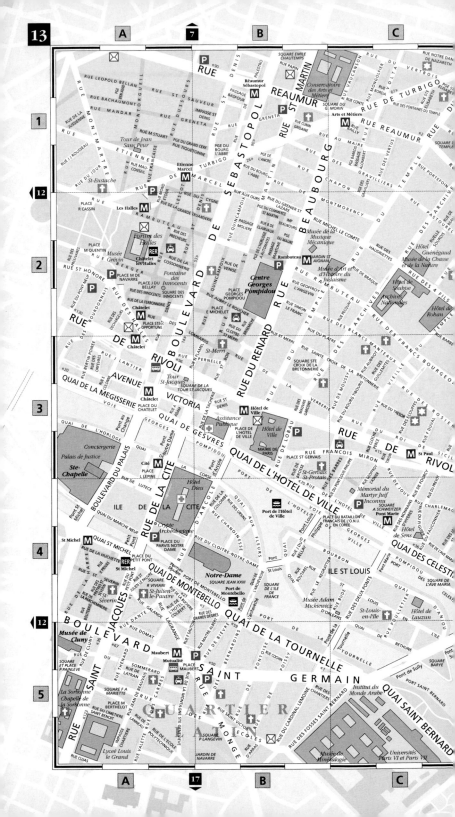

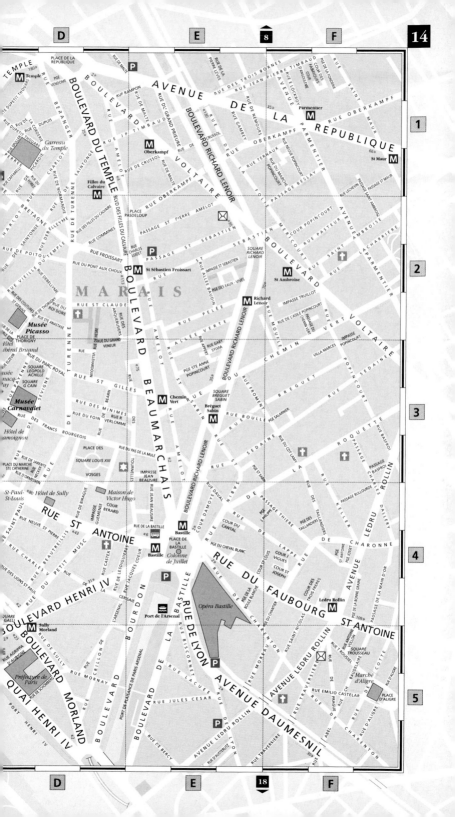

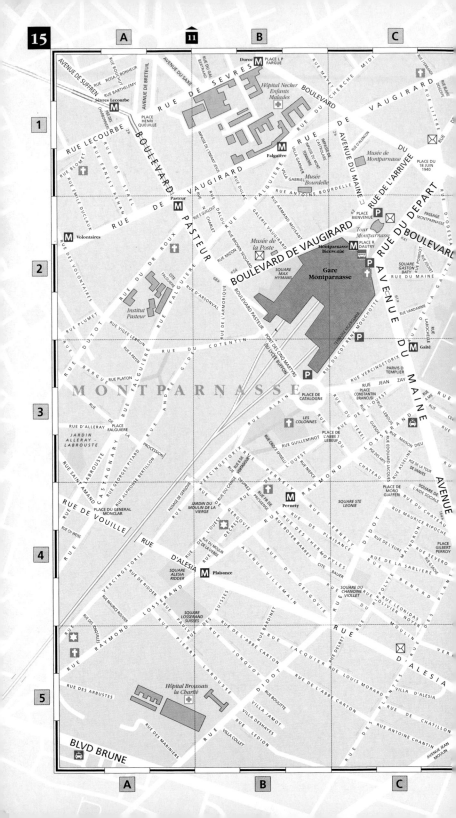

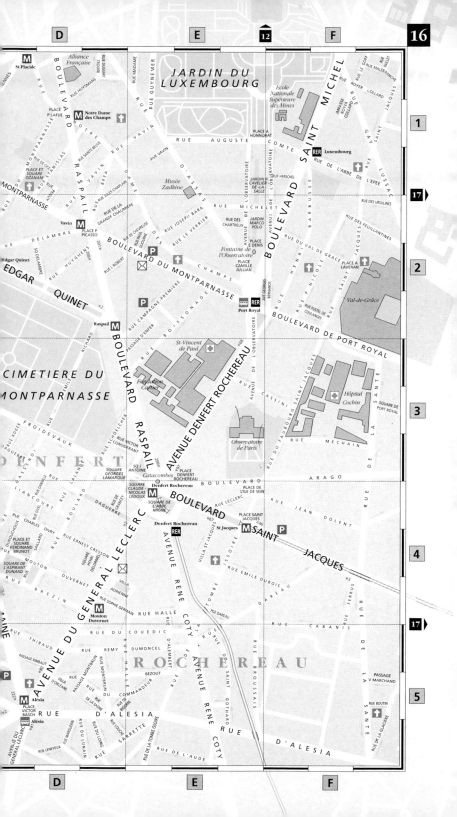

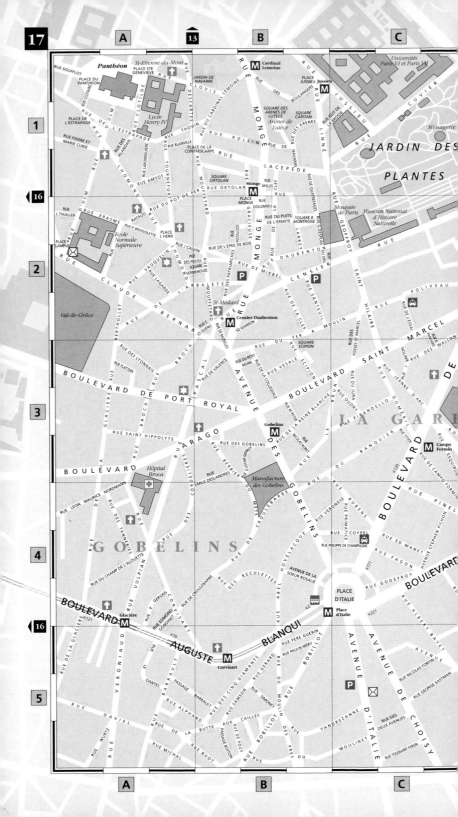

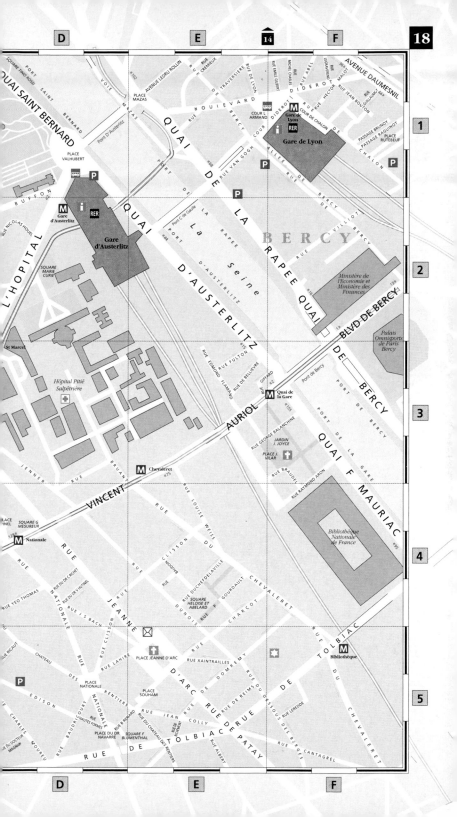

General Index

Acknowledgments

DORLING KINDERSLEY would like to thank the many people whose help and assistance contributed to the preparation of this book.

MAIN CONTRIBUTOR
Alan Tillier has lived in all the main areas of Paris for 25 years, during which time he has been Paris correspondent for several journals including *Newsweek, The Times,* and the *International Herald Tribune.* He is the author of several *Herald Tribune* guides for business travellers to Europe.

CONTRIBUTORS
Lenny Borger, Karen Burshtein, Thomas Quinn Curtiss, David Downie, Fiona Dunlop, Heidi Ellison, Alexandre Lazareff, Robert Noah, Martha Rose Shulman, David Stevens, Jude Welton.

DORLING KINDERSLEY wishes to thank the following editors and researchers at Websters International Publishers: Sandy Carr, Siobhan Bremner, Valeria Fabbri, Gemma Hancock, Sara Harper, Annie Hubert, Celia Woolfrey.

ADDITIONAL PHOTOGRAPHY
Andy Crawford, Michael Crockett, Lucy Davies, Mike Dunning, Philip Gatward, Steve Gorton, Alison Harris, Chas Howson, Dave King, Ranald MacKechnie, Eric Meacher, Neil Mersh, Stephen Oliver, Poppy, Susannah Price, Tim Ridley, Philippe Sebert, Steve Shott, Peter Wilson, Steven Wooster.

ADDITIONAL ILLUSTRATIONS
John Fox, Nick Gibbard, David Harris, Kevin Jones Associates, John Woodcock.

CARTOGRAPHY
Andrew Heritage, James Mills-Hicks, John Plumer, Chez Picthall (DK Cartography). Advanced Illustration (Cheshire), Contour Publishing (Derby), Euromap Limited (Berkshire). Street Finder maps: ERA-Maptec Ltd (Dublin) adapted with permission from original survey and mapping by Shobunsha (Japan).

CARTOGRAPHIC RESEARCH
Roger Bullen, Tony Chambers, Paul Dempsey, Ruth Duxbury, Ailsa Heritage, Margeret Hynes, Jayne Parsons, Donna Rispoli, Andrew Thompson.

DESIGN AND EDITORIAL
MANAGING EDITOR Douglas Amrine
MANAGING ART EDITOR Geoff Manders
SENIOR EDITOR Georgina Matthews
SERIES DESIGN CONSULTANT Peter Luff
EDITORIAL DIRECTOR David Lamb
ART DIRECTOR Anne-Marie Bulat

PRODUCTION CONTROLLER Hilary Stephens
PICTURE RESEARCH Naomi Peck
DTP DESIGNER Andy Wilkinson
Janet Abbott, Emma Ainsworth, Hilary Bird, Vanessa Courtier, Maggie Crowley, Guy Dimond, Simon Farbrother, Fay Franklin, Graham Green, Alison Harris, Paul Hines, Fiona Holman, Gail Jones, Nancy Jones, Stephen Knowlden, Chris Lascelles, Rebecca Milner, Fiona Morgan, Earl Neish, Lyn Parry, Shirin Patel, Stephanie Rees, Simon Ryder, Andrew Szudek, Andy Willmore.

SPECIAL ASSISTANCE
Miranda Dewer at Bridgeman Art Library, Editions Gallimard, Lindsay Hunt, Emma Hutton at Cooling Brown, Janet Todd at DACS, Oddbins Ltd.

PHOTOGRAPHIC REFERENCE
Musée Carnavalet, Thomas d'Hoste.

PHOTOGRAPHY PERMISSIONS
DORLING KINDERSLEY would like to thank the following for their kind permission to photograph at their establishments: Aéroports de Paris, Basilique du Sacré-Coeur de Montmartre, Beauvilliers, Benoit, Bibliothèque Historique de la Ville de Paris, Bibliothèque Polonaise, Bofinger, Brasserie Lipp, Café de Flore, Caisse Nationale des Monuments Historiques et des Sites, Les Catacombes, Centre National d'Art et de Culture Georges Pompidou, Chartier, Chiberta, La Cité des Sciences et de l'Industrie and L'EPPV, La Coupole, Les Deux Magots, Fondation Cousteau, Le Grand Colbert, Hôtel Atala, Hôtel Liberal Bruand, Hôtel Meurice, Hôtel Relais Christine, Kenzo, Lucas-Carton, La Madeleine, Mariage Frères, Memorial du Martyr Juif Inconnu, Thierry Mugler, Musée Armenien de France, Musée de l'Art Juif, Musée Bourdelle, Musée du Cabinet des Medailles, Musée Carnavalet, Musée Cernuschi: Ville de Paris, Musée du Cinema Henri Langlois, Musée Cognacq-Jay, Musée de Cristal de Baccarat, Musée d'Ennery, Musée Grévin, Musée Jacquemart-André, Musée de la Musique Méchanique, Musée National des Châteaux de Malmaison et Bois-Préau, Collections du Musée National de la Légion d'Honneur, Musée National du Moyen Age-Thermes de Cluny, Musée de Notre-Dame de Paris, Musée de l'Opéra, Musée de l'Ordre de la Libération, Musée d'Orsay, Musée de la Préfecture de la Police, Musée de Radio France, Musée Rodin, Musée des Transports Urbains, Musée du Vin, Musée Zadkine, Notre-Dame du Travail, A l'Olivier,

Palais de la Découverte, Palais de Luxembourg, Pharamond, Pied de Cochon, Lionel Poilaîne, St. Germain-des-Prés, St. Louis en l'Ile, St. Médard, St. Merry, St-Paul– St-Louis, St-Roch, St-Sulpice, La Société Nouvelle d'Exploitation de La Tour Eiffel, La Tour Montparnasse, UNESCO, and all the other museums, churches, hotels, restaurants, shops, galleries and sights too numerous to thank individually.

PICTURE CREDITS

t=top; tc=top center; tr=top right; cla=center left above; ca=center above; cra=center right above; cl=center left; c=center; cr=center right; clb=center left below; cb=center below; crb=center right below; bl=bottom left; bc=bottom center; br=bottom right.

Works of art have been reproduced with the permission of the following copyright holders: © SUCCESSION H MATISSE/DACS 1993: 111ca; © ADAGP/SPADEM, Paris and DACS, London 1993: 44cl; © ADAGP, Paris and DACS, London 1993: 61br, 61tr, 105tc, 107cb, 109b, 111cb, 111cb, 112bl, 112t, 112br, 113bl, 113br, 119c, 120b, 179tl, 180bc, 181cr, 211tc; © DACS 1993: 13cra, 36tl, 43cra, 45cr, 50br, 55cr, 57tl, 100t, 100br, 100clb, 100cl, 100ca, 101t, 101ca, 101cr, 101bl, 104, 107cra, 113c, 137tl, 178cl, 178ca, 208br.

CHRISTO–THE PONT NEUF WRAPPED, Paris, 1975-85: 38cla; © CHRISTO 1985, by kind permission of the artist. Photos achieved with the assistance of the EPPV and the CSI pp 234-9; Courtesy of ERBEN OTTO DIX: 110bl; Photos of EURO DISNEYLAND ® PARK and the EURO DISNEY RESORT ®: 233b, 242tl, 242cl, 242b, 243tc, 243cr, 243bl, 244t, 244cl, 244b, 245t, 245c, 245bl, 245br, 346cl. The characters, architectural works and trademarks are the property of THE WALT DISNEY COMPANY. All rights reserved; FONDATION LE CORBUSIER: 59t, 254b; Courtesy of THE ESTATE OF JOAN MITCHELL: 113t; © HENRY MOORE FOUNDATION 1993: 191b. Reproduced by kind permission of the Henry Moore Foundation; BETH LIPKIN: 241t; Courtesy of the MAISON VICTOR HUGO, VILLE DE PARIS: 95cl; Courtesy of the MUSÉE D'ART NAIF MAX FOURNY PARIS: 221b, 223b; MUSÉE CARNAVALET: 212b; MUSÉE DE L'HISTOIRE CONTEMPORAINE (BDIC), PARIS: 208br; MUSÉE DE L'ORANGERIE: 130tr; MUSÉE DU LOUVRE: 125br, 128c; MUSÉE NATIONAL DES CHÂTEAUX DE MALMAISON ET BOIS-PRÉAU: 255cr; MUSÉE MARMOTTAN: 58c, 58cb, 59c, 60tl, 131tr; MUSÉE DE LA MODE ET DU COSTUME PALAIS GALLIERA: 57br; MUSÉE DE MONTMARTRE, PARIS: 221t; MUSÉE DES MONUMENTS FRANÇAIS: 197tc,

198cr; MUSÉE NATIONAL DE LA LÉGION D'HONNEUR: 30bc, 143bl; MUSÉE DE LA VILLE DE PARIS: MUSÉE DU PETIT PALAIS: 54cl, 205cb; © SUNDANCER: 346bl.

The Publishers are grateful to the following individuals, companies and picture libraries for permission to reproduce their photographs:

ADP: 361b; ALLSPORT UK: Sean Botterill 39br; ALLVEY & TOWERS: 362bl; THE ANCIENT ART AND ARCHITECTURE COLLECTION: 20clb; JAMES AUSTIN: 88t.

BANQUE DE FRANCE: 133t; NELLY BARIAND: 165c; GÉRARD BOULLAY: 84tl, 84tr, 84bl, 84br, 85t, 85cra, 85crb, 85br, 85bl; BRIDGEMAN ART LIBRARY, LONDON: (detail) 19br, 20cr, 21cl, 28cr–29cl, (detail) 33br; British Library, London (detail) 16br, (detail) 21bl, (detail) 22tl, (detail) 29tl; B N, Paris 17bl, (detail) 21tc, (detail) 21cr; Château de Versailles, France 17tr, 17bc, (detail) 17br, (detail) 28br, (detail) 155b; Christie's, London 8–9, (detail) 22cb, 32cla, 34tl, 44c; Delomosne, London 30clb; Detroit Institute of Art, Michigan 43ca; Giraudon 14, (detail) 24bl, (detail) 24clb, (detail) 25br, (detail) 28bl, (detail) 28cla, (detail) 29bl, 31cb, 58br, (detail) 60bl, 60ca, 60c; Lauros– Giraudon 21tr; Louvre, Paris 56t, 60br, 61bl, 61tl; Roy Miles Gallery 25tr; Musée de L'Armée, Paris (detail) 83br; Musée Condé, Chantilly (detail) 4tr, 16bl, 17cl, (detail) 17tcr, (detail) 17c, (detail) 20tl, (detail) 24bc; Musée Crozatier, Le Puy en Velay, France (detail) 23bl; Musée Gustave Moreau, Paris 56b, 231t; National Gallery (detail) 27tl, (detail) 44b; Musée d'Orsay, Paris 43br; Musée de la Ville de Paris, Musée Carnavalet (detail) 28bc, (detail) 29tr, 29crb; Collection Painton Cowen 38cla; Palais du Tokyo, Paris 59b; Philadelphia Museum of Modern Art, Pennsylvania 43cra; Temples Newsham House, Leeds 23cr; Uffizi Gallery, Florence (detail) 22br; © THE BRITISH MUSEUM: 29tc.

CIA: G Cousseau 232crb; CITÉ DE LA MUSIQUE: Eric Mahondieu 235br; CITÉ DES SCIENCES ET DE L'INDUSTRIE: Michel Lamoureux 236cb, 236b, 238t; Michel Virad 237tl, 238br; CSI: Pascal Prieur 238cl, 238cb.

© DISNEY: 242tr, 243br, 346t. The characters, architectural works and trademarks of EURO DISNEYLAND ® PARK and the EURO DISNEY RESORT ® are the property of THE WALT DISNEY COMPANY. All rights reserved; R Doisneau: RAPHO 143t. ESPACE MONTMARTRE: 220bl; MARY EVANS PICTURE LIBRARY: 36bl, 42br, 81br, 89tl, 94b, 130b, 141cl, 191c, 192cr, 193crb, 209b, 224bl, 247br, 251t, 253b, 372t.

GIRAUDON: (detail) 20bl, (detail) 21crb; Lauros–Giraudon (detail) 31bl; Musée de la Ville de Paris: Musée Carnavalet (detail) 211t; LE GRAND VÉFOUR: 287t.

ROBERT HARDING PICTURE LIBRARY: 20br, 24tl, 27ca, 27br, 34cla, 36tl, 39tl, 45cr, 65br, 240cb, 365cr; B M 25ca; B N 191tr, 208bc; Biblioteco Reale, Turin 127t; Bulloz 208cb; P Craven 364b; R Francis 82clb; I Griffiths 360t; H Josse 208br; Musée National des Châteaux de Malmaison et Bois-Préau 31tc; Musée de Versailles 24cl; R Poinot 345b; P Tetrel 251crb; Explorer 10bl; F. Chazot 329b; Girard 65c; P Gleizes 62bl; F Jalain 362b; J Moatti 328bl, 328cl; Walter Rawlings 41bc; A Wolf 123br, 123tl; ALISON HARRIS: Musée de Montparnasse 179cl; Pavillon des Arts 108br; Le Village Royale 132tl; JOHN HESELTINE PHOTOGRAPHY: 12br, 174; THE HULTON DEUTSCH COLLECTION: 42cl, 43bl, 43cr, 43t, 45cl, 101br; HULTON GETTY: 231bl; Charles Hewitt 38clb; Lancaster 181tc.

© IGN PARIS 1990 Authorisation Nº 90–2067: 11b; INSTITUT DU MONDE ARABE: Georges Fessey 165tr.

THE KOBAL COLLECTION: 42t, 44t, 140b; Columbia Pictures 181br; Société Générale de Films 36tc; Paramount Studios 42bl; Les Films du Carrosse 109t; Montsouris 197cra; Georges Méliès 198bl.

THE LEBRECHT COLLECTION: 227br.

MAGNUM: Bruno Barbey 64b; Philippe Halsmann 45b; MINISTERE DE L'ECONOMIE ET DES FINANCES: 355c; MINISTERE DE L'INTÉRIEUR SGAP DE PARIS: 352bc, 352br, 353t; COLLECTIONS DU MOBILIER NATIONAL-CLICHÉ DU MOBILIER NATIONAL: 167cr; © photo MUSÉE DE L'ARMÉE, PARIS: 189cr; MUSÉE DES ARTS DÉCORATIFS, PARIS: L Sully Jaulmes 54t; MUSÉE DES ARTS DE LA MODE–Collection UCAD– UFAC: 121b; MUSÉE BOUILHET-CHRISTOFLE: 57tr, 132t; MUSÉE CANTONAL DES BEAUX-ARTS, LAUSANNE: 115b; MUSÉE CARNAVALET: Dac Karin Maucotel 97b; MUSÉE NATIONAL DE L'HISTOIRE NATURELLE: D Serrette 167cl; MUSÉE DE L'HOLOGRAPHIE: 109cl; © MUSÉE DE L'HOMME, PARIS: D Ponsard 196cb, 199cl; © PHOTO

MUSÉE DE LA MARINE, PARIS: 30bl, 196cl; MUSÉE NATIONAL D'ART MODERN–CENTRE GEORGES POMPIDOU, PARIS: 61tr, 110br, 110bl, 111t, 111ca, 111cb, 112t, 112bl, 112br, 113t, 113c, 113bl, 113br; MUSÉE DES PLANS-RELIEFS, PARIS: 186crb; MUSÉE DE LA POSTE, PARIS: 179tl; MUSÉE DE LA SEITA, PARIS: D Dado 190t.

PHILIPPE PERDEREAU: 132b, 133b; CLICHÉ PHOTOTHEQUE DES MUSÉES DE LA VILLE DE PARIS – © DACS 1993: 19ca, 19crb, 26cr–27cl, 96tr; POPPERFOTO: 227t.

RATP.SG/G.I.E. TOTHEME 54; 370; REDFERNS: W Gottlieb 36clb; © PHOTO RÉUNION DES MUSÉES NATIONAUX: Grand Trianon 24crb; Musée Guimet 54cb; Musée du Louvre: 25cb, (detail) 30cr–31cl, 55tl, 123bl, 124t, 124c, 124b, 125t, 125c, 126c, 126bl, 126br, 127b, 128t, 128b, 129t, 129c; Musée Picasso 55cr, 100t, 100c, 100cl, 100clb, 100br, 101bl, 101cr, 101ca, 101t; ROGER-VIOLLET: (detail) 22clb, (detail) 37bl, (detail) 192bc, (detail) 209t; ANN RONAN PICTURE LIBRARY: 173cr; PHILIPPE RUAULT: Fondation Cartier 179bl.

LA SAMARITAINE, PARIS: 115c; SEALINK PLC: 362cl; SIPAPRESS: 222c; FRANK SPOONER PICTURES: F Reglain 64ca; P Renault 64c; SYGMA: 33crb, 240cl; F Poincet 38tl; Keystone 38bc, 241cra; J Langevin 39br; Keler 39crb; J Van Hasselt 39tr; P. Habans 62c; A Gyori 63cr; P Vauthey 65bl; Y Forestier 188t; Sunset Boulevard 241br; Water Carone 328t.

TALLANDIER: 23cb, 23tl, 26cl, 26clb, 26bl, 27bl, 28tl, 29cr, 29ca, 30tl, 30cb, 30br, 36cla, 37ca, 37br, 38cb, 52cla; B N 26br, 30crb, 36bc; Brigaud 37crb; Brimeur 32bl; Charmet 34cb; Dubout 15b, 18br, 22ca, 23br, 24br, 28c, 31cr, 31tr, 32br, 33bl, 34clb, 34bl, 34br, 35bl, 35br, 35clb, 35tl, 36crb; Josse 18cla, 18tc, 18c, 18clb, 19tl, 34bc; Josse-B N 18bl; Joubert 36c; Tildier 35ca; Vigne 32clb; LE TRAIN BLEU: 289t.

VIDÉOTHÈQUE DE PARIS: Hoi Pham Dinh 106lb

AGENCE VU: Didier Lefèvre 328cr.

Front Endpaper: RÉUNION DES MUSÉES NATIONAUX: Musée Picasso cr.Back endpaper: RATP CML AGENCE CARTOGRAPHIQUE.

Phrase Book

IN EMERGENCY

Help!	Au secours!	oh sekoor
Stop!	Arrêtez!	aret-ay
Call a doctor!	Appelez un médecin!	apuh-lay uñ medsañ
Call an ambulance!	Appelez une ambulance!	apuh-lay oon oñboo-loñs
Call the police!	Appelez la police!	apuh-lay lah pob-lees
Call the fire department!	Appelez les pompiers!	apuh-lay leb poñ-peeyay
Where is the nearest telephone?	Où est le téléphone le plus proche?	oo ay luh tehlehfon luh ploo prosh
Where is the nearest hospital?	Où est l'hôpital le plus proche?	oo ay l'opeetal luh ploo prosh

COMMUNICATION ESSENTIALS

Yes	Oui	wee
No	Non	noñ
Please	S'il vous plaît	seel voo play
Thank you	Merci	mer-see
Excuse me	Excusez-moi	exkoo-zay mwah
Hello	Bonjour	boñzboor
Goodbye	Au revoir	oh rub-vwar
Good night	Bonsoir	boñ-swar
Morning	Le matin	matañ
Afternoon	L'après-midi	l'apreb-meedee
Evening	Le soir	swar
Yesterday	Hier	eeyebr
Today	Aujourd'hui	oh-zboor-dwee
Tomorrow	Demain	dubmañ
Here	Ici	ee-see
There	Là	lah
What?	Quel, quelle?	kel, kel
When?	Quand?	koñ
Why?	Pourquoi?	poor-kwah
Where?	Où?	oo

USEFUL PHRASES

How are you?	Comment allez-vous?	kom-moñ talay voo
Very well, thank you.	Très bien, merci.	treb byañ, mer-see
Pleased to meet you.	Enchanté de faire votre connaissance.	oñshoñ-tay dub febr votr kon-ay-sans
See you soon.	A bientôt.	byañ-toh
That's fine	Voilà qui est parfait	vwalah kee ay par-fay
Where is/are...?	Où est/sont...?	oo ay/soñ
How far is it to...?	Combien de kilometres d'ici à...?	kom-byañ dub keelo-metr d'ee-see ah
Which way to...?	Quelle est la direction pour...?	kel ay lah deer-ek-syoñ poor
Do you speak English?	Parlez-vous anglais?	par-lay voo oñg-lay
I don't understand.	Je ne comprends pas.	zbuh nuh kom-proñ pah
Could you speak slowly please?	Pouvez-vous parler moins vite s'il vous plaît?	poo-vay voo par-lay mwañ veet seel voo play
I'm sorry.	Excusez-moi.	exkoo-zay mwah

USEFUL WORDS

big	grand	groñ
small	petit	pub-tee
hot	chaud	show
cold	froid	frwah
good	bon	boñ
bad	mauvais	moh-veh
enough	assez	assay
well	bien	byañ
open	ouvert	oo-ver
closed	fermé	fer-meb
left	gauche	gobsh
right	droit	drwah
straight ahead	tout droit	too drwah
near	près	preh
far	loin	lwañ
up	en haut	oñ ob
down	en bas	oñ bah
early	de bonne heure	dub bon urr
late	en retard	oñ rub-tar
entrance	l'entrée	l'on-tray
exit	la sortie	sor-tee
toilet	la toilette, le WC	twab-let, vay-see
free, unoccupied	libre	leebr
free, no charge	gratuit	grab-twee

MAKING A TELEPHONE CALL

I'd like to place a long-distance call.	Je voudrais faire un interurbain.	zhub voo-dreb febr uñ añter-oorbañ
I'd like to make a collect call.	Je voudrais faire une communication avec PCV.	zhub voo-dreb febr oon komoonikah-syoñavek peb-seb-veb
I'll try again later.	Je rappelerai plus tard.	zhub rapel-eray ploo tar
Can I leave a message?	Est-ce que je peux laisser un message?	es-keb zhub pub leh-say uñ mehsazb
Hold on.	Ne quittez pas, s'il vous plaît.	nuh kee-tay pab seel voo play
Could you speak up a little please?	Pouvez-vous parler un peu plus fort?	poo-vay voo par-lay uñ puh ploo for
local call	la communication locale	komoonikah-syoñ low-kal

SHOPPING

How much does this cost?	C'est combien s'il vous plaît?	say kom-byañ seel voo play
I would like ...	je voudrais...	zhub voo-dray
Do you have?	Est-ce que vous avez?	es-kuh voo zavay
I'm just looking.	Je regarde seulement.	zhub rubgar sublmoñ
Do you take credit cards?	Est-ce que vous acceptez les cartes de crédit?	es-kuh voo zaksept-ay leb kart duh kreb-dee
Do you take traveler's cheques?	Est-ce que vous acceptez les cheques de voyages?	es-kuh voo zaksept-ay leb shek duh vwayazb
What time do you open?	A quelle heure vous êtes ouvert?	ah kel urr voo zet oo-ver
What time do you close?	A quelle heure vous êtes fermé?	ah kel urr voo zet fer-may
This one.	Celui-ci.	suhl-wee-see
That one.	Celui-là.	suhl-wee-lah
expensive	cher	shebr
cheap	pas cher, bon marché	pah shebr, boñ mar-shay
size, clothes	la taille	tye
size, shoes	la pointure	pwañ-tur
white	blanc	bloñ
black	noir	nwahr
red	rouge	roozh
yellow	jaune	zhobwn
green	vert	vebr
blue	bleu	bluh

TYPES OF SHOP

antiques shop	le magasin d'antiquités	maga-zañ d'oñteekee-tay
bakery	la boulangerie	booloñ-zhuree
bank	la banque	boñk
bookstore	la librairie	lee-brebree
butcher	la boucherie	boo-shebree
cake shop	la pâtisserie	patee-sree
cheese shop	la fromagerie	fromazb-ree
dairy	la crémerie	krem-ree
department store	le grand magasin	groñ maga-zañ
delicatessen	la charcuterie	sharkoot-ree
drugstore	la pharmacie	farmab-see
fish seller	la poissonnerie	pwasson-ree
gift shop	le magasin de cadeaux	maga-zañ duh kadoh
greengrocer	le marchand de légumes	mar-shoñ duh lay-goom
grocery	l'alimentation	alee-moñta-syoñ
hairdresser	le coiffeur	kwafubr
market	le marché	marsh-ay
newsstand	le magasin de journaux	maga-zañ duh zboor-no
post office	la poste, le bureau de poste, le PTT	pobst, booroh dub pobst, peb-teb-teb
shoe store	le magasin de chaussures	maga-zañ duh show-soor
supermarket	le supermarché	soo pebr-marshay
tobacconist	le tabac	tabab
travel agent	l'agence de voyages	l'azboñs dub vwayazb

SIGHTSEEING

abbey	l'abbaye	l'abay-ee
art gallery	le galerie d'art	galer-ree dart
bus station	la gare routière	gabr roo-tee-yebr

cathedral	la cathédrale	katay-dral
church	l'église	l'aygleez
garden	le jardin	zhar-dañ
library	la bibliothèque	beebleeo-tek
museum	le musée	moo-zay
railway station	la gare (SNCF)	gahr (es-en-say-ef)
tourist information office	les renseignements touristiques, le syndicat d'initiative	roñsayn-moñ toorees-teek, sandee-ka d'eenee-syateev
town hall	l'hôtel de ville	l'obtel dub veel
closed for public holiday	fermeture jour férié	febrmeb-tur zhoor febree-ay

STAYING IN A HOTEL

Do you have a vacant room?	Est-ce que vous avez une chambre?	es-kuh voo-zavay oon shambr
double room, with double bed	la chambre à deux personnes, avec un grand lit	shambr ab dub pebr-son avek un gronñ lee
twin room	la chambre à deux lits	shambr ab dub lee
single room	la chambre à une personne	shambr ab oon pebr-son
room with a bath, shower	la chambre avec salle de bains, une douche	shambr avek sal dub bañ, oon doosh
porter	le garçon	gar-soñ
key	la clef	klay
I have a reservation.	J'ai fait une réservation.	zhay fay oon rayzebrva-syoñ

EATING OUT

Have you got a table?	Avez-vous une table de libre?	avay-voo oon tabbl duh leebr
I want to reserve a table.	Je voudrais réserver une table.	zhub voo-dray rayzebr-vay oon tabbl
The bill please.	L'addition s'il vous plaît.	l'adee-syoñ seel voo play
I am a vegetarian.	Je suis végétarien.	zhub swee vezhay-tehryañ
Waitress/ Waiter	Madame, Mademoiselle/ Monsieur	mab-dam, mab-demwahzel/ mub-syub
menu	le menu, la carte	men-oo, kart
fixed-price menu	le menu à prix fixe	men-oo ab pree feeks
cover charge	le couvert	koo-vehr
wine list	la carte des vins	kart-deb vañ
glass	le verre	vehr
bottle	la bouteille	boo-tay
knife	le couteau	koo-tob
fork	la fourchette	for-shet
spoon	la cuillère	kwee-yehr
breakfast	le petit déjeuner	pub-tee deb-zhub-nay
lunch	le déjeuner	deb-zhub-nay
dinner	le dîner	dee-nay
main course	le plat principal	plab praïsee-pal
starter, first course	l'entrée, le hors d'oeuvre	l'oñ-tray. or- dubvr
dish of the day	le plat du jour	plab doo zhoor
wine bar	le bar à vin	bar ab vañ
café	le café	ka-fay
rare	saignant	say-noñ
medium	à point	ab pwañ
well done	bien cuit	byañ kwee

MENU DECODER

apple	la pomme	pom
baked	cuit au four	kweet ob foor
banana	la banane	banan
beef	le boeuf	buhf
beer, draught	la bière, bière	bee-yehr, bee-yehr
beer	à la pression	ab lab pres-syoñ
boiled	bouilli	boo-yee
bread	le pain	pan
butter	le beurre	burr
cake	le gâteau	gab-tob
cheese	le fromage	from-azb
chicken	le poulet	poo-lay
chocolate	le chocolat	shoko-lab
cocktail	le cocktail	cocktail
coffee	le café	kab-fay
dessert	le dessert	deb-ser
dry	sec	sek
duck	le canard	kanar
egg	l'oeuf	l'uf

fish	le poisson	pwab-ssoñ
French fries	le frites	freet
fresh fruit	le fruit frais	fruee freb
garlic	l'ail	l'eye
grilled	grillé	gree-yay
ham	le jambon	zboñ-boñ
ice, ice cream	la glace	glas
lamb	l'agneau	l'anyob
lemon	le citron	see-troñ
lobster	le homard	omabr
meat	la viande	vee-yand
milk	le lait	leb
mineral water	l'eau minérale	l'ob meeney-ral
mustard	la moutarde	moo-tard
oil	l'huile	l'weel
olives	les olives	leb zoleev
onions	les oignons	leb zonyoñ
orange	l'orange	l'oroñzb
fresh orange juice	l'orange pressée	l'oroñzb press-eb
fresh lemon juice	le citron pressé	see-troñ press-eb
pepper	le poivre	pwavr
poached	poché	posb-ay
pork	le porc	por
potatoes	les pommes de terre	pom-dub tebr
prawns	les crevettes	krub-vet
rice	le riz	ree
roast	rôti	row-tee
roll	le petit pain	pub-tee pañ
salt	le sel	sel
sauce	la sauce	sobs
sausage, fresh	la saucisse	sobsees
seafood	les fruits de mer	fruee dub mer
shellfish	les crustaces	kroos-tas
snails	les escargots	leb zes-kar-gob
soup	la soupe, le potage	soop, pob-tazb
steak	le bifteck, le steack	beef-tek, stek
sugar	le sucre	sookr
tea	le thé	tay
toast	le toast	toast
vegetables	les légumes	lay-goom
vinegar	le vinaigre	veenaygr
water	l'eau	l'ob
red wine	le vin rouge	vañ roozb
white wine	le vin blanc	vañ bloñ

NUMBERS

0	zéro	zeb-rob
1	un, une	uñ, oon
2	deux	dub
3	trois	trwab
4	quatre	katr
5	cinq	sañk
6	six	sees
7	sept	set
8	huit	weet
9	neuf	nerf
10	dix	dees
11	onze	oñz
12	douze	dooz
13	treize	trebz
14	quatorze	katorz
15	quinze	kañz
16	seize	sebz
17	dix-sept	dees-set
18	dix-huit	dees-weet
19	dix-neuf	dees-nerf
20	vingt	vañ
30	trente	tront
40	quarante	karoñt
50	cinquante	sañkoñt
60	soixante	swasoñt
70	soixante-dix	swasoñt-dees
80	quatre-vingts	katr-vañ
90	quatre-vingts-dix	katr-vañ-dees
100	cent	soñ
1,000	mille	meel

TIME

one minute	une minute	oon mee-noot
one hour	une heure	oon urr
half an hour	une demi-heure	oon dub-mee urr
Monday	lundi	luñ-dee
Tuesday	mardi	mar-dee
Wednesday	mercredi	mehrkrub-dee
Thursday	jeudi	zhub-dee
Friday	vendredi	voñdrub-dee
Saturday	samedi	sam-dee
Sunday	dimanche	dee-moñsb

DORLING KINDERSLEY *TRAVEL GUIDES*

TITLES AVAILABLE

THE GUIDES THAT SHOW YOU WHAT OTHERS ONLY TELL YOU

COUNTRY GUIDES

AUSTRALIA • CANADA • FRANCE • GREAT BRITAIN
GREECE: ATHENS & THE MAINLAND • THE GREEK ISLANDS
IRELAND • ITALY • MEXICO • PORTUGAL • SCOTLAND
SOUTH AFRICA • SPAIN • THAILAND

REGIONAL GUIDES

BARCELONA & CATALONIA • CALIFORNIA
FLORENCE & TUSCANY • FLORIDA • HAWAII
JERUSALEM & THE HOLY LAND • LOIRE VALLEY
MILAN & THE LAKES • NAPLES WITH POMPEII & THE
AMALFI COAST • PROVENCE & THE COTE d'AZUR • SARDINIA
SEVILLE & ANDALUSIA • SICILY • VENICE & THE VENETO
GREAT PLACES TO STAY IN EUROPE

CITY GUIDES

AMSTERDAM • BERLIN • BUDAPEST • DUBLIN • ISTANBUL
LISBON • LONDON • MADRID • MOSCOW • NEW YORK
PARIS • PRAGUE • ROME • SAN FRANCISCO
ST PETERSBURG • SYDNEY • VIENNA • WARSAW

TRAVEL PLANNERS

AUSTRALIA • FRANCE • FLORIDA
GREAT BRITAIN & IRELAND • ITALY • SPAIN

DK TRAVEL GUIDES CITY MAPS

LONDON • NEW YORK • PARIS • ROME
SAN FRANCISCO • SYDNEY

DK TRAVEL GUIDES PHRASE BOOKS

Paris Metro and Regional Express Railway (RER)

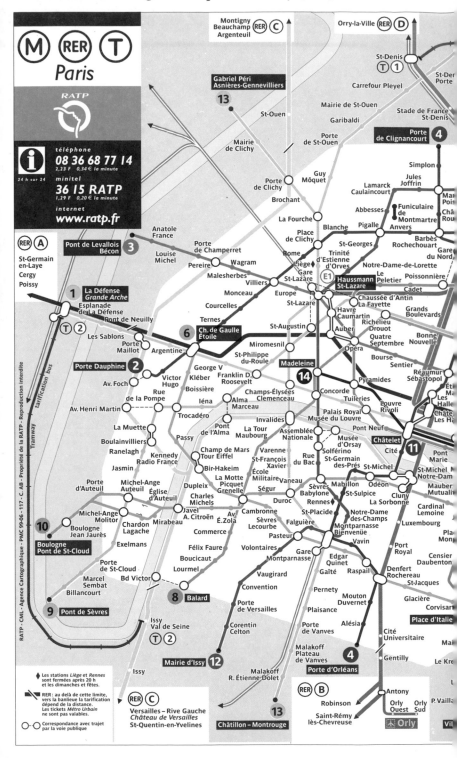